W9-BMZ-825

THE JOURNEY
OF ADULTHOOD

FOURTH EDITION

THE JOURNEY
OF ADULTHOOD

FOURTH EDITION

HELEN L. BEE
BARBARA R. BJORKLUND

PRENTICE HALL
Upper Saddle River, New Jersey 07458

Library of Congress Cataloging-in-Publication Data
Bee, Helen, L.,
    The journey of adulthood/Helen L. Bee, Barbara R. Bjorklund.—4th ed.
      p. cm.
    Includes bibliographical references and indexes.
    ISBN 0-13-010953-3
    1. Adulthood–Psychological aspects.   2. Aging–Psychological
    aspects. 3. Adulthood. 4. Aging. I. Bjorklund, Barbara R.
    II. Title.
    BF724.5.B44   2000   99-24184
    155.6—DC21   CIP

To my father, Justin E. Bee,

whose own journey through

adulthood has always been

an inspiration to me

Editor-in-Chief: Nancy Roberts
Executive Editor: Bill Webber
Acquisition Editor: Jennifer Gilliland
Assistant Editor: Anita Castro
Editorial Assistant: Jessica Spillers
AVP, Director of Manufacturing
  and Production: Barbara Kittle
Senior Managing Editor: Mary Rottino
Production Liaison: Fran Russello
Project Manager: Kerry Reardon
Manufacturing Manager: Nick Sklitsis
Prepress and Manufacturing Buyer: Tricia Kenny

Creative Design Director: Leslie Osher
Cover and Interior Design: Ann DeMarinis
Associate Creative Director: Carole Anson
Cover Art: Comstock Stock Photography
Director, Image Resource Center: Melinda Lee Reo
Manager, Rights & Permissions: Kay Dellosa
Image Specialist: Beth Boyd
Photo Researcher: Anthony Arabia
Text Permission Specialist: Lisa Black
Line Art Coordinator: Guy Ruggiero
Artist: Maria Piper
Director of Marketing: Gina Sluss

This book was set in 11/12.5 Adobe Garamond Type face by Laurel Road Publishing Services
and was printed and bound by Courier Companies, Inc., Westford, Massachussetts
The cover was printed by Lehigh Press, Inc.

©2000, 1996, 1992, 1986 Prentice-Hall, Inc.
Upper Saddle River, New Jersey 07458

Printed in the United States of America
10 9 8 7 6 5

ISBN 0-13-010953-3

Prentice-Hall International (UK) Limited, *London*
Prentice-Hall of Australia Pty. Limited, *Sydney*
Prentice-Hall Canada Inc., *Toronto*
Prentice-Hall Hispanoamericana, S.A., *Mexico*
Prentice-Hall of India Private Limited, *New Delhi*
Prentice-Hall of Japan, Inc., *Tokyo*
Pearson Education Asia Pte. Ltd., *Singapore*
Editora Prentice-Hall do Brasil, Ltda., *Rio de Janeiro*

BRIEF CONTENTS

CONTENTS

3

PHYSICAL CHANGES 62

4

CHANGES IN HEALTH AND HEALTH HABITS 98

5

COGNITIVE CHANGES   128

6

SOCIAL ROLES IN ADULTHOOD   160

7

DEVELOPMENT OF RELATIONSHIPS   194

8

WORK AND WORK ROLES IN ADULTHOOD   232

9

CHANGES IN PERSONALITY AND MOTIVES 272

10

THE GROWTH OF MEANING 304

11

DEALING WITH THE STRESSES OF ADULT LIFE   332

12

THEMES OF ADULT DEVELOPMENT: AN OVERVIEW   360

13

THE FINAL STAGE: DEATH AND DYING 378

14

THE SUCCESSFUL JOURNEY: PATHWAYS, TRAJECTORIES, AND GULLIES 400

PREFACE

The fourth edition of *The Journey of Adulthood* continues to be about the *process* of adult development, the way people change all along the way from early adulthood to old old age. I have cut through the large-scale findings by including cultural differences, gender differences, and individual differences. To avoid presenting a catalog of disease and decline, much new material has been included on compensation, prevention, and gains that come with age. I have sought out work conducted by researchers around the world dealing with diverse populations and have balanced up-to-date research findings with sound theoretical concepts both new and old. Throughout, I have endeavored to cushion scientific information with warmth and humor.

The chapters in the book fall into three main categories. The first two chapters lay the groundwork for the book: defining terms, describing key concepts, and presenting major theories of adult development. The next chapters are based on empirical findings from a variety of fields, including health and medicine, behavior genetics, cognitive development, social psychology, sociology, economics, social development, and other areas that deal with all the aspects of adult development. In the last five chapters, I cover some topics that are not so easily pigeonholed into one or another field of science but are nevertheless important parts of adulthood, such as the growth of meaning, dealing with stress, the debate about how best to conceptualize the transitions of adulthood, and confronting death. In these last chapters, I try to pull the threads together and tie up some loose ends.

NEW IN THIS EDITION

First and most important, every chapter has been updated to reflect substantial changes in this field in the past few years. Due to the increasing number of people in the world who are living into their 70s, 80s, and later, the study of adult development and aging has become extremely popular in both the academic world and among the general public. There has been an increase in research and publications, and an increase in college and university programs for students who are interested in working with aging adults. The increase in research interest and funding has resulted in the development of new technologies, new research paradigms, and new subfields of study. Although it is dizzying to keep up with all the changes, it is exciting to be part of it, and I have included some of the most interesting new work in this edition of the book.

Some of the changes that have occurred since the last edition have been in the classroom. Students taking adulthood and aging courses these days are more diverse. They come from a variety of countries and a variety of cultural groups within the United States. For many, English is often a second language. Classes are no longer made up mostly of psychology majors. To respond to these changes, I have included a little more explanation of basic terms within the text and almost doubled the number of glossary entries while keeping the level of writing and content the same as before. Another change I have found in the classroom is that many students taking these courses have a personal interest in the topic, being either aging adults themselves or family members of aging adults. Because of this, I have included some self-help books in the selected readings section and added more applied research in some of the chapters. The chapter divisions have stayed basically the same as in the third edition, but the chapter on individual differences is gone, with the material being dispersed throughout the relevant chapters.

There has also been a personnel change with this edition, although I hope you will find it a minor change. Helen L. Bee has found that her journey of adulthood has brought her so many new roles as she approached retirement that she has decided to devote more time to those adventures and less to writing. Although the book is still clearly her book, I was asked to revise it for this edition. I have used Dr. Bee's books both as a student and as a professor, and I have tried above all to preserve her basic framework, philosophy, and tone. I would welcome your comments.

HIGHLIGHTS OF CHANGES AND ADDITIONS

Theories of aging have been updated to exclude some that have fallen into disuse and to include updated research findings on the most promising theories. This section is no longer divided into categories of theories because new research findings have blurred those boundaries.

The section on **body changes** has been expanded to include some of the ways in which these changes can be prevented or remedied. A table on **body weight** is included to allow easy calculation of body mass index, and new USDA recommendations on weight gain are given.

Information on **sexual activity** has been expanded to include new information that shows exactly which sexual responses change with age and what those changes are. This section also includes a model of factors that determine whether or not older adults will be sexually active or not.

The table on **calculating your own longevity** has been updated or reflect recent research. A section on residential options for older adults has been added.

The section on health and aging has more information on **Alzheimer's disease**, and the mental health section has expanded coverage of mental disorders that occur at various ages. There is also updated information on individual differences in health.

The chapter formerly known as Intellectual Changes, expanded and renamed Cognitive Changes, now includes new research on **adult cognition**. In addition, a section has been added on **human factors research**, and a recent theoretical approach to the study of wisdom using a **theory of mind** explanation is included.

There is an update on gender roles and stereotypes to include Bem's **social schema theory**, and also a new framework for **theories of love**, new research on **adult attachment**, more research on **homosexual partnerships** in middle and late adulthood, and a new section on **sibling relationships** across adulthood.

The chapter on career paths includes new research on change (or lack of change) in **job performance** with age, and new theoretical ideas about **women's career paths**, **women and retirement**, and the **economic problems of older women**.

The chapter on personality includes some new **behavior genetic research**, and the chapter on stress has new health psychology findings on **stress and social support** as factors in health and healing.

I have continued to use **critical thinking questions** throughout the chapters and also **summary tables** of empirical findings that show principal changes or continuities of different abilities or attributes with age, **chapter-ending summaries**, highlighted terms that are defined in the **glossary**, and an annotated list of **suggested readings** at the end of each chapter.

SOME BOUQUETS

I appreciate the comments and the suggestions of the reviewers who have offered their wisdom at various stages of the writing process. Their insights have been invaluable. Thanks go to: Leslie D. Frazier, *Florida International University;* Paul W. Foos, *The University of North Carolina at Charlotte;* Roger Baumgarte, *Withrop University;* Donna Frick-Horbury, *Appalachian State University;* Andrea D. Clements, *East Tennesse State Univeristy;* Kathleen V. Fox, *Salisbury State University;* Samuel W. Cochran, *University of Texas at San Antonio;* and Virginai G. Gonzalez, *Columbia University.*

A huge bouquet goes to Helen L. Bee, who has been helpful, supportive, encouraging, trusting, and every bit as warm and witty in person as she is on the pages of her books. When I began this revision project, I thought of it as "a piece of cake" because of the strong reader approval the book enjoys, but partway into the revision I realized how difficult the job would be. For a long time I simply added new research, which of course made the book much too long. The Helen gave her advice: *Don't hesitate cutting whole sections; that's as important as adding new material.* So I did, although the first time was difficult. I truly hope the book now reflects the best of both of us.

Thanks also go to my family, who were patient and helpful through the last year, especially my husband, David Bjorklund, who managed to be enthusiastically supportive of this project even though he was revising his own textbook at the time.

Two students, Monique Agnieszka Yenke and Sylvia Baquerizo, helped me with the library research during the summer term and gave me feedback on various chapters as undergraduate readers. I also freely tapped the brain of a former high school science teacher who is currently a graduate student in neuropsychology, Mary Alice Ross. She gave me great suggestions on the more technical chapters which allowed me to be more accurate and use smaller words. Jean Bernholtz, good friend and clinical psychologist, advised me on the sections about mental health.

Finally, much thanks goes to my editor, Anita Castro, who has been a combination cheerleader and counselor throughout the project.

Barbara R. Bjorklund
Ft. Lauderdale, Florida

DEFINING THE JOURNEY: SOME ASSUMPTIONS, DEFINITIONS, AND METHODS

CHAPTER 1

Some of you reading this are just beginning the journey of your own adult life; some of you are partway along the road, having traveled through your 20s, 30s, or perhaps 40s, 50s, or beyond. Whatever your age, you *are* traveling, moving through the years and through the changes and transformations that come with the years. We do not all follow the same itinerary on this journey; you may spend a long time in one country that I do not visit at all; I may make an unusual side trip. Or we may visit the same places but experience them very differently. If you and I both visited Paris, we would not see precisely the same sights or eat the same food or—more important—come away with precisely the same impressions or understandings. You might be impressed by the beauty of the city but be negatively affected by one encounter with a rude waiter. I might find the people charming and the city remarkable but have my impression colored by my frustration at trying to use my limited French.

Every journey is unique. No two adult lives are exactly alike. Still, there have to be some common themes or there would be no reason for a book on adult development. Amidst the variability, there are some typical itineraries, some commonly shared experiences, some shared lessons or tasks. My task is to explore both—both the uniqueness and the common ground of adult lives. One person's journey can perhaps help illustrate both:

> It seems in retrospect that I have uprooted myself every five to seven years and gone off in a different direction. Sometimes these changes have been physical, moving from place to place; sometimes they have been inner changes.

> After college, I completed a Ph.D. in four years and started off on a traditional academic career with a first job at Clark University in Worcester, Massachusetts, and then a shift to the University of Washington, in Seattle, changing jobs mostly because I was dying to get back to the Pacific Northwest, where I had been raised and where my friends and family all were. I spent a total of eight years being a young professor, doing all the customary things: teaching huge classes as well as seminars, "doing" research, sitting on endless committees, and having anxiety attacks about whether I'd get tenure or not (I did). I loved the teaching, eventually enjoyed the research, loathed the committee meetings and the anxiety, and in the end disliked the life of a professor as a whole. After a year's sabbatical during which I went around the world looking at child care arrangements in other countries (Russia, Israel, Scandinavia, France, and spots in between), I resigned my tenured job. For me, the "average day" of a professor

contained too many things I did not like and too few that brought pleasure or satisfaction. And it was too much the life of the mind, too narrow a preoccupation. So at the age of 32, to the astonishment and consternation of a great many people, I quit, having no clear idea of how I would make a living, but knowing that whatever it was, it would not be a traditional academic job.

Shortly afterward I married and moved with my husband and his two children (aged 3 and 11 at the time) to a small island north of Seattle, where we lived for six years. I adopted the children and settled into full-time motherhood as well as into marriage. In retrospect, I also think of this as my *back to the land* phase, although it was much more than that. I began to write books as a way to earn a living, which turned out to be both enjoyable and successful. I spent three years at the thankless but fascinating community job of school board director, grew a huge garden, learned how to can and how to make bread and butter and jam. It is difficult to exaggerate the pleasure I felt each fall at the sight of the shelves all stacked with canning jars filled with colorful produce—green beans, tomatoes, peaches, blackberry and raspberry jam, applesauce. In those same years I also grew up in some quite different ways and discovered some parts of myself that logic didn't touch.

Unfortunately, the marriage did not hold together. Eventually, I moved back to Seattle, where I began work on some research with colleagues, began teaching again part time, and generally stuck my toe back into the traditional academic waters. At the same time I became much more interested in what I now think of as the *inner journey,* the search for understanding of what each of us is all about. Over the next few years I began to read the literature of mysticism, meditation became part of my daily routine, and I struggled with the problem of applying fundamental ethical principles to my everyday living. My friendships deepened, my capacity to care for others seemed to grow, my willingness to make commitments to others expanded.

And just when I was sure that there would be no more romance in my life, sure that I would be able to find much contentment in solitude, I fell in love again and moved to the Midwest to live with this new love—a man who is, ironically, a university professor. This shift has not only taken me away from my beloved Northwest and my family, it has brought a whole new set of lessons about intimacy, about friendships, about independence and dependence.

Something else began to happen, too, in my middle 50s. I felt a whole lot freer from the constraints of all those expectations that seemed to dominate my earlier life. Of course, it helped that my youngest child was through with college and launched into independence, so some of the responsibilities of being a parent were almost completed. But it was more than that. It was a sense that I *know* better who I was, and could *be* that person with greater freedom and ease. I no longer felt that I needed to bend myself into some other sort of shape to fit into the expected molds—whether it is the mold of "young professor" or the mold of "wife" or "mother." When I turned 50 I decided I was old enough to start being seriously eccentric—and then had to laugh when my friends all told me that I had been eccentric for quite some time!

Having freed myself this way from molds and expectations, I chose in my 50s to devote more and more of my time working as a volunteer for various nonprofit groups, including the choir I have sung with for many years, several other arts groups, political candidates, and a spiritual camp in Washington State. This work brings me deep satisfaction on many levels, not the least of which is the delight at being able to help make things run better. In the role of manager of my choir, I have helped put the group in the black by writing successful grants, commissioning new music, and making a first CD. It feels quite wonderful. It also feels a lot like a full-time job! So rather than give up the pleasure of volunteering, I have chosen to reduce my professional work by bringing colleagues into the job of text writing. For this edition of *The Journey of Adulthood*, I have had a fine (younger!) collaborator, Barbara Bjorklund, who has taken to the task as a duck to water.

Next spring I turn 60 and will retire from my full-time writing job, leaving all my time for whatever volunteer work I may choose, as well as time for naps, reading trashy books, and taking more walks with friends. I plan to celebrate with a huge party full of singing. I am sure that I have vastly more growing to do, but I am looking forward with relish to the many good years still ahead of me.

As you may well have guessed, this is my own life I am describing. Most of this is taken from the description I wrote for my college twenty-fifth reunion yearbook, with some updating for the years since. Since the women in my family live to be *very* old (typically, into their late 90s), I am past the middle of my expected span of years, but with the likelihood of many more years ahead.

Chances are good that my journey and yours have many differences. I chose a fairly high-powered career at a time when it was not so common for women to do that, and then I changed gears professionally in an unusually radical way. I married late and have no natural-born children. These deviations from the norm are obvious. Describing them may be useful for introducing myself to you so that you can have at least a brief acquain-

BETWEEN HER 40s AND HER 80s, this woman (who happens to have been my grandmother) changed in many outward ways. But are there ways in which she also stayed the same? Certainly *she* had a sense of continuity, of taking herself along through the years.

tance with the person who will be talking to you in these pages, but they are not important in themselves. What is much more interesting, to me at least, are the possible common themes and key issues about adult development that may be hidden behind the obvious variability of our experiences. Let me point to a few of those issues.

First, when I think about myself, and read what I wrote, I experience both a sense of continuity and a sense of change. I'm still very much an intellectual, so that is constant. Yet I feel that my relationships with others have changed greatly. Is this typical? How much do people really change in adulthood? Most of us like to *think* that we are growing and maturing. But are we really? How much do we just take ourselves with us through the years, bringing the same patterns, the same styles to each new situation? This issue of continuity versus change will form one of the major themes of this book.

A second issue that may have struck you as you read my brief life history is the occurrence of episodes, phases, or even stages. I established stable life patterns, then reassessed them and changed, only to establish a new life pattern for a number of years. And each of these periods or stages seemed to be focused on a different set of tasks, goals, or issues: getting a career started and achieving success; rearing a family and exploring the tenderer side of myself; searching for the reasons, the meaning; accepting myself as I am. Is this type of life pattern typical? Is adult life made up of phases or stages? If it is, are these stages shared by all adults? Are the tasks and issues the same for all 20-year-olds, or all 40-year-olds, or all 70-year-olds? Is there, in other words, a predictable or expectable rhythm to adult life? This theme, too, will recur repeatedly in the pages ahead.

Still a third theme has to do with inner versus outer changes. My life has gone through a variety of "outer" changes—shifts in the jobs I held, in the people I lived with, the roles I tried to fill with those people. I went from student to professor to wife and parent to author and researcher, and again to wife. At the same time I changed physically: my hair turned prematurely white, I gained and then lost weight, I lost fitness and then regained it (several times!). All of these changes can be seen by someone observing from the outside, and represent, in a sense, an "outer journey" through the adult years.

But we can talk about an inner journey as well—a set of changes that are experienced by the individual but that may not be so obvious to someone on the outside. My own sense of growing up is one such inner change, as is the shift I experienced from a preoccupation with success to a preoccupation with inner growth and spiritual development.

I do not at all mean to imply that these inner and outer changes are independent of one another. They are not, as we will see again and again through the book. The shifts we all experience in the roles we fill (e.g., student, spouse, parent, young worker, older worker, mentor, friend) affect the way we feel about ourselves and the issues that concern us. I am freer now to "be myself" in part precisely because my youngest child is grown and flown, not because I am in my 60s. Yet physical aging, too, can influence our inner processing. The moment at age 38 when I realized that walking up a flight of stairs made me puff was not just a recognition of a physical change; it was a shock to my image of myself. I felt middle-aged for the first time, and that realization changed my inner perspective.

The influences go the other way, too. The inner shifts influence our outward behavior in important ways as well. Thinking of myself as middle-aged resulted in a new exercise program, weight loss, and a significant change in my appearance. Another adult may change jobs at age 30 or at 40 because of a major shift in the issues that preoccupy him or her. One of my tasks in this book is to try to sort out the causal links between the inner and outer threads of change.

DESCRIPTION AND EXPLANATION

I can also cast the issues to be dealt with in this book in terms of two types of questions: descriptive and explanatory. The first task with any scientific endeavor is description. What happens? What kinds of changes occur over the adult years? What kinds of continuities exist? Are these changes or continuities widely shared or universal, or alternatively, are there subgroups that seem to share distinctive patterns of change and continuity? To understand development, we must be able to answer such questions about each facet or aspect of human functioning: the way the body works; the way the mind works; the kinds of roles and relationships adults have; the inner patterns, such as personality or temperament. Merely describing such change and continuity is no small task. And as you will discover very quickly, we lack the data to provide good, basic description in a great many areas. Still, we can begin.

Equally important are questions that ask "how" or "why." We will be searching for causes, both for shared patterns of change and for individual variations. For example, one of the clear pieces of descriptive information we now have is that adults experience some decline in the speed with which they can do mental tasks, beginning sometime in their 40s or 50s. By age 60 or 70, this difference in speed is quite noticeable. How can we account for this? Such a loss of speed could certainly be the result of one or more physical changes, such as the speed with which the nervous system conducts signals. But slower performance of mental tasks could also result from a change in the amount of time that older adults, compared to younger adults, spend doing complex mental tasks. Maybe they are just out of practice. Still a third possibility is that older adults may be much less motivated to compete or to strive to succeed at such tasks. Working quickly may simply not be a high value.

Virtually every pattern of change over adulthood that we can identify or describe has such multiple possible explanations. In most instances we are a very long way from understanding the causes of the patterns we observe. But psychologists and sociologists who study adult development have at least reached some preliminary agreement on three major categories of influences that help to explain both the ways in which we tend to be alike in our adult journeys and the ways in which we differ from one another: (1) shared, age-graded change; (2) cohort effects; and (3) unique experiences (Baltes, Reese, & Lipsitt, 1980).

EXPLAINING CHANGE IN ADULTHOOD

Shared, Age-Graded Changes

Shared, age-graded change is probably what you assume is meant when you hear the phrase *adult development*. These are changes linked to age in some way and shared by most or all adults in every generation. There are at least three factors or processes that might produce such age-graded changes.

Biologically Influenced Changes. Some of the changes we see in adults are shared by all of us because we are all biological organisms undergoing natural aging processes. Many such changes are easy to see, such as hair gradually turning gray or skin becoming wrinklier. Others are not visible directly from the outside but occur inwardly, such as the loss of muscle tissue, which results in a gradual loss of physical strength, or reduced efficiency of the neural connections in the brain. The *rate* at which such physical changes occur varies quite a lot from one adult to another, but the *sequence* seems to be highly similar.

Such biological explanations of adult change have not been terribly popular, perhaps because most of us, including the researchers and the theorists, don't like to think about our own physical aging. But we need to keep in mind that we each have an aging body—that there are common chemical and biological changes that occur with aging, a kind of **biological clock,** ticking away in the background.

These biological changes affect us indirectly as well as directly. For example, my loss of fitness in my late 30s contributed to my sense of being "middle-aged." To be sure, I was able to improve my fitness, but the very fact that I could stay fit with little effort at 20 but had to take up an exercise program to maintain my aerobic capacity when I was 38 made it clear to me that some underlying change had occurred and that awareness had a psychological effect.

Shared Experiences. There is also a **social clock** that operates to produce shared change (Helson, Mitchell, & Moane, 1984). In any given culture, the social clock defines a sequence of normal adult-life experiences, such as the timing of marriage and childbearing, or the typical timing of retirement. Sociologist Matilda White Riley (1976, 1986) points out that virtually all societies are organized into **age strata,** periods in the life span that have shared demands, expectations, or privileges. In any culture, adults have quite different expectations of, and attitudes toward, 18, 35, and 60-year-olds. They are expected to do different things, to form different types of relationships, to have different pleasures. They are afforded different amounts of recognition, responsibility, or power.

CRITICAL THINKING

Pause for a moment and think about these three age groups. How would you describe each group? What expectations do you have about each? What privileges do you think they each have in your culture or subculture?

In American culture, for example, attitudes about the elderly are generally negative, a form of what gerontologists call **ageism**—analogous to sexism or racism (Palmore, 1990): "out to pasture," "over the hill," "washed up." Older adults are routinely described or perceived as infirm, cranky, sexless, childlike, senile, or useless, and these stereotypes are held by young and old alike. These views have changed somewhat in recent years as health and vigor among the older groups has improved and their political power has increased. But these attitudes have been an integral part of this culture and others for many decades. In sharp contrast are cultures such as those of Japan and China, in which older adults are by tradition afforded the status of *elder,* and treated with *more* respect than other age groups, a form of positive ageism (Maeda, 1993). These differences in attitude help to shape each culture's social structure and its social policies, as well as affecting individual relationships between adults of different ages. Such collections of attitudes toward and expectations and responsibilities for each age constitute the **age norms** for a given culture or subculture. Over the course of adulthood, each person passes through such a sequence of age strata, and this shared pathway tends to shape all adult lives into common trajectories.

Other than ageism, one of the most significant elements in age stratification and age norms in virtually all cultures is the pattern of experiences associated with marriage and family life—what sociologists call the **family life cycle.** In the United States and most countries of Western Europe, for example, about 90 percent of adults marry (Goldman, 1993; Popenoe, 1993). The great majority (about 90 percent) also have children. Once the first child is born, most parents are locked into a sequence of experiences linked to the child's developmental stage: infancy, toddlerhood, school age, adolescence, and finally, departure from home. Each of these periods in the child's life makes a different set of demands on parents, and this sequence of demands shapes 20 or 30 years of most adults' lives.

Other widely shared age-related cultural patterns may also be powerful influences on adult life. To take just one more example: For the past several generations at least,

THE MANY GENERATIONS of the Limon family gather every year for a reunion. What age strata are represented here? What different roles or expectations do you associate with each of these age strata?

adults in industrialized countries have become more physically and mentally sedentary with age. Our jobs are becoming more automated, we read less, move less. So the common experience of lowered fitness in one's 30s or 40s may be caused not by inevitable body changes but rather, may be a side effect of the age norm of a more sedentary life in middle age.

Obviously, shared developmental changes based on the social clock are much less likely to be universal than are those based on the biological clock. But *within* any given culture, shared age-graded experiences can help us explain the common threads of adult development.

Internal Change Processes. At a deeper level, there may be shared inner changes resulting from the way we respond to the pressures of the biological and social clocks. An example from childhood development makes the point particularly clearly: A baby begins to walk at about 12 months of age as the result of a whole series of universally shared biological changes. But learning to walk, in turn, triggers a set of psychological changes, including a greater sense of independence. In a similar way, the common tasks of adult life, and the common biological changes, may create a kind of agenda for inner psychological change.

For example, one theory suggests that in early adulthood, particularly after the birth of children, traditional masculine or feminine qualities are exaggerated and emphasized. Then at midlife, after the children are grown and gone, men and women both seek to "balance" their feminine and masculine qualities more completely (Giele, 1982; Gutmann, 1987). For most of us, this would mean expanding the expression of the less practiced aspect. If this is true, we might find that men at midlife become more emotionally expressive and warm while women become more assertive and independent. In fact, there is some evidence that such a gender-role crossover does occur in many cultures, as I'll describe more fully later. For now my point is simply that this is an example of the kind of internal change that many theorists have both searched for and found most intriguing: one linked to age but neither caused by biological change nor entirely defined by age norms.

If we are to understand adult development, we must eventually be able to sort out the effects of and interactions among these several types of age-graded changes. If we observe the same pattern of change between ages 20 and 60 in many cultures, and in many generations in the same culture, we still will not know whether that particular change is biologically based, culturally defined, or results from some natural or inevitable internal psychological change, or some combination of the three.

Cultural and Cohort Effects

Less universally shared experiences may also shape adult development for subgroups, such as different cultures or generations within a culture. Cultures vary enormously in the ways in which they structure the expected life pattern: the typical age of marriage or childbearing, the typical number of children, the roles of men and women, caste or class structures, and the like. As one example, cultures in which marriage is virtually universal, such as Japan (where 97 percent of adults marry) (Goldman, 1993), will have a different effect on individual adult lives than will cultures in which patterns of marriage and childbearing are more varied. I am well aware of the fact that virtually all of the research and theorizing we have about adult development is based on studies of only a few cultures—especially, Western cultures. It is quite likely that some of the patterns of change or development that we have come to think of as universal are in fact culture specific, a possibility that I will return to again and again throughout this book.

THE VIETNAM WAR MEMORIAL has helped to heal some cultural wounds, but the cohort that came to adulthood during that war time were strongly marked by the experience. Is there any equivalent current-day circumstance that you think has as powerful an effect on today's 20-year-olds?

But even *within* a culture there are significant variations in adult life experience from one generation to the next. The key concept is that of a **cohort,** a term used by social scientists to describe a group of persons born within some narrow band of years, who thus share certain cultural influences and historical experiences. The term is roughly synonymous with the word *generation,* except that a generation normally refers to a 20-year span, whereas a cohort can refer to a much smaller band of years.

For our purposes, the concept of a cohort is important for two reasons: (1) It helps to explain how and why adults of any given era will be like one another in their values, life experiences, or attitudes; and (2) it can help explain *differences* in attitudes, values, skills, or life experiences that we may see between groups of adults of different ages. I can make both these points clearer with some examples.

One relatively easy way to see the effect of variations in the experiences of adjacent cohorts is to look at major social upheavals, such as (in our culture) the Great Depression of the 1930s, World War II, or the Vietnam War. To be sure, everyone who was alive during one of these eras was affected in *some* way by each event, but because these events hit each cohort at a different age, the effects are remarkably cohort specific. Glen Elder's research on the Great Depression is a wonderful example (Elder, 1974, 1978; Elder, Liker, & Cross, 1984). He has found that those who were teenagers in the depths of the Depression showed fewer long-term effects than did those who had been in early elementary school when the Depression struck full force. The younger cohort spent a greater portion of their childhood under conditions of economic hardship. The hardship altered family interaction patterns, educational opportunities, and even the personalities of the children, so that the negative effects could still be detected in adulthood. Those who were teenagers during the Depression did not show negative effects in adult life; on the contrary, some of them seemed to have grown from the experience of hardship and to show more independence and initiative as adults as a result. Thus two cohorts, rather close in actual age, experienced the same historical event differently because they were different ages at the time.

The same point emerges from a study by Abigail Stewart and Joseph Healy, Jr. (1989) of a group of women who had all been in graduate school between 1945 and 1951 but who actually represented three different cohorts: those who were fully grown before World War II (born between 1906 and 1914), those who reached adulthood *during* the war (born 1918 to 1922), and those who reached adulthood *after* the war (born 1925 to 1929). Those in the oldest group had grown up during the Depression, when self-reliance and financial security were strongly valued but when traditional family values were also very strong. But the value structure of that era also included the belief that a woman must choose between a career and a home; she could not do both and do justice to the important family values. In contrast, the women from the last of the three cohorts had been adolescents during the war, at a time when it was very common for women to work. This cohort then spent their young adulthood in the postwar period when women were expected to devote themselves gladly to family life. Stewart and Healy argued that these women, conditioned by both experiences, fully expected to marry and have children but also valued work and thought it "natural" for women. Women of this cohort believed that one could have both career and family. When the life histories of these women were examined, the contrast was clear: Only one-fourth of those in the earliest cohort ever had children, whereas 88 percent of those in the latest cohort gave birth to at least one child.

An example that may be a bit closer to home for many of you would be the effect of the Baby Boom—that major increase in birth rate after World War II that peaked in

CRITICAL THINKING

What formative experiences do you think shaped or are shaping your own cohort? Or to put it another way, how is the experience of your cohort different in formative ways from the experiences of older and younger cohorts?

the United States between 1955 and 1965. The unusual size of this cohort has made a significant difference in many arenas of adult life. For example, those in this group have experienced greater competition for spaces in college and for jobs. My own cohort, which came just before the Baby Boom, is far smaller. Thus when I finished graduate school, colleges and universities were expanding rapidly in anticipation of the increased student population to come. Job opportunities were numerous. But when those born in the later stages of the Baby Boom hit the job market, jobs were scarce. A particular cohort, then, has not only lived through specific historical or cultural events but has lived through them *at the same time in their lives.* The timing of the events interacts with the tasks, issues, or age norms for that age, producing unique patterns of influence for each cohort and helping to create common adult-life trajectories for those born into the same cohort. Thus the concept gives us a powerful tool in understanding the similarities in adult lives.

At the same time, the concept of a cohort has been enormously helpful in explaining differences as well. In particular, it helps us to differentiate between *real* developmental change, universal or nearly universal changes with age that are grounded in basic biology or in common psychological processes, and *apparent* change, which is really not individual change at all but merely cohort differences.

Examples of Cohort Effects. One well-known example comes from studies of IQ in adulthood. Does IQ change (go up or down) as we age, or is it stable? Early researchers studying IQ in adulthood (Matarazzo, 1972; Wechsler, 1955) compared average IQ scores of adults of different ages. They found that the older the group, the lower the average score. Alas, it looked as if we all declined in mental power as we got older. But there is a cohort effect lurking in the data: Each successively older cohort in our culture has had fewer average years of education than did the preceding cohort. So it could be education, not age, that is related to performance on IQ tests. Indeed, as you'll see in Chapter 5, there is a good deal of evidence to support such an interpretation.

Take a look at Figure 1.1 for a second example. The data for this figure come from interviews in 1976 with a nationally representative sample of U.S. adults (Veroff, Douvan, & Kulka, 1981). Among other things, each subject was asked a set of questions about

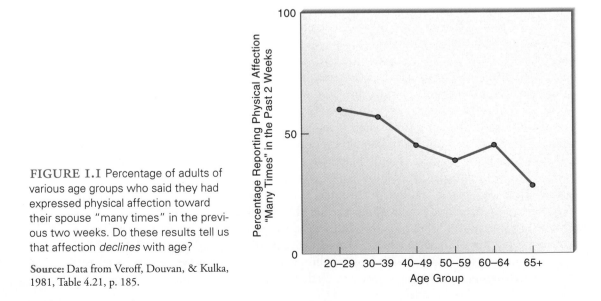

FIGURE 1.1 Percentage of adults of various age groups who said they had expressed physical affection toward their spouse "many times" in the previous two weeks. Do these results tell us that affection *declines* with age?

Source: Data from Veroff, Douvan, & Kulka, 1981, Table 4.21, p. 185.

his or her marriage, including a question about how frequently he or she had expressed physical affection toward his or her spouse in the past two weeks. The figure shows the percentage in each age group who choose the option "many times" in answer to this question. You can see that fewer older adults than younger ones reported that such affection was frequent.

How should we interpret such a result? Does it mean that marriages become less affectionate over time? That's certainly one option, and it may well be true. But it is also possible that there is a cohort effect involved. The older groups in this study are not just older, they are also members of cohorts who grew up in an era when physical affection was perhaps more constrained than it is in more recent cohorts. With these data alone, we simply cannot choose between these alternatives.

A **cohort effect,** in general, is any difference between groups of adults of varying ages that is due not to age or aging or to any other developmental process but simply to the fact that the different age groups have grown up in different historical or cultural circumstances. As we look at descriptions of age-related differences in adulthood in the remainder of this book, we need to be steadily alert for possible cohort effects. Cohort differences make it harder to develop broad, general statements or universal principles about adult development. But such differences are not just "noise" in the system. They are interesting in and of themselves. They tell us something about how major social forces shift the developmental patterns for adults, knowledge that adds to our growing information about the way in which specific experience affects the journey of adulthood.

Unique, Nonshared Events

If we take this argument one step further, it is clear that we also need to understand the impact of those *individual* experiences that may be formative in the adult life of any one person. Having your parents die when you are in your 20s or 30s, a significant illness early in life, the early death of a spouse or a child, losing a job, marrying very early or very late (or not at all), having a special teacher in high school who inspires you to go on for a specific kind of training—all of these and hundreds of experiences like them can alter the pathway a particular person will follow through adulthood. Even such experiences as marital separation or divorce, which are now widely shared, belong in this category of "unique or nonshared events," since divorce is neither universal nor age-graded.

Timing of Experience. Many psychologists and sociologists have suggested that the *timing* of such unique events is a particularly salient element in the equation. Bernice Neugarten (1979), for example, argued that events that are *on-time,* that follow a normal expectable life cycle, are less disruptive or difficult than those that are *off-time.* So having your parents die when you are in your 20s (which is off-time) is more difficult to deal with, more likely to lead to significant life disruption, than is the death of your parents when you are in your 40s or 50s. Similarly, losing your job in your 30s is harder to handle than is retirement at 65. In some sense, this is another way of saying that those adults who deviate in significant ways from the age norms of their culture or their cohort are likely to show more distinctive or unusual patterns of development than do those whose lives more closely follow the culturally defined age norms.

Obviously, in a book like this I cannot begin to explore the effects of every possible combination of unique and shared experiences in the lives of adults. But I can and will try to search for any underlying patterns that may exist that will help us understand types of unique events, their timing, and their combined effects.

CRITICAL THINKING

Does this hypothesis about the effects of on-timeness and off-timeness make sense to you? Can you think of examples in your own life or in the lives of others you know?

EXPLAINING CONTINUITY IN ADULTHOOD

In my discussion so far, I have been focusing on the alternative explanations of *change*. Such an emphasis is entirely reasonable, since, after all, the subject of this book is adult *development*. But each of us also has a profound sense of continuity, a sense of "staying the same," throughout our adult years. To understand adulthood, we must also explore and understand such continuity. Not surprisingly, just as there are both biological and environmental explanations of change over time, so we have both physical and experiential explanations of continuity as well.

Biological Explanations of Continuity: Behavior Genetics

Each of us inherits, at conception, a unique combination of genes. A very large percentage of these genes is identical from one member of the species to the next, which is why our developmental patterns are alike—why children all over the world walk at about 12 months, why we go through puberty in our early teens and menopause in our 40s or 50s. But our genetic inheritance is individual as well as collective. The study of genetic contributions to individual behavior, called **behavior genetics,** has been a particularly hot research topic in recent years. We now know that specific heredity affects a remarkably broad range of behaviors, including cognitive abilities such as IQ, physical characteristics such as height or body shape or a tendency to fatness or leanness, personality characteristics, and even pathological behavior, such as a tendency toward alcoholism, schizophrenia, or depression (Plomin, DeFries, McClearn, & Rutter, 1997).

In searching for such genetic influences on variations in adult behavior, behavior geneticists rely primarily on studies of identical and fraternal twins. Identical twins develop from the same sperm and ovum and thus share exactly the same genetic patterning; fraternal twins, in contrast, each develop from a separate sperm and ovum. They are therefore no more alike than are any other pair of siblings, except that they have shared the same prenatal environment and grew up in the same sequential niche within the family. If identical twins are more like one another on any given trait than are fraternal twins, that would demonstrate the influence of heredity on that trait.

An especially useful version of the twin study is to compare identical and fraternal twins who have been reared apart from one another. If identical twins are still more like one another on some dimension, despite having grown up in different environments, we have even clearer evidence of a genetic contribution for that trait.

One particularly rich set of data has come from Sweden, where a twin registry has been maintained since 1886. Over 25,000 pairs of twins born between 1886 and 1958 are listed, including some who were reared apart. In one recent analysis, for example, Bergeman et al. (1993), had 214 pairs of identical twins and 338 pairs of fraternal twins complete a questionnaire that measures various facets of personality. The strategy is then to use a statistic called a *correlation* (which I will describe in more detail shortly) to look at the degree of similarity of each pair of twins on the various dimensions of personality. The closer the correlation is to +1.00, the more similar the two sets of scores are. Table 1.1 gives the results for two of the dimensions they studied, **openness to experience,** which reflects aspects of curiosity, imagination, and intellect, and **conscientiousness,** which reflects aspects of planfulness, efficiency, and organization. You can see that identical twins, whether reared together or apart, were more alike than were fraternal twins on both dimensions, particularly on openness to experience, showing that there is a genetic component to those personality dimensions.

None of these characteristics is totally fixed by heredity. The environment in which a child grows up has a good deal of influence as well. But to the extent that such qualities are stable over the life course—and they are, as you'll see in Chapter 9—such inherited characteristics create a base of consistency over time. No matter

TABLE 1.1 **Correlations Between the Personalities Test Scores of Identical and Fraternal Twins: A Behavior–Genetic Approach**

	Openness to Experience	Conscientiousness
Identical twins reared together	.51	.47
Identical twins reared apart	.43	.19
Fraternal twins reared together	.14	.11
Fraternal twins reared apart	.23	.10

Source: Bergeman et al., 1993, Table 3, p. 168.

what time it is on the "biological clock" or the "social clock," each of us will bring his or her own array of inborn characteristics or tendencies to the tasks and problems confronting him, or her.

Environmental Sources of Continuity

Such consistent qualities then interact with the environment in various ways to promote still more individual consistency. For example, each of us tends to choose occupations or activities that match our personality or our skills, and we avoid those activities we think we will be bad at. In this way we reinforce the initial patterns and protect ourselves from pressure to modify our behavior.

Our habitual patterns also trigger reactions from others around us that tend to perpetuate the patterns still further. An adult who complains and criticizes is likely to draw negative reactions from others, which may further strengthen the person's complaining behavior. A person with a more positive attitude elicits positive responses, thus strengthening the original attitude and fostering continuity over time.

A wonderful illustration of how various pressures toward continuity can operate jointly comes from research by Avshalom Caspi and his colleagues (Caspi & Elder, 1988; Caspi, Elder, & Bem, 1987, 1988). Caspi has studied the life histories of 284 children born in the 1920s—the same group of subjects, by the way, that Elder studied in his research on the effects of the Great Depression. Among these subjects was a group who had been rated as "ill-tempered" as children. Caspi wanted to know what happened to these children as they moved into adulthood compared to more "even-tempered" boys.

It turned out that they had quite distinctive adult lives. They were twice as likely to be divorced by age 40 and completed fewer years of school than did their more even-tempered peers. Among those who had been drafted into the military, the ill-tempered boys had a lower military rank at the time of their discharge than did the even-tempered boys. They also had lower-status jobs and changed jobs more often. Interestingly, however, the pattern of greater job change turned out to be true only for those ill-tempered men in low-status jobs. Ill-tempered boys who achieved high-status jobs had no more difficulty in holding such a job than did their even-tempered peers. Where might such a difference come from? Caspi offers one explanation. He suggests that the major difficulty these men have is in dealing with any kind of authority figure. Higher-status jobs are likely to involve less supervision and thus less chance of eliciting the pattern of ill-temper. Those in low-status jobs, in contrast, have many opportunities for conflict with authority figures and tend to move from job to job.

Here we can see the operation of all the various types of pressures for continuity. Heredity doubtless plays some role in creating the initial pattern of ill-temper. But the pat-

CRITICAL THINKING

Can you think of examples in your own life that would illustrate this point? Do you choose activities that allow you to stay the same, or do you challenge yourself with new experiences?

tern persists because of the choices the person makes and because of environmental forces toward continuity. However, when the environment does *not* sustain the initial pattern, change can and does occur.

SOME DEFINITIONS

In these first pages, to get the discussion moving, I have used a variety of terms without defining them precisely: words such as *development, change, aging,* and *maturing.* Before I go further I need to pause and define some of these terms. At the very least we need terms for the following processes or concepts: (1) basic physiological change that is an inevitable accompaniment of the passage of years; (2) "improvements" that occur with age, such as greater personality flexibility or successful completion of a series of tasks or dilemmas; (3) "declines" that may occur with age (that may or may not be physiologically based), and (4) all other patterns of variation in behavior or attitudes that are associated or linked with age but that don't fit the other categories.

My choices for terms to describe these different patterns may not exactly fit your pre-conceived notions, but I will use these terms consistently throughout the book.

Adulthood. I will define adulthood as that period from age 18 to death. Eighteen is an arbitrary age, but it represents (in our culture at least) the time when young people graduate from high school, and many then immediately take on the duties and responsibilities of adulthood. I will use the phrase **young adulthood** to refer to the period between 18 and 40, **middle adulthood** to refer to the period between 40 and 65, and **old age** to refer to the remaining years. I will also follow the pattern now common among gerontologists and subdivide this final period into the **young old,** which refers to those between 65 and 75, and the **old old,** referring to those 75 and older, and the **oldest old,** describing those over 85.

THIS GREAT GRANDMOTHER is part of the fastest-growing age group in most Western countries—those over 85, who are often called the "oldest old."

Aging. To be consistent, I will use this term to describe simply the passage of years, although the everyday meaning also includes the notion of decline or "getting worse," as in "She's certainly aged since we saw her last, hasn't she?" I will make every effort to avoid that sort of implication for the word *aging*.

Maturation. This is a term used commonly in the study of children's development to refer to those process of change with age that are governed by underlying physiological processes, determined largely by the genetic code. We can speak, for example, of the maturational changes that underlie the infant's progression from sitting to crawling to walking, or the maturational changes of puberty. I will use the term in the same way in this book to describe any sequence of physical changes that appears to be governed by systematic, shared genetic or other biological processes. For example, the complex sequence of changes in sexual and reproductive functioning between age 40 and 60 (referred to most generally as the *climacteric* in both men and women, also called *menopause* in women) is a maturational change parallel to the changes of puberty. Note that *maturation,* in this sense, is quite different from the common parlance word *maturing,* which often connotes "becoming wiser" or "becoming psychologically better balanced." Any increase in wisdom or balance *might* be the result of fundamental maturational (physiological) processes but could also reflect any one of a host of other growth or development processes as well. Note also that a maturational change might involve either gain or loss. With increasing age, adults lose muscle tissue but gain ear size; we lose speed in nerve synapses but gain plaque in our blood vessels.

Development. In my use of the term *development* I am following, at least roughly, the definitions given by Heinz Werner and Bernard Kaplan (Kaplan, 1983; Werner & Kaplan, 1956), who define development in terms of increasingly higher, more integrated levels of functioning. Whether development in this sense of the word actually exists or not in adulthood is one of the key questions I will be asking in this book. Do some adults, or all adults, become "more mature," "wiser," more altruistic and compassionate? Obviously, the decision of what constitutes "better" or "more mature" is a question as much of values and philosophy as fact. But I am not content merely to describe strings of changes with age without at least addressing the question of value or "growth."

This use of the word *development,* I realize, does not fit well with common parlance. The word is used in normal conversation, and even among psychologists, to mean roughly "change with age" or "change over time." So you will have to make an effort to remember that when I use the term I do not mean it in this looser way, but much more narrowly to refer to only a subset of changes with age—those changes that arguably reflect the emergence of some more complex or more integrated system or structure.

Gain and Decline. These two terms I will use, as nonpejoratively as possible, to describe changes that involve increases or decreases in some function or skill over age. It is important to be clear about the fact that *development,* as I have defined it here, may result from either gains or declines. It is possible, for example, to gain in wisdom as a result of loss of health: illness causes some people to examine themselves and their lives in constructive and beneficial ways.

Change. Where it is not clear whether a pattern of variation with age is a gain, or a loss, or reflects some development, I will simply talk about change. Descriptions of change or stability will nearly always be the beginning point in our explorations of adulthood. What is the pattern of frequency and depth of friendship over the adult years? What is the pattern of change in visual acuity in older adults? What happens to scores on IQ tests over time in adulthood? All of these are questions at the descriptive level that call for data on change or stability over age. It is when we turn to the task of explanation that terms such as *maturation* or *development* are likely to enter the discussion. Is some observed change the result of biological maturation? Does it reflect some basic inner restructuring, some development? Or, might the difference that we observe between old and young be some kind of cohort effect?

FINDING THE ANSWERS: RESEARCH ON ADULT DEVELOPMENT

To answer questions like these is no simple task. Furthermore, as in any field, the specific decisions the investigator makes in designing any given study affect the breadth or clarity of the conclusions that can be drawn from that research. So it is important for you to know something about research methodology, if only so that you can be an intelligent consumer of research.

Suppose, for example, that I want to know something about changes or continuities in personal relationships over the adult years—relationships with the spouse, with other family members, or with friends. Or, suppose that I wanted to study memory over adulthood. Older adults frequently complain that they can't remember things as well any more. Is this a valid perception? Is there really a *loss* in memory in old age, or earlier?

How would I go about designing research to answer such questions? In every instance, there is a set of decisions:

* Should I study groups of people of different ages, or should I study the same group of people over time, or some combination of the two? This is a question dealing with basic **research design.**

* How will I measure memory, or the quality of relationships? Should I simply ask people to tell me how much difficulty they have remembering a new telephone number, or will I need a standardized instrument? How can I best inquire about relationships—with a questionnaire, or in an interview? These are questions of **research methodology.**

* How will I interpret the results? Is it enough merely to determine the average number of friends, or the average relationship satisfaction described by subjects of each age group? What else would I want to do to tease out some of the possible explanations? These are questions of **research analysis.**

RESEARCH DESIGN

Choosing a research design is perhaps the most crucial decision the researcher makes. This is true in any area of psychology or sociology, but there are special considerations when the subject of study is change or development with age. There are essentially three choices: (1) You can choose different groups of subjects at each of a series of ages and compare their responses, which is called a **cross-sectional design;** (2) you can study the *same* subjects over a period of time, observing whether their responses remain the same or change in systematic ways, which is called a **longitudinal design;** or (3) you can combine the two in any of several ways, collectively called **sequential designs.**

Cross-Sectional Designs

The essential characteristic of cross-sectional studies is that they include *different* groups of subjects at *different* ages. Each subject is tested only once. Such comparisons tell us about age *differences,* but—as you may have figured out from my discussion of cohort effects—they do not tell us directly about age *change.*

You've already seen one example in Figure 1.1. Figure 1.2 offers a second, based on results of several memory tests given to adults of various ages (Salthouse, 1991). In the digit span test they were read lists of numbers, one number per second, and then had to try to write the numbers down in the order they had heard them—a task rather like what you do when someone gives you a phone number and you try to remember it long enough to write it down or dial it. In the word span test, they heard a list of words (e.g., *dog, crayon, school*) and then had to write the words down in the order given. In reporting the results, Salthouse uses the performance of the 20-year-olds as a standard and then compares each succeeding age group to that norm, using standard deviation units. To give you some idea of the meaning of such a scale, a score 1 standard deviation below the 20-year-old norm would indicate a performance worse than all but 17 percent of the young group. These results appear to show a clear decline in memory with age. But because these are cross-sectional data, we cannot be sure of this conclusion. It is also possible that there are cohort effects at work, such as education differences among the cohorts.

Sociologists frequently use a variation of the cross-sectional design in which subjects are grouped not by age but by their stage in the family life cycle, such as comparing newlyweds, those with young children, and retired couples whose children are all launched. But because life-cycle stage and cohort are so strongly linked, any results from such comparisons leave us with the same kind of difficulty of interpretation.

Cross-sectional studies of either type can be extremely useful. They are relatively quick to do and can give us a glimpse of possible age differences. In this way, we may generate new hypotheses about the processes of continuity and change over adulthood. But in any cross-sectional design, age and cohort are totally *confounded*—that is, they vary simultaneously, so we cannot sort out their independent effects. Furthermore, cross-sectional research cannot tell us anything about *individual* consistency over time, because each subject is tested or interviewed only once. If what you want to know is whether 20-year-olds with especially good memories are still going to be among the best when they are 60 or 80, a cross-sectional study will be useless.

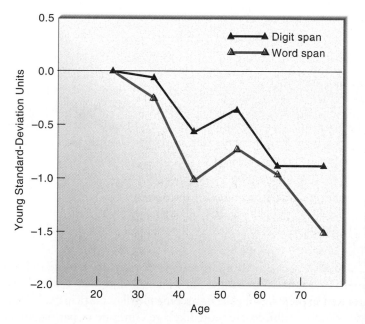

FIGURE 1.2 In this cross-sectional study, Salthouse measured both digit span (the number of numbers that can be correctly recalled in order) and word span. These results seem to indicate a decline in memory with age, but cross-sectional data like this can't tell us that for sure.

Source: Salthouse, 1991, Fig. 6.2, p. 224.

Longitudinal Designs

Longitudinal studies solve many of these problems because they follow the *same* subjects over time. They therefore allow us to look at change or consistency within the same individual. The typical procedure is to select a relatively small group of children or adults who are all roughly the same age at the beginning of the study, and then study them intensively and repeatedly as they move through some interesting period of years. Short-term longitudinal studies, following people over periods of several years, have become extremely common in research on both children and adults. Researchers studying grief reactions, for instance, frequently study newly widowed adults over several years to try to understand the changes in grieving over time (F. H. Norris & Murrell, 1990). Or researchers interested in marital relationships may study a group of newlywed pairs through the first year or two of marriage to study changes in interaction patterns or attitudes (Gottman, 1994a; Huston, McHale, & Crouter, 1986).

There are also a few very long-term longitudinal studies in which subjects have been followed from childhood into adulthood, or from early to middle adulthood, or from middle adulthood to old age. One of the most famous of these very long-term studies is the Berkeley Intergenerational Study, in which several hundred children born between 1918 and 1928 were followed until they were in their 50s or 60s (Eichorn, Clausen, Haan, Honzik, & Mussen, 1981). Data from this study have been used by many investigators to explore various hypotheses, including Elder in his studies of the Great Depression and Caspi in his studies of shy and ill-tempered boys. Other long-term studies include the Grant study of a group of Harvard men who attended college in the late 1930s and who were studied from college age into their 60s (Vaillant, 1977), a study by Helson (Helson & Moan, 1987; Helson & Stewart, 1994; Helson & Wink, 1992; Wink & Helson 1993) of a group of 1958 and 1960 graduates of Mills College followed from college age into their 50s, and studies of AT&T managers over a 20-year period in early adulthood (Bray & Howard, 1983). Each of these studies offers a remarkably rich body of information, albeit on a small (and not necessarily representative) group of individuals.

Longitudinal studies have many obvious advantages over cross-sectional designs. Most specifically because age and cohort are not confounded, any changes that we see are real changes, not just cohort differences, and nonchange represents real stability. For example, look at the data in Figure 1.3, from the Berkeley Intergenerational Study. In this case, Laura Carstensen (1992) went back to the transcripts of interviews conducted with these subjects when they were age 30, 40, and 50. Based on the transcripts, she rated each subject's comments about her (or his) relationship with her spouse along several dimensions, including frequency of interaction, satisfaction, and emotional closeness. You can see in the figure that all three were essentially stable over the 20-year period. When you compare these results to the data in Figure 1.1, you can see why cross-sectional data alone will never be sufficient to answer questions about change or continuity over time. To be sure, quite different measures are used in the two cases. It may be that physical affection does decline but that satisfaction and closeness do not. But the conclusions we are tempted to draw about the quality of marital interactions over adulthood are quite different in the two cases.

Despite the obvious advantages of longitudinal designs for answering the sort of questions we want to answer about adulthood, longitudinal studies are not the be-all and end-all. They suffer from several significant problems.

Selective Attrition and Dropout. One obvious difficulty is that it is impossible to keep in touch with all of the subjects over time. Some move and you can't find them again. Some decline to participate at later testing points. Some die or become too ill to participate. In general, the healthiest and best educated subjects are more likely to continue to participate in

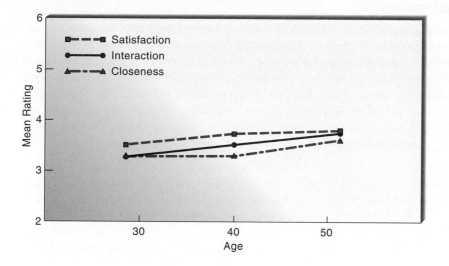

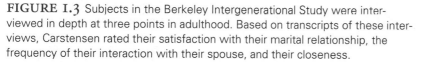

FIGURE 1.3 Subjects in the Berkeley Intergenerational Study were interviewed in depth at three points in adulthood. Based on transcripts of these interviews, Carstensen rated their satisfaction with their marital relationship, the frequency of their interaction with their spouse, and their closeness.

Source: Carstensen, 1992, Fig. 5, p. 336.

longitudinal research, so that over time your sample becomes more and more biased toward those with the best functioning, a type of **selective attrition.** This is a problem with all longitudinal research but is particularly troublesome in studies of the final decades of life. Since the least healthy older adults die, we may underestimate the degree of actual decline in some function (such as memory speed, or IQ, or whatever) because each succeeding test includes only those healthy enough to have survived (Siegler, McCarty, & Logue, 1982).

Analyses from Warner Schaie's Seattle Longitudinal Study suggest that not all types of dropouts are equally problematical. Schaie found that those subjects who dropped out because they were no longer interested had had about the same initial qualities as did those who remained in the study all along. It was those who dropped out because they died or who were too ill to continue who led to biased results because they had differed from the continuing subjects at the beginning (Cooney, Schaie, & Willis, 1988). Because of such difficulties, we must be cautious about drawing overly optimistic conclusions from longitudinal studies that appear to show that skills are retained or even improved in old age.

Time of Measurement Effects. More important, longitudinal studies don't get around the cohort problem completely. Each longitudinal study includes only subjects from a single cohort. Both the Berkeley subjects and those involved in the Grant study, for example, were born between 1918 and 1928. This is in some respects a highly atypical group. They grew up during the Depression, lived through World War II, formed their families during that unusual time immediately following the war when women returned to full-time homemaking and birthrates soared. Both preceding and succeeding cohorts had very different life experiences. Longitudinal data on this cohort *may* point to basic developmental processes in adult life; or they may tell us only something about adult-life patterns in this cohort. Indeed, *any* longitudinal study of this type can inform us about changes or continuities only in the particular cohort studied. This is referred to as a **time of measurement effect,** because the time at which you study a particular group affects the results you obtain.

Sequential Designs

The way around this problem is with one or another form of sequential design. The easiest way for me to make the variations in sequential design clear to you is with Figure 1.4. At the top of the figure is the year of birth of each of several cohorts. On the left are the years in which a sample of people from any given cohort might have been tested. Each entry in the table represents the *age* that that cohort would have been at the time of testing. Within this matrix you can see that a cross-sectional study involves comparisons along any *row*, while a longitudinal study represents comparisons along any one *column*. Sequential designs involve combinations of these two. There are several possibilities.

1. **Time-lag design.** One simple alternative is to compare along the diagonal, such as the circled entries. This involves comparing several cohorts, each of which was the *same age* at the time of testing. This is a very good way to look quite specifically for cohort effects. When the government asks a new sample of teenagers every few years about their drug use, they are using a time-lag design. Their intent is not only to discover how many current youth are using drugs, but also to find any trends over time—any cohort changes.

2. **Time-sequential design.** A second alternative is to do several cross-sectional studies a few years apart. In Figure 1.4, this means completing parts of two or more rows. A good example of this is the same study by Veroff and his colleagues represented in Figure 1.1. Veroff has parallel data from two large national samples, one interviewed in 1957 and one in 1976. At both time points, he asked each married subject whether he or she had experienced marital problems. Figure 1.5 shows the percentage of respondents at each age, at each testing point, who said they had had such marital problems. You can see in the results both a time of measurement effect and a replication of an apparent change with age. Subjects included in the 1976 samples were all more likely to report problems, no matter what their age. But at both testing points, Veroff found a clear drop with age in the incidence of reported problems. The fact that this pattern occurs twice, over two sets of cross-sectional comparisons, makes it seem more likely that there is a "real" change with age involved here.

FIGURE I.4 It's worth the effort to study this figure carefully. Each entry in the table is the age of a group of subjects who were tested at a particular historical time. Cross-sectional research designs involve comparisons of entries across any row; longitudinal designs involve comparisons down any column; sequential designs involve a combination of rows and columns. The shaded square represents the most complex combination, a cohort-sequential design, while the circles represent the simplest, a time-lag design.

Year of Birth of Each Cohort

Year in Which Measurement Was Obtained	1910	1920	1930	1940	1950	1960	1970	1980	1990
1925	15								
1935	25	15							
1945	35	25	15						
1955	45	35	(25)	15					
1965	55	45	35	(25)	15				
1975	65	55	45	35	(25)	15			
1985	75	65	55	45	35	(25)	15		
1995	85	75	65	55	45	35	25	15	
2005	95	85	75	65	55	45	35	25	15

3. **Cohort-sequential design.** The obvious next possibility would be a design involving several columns in Figure 1.4, which means doing two or more equivalent longitudinal studies, each with a different cohort. If later investigators, for example, had duplicated the Berkeley Intergenerational Study with a group born in the 1940s or 1950s, that would be a cohort-sequential study.

4. **Cross-sequential design.** The most complex of the sequential designs is a cross-sequential design, involving multiple rows and columns in Figure 1.4, such as the shaded box. A good example of this is one of the Duke Longitudinal Studies of Aging (Palmore, 1981), in which the researchers began by testing a sample of subjects from each of five age groups: 45-, 50-, 55-, 60-, and 65-year-olds. All five groups were then followed over a period of six years, with testing every two years.

5. **Panel studies.** A variant of the cross-sequential design, called a panel study, is common in sociological research. The researcher, aiming for greater representativeness than is often found in the small-sample studies done by psychologists, begins with a large sample of people, usually chosen so as to be statistically representative of the national population or a subgroup of the population, such as heads of households, or single mothers, or whatever. Usually, the initial sample varies quite widely in age. All of these subjects are then reinterviewed on a regular schedule over the succeeding years. In long-term panel studies, as subjects drop out or die they are replaced, so that in any given year the entire sample is still representative of the population from which it was drawn, even though the sample does not now include precisely the same people from year to year. Still, the lives or experiences of those who do remain in the study can be traced over time.

One of the richest and most influential of the panel studies of adult development is the Michigan Panel Study of Income Dynamics (Duncan & Morgan, 1985),

CRITICAL THINKING

Can you think of any reason why the incidence of reported marital problems would be higher in 1976 than in 1957?

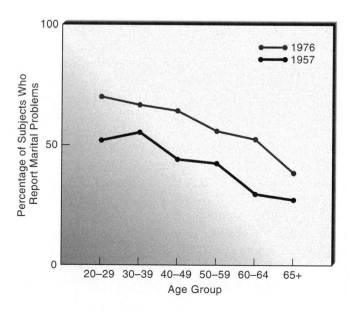

FIGURE 1.5 Example of a time-sequential study. Veroff completed two cross-sectional studies, 19 years apart. At each time period, the percentage who reported marital problems declined with age.

Source: Data from Veroff, Douvan, & Kulka, 1981, Table 4.20, p. 183.

which began with a nationally representative sample of 5000 *families* in 1968, and has followed not only the members of those original families, but also the families formed by the grown children and the families formed by remarriages of the original spouses. At the moment, about 6500 families (over 16,000 persons) are included. Each year, one member of each family is interviewed in detail, and that person gives information not only about himself or herself but also about other members of the family.

When several of these types of sequential designs are combined, as Schaie has done in the Seattle Longitudinal Study (1983a, 1993), remarkably rich and powerful data may emerge. Schaie began in 1956 by giving IQ tests to subjects in a series of cohorts seven years apart in age, ranging from 25 to 67 at the start of the study. This first study was thus cross-sectional. Then some of the subjects *of each age* were followed longitudinally, with retesting at seven-year intervals. The most recent retesting of this group, in 1991, was the sixth retesting, so a period of 35 years is involved. This now gives him a cross-sequential analysis, essentially like the Duke studies but over a longer period of time.

Not content with that, however, every seven years Schaie also selected *another* set of cross-sectional samples with new 25-year-olds, new 32-year-olds, and so on, and followed some of them longitudinally, which gives him a cohort-sequential design as well. At this point he has one set of longitudinal subjects he has followed for 35 years, another set he has followed for 28 years, and so on. He also has six full cross-sectional studies, seven years apart. It is a remarkable study. Few researchers have had either the patience or the resources to complete designs of this complexity. But all the sequential designs allow us to shift from talking merely about age differences to analysis of age *changes* and their variations. They also allow us to separate out the impact of unique cohort experiences (time of measurement effects) from that of more enduring developmental patterns.

RESEARCH METHODS

Selecting an appropriate research design is only the first decision. The next set of choices involves selecting the subjects to study and deciding how to study them.

Choosing the Subjects

Ideally, of course, if we want to be able to generalize the results of a given study to all adults, we would need a representative sample of all the adults in the world. Given the obvious impossibility of such a goal, researchers make a variety of compromises in selecting subjects, each of which may affect the generalizability of the findings. Sociologists and epidemiologists often try to get around the problem by selecting large, statistically representative samples of the group of interest. The National Survey of Black Americans, for example, involves a nationally representative sample of over 2000 black adults in the United States, interviewed in 1979 and 1980. The trade-off in such very large studies is often depth.

Psychologists, in contrast, more often choose to study small samples of subjects in greater depth, hoping to uncover basic processes. Many of the samples that have been studied the longest and in greatest depth are not only small but are also nonrepresentative in other respects. Often, they are made up primarily of white, well-educated, middle-class adults, sometimes only men. While it is true that detailed studies of such groups may give us insights into basic developmental processes, we need to be very careful about generalizing too broadly from such research without parallel studies in other social-class, ethnic, or cultural groups.

Collecting Information from Your Subjects

Once the research design is determined, the next major set of decisions has to do with the ways in which information will be collected from subjects. Each of the basic strategies has distinct advantages. Since you have encountered descriptions of these techniques in earlier courses, I will assume that each of you has at least some knowledge of the pros and cons of the alternatives, and describe them only very briefly.

Observation. The most open-ended way to explore behavior is to observe your subjects in natural surroundings. This is a common technique in studies of children but is rarely done with adults. Even structured observations, observations of adults in specially created or artificial situations, are relatively rare. Most of what we know about adulthood comes from asking people about themselves in one way or another.

Interviews. One of the most common way to "ask" is with an interview. All the major longitudinal studies I've described so far, for example, included extensive interviews in their test procedures; many sociological studies of aspects of adult life also involve structured interviews. Sometimes the transcripts of subjects' responses to interview questions are later rated on broad dimensions by other psychologists or researchers, as Carstensen did in the data in Figure 1.3; sometimes the data from the interviews are coded in a more direct fashion.

Questionnaires. Still more structured is a questionnaire in which the alternative answers are provided. The questions may request factual information about the subject (age, occupation, number of friends of various types, marital status, income, etc.) or about attitudes or beliefs. In-depth interviews may also involve extended conversations about the impact of individual experiences.

Other Standardized Tests. IQ tests and tests of other specific abilities are also used widely, as are standardized tests of personality such as those used in the Bergeman study represented in Table 1.1. Such tests are sometimes administered individually, sometimes given in groups.

Many of the long-term longitudinal studies have included all or most of these techniques in their testing procedures, yielding a very rich body of data. Most of the shorter-term longitudinal studies or cross-sectional studies involve a more focused set of questions and a narrower range of assessment techniques.

UNDERSTANDING THE ANSWERS: ANALYSIS OF RESEARCH FINDINGS

Once the data have been collected, researchers must make another set of decisions about how to analyze the findings. Some of the statistical methods now being used are extremely sophisticated and complex. I'll be describing a few of these in later chapters when I discuss specific studies that include them. At this early point, all I want to do is talk about the two most common ways of looking at the results of studies of adult change and continuity.

The most common way to describe age differences is simply a comparison of **mean scores** on some measure for each of several different age groups. Then the means (averages) are compared in some fashion, just as you have seen in many of the figures so far in this chapter. When longitudinal data are available, we are comparing average scores for the same people at different ages, but the basic strategy is the same. In each case we are usually looking for a trend, a pattern of scores linked to age.

If the sample studied is large enough, it is often possible to subdivide it and look for age differences or continuities in various subgroups, such as women versus men, working class versus middle class, those with young children versus those without young children, and the like. If every group shows essentially the same pattern over age, and if the same pattern occurs in longitudinal studies as well as cross-sectional comparisons, we'd be much more likely to conclude that this is a significant age-linked pattern. However, if the changes and continuities are very different for different subgroups (as is often the case), we are led to ask other kinds of follow-up questions: Why might the groups differ? What do the differences tell us about the possible pathways through adulthood?

Let me give you a quick example. A consistent finding in sociological research on families is that marital satisfaction is related to the presence and age of children. Figure 1.6 shows the results from one of the early studies (Rollins & Feldman, 1970), although this pattern has frequently been replicated in other cohorts (Glenn, 1990). You can see that the percentage of couples who say they are happy "all the time" goes down with the birth of the first child and stays relatively low until retirement age. I'll be talking more about this intriguing pattern in Chapter 6. For now I merely want to have you think about the way in which these findings are analyzed and interpreted. Even though this cross-sectional pattern has been widely replicated, this way of analyzing the data doesn't tell us whether every family goes through something similar.

In fact, when researchers have looked at subgroups, they have found that not everyone experiences this same drop in satisfaction after the birth of the first child. For exam-

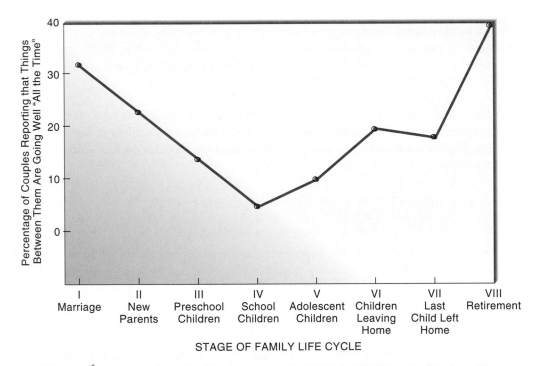

FIGURE 1.6 These cross-sectional findings are typical of studies of this type: Couples with young children are less satisfied with their marriages than are couples with no children or couples whose children have left home.

Source: B. C. Rollins & H. Feldman, 1970, Marital satisfaction over the family life cycle, *Journal of Marriage and the Family, 32,* 20–28. Data from Tables 2 and 3, p. 24. Copyright 1970 by the National Council on Family Relations, 3989 Central Avenue, NE, Suite 550, Minneapolis, MN 55421. Reprinted by permission.

ple, Estes and Wilensky (1978) have found that families with low levels of financial worry show little change in marital satisfaction over the family life cycle, whereas those who experienced financial strain showed a curvilinear pattern like the one shown in Figure 1.6. Such a finding points us in a new direction, suggesting that it is not the family life-cycle stage *per se* that is causal, but some other factor that is correlated with family stage, such as economic strain.

Comparisons of means for different age groups, either cross-sectionally or longitudinally, can give us some insights about possible age changes or developmental patterns, but they cannot tell us whether there has been continuity or change *within individuals.* For this, a different type of analysis is required, that of correlational techniques. A **correlation** is simply a statistic that tells us the extent to which two sets of scores on the same people tend to vary together. Correlations (symbolized r) can range from +1.00 to -1.00, with a positive correlation showing that high scores on the two dimensions occur together. A negative correlation tells us that high scores on one dimension go with low scores on the other. The closer the number is to 1.00, the stronger the relationship. A correlation of 0.00 indicates no relationship.

For example, height and weight are positively correlated: Taller people generally weigh more, shorter people less. But the correlation is not perfect (not 1.00) because there are some short, heavy people, and some tall, light people. If you are on a diet, the number of pounds you lose is *negatively* correlated with the number of calories you eat: High calories go with low weight loss. But this correlation, too, is not perfect (as any of you who have dieted know full well!).

When we go searching for continuities or discontinuities in individual patterns over adulthood, the correlation is the main tool we use. A researcher will typically measure some skill or quality in each member of a sample at several time points and then use the correlation statistic to describe the degree to which the scores at any two time points are similar to one another. For example, do adults who have high IQs at 20 still have high IQs at 40? Yes. In one study, Dorothy Eichorn and her colleagues (Eichorn, Hunt, & Honzik, 1981) found a correlation between IQ at 18 and at 40 of about 0.80, which is very high indeed.

Correlations are also used to reveal patterns of change or continuity. If we were interested in knowing more about adults who remain satisfied with their lives into old age (as Palmore, 1981, has seen), we could look at the correlations between life satisfaction at different ages and a wide range of other measures, such as education, income, presence of family members, availability of friends, and health. Ultimately, however, correlations can tell us only about relationship; they cannot tell us about causality, even though it is often very tempting to make the conceptual leap from a correlation to a cause. Some cases are easy. If I told you that there was a negative correlation between the per capita incidence of refrigerators in the countries of the world and the infant mortality rates in those countries, you would not be tempted to conclude that the presence of refrigerators causes lower infant mortality. You'd look for other kinds of societal changes that might explain the link between the two events. But if I tell you that there is a correlation between the amount of time that adults spend with friends and family and the overall life happiness that those adults report, you would be much more tempted to jump to the conclusion that greater happiness is caused by contact with friends and family. And it may be. But the correlation, by itself, doesn't tell us that; it only tells us that there is a relationship. It remains for further research and theorizing to uncover the causal links, if any.

There are many variations on these analytical themes, but nearly all the research on adult development involves one or the other (or both) of these basic techniques.

CRITICAL THINKING

What other explanations for such a correlation can you think of?

EXPERIMENTAL DESIGNS

The type of research design I have not mentioned thus far (an omission you may have noted, particularly if you are familiar with research in other areas of psychology) is the **experimental design.** In a true experiment, the researcher controls or manipulates one or more variables systematically, assigning subjects randomly to either treatment or non-treatment groups. Because the questions we are interested in when we study development have to do with differences between groups of people of different ages, the subjects cannot be assigned randomly to those groups. Such studies that lack random assignment are designated **quasi-experimental designs,** and the experimenter forfeits the right to claim that age itself is the *causal factor* in the changes found. But there are important ways in which experiments can help to explore alternative explanations of age-related patterns that may be observed in quasi-experimental studies. For example, take the observation that older adults perform many intellectual tasks at a slower speed than do younger adults. There are several possible explanations of this pattern, some of which I sketched earlier: It could reflect fundamental maturational changes in the brain or nervous system; it could reflect differences in practice at such tasks; it could reflect differences in motivation to compete or achieve; it could reflect the differences in years of education between young and old cohorts.

True experiments might help us choose among these alternatives. For example, we could select groups of young, middle-aged, and older subjects and randomly assign half of each age group to a special training group in which extra practice was given on some particular intellectual task. The other half of the subjects at each age might be given no training, or might be given training at some other kind of task altogether. If we then tested all the subjects before and after training, we could determine whether the older group benefited more, equally, or less from training than did the younger groups. If they benefited more, it would provide support for the "lack of practice" explanation for speed differences. If they benefited less, it would provide some support (although not conclusive) for a biological or maturational explanation of the basic difference observed.

Perhaps there are so few experiments of this kind in the study of adult development because we are still concerned primarily with problems of description rather than explanation. In those areas in which the basic descriptive research is more complete, such as the study of changes in intellectual performance over adulthood, experiments like this are done, and we will encounter a few as we go along. But at the moment, systematic, controlled experimentation is not one of the major modes of research in this field.

A FINAL WORD

Since I began this chapter on a personal note, let me end it the same way. I approach the topic of this book both as a psychologist and as an adult. My interest is both scientific and personal. I want to understand how it all works and why, both because that is inherently interesting to me, and because it may help me to understand and deepen my own development. Your own journey through adulthood will be like my own in many ways and very unlike it in others. What I am searching for in this book are the basic rules or processes that account for both those similarities and differences. I hope you can share with me the sense of adventure in the scientific search as well as in the personal journey.

1. Several key themes run through the study of adult development: Is there continuity, or is there change within the individual? Are there stages or phases? Is there both inner and outer change? In each instance it is important to look at both descriptive and explanatory evidence.

2. Three major kinds of influences help to foster change over adulthood. The first are shared, age-graded experiences, which can be further subdivided into three types: shared, inevitable biological changes that are part of aging; shared cultural experiences, such as those associated with the family life cycle; and internal changes that may be common to all adults.

3. Experiences unique to individual cohorts—such as the impact of the Great Depression or the Vietnam War or the women's movement—may also serve to shape adult life trajectories in similar ways for all members of each cohort.

4. Unique experiences encountered by each adult, shared neither within a cohort nor across cohorts, form a third source of pressure for change. Examples: the unexpectedly early death of a parent; losing your job in middle age; serious illness or disability at an early age; divorce; winning the lottery.

5. To understand adulthood, we must also understand continuity or consistency over time. One major source of such consistency is heredity, which affects personality patterns, susceptibilities toward various pathologies, and specific patterns of physical aging.

6. The term *maturation* will be used to describe age-graded changes due to fundamental, universally shared biological changes. The term *development* will be used to describe changes with age that involve improvement or growth.

7. Dividing up the adult years somewhat arbitrarily, we can refer to those between 18 and 40 as *young adults,* those between 40 and 65 as *middle adults,* those between 65 and 75 as *young old,* and those over 75 as *old old.*

8. Researchers exploring questions of adult continuity and change must choose one of several basic research designs. Cross-sectional designs involve studying separate groups at each of several ages or stages; longitudinal designs involve repeated study of the same individuals over time; sequential designs involve some combination of the two, such as repeated cross-sectional studies (time-sequential design), replications of longitudinal studies (cohort-sequential design), or both (cross-sequential design).

9. Cross-sectional designs inevitably confound age and cohort; longitudinal studies, which involve assessment of individuals from a single cohort over time, confound age change and time of testing. Longitudinal designs also suffer from problems of selective attrition. Sequential designs can help sort out some of the differing effects.

10. A researcher must also decide how to collect information from subjects. The most common strategies in adult research are individual interviews (in person or over the phone), questionnaires, and standardized tests, such as measures of depression or life satisfaction.

11. Analysis of findings typically involve one of two techniques: comparison of means for groups of different ages (or for the same people across age); or calculation of correlations between scores for the same people at different ages (to check for individual consistency) or for the same people at the same time on different measures.

12. True experiments, in which the experimenter systematically manipulates one or more variables and assigns subjects at random to experimental and control groups, are not common in the study of adult development, although they can help us to choose among competing explanations for patterns of change or continuity over age.

KEY TERMS

biological clock

social clock

age strata

ageism

age norms

family life cycle

cohort

cohort effect

behavior genetics

openness to experiences

conscientiousness

adulthood

young adulthood

middle adulthood

old age

young old

old old

oldest old

aging

maturation

development

gain

decline

change

research design

research methodology

research analysis

cross-sectional design

longitudinal design

sequential design

selective attrition

time of measurement ef-

fect

time-lag design

time-sequential design

cohort-sequential design

cross-sequential design

panel studies

observation

interviews

questionnaires

correlation *(r)*

comparison of mean
  scores

experimental design

quasi-experimental
  design

SUGGESTED READINGS

Myers, G. C. (1996). Aging and the social sciences: Research directions and unresolved issues. In R. H. Binstock & L. K. George (Eds.), *Handbook of aging and the social sciences (4th ed.* pp. 1–11. San Diego, CA: Academic Press.

This concise, well-written article tells about the current state of research in adult development and aging and predicts future research trends, such as more interdisciplinary research and more research aimed at intervention into the aging process.

Rowe, J. W., Wang, S. Y., & Elahi, D. (1990). Design, conduct, and analysis of human aging research. In E. R. Schneider & J. W. Rowe (Eds.), *Handbook of the biology of aging* (3rd ed., pp. 63–71). San Diego, CA: Academic Press.

This paper includes a particularly good discussion of the pros and cons of longitudinal research in the study of aging.

Schaie, K. W. (1983). What can we learn from the longitudinal study of adult psychological development? In K. W. Schaie (Ed.), *Longitudinal studies of adult psychological development.* New York: Guilford Press.

Schaie has been one of the foremost advocates of the use of complex and elegant sequential designs for studying adult development. Many of his writings on the subject are quite dense and difficult, but this particular chapter is reasonably readable.

Stanovich, K. E. (1998). How to think straight about psychology. Reading MA: Addison Wesley Longman.

This book is not focused on developmental research, but it is a good one, nevertheless, offering a nice basic understanding of research in psychology. (This is especially good for the nonpsychology student.)

Vaillant, G. E. (1977). *Adaptation to life.* Boston: Little, Brown.

If you are dying to get started reading about some real people actually moving through adulthood, try this book. I have found it to be one of the most intriguing of the descriptions of longitudinal evidence, full of fascinating case studies as well as provocative theory.

THEORIES
OF ADULT CHANGE
OR DEVELOPMENT

CHAPTER 2

Having just spent an entire chapter trying to persuade you that adult life is powerfully shaped by persistent, durable characteristics of individuals, it may seem contradictory to turn now to an examination of the ways in which adult lives move in the same directions, or share similar patterns. But the fact that both of these ways of looking at adulthood are true simultaneously is one of the basic points I want to make in this book. Each of us may enter and move through adulthood on a somewhat different trajectory, but all adult trajectories may still have important elements in common. We are both all alike and all different.

The empirical search for the common elements is the subject of the nine chapters in the next section. Before looking at the data, though, I want to lay the groundwork by talking about theories of adult continuity and change. I find these theories fascinating in themselves. But they also serve to point us at some of the critical questions that research might answer and to illustrate the variety of ways of thinking about adulthood.

VARIETIES OF THEORIES

Twenty-five years ago, any discussion of theories of adult development would have been almost totally dominated by one theory: Erik Erikson's model of psychosocial development. Erikson's view is still highly influential, but today there has been a real flowering of ideas, some of them distinctly different from Erikson's model. This wide variety of existing theories will form a better framework for later discussions if I organize the approaches along several dimensions, as I have done in Figure 2.1. Any categorization scheme, including this one, is inevitably an oversimplification. Each theory contains its own unique combination of ideas. But I can still use the two dimensions shown in Figure 2.1 as one helpful basis for organizing the options.

The first dimension on which theories may be organized is their relative emphasis on development versus change. The fundamental difference—as I am using the terms *development* and *change* in this book—is that a **theory of adult development** assumes that there is some goal or endpoint toward which the adult moves, and that this endpoint is potentially "better" or more mature than what is seen at earlier ages. A **theory of adult change,** in contrast, assumes no such endpoint or goal nor any "improvement" or growth. Among developmental theorists, for example, Erikson talks about *ego integrity* as being the final stage, accompanied by wisdom. Vaillant describes a developmental continuum from immature to more mature forms of defense mechanisms. Other theorists, such as Levinson and Pearlin, while agreeing that significant changes take place

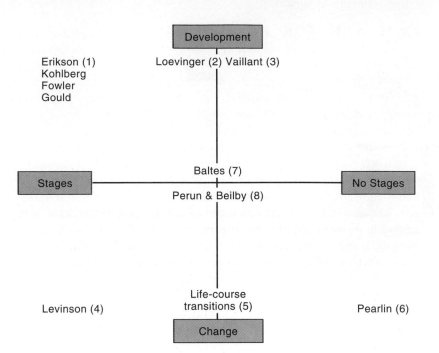

FIGURE 2.1 This two-dimensional grid, with development versus change as one dimension and stage versus nonstage theories as the other, allows us to contrast several of the major theories of development. (The numbers in parentheses indicate the sequence in which these theories are discussed in the chapter.)

over the adult years, do not see those changes as leading to more integrating or more wisdom. Your great aunt Elsie is different from you in specific, predictable ways, but she is not necessarily better (or worse).

The presence or absence of stages in each theory is the second dimension I have used to categorize theories of adulthood. This is a somewhat risky organizational rubric, since the term *stage* is used to describe several different concepts. Most broadly, **stages** refer to fixed sequences of experiences or events over time, such as the family life-cycle stages I mentioned briefly in Chapter 1. More narrowly (and more commonly in psychological theories), stages imply systematic, sequential, *qualitative* changes in a skill or underlying psychological structure. When Jean Piaget talks about stages in children's cognitive development, for example, he does not mean merely that children learn to add and subtract before they learn to multiply and divide, but rather, that the ability to multiply and divide requires fundamentally different understanding, logic, or mental structures. Each stage is thought of as being a structural whole, as having its own logic. Most (but not all) stage theories of adult development make similar assumptions about the nature of changes in adulthood.

Stage theorists also differ on the extent to which they argue that the various stages are age linked. Levinson's stages are strongly connected to specific ages, for example, whereas Loevinger's are not. At the other end of the continuum are those theorists who see no stages in adult development at all, in any sense of the term *stage*. Sociologist Orville Brim represents this **antistage** point of view when he says that stage theories "are a little like horoscopes. They are vague enough so that everyone can see something of themselves in them. That's why they're so popular" (quoted in Rosenfeld & Stark, 1987, p. 68). Theorists who argue against stages assert that there are no shared "midlife crises," no expectable "integrity" in old age. Instead, there are many pathways, many patterns, with adult life a process of constant change and flux. In between these two extremes lie a number of theorists who argue that there are **sequences** but not stages. That is, there may be predictable orders or arrangements of experiences in adulthood, but these changes may not be integrated into inclusive, shared internal or external structures.

When we put these two dimensions together, as in Figure 2.1, some combinations are obviously more common than others. Stage theories of development (the upper left quadrant) have been particularly influential and continue to form an important backdrop for much of our current thinking, although they have waned somewhat in direct influence in recent years. Many current theories are to be found more toward the middle, such as the life-span perspective represented by Baltes. Indeed, a growing number of theorists and researchers have gone even further, shifting to the opposite corner, as in Pearlin's theory of psychological distress.

Because of their historical and conceptual importance, let me start a detailed discussion of the theoretical alternatives in the upper left corner of Figure 2.1, and then work my way slowly toward the theories that lie in the middle. (The sequence I will use is indicated in Figure 2.1 by the numbers in parentheses after each theorist's name.)

DEVELOPMENTAL STAGE THEORIES OF ADULTHOOD

Erikson's Theory of Identity Development

Erik Erikson's theory (1950, 1959,1980, 1982; Erikson, Erikson, & Kivnick, 1986; R.I. Evans, 1969) has clearly been the most influential view of adult development proposed thus far. There are traces of this theory in most if not all other stage theories of adulthood, and his terminology has been widely adopted. He proposes that psychosocial development continues over the entire life span, resulting from the interaction between inner instincts and drives and outer cultural and social demands. For Erikson, a key concept is the gradual, stepwise emergence of a sense of **identity.** Erikson explicitly stated that development follows a basic, built-in "ground plan" (1959, p. 53), which shapes a sequence of "potentialities for significant interaction" with those around the child or the adult. To develop a complete, stable identity, the person must move through and successfully resolve eight "crises" or "dilemmas" over the course of a lifetime (see Table 2.1). Each dilemma emerges as the child or adult is challenged by new relationships, tasks, or demands. The fourth stage, "industry versus inferiority" for example, begins when the child starts school and is challenged by the demand to learn to read and write and absorb great chunks of new information.

Each dilemma or stage is defined by a pair of opposing possibilities, one of which describes the optimum outcome of that dilemma, the other the potential negative or less healthy outcome, such as trust versus mistrust, or integrity versus despair. In his later writings, Erikson also talked about the potential *strength* to be gained from a healthy resolution of each dilemma, as you can see in Table 2.1. A "healthy resolution," however, does not mean moving totally to the apparently positive end of any one of the continua that Erikson describes. An infant can have too much trust; too much industriousness can lead to narrow virtuosity; too much identity cohesion in adolescence can result in fanaticism. The best resolution, in this view, is a balance.

Another key point about Erikson's theory that bears emphasis is his contention that these dilemmas/crises are forced on each of us as we move through the life cycle. Unlike some other stage theorists, such as Loevinger, Erikson does not think that you simply stay at a given stage until you have completed it before going on to the next. He argues instead that each person is pushed through this sequence of dilemmas by biological maturation, by social pressures, and by the demands of the roles that he or she adopts. You can't stay a 20-year-old until you get it right! On that next birthday you are 21, and then 22, whether or not you are ready. And with increasing age there are new demands, new dilemmas. When you arrive at 60 or 70, the tasks you didn't deal with fully will remain as unresolved issues, interfering with your ability to find true integrity. Erikson's theory thus belongs in the upper corner of this quadrant of the diagram because he not only thinks that the ultimate result of coping with these dilemmas *can* be maturity and wisdom, but because he thinks that the stages come along at roughly the same ages for all of us, and must be dealt with in sequence, regardless of how well or poorly we may have resolved the preceding stages.

The Dilemmas of Adult Life. As you can see in Table 2.1, there are four dilemmas that describe adulthood, beginning with stage V, **identity versus role confusion,** which is the central task of adolescence and the early 20s. The young person must develop a specific ideology, a set of personal values and goals. In part, this is a shift from the here-and-now orientation of the child to a future orientation; teenagers must not only consider what or who they *are* but who or what they *will be.* Erikson [and others who have explored this stage

TABLE 2.1 **Erikson's Stages of Psychosocial Development**

Approximate Age (Years)	Stage	Potential Strength to Be Gained	Description
0–1	I. Basic trust versus mistrust	Hope	The infant must form a first, loving, trusting relationship with the caregiver, or risk a persisting sense of mistrust.
2–3	II. Autonomy versus shame and doubt	Will	The child's energies are directed toward the development of key physical skills, including walking and grasping and sphincter control. The child learns control but may develop shame if not handled properly.
4–5	III. Initiative versus guilt	Purpose	The child continues to become more assertive, to take more initiative, but may be too forceful and injure others or objects, which leads to guilt.
6–12	IV. Industry versus inferiority	Competence	The school-aged child must deal with the demands to learn new, complex skills, or risk a sense of inferiority.
13–18	V. Identity versus role confusion	Fidelity	The teenager (or young adult) must achieve a sense of identity—both who he or she is and what he or she will be—in several areas, including occupation, gender role, politics, and religion.
19–25	VI. Intimacy versus isolation	Love	The young adult must risk the immersion of self in a sense of "we," creating one or more truly intimate relationships, or suffer feelings of isolation.
25–65	VII. Generativity versus self-absorption and stagnation	Care	In early and middle adulthood, each adult must find some way to satisfy the need to be generative, to support the next generation or turn outward from the self toward others.
65+	VII. Ego integrity versus despair	Wisdom	If all previous stages have been dealt with reasonably well, the culmination is an acceptance of oneself as one is.

Source: Data from Erikson, 1950, 1959, 1980; Erikson, Erikson, & Kivnick, 1986.

following Erikson's lead, such as James Marcia (1980) or Alan Waterman (Waterman & Archer, 1990)] suggests that the teenager or young adult must develop several linked identities: an occupational identity (what work will I do?), a gender or gender-role identity (how do I go about being a man or a woman?), and political and religious identities (what do I believe in?). If these identities are not worked out, the young person suffers from a sense of confusion, a sense of not knowing what or who he is.

Stage VI, **intimacy versus isolation,** builds on the newly forged identity of adolescence. Erikson says: "[I]t is only after a reasonable sense of identity has been established that real *intimacy* with the other sex (or, for that matter, with any other person or even with oneself) is possible. Sexual intimacy is only part of what I have in mind.... The youth who is not sure of his identity shies away from interpersonal intimacy; but the surer he becomes of himself, the more he seeks it in the form of friendship, combat, leadership, love, and inspiration" (1959, p. 101). Intimacy is "the ability to fuse your identity with somebody else's without fear that you're going to lose something yourself" (Erikson, in R.I. Evans, 1969). Many young people, Erikson thought, make the mistake of thinking they will find their identity in a relationship, but in his view, it is only those who have already formed (or are well on the way to forming) a clear identity who can successfully enter this fusion of identities that he calls intimacy. For those whose identities are weak or unformed, relationships will remain shallow and the young person will experience a sense of isolation or loneliness.

Although in his earliest descriptions of the stages, Erikson had assumed that everyone passes through these stages in the same order, in later writings he suggested that the sequence of identity formation followed by intimacy may not be true for many women, for whom identity may be *created* in a network of relationships. Other authors (Sangiuliano, 1978) argue that many women simply reverse the sequence of the tasks of identity and intimacy, while Carol Gilligan (1982) argues that women's identity development is, from the beginning, *inter*dependent rather than *in*dependent. Women define themselves, and think about their choices and dilemmas, in terms of relationships, while men appear to define themselves more by what they do or what they are, separate from their relationships. For women, then, there may simply not be a separate stage of intimacy; rather, intimacy may form the backdrop for all women's stages.

Whatever the resolution of the controversy concerning the stage of intimacy, there is reasonably good agreement among Eriksonian theorists that the next stage for both men and women is **generativity versus self-absorption and stagnation.** Generativity "is primarily the concern in establishing and guiding the next generation" (Erikson, 1963, p. 267), and it "encompasses *procreativity, productivity,* and *creativity*" (Erikson, 1982, p. 67). This stage builds on those that came before. During the fifth stage (identity) young adults develop a sense of who they are; in the sixth stage (intimacy), they establish long-term bonds of intimacy through marriage or friendships. At that point they are ready to make a commitment to society as a whole in the sense of continuing that society through its next generation. "In generativity, the adult nurtures, teaches, leads, and promotes the next generation while generating life products and outcomes that benefit the social system and promote its continuity from one generation to the next" (McAdams, & de St. Aubin, 1992, p. 1003).

✳ CRITICAL THINKING

Do you think that Gilligan is correct in this proposal, or correct only for some cultures and some cohorts? What about current cohorts of young people in the United States?

The bearing and rearing of children is clearly a key element in Erikson's view of generativity, but it is not the only element. Serving as mentor for younger colleagues, doing charitable work in society, or the like, are also expressions of generativity. But neither rearing children nor teaching nor mentoring automatically creates a satisfying sense of generativity, just as being married is not a guarantee of successful resolution of the crisis of

GENERATIVITY can be expressed in many ways, including through the role of tutor.

intimacy. Those adults who do not find some avenue for successful expression of generativity may become self-absorbed or experience a sense of stagnation.

The virtue or strength that can emerge from this stage, according to Erikson, is *care,* which implies both taking care *of* and caring *for* or *about* others or society. The opposite quality, the weakness of this stage, if you will, is *rejectivity,* that is, the "unwillingness to include specified persons or groups in one's generative concern" (1982, p. 68). In its most extreme form, it involves rejection of all others as legitimate recipients of care. But even in most generative adults, Erikson believes, there is still some rejectivity, some "us" and "them" thinking, some designation of groups that are outside the range of caring.

Dan McAdams and his colleagues (McAdams & de St. Aubin, 1992; McAdams, de St. Aubin, & Logan, 1993) have recently expanded on Erikson's ideas about this stage, proposing that generativity is motivated both by individual inner desires and by social demand. In virtually all cultures, the social demand takes the form not only of pressure to bear children, but also pressure to take up the key roles in the social system, to produce, to carry on traditions. The two motivating inner desires, McAdams et al. argue, are both the "communal need to be nurturant" and the "agentic desire to do something or be something that transcends death" (1993, p. 222). These inner and outer pressures jointly lead to a concern for the next generation and to specific generative commitments and actions, such as deciding to have children, or working for a charitable organization, or teaching.

Erikson's thinking about his final proposed stage, **ego integrity versus despair,** has undergone some interesting changes. He was himself in his middle years when he first described it, and at that time he saw it in somewhat rosy terms, such as the following: "Only he who in some way has taken care of things and people and has adapted himself to the triumphs and disappointments of being, by necessity, the originator of others and the generator of things and ideas—only he may gradually grow the fruit of the seven stages. I know no better word for it than *integrity*" (1959, p. 104). Later, when he himself was in his 70s and 80s, he saw this last stage more negatively. Wisdom, which he defines as "informed and detached concern with life itself in the face of death" (1982, p. 61), may be the virtue or strength of this stage. But the antithesis, the weakness of the stage, is disdain, which flows from the feeling of helplessness or confusion that is likely as death approaches. The sense of physical limitation, of loss, contributes often to an increased self-centeredness, a quality that is in sharp contrast to the universalism or altruism that Erikson emphasized in his earlier writings on this final stage. Here is one of his recent descriptions: "Burdened by physical limitations and confronting a personal future that may seem more inescapably finite than ever before, those nearing the end of the life cycle find themselves struggling to accept the inalterability of the past and the unknowability of the future, to acknowledge possible mistakes and omissions, and to balance consequent despair with the sense of overall integrity that is essential to carrying on" (Erikson et al., 1986, p. 56).

Those adults who cannot achieve a sense of integrity, perhaps because they carry forward a residue of distrust, guilt, diffusion, isolation, or self-absorption from earlier stages, experience a sense of despair. They feel that time is too short, or that their life has been a failure, or that they wish they had it to do over again. Let me emphasize yet again that in Erikson's view, all the stages build on and affect one another. The unsuccessful resolution of any one stage leaves the person with "unfinished business," unresolved conflicts, that are carried forward to the next stage, making it then more difficult to resolve the next stage successfully. Thus Erikson is proposing a set of stages that are not only inevitable and in a fixed sequence, but are also cumulative.

Erikson's theory can also provide a theoretical rationale for the impact of being *off-time* in adult tasks, a notion that I mentioned in Chapter 1 (McAdams & de St. Aubin, 1992). If Erikson is correct, these stages need to be completed in the order specified. To be off-time is to address any one dilemma or crisis out of order, such as a teenage parent who faces the demands of generativity before coping with either identity or intimacy. In this view, being off-time is not just a question of being different from one's peers, but of being psychologically off-time for the task involved.

Loevinger's Theory of Ego Development

A second stage theory of development, Jane Loevinger's theory of ego development (1976), is in some ways similar to Erikson's, but in Loevinger's model the stages are sequential and cumulative but *not* inevitable. For this reason, I have placed her theory more toward the middle of the dimension of stages/no stages in Figure 2.1. She proposes 10 stages from birth through adulthood, summarized in Table 2.2. As in Erikson's theory, each stage builds on the one that precedes. But in Loevinger's view, a shift to the next stage occurs *only* when a person has completed the development of the current stage. Although the first few stages are typically completed in childhood, the stages have only very loose connections to particular ages. Among a group of adults of any given age, a wide range of stages of ego development would be visible. What Loevinger is describing, in essence, is a pathway (or, perhaps a better image, a flight of stairs) along which she thinks we all must move. But the rate of movement, and the final stage (step) achieved, differ widely from one person to the next.

Loevinger suggests that virtually all adults move successfully through the first three stages. Some then get stuck at the **self-protective stage**, while others move to the **conformist stage** and no further. Most adults, however, reach at least the transition that she calls the **self-aware level**, and many go beyond this to the **conscientious stage** or further. The final four stages are particularly interesting for a study of adulthood. The conscientious stage is really defined by the emergence of a set of self-chosen and self-evaluated rules. It is thus in some ways like Erikson's stage of identity versus diffusion, except that Loevinger argues that the transition to the conscientious stage often occurs well past adolescence, if it occurs

CRITICAL
THINKING

Can you recognize yourself, close friends, or members of your family in Loevinger's stages? Does it seem to you that you have moved through the stages in the order she lists?

TABLE 2.2 **Loevinger's Stages of Ego Development**

Stage or Level	Description
Presocial stage	Babies must learn to differentiate themselves from their surroundings to develop object constancy.
Symbiotic stage	Babies retain symbiotic relationships with their mothers (or other major caregivers). Major task is to emerge from that symbiosis, in part through language.
Impulsive stage	Children assert their separate identity, partly by giving free rein to impulses. Others are valued in terms of what they can give. Those remaining too long at this stage may be "uncontrollable" or "incorrigible."
Self-protective stage	Children learn self-control of impulses by anticipating immediate short-term rewards or punishments. Children understand the existence of rules but try always to maximize their own gain. Some adults function at this stage.
Conformist stage	Children (or adults) identify their own welfare with that of the group and attempt to model their behavior along the lines of group expectations. Individuals in this stage tend to be insensitive to individual differences, to be highly stereotyped in response, particularly about gender roles. Inner life is seen in black and white: happy/sad, good/bad.
Self-aware level	This is a transition level between conformist and conscientious stages. Self-awareness increases, as does acceptance of individual differences and shadings of feelings and opinions. Stereotypic categories such as gender, marital status, and education, however, are likely to be the basis of judgments, rather than other people's individual traits or needs.
Conscientious stage	Individually created rules and ideals have now been formed, and the person attempts to live by them. Adults at this stage have a richer inner life, with many more shadings of feelings; similarly, the view of other people becomes more individualistic, the relationships more mutual.
Individualistic level	This is a transition level between the conscientious and autonomous stages. Persons at this level are focused heavily on the question of independence and dependence. They are also more aware of inner conflict.
Autonomous stage	Adults in this stage (comparatively rare) are fully independent, with a capacity to acknowledge and deal with inner conflict. Other people are accepted and cherished for what and who they are, with no attempt to make them over.
Integrated stage	This final stage, which is extremely rare, transcends the conflict of the autonomous stage.

Source: Adapted from Loevinger, 1976.

at all. Another aspect of the conscientious stage is the ability to see other people in complex three-dimensional terms, in contrast to the greater stereotyping and two-dimensionality of relationships of earlier stages. "With the deepened understanding of other people's viewpoints, mutuality in interpersonal relations becomes possible" (Loevinger, 1976, p. 22). An adult at this stage would no longer describe (or think of) a particular friend as "a stockbroker who grew up in New York," but perhaps as "a highly achievement oriented, determined, but somewhat lonely man."

The key to the **individualistic level,** which represents a transition stage between the conscientious and the autonomous, is the development of greater tolerance for both self and others. Individuals are experienced as unique; their flaws and their virtues are seen clearly. There is also a renewed struggle with the problem of dependence on others. The individualistic adult realizes that independence is not achieved merely by earning your own money or having your own house. There is an inner level of independence as well. The individualistic person has not yet reached the point of full independence, but knows that it is possible.

The next full stage in Loevinger's model is the **autonomous stage,** when that inner independence has been reached. Autonomy does not at all imply indifference toward others. On the contrary, the autonomous adult cherishes the individuality of others and finds richness in personal relationships. But he or she is willing to let friends and family be themselves. A man has let his wife step off her pedestal, or has realized that his father had been a partial failure in his business, but loves them both the more deeply for his acceptance of their flaws and failings.

Another key to this stage is the acceptance of the fact of conflict and paradox in human lives. The autonomous adult no longer sees the world in terms of opposites (good and bad, right and wrong) as the conscientious person tends to do; rather he or she sees gradations, exceptions, complexities.

The highest stage in this model is the **integrated stage.** On the surface it is somewhat like Erikson's early conceptualization of the stage of ego integrity, but Loevinger thinks that it is a more developed stage than integrity. The integrated person arrives at a personal reconciliation of the conflicts examined at the autonomous stage and gives up the quest for the unattainable.

Loevinger's theory has become more influential in recent years, for several reasons. First, the fact that the stages are not linked to specific ages can be a real strength. As our empirical information about adult development has grown, it has become increasingly clear that strict age-linked stages, although tidy and appealing, do not match the variability of real life. Adults of any one age differ widely from one another. Loevinger's theory can help to describe those differences. Second, Loevinger and her colleagues have developed an instrument, the Washington University Sentence Completion Test, to measure a subject's position in the stage continuum. It includes such items as: "A woman feels good when _____" and "My main problem is _____." Subjects' answers are then evaluated according to well-defined criteria and to yield a stage score. The existence of such a measure has made it possible for Loevinger's model to be used in research on a range of aspects of adult development, as you will see as you move through this book.

Other Developmental Stage Theories

There are many other theories in this same group that describe narrower dimensions of development, such as Lawrence Kohlberg's theory of moral development (Kohlberg, 1964, 1981, 1984) or James Fowler's theory of faith development (1981), both of which I will talk about in Chapter 10. Still other theories in this group, while broad in scope, cover a narrower age range than do Erikson's or Loevinger's, such as Roger Gould's extremely interesting theory of personal transformation (1978, 1980). Gould's theory effectively covers only the period from about 20 to about 45, and says nothing about the later years. He proposes, in essence, that the process of adult development is one of identifying, and then giving up, a series of "myths" about the world and your place in it. Some of these myths are individual, but Gould argues that there are also shared age-linked myths, such as the one common in one's early and middle 20s that says something like "as long as I follow the rules, I will be rewarded and be happy." In midlife there is the myth of immortality that must be faced and abandoned if full adult psychological potential is to be achieved.

Whether narrow or broad, covering all ages or only a portion of the age span, all of these theories share the basic assumption that adults actually develop—that we can become more mature, or can create more complex or higher orders of understanding—and that the development occurs in stages or steps or sequences.

DEVELOPMENT WITHOUT STAGES: VAILLANT'S VIEW OF ADAPTATION IN ADULT LIFE

One of the few theorists whose proposals could arguably be placed in the upper right quadrant of Figure 2.1 is George Vaillant. There are some important stagelike elements in his theory, but the most central concept in this model relies little on the concept of stage. Vaillant (1977) begins by accepting Erikson's stages as the basic framework of development, although he inserts an additional stage, which he calls **career consolidation,** between Erikson's stages of intimacy and generativity, some time at about age 30. Adults in this career consolidation stage, as Vaillant sees them, are intent on establishing their own competence, on mastering a craft, on acquiring higher status or a positive reputation.

Despite his acknowledgment of these stages, however, Vaillant's theory is in many respects more like Loevinger's than like Erikson's. Like Loevinger, Vaillant describes a direction in which growth or development *may* occur but does not assume that everyone moves the same distance in this direction. In particular, Vaillant has been interested in potential progressive change in the ways in which adults adapt psychologically to the trials and tribulations they face. The major form of adaptation he discusses is the **defense mechanism,** Freud's term for a set of normal, unconscious strategies used for dealing with anxiety. Everyone has some anxiety, so everyone uses some kinds of defense mechanisms. All involve some type of self-deception or distortion of reality. We forget things that make us uncomfortable, or remember them in a way that is not so unpleasant; we give ourselves reasons for doing something we know we shouldn't do; we project our unacceptable feelings onto others rather than acknowledging them in ourselves. What Vaillant has added to Freud's concept is the notion that some defense mechanisms are more mature than others.

Table 2.3 lists the four levels of defense mechanisms in Vaillant's classification. In general, mature defenses involve less distortion of reality. They reflect more graceful, less uncomfortable ways of coping with difficulties. Vaillant's central thesis is that for an adult to be able to cope effectively with the slings and arrows of normal life, his or her defense mechanisms must mature. The term *level* to describe these groupings of defense mechanisms may be somewhat confusing. Vaillant is not saying that an adult, at any one moment, uses only defenses at a single level. On the contrary, most of us use a wide range of defenses, covering several levels. And most of us show "regression" to less mature kinds of defenses when we are under stress. Facing a serious operation, most of us go through repression (of fear), or intellectualization (such as studying the details of the operation very abstractly), or projection ("My husband is the one who's afraid, I'm not"), or acting out (getting furious with the nurse for needing to jab you twice to get blood). Despite such regressions, Vaillant argues that in the normal course of adult life most adults add some of the more mature mechanisms or use them more frequently, and at the same time use the less mature mechanisms less often. Furthermore, Vaillant argues that individuals vary in the extent to which they show such maturing. It is those who move most toward mature defenses who will be most successful in their personal and professional lives.

CRITICAL THINKING

Think about the last time you faced a major stressful situation. What defense mechanisms do you think you used to handle your anxiety?

Vaillant's theory is thus clearly *developmental* in emphasis, since he is charting the progress each adult makes toward higher levels of maturity. But the move from immature to mature defenses is gradual rather than stagelike, more like a slope than a flight of stairs. And like Loevinger, Vaillant assumes that the more mature levels are not achieved by all adults.

TABLE 2.3 **Levels of Defense Mechanisms Proposed by Vaillant**

Level	Description
I. "Psychotic" mechanisms	*Delusional projection:* frank delusions, such as delusions of persecution.
	Denial: denial of external reality.
	Distortion: grossly reshaping external reality to suit inner needs, including hallucinations and wish-fulfilling delusions.
II. Immature mechanisms	*Projection:* attributing one's own unacknowledged feelings to others ("You're the one who's afraid, not me").
	Schizoid fantasy: the use of fantasy or inner retreat to resolve conflict.
	Hypochondriasis: reproach toward others turned into complaints of physical illness; often used to avoid making dependency demands directly or to avoid complaining directly about being ignored.
	Passive-aggressive behavior: aggression toward others expressed indirectly and effectively through passivity or directed toward the self.
	Acting out: direct expression of an unconscious wish but without acknowledging the emotion that goes with it; includes delinquent behavior, but also "tempers."
III. "Neurotic" mechanisms	*Intellectualization:* thinking about wishes or desires in formal, emotionally bland terms and not acting on them.
	Repression: memory lapses or failure to acknowledge some information; putting out of conscious memory.
	Displacement: directing your feelings toward something or someone other than the original object (e.g., cuddling your cat when you really want to hold a lover).
	Reaction formation: behaving in a fashion directly opposite to what you would really (unconsciously) like to do, such as being exceptionally nice to a co-worker you detest, since you cannot acknowledge your hatred to yourself.
	Dissociation: temporary, drastic modification of one's sense of character, such as a sudden devil-may-care attitude, or periods of irresponsibility.
IV. Mature mechanisms	*Altruism:* vicarious but constructive service to others.
	Humor: overt expression of anxiety-provoking ideas or feelings but without discomfort and without unpleasant effects on others; does not include sarcasm.
	Suppression: conscious or semiconscious decision to postpone dealing with an impulse or conflict.
	Anticipation: realistic expectation of future problem or discomfort, and planning for it.
	Sublimation: indirect expression of some desire or need but without loss of pleasure or adverse consequences, such as expressing aggression through sports; instincts are channeled rather than being dammed up.

Source: Data from Vaillant, 1977, pp. 383–386.

Stage Theories of Adult Change

When we move to the group of theories in the lower left quadrant of Figure 2.1, the concept of stages or sequences remains. What is eliminated is the assumption that movement through these stages involves "development." One of the most famous and often-quoted theories of this type is Daniel Levinson's model of the *seasons of adulthood.*

Levinson's Theory of Seasons of Adulthood

Daniel Levinson began his pioneering work in adult development in 1967 with a study of 40 men, using a new method he had developed called the *intensive biographical interview.* He intentionally limited his population to men because "[i]t seemed to me that there were significant gender differences in adult life and development. To include twenty men and twenty women would do justice to neither and might result—as it often has in the past—in an allegedly "general" theory based primarily on the evidence from men. My final decision to study men rather than women was based largely on personal considerations: I had an intense desire to understand my own adult development" (1996, p. ix). Levinson later fulfilled the promise he made to himself to study a group of women also, but he died before publishing the results. In 1996 his wife and colleague, Judy Levinson, compiled his findings and published it as *The Seasons of a Woman's Life,* which is discussed in more detail in Chapter 8.

The central concept in Levinson's theory of adult change (1978; 1980, 1986, 1990) is that of the **life structure,** which is the "underlying pattern or design of a person's life at a given time" (1986, p. 6). The key components of the life structure are *relationships* with various others: spouse or partner, children, boss or work subordinates, or a significant group or social structure, such as a church or club, or even with some part of nature, or with a specific inanimate object. "These relationships are the stuff of which our lives are made. They give shape and substance to the life course" (1990, p. 42). At the same time, the life structure each of us creates is also affected by our personality, our style. Two individuals apparently dealing with similar life circumstances will not create precisely the same life structure. And because relationships necessarily change over the course of adult life—as your children get older, or as your own parents require more assistance, or as you move from subordinate to boss at work—life structures cannot remain stable throughout life. Levinson proposes, therefore, that adult life, at least for men, is made up of alternating periods of stable life structures and transition periods during which the old life structure is reexamined, adjusted, or altered.

The overall sequence that he suggests is fairly complex, as you can see in Figure 2.2. He first divides adult life into a sequence of broad *eras,* each lasting roughly 25 years, and each marked with a distinct *biopsychosocial character* (1990, p. 39). Between eras there are major transitions, such as the early adulthood transition or the midlife transition. Within each era, there are further steps or stages, beginning with a **novice phase,** during which a person tries out an initial life structure designed to deal with the new demands of that era. This first try at a suitable life structure is then reassessed in a **midera transition,** after which there is a **culminating phase,** in which an improved or more adaptive life structure is created, bringing the efforts of that era to fruition. This culminating life structure is itself reassessed and modified at the end of the era, when the major transition to the new era begins.

Levinson suggests that each era, each stable period within an era, and each transition has a particular content, some of which I have summarized in Table 2.4. The **early adult transition** deals with the problem of independence, of establishing an identity and a life separate from one's family (thus it is similar in some respects to Erikson's stage of identity versus role confusion). Young adults must explore the adult world, find work, create

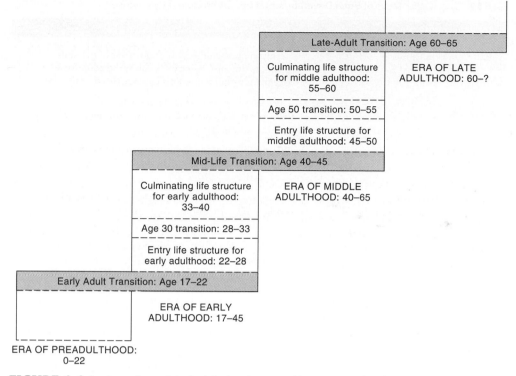

FIGURE 2.2 Levinson's model of adult development. You can see the alternation of periods of stable life structures with periods of transition. Transitions between one era and the next are likely to be more pervasive than are those within any given era.

Source: Levinson, 1986. Adapted from *The seasons of a man's life* by Daniel J. Levinson et al., 1978. Copyright © 1978 by Daniel J. Levinson. Reprinted by permission of Alfred A. Knopf, Inc.

relationships. This first inner and outer exploration leads to the creation of a first life structure in the 20s.

This "novice" life structure of early adulthood is commonly distinguished by two elements that Levinson thinks play a critical part in an adult's life: the creation of a relationship with a **mentor,** and the establishment of the **dream.** The dream is a sort of fantasy or a set of imagined possibilities showing what one wants to become: a picture of oneself winning the Nobel prize, or breaking Mark McGwire's batting record, or bringing about racial equality in the country (Martin Luther King's "I have a dream" speech). Many young adults dream of becoming rich, or finding the perfect mate, or living happily ever after in a lovely house in a nice neighborhood with two well-behaved children. As a young man pursues this dream, for example, he may establish a mentor relationship. The mentor is ordinarily a male who is 8 to 15 years older (someone, perhaps, in his own stage of generativity) who takes the young person under his wing, who teaches, advises, sponsors, supports, and serves as a model for the young person. A mentor is often found in a work setting, but the mentor could also be an older relative or a friend. He (or rarely she) is both a parent figure and a peer, and must be both if the relationship is going to work. The role of the mentor is to help the young person make the transition from reliance on the parents and their world to reliance on himself.

CRITICAL THINKING

**What is or was your dream
at this age?**

TABLE 2.4 **Major Tasks of Each Developmental Period Proposed by Levinson**

Developmental Period	Age	Tasks
Early adult transition	17–22	Terminate preadulthood and move out of preadult world, taking preliminary steps into the adult world. Explore possibilities and make tentative commitments.
Entering the adult world	22–28	Create a first major life structure, which may include marriage and a separate home, a mentoring relationship, and the dream. Attempt to pursue the dream.
Age-30 transition	28–33	Become aware of the flaws in the first life structure and reassess it. Reconsider earlier choices and make new ones as needed.
Culmination of early adulthood: settling down	33–40	Create a second adult life structure; invest yourself in work, family, friendships, community. Establish a niche in society and strive to "make it," to achieve the dream.
Midlife transition	40–45	A bridge from early to middle adulthood: Ask basic questions, such as "What have I done with my life?" or "What do I want for myself and others?" May or may not involve crisis.
Entering middle adulthood	45–50	Create a new life structure, often (but not always) with a new job, or a new marriage, or a change in nature of work life.
Age-50 transition	50–55	Similar in function to the age-30 transition; a more minor adjustment to the middl- adult life structure. However, if no crisis occurred at midlife transition, one is likely to occur now.
Culmination of middle adulthood	55–60	Build a second midlife structure, analogous to settling down in middle adulthood. May be a particularly satisfying time if the adult has successfully adapted the life structures to changes in roles and self.
Late-adult transition	60–65	Termination of middle adulthood and bridge to late adulthood. Conclude the efforts of middle adulthood, prepare for retirement and the physical declines of old age. A major turning point in the life cycle.
Late adulthood	65+	Create a new life structure that will suit the new patterns in retirement and the increasing physical declines. Cope with illness. Deal with the psychological issue of loss of youth.

Source: Levinson, 1978.

The life structure of the 20s, including both the dream and (for some) a mentor, does not last, in part because the goals may not be reached, but also because the relationships and social demands change. At the very least, the novice-phase life structure of the 20s must be reexamined to see if it still fits, if the goals are still the same, if the strategies are working. In Levinson's view, the **age-30 transition** is focused on just such a reassessment, and it is followed by the culminating phase of this era, which he sometimes calls **settling down.**

The **midlife transition** in the early 40s deals with another set of issues—with awareness of mortality, with the realization that the dream may not have been fulfilled. A further major transition, at around age 60 to 65, is focused on the sense of loss of physical powers or possible illness, on accepting that one has achieved as much as one can.

Levinson is not saying that all adult lives are exactly alike. Indeed, he emphasizes that the specific life structures created in these various stages and eras will be widely different. But he is saying that the underlying sequence of eras, of stable and transitional stages, holds for all adults in all cultures: "It is abundantly evident that, at the level of events, roles, or personality, individual lives unfold in myriad ways. There is not much order in the concrete individual life course.… I do propose, however, that there is an *underlying* order in the human life course, an order shaped by the eras and by the periods in life structure development.… It is my hypothesis… that the basic nature and timing of life structure development are given in the life cycle at this time in human evolution" (1990, p. 43).

At the same time, Levinson explicitly rejects the idea that these sequences of life structures, these "seasons of a man's life," involve any movement from worse to better or less mature to more mature. He assumes change, even systematic change, with age, but not development. As he says: "The tasks of one period are not better or more advanced than those of another, except in the general sense that each period builds upon the work of the earlier ones and represents a later phase in the cycle. There are losses as well as gains in the shift from every period or era to the next" (1978, p. 320).

Levinson's view has been at least partially supported by the existing research on women (Levinson, 1996; Roberts & Newton, 1987). The majority of women studied intensively do go through an age-30 transition, for example. On the other side of the ledger, there is little support for Levinson's notions of the universality of the dream or the mentor role. A distinct subset of the women studied have described no dream, and only a fraction of them have had a mentor. Still, at the deepest level that Levinson describes, the level at which there are alternating periods of stable life structures and transitions, there is some support for his view.

Life-Course Transitions: A Sociological Perspective

In the same approximate place in the theoretical matrix, although shifted toward the middle on the stage/no stage continuum, lies a composite sociological perspective focused on **life-course transitions** (George, 1993). I use the word *perspective* rather than *theory* quite deliberately. Sociologists, whose thinking about the adult life course was shaped for many years by a strongly stage-based theory, the model of family life stages, have been struggling to come to terms with the obvious variability in adult life pathways. The current perspective has several important theoretical roots.

Role Theory. One important precursor to the current sociological views is the concept of a **role.** Sociologists describe social systems as being made up of linked or interlocking **positions** (also called *statuses),* such as teacher and student, parent and child, or employer and employee. The **content** of a particular position is called a *role.* A role is thus a kind of job description for a particular position, a set of skills or qualities expected in a person who occupies that position. The person who fills the role of Girl Scout leader, for example, is expected to know about camping, cooking, and crafts, and about organizing activities that will keep young children interested. Such a person is also expected to be friendly and cheerful.

The concept of role has proven to be highly useful in descriptions of adult life. In fact, we can describe (or even define) any one adult's life in terms of the roles that he or she performs. I am a mother, a daughter, a sister, a partner (a role I often refer to as "spouselike person"), a psychologist, an author, a friend, a school board member, and so on. Collectively, the roles any one of us occupies at any one time in our life make up a kind of framework for what Levinson calls the life structure.

We can also examine the frictions that emerge when a person attempts to fulfill the demands of two or more roles simultaneously (as virtually all of us do). **Role conflict** occurs when two or more roles are partially or wholly incompatible, logistically or psychologically. When you are trying to juggle the competing demands of your schoolwork, your job, and your family, you are experiencing role conflict. There are not enough hours in the day to fulfill the expectations of all three roles. **Role strain** occurs when a person's own qualities or skills are a poor match for the demands of any one role. If you have been out of school for awhile, so that your study skills are rusty, you may experience role strain when you go back to school. If you are promoted to a job for which you are only marginally prepared, you will feel role strain.

CRITICAL THINKING

Make a list of all the roles you presently occupy. Which combination(s) of roles creates role conflict, or role strain, for you?

The concept of roles can also help us understand changes over adult life, because there are certain roles that shift predictably with age. As I pointed out in Chapter 1, there are age strata in any society which have accompanying roles. In our culture, teenagers have one role, young adults another, retired persons still another. Work roles also change with age, as I'll detail in Chapter 8. And, of course, roles within a family change, as I pointed out in Chapter 1.

Family Life Stages. This last fact lies at the heart of a theory or model that shaped sociological thinking for many years. Evelyn Duvall (1962), among others, proposed that adult life could be understood in terms of a set of systematic changes in family roles. At least for those adults who marry and have children (the vast majority of adults), adult life marches to the rhythm of shifts in family roles. As you can see in Table 2.5, Duvall proposed eight such **family life stages,** each reflecting either additions or deletions to the family (new child, or children leaving) or changes in the content of the parent role as the children shift from infancy to toddlerhood to school age to adolescence.

This conceptualization has served as an organizing model for a great deal of sociological research on adulthood. Instead of comparing adults of different ages, researchers compare adults in different life-cycle stages, creating a variant of the cross-sectional design. You have already seen an example of this in Chapter 1 (Figure 1.6), and there will be more examples throughout the book. The basic idea, obviously, is that a person's behavior and attitudes are shaped by the roles he or she occupies. And since these roles change with age in systematic and predictable ways, adults will also change systematically and

TABLE 2.5 **Stages in Family Life Cycle Proposed by Duvall and Others**

Stage	Description
1	*Newly married with no children;* the role of spouse has been added.
2	*New parents;* first child is an infant, so the new role of parent has been added.
3	*Family with preschool children;* oldest child is between 2 and 6; other younger children may also be in the family.
4	*Families with school-age children;* oldest child is between 6 and 12; there may be younger children as well.
5	*Families with adolescent children;* oldest child is now a teenager, which changes the parental role in specific ways.
6	*Families with the oldest child gone from home;* there may well be other children still at home, but the "launching center" role of the family has begun.
7	*Families in which all children have left home;* this is often called the "postparental" stage.
8	*Aging families;* one or both spouses has retired.

Source: Duvall, 1962.

predictably. There is no notion here that some roles are better than others or that the family life cycle (or any other age-related change in roles) leads to "growth" or "improvement" in some fashion. But there are definable stages, widely shared in this and other cultures. Knowing that a person has a new infant tells you something about his or her life. If you knew that another person's youngest child had just gone off to college, you would quite correctly infer very different things about his or her daily existence.

But this conception, at least in the simplified form represented in Table 2.5, has been set aside because of two types of major flaws. First, there are a number of important roles totally omitted from the model, such as the role of grandparent, or the role of caregiver to one's own aging parents. There is also no differentiation of the postparental period, as if once the children were gone, there were no further changes in roles or life patterns. The more we learn about the young old, the old old, and the oldest old, the more it is clear that these groups have quite different roles, different life structures.

The second and even more telling problem with family life-cycle stages as a theory of adult life is that in today's industrialized societies, a great many people simply don't move through this sequence of roles in the order given. Many adults today do not marry; a growing number do not have children; many (perhaps even half in the United States) divorce and move through complex combinations of family roles. To use myself as an example again, I did not marry until I was 32, then became the instant mother of two stepchildren (aged 3 and 11 then) with whom I lived for seven years. Then I was alone for four years, then lived for one year with my newly adult son, and then remarried, becoming stepmother to four more children, all more or less grown and flown. I cannot find my life in Duvall's model, and neither can a growing number of adults.

Current Conceptualizations. Yet there are important elements to the concept of the family life cycle that both sociologists and psychologists would like to retain. Although the sequence and timing may vary, it is clear that the particular family life cycle a person experiences has an important effect on his or her life pattern. And in any given culture or cohort, there may nonetheless be some shared markers, some common transition points, such as retirement in the 60s in most industrialized countries.

Out of these concepts has now emerged a new sociology of the life course. According to Linda George (1993), it includes a number of key elements. First, the **life course** is seen as a social phenomenon, distinct from the life span. It is unique for each person, but nonetheless occurs within a given social and historical context which may impose some commonalities. Second, any life course contains a number of **transitions,** defined as "changes in status that are discrete and bounded in duration" (p. 358), such as shifting from being single to being married, or from working to being retired. Transitions that are highly predictable and widely shared in any given culture or cohort are called **life-course markers.** In recent cohorts, many of the family life transitions that are concentrated in early adulthood—such as marriage and first parenthood—have become less predictable, with highly variable timing and sequence. At the same time, some transitions in middle and late adulthood have become more prevalent and predictable, such as the death of a parent while one is in middle age, or voluntary retirement in one's 60s.

Sociologists and psychologists who study the life course continue to be especially interested in those age-linked socially recognized sequences of transitions that may be widely shared within a given cohort. As Avshalom Caspi and Glen Elder say, "successful transitions and adjustments to age-graded roles are the core developmental tasks faced by the individual across the life course" (1988, pp. 120–121). But the new emphasis on life transitions points to different questions than those provoked by the Duvall model. For example, what are the effects of variations in sequence, or variations in the timing of specific sequences of transitions?

What both George and Caspi and Elder are saying, then, is that family life stages need not be precisely the same for all adults for some aspects of basic theoretical perspective to remain useful. The specific sequence of roles, or the timing of those roles, may change from one cohort to the next, from one culture to the next, or even for different subgroups within a given culture, but dealing with *some* normative sequence of roles is the very stuff of adult life.

THEORIES OF CHANGE WITHOUT STAGES

Clearly, many sociologists (and many psychologists) have been pushed away from strict stagelike theories by the obvious variability in adult lives. Others have taken the argument to the logical extreme and abandoned the notion of shared stages altogether. In the view of these theorists, it is more fruitful to examine the ways that adults adapt to the unique constellations of life experiences they may face rather than to search for elusive (or nonexistent) patterns of shared stages.

Many of the theories in this group are really preliminary models rather than complete theories, proposed by researchers who have struggled to apply earlier, stagelike concepts to their observations of adult life and who have found the stage theories wanting. These theories could best be described as **eclectic.** What they have in common, other than their strong data-based orientation, is skepticism about the usefulness of simple stage models of adult development, and similar doubt about conceptualizing changes in adulthood as "development." Leonard Pearlin's approach is a good example of a theory of this type.

Pearlin's Model of Psychological Distress In Adults

Leonard Pearlin (1980, 1982a, 1982b) has offered a useful synthesis of concepts from both psychology and sociology. His major interest has been in sources of distress over the adult years and in people's methods of coping with such distress. But his suggestions about the adult years are not limited to the domain of distress. Pearlin grants that there may be life tasks or psychological issues that are characteristic of particular age periods. But in his view, such age-related issues form only a minor part of the experience of aging. Pearlin is much more struck by the diversity of pathways: "Because people are at the same age or life cycle phase, it cannot be assumed that they have either traveled the same route to reach their present locations or that they are headed in the same future directions" (1982a, p. 64).

The elements in individual lives that determine the route a person follows, in Pearlin's view, are several: (1) dimensions of individual difference, particularly the social or economic class in which the person finds himself or herself; (2) the range of skills the person has for coping with stress or life change (the wider the range of such coping skills, the less distress the person will feel, (3) the availability and usefulness of social support networks (adults with strongly supportive networks experience any form of potential distress less acutely); and (4) the nature and timing of the sources of stress or distress the person must face.

Pearlin divides sources of distress into three types. First there are the **daily life strains** that are built into any life: chronic and durable distress such as the complaining mother-in-law, the boring job, the role conflict inherent in trying to work and care for a family at the same time, the need to stretch the budget to meet inflation. Second, there are **scheduled life strains,** predictable events such as the birth of a child, the

CRITICAL THINKING

Can you think of examples of scheduled and unscheduled changes in your own life or in your parents' lives? Do your or their experiences with these changes appear to match Pearlin's model?

departure of a young adult from home, or retirement. These are all anticipated role changes. Finally, there are the **unscheduled life strains,** unexpected changes such as being laid off from work, or an automobile accident, or the unexpected death of a parent or close friend—a concept rather similar to Neugarten's notion of on-time and off-time life events.

Pearlin's research findings persuade him that scheduled changes have relatively little effect on feelings of distress or well-being, whereas unscheduled changes frequently have major effects. But even unscheduled events have most of their impact indirectly, by increasing the daily life strains. Being widowed, for example, has a relatively small impact on adults who have adequate financial and emotional resources. Those adults who are forced to change their daily lives sharply, however—go to work, or live at a lower economic level, or cope with rearing children alone—show far more distress, depression, and anxiety. Pearlin appears to be saying that the unplanned disruption of a life structure (to borrow Levinson's concept) is what causes maximum distress.

It should be clear from even this limited description of Pearlin's work that while this is a theory about *changes* in adult lives, it is definitely not a theory about development. Pearlin specifically rejects the idea that there is any inner unfolding, any "growth." "We hold, first, that adult emotional development does not represent the gradual surfacing of conditions that happen to reside within individuals. Instead, we see it as a continuing process of adjustment to external circumstances…. (1980, p. 180]. Since adults of any given age are likely to share certain external circumstances, there *may* be common experiences at different points in the life course, at least for subgroups within any given cohort. But Pearlin is arguing that real understanding of adult lives will be found not in defining those shared experiences as universal stages, but in searching for those principles that govern the way that individual adults cope with the changing demands of adult life.

ACCORDING TO PEARLIN'S THEORY, which is likely to be more stressful in an adult's life: retiring at 65, or losing your job when you are in the middle of adulthood like these adults?

ADDITIONAL THEORETICAL COMPLEXITIES

The classification of theories I have offered in Figure 2.1 highlights two dimensions on which theories of adulthood differ from one another. But even the brief descriptions I have given of these theories point to other important dimensions on which theories of adult lives might be arrayed. Two such additional dimensions seem to me to be especially critical.

First, there is the question of **universality versus diversity.** Are there ways in which *all* adults change or develop in the same way, in the same sequences, or at the same rates? Some theorists, such as Erikson or Loevinger or Levinson, obviously think so. They are searching for underlying sameness in the face of apparent difference. Other researchers, including Pearlin and even Vaillant, have been much more struck by the diversity of adult pathways, sequences, and coping strategies. For theorists in this second group, understanding adulthood means to understand *why* people develop differently, or in different sequences, or more or less fully. What are the characteristics of the person—the background characteristics or the life experiences—that lead one adult to an integrated, satisfied old age, and another to a bitter, maladaptive, or lonely old age?

A second key issue that separates the theorists I have talked about is whether they see change (or development) as resulting primarily from some kind of internal "psychological clock," or from primarily external influences, such as social roles, subcultural norms, or cohort experiences. To some degree this particular debate has divided the psychologists and the sociologists who study adulthood. As sociologist Dale Dannefer has pointed out somewhat scathingly (1984a, 1984b, 1988), a psychologist faced with any research results that look even remotely like a common pattern is very likely to assume that he or she has uncovered a basic, normative process of aging. Dannefer describes the psychologists' typical assumption as the **ontogenetic fallacy:** The assumption that "change in adulthood [is] a natural property of the individual which tends to be uniform across individuals and relatively unaffected by context" (1984a, p. 109).

In contrast, many theorists emerging from a sociological tradition have been more interested in understanding the impact on adult lives of such contextual forces as cohort differences and subcultural norms, such as the differences in life expectations for working-class and middle-class adults in any cohort. To psychologists searching for internal orderliness, cohort or cultural differences are "noise" in the system; they want to look beyond or behind such variation for the common pattern they assume is there. To sociologists, cohort and subcultural differences are precisely the data of interest.

Clearly, such a difference in basic assumptions is going to lead theorists of the several persuasions to study very different aspects of individual lives. Psychologists typically focus on measuring internal states, such as personality, coping skills, or mental abilities. Sociologists are much more likely to focus on changes in roles, such as retirement or the birth of the first child. Even when the same event is studied, the two groups ask very different questions. A psychologist looking at the impact of the birth of an adult's first child is likely to study the impact on his or her personality or on gender-role attitudes; the sociologist is likely to look at structural changes in family roles resulting from the child's inclusion in the family system.

To be sure, this demarkation line between the two disciplines is often crossed. Nonetheless, this disagreement about which aspects of adulthood should be studied, and about whether we should search for understanding in internal or in external forces, runs through all the literature on adulthood and makes synthesis of theory and data extremely difficult. Undaunted, a number of recent authors have attempted such syntheses, some of which I find intriguing. Let me describe two such attempts and then add several suggestions of my own.

Baltes's Life-Span Perspective

Paul Baltes, along with colleagues such as Richard Lerner and David Featherman, is quick to point out that the **life-span perspective** is a perspective and not a theory (Baltes, 1987; Baltes, & Reese, 1984; Dixon & Lerner, 1988, 1992; Featherman, 1983; Lerner, 1986). As Dixon and Lerner put it: "What is the life-span perspective? It should be noted immediately that it does not constitute a theory, a collection of theories, or a metatheory of development; rather, it offers a perspective on psychology based on the proposition that the changes (growth, development, aging) shown by people from the time of their conception, throughout their lives, and until the time of their death are usefully conceptualized as developmental" (1988, p. 34).

In some respects, this perspective is an antidote to the common assumption two decades ago that "development" occurred only in childhood and adolescence. Among other things, we know that development in childhood clearly had at least some biological, maturational base. Children and adolescents are clearly growing and changing physically, and those physical changes affect everything else. When we applied the same model to adulthood, all we saw in the way of change was the decay of the physical organism. Baltes and those of like mind see this as a very narrow view. He argues that development continues over one's lifetime and is influenced not just by biological change but by a whole set of other factors, including age-graded changes dictated by culture, historical (cohort) effects, and unique individual experiences.

The starting point for the life-span perspective, then, was simply the assumption that there is more to study in adult development than physical decline. Over the past two decades, however, this perspective has become richer. As Baltes describes it in his more recent writings, it now includes the set of assumptions, propositions, or "family of beliefs" listed in Table 2.6, that guide both thinking and programs of research. When you read through these propositions you'll see that Baltes and his colleagues are not rejecting totally the notion that there may be shared stages of development. There might even be many different sets of stages or sequences, each connected to or characteristic of one facet of development, such as changes in certain kinds of intellectual skills, or changes in levels of rigidity. But researchers and theorists such as Baltes, working within this general perspective, also assume **plasticity.** The human organism, throughout the life span, is capable of change. Plasticity clearly has some limits, and it may be that those limits get narrower as we get older—an empirical question of great interest to Baltes—but he assumes that there is at least some plasticity at all times. Stage theorists such as Loevinger or Erikson also assume the potential for change, but in many stage theories, change is unidirectional. Those who follow a life-span development perspective do not make such an assumption; in their view, change can go in many directions.

If, after reading the list in Table 2.6, and after reading my brief description of this perspective, you have a sense of fuzziness, you are not alone. In some sense the life-span developmental perspective offers a theoretical synthesis simply by taking a great many things in under the tent. At first, this may seem like trying to be all things to all people. But there is more to it than that. Baltes and his colleagues are assuming that there is *lawfulness* to the changes we see in adult life and that those laws go beyond processes of physiological decline. Our task as psychologists (or sociologists or anthropologists or biologists) is to uncover and understand the nature of that lawfulness. They do *not* assume that the specific pathways followed by adults will necessarily be all the same; they do not assume that all pathways lead toward either decline or toward higher efficacy. They do assume that the underlying lawfulness will create many different surface patterns, just as Levinson as-

TABLE 2.6 **Major Theoretical Propositions of the Life-Span Perspective**

Concepts	Propositions
Life-span development	Development is a lifelong process. No age period holds supremacy in regulating the nature of development. At all stages of the life span, continuous (cumulative) and discontinuous processes are at work.
Multidirectionality	There is no single direction of change in development even within the same domain (such as intellectual development). Some functions show increases, some decreases. And at any given age, some systems of behavior show increases, whereas others show declines.
Development as gain/loss	The process of development is not a simple move toward higher efficacy, such as incremental gain. Rather, throughout life, development always consists of the joint occurrence of gain (growth) and loss (decline).
Plasticity	There is considerable capacity for change (either growth or decline) within each person at any point in the life course. Thus, depending on the conditions and experiences, the developmental course of a given person can take many forms.
Historical embeddedness	Life-span development can also vary substantially in accordance with historical–cultural conditions, cohort differences, differences within cohorts in the same culture, and differences between cultures.
Contextualism	Any particular course of individual development is understood as the outcome of the interactions of three systems of developmental influences: age-graded, history-graded, and nonnormative.
Multidisciplinary approach	Understanding of human development will be furthered by collaborative work among several disciplines, including anthropology, biology, and sociology as well as psychology.

Source: Adapted from Baltes, 1987, Table 1, p. 613.

sumes that myriad specific life patterns can reflect the same underlying sequence of basic eras and periods of transition. Thus though it is true that the life-span perspective offers a very large tent, the tent is not unlimited.

Within the broad category of the life-span perspective, we can find much more specific theoretical proposals, some of which also offer potential theoretical synthesis. One such is Pamela Perun and Denise Bielby's (1980) timing model of development, a theory that has not become widely known, but that I find to be a clear and helpful model.

Perun and Bielby's Timing Model Of Adult Development

Perun and Bielby (1980) conceive of adult life as made up of a large number of **temporal progressions,** sequences of experiences or internal changes each of which follows some timetable. The physical changes in the body over adulthood represent one such temporal progression, as do the changes in the family life cycle, or the ego developments described by Loevinger, or alterations in work roles or gender roles. Figure 2.3 shows this model graphically, which may help to convey the complexity. Each of these disks, rather like machine gears moving at different rates, represents a single temporal progression, such as the life cycle within a nuclear family (marrying, having children, having those children grow up), or a separate life cycle within the extended family (such as the timing of one's parents' deaths). Each of these progressions moves at a different rate for each person, thus creating a unique pattern for each adult. A young adult who marries at 16, has speeded up the family life-cycle progression; another adult who exercises three times a week for his en-

SOME POSSIBLE TEMPORAL PROGRESSIONS

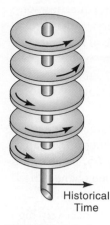

Physical changes over adulthood

Changes in nuclear family roles
   (family life cycle)

Changes in other family roles
   (such as roles with one's parents)

Changes in work roles

Changes in emotional/personal tasks
   of adulthood

Historical
Time

FIGURE 2.3 Perun and Bielby's timing model of the life course. Each of these disks represents one "temporal progression," a set of sequential changes in one aspect of adult functioning. Each moves along on its own timetable, at its own speed, with both speed and timetable affected by cohort, culture, gender, race, and so on, creating a unique pattern of interlocking changes for each person.

Source: Perun & Bielby, 1980, Fig. 1, p. 102. Reprinted by permission of Westview Press, Boulder, Colorado.

tire adult life may slow down the rate of the physical change progression. Furthermore, this entire process is embedded within a particular period of historical time (a cohort), which will affect the process as well. For each of us, this collection of temporal progressions forms a whole. We do not experience this as a set of independent gears, crunching away inside. What we experience are the interrelationships among these progressions.

Perun and Bielby suggest that one of the key interrelationships is the **synchrony** or **asynchrony** of these temporal progressions. Do the several timetables dovetail, support one another, match? If so, synchrony exists and the person will experience low levels of stress. In Levinson's terms, when there is synchrony, a stable life structure exists. "Asynchrony occurs when one or more dimensions is off-time in relation to others" (Perun & Bielby, 1980, p. 105). This creates friction, as if the gears did not quite mesh. We experience such friction as stress, or as a crisis, and strive to change in one or more dimensions until synchrony is again achieved. To get the gears to mesh again, you may have to move one of the other gears to a new position. The man who, at 45, finds that he puffs when he walks up a flight of stairs, or can no longer beat his younger colleagues at tennis, may well experience this as asynchronous with his sense of increased effectiveness and responsibility at work. He could deal with this asynchrony in several ways, each of which involves "moving another gear." He might get into better physical shape (moving back or slowing down the rate of change of the progression of physical changes). Or he might go through some sort of internal reappraisal that would change the way he perceived the importance of physical competition. In coming to terms with his physical aging, he might shift to a higher level of ego development and again experience relative synchrony.

Thus there are two sources of change within this model: First, the basic temporal progressions themselves describe changes, some of which are either inevitable or widely shared and some of which may be stagelike. Second, asynchrony triggers additional change. Several intriguing and potentially useful implications or expansions of this model occur to me.

1. The rate of movement along any one temporal dimension may be influenced by individual differences: by gender, race, intelligence, temperament, education, or social class. For example, women from working-class families marry earlier and have their children earlier. This changes the timing of at least one of the gears in the model, which will in turn alter the points at which asynchrony will be experienced. If we could add to this model some equations describing factors that affect the rate of change in each progression, we could come closer to being able to predict individual life patterns.

2. Following Pearlin's lead, we might also hypothesize that anticipated or scheduled shifts on any one progression will create less disrupting asynchrony than will unanticipated or unscheduled changes. If I plan to retire at 65, I can think about the changes that will be involved and partially adjust to the change ahead of time.

3. Being significantly off-time in any one progression should produce relatively high rates of asynchrony throughout the life course. Women who have children in their teens, or those who do not have their first child until they are in their late 30s, would be two examples of such off-time patterns. But Perun and Bielby's model also suggests that there is a potential reward to be reaped from off-timeness as well, since coping with the asynchrony produced by the off-time pattern *may* lead to higher levels of personal adaptation or growth.

4. Despite individual differences in the rate of movement along the several progressions, there are still widely shared (although not universal) points of asynchrony. At midlife, for example, those adults who follow a modal pattern are likely to have their children begin leaving home, their parents begin to fail in health, their own bodies begin to show signs of decline, and their jobs "peak out," all at approximately the same time. Such shared asynchronies may produce the somewhat illusory appearance of broad stages in adult lives.

5. If asynchrony is one of the keys to personal change (and possibly to personal growth), adults who find themselves in situations that force change are also likely to show the greatest growth. As an example, Melvin Kohn (1980) (whose work I'll describe more fully in Chapter 8) has found that adults in complex jobs show greater growth in intellectual skill than do adults who have more routine jobs. Some of this is self-selection, of course: Adults with less intellectual skill to start with are more likely to end up with less complex jobs. But Kohn has shown that job complexity has an independent effect. High job complexity pushes everyone toward more complex and elaborated ways of thinking.

6. Given asynchrony, growth is not the only possible outcome. Synchrony can be recreated by regression or retreat in some progression. For example, if a new job requires you to learn a whole new set of complex skills, thus creating asynchrony, you could give up the job and go back to something more familiar. A midlife man may respond to the asynchronies of that age not by becoming physically fit, or accepting limitations, but by increased drinking, or by depression. Each of these is a kind of adaptation. In Vaillant's terms, each of these is a defense against the anxiety produced by the asynchrony.

These implications and expansions illustrate, I hope, the potential richness of this model, or models like it. An approach like this goes beyond the broadness of the life-span perspective and suggests several of the basic laws that may govern adult life change and development. Nonetheless, there is clearly a great deal that is not dealt with in such a model. As an example, when a person is faced with asynchrony, what determines the coping method that he or she uses? Given what appears to be the same crisis, why do some people respond constructively, others destructively? And what determines the form that a new life structure will take? If we think of each of these asynchronies as a large freeway cloverleaf intersection, then each represents a set of choices. You can choose to continue along the same road; you can turn off onto a new road, or you can turn around and go back on the road you came on. What determines such choices? Is there lawfulness here, too? Are these choices affected by personality, by social class, by ethnicity or gender?

Erikson would undoubtedly suggest that each choice affects all that follow it. So unsuccessful resolutions of early dilemmas (perhaps particularly the very first dilemma of trust versus mistrust) will increase the chances that later dilemmas will be unsuccessfully, or even destructively, resolved. To predict the future life course of any one person, then, we would need to know his or her life history in detail—a very tall order indeed.

TABLE 2.7 Major Sources of Data on Which the Several Theories of Adult Development Are Based

Theorist	Database
Erikson	Primarily Erikson's own clinical observations as a child analyst and extensive reading of anthropological descriptions of other cultures.
Loevinger	Loevinger's own clinical judgment, supplemented and supported by fairly extensive research with the Sentence Completion Test of Ego Development, including studies of both black and white children, high school and college students studied longitudinally over four to six years, numerous college samples, and many studies relating this measure to other assessments. Less extensive evidence on the higher stages.
Vaillant	Vaillant's own clinical judgment as a psychiatrist, but based primarily on interviews with 100 of the all-male Grant study participants at about age 50, plus all other information on these Harvard men in the Grant study files.
Levinson	Original source was an extensive set of interviews and assessments of 40 men between the ages of 35 and 45, equally divided into four occupations: hourly industrial workers, executives, university biologists, and novelists. Samples of women have since been studied by both Levinson and several others, but few data published.
Life-Course Transitions	Proposed by several sociologists as a synthesizing concept, based on hundreds of studies of families in earlier decades, and since used as an organizational rubric and theoretical concept in hundreds more studies. Very extensive database.
Pearlin	Major source is a short-term longitudinal study of adults from a wide range of socioeconomic levels, both male and female, ages 18 to 65; 2,300 adults were interviewed once, and a subset reinterviewed four years later, covering all aspects of work and love.
Baltes	A theoretical approach not based on a specific study, although research on changes in adult intellectual functioning has been especially influential.
Perun and Bielby	A theoretical synthesis based on both theory and empirical evidence from others, but applied principally to a sample of 41 married women with Ph.D.s.

SOME SHARED FLAWS AND WEAKNESSES IN THE THEORIES

Before leaving this excursion through the research landscape and beginning our much longer journey through the empirical evidence on changes and continuities in adulthood, I would be remiss if I did not point out several major weaknesses shared by most or all of these theories. First, the database for these theories is typically extremely small. In Table 2.7 I have described briefly the major studies or clinical data from which these several theories have emerged. As you can see, most of the theories—particularly those offered by psychologists—are based on very limited observations of actual adults. Vaillant interviewed 100 middle-aged men; Erikson's theory is based primarily on his own clinical observations. Of course, this need not mean that the theories are wrong. Many remarkable theoretical insights have been based on only a few clinical observations (Freud's work and that of Piaget come immediately to mind). But it does mean that the wide applicability of any one theory has not been well tested.

Second, there are several marked biases built into many (but not all) of the data sources and the theories themselves. Most theorists have studied primarily white middle-class, adults. All have studied only Western culture. In addition, several of the major theories are based largely or entirely on interviews with or observations only of men. Whether any theory emerging from such observations will be applicable to women, to working-class adults, or to adults of other cultures is open to real question. More particularly, any theory based on such limited observations that proposes that all adults develop in the same way or in precisely the same sequence seems to me to be particularly suspect, precisely the point made by sociologist Dale Dannefer in his critique of psychological theories of adulthood. That does not mean that we cannot learn from such theories, but it does mean that we should be suitably skeptical about their wide applicability.

What I need to do now is to look at each of the gears or cogs shown in Figure 2.3 one at a time, so that you can get some sense of the kinds of changes that occur in each dimension over the adult years. I will then come back to the task of putting the pieces together in Chapter 14, where I will attempt another synthesis.

SUMMARY

1. Theories of adulthood differ on a number of important dimensions, among them the distinction between development and change, and between stagelike and non-stagelike change. Theorists who assume that there is some common direction in which adults move can be described as *development* theorists; those who assume change without shared direction can be described as *change* theorists. Some in each group further assume that the movement (change or development) occurs in fixed stages of some kind; others assume no such stages.

2. Developmental-stage theorists include Erik Erikson, Jane Loevinger, Roger Gould, and many others.

3. Erikson's theory of identity development describes eight stages or dilemmas, spread over the entire life span, each of which is linked to a particular age. The person moves into a new stage because of changes in cultural or role demands, or physical changes, and must then resolve the dilemma associated with that stage.

4. Incomplete or imperfect resolution of a dilemma leaves unfinished business to be carried forward to the next stage, increasing the likelihood that the next stage, too, will be resolved imperfectly.

5. The four stages Erikson describes that are part of adulthood are identity versus role diffusion, intimacy versus isolation, generativity versus stagnation, and integrity versus despair.

6. The stages in Loevinger's theory are not tied to age. Children and adults move along a progression of 10 steps or levels, each built on the preceding ones, with movement occurring only when the preceding stage has been completed. A group of adults of a given age will thus contain individuals who may be functioning at any one of several different levels.

7. The stages in Loevinger's theory that are particularly relevant to the study of adulthood are the conformist, the self-aware, the conscientious, the individualistic, the autonomous, and the integrated.

8. George Vaillant assumes the validity of Erikson's stages but adds the concept of maturing defense mechanisms. He describes several levels of maturity of defenses, and suggests that (a) as a group adults move toward more and more mature defenses, and (b) that adults vary in the degree to which that movement occurs.

9. Another group of theories retains the concept of stage but eliminates the concept of directional development. Prominent in this group is Levinson's theory of seasons of life. Present-day sociological models of adult life transitions also can be located roughly here.

10. Levinson proposes a universally shared rhythm of stable life structures alternating with periods of transition. These alternations occur at particular ages, as adults come to terms with particular issues that are relevant for those ages.

11. Current adult-life transition theories are based heavily on the concept of role and have as theoretical progenitors the older theories of the family life cycle. The emphasis is on the individual life course and on the impact of timing and sequence of both shared and individual transitions.

12. More eclectic models, assuming neither development nor stages, also exist, such as Leonard's Pearlin's model of methods of handling distress in adulthood.

13. These theories also differ on other dimensions, such as whether they assume universality or diversity of patterns, and whether they focus on internal or external change. As a general rule, sociologists have emphasized the potency of such external forces as cohort effects and subcultural influences; psychologists have emphasized the importance of some kind of shared psychological clock that leads to common inner changes.

14. Several attempts at synthesis involve intermediate positions on the two key theoretical dimensions. Baltes's life-span perspective is a broad view that emphasizes the importance of both internal and external forces, both development and change. He assumes that some type of development continues over the whole lifetime, that the process is lawful, but that individual pathways may diverge sharply.

15. Perun and Bielby's timing model is a second form of synthesis. They assume that within each adult there is a series of separate temporal progressions, each moving at its own speed. Asynchrony among these several progressions produces stress, which

each person resolves by some kind of change in one or more progression. This theory appears to provide a better (albeit much more complex) view of adult development than do many of the previous theories.

16. All of these theories, to a greater or lesser extent, share two weaknesses: They are based on a paucity of data, and they tend to be biased toward descriptions of the adult lives of white, middle-class, American males.

KEY TERMS

theory of adult development

theory of adult change

stages

antistages

sequences

identity

identity versus role confusion

intimacy versus isolation

generativity versus self-absorption and stagnation

ego integrity versus despair

self-protective stage

conformist stage

self-aware level

conscientious stage

individualistic level

autonomous stage

integrated stage

career consolidation

defense mechanism

life structure

novice phase

midera transition

culminating phase

early adult transition

mentor

the dream

age-30 transition

settling down

midlife transition

life-course transitions

role

positions

content

role conflict

role strain

family life stages

life course

transitions

life-course markers

eclectic theories

daily life strain

scheduled life strains

unscheduled life strains

universality versus diversity

ontogenetic fallacy

life-span perspective

plasticity

temporal progression

synchrony

asynchrony

SUGGESTED READINGS

Baltes, P. B. (1987). Theoretical propositions of life-span developmental psychology: On the dynamics between growth and decline. *Developmental Psychology, 3,* 611–626.

In the past I have found the life-span perspective difficult to grasp. It seemed unbearably broad and fuzzy. But in this systematic statement, Baltes has made it much clearer.

Gould, R. (1978). *Transformations. Growth and change in adult life.* New York: Simon & Schuster.

I am particularly fond of this book, since it is written in an unusually engaging and clear style, with a great deal of clinical case material. It is perhaps the least technical and complex of the series of theoretical books (including Vaillant's and Levinson's) that came out at about that same time.

Lerner, R. M. (1986). *Concepts and theories of human development* (2nd ed.). New York: Random House.

If you are looking for a book that will give you more detail and depth on many of the basic theories of development, in both childhood and adulthood, this is an excellent source.

Levinson, D. J. (1990). A theory of life structure development in adulthood. In C. N. Alexander & E. J. Langer (Eds.), *Higher stages of human development. Perspectives on adult growth* (pp. 35–53). New York: Oxford University Press.

This is a very good brief description of Levinson's theory.

Smelser, N. J., & Erikson, E. H. (1980). *Themes of work and love in adulthood.* Cambridge, MA: Harvard University Press.

This is a wonderful collection of papers by many of the major theoretical figures I have talked about in this chapter, including Levinson, Gould, and Pearlin. The chapters are not overly technical, but each gives a good overview of that particular approach.

Turner, B. F., & Troll, L. E. (Eds.). (1994). *Women growing older. Psychological perspectives.* Thousand Oaks, CA: Sage.

This is also a wonderful collection of papers. Although the focus is on the experiences of older women, many of the selections offer general theoretical models as well.

PHYSICAL
CHANGES

C H A P T E R

3

My maternal grandparents both lived into their 90s and were physically in quite good shape until their final few years. They remained active and vital people through the final decades, keeping house for themselves and each keeping up an extensive correspondence with friends and family. (My grandfather, in fact, always tried to answer letters the day he got them. No matter how hard I tried, I always seemed to owe him a letter!). My grandmother was working on her third book in her late 80s and early 90s. Despite their continuing productivity and enjoyment of life, though, they were both acutely aware of the physical changes that had significantly altered their lives in the final decade or so. They reported loss of energy and vitality; they had increasing difficulty following conversations in large groups; they lost quite a lot of physical coordination in the last years, and both became extremely thin. How typical are these changes? We all know that adults get grayer and wrinklier and a bit slower as they age. But what other changes take place?

More important, what changes will we all experience if we are lucky enough to live to be very old, and what changes will happen to only some of us? There is an important distinction between **primary aging** and **secondary aging** (Busse, 1987). Primary aging is the gradual, shared, inevitable set of gains or declines that begins early in adulthood and continues over the years. Secondary aging, in contrast, is the product of environmental influences, health habits, or disease, and is neither inevitable nor shared by all adults.

Distinguishing between the effects of primary and secondary aging is a very tricky process indeed. In particular, sorting out the effects of disease from the effects of normal aging has proven to be highly complicated. Suppose, for example, that we want to know about the normal maturational changes in heart function over the years of adulthood. Does the heart become less efficient? What happens to blood pressure or to blood cholesterol? Whether we use a cross-sectional or a longitudinal design to try to answer such questions, we will have the same problem: *with increasing age, more and more adults in the sample are likely to suffer some effects of heart disease.* If we then average the scores for each age group on any measure of physical function, we are likely to find what looks like a steady decline or deterioration. But many healthy adults show no such changes, while those with disease show a lot of decline. To understand what kinds of changes in the circulatory system are part of primary aging, we must study only people free of heart disease.

This has been more easily said than done in the past. At the beginning of the Baltimore Study of Aging, participants with signs of heart disease were screened out using stress tests, but remaining participants showed significant declines with age. Then experimenters used sensitive thallium scans along with stress tests to screen out participants with less apparent signs of heart disease. Once these persons were removed, the remaining group showed no declines in cardiac output well into their 70s and 80s (Baker & Martin, 1997). As screening techniques become more and more exact, the examination of other types of primary aging, independent of disease, will be possible.

In this chapter I will discuss primary aging, leaving secondary aging for Chapter 4. As I talk about these shared, inevitable changes that comprise normal physical aging, I need to try to find some kind of balance. On the one hand, I want to avoid an unrealistic kind of optimism which implies that virtually all changes with age are either illusory or insignificant. On the other hand, I need to avoid creating an overly pessimistic picture, with long descriptions of declines and deteriorations, some of which are secondary rather than primary aging. In an effort to create a foundation for such a balanced view, let me begin by looking at various theories about the basic, underlying processes of normal aging. Why is it that we don't live forever? What is going on in the body at one level or another that may produce the pattern we think of as aging?

EXPLANATIONS OF PRIMARY AGING

Why our bodies age has been the subject of speculation for centuries, but the technology necessary to evaluate those ideas is fairly new. The result is that biology of aging is a relatively young field and has no grand theories on which a significant number of scientists agree (Schaie & Willis, 1996). Instead, there are a dozen or so fledgling theories that have been offered by various biologists. Some of these theories have received a lot of research attention, and some have received little. Some are even untestable! I have selected a few of the more recent theories to describe here, along with support and criticism for each. Please keep in mind that probably no single theory will ever explain all the changes that occur in primary aging, and that several of the proposed mechanisms may be simply the same process being viewed at different levels.

Free Radicals. One theory of aging is based on random damage that takes place on the cellular level. **Free radicals** are molecules or atoms that possess an unpaired electron. They are the by-products of normal body metabolism as well as a response to diet, sunlight, x-rays, and air pollution. These molecules enter into many potentially damaging chemical reactions, resulting in some irreparable cellular damage that accumulates with age. For example, oxidation reactions caused by free radicals can damage cell membranes, in turn reducing the cell's protection against toxins and carcinogens. Free radicals are associated with many diseases of old age, such as cardiovascular disease, cancer, vision problems, and changes in the immune and pulmonary systems, but whether they *cause* the diseases or simply co-occur with them is still in question. It is thought that some vitamins and minerals, such as vitamins C and E, beta-carotene, and selenium, act as **antioxidants** by inhibiting the formation of free radicals or providing

THE EFFECTS OF PHYSICAL AGING are clear here, including wrinkling of the skin. But what causes such changes? What are the underlying physiological processes that lie behind what we see as primary aging?

protection from them. Research findings are mixed, and more work is needed to substantiate the effects of antioxidants on aging individuals (Rowe & Kahn, 1998).

In related research, geneticists have recently identified a genetic mutation in roundworms that might produce natural antioxidant effects. When these worms, which had been selectively bred to have a life span twice that of normal roundworms, were exposed to chemicals that generate free radicals, they proved to be much more resistant to the damaging effects than worms with normal life spans. The scientists identified two enzymes produced by the mutant genes in the long-lived roundworms that were capable of converting free radicals into more benign molecules. Whether or not these genetic mutations occur in humans and whether they are associated with longer individual life spans is now the focus of new research (Hamer & Copeland, 1998).

DNA Repair. Another candidate for explaining physical aging is based on the cell's ability to repair DNA damage. Some breaks in DNA strands are common daily events, resulting from environmental assaults such as background radiation and heat. According to this theory, the cell's ability to make these repairs decreases with age, and the damage that builds up over time causes physical aging. How does this theory hold up to evaluation? Research has shown that DNA repair does take place in cells, but the question of whether long-lived species have more active and efficient repair mechanisms than species with shorter lives is still being investigated. So far this question has brought mixed results. Furthermore, it has not been established that there is a relationship between repair ability and age of individuals within a species, and there is no evidence that DNA repair declines with normal aging (Shulz-Aellen, 1997).

Natural Selection. This idea, based on evolutionary theory, argues that aging is programmed into our biology because once we have reproduced and the new generation is assured, there is no reason for us to continue. In other words, natural selection only favors genetic traits that contribute to good health and survival through young adulthood and the prime reproductive years. Genes that contribute to good health and survival in middle and late adulthood are not necessarily passed on to the next generation. Conversely, genes that contribute to infirmity and premature death in middle and late adulthood, such as genes for Alzheimer's disease, are not reduced in the population by natural selection but are passed along to the next generation. In other words, once young adulthood is over, there is no evolutionary advantage to having genes for good health and no evolutionary disadvantage to having genes for poor health.

Like most evolutionary theories, this theory is difficult to test empirically, but some evidence exists both for and against it. First is the evidence that genetic diseases that cause early death or otherwise limit reproduction are very rare, whereas those that have their effect in later adulthood are relatively common, implying that natural selection works less on us after we are past the reproductive years and into middle adulthood and old age. An example given by evolutionary biologist Steven Austad (1997) compares *progeria*, a fatal genetic disorder that occurs in childhood, and *Huntington's disease*, another fatal genetic disorder, which occurs in middle adulthood. Although both are carried by dominant genes, meaning that only a single copy of the gene is necessary for the disease to be expressed, Huntington's disease runs in families and is 500 times more common than progeria, which occurs only as a spontaneous mutation. The difference, according to Austad, is that progeria has been all but obliterated from the human genome by natural selection because it limits its victims' reproductive abilities by causing early death. Huntington's has not been affected in this way because its victims usually have survived past reproductive age before the disease strikes. Evolutionary biologists believe that many of the physical declines we experience as we age are due to harmful genes that have escaped the effects of natural selection because they are timed to be expressed later in life, after we have passed on our genes to the next generation.

The second piece of evidence does not lend much support to the theory because it tells us that only about 35 percent of the variability in longevity among humans is due to genetics. The message is that even if natural selection plays a part in aging, it is a small part. Other theories are necessary to explain the other 65 percent of variability (Rowe & Kahn, 1998).

Genetic Limits. This theory centers around the observation that each species has a characteristic maximum life span. Something between 110 and 120 years appears to be the effective maximum life span for humans, while for turtles it is far longer, and for chickens (or dogs, or cats, or cows, or most other mammals) it is far shorter. Such observations indicated to cellular biologists such as Leonard Hayflick (1977, 1994) that there is a genetic program setting the upper age limit of each species. Hayflick showed that when human embryo cells (such as cells from the skin) are placed in nutrient solutions and observed over a period of time, the cells divide only about 50 times, after which they stop dividing and enter a state known as **senescence.** When cells are taken from human adults, they double fewer times (perhaps 20 times). Furthermore, cells from the embryos of longer-lived creatures such as the Galápagos tortoise double perhaps 100 times, while chicken embryo cells double only about 25 times. Thus there appears to be a correlation between the longevity of each species and the number of times their cells will divide. According to this theory, aging, or at least ultimate death, may result from reaching the *Hayflick limit* and exhausting the ability of the cells to replicate themselves.

Support for this theory is found in the discovery that all chromosomes in the human body (and presumably in other species, too) have, at their tips, lengths of repeating DNA called **telomeres.** Telomeres appear to serve as a timekeeping mechanism for the organism. Similar to Hayflick limits, the length of the telomeres of an infant is much longer than that of an adult. The telomeres in old people's cells are very short and worn down. It has been shown in lab demonstrations that once the telomeres are gone, the cell enters senescence. Telomeres are thought to be the mechanisms that dictate the genetic limits observed by Hayflick and others.

Evidence against this theory is that cultured cells with depleted telomeres may stop dividing, but they don't necessarily die. Improved lab methods have allowed nondividing cells to stay alive for at least several years after reaching senescence. Another argument is that this theory can't explain all forms of aging, because aging occurs in many cells that never divide, such as those in muscles, eyes, and the brain. Instead of being the *cause* of aging, critics believed that genetic limits may be an integral part of normal development for some types of cells (Austad, 1997).

Caloric Restriction. This theory is based on the premise that the hypothalamus serves as a glandular clock of some kind that measures age in number of calories metabolized by the body. This idea was first suggested half a century ago when researchers studied the effects of feeding lab rats diets drastically reduced in calories but containing all the necessary nutrients. The animals stayed youthful longer, suffered fewer late-life diseases, and lived significantly longer than did their normally fed counterparts. More recent longitudinal studies on monkeys have shown similar results in preliminary reports. After about eight years of caloric restriction, the animals are happy and healthy and don't show the signs of middle age that the control animals show (Weindruch, 1996).

Would this work for humans? No formal studies have been done, but proponents give evidence from "natural" studies showing that longevity and caloric restriction are related. For example, residents of the Japanese island of Okinawa have significantly reduced diets com-

C RITICAL
T HINKING

What would a diet of 1200 calories a day be like? Do you think you would choose to restrict your food intake this way in order to add five years to your life? What about 10 years? Do you think many people would agree with you?

pared to Japanese living in other parts of Japan. Okinawans are significantly smaller, but they also live longer; Okinawa has four times the number of people over 100 years of age than the rest of Japan does (Austad, 1997). It is thought their natural caloric restrictions contribute to their longevity.

Critics of this theory point out that severe food restriction can have serious implications in humans, such as decreased immune defenses, infertility, and loss of muscle and bone mass, not to mention the less severe symptoms of hunger pangs and food fantasies. With a large percentage of our population finding it difficult to keep our weight down to a healthy level, it seems improbable that many of us could restrict our diets permanently to the 1200 or so calories a day that might extend our lives. The plain truth may be that not many of us are willing to trade the pleasure we get from eating good food for the chance of increasing our longevity (Medina, 1996).

One Last Word on Theories of Aging

I will repeat the warning that it is not likely that any single theory will be proven to be the one and only correct answer to the question, "Why do we age?" In fact, it is possible that most of them will prove to be useful in the near future as building blocks for constructing a full and clear explanation of the primary aging process.

LONGEVITY, LIFE EXPECTANCY, AND LIFE SPAN

Let me begin with the most basic question: *Just how long do people live?* To answer this, we need some terminology. **Life span** refers to the upper boundary of years a given species can expect to live. For cats, this upper boundary is roughly 20 years; for humans it appears to be roughly 110 to 120 years. **Longevity** refers to the average expected length of life at any particular time in history, in a particular culture. Finally, the related concept of **life expectancy** refers to the average number of years a person of a given age can still expect to live. We can talk about life expectancy at birth, or life expectancy at age 40, or 65, or 80.

One of the most striking facts about physical aging at this point in history is that longevity has increased significantly in most of the world. For a person born in the United States in 1900, life expectancy at birth was only 48 years; by the end of the century it will be more than 75 years (Austad, 1997). This startling change has occurred in part because far fewer people die in infancy and early childhood than was true several generations ago. But in the last few decades, life expectancy has risen dramatically because years have been added at the upper end of the life span, primarily through the virtual elimination of infectious disease and through reduction of life-style risks of major disorders such as heart disease. Life expectancy at birth for people born in each decade of this century is shown in Table 3.1.

The result of this increased longevity has been a rapid rise in the number and percentage of older adults in the population, and this is expected to continue well into the next century. By the year 2020, the Census Bureau estimates there will be 6.7 million Americans age 85 and older, and fully 18 percent of the total population will be over age 65, compared to about

TABLE 3.1 **Life Expectancy for U.S. Men and Women Born in Various Decades from 1900 to 2000**

	Life Expectancy	
Decade of Birth	Men	Women
1900	49.6	49.1
1910	50.2	53.7
1920	54.6	56.3
1930	58.0	61.4
1940	60.9	65.3
1950	65.3	70.9
1960	66.6	73.2
1970	67.1	74.8
1980	69.9	77.5
1990	71.8	78.6
2000	73.4	81.1

Source: National Center for Health Statistics, 1992.

11.5 percent today (Schneider & Guralnik, 1990; U.S. Bureau of the Census, 1993). In part, this "graying" of the population is due to the Baby Boom generation, the large number of babies born to returning veterans after World War II. Those former "babies" will be in their mid-50s at the beginning of the new century and will move into retirement and old age beginning in roughly the year 2010. But the increase in life expectancy has also contributed greatly to the steady increase in the percentage of adults over 65—a pattern found all over the world, as you can see in Figure 3.1.

Despite these advances, however, the life span probably has not changed at all. A few people have always lived to be 100 or a bit older; now, by postponing death and alleviating the disabling effects of many chronic diseases, we have enabled more people to approach the maximum potential span of years and to remain in far better health during late adulthood. But all the improvements in health care and disease prevention have not stretched the upper boundary—yet.

CRITICAL THINKING

Suppose that advances in genetic engineering make it possible to extend the normal life expectancy to 150 years. What changes would that bring about?

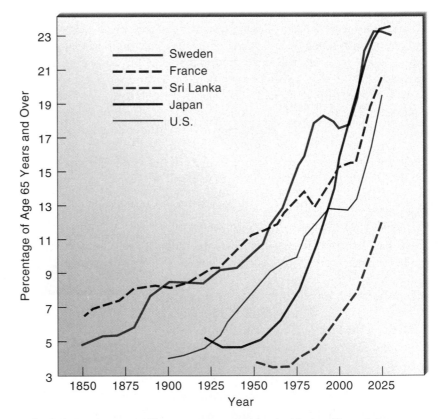

FIGURE 3.1 Increased life expectancy, combined with the effect of the post–World War II Baby Boom worldwide, has already meant a major increase in the percentage of the population in most countries over age 65. This trend will become much more marked in the early part of the next century.

Source: Myers, 1990, Fig 2-2, p. 27. Reprinted by permission of Academic Press, San Diego, California, and the author.

Sex Differences in Longevity

Another fact about longevity and life expectancy is worth discussion: In almost all the countries in the world, women live longer than men do, a point apparent in Table 3.1. Several possible reasons for this sex difference have been compiled by Hilary Lips (1997): (1) women are less likely to inherit a variety of sex-linked genetic disorders; (2) women are naturally protected from some diseases by relatively higher estrogen levels during their reproductive years; (3) women survive difficult conditions better, due to their lower metabolic rate and greater percentage of body fat; (4) women are less likely to participate in high-risk behaviors such as waging war and driving race cars; (5) women are more apt to have jobs with lower rates of injury and health hazards; and (6) women are more knowledgeable about health and engage in more health-oriented behaviors—ideas we will be returning to again and again in later chapters.

Taking all of these facts together I can quite confidently predict that the vast majority of you can expect to live to be 60 or older, and a large percentage of you will live well into your 80s or even 90s. Just what will your bodies be like in those later years of adulthood?

Physical Changes Over Adulthood

Appearance

For many adults, the most obvious changes with age are the ones they see in their mirror every day—those changes in physical shape and contour, in skin and hair, that visibly chart the passage of years.

Weight and Height. Longitudinal research of healthy adults, such as those in the Baltimore Longitudinal Study of Aging, shows that adults lose 1 to 2 inches in height over their lifetimes, with the change beginning at about age 40 (Rossman, 1980; Shock, 1985). Most of this loss occurs in the spine, where the disks between vertebrae first shrink. Later, the vertebrae themselves lose height. The overall effect is that the trunk becomes shorter while the arms and legs remain about the same length.

Changes in weight over adulthood follow a different pattern, first rising in the 30s and 40s, then declining by about 10 pounds, beginning sometime in the 50s, following approximately the shape of an inverted U (Shock, 1985). Much of this weight loss occurs when the fat deposits in the body shift locations and take the place of former muscles. Past about age 50, fat is lost in the face and in the legs and lower arms, while it is added in the upper arm, the thighs, belly, and buttocks (Shimokata et al., 1989). A hopeful note is that this "middle-age spread" is not inevitable, and that exercise and diet can go a long way in its prevention (or correction). Adults who stay active in sports don't show the same loss of muscle and gain of fat, and those who are more sedentary can still strengthen muscles and reduce fat by regular walking or swimming (Spirduso, 1995). More extreme measures are being taken by an increasing number of middle-aged and older adults who wish to maintain their younger-looking body shapes. Cosmetic surgery and liposuction are becoming common procedures to correct sagging body parts and remove unwanted fat deposits.

Critical Thinking

What cultural explanation of such a U-shaped weight curve might you think of?

Beyond the concerns of appearance, increased weight has serious health implications. In a 30-year longitudinal study of over 300,000 men and women, June Stevens and her colleagues found that until age 75, higher weight, as measured by body mass index was associated with a greater risk of premature death from all causes, including heart disease (Stevens et al., 1998). This study and others has caused the U.S. Department of Agriculture to reconsider their 1990 guidelines that allowed for a "safe" increase of weight as one aged (Fackelman, 1998). Figure 3.2 shows the body mass index (BMI) for people of various heights and weights. Optimal BMI scores of 19 to 25 are shown in the white boxes that run diagonally across the chart. These are the scores we should strive for no matter what our age. Borderline scores of 26 and 27 are the scores that should signal us not to gain any more weight. People of any age whose scores are 28 and above are advised to take measures to start controlling their calories and begin building exercise into their lives (Fackelman, 1998).

Skin and Hair. Wrinkles of the skin, which become particularly evident beginning at 40 or 50, result in part from the redistribution of fat I've just described because some of the layer of fat beneath the skin is lost in the face, neck, and arms. It also occurs because of a loss of elasticity in the skin itself, part of a pervasive loss of elasticity that affects muscles, tendons, blood vessels, and internal organs as well as skin. Such a loss of elasticity is especially noticeable in skin that has been continually exposed to the sun, such as the skin of the face and hands.

From a quick trip down the beauty aisle of a drugstore or a look at the annual earnings of a cosmetic company, you would get the impression that many miracle cures are available for aging skin. However, the only effective products available over the counter are those that will cover up the wrinkles and age spots. One product available by prescription seems to be effective in reversing skin damage due to exposure to the sun. Several well-designed lab studies have shown that applying tretinoin (or Retin-A) to the skin for several months not only changed the appearance of damaged skin but also reversed some of the underlying changes that had occurred (Rowe & Kahn, 1998).

WEIGHT / HEIGHT	100	105	110	115	120	125	130	135	140	145	150	155	160	165	170	175	180	185	190	195	200	205	210	215	220	225	230	235	240	245	250
5'0"	20	21	21	22	23	24	25	26	27	28	29	30	31	32	33	34	35	36	37	38	39	40	41	42	43	44	45	46	47	48	49
5'1"	19	20	21	22	23	24	25	26	26	27	28	29	30	31	32	33	34	35	36	37	38	39	40	41	42	43	43	44	45	46	47
5'2"	18	19	20	21	22	23	24	25	26	27	27	28	29	30	31	32	33	34	35	36	37	37	38	39	40	41	42	43	44	45	46
5'3"	18	19	19	20	21	22	23	24	25	26	27	27	28	29	30	31	32	33	34	35	35	36	37	38	39	40	41	42	43	43	44
5'4"	17	18	19	20	21	21	22	23	24	25	26	27	27	28	29	30	31	32	33	33	34	35	36	37	38	39	39	40	41	42	43
5'5"	17	17	18	19	20	21	22	22	23	24	25	26	27	27	28	29	30	31	32	32	33	34	35	36	37	37	38	39	40	41	42
5'6"	16	17	18	19	19	20	21	22	23	23	24	25	26	27	27	28	29	30	31	31	32	33	34	35	36	36	37	38	39	40	40
5'7"	16	16	17	18	19	20	20	21	22	23	23	24	25	26	27	27	28	29	30	31	31	32	33	34	34	35	36	37	38	38	39
5'8"	15	16	17	17	18	19	20	21	21	22	23	24	24	25	26	27	27	28	29	30	30	31	32	33	33	34	35	36	36	37	38
5'9"	15	16	16	17	18	18	19	20	21	21	22	23	24	24	25	26	27	27	28	29	30	30	31	32	32	33	34	35	35	36	37
5'10"	14	15	16	16	17	18	19	19	20	21	22	22	23	24	24	25	26	27	27	28	29	29	30	31	32	32	33	34	34	35	36
5'11"	14	15	15	16	17	17	18	19	20	20	21	22	22	23	24	24	25	26	26	27	28	29	29	30	31	31	32	33	33	34	35
6'0"	14	14	15	16	16	17	18	18	19	20	20	21	22	22	23	24	24	25	26	26	27	28	28	29	30	31	31	32	33	33	34
6'1"	13	14	15	15	16	16	17	18	18	19	20	20	21	22	22	23	24	24	25	26	26	27	28	28	29	30	30	31	32	32	33
6'2"	13	13	14	15	15	16	17	17	18	19	19	20	21	21	22	22	23	24	24	25	26	26	27	28	28	29	30	30	31	31	32
6'3"	12	13	14	14	15	16	16	17	17	18	19	19	20	21	21	22	22	23	24	24	25	26	26	27	27	28	29	29	30	31	31
6'4"	12	13	13	14	15	15	16	16	17	18	18	19	19	20	21	21	22	23	23	24	24	25	26	26	27	27	28	29	29	30	30

FIGURE 3.2 An easy way to check your body mass index (BMI) is to look it up on this chart. Find your weight across the top of the chart and your height down the left side. The square on the chart where they intersect is your BMI. A score of 19 to 25 is optimal regardless of your age. Scores of 28 or more means that you should change your lifestyle to include at least 30 minutes of continuous physical activity each day and eat a healthful diet.

Source: Fackelman, 1998, p. 285.

Skin damage that is too severe to be remedied by prescription creams can be treated by more extreme techniques, such as chemical peels or laser treatment. Several new types of lasers are being used to reverse deep wrinkles and dark discolorations. As you might expect, this type of treatment is more expensive than skin creams and carries more risks. It is usually done at an outpatient facility, but the redness, swelling, and oozing of treated skin areas can take weeks to heal. Nevertheless, many people have been pleased with the results and find that when they look younger they feel younger (Rowe & Kahn, 1998).

Hair loss is also a common characteristic of aging for men and, to a lesser extent, women. Some men begin to lose hair very early in adulthood, but virtually all adults experience thinning of hair beginning in the 50s or 60s (postmenopausally for women). Graying of hair differs widely among ethnic groups and among individuals within any one group. Asians, collectively, gray much less than Caucasians, for example. But most adults show some graying.

Men and women have used chemical and natural dyes to conceal their hair throughout history, and it is still a big practice today. Other old solutions in new boxes are wigs and hairpieces, and hair replacement "systems" for men. In addition, new drugs have become available that slow down or reverse hair loss, some over the counter for men and women (monoxidil, or Rogaine) and others by prescription for men only (finasteride, or Progera). The most extreme solution to hair loss is hair transplant, a surgical procedure in which small plugs of hair and skin are transplanted from a high-hair-growth area of the body to the hairless part of the scalp. Again, none of these antiaging measures actually turns back the clock, but when they are done by experienced professionals and the patients have realistic expectations, they can be a good morale boost for those who need one.

Senses

A second series of body changes noted by many adults as they age affects the senses of vision, hearing, tasting, and smelling.

Vision. Vision is the last sense to develop and the first to show signs of aging. It is also the sensory system that has the most complex structure and function and, as you might guess, has the most to go wrong. During normal aging, the lens of the eye gradually thickens and yellows, and the pupil of the eye loses its ability to open in response to reduced light. The result is that the older we get, the less light gets to our retinas. In fact by 60, our retinas are getting only 30 percent of the light they did in our 20s. One of the changes we experience as a result of this is a gradual loss of **visual acuity,** the ability to perceive detail in a visual pattern. The Baltimore Study of Aging has shown that every 10 years between the ages of 20 and 80, there are significant changes in visual acuity due to this gradual decrease in light available to the retina (Woodruff-Pak, 1997). To test this yourself, try reading a small-print book both indoors where you usually study and then outdoors in the full sunlight. If you are like most of us, you will notice that the clarity of the print is better in the bright sunlight.

Around the age of 45 or so, the lens of the eye, which has been accumulating layers of cells since childhood and gradually losing elasticity, shows a sharp decrease in its ability to **accommodate,** or to change shape to focus on near objects or small print. This loss of accommodation further reduces overall visual acuity in middle-aged and older adults. Most people with reduced visual acuity or loss of near vision can function quite well with prescription glasses or contact lenses.

Another visual change that takes place throughout adulthood is a gradual loss of ability for **dark adaptation,** with a marked decline after the age of 60. This has minor implications such as difficulty reading menus in dimly lit restaurants or finding seats in darkened movie theaters. It also has more dangerous ones, such as problems seeing road signs at night or recovering from the sudden glare of oncoming headlights. This is one of the reasons older people prefer attending matinee performances, making "early bird" dinner reservations, and taking daytime classes at the university or adult education center.

Two more conditions of aging in the visual system may or may not be part of normal aging, but they are so common that I will include them here. The first is **cataracts,** a gradual clouding of the lens of the eye, as seen in Figure 3.3, so that images are no longer transmitted sharply to the retina. The bad news about cataracts is that they happen to most people who are over the age of 60; the good news is that they are usually quickly and safely corrected with outpatient surgery under local anesthetic. This surgery involves removing the cloudy part of the lens and implanting an artificial lens that can even be designed to correct for visual acuity. Cataract surgery has become the most common type of surgical procedure done on people over 65 (Mattox, Wu, & Schuman, 1995), with over 1.3 million extractions done each year (Ernest, 1997).

The second common condition of the visual system is **glaucoma,** the dangerous buildup of pressure inside the eye which ultimately can destroy the optic nerve and lead to blindness. Glaucoma is the second-leading cause of blindness for all people in the United States and the leading cause of blindness for African-Americans. Glaucoma is easily treated with eyedrops, laser treatment, or surgery, but first it has to be detected. What are the warning signs of glaucoma? Like other hypertension problems, there are none. It is estimated that 2 million people in the United States currently have glaucoma, but half are not aware that they have it. Glaucoma can be detected as part of a routine eye examination, and it is recommended that people over 40 be screened for this yearly (Woodruff-Pak, 1997).

Hearing. Most adults in the decade of their 30s begin to experience some hearing loss, mainly of higher tones. There is also shortening of the loudness scale, meaning that there is confusion between loud tones that are not being heard as well as before and softer tones that are still being heard accurately (Woodruff-Pak, 1997). Without the loud–soft discrimination, it is difficult to perceive which sounds are coming from nearby and which are from across a noisy room—which words are coming from your dinner partner and which are coming from the waitress two tables over. Understandably, any type of hearing loss can interfere with social interactions, especially conversations with softer, higher-voiced women and children, and the enjoyment of music, television, and telephone conversations. However, it is not the case that hearing-impaired elderly are necessarily socially isolated or distressed. Mild to moderate hearing loss, even if uncorrected with a hearing aid, is not correlated with measures of life satisfaction or psychological health. Only among those with severe hearing loss do we find heightened levels of depression (Schieber, 1992).

By age 65, as you can see in Table 3.2, roughly a fourth of adults have some significant hearing impairment, and 5.7 percent require hearing aids. Among the old old and the oldest old, these figures rise sharply. It is also

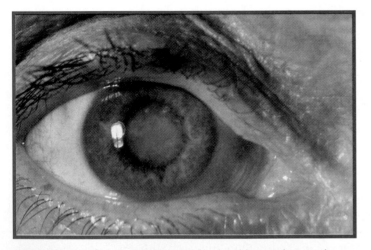

FIGURE 3.3 Cataracts appear as cloudy white patches on the lens of the eye.

Source: J. T. Ernest, 1997, Changes and diseases of the aging eye. In C. K. Cassel et al. (Eds.), *Geriatric medicine* (3rd ed., p. 685). New York: Springer.

TABLE 3.2 **Percentage of Hearing Impairment Among Older Adults**

Age Group	Those with Hearing Impairment			Those Using Hearing Aids		
	Total	Male	Female	Total	Male	Female
65–74	23.2	30.3	17.7	5.7	7.0	4.7
75–84	34.3	43.2	29.5	10.7	13.6	8.9
85+	51.4	a	a	19.0	a	a

aNo separate gender data are available for this age group.

Source: U.S. Bureau of the Census, 1990, Table 192, p. 1199.

clear from the table that men are more likely than women to suffer significant hearing loss, a pattern that is not true of visual loss. I'll have more to say about this difference a bit later in the chapter when I talk about individual differences.

Smell and Taste. There is little or no loss of ability to taste the four basic flavors (salty, bitter, sweet, and sour) over the years of adulthood. Taste receptor cells have short lives and are constantly replaced (Bornstein, 1992). There is some decline in the amount of saliva secreted, producing a sensation of "wooly mouth" for some older adults, and older adults appear to experience many flavors less intensely than is true of younger adults, leading them to prefer more intense concentrations of flavors such as sweetness (de Graaf, Polet, & van Staveren, 1994). These changes are not insignificant, especially since they may affect food choices and eating behavior. Still, a far larger change is in smell. One particularly comprehensive cross-sectional study is by Richard Doty and his colleagues (Doty et al., 1984), who tested nearly 2000 children and adults, using 40 different smells, ranging from pizza to mint to gasoline. He found that peak olfactory ability (best and most rapid discrimination) was in early adulthood, between about ages 20 and 40. The sense of smell dropped slightly between ages 40 and 70, and then dropped markedly among those over 70. The oldest group in this study, in their 80s, identified only about half the smells, while those in their 40s identified 37 of the 40 smells. About 60 percent of adults in this study who were between ages 65 and 80 had severe losses in the sense of smell; about a fourth had lost all sense of smell. (Incidentally, smokers lost their sense of smell to a greater degree than nonsmokers.)

✳ CRITICAL THINKING

Do you think it matters, in any practical way, whether older adults still have a good sense of smell? What real-life ramifications might there be of a loss of this sense?

Many of these changes in both appearance and sensory acuity are related to a much broader set of changes with age in internal organs or body systems, including muscles, bones, heart and lungs, the nervous system, the immune system, and the neuroendocrine system.

Muscles and Bones

Muscles. Studies of healthy adults show a significant loss of muscle tissue over the adult years, with the most rapid decline occurring after age 50 (Fiatarone & Evans, 1993). The major effect of this loss of muscle mass with age is a steady reduction in physical strength, a pattern found in both cross-sectional and longitudinal data. Figure 3.4 shows both, drawn from the results of the Baltimore Longitudinal Study of Aging. In this sample, the decline in strength began around the age of 50.

There is some debate over whether this loss of muscle mass and strength is part of primary aging or simply the result of inactivity as we age. Studies have shown that older men and women who take part in weight training for three months show increases in muscle mass and strength (Fiatarone & Evans, 1993; Pyka, Lindenberger, Charette, &

Marcus, 1994), so it may be true that some types of inactivity take a toll on muscles of aging adults, but no other type of physical training seems to have this effect. Aerobic training such as fast walking or running, or vigorous activity such as gardening or housework, have no such effects on the elderly (Phillips, Bruce, Newton, and Woledge, 1992). My conclusion from this evidence is that there is a basic primary aging process in the muscle tissue that occurs despite high levels of normal activity but that this process can be compensated for to some extent by weight training.

Bones. Changes in the bones are also an aspect of primary aging. Several significant changes are involved. First, bone marrow (in which blood cells are made) gradually disappears from the bones of the arms and legs and becomes concentrated in the bones of the trunk. Second, calcium is lost from the bones, which reduces bone mass and leaves bones more brittle and porous. As you can see in Figure 3.5, this process begins around the 30s for both men and women, but the overall effect of this bone loss is greater for women for several reasons. First, women's bones are smaller and contain less calcium—in other words, even if the decline is equal, women have started out at a disadvantage. Second, the decline is not equal; as can be seen in Figure 3.5, women's bone loss rate shows a marked acceleration between the ages of 40 and 50, resulting in a significant increase in the risk of fractures several decades earlier than in men.

When bone loss exceeds that of normal aging and puts a person at significant risk for bone fracture, it is considered **osteoporosis.** There is controversy over whether osteoporosis is a disease or not because it is so predictable and because the process is not distinguishable from normal aging of the bones except in degree of severity (Medina, 1996). Osteoporosis affects half of all women over 50 and almost all women over 70. The biggest problem caused by osteoporosis is the increased risk of injury after a fall. Diminished eyesight and a decreased sense of balance result in an increased number of falls as we get older. Over the period of a year, one in three people over 65 will experience a fall, and the proportion of those over 80 who fall will be one in two (Tinetti et al., 1997). When

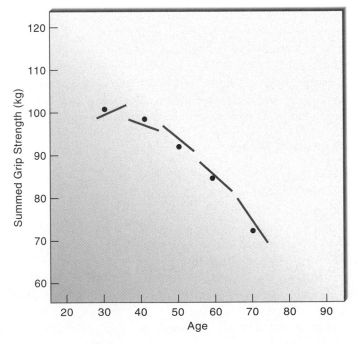

FIGURE 3.4 Grip strength declines with increasing age. The dots represent cross-sectional comparisons of 847 men in the Baltimore Longitudinal Study of Aging. The lines represent longitudinal data from the same study for 342 men followed for an average of nine years.

Source: Kallman, Plato, & Tobin, 1990, Fig. 2, p. M84.

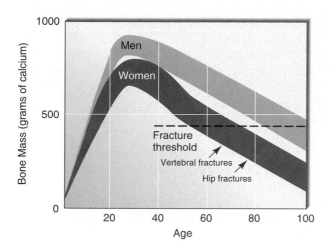

FIGURE 3.5 Changes in bone mass with age. The indications of vertebral fractures and hip fractures do not mean that all women whose bone mass falls to this level will suffer such fractures, only that the likelihood is greatly increased.

Source: Mundy, 1994, p. 216. Reprinted with permission from *Nature, 367.* Copyright 1994 Macmillan Magazines Limited.

brittle bones are entered into the equation, those falls can result in serious injury, disability, loss of independent living, and even death. Five percent of falls result in bone fracture, most commonly at the wrist and pelvis (Baker & Martin, 1997).

Because of the rapid acceleration of bone loss in women during menopause, and because estrogen promotes production of growth hormones and other bone-related hormones, researchers have investigated the role of **estrogen** in osteoporosis. There is now well-documented evidence that **hormone replacement therapy** prevents the acceleration of bone loss in middle-aged women and increases bone mineral density in older women who have not used hormones previously (Writing Group for the PEPI Trial, 1996). I will discuss this in more detail later in the chapter.

Another important factor in maintaining strong bones for both men and women is the calcium and vitamin D connection. Calcium is critical for maintaining bone strength, and vitamin D is critical for efficient calcium use. For a variety of reasons, older adults in the United States do not get enough of either of these compounds in their diets (Dawson-Hughes, Harris, Kroll, & Dallal, 1997). In a well-controlled study that supplied calcium and vitamin D to randomized, placebo-controlled groups of older adults (70 to 101 years of age), participants in the treatment groups showed significantly less bone loss and fewer subsequent fractures than the placebo groups (Murray, Luckey, & Meier, 1996).

Recent studies show that bone density may be linked to a specific gene that affects vitamin D absorption. People with two copies of this recessive gene have lower bone density in adolescence, and the women show a greater rate of bone loss at menopause, putting them at greater risk for

WATER EXERCISE CLASSES are popular because they increase strength and flexibility without putting undue stress on the joints.

osteoporosis and bone fractures (Baker & Martin, 1997). Other major known risk factors for osteoporosis are given in Table 3.3.

Another important change in the bones occurs at the joints. Everyone appears to experience some wear and tear in the joints as a result of years of ordinary body movements. When such changes become marked, they are called **osteoarthritis.** When asked in national surveys, roughly a third of men and half of women over 65 report having "arthritis" of some form (Brock, Guralnik, & Brody, 1990; U.S. Bureau of the Census, 1993). It is a popular misconception that the best remedy for arthritis is to rest those joints. Exercise that increases strength and flexibility without exerting undue stress on the joints can be an important part of treatment. This includes swimming, bicycling, walking, and other low-impact exercises (Ettinger, 1997).

Over the years of adulthood, these several changes in bones and muscles can have significant effects on people's daily lives affecting the tasks that can be accomplished readily, degree of discomfort, and the risk of disability.

Cardiovascular and Respiratory Systems

Physicians and physiologists measure overall aerobic capacity by assessing maximum oxygen uptake (**VO$_{2\,max}$**), which reflects the body's ability to take in and utilize oxygen during dynamic aerobic exercise (such as fast walking or running). Recent longitudinal research with healthy adults indicates that VO$_{2\,max}$ reaches a peak in adolescence and declines steadily with age over the adult years. However, there is a significant difference between the VO$_{2\,max}$ values attained by active adults versus those of sedentary adults. As you can

TABLE 3.3 **Risk Factors for Osteoporosis**

Factor	Risk
Age	Bone density decreases with age for both men and women, but women have a steep decline at menopause.
Sex	Women have less bone density than men, they lose bone density more quickly than men once they reach menopause, and they spend more years in advanced age than men do, all contributing to the large number of osteoporosis cases among women.
Race	Whites and Asians have higher risk than African-Americans.
Menopausal status	Postmenopausal women are at far higher risk; estrogen replacement therapy postmenopausally reduces the risk significantly.
Weight	Those who are light for their height have higher risk.
Timing of climacteric	Women with early menopause or those who have had their ovaries removed are at higher risk.
Heredity	Bone density is strongly influenced by heredity; specifically to the gene that affects the ability of the body to absorb vitamin D. Thus those with a family history of osteoporosis have higher risk.
Diet	Diet low in calcium and high in caffeine leads to higher risk.
Exercise	Sedentary lifestyle associated with higher risk; increasing the level of exercise reduces the risk, even among older women.
Lifestyle choices	Smokers are at greater risk than nonsmokers.

Source: Data from Duursma, Raymakers, Boereboom, & Scheven, 1991; N. A. Morrison et al., 1994; Murray, Luckey, & Maier, 1996.

see in Figure 3.6, declines occur in both groups, but far less in active adults than in sedentary ones. In fact, for men in their 50s, being active gives one a 10-year advantage over his or her sedentary peers (E. B. Larson & Bruce, 1997).

This may be all well and good for senior athletes and fitness buffs, but what about the average adult? Does $VO_{2\,max}$ have anything to do with daily living? The answer is a resounding "yes"! Everything we do is fueled by our body's ability to take in and utilize oxygen. The higher the $VO_{2\,max}$ levels, the more energy we have, the less effort we need to do daily tasks, the less apt we are to be disabled from chronic illnesses, and the more years of *active* life expectancy we have (E. B. Larson & Bruce, 1997). So while age-related decline in the cardiovascular and respiratory systems is undeniably a part of primary aging, some of it is under our control and the decisions we make every day can have a tremendous effect on what our lives will be like in later adulthood.

Nervous System

Many people believe that old age means deterioration of the brain. This is not surprising considering the scientific evidence available a few decades ago. For example, for many years textbooks told us that during adulthood, we lose 100,000 neurons per day. It now appears that this conclusion, like many such conclusions about primary aging, is a considerable overestimation. Newer technologies have shown that loss of brain cells, or **neurons,** in primary aging is much less than projected in older estimates; it is confined to certain parts of the brain; it signifies in some cases an improvement in function instead of a loss in function; and it varies considerably from person to person (Woodruff-Pak, 1997).

Although most neurons never divide and replace themselves, the nervous system is characterized by life-long **plasticity,** meaning that neurons are capable of making changes with age. Examples of this plasticity are growing new projections, known as

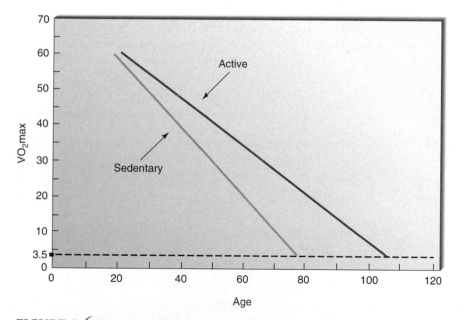

FIGURE 3.6 Age-related decline in $VO_{2\,max}$ for sendentary and active adults. Adults who lead an active lifestyle tend to retain their oxygen utilization efficiency later in life compared to those who live a sedentary life. (The dashed line at the 3.5 level is the minimum $VO_{2\,max}$ necessary to sustain life.)
Source: E. B. Larson & Bruce, 1997, p. 55.

dendrites, to make new connections with other neurons, changing response rates and thresholds to neurotransmitters, and taking over the function of nearby neurons that have been damaged.

Paul Coleman and colleagues compared brain autopsy tissue for healthy middle-aged and older adults, and older adults with Alzheimer's disease. They found evidence of neuron loss in the healthy older adults but also evidence of new growth of surrounding dendrites. This was not the case for older adults with Alzheimer's disease (Coleman & Flood, 1987).

Another example of plasticity in the brain is **pruning,** the ability to shut down neurons that are not needed in order to "fine tune" the system and improve functioning of the remaining neurons. Most pruning takes place in early infancy, but there is also evidence to suggest that some neuron loss in old age could reflect this process (Woodruff-Pak, 1997). So although there is a loss in the total number of neurons with age, not all of the loss translates to functional decline.

It has been shown, at least in animal studies, that aging brains can show a sharp increase in dendritic spikes as a result of being exposed to enriched environments (Greenough, Black, & Wallace, 1987). Related human studies have demonstrated that for people in their 70s, regular, strenuous physical activity such as gardening is related to significantly higher scores on a variety of cognitive and memory tests (Berkman et al., 1993), and that physical activity in older subjects is correlated with quicker reaction time and better cognitive and memory function, compared to people the same age who were not active. So although it is not possible to assign human subjects randomly to enriched and impoverished environments, considerable evidence exists that physical exercise brings changes in human behavior that correspond to underlying retention of neural structures during old age (Cotman & Neeper, 1996).

Research interest in primary aging has moved away from simply counting neurons and has begun to focus on other factors. John Morrison and Patrick Hof (1997) reviewed some of the research on neuronal loss and concluded that the normal physical and mental slowing with age that we experience is more likely due to changes in the structure and function of specific neurons and circuits, and peripheral changes in the body such as decreased production of nerve growth factors and hardening of the arteries, than it is to

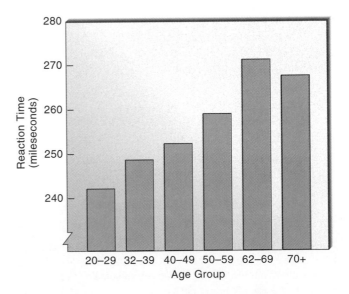

FIGURE 3.7 Average reaction time, by age, on the Wilkinson and Allison apparatus.

Source: Wilkinson & Allison, 1989, Fig. 2, p. P31. Copyright 1989 Gerontological Society of America. Reprinted by permission.

neuron loss. (Age-related changes in thought processes that accompany changes in the nervous system will be discussed in Chapter 5.)

One widespread and significant effect of primary aging is a slowing of transmission of information across the synapses between neurons (Woodruff-Pak, 1997). At a behavioral level you can see the effect of this slowing in measures of reaction time, which is the time between the onset of a stimulus and a person's response. For example, in one large cross-sectional study in England involving over 5000 subjects ranging in age from children through adults over 70, Robert Wilkinson and Sue Allison (1989) had subjects watch a number display that originally showed 0000. Subjects were told that as soon as they saw numbers begin to appear in the number window, they were to stop them as quickly as possible by pressing a red button. Subjects then repeated this same sequence of watching/red button pushing for 1 minute. The results are shown in Figure 3.7.

You can see that with increasing age the average reaction time got slower and slower. Eight-year follow-ups from the Baltimore Longitudinal Study of Aging show the same kind of slowing with age longitudinally (Fozard, Vercruyssen, Reynolds, Hancock, & Quilter, 1994). Furthermore, the Baltimore studies indicate that the more complex the task, the greater the slowing of reaction that occurs with age. And older adults generally make more errors as well, so they are not trading off speed for accuracy. All in all, findings like these strongly reinforce the conclusion that we are looking here at a basic primary aging pattern.

Immune System

The immune system protects the body in two ways: The **B cells,** produced in the bone marrow, make proteins called **antibodies,** which react to foreign organisms (such as viruses and other infectious agents), and the **T cells,** produced in the thymus gland, reject and consume harmful or foreign cells such as bacteria or transplanted organs. With age, the thymus gland decreases dramatically in size and mass. By age 45 or 50, adults retain only about 10 percent of the cellular mass of thymus gland they had at puberty (Burns & Goodwin, 1997). It is hypothesized that this smaller, less functional thymus then becomes less able to turn the immature T cells produced by the bone marrow into fully "adult" cells. Adults produce fewer antibodies than do children or teenagers. In addition, T cells partially lose the ability to "recognize" a foreign cell, so that some disease cells (e.g., cancer cells) may not be fought. This may account for an apparent age-related susceptibility to certain diseases.

It has been difficult to establish that the aging body's decreasing ability to defend itself from disease is a process of primary aging. To show this for humans, it would be necessary to show not only that decreased immunity led to increased disease in later years, but that preexisting diseases didn't *cause* the decreased immunity in the first place—a project that would involve following closely a great number of research participants for many years. Of the few studies that have attempted this, the best found a close but not significant association between immune system function and longevity in a group of 273 initially healthy people (Wayne et al., 1990). However, animal studies, which can be accomplished in far less time, have lent "suggestive, but not compelling" support for the argument that decline of immunity is primary aging, leading to increased susceptibility to disease (secondary aging) in later life (R. A. Miller, 1996a).

From another viewpoint, we have growing evidence that the functioning of the immune system is responsive to psychological stress and depression (Weisse, 1992). Medical students, for example, show lower levels of one variety of T cells in the month before their final exams than in the month after (Kiecolt-Glaser & Glaser, 1988), and adults who have recently been widowed show a sharp drop in immune system functioning (Irwin & Pike,

1993). Furthermore, stressed-out older adults who do relaxation exercises or write about the events causing their stress show an increase in immune function, although the reason this happens and the long-term effects have not been explored (Burns & Goodwin, 1997). Nevertheless, the increased stress that older adults experience is a likely candidate for at least part of the decline we see in immune system function over time, and one that at least has a potential remedy.

Regardless of the cause of the decline in immune function with age, it has been the focus of some interesting research lately on nutrient supplements (R. A. Miller, 1996b). Based on several well-designed studies of the effects of nutrient supplements such as vitamin E on the immune function of older adults, the medical community has begun to change its long-held belief that all nutritional needs can be met by a balanced diet. In a commentary in the *Journal of the American Medical Association,* Newfoundland's Ranjit Chandra (1997) announced that there is an abundance of evidence that nutrient supplements can enhance immune system functioning for the elderly. Due to the finding that almost one-third of all elderly individuals in the United States have nutritional deficiencies, Chandra recommends that modest amounts of nutritional supplements be prescribed for all elderly patients. In addition, because the cost of a year's supply of supplement is less than the cost of three visits to a physician and far less than the cost of one day in the hospital, this recommendation makes economic sense as well. "The era of nutrient supplements to promote health and reduce illness is here to stay" (p. 1399).

Critical Thinking

If cumulative stress causes the deteriorative changes in the immune system, that ought to mean that the least stressed adults should live longer. Can you think of any evidence you have already read that would support such a conclusion? How might you test this hypothesis more fully?

Neuroendocrine System

Both men and women experience changes in their neuroendocrine systems over the course of adult life, the most obvious being the **climacteric,** the age-related loss of reproductive ability. The climacteric takes place gradually for men over middle and late adulthood, and more abruptly for women around the late 40s and early 50s.

The Climacteric in Men. Research with healthy adults suggests that the quantity of viable sperm produced begins to decline in a man's 40s, but the decline is not rapid, and there are documented cases of men in their 80s fathering children. The **testes** shrink gradually, and after about age 60, the volume of **seminal fluid** begins to decline. These changes are associated in part with testicular failure and the resulting gradual decline in **testosterone,** the major male hormone, beginning in early adulthood and extending into old age (Mobbs, 1996). Declining hormone levels in men are also associated with decreases in muscle mass, sexual desire, appetite, facial hair, bone mass, and red blood cells, and increases in body fat (L. E. Johnson, Kaiser, & Morley, 1997).

Just how large this decline in testosterone may be is not yet clear. Early research, which included older adults who were less healthy, showed a drop of as much as 60 percent. This was followed by a number of studies that showed no decline at all (Harman & Talbert, 1985). One typical conclusion, based on careful cross-sectional studies, is that there is a small decline (Gray, Berlin, McKinlay, & Longcope, 1991) and that this decline is part of primary aging. I am sure the data are not all in on this one; long-term longitudinal data are obviously needed. At the very least, it appears that the hormone changes that are part of the climacteric in men are more complex than first supposed and involve changes in the hormones secreted by the hypothalamus and the pituitary, as well as testosterone created in the testes.

Along with the decline in fertility that men experience with age, there is also a decline in sexual response. Although most men experience erection problems from time to time, this condition is not considered **erectile dysfunction** unless the man reports that he is unable to get an erection adequate for satisfactory sexual performance. This problem occurs in an estimated 30 million men in the United States, half of them over 65. Thus, erectile dysfunction is associated with age, occurring in 5 percent of men between 40 and 65, and 25 percent of men over 65 (National Institutes of Health, 1992). Although erectile dysfunction occurs for many reasons (heart disease, diabetes, excessive alcohol consumption, medication, smoking), the underlying mechanism seems to be similar in most cases—a shortage of **cyclic GMP,** a substance that is released by the brain during sexual arousal. Part of the job of cyclic GMP is to close down the veins of the penis that normally drain away blood so that the blood supply increases and the tissues become engorged and erect. When cyclic GMP is in short supply, regardless of the reason, the result is erectile dysfunction. Recently, drugs have been developed that magnify the effects of cyclic GMP, making erections possible if even a small amount of the substance is present. One of these drugs, Viagra, was approved in 1997 and during the first two weeks it was available to pharmacies, it was prescribed to a record number (36,000) of patients (Handy, 1998).

The Climacteric in Women. During middle adulthood women's menstrual periods gradually end, signaling an end to the ability to reproduce, an event known as **menopause.** The main cause of menopause is ovarian failure, leading to a drop in a key hormone, estrogen, although there are complex changes in other hormones as well. Table 3.4 summarizes the changes from premenopause to postmenopause in two forms of estrogen, and in progesterone, which is an important ingredient in the menstrual cycle, triggering the sloughing off of the material accumulated in the uterus. As these hormones decline, the menstrual cycle becomes less regular and finally stops altogether. This transition takes from two to seven years for most women. The average age of menopause for both blacks and whites in the United States is approximately 51, although it is still considered normal for women to experience menopause as early as 40 and as late as 60 years of age. Considering that many women today can expect to live well into their 70s, a woman experiencing menopause has more than one-third of her life ahead of her (Bellatoni & Blackman, 1996).

As with men, this series of hormone changes is accompanied by changes in more than reproductive ability. There is some loss of tissue in the genitals and the breasts, and breast tissue becomes less dense and firm. The ovaries and uterus become smaller, the vagina becomes shorter and smaller in diameter with thinner and less elastic walls, and there is less lubrication produced in response to sexual stimulation—the latter being a direct result of insufficient estrogen, not an indirect result of the changes in the vaginal walls (Harman & Talbert, 1985).

The other major physical symptom experienced by the majority of women around the time of menopause is the **hot flash,** a brief, abrupt rise in body temperature that may be accompanied by sudden sweating and skin flushing. (I first experienced this somewhat startling phenomenon at age 46 when I happened to be on a trip to China. The flashes then recurred as often as 30 or 40 times per day, and I was continually flushed and damp with sweat. I came to think of the entire trip as "Hot Flashing Through China.")

TABLE 3.4 **Levels of Estrogens and Progesterone Before and After Menopause[a]**

	Estradiol	Estrone	Progesterone
Premenopausal women	50–200	35–500	300–20,000
Postmenopausal women	35–54	12–21	160–220

[a]All values here are picograms per milliliter of plasma.

Source: Harman & Talbert, 1985, Table 3, p. 466.

About two-thirds of women experience hot flashes within the two-year period surrounding their final menstrual period, and these symptoms typically continue to occur for about a year. However, about one third of women will have them for five years or more (Bellatoni & Blackman, 1996)—a group of which I am one. The most serious side effect of hot flashes, aside from the occasional social discomfort they may cause, is that when frequent or severe, they interfere with normal sleep patterns and can thus contribute to daytime fatigue and low productivity (Matthews, 1992). The causes of hot flashes are not yet well understood. The most favored theory currently is that the difficulty is caused by changes in levels of neurotransmitters and natural opiates in the brain (Bellatoni & Blackman, 1996; Gannon, 1990).

Psychological Correlates of Menopause: Fact or Fallacy? One other aspect of the female climacteric deserves emphasis: Until quite recently, it was widely assumed that depression and other psychological symptoms were a standard accompaniment of the climacteric in women. The available evidence refutes this conclusion. Four relevant, well-designed studies exist, three in the United States and one in Sweden, all longitudinal. In none of these studies is any connection found between menopausal status, or a change from premenopausal to menopausal status, found to be associated with a rise in depression or other psychological symptoms (Busch, Zonderman, & Costa, 1994; Hallström & Samuelson, 1985; Matthews et al., 1990; McKinlay, McKinlay, & Brambilla, 1987). In the largest and most recent of these, a group of 3049 women aged 40 to 60 who have been part of the National Health Examination Follow-up Study were studied over a 10-year period (Busch et al., 1994). The researchers divided these women into four groups, based on their initial menopausal status: premenopausal, in the midst of, and postmenopausal, with the latter group divided into those who had surgical menopause and those with natural menopause. When they compared these four groups cross-sectionally, they found essentially no differences in depression, well-being, or sleep disturbance. And for those women whose menopausal status had changed over the 10 years of the study, they found no indication of a change in any of these characteristics linked to menopause.

The clear truth is that a small minority of women experience significantly unpleasant physical symptoms associated with menopause, such as frequent hot flashes. Matthews estimates that perhaps only 1 in 10 women experience some rise in depression or irritability as a result of these symptoms, while the remaining 9 in 10 do not. Thus the myth of women's inevitable distress during menopause can be dispelled.

Hormone Replacement Therapy. *If aging of the various neuroendocrine systems in men and women is due to a decline in hormone production, why not replace those hormones and reverse the process?* This is not a new or novel suggestion, and has been the impetus behind many failed "fountain of youth" therapies throughout history, including the injection of pulverized sheep testicles into patients in the 1890s and testicle transplants from cadavers in the 1920s (Hayflick, 1994). Needless to say, none of these restored youth, but more recent attempts to replace diminished hormone supplies in aging adults have met with more success. Although none reverse the aging process, they do slow it down somewhat.

Estrogen and Progesterone Replacement. The various symptoms of the climacteric in women can be sharply reduced by replacing the estrogen their ovaries no longer produce with synthetic estrogen taken orally in pills (along with progesterone) or through the skin in a transdermal patch. This **hormone replacement therapy** (HRT) is controversial today because in decades before, only estrogen was used and it was found to be linked to higher levels of endometrial cancer (Whitehead & Fraser, 1987). Subsequently, researchers found that a combination of low dosages of both estrogen and progesterone eliminated the increased risk of endometrial cancer. Furthermore, new studies also made clear that the use of replacement estrogen has important additional benefits: It substantially reduces the risk of coronary heart disease (Stampfer & Colditz, 1991), increases bone mineral density (Writing Group for the PEPI Trial, 1996), improves memory, and may prevent cognitive losses associated with both normal aging and Alzheimer's disease (Wickelgren, 1997)

A few cautionary notes are warranted here: Some of this research is based on studies of women who took only estrogen, not the newer, safer estrogen/progesterone combination. Preliminary studies show that the benefit of the hormone combination therapy might not be as strong as that for estrogen alone. A few studies (but not the majority of studies) have found that women who have taken hormone replacement therapy have an increased risk of breast cancer. Longitudinal studies with placebo controls are needed to clarify this issue (Staffa, Newschaffer, Jones, and Miller, 1992). Most physicians today recommend against hormone replacement for women with a family or personal history of breast cancer. In addition, estrogen replacement therapy can produce unwanted side effects such as breast tenderness and vaginal bleeding. Half of the women who begin hormone replacement therapy quit during the first year due to concerns about the long-term hazards and side effects.

Recently, a variety of synthetic estrogens have been developed that provide protection against heart disease, osteoporosis, and breast cancer without the risks and side effects of current hormone replacement therapy (Rifkind & Rossouw, 1998). Although these "designer estrogens" don't provide relief from hot flashes and other symptoms of menopause, they give women yet another option in this important decision.

DHEA and Growth Hormone Replacement. Age-related declines for both sexes have been documented for two other hormones, **DHEA** and **growth hormone.** Not only do these hormones decline with age, but animal studies have shown that replacing these hormones reverses aging and provides protection against disease. What about humans? The findings are mixed. Human studies with DHEA replacement have shown "remarkable" increases in self-reported physical and psychological well-being. They have also shown increased lean body mass for both sexes and increased muscle strength for men (Lamberts, van den Beld, & van der Lely, 1997). However, although DHEA is currently available over the counter and used widely in the United States as a treatment for aging, the scientific verdict on its effectiveness and safety is still out.

Growth hormone replacement therapy in humans has shown to increase muscle mass, muscle strength, bone mass, and quality of life for adults of a wide range of ages. Recent studies have shown that replacing growth hormone in adults over 75 years of age who had suffered acute hip fractures resulted in significantly earlier return to independent living. Caution is still advised because researchers have not uniformly proven the safety of long-term administration of growth hormone because of its implication with malignant tumors (Lamberts et al., 1997).

THE EFFECTS OF PHYSICAL AGING ON BEHAVIOR

The changes discussed so far form the foundation for age-related changes in more complex behaviors and day-to-day activities.

Slowing Down

For most of us, the most pervasive change is a quite distinct (and accurate) feeling of becoming slower and slower as we get older. This is not an illusion, and it is not restricted to the last years of adulthood. The process of slowing begins much earlier, although it may be detected only by those who are operating at or near peak physical capacity, such as athletes. In any sport, the top performers are in their teens or 20, especially in any sport involving speed. Swimmers often peak in their teens; short-distance runners in their early 20s, baseball players at about 27 (R. Schulz, Musa, Staszewski, & Siegler, 1994). As endurance rather than speed becomes more involved in performance, such as for longer-distance running, the peak performance ages rise, but the top performers are still in their 20s (Ericsson, 1990; R. Schulz & Curnow, 1988).

Cross-sectional comparisons of athletes involved in "masters" swimming and running events (usually defined as competitions for those age 30 or 35 and older) show the same kind of pattern: a steady drop in speed with increasing age (Ericsson, 1990). You can see one example in Figure 3.8, which shows the average times for the 50-meter free-style swimming event from German masters championships. Of course, these are cross-sectional comparisons. Perhaps the younger groups had benefited from better training, or trained more vigorously. Longitudinal data on a few world-class athletes who continued competition throughout their 30s suggest that the slope of the line may be somewhat less steep, at least up to age 40 or so. But there is absolutely no doubt about the basic shape of the curve: We slow down as we get older.

Stamina, Dexterity, and Balance

In addition to loss of speed, all the physical changes associated with aging combine to produce a reduction in stamina, dexterity, and balance. The loss of **stamina,** which is the ability to sustain moderate or strenuous activity over a period of time, clearly arises in large part from the changes in the circulatory system, as well as from changes in muscles. **Dexterity,** the ability to use the hands or body in a skillful way, is lost primarily as a result of arthritic changes in the joints.

Another significant change, one with clear practical ramifications, is a gradual loss of **balance,** the ability to adapt body position to change (Guralnik et al., 1994). Older adults are likely to have greater difficulty handling uneven sidewalks or snowy streets, or in adapting their body to a swaying bus. All of these situations require flexibility and muscular strength, both of which decline in old age (Woollacott,1993). One result of the less steady balance is a greater incidence of falls among the elderly. As mentioned before, declining eyesight and brittle bones combine with this decline in balance to produce a serious health risk for older adults.

Sleep

Another consequence of the changes in the neurological system is an increased likelihood of **insomnia,** or problems with sleeping. William Dement and his colleagues reports that with increasing age, especially after perhaps age 50 or 60, older adults wake up more often

FIGURE 3.8 Average times for the 50-meter free-style swimming event at the German masters championships between 1971 and 1983.

Source: Ericsson, 1990, Fig. 6.3, p. 173. Adapted from Letzelter, Jungermann, & Freitag, 1986, p. 391.

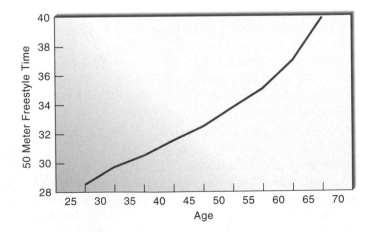

during the night and have fewer total hours of the type of sleep associated with the slowest brain waves—what in layman's terms we would call deep sleep (Bliwise, Carey & Dement, 1983; Bliwise, Carskadon, Carey & Dement, 1984; Miles & Dement, 1980). Breathing disturbances during sleep also becomes more common (Woodruff-Pak, 1997). Since repeated wakefulness in the night and lessened deep sleep mean that older adults are often not getting enough sleep at night, daytime napping becomes much more frequent. This need for daytime naps, in turn, can have a major impact on the rhythm and pattern of a person's daily life (Lamberg, 1997).

Some of the sleep problems among older people are due to health problems and medications, factors that are part of secondary aging. But some of the difficulties in sleep seem to be primary aging. Donald Bliwise, who has been conducting a longitudinal study of the sleep patterns of 256 older adults in the Bay Area Sleep Cohort (BASC), has found that the sleep of the older adult seems to be intrinsically lighter, making other factors such as pain, coughing, urge to urinate, and hot flashes more likely to cause sleep disruption (Bliwise, 1997). Sleep problems in older adults are also caused by psychological factors such as depression and anxiety. For example, bereavement can cause sleep disturbance in older adults for as long as two years after the death of a loved one (Reynolds et al., 1993). Pharmaceutical remedies for sleep problems range from hypnotics to antidepressants, but most recent recommendations involve life-style changes such as limiting the time spent in bed, increasing the time spent outdoors in daylight, and increasing physical exercise (Lamberg, 1997).

CRITICAL THINKING

Think about it a minute. What changes would it mean in your life if you needed at least one nap every day to stay functional?

Sexual Activity

Sexual activity, too, shows the effects of all the physical changes of aging. The key observation is that the frequency of sexual activity—among adults with a regular partner—drops from a high of perhaps 10 or more times per month in the early 20s to about three times a month at age 65. The absolute numbers have varied from one study to the next, but the pattern of decline in frequency has been found in all studies, both cross-sectional and longitudinal. Data from one study of each kind are combined in Figure 3.9. The longitudinal data in the figure come from the Duke Longitudinal Study (Palmore, 1981), an investigation I have described before. The cross-sectional data come from a nationally representative sample interviewed in 1987–1988, the National Survey of Families and Households, which included 807 respondents who were 60 or older (Marsiglio & Donnelly, 1991). The left-hand side of the figure shows the percentage of married adults, at various ages, who reported that they were still sexually active. In the case of the cross-sectional data, the respondents were asked if they had had intercourse at least once in the past month, while the Duke subjects were counted as sexually active if they said they had had any sexual activity at all. Despite these differences, the two sets of data obviously match remarkably well. The right-hand side of the figure shows the frequency of intercourse per month among those who said they were sexually active. Sexual activity obviously declines with age, particularly after age 70 or 75, but among adults with an available sexual partner, roughly half are still sexually active into their 70s, most on a regular basis.

I think it is important to mention here that almost all research on sexual activity is done in survey form, which has several important limitations. First, the numbers represent what people *say* they do, not what they actually do. Second, the sample is always biased toward people who are willing to discuss their sexual activity. Third, cohort effects exist that would make young people more likely than older people to report certain types of sexual activity, regardless of what is actually practiced. A last problem with this research is that the variables of interest are almost always frequency counts—how many times dif-

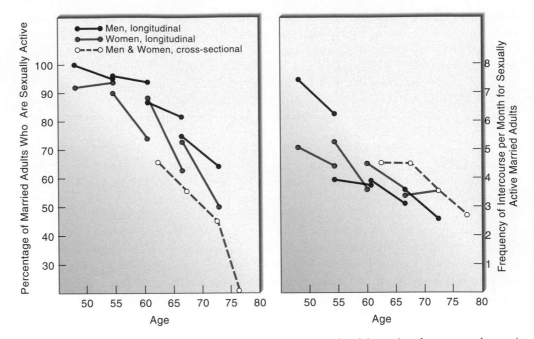

FIGURE 3.9 Longitudinal and cross-sectional data on sexual activity and on frequency of sexual intercourse among sexually active married adults. For the longitudinal data, each line represents one group of men or women who were followed for a period of six years.

Source: E. Palmore, *Social patterns in normal aging,* Fig. 6-4, p. 88. Copyright 1981 Duke University Press. Data from Marsiglio & Donnelly, 1991, Table 2, p. S341.

ferent sexual events occur. This gives us a lot of information about age changes in *quantity* of sexual activity but not much about age changes in *quality*. Keeping all these warnings in mind, we look next at how sexual activity changes with age and some speculation about why.

Judith Levy (1994) lists four factors, one biological and three social, that affect the probability that an older person will have sexual relations or not: (1) physical ability to participate in sexual relations, (2) desire to engage in sexual relations, (3) availability of a willing partner, and (4) access to physical and social space in which sexual relations can take place.

Physical Ability. Primary aging can translate into age-related changes in sexual response for both men and women. Before we look into how physical abilities affect sexual relationships, let's find out what those changes are. Studies of the physiological components of sexual responses of younger men and women (aged 20 to 40) compared to older men and women (aged 50 to 78) show that there are changes in four stages of sexual response (Medina, 1996). These changes, which are described in Table 3.5, show that sexual responses of older men and women are a little slower, a little less intense, and, at least for women, can be a little more painful. Although most of the changes result in less sexual activity with age, some of the changes, such as an end to concerns about pregnancy, can have the opposite result.

In addition, secondary aging has a profound effect on sexual activity, not only the diseases that directly affect sexual function (diabetes, heart disease, prostate disease), but also those that have indirect effects (arthritis, stroke, dementia) as well as some medications. Couples who are not able to participate in genital intercourse as they get older find other ways to have sexual relations or intimate physical contact, and those for whom intercourse is awkward or painful often develop new sexual strategies to overcome the limitations (Kennedy, Haque, & Zarankow, 1997).

Desire to Engage in Sexual Relations. Many older people (and younger ones also) believe that sexuality is only for the young and those with perfect bodies. As they age, they feel less and less attractive. In addition, older people today are more apt to have grown up with few role models for sexually active seniors. (Fortunately, today's youths have role models such as Paul Newman and Sophia Loren, who portray attractive, sexually active seniors in films.) For some people, lack of sexual desire is due to monotony. Many studies have shown that after the first year of marriage, the average frequency of intercourse drops by half and then declines gradually for the next 20 years. However, this research also shows great variability among couples, with some couples at all ages continuing to have high frequencies of intercourse (Edwards & Booth, 1994). For others, though, marriage brings overfamiliarity and predictability, which lead to a decline in desire for sexual relations.

Availability of a Partner. The major factor cited in many studies for an age-related decline in frequency of sexual relations is the availability of a partner. With age, social losses (loss of spouse through death or divorce, disability of spouse, reduced social contacts) overtake social gains (marriage, remarriage, new social contacts), and older adults find themselves less likely to have an available partner even if they are willing and able to have a sexual relationship. This is especially true for women. Due to the their greater longevity, the practice in our culture of women marrying older men, and the age-old double standard that does not condone casual sexual encounters for women, many more women than men find themselves without a sexual partner in later years.

Another barrier to finding a sexual partner for older adults can be their adult children, who resent or otherwise discourage their single parents from forming new romantic partnerships. Some adult children worry about losing their inheritances to new spouses or taking care of additional aging family members, and others simply refuse to acknowledge their parents' sexuality in late adulthood (Alexander & Allison, 1995).

TABLE 3.5 **Sexual Responses in Older Women and Men Aged 50 to 78 (Compared to Younger Women and Men Aged 20 to 40)**

Phase	Women	Men
Excitement	Vaginal lubrication takes 1–5 minutes (compared to 15–30 seconds in younger women).	Erection after stimulation takes 10 seconds to several minutes (compared to 3–5 seconds in younger men).
Plateau	Vagina does not expand as much, the minor labia do not redden as much due to increased blood flow, and the clitoris does not elevate and flatten against the body as much (compared to the response of younger women).	Pressure for ejaculation is not felt as quickly (compared to younger men).
Orgasm	Vagina contracts and expands in 4 to 5 smooth, rhythmic waves occurring at 0.8-second intervals (compared to 8 to 10 waves occurring at 0.8-second intervals in younger women). Uterus contracts and is sometimes more painful (compared to younger women).	Urethra contracts in 1 to 2 waves at 0.8-second intervals compared to 3 to 4 times at 0.8-second intervals for younger men), and the semen can travel 3 to 5 inches after expulsion (compared to 12 to 24 inches in younger men).
Resolution	Return to prearousal state is more rapid (compared to younger women).	Return to prearousal is in one stage and takes only a few seconds (compared to two stages in younger men which takes from minutes to hours).

Source: Data from Medina, 1996, pp. 215, 223.

Access to a Conducive Environment. This may not be a concern of most older adults, but for the 5 percent who are in nursing homes and the larger number who live with their adult children, it is a major stumbling block to sexual relations, even if they have the desire, the ability, and a willing partner. Before the Patients' Rights Act of 1980, nursing homes routinely separated men and women, even married couples who were still sexually active. And contact between unmarried residents was monitored and restricted to hugging and kissing on the cheek in many facilities (L. H. Levy, Martinkowski, & Derby, 1994). Conditions are somewhat better today for heterosexual couples, but homophobic attitudes make it very difficult for older gay and lesbian adults to establish or maintain relationships in nursing homes or homes of their adult children (Kelly & Rice, 1986).

Other Forms of Sensuous Activity. Not all types of sensual pleasure entail all of these requirements. Erotic dreams and sexual fantasies can be sources of arousal and pleasure for older adults who lack partners or the physical capabilities to have intercourse. In a survey of healthy people between 80 to 102 years of age, 88 percent of the men and 72 percent of the women reported fantasizing about sex (Crooks and Baur, 1990). Masturbation is practiced by many older adults without sexual partners, and besides serving as a sexual release, it also stimulates sexual appetite and contributes to maintaining genital health and function (Weg, 1983). According to one study, almost 50 percent of healthy women over the age of 60 reported that they practice masturbation (Kaiser, Wilson, & Morley, 1997). Together these findings clearly indicate that sexuality is an integral part of most adults' lives throughout the life span, whether in partnered intercourse or other forms of sensuous activity.

PULLING THE THREADS TOGETHER: AN OVERVIEW OF BODY CHANGES IN ADULTHOOD

I have summarized the myriad details of primary aging in Table 3.6, showing the physical characteristics of young, middle-aged, and older adults. When you look at the information this way, you can see that adults are clearly at their physical peak in the years from 20 to 35 or 40. In the years of midlife, from 40 to 60 or 65, the rate of physical change varies widely from one person to the next, with some experiencing a loss of physical function quite early, others much later. From age 65 onward, the loss of some abilities continues, along with significant increases in chronic diseases—both trends that accelerate among the old old. But here, too, there are wide individual differences in the rate of change and effective compensations that can maintain perfectly adequate (or even excellent) physical functioning for many adults well into their 70s or 80s. Among the old old and the oldest old, however, all these changes accelerate and compensations become more and more difficult to maintain.

I am sure that summaries like this one are helpful; no doubt this is the section you will come back to when you are reviewing for examinations. But I don't want to end here. Given the fast-changing state of our knowledge about physical aging, these summaries are too tidy. So let me end this chapter by commenting on some of the recurrent questions and themes about physical aging.

SOME RECURRENT THEMES AND REMAINING QUESTIONS

Are the Changes Gradual?

In this chapter I've described a great many changes that take place in our bodies, usually including some phrase such as "the change begins at roughly age 50 and continues thereafter." Such statements imply that physical aging, once it begins, takes place at a constant rate. This is not entirely accurate.

Certainly it is not true for every aspect of physical aging. In some cases, such as the loss of smell sensitivity, there seems to be a very gradual decline until roughly age 65 or 70, after which the decline becomes much more marked. In Chapter 5 you'll see that declines in many cognitive abilities follow a similar trajectory. In other cases there may be a more steady change beginning in early adulthood, much as the yellowing of the lens of the eye. The truth seems to be that different body systems "age" at widely different rates. And sometimes the changes occur early in life but have no effect on function until later, such as the case of loss of bone mass in middle adulthood that shows up as brittle bones decades later. So it is a mistake for us to think of "aging" as a uniform process.

Which Changes Represent Primary Aging and Which Represent Secondary Aging?

I've already given you examples of a number of widely accepted "facts" about aging that have been called into question, as studies of healthy adults have pointed to very different conclusions. Loss of neurons is much less than originally estimated; testosterone levels decline very slowly in healthy men well into old age; depression and other mental disorders are not part of menopause for the vast majority of women.

TABLE 3.6 **Summary of Primary Age Changes in the Body**

Age 20–40	Age 40–65	Age 65–75	Age 75+
Maximum height; the head grows and changes shape.	Height is lost slowly; skin and other tissues begin to lose elasticity.	Height continues to be lost; continuation of loss of elasticity.	Probably a slight acceleration of these same changes.
Peak of sensory acuity.	Senses begin to be less acute starting at about age 50, but these changes are still small enough to make little difference in daily life, except for the need for glasses.	Loss of auditory acuity becomes more noticeable for many; some loss of smell sensitivity.	Accelerated loss of acuity in most senses, most noticeably smell and hearing.
Peak of physical strength, stamina, aerobic fitness, and athletic skill.	Beginning decline in strength and in heart and lung function under work conditions. Large individual differences and little effect on everyday life.	Continued decline in strength and aerobic fitness, with less change in physically active adults. These losses begin to have some effect on daily life.	Losses in strength and fitness now very likely to affect daily life, although there are large individual variations.
Nervous system at maximum efficiency.	Slight loss of dendritic density.	Further loss of dendrites and nerve conductance speed; probably some loss of neurons.	Probably, further loss of neurons; reduced weight of brain; marked loss of dendrites and slower speed of reaction.
Optimum reproductive period; for women, optimum period is in the 20s.	Climacteric, with accompanying changes in hormones and genitalia.	Continued slow drop in level of testosterone for men.	Little further change, although probably additional reduction in testosterone for men.
Immune system at peak efficiency.	Loss of size of thymus; loss of efficiency of immune system.	Significant increase in susceptibility to disease as immune system declines further.	Pattern of changes continues, possibly at an accelerated rate.
Peak of sexual activity.	Frequency of sexual activity declines, but virtually all adults are still sexually active.	Roughly half of adults still sexually active, but frequency declines.	Perhaps only a quarter or less of adults still sexually active.

Clearly, we need to know a good deal more about healthy aging before we can be sure just how much change reflects primary aging. At the same time, we also need to understand the way in which specific environments may interact with primary aging processes. A very nice example of this kind of interaction comes from studies of hearing loss. Figure 3.10 shows in simplified form both the basic descriptive evidence on the relationship between age and hearing loss, and explanatory evidence exploring the role of environmental influences. What this suggests is that while some hearing loss is a normal aspect of aging—since even adults in very quiet environments have some wear and tear on the auditory system—a great deal of the loss we associate with aging in industrialized countries is linked not just to age but to exposure to noise. Within U.S. samples, men with greater noise exposure have far more hearing loss than do those with less exposure. Women, with even less exposure to high-decibel noise in their workplaces, show still less, while samples from other cultures in which there is very low noise level show still less. Similarly, the data on the impact of stress on immune system functioning fit into this model.

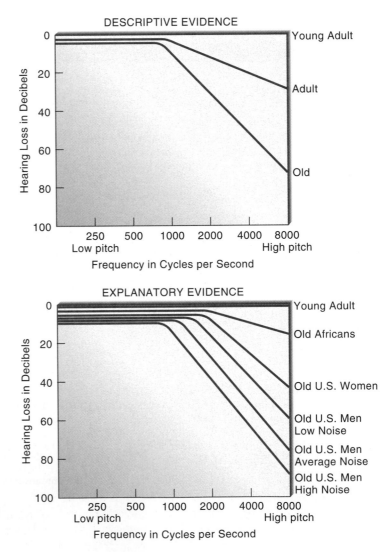

FIGURE 3.10 The upper figure shows the general pattern of age changes in hearing loss at various pitches. The lower figure explores one set of explanatory possibilities: that the hearing loss is caused by noise exposure. Not only do these results tell us something about how much of hearing loss is a result of primary and how much of secondary aging, they also illustrate the usefulness of comparing aging patterns in different subgroups of adults who have had different life experiences.

Source: Baltes, Reese, & Nesselroade, 1977. Copyright Wadsworth Publishing Company. Reprinted with permission.

At the other end of the spectrum, some environments may retard the primary aging changes or even reverse them. Adult animals placed in visually enriched environments show increases in the number of neuron connections in the brain. And in humans it is shown that adults who remain physically active and who choose more stimulating activities and environments appear to "age" more slowly—a point that I will come back to repeatedly.

Recently, many researchers have begun to study "successful" aging instead of having "a preoccupation with disability, disease, and chronological age" (Rowe & Kahn, 1998, p. xi). Earlier thinking has been that primary aging is "inevitable" and that we should just "deal with it," saving our efforts to fight against secondary aging, which could be warded off somewhat by lifestyle changes. However, as can be seen in some of the new research discussed in this chapter, scientists are beginning to understand the primary aging process and find ways to slow it down (Rowe, 1997). Even though we may never extend the maximum life span for our species, an increasing number of scientists are beginning to believe that we can extend our individual life expectancy and the number of *healthy* years we live by methods such as hormone replacement therapy (Lamberts et al., 1997), aerobic and weight training exercise programs (E. B. Larson & Bruce, 1997), and dietary supplements (Chandra, 1997).

CRITICAL THINKING

Since adults who choose to be more physically or mentally active are different from those who choose not to, how can we ever sort out the effect of activity on aging?

Individual Differences in Aging Patterns and Rate

When we look directly at individual differences, it becomes even more clear that sweeping generalizations about aging are very difficult to make. When we study groups, whether cross-sectionally or longitudinally, and then display the results as averages for each age range (as I have done repeatedly in figures in this chapter), we run the risk of conveying the impression that each person's pattern or trajectory is roughly the same as the overall curve. What we are discovering from the ongoing longitudinal studies is that there are really huge individual differences in the pattern and rate of physical changes with age. Nathan Shock, who has been involved in the Baltimore Longitudinal Studies of Aging, puts it this way: "[R]elatively few individuals follow the pattern of age changes predicted from averages based on measurements made on different subjects. Aging is so highly individual that average curves [even from longitudinal data] give only a rough approximation of the pattern of aging followed by individuals" (1985, p. 740). He goes on to point out that because of the wide variability at any one age, age itself is actually a poor predictor of performance. That is, if all you know about someone is his or her age, you could not make a very good prediction of the person's blood pressure, or weight, or hormone levels, or immune system response. Thus physical development in adulthood is not nearly as uniform as it is in childhood. Most 2-year-olds have similar physical features and abilities, but there is more diversity among 30-year-olds, and even more among the physical features and abilities of 80-year-olds.

What could account for such differences in later adulthood? A number of obvious possibilities come immediately to mind.

Specific Experience. The most obvious possibility is that our specific experiences affect the rate, or even the pattern, of physical aging. I've already given a number of examples of environmental factors that we know make a difference, including noise level, emotional stress, and general level of stimulation. One that I have not talked about, but that appears to be a highly significant factor, is exercise. My interest in this particular aspect of aging stems in part, I am sure, from my own decision at the age of 38 to begin exercising and running regularly. Nowadays, my knees no longer appreciate a regular running regimen, but I continue to walk two to three miles a day. Like most "converts" (such as ex-smokers), I can be a bit of a bore on the subject. But in this case my point is well buttressed by research.

For example, I pointed out earlier that maximum oxygen uptake ($VO_{2\,max}$) typically declines in adulthood, which means that older adults are getting less oxygen to the brain, the muscles, and all other parts of the body. At any age, however—even among the oldest old—$VO_{2\,max}$ can be increased significantly with exercise, a process referred to generally as a **training effect** (Blumenthal et al., 1991; Buchner, Beresford, Larson, LaCroix, & Wagner, 1992). In addition, I also pointed out the importance of weight training exercise to maintain or increase bone density, and low-impact exercise to alleviate the symptoms of osteoarthritis.

In summary, it seems that a program of regular aerobic activity combined with weight training exercises is beneficial for adults of all ages. Not only does it slow down primary aging, it prevents some aspects of secondary aging and may even increase life expectancy (E. B. Larson & Bruce, 1997). As the adage goes, "use it or lose it."

Heredity. We each inherit genes that help to shape the pattern and rate of our physical aging. Twin studies and other family studies show that longevity itself is moderately heritable (Herskind et al., 1996; Plomin & McClearn, 1990). Those who come from long-lived families also seem to have lower risk of disease in late adulthood. For example, in his studies of the Harvard men in the Grant study sample, George Vaillant finds that those men whose oldest grandparent had lived past 90 had only about a one-in-four chance of suffering from any kind of chronic illness at age 65. In contrast, nearly three-fourths of those whose oldest grandparent had died before age 78 suffered from a chronic illness in young old age (Vaillant, 1991).

As you will see in the next chapter, susceptibility to some diseases runs in families as well, something you are likely to be aware of if you have had a complete physical exam lately. Most physicians today will ask you about the disease history of your parents, your grandparents, even your aunts and uncles. In particular, they are likely to ask you about the family patterns of heart disease, cancer (particularly breast cancer), Alzheimer's disease, and osteoporosis, each of which is thought to be genetically influenced (Baker & Martin, 1997).

You can add up many of these factors in making a prediction of your own longevity using the list in Table 3.7. After you have filled out all the items in the table, add the resulting number to the appropriate life expectancy figure from Table 3.1, and you'll get a rough prediction of your own longevity. As you do this, you'll notice that while some of the items are factors over which you have no control, many of the most significant ones are controllable, or partially controllable, such as smoking and body weight. If you wish to "live long and prosper," as Mr. Spock of *Star Trek* would say, it pays to make good choices now.

TABLE 3.7 **Calculating Your Own Longevity**

Respond to each item honestly and sum the various positive and negative factors to arrive at the approximate number of years more (or less) than average you are likely to live.
Heredity
For each grandparent who lived past 80, add 1 year.
For each grandparent who lived to 70, but not 80, add 1/2 year.
If your mother lived past 80, add 4 years.

TABLE 3.7 **Calculating Your Own Longevity (continued)**

Respond to each item honestly and sum the various positive and negative factors to arrive at the approximate number of years more (or less) than average you are likely to live.

If your father lived past 80, add 2 years.

For each grandparent, parent or sibling who died of any type of heart disease before age 50, subtract 4 years.

For each such relative dying of heart disease between age 50 or 60, subtract 2 years.

For each grandparent, parent, or sibling who died of diabetes or ulcers before age 60, subtract 3 years.

Women: For each sister or mother who died of breast cancer before age 60, subtract 1 year.

If your intelligence is superior, add 2 years.

Health History

If your mother was younger than 18 or older than 35 at your birth, subtract 1 year.

If you are the first born in your family, add 1 year.

Women: If you have had no children (or plan no children), subtract 1/2 year.

If you have an annual physical exam, add 2 years.

If your weight is 10 to 30 percent above ideal weight shown in standard tables, the amount you must subtract depends on your age and gender. *Women:* Subtract 5 years if you are between 20 and 30, 4 years if you are between 30 and 50, and 2 years if you are over 50. *Men:* Subtract 10 years if you are between 20 and 30, 4 years if you are between 30 and 45, and 2 years for any age over that.

If your weight is more than 30 percent above the standard tables: *Women:* Subtract 6 1/2 years if you are between 20 and 30, 5 years if you are between 30 and 50, and 4 years thereafter. *Men:* Subtract 13 if you are between 20 and 30, 6 if you are between 30 and 40, and 4 years thereafter.

If your diet is genuinely low in fat and sugar, and you never eat past the feeling of fullness, add 1 year.

If you smoke 2 packs or more per day, subtract 12 years; if you smoke 1 to 2 packs a day, subtract 7 years; if you smoke, but less than 1 pack a day, subtract 2 years.

If you never drink, neither add nor subtract; if you are a heavy drinker, subtract 8; if you are a moderate drinker, add 3. If you are a light drinker, add 1 1/2.

If you do some aerobic exercise at least 3 times a week, add 3.

If you sleep more than 10 hours or less than 6 hours per night, subtract 2.

If you have intimate sexual relations once or twice a week, add 2.

If you have a chronic health condition (e.g., high blood pressure, diabetes, ulcers, cancer) or are frequently ill, subtract 5.

Your Current Life

If you have 4 or more years of college, add 3; if you have 1 to 3 years of college, add 2; if you have completed high school and gone no further, add 1; if you have completed less than eighth grade, subtract 2.

If your occupation is at a professional, technical, or managerial level, add 1 year; if you work at unskilled work, subtract 4.

If your family income is above average for your education and occupation, add one year; if it is below average, subtract 1.

If you job is physically active, add 1; if it is sedentary, subtract 2.

If you now live in an urban area and have lived in urban areas most of you life, subtract 1; if you have spent most of your life in a rural area, add 1.

TABLE 3.7 **Calculating Your Own Longevity (continued)**

Respond to each item honestly and sum the various positive and negative factors to arrive at the approximate number of years more (or less) than average you are likely to live.

If you are married and living with your spouse, add 1.

If you are separated or divorced, subtract 9 if you are a man, 4 if you are a woman.

If you are widowed, subtract 7 if you are a man, 4 if you are a woman.

If you are a never-married woman, subtract 1 for each decade unmarried past age 25.

If you are a never-married man and living with your family, subtract 1 year for each decade unmarried past 25; if you live alone, subtract 2 for each decade unmarried past 25.

If you have at least two close friends in whom you can confide, add 1.

If your personality is noticeably aggressive and hostile, subtract 2 to 5, depending on how much the description fits.

If you are a basically happy person and have a lot of fun in life, add 2 years.

If you have had an episode of being depressed or very tense, guilty, or worried that lasted as long as a year or more, subtract 1 to 3, depending on how severe the depression was.

If you take a lot of risks or live in a high-crime neighborhood, subtract 2 years; if you use seat belts regularly and generally avoid risks, add 1 year.

Source: Adapted from Woodruff-Pak, 1988, pp. 145–154; 1997, pp. 278–283.

SUMMARY

1. An important distinction is between primary and secondary aging. The former refers to universal, unavoidable, maturationally based changes with age; the latter refers to changes resulting from specific experience, disease, or environment.

2. There are quite a few answers available to the question, "Why do we age?" None is an all-encompassing grand theory like we find in some other fields of science. Instead, they are mostly small theories and apply to limited aspects of the aging process.

3. One explanation of aging is that free radicals released during cell metabolism build up and begin to interfere with normal cellular activity.

4. Another explanation of aging is that cells lose their ability to repair DNA over the years and the buildup of damaged DNA is the cause of aging.

5. Evolutionary theory explains that natural selection protects us in childhood and through our prime reproductive years but that after that there is no reproductive advantage to genes for good health or longevity.

6. The theory of genetic limits explains that aging happens because each species has a genetically determined limit as to how many times its cells can divide, and when that limit is reached, life ends.

7. Proponents of caloric restriction theory claim that the days of our lives are measured by the number of calories that our bodies metabolize. If we use up our allotted number of calories slowly by eating less, we extend our lives and postpone many of the physical effects of aging.

8. Although the average life expectancy has been increasing steadily over the past decades, now reaching approximately 78 years for women and 71 years for men in the United States, the maximum life span appears to have remained the same, at about 110 or 120 years.

9. Body changes in adulthood include changes in external appearance such as loss of height, redistribution of fat, loss of hair, loss of elasticity in skin and other organs. Although many products that claim to reverse physical aging are available, only a few have been found effective by researchers.

10. Loss of acuity in the senses also occurs, so that by age 65 or 70, 70 percent of adults have some visual loss, and 30 percent or more have significant hearing loss. Most visual and hearing losses are correctable by glasses, contact lenses, and hearing aids. Taste perception changes little, but the sense of smell becomes markedly less acute.

11. Two visual disorders that occur in later adulthood are so common that there is debate over whether they are primary or secondary aging. Cataracts, a gradual clouding of the lens of the eye, can be removed by simple surgery. Glaucoma, a buildup of pressure in the eye, is a major cause of blindness but can be controlled if diagnosed by routine eye exam.

12. A loss of muscle tissue is another body change, as is a loss of bone mass. Osteoporosis is the condition in which loss of bone mass is so great as to put one at risk for fracture; it occurs more frequently in women due to smaller bones and menopause. Hormone replacement therapy, supplementary calcium and vitamin D, and exercise can slow bone loss and even reverse it.

13. The cardiovascular system shows a steady decrease with age in maximum oxygen uptake and utilization ($VO_{2\,max}$) beginning after adolescence. People who exercise regularly have significantly slower rates of decline than do those who are sedentary.

14. Neurons appear to decline in number in certain parts of the brain with age; the larger change is a loss of dendrites and a reduction of function of individual neurons, and thus a loss of synaptic efficiency and speed.

15. The immune system declines in efficiency with age as the thymus gland decreases in size and in ability to support the growth of T cells and antibodies. This is related to (and probably the cause of) an age-related increase in disease. The immune response is also strongly affected by stress, and stress-reduction techniques increase immune function.

16. Both men and women experience a loss of reproductive capacity in middle and old age through a series of changes in hormones called the climacteric. In men, there is a decrease in production of viable sperm, genital tissue, muscle mass, sexual desire, ability to achieve and sustain an erection, facial hair, bone mass, and an increase in body fat. In women, menstruation ceases at about age 51 (on average), and this change is accompanied by loss of breast tissue and changes in the genitals that can make intercourse painful. Many women also experience hot flashes during the years leading up to menopause. Many symptoms of menopause can be alleviated by hormone replacement therapy.

17. Hormone replacement therapy is thought to decrease woman's risk of heart disease, osteoporosis, and Alzheimer's disease; hormone replacement therapy is not recommended for women with a personal or family history of breast cancer, although synthetic hormones are being developed that may bypass this risk. Psychological symptoms are not part of menopause for the vast majority of women.

18. Other hormones that decrease with age include DHEA and growth hormone. Research on replacing these hormones in aging people have brought mixed results, and the effectiveness and safety has not been determined for either hormone.

19. All the physical changes listed combine to affect daily behavior. The most widespread effect is a general slowing.

20. As people age they spend more time in the lighter stages of sleep. This makes any disturbance (internal or external) more apt to wake them up during the night.

21. There is an age-related decline in frequency of sexual activity, but the sharpest rate in decline is between the first and second years of marriage. There is great variation in sexual practices of older adults, and whether they have a sexual relationship or not depends on many factors, the biggest being availability of a partner.

22. Not all changes in the physical body that we associate with aging are gradual over the adult years. Some only begin late in life; some start early but have an impact on behavior only much later.

23. Individual differences in rate and pattern of aging are extremely large, affected not only by differing heredity but by differing experiences, including exercise.

24. Exercise or physical activity has been linked to slower aging processes in several systems, lowered risk of disease, and greater capacity for physical exertion. At least some of the body changes normally thought of as "aging" may thus be the result of disuse.

KEY TERMS

primary aging	osteoporosis	testes
secondary aging	estrogen	seminal fluid
free radicals	hormone replacement therapy	testosterone
antioxidants		erectile dysfunction
senescence	osteoarthritis	cyclic GMP
telomeres	$VO_{2\,max}$	menopause
life span	neurons	hot flash
longevity	plasticity	DHEA
life expectancy	dendrites	growth hormone
visual acuity	pruning	stamina
accommodate	B cells	dexterity
dark adaptation	antibodies	balance
cataracts	T cells	insomnia
glaucoma	climacteric	training effect

Austad, S. N. (1997). *Why we age: What science is discovering about the body's journey through life.* New York: Wiley.

Biologist Steve Austad has written this book to tell the nonbiologist about a new viewpoint of aging. He does this by giving an interesting account about the history, theories, experiments, and personalities of the people involved in the field of aging research. The writing is understandable and funny, and he dismisses a lot of popular myths and misinformation about aging, leaving the facts well organized and easy to understand.

Hayflick, L. (1994). *How and why we age.* New York: Ballantine Books.

Hayflick is a pioneer in the field of gerontological biology, but this book is aimed at the layperson. It is a mixture of science and trivia written in clear, nontechnical language. It tells about the biology and psychology of aging and gives some courageous statements about such controversial subjects as caloric restriction, hormone replacement therapy, and nutritional supplements.

Medina, J. J. (1996). *The clock of ages: Why we age, how we age, winding back the clock.* Cambridge, England: Cambridge University Press.

Medina is a molecular biologist, but that shouldn't scare you away. He is also a gifted storyteller, and in this book he tells the story of the science of aging. He includes all the facts about physical aging and all the theories, but also weaves in stories about Billy the Kid, Francisco de Goya, and Jane Austen. He also includes illustrations and section headings like "Wrinkle Wrinkle Little Star."

Rowe, J. W., & Kahn, R. L. (1998). *Successful aging.* New York: Pantheon.

The authors summarize 10 years of research showing that successful aging is determined more by individual lifestyle choices than by genetic inheritance. This research project, sponsored by the MacArthur Foundation, has been the first to reject the established approach of studying decline and to institute the practice of studying aging persons who had preserved and even enhanced their mental and physical abilities. This book is written for the general public and gives a clear explanation of what has become known as the "new gerontology." If you read only one book about aging, this should be it.

CHANGES IN HEALTH AND HEALTH HABITS

CHAPTER 4

One of the most pervasive myths about adult life in our culture is "to be old is to be sick" (Rowe & Kahn, 1998, p. 13). This might have been true at the beginning of this century, but it does not reflect the facts about aging today in most of the world. A more accurate picture shows us that over 94 percent of people over 65 in the United States today are living independently in their own homes. Of older adults between 65 and 74, almost 90 percent report having no disability whatsoever. And of those between 75 and 84, 73 percent say they are without disability. In fact, even among those over 85 years of age, 40 percent is fully functioning.

The reason for this change is an increase in health practices and a decrease in many diseases. In Chapter 3, I talked about primary aging, changes that happen to most people as they get older. Some of the changes of primary aging can be slowed down or even reversed for a time; other changes can be corrected or skillfully covered up. But the fact remains that the changes of primary aging happen to all of us eventually, even to the healthiest among us. In this chapter I want to talk about secondary aging, the changes that happen to only some people as they age and that can be prevented and even cured in many cases. Although the topic is death and disease, I will remind you frequently that secondary aging, by definition, is often preventable and curable. Today more than ever, each person's quality of life in old age is, to a large extent, under his or her own control, and much of that control is in the form of health practices that begin in young and middle adulthood.

OVERALL AGE PATTERNS IN HEALTH AND DISEASE

Let's begin at the simplest descriptive level: At what age do most adults die? What are the most common causes of death at various ages? What other diseases are prevalent among adults?

Mortality: Causes of Death

Figure 4.1 shows the **mortality rate,** or the probability of dying in any one year, for all adults in that age range. You can see that less than one-tenth of 1 percent of adults aged 15 to 24 die in any given year, while over 15 percent of adults over 85 die each year. The fact that older people are more likely to die is surely no great surprise (although you may be comforted to see how flat the curve is into the 60s).

Table 4.1 tells about the causes of death for people at different ages. For young adults (24 to 44) two of the causes in the top five aren't even diseases—accidents and suicide. By middle adulthood (45 to 65) accidents are

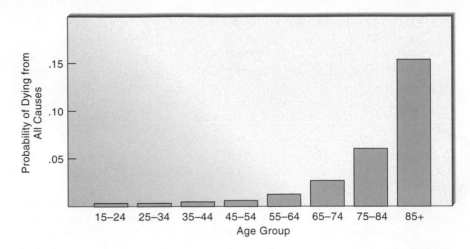

FIGURE 4.1 The probability of dying of any cause increases with age, especially after 60.

Source: Data from U.S. Bureau of the Census, 1993, Table 14, p. 15.

down to third place, behind cancer and cardiovascular disease, while HIV is in fifth place, tied with chronic liver disease. Older adults (65 to 74) die from heart disease, cancer, and chronic obstructive pulmonary diseases, which are also found on the list for middle-aged adults, but now diabetes and pneumonia/influenza have appeared. Finally, the older group (75 and above) shows the same top five causes of death with some change in order for the last three (American Heart Association, 1998).

Morbidity: The General Pattern of Illness with Age

Chronic and Acute Diseases. You might assume that a similar age pattern would emerge for **morbidity,** or illness rate, with older adults suffering from more of all types of diseases. But that is not the case. Younger adults are actually about twice as likely as are those over 65 to suffer from those short-term illnesses physicians call **acute illnesses,** including colds, the flu, infections, or short-term intestinal upsets. It is only the rates of **chronic illnesses**— those longer-lasting disorders such as heart disease, arthritis, or high blood pressure—

TABLE 4.1 **Top Five Causes of Death for U.S. Adults in Four Age Groups**

Age 24–44	Age 45–64	Age 65–74	Age 75+
1. Accidents	1. Cancer	1. Cardiovascular disease	1. Cardiovascular disease
2. Cardiovascular disease	2. Cardiovascular disease	2. Cancer	2. Cancer
3. Cancer	3. Accidents	3. Chronic obstructive pulmonary disease	3. Pneumonia/ influenza
4. Suicide	4. Chronic obstructive pulmonary disease	4. Diabetes	4. Chronic obstructive pulmonary disease
5. HIV	5. HIV/chronic liver disease	5. Pneumonia/influenza	5. Diabetes

Source: American Heart Association (1998).

that show an age-related increase. Older adults have two to three times the likelihood of suffering from such disorders compared to adults in their 20s and 30s (U.S. Bureau of the Census, 1993).

Furthermore, when young adults do have chronic disorders, they aren't the same ones you see in older adults, as you can see in Figure 4.2. Among those under 45, the single most common chronic illness is sinusitis, with hay fever or allergies also common. Both of these problems remain frequent in older adults but become proportionately much less significant. In these older groups it is arthritis, high blood pressure, and heart disease that are the most common chronic illnesses—all problems with low rates among younger adults. At the same time, in my usual search for a balanced view of aging, it is important to point out that roughly a fifth of adults over age 65 in the United States have no chronic ailment at all (Guralnik & Kaplan, 1989). So although the probability of chronic illness rises with age, it never reaches 100 percent.

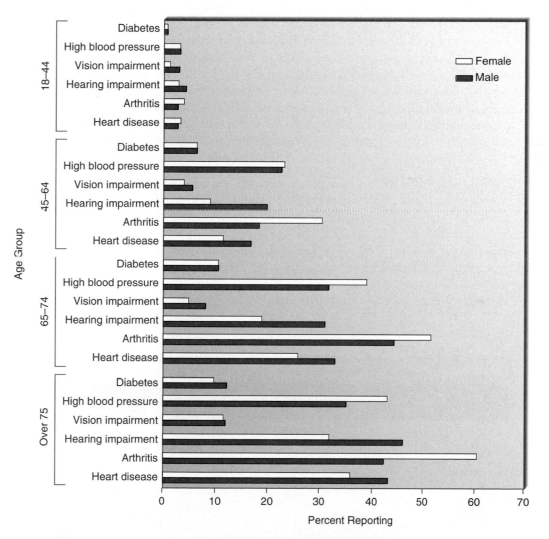

FIGURE 4.2 U.S. men and women who lived in households in the community were surveyed about chronic illnesses. All six illnesses shown increased with age. More women of all ages reported having arthritis; more men of all ages reported having hearing impairment. But even in the oldest age, many people reported no chronic disease at all.

Source: Data from U.S. Bureau of the Census, 1994.

Disabilities. It is quite possible to have one or more chronic diseases without experiencing significant disability. I have a chronic lower back problem that requires thought and good sense but restricts me very little; another adult may have mild arthritis that responds well to aspirin and requires no limitation in major activities. For most adults, the crucial issue is not whether you have a chronic ailment but whether that ailment or disease has an impact on daily life, requiring restriction in daily activities or reducing your ability to care for yourself.

Psychologists, epidemiologists, gerontologists, and even lawyers who deal with guardianship cases all measure disability by inquiring about a person's ability to perform two groups of activities: (1) basic self-care activities, such as bathing, dressing, walking a short distance, shifting from a bed to a chair, using the toilet, and eating, collectively called **activities of daily living** (ADLs), and (2) more complex everyday tasks, such as preparing meals, shopping for personal items, doing light housework, doing the laundry, using transportation, handling finances, using the telephone, and taking medications, referred to as **instrumental activities of daily living** (IADLs). Older adults in the United States and several other countries reported spending more time each day on IADLs than any other activity, some 5 to 6 hours (S. L. Willis, 1996).

You can get some sense of how many older adults have such disabilities from Table 4.2, which reflects responses to two large surveys in the 1980s, one in the United States and one in Canada (Kunkel & Applebaum, 1992). In this case, the category of "little or no disability" means that the person has problems with at most one of these listed activities. A "moderate disability" means problems with at least one ADL or two IADLs, while "severe disability" means problems with two or more ADLs. Figure 4.3, based on U.S. data from the same period, will give you some sense of the proportion of older adults who have problems with one specific task, in this case preparing meals.

Self-Ratings of Health. Another way we might measure adults' health, other than asking about activities of daily living, would be quite simply to ask adults to rate their own health on some simple scale. We know that such self-ratings have some validity, because longitudinal data tell us that those who rate their own health as "poor" are indeed more likely to die over the succeeding few years than are those who rate their health as excellent (Schoenfeld, Malmrose, Blazer, Gold, & Seeman, 1994). Not surprisingly, when adults of various ages are asked about their health, young adults are far more likely to rate themselves as in excellent health than are older adults, as you can see in Table 4.3, which

TABLE 4.2 **Percentage of Older Adults in the United States and Canada Who Experience Little, Moderate, or Severe Disability**

	Age Group		
Disability Category	**65–74**	**75–84**	**85+**
Little or none			
Males	90.9%	82.7%	58.3%
Females	89.0	79.2	49.8
Moderate			
Males	5.1	9.1	19.9
Females	6.3	12.1	21.8
Severe			
Males	4.0	8.2	21.7
Females	4.6	10.8	31.7

Source: Kunkel & Applebaum, 1992, Table 3, p. S257.

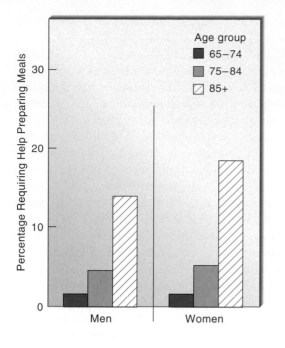

FIGURE 4.3 Percentage of the young old, old old, and oldest old who require assistance in preparing meals—one of the traditional "independent activities of daily living."

Source: Guralnik & Simonsick, 1993, Fig. 2, p. 5.

is drawn from a nationally representative sample in the United States (Verbrugge, 1989). At the same time, it's also clear that more than two-thirds of adults over 65 think of themselves as having good, very good, or excellent health. This does not mean, of course, that a 70-year-old who describes himself or herself as in "very good health" has the same physical functioning as a 27-year-old who chooses the same overall description. We adjust our expectations of health as we get older, so when we are asked how good our health is, we are answering not on an absolute scale but to at least some degree on a relative one ("my health is excellent for someone my age"), and this is more true as we get into old age. Nonetheless, it is still striking that so many older adults describe their health as good, very good, or excellent.

Institutionalization. For those whose health is poor, especially those with many disabilities, one of the possible outcomes is institutionalization—a result already clear from Figure 4.3. In the United States on any given day, roughly 5 percent of adults over 65 are cared for in a nursing home of some kind. Among the oldest old, however, this figure is 22 percent.

Men are likely to spend less time in nursing homes than women, and married people are likely to spend less time than single people, especially single women with few or no children, few social contacts, and significant disability. If the disability is such that older persons can no longer toilet or feed themselves, or if they suffer from significant men-

TABLE 4.3 **Ratings of Their Own Health Given by Adults in the United States (Percent)**

	Age Group		
Rating	25–44	45–64	65+
Excellent or very good	72.6	52.3	35.2
Good	21.0	29.1	32.3
Fair or poor	5.0	12.4	21.5

Source: Verbrugge, 1989, Table 2.13, p. 48.

tal confusion, institutionalization is particularly likely (Steinbach, 1992; Wolinsky, Calahan, Fitzgerald, & Johnson, 1993; Montgomery & Kosloski, 1994).

Among ethnic subgroups in the United States, nursing home care is most likely among Caucasians, and less likely among African-Americans, Hispanics, or Asian-Americans. For example, in the 1982 National Long-Term Care Survey of frail elders (the same group studied by Manton and shown in Figure 4.3), 8.3 percent of the whites were in institutions, compared to 3.8 percent of African-Americans, even though the groups were equivalently disabled (B. Miller, McFall, & Campbell, 1994). Similarly, the 1980 U.S. Census shows that 2.7 percent of unmarried Hispanic women over 55 in 1980 were in institutions, as were 4.6 percent of Japanese-Americans, and 2.9 percent of Chinese-Americans, compared to 7.8 percent of unmarried white women of the same age (Burr & Mutchler, 1992, 1993).

Critical Thinking

What other cultural values or beliefs besides variations in the centrality of family interactions might contribute to this difference among ethnic groups in the rate of nursing home care for older adults? Can you think of other explanations of this difference?

The usual explanation of these ethnic group differences is that the majority white culture places more emphasis on independence and less emphasis on family solidarity than is true in any of the other three groups. Thus more single older white adults live alone than is true for African-Americans, Asians, or Hispanics, and when they become too frail to live alone, more whites shift to nursing home care. But in all these groups, nursing home care is virtually always the choice of last resort for either the elders themselves or their families. If you ask older adults what kind of care they would like should they become sick or disabled, the majority say they would like to be cared for in their own home either by a relative or by paid helpers. The two least preferred choices are being cared for in the home of a child or other relative, or nursing home care (W. J. McAuley & Blieszner, 1985). Yet the economics of care in the United States and the burden of caring for a significantly physically or mentally disabled elder are such that institutional care is sometimes the only reasonable choice—a point I come back to later in this chapter and in Chapter 6.

Aging in Place. The new trend in living arrangements for the elderly is **aging in place,** meaning that the first option in living arrangements for an older person is the place where they currently reside. In a recent survey by the Association for the Advancement of Retired Persons, 86 percent of older people questioned expressed the desire to continue living in their own homes. They feel that their own homes symbolize independence, the family's center, a history of pleasant memories, and their remaining status (Glassman, 1995). This way of thinking is reflected in federal policy that extends Medicare and Medicaid payment for nursing home services to home care and assisted living services.

The concept of aging in place means that many older adults with disabilities are still able to live in their own homes, due to programs that provide meals, housekeeping assistance, personal care assistance, adult day care programs, and transportation. Homes are modified for wheelchair access, bathrooms have grab rails and tub seats added, and small changes are made, such as getting rid of loose rugs, slippery tile, and dim lighting, all of which help to assure as much independence as possible for as long as possible.

Other Housing Options. Older adults who are still independent but do not wish to remain in their former homes often move into **retirement communities,** which consist of individual houses and apartments with community centers featuring swimming pools, golf courses, planned activities, and group transportation for shopping and entertainment. Those who need more assistance can choose **congregate living facilities,** where they live in their own apartments but have one or more meals in a community dining room. Housekeeping services and medical services are available as needed. The next level of care is **assisted living** (also known as nursing homes), which offers more intensive help with personal needs and 24-hour custodial supervision (Glassman, 1995).

A new option is the **continuing care retirement community.** Residents begin in independent living quarters and then can move to facilities offering more care if and when it becomes necessary. Since everyone enters in good health and pays the same fees whether or not they need assistance it operates similar to group insurance plans.

Disabilities and Institutionalization in Context. It is important for me to put the information on overall rates of disease and disabilities into some kind of context, so that you do not take away from this section the impression that all older adults suffer from severe disabilities. So let me reemphasize some basics: Roughly three-fourths of all adults over 65 (in the United States and Canada) show *no* disability at all (Manton, Corder, & Stallard, 1993). It is really only among the oldest old that disability is found in as many as half of adults, as you can see with another look at Table 4.2. Furthermore, Manton finds that the incidence of disability is *declining* among older adults in the United States. So although it is true that some form of disability becomes more common in old age, it is not a typical part of the aging experience until late old age, and even then, roughly half of elders are able to continue to care for themselves and to perform ordinary activities of daily living.

AGE CHANGES IN SPECIFIC DISEASES

Heart Disease

The death rate from **coronary heart disease** (CHD) has been dropping rapidly in the past two decades in the United States and most other industrialized countries. Yet CHD remains the leading cause of death and disability among both men and women in the United States and throughout the developed world (American Heart Association, 1998). Although the phrase *coronary heart disease* covers a number of physical deteriorations, the key change is in the coronary arteries, which slowly become blocked with fibrous and calcified tissue, a process called **atherosclerosis.** Atherosclerosis is *not* a normal part of aging. It is a disease, and not everyone has it.

Some people are at greater risk of contracting this disease than others. Most of what we know about the risks contributing to cardiovascular disease comes from several longitudinal epidemiological studies, of which the most famous is the Framingham Study (e.g., K. M. Anderson, Castelli, & Levy, 1987; Dawber, Kannel, & Lyell, 1963; Garrison, Gold, Wilson, & Kannel, 1993; Kannel & Gordon, 1980). The Framingham researchers began in 1948 with a sample of 5209 adults, then aged 30 to 59, all residents of Framingham, Massachusetts. These adults have been reassessed roughly every two years since then, as have many of their children, a process that has enabled the researchers to track the long-term health of adults who had various physical characteristics or personal habits and thus to identify risk factors for heart disease. The risks they identified are listed on the right-hand side of Table 4.4.

Because equivalent lists have appeared in innumerable newspapers and magazines, I suspect this catalog of risks is highly familiar to you by now. What is not usually emphasized, and what is very important for you to understand, is that the risks listed are cumulative. The more risk factors in your profile, the higher the chance that you have, or will develop, CHD. Further, the effects are not just additive. Some combinations multiply the risk. For example, high cholesterol is three times as risky in a heavy smoker as in a nonsmoker (Tunstall-Pedoe & Smith, 1990). Let me also point out that many of the items on this list are under your control. To be sure, you have no control over your genes. But you do have some control over smoking, weight, diet, and exercise.

CRITICAL THINKING

Be honest with yourself now: How many of these risks describe you? Which ones could you readily change? Which would be hardest to change?

TABLE 4.4 **Risk Factors for Heart Disease and Cancer**

Risk Factor	Cancer	Heart Disease
Blood pressure	No known risk.	Systolic pressure above 140 is linked to higher risk; the higher the BP, the higher the risk.
Smoking	A major risk for lung cancer, perhaps also pancreatic cancer.	A major risk factor; the more you smoke, the greater the risk. Stopping smoking reduces the risk.
Cholesterol	No known risk.	Clear risk for total cholesterol of 200 or more; the culprit appears to be elevated levels of low-density lipoproteins.
Exercise	Inactivity is associated in some studies with higher risk of colon cancer.	Inactivity appears to roughly double the risk of CHD.
Diet	High-fat diet appears to increase the risk, although there is still dispute; high-fiber diet may reduce the risk.	High-fat diet is linked to increased risk, but there is not uniform agreement on the effects.
Weight (obesity)	Greater weight linked to increased risk of several cancers, including breast cancer, although the effect is smaller than for CHD.	Any weight more than 30% above the recommended level for height is associated with increased risk, and extreme slimness is associated with lower risk.
Heredity	Some forms of cancer clearly run in families; mechanism is not yet entirely clear.	Those with first-degree relatives with CHD have 7 to 10 times the risk of CHD themselves.

Source: Data from Benfante, & Reed, 1990; Berlin & Colditz, 1990; Chamberlain & Galton, 1990; Fozard, Metter, & Brant, 1990; Kannel & Gordon, 1980; Kritchevsky, 1990; I. Lee, Manson, Hennekens, & Paffenbarger, 1993; McGandy, 1988; Rose, 1993; Shipley, Pocock, & Marmot, 1991.

Women and Coronary Heart Disease. I feel I should emphasize something here: *Coronary heart disease is the number one killer of women in the United States and in all industrialized countries.* The numbers can be misleading because the average age that men have heart attacks and die from heart disease is younger than it is for women. When heart disease rates are compared within age groups, it can give the impression that women are at a lower risk than men. This is not true; in fact, there is some evidence to the contrary. Research shows that women are almost twice as apt to die than men in the year following their first heart attack, and several explanations have been suggested for this, including the fact that women having a first heart attack are usually older than men and more apt to have other health problems, too (Shumaker & Smith, 1995). However, a recent study done in Spain of 331 women admitted to hospitals with their first heart attacks showed that compared to a control group of men, the women had more severe heart attacks regardless of age or the presence of other health problems (Marragut et al., 1998).

It is a popular misconception that breast cancer is the biggest health enemy for women, but this is far from true. A woman has a 4 percent chance of dying of breast cancer compared to a 50 percent chance of dying of some type of heart disease. The risk is even higher for African-American women because they have a higher incidence of hypertension (American Heart Association, 1998). My message here is that warnings about cholesterol level, exercise, and smoking should be heeded by women as much as by men.

Cancer

Between 1990 and 1995, the incidence and death rate from cancer declined by nearly 3 percent, the first time there had been a sustained decline since national record keeping began in 1930 (Wingo, Ries, Edwards, Rosenberg, & Miller, 1998). Nevertheless, cancer remains the second-leading cause of death for adults in the United States, and the incidence of cancer increases with age, meaning that more older people than younger people contract cancer. Another change with age is in the type of cancer one is likely to have. Breast cancer is the most frequent cause of cancer death for women under 55, while leukemia is most frequent for young adult men, and lung cancer is most frequent for middle-aged men. Once men and women reach 55, lung cancer remains the top cancer killer and stays there through the rest of the life span. Another age-linked pattern occurs for survival rates from cancer: Five-year survival rates for cancers of various types remain fairly steady throughout adulthood but then decline after age 75 (List, 1988).

Breast cancer and leukemia are top causes of death for those under 55; lung cancer is the top cause for those over 55.

Cancer is rapidly accelerated, uncontrolled cell division and is caused by a series of genetic errors, or **mutations,** at the cellular level. Usually, enzymes repair these errors before the cell divides, but when these mechanisms fail, the mutations can lay the groundwork for cancer. Fortunately for us, it requires a number of independent mutations for cancer to develop; for example, colon cancer seems to require at least four (Austad, 1997). However, this gives you an idea of why older people are more likely to develop cancer—because they have had more cell divisions and more time for errors to occur. It tells why some parts of the body are more vulnerable to cancer, such as the breast and colon, where cells divide more times during the lifetime. And this also gives you a clue about how the environment can affect the development of cancer; why people whose lungs are continually irritated by tobacco smoke or industrial pollution are more apt to get lung cancer (Ershler, 1997).

Like heart disease, there are some identifiable risk factors for various forms of cancer, summarized in the center column of Table 4.4. Note that here, too, as with heart disease, personal choices made in your 20s and 30s may either forestall, or help set into motion, disease processes that will become manifest only several decades later.

Alzheimer's Disease

Alzheimer's disease is a progressive, incurable deterioration of key areas of the brain. Unlike coronary heart disease and cancer, which can occur throughout adulthood, Alzheimer's disease is truly a disease of old age, with 90 percent of cases developing after the age of 65. Once considered a rare disorder, Alzheimer's disease has become a major public health problem in the United States and throughout the world, primarily because of the increase in longevity and the greater proportion of older people in our population. Alzheimer's disease afflicts one-tenth of Americans over 65 and almost one-half of those over 85—some 4 million people. If you are like 20 million other people in the United States, you are acutely aware of this problem because you have a family member with Alzheimer's disease and are experiencing its effects firsthand.

Alzheimer's disease is the fourth leading cause of death in the U.S. and the major type of **dementia** among older adults, meaning that it involves global deterioration in intellectual abilities and causes functional impairment. It involves significant impairment of memory, judgment, social functioning, and control of emotions. Other types of dementia can be caused by multiple small strokes, Parkinson's disease, multiple blows to the head (as among boxers), a single head trauma, advanced stages of AIDS, depression, drug intoxication, hypothyroidism, some kinds of tumors, vitamin B_{12} deficiency, anemia, and alcohol abuse. I give you this list not because I expect you to memorize it, but because I want you to realize that a loss of cognitive functioning in an older person is not necessarily Alzheimer's disease. About 10 percent of patients with symptoms of dementia have a condition that can be treated, such as depression, drug intoxication, vitamin B$_{12}$ deficiency, nervous system infection, and hypothyroidism (Morrison-Bogorad, Phelps, & Buckholtz, 1997).

There is no cure at this time for Alzheimer's disease, but progress is being made in several areas. Some of the new advances have been in diagnosing the disease and predicting its course. Until recently, Alzheimer's disease could only be diagnosed with certainty at autopsy, but recently, clinicians have developed guidelines for delineating between Alzheimer's and other dementias and can now diagnosis the disorder in living patients with 85 percent accuracy (Cullum & Rosenberg, 1998). Other research has made it possible to predict the probable course of the illness for individual patients, making it possible for them and their families to have some control over their lives by making plans for the future (Stern et al., 1997).

Genetic researchers are making advances in identifying the causes of Alzheimer's disease, the first step toward a cure. It has been known since the early part of this century that many of the people who die of dementia have abnormalities in the brain tissue called plaques and tangles. The plaques, first identified by Alois Alzheimer in 1907, are small, circular deposits of a dense protein, **beta-amyloid;** the tangles are webs of degenerating neurons, as illustrated in Figure 4.4. However, it was only recently that researchers identified some of the genes that caused the buildup of protein in the brain (Selkoe, 1997). I say "some of the genes" because it is now thought that a number of different genes can cause Alzheimer's disease.

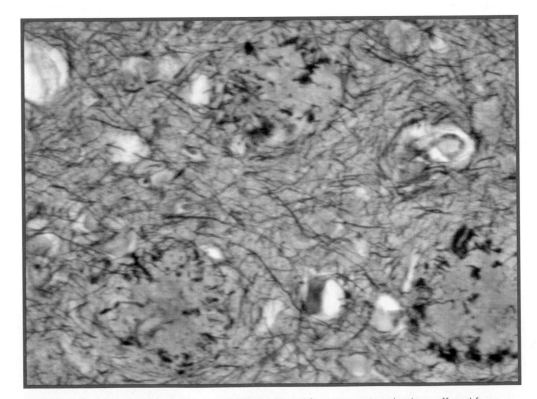

FIGURE 4.4 This neuron is from a patient diagnosed from autopsy as having suffered from Alzheimer's disease. You can see how tangled and fragmented the dendrites have become.

Ironically, we know the most about early-onset Alzheimer's, the type that accounts for the fewest number of cases, about 10 percent. Working with families who have an unusually large number of members with early-onset Alzheimer's, researchers have identified three genes: APP, PS1, and PS2, any one of which can cause overproduction of the beta-amyloid protein found in the brains of Alzheimer's victims. A panel of experts from the National Institutes of Health and the Human Genome Project has recommended that genetic testing is appropriate for healthy people in families with a high incidence of the early-onset type of this disease, if they request it, and that it should be confidential and accompanied by counseling before testing is done, at the time the results are given, and again in a follow-up session (Post et al., 1997).

The causes of late-onset Alzheimer's disease are less clear, although this type accounts for 90 percent of cases. Some cases are thought to have a genetic cause, and researchers have been working to identify the gene or genes responsible. So far, only one gene has been implicated: *apoE.* This gene can take one of four forms, designated *apoE1, apoE2, apoE3,* and *apoE4.* Only the last one, *apoE4,* is associated with Alzheimer's disease; people who have one copy of *apoE4* have 2 to 4 times the chance of developing the disease as do people with other forms of the gene, and people who have two copies of it have 5 to 18 times the chance of developing Alzheimer's disease.

Although this sounds encouraging, there is more to the story. Most people with Alzheimer's disease do not have the *apoE4* gene at all. Some people with one or even two copies of *apoE4* remain healthy well into old age. In addition, the probabilities for contracting the disease if you have the *apoE4* gene don't seem to hold true for all racial and ethnic groups (Farrer et al., 1997). So although this information is valuable for future research, and genetic testing can be part of the diagnostic process for patients already showing symptoms of dementia, testing of healthy persons is not recommended at this time by experts because it would not give an accurate prediction of whether they would develop the disease (Post et al., 1997).

Alzheimer's Disease and Normal Aging of the Brain. Let me go back for a moment to primary aging of the nervous system, information I wrote about in Chapter 3. With normal aging there is some neuronal loss in some parts of the brain, decrease in dendrites, and evidence of a change in neurotransmitter function. As you will see in Chapter 5, the memory of an older adult is not as sharp or as quick as it once was, and it becomes more difficult to learn new information. This might lead you to believe that Alzheimer's disease is just an extreme form of normal aging, but this is definitely not true. Alzheimer's disease is a different creature entirely. The types of mental losses are different. With normal aging, we might forget the zip code for a close friend to whom we are mailing a letter; with Alzheimer's disease, we don't know which line to put the address on and where to stick the stamp. With normal aging we might forget where we put our car keys, but with Alzheimer's we confuse red and green traffic lights—which means to stop and which means to go.

On a cellular level, the brains of people with Alzheimer's disease have extensive degeneration of neurons in selected parts of the brain, mainly the circuits involved in memory and attention, while healthy people of the same age have little loss in those areas. Furthermore, the types of losses are different, with Alzheimer's disease causing cell death and destruction of the neurons, and normal aging causing more subtle changes in the molecules and structure of the neurons (Morrison & Hof, 1997).

It is important to distinguish between primary aging and secondary aging in mental processes. Recent research has shown that about 1 in 5 primary caregivers of older people with dementia do not recognize that there is a problem, including 1 in 10 caregivers of peo-

**CRITICAL
THINKING**

What are some of the pros and cons of being tested for early onset Alzheimer's disease? If you were a candidate for this type of genetic testing, would you choose to have it? Why or why not?

ple with severe dementia. One of the most frequently cited reasons for this is that they believed that their family member was "just getting old." This is unfortunate for the 10 percent of dementia cases that can be treated and also for the younger caregivers who believe that these conditions are normal and that they, too, will experience the same as they age.

A Word About Caregivers of Alzheimer's Patients. The average person with Alzheimer's disease lives for eight years after diagnosis, and some live as many as 20 years. Most Alzheimer's patients live at home and are taken care of by family members—their spouse, daughters, daughters-in-law. Nearly half of the caregivers suffer from symptoms of depression (Small et al., 1997), producing another 2 million secondary victims of this disease. New guidelines by the medical community call for treatment of the family unit instead of the individual patient. As the number of families affected by this disease increases, more services have become available, including day care centers and support groups (Merrill, 1997).

Aging and Physical Disease: An Overview

Before I go on to other subjects, I need to underline yet again a key point about what I have said so far concerning both specific diseases and disease in general: Although the risk of having *some* disease increases with age, no one of these specific diseases is an inevitable part of aging. It may be common to develop some atherosclerosis as you get older, but it is not a normal part of aging; Alzheimer's disease increases in frequency in the later years of life, but dementia (of any type) is not a normal part of aging in the same sense that puberty is a normal part of physical development in childhood, or that menopause is part of normal aging for middle-aged women.

Of course, the physiological changes in the immune system, the neurological system, and the cardiovascular system that do appear to be part of primary aging obviously contribute to the increased vulnerability to disease as we get older. But that general statement does not explain why one person gets cancer, another heart disease, and another remains essentially disease-free into old age.

AGE CHANGES IN MENTAL HEALTH

A decade or two ago, summary statements about the relationship of age and mental health would have sounded a lot like the summaries of changes in physical health: Things get worse as you age. Indeed, most gerontological texts and most government documents emphasized that a great number of mental disorders, but particularly depression, increased steadily with age and were a special problem among those over 65. More recent research makes it pretty clear that this conclusion is incorrect, but it is still difficult to tell what the real picture is because of changing diagnoses of mental disorders, the inclusion of institutionalized older adults in studies, and the limitations of cross-sectional data.

In an extensive review of the available literature, Margaret Gatz and her colleagues (Gatz, Kasl-Godley, & Karel, 1996) concluded that the proportion of people in the United States over 65 who can be diagnosed with a mental disorder (22 percent) is identical to the proportion of all adults in the United States with mental disorders (22 percent), and very close to the proportion of people under 18 who have mental disorders (17 to 22 percent). Thus the prevalence of mental disorders seems to be constant across age groups, although different disorders are predominant at different ages.

Even if the rate of mental disorders stays constant across the life span, questions remain. Are there certain types of mental disorders that are more prevalent in later adulthood? Are the symptoms the same in people of different ages? Is treatment as successful in older patients? I have selected two disorders that are common in older adults—depression and anxiety—to answer some of these questions.

Depression

The basic question here is whether older adults suffer more than younger adults from depression. It seems like an easy question, but it is not. First, we need to define what we mean by **depression.** There are two ways of measuring depression: One is using the criteria that therapists use when diagnosing mental disorders, the **Diagnostic and Statistical Manual of Mental Disorders, 4th Edition** (DSM-IV) published by the American Psychiatric Association in 1994, and the other is using one of many available symptoms checklists. The DSM-IV requires that before a person is diagnosed as suffering from a **major depressive disorder,** he or she must exhibit depressed mood (of course) and/or loss of interest or pleasure in activities along with several additional symptoms, as shown in Table 4.5. Using this definition, longitudinal research shows that about 1 percent of adults over 65 suffer from depression (Regier et al., 1988).

The second method of defining depression is using a symptoms checklist. Respondents are usually asked to read a list of symptoms and indicate which ones they have experienced within some time frame, how frequently they have experienced them, and how severe the symptoms were. Sample questions from a symptoms checklist are shown in Table 4.6. As you might imagine, it is possible for a person to score high on depression when a symptom checklist is used but not fit the DSM-IV clinical diagnosis for major depressive episode. Using the symptom checklist criteria, Koenig and Blazer (1992) reanalyzed the data used by Regier in the study cited above and found that over one-fourth (27 percent) of the respondents aged 65 and older were depressed. So depending on the method of measuring depression, the same group of people can have as few as 1 percent of their members depressed or as many as 27 percent. In more recent research, a distinction is made between **clinical depression,** as diagnosed by the DSM-IV, and **subclinical depression,** as diagnosed by a symptoms checklist.

Studies comparing adults of different ages using the DSM-IV criteria show that the rate of clinical depression *does not* change much with age. By contrast, other studies using the symptom checklist to measure depression show that the rate of subclinical depression *does* change with age. Figure 4.5 shows that very young adults and very old adults (over 75 years of age) have higher rates than those in the middle of the life span (Kessler, Foster,

TABLE 4.5 **Diagnostic Features of a Major Depressive Episode**

Five of the following items must be present during the same two-week period, including one of the two items marked with an asterisk.
1. Depressed mood for most of the day.*
2. Loss of interest or pleasure in all, or almost all, activities.*
3. Significant weight change when not dieting (loss or gain).
4. Significant change in sleep habits (insomnia or hypersomnia).
5. Psychomotor agitation or retardation almost daily.
6. Fatigue or loss of energy almost daily.
7. Feelings of worthlessness or excessive or inappropriate guilt almost daily.
8. Diminished ability to think or concentrate, or indecisiveness almost daily.
9. Frequent thoughts of death or suicide without a specific plan, or a suicide attempt, or a specific plan for committing suicide.

Source: Adapted from the *Diagnostic and Statistical Manual, 4th Edition,* of the American Pyschological Association, 1994.

TABLE 4.6 **Examples of Symptom Checklist Questions for Evaluating Depression**

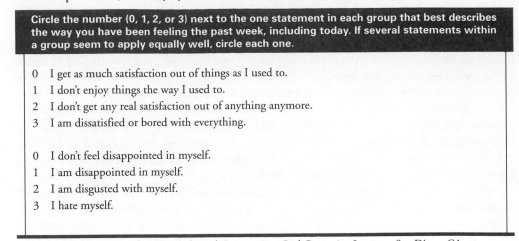

Circle the number (0, 1, 2, or 3) next to the one statement in each group that best describes the way you have been feeling the past week, including today. If several statements within a group seem to apply equally well, circle each one.

0   I get as much satisfaction out of things as I used to.
1   I don't enjoy things the way I used to.
2   I don't get any real satisfaction out of anything anymore.
3   I am dissatisfied or bored with everything.

0   I don't feel disappointed in myself.
1   I am disappointed in myself.
2   I am disgusted with myself.
3   I hate myself.

Source: Selected items from Psychological Corporation, *Beck Depression Inventory,* San Diego, CA: Harcourt Brace Jovanovich.

Webster, & House, 1992), and this is true even when the increased physical symptoms of older people are considered (Gatz et al., 1996).

Is depression in older adults a different disorder than depression in younger adults? In other words, do health care professionals need to look for different warning signs or consider different treatment depending on the age of their patients? Again, it depends on how severe the depression is. Researchers compared middle-aged and older adults who were hospitalized for clinical depression and found that their family histories, response to treatment, and most of their symptoms were remarkably similar. The only exceptions were

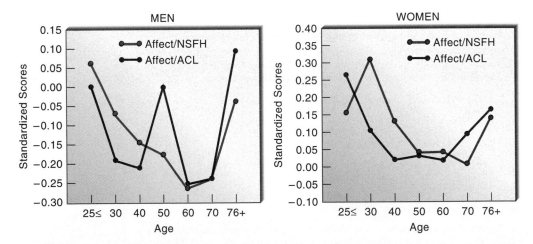

FIGURE 4.5 Rate of self-reported depressive feelings for adults of various ages from two large, nationally representative, cross-sectional studies, the Americans Changing Lives (ACL) survey (1986) and the National Survey of Families and Households (NSFH) in 1987–1988.

Source: Kessler, Foster, Webster, & House, 1992, Figs. 1 and 2, 123. Copyright 1992 by the American Psychological Association. Reprinted by permission.

that the older patients were more apt than younger patients to show weight loss and constipation, and less apt to have suicidal thoughts (Blazer, Hughes, & George, 1987).

A slightly different situation emerges when patients with subclinical depression are compared. This was the focus of research by Blazer and colleagues (Blazer, Hughes, & George, 1987) when they compared older adults with middle-aged adults, both groups being treated for depression as outpatients. In this study of less depressed adults, differences in symptoms did emerge. Older patients reported significantly more physical symptoms, such as abdominal complaints, sleep disturbances, lethargy, and constipation, as well as more thoughts of death. However, response to treatment did not differ between the two age groups.

One last word about depression. Think for a moment about the symptoms of depression outlined above: loss of appetite, sleeplessness, loss of energy, loss of interest and enjoyment of the normal pursuits of life. Do these remind you of the false stereotypes of normal aging? Unfortunately, some health care professionals, family members, and older adults themselves make the mistake of thinking that these symptoms are part of normal aging. This is why it is so important to distinguish between primary and secondary aging. Depression in the elderly is not normal; it is a disease, it can be diagnosed, and in most cases it can be treated safely and effectively with antidepressants and brief therapy.

Suicide. There is one form of disturbance, at least in the United States, that shows a clear increase with age: suicide. In 1992, people over 65 made up 20 percent of the suicides in the United States but comprised only 13 percent of the population. Between 1980 and 1992, suicide rates increased 9 percent for people over 65 and 35 percent for people over 80. These numbers can be somewhat misleading. As you can see in Figure 4.6, the heightened suicide rates do not occur among all older adults. This sharp increase with age is carried by a single subgroup in the United States: white males. African-American males and women in general show no such rise with age, but white men over 65 have three

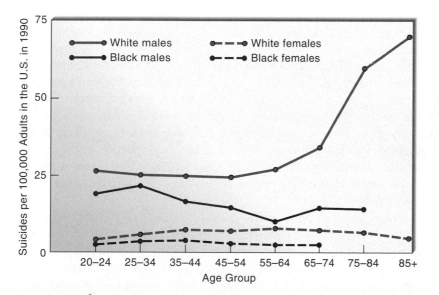

FIGURE 4.6 Suicide rates in the United States in 1990. Only among white males is there an increase with age.

Source: Data from U.S. Bureau of the Census, 1993, Table 137, p. 99.

times the suicide rate as that of the general population, and white men over 85 have six times the suicide rate of the general population (Lebowitz et al., 1997).

What might account for such a pattern? Why is the rate so high among older white men? The pattern for white elderly males has existed throughout this century in the United States (although it was higher in the first half of the century than it is now), so this is not a temporary phenomenon or something unique to current cohorts of older men (Posner, 1996). Similar statistics are also found in all countries that keep reliable records (Butler et al., 1997). Yet I can find no good explanation. One possibility is that white men in this group experience a loss of status in their lives as they age. Their earning ability is usually lower than when they were at the peak of their careers, and if they have retired, they no longer have the power and prestige that came with their jobs (McCall, 1991). Although many women also go through the same experience, they have had the benefit of multiple roles in their lives and haven't depended on any one part of their lives to define themselves. According to this explanation, older black men are not as likely to have had power and status in their jobs and were more likely to base their self-esteem on individual abilities and achievements that would continue after retirement.

Other possible explanations might be constructed from the few clues that we have about older white men who commit suicide. The strongest predictor is depression. Other factors are living alone and having anxiety disorders, emotional disturbances, medical problems, family conflict, financial problems, and relationship loss (Florio et al., 1997; Koenig, Blazer, & Hocking, 1997). However, the cause of this inequality in late-life suicides remains a mystery. It is one of the few areas in which there is a greater difference between men and women in old age than at earlier ages.

Anxiety

Some researchers argue that anxiety is more common than depression in later life (Schramke, 1997), but again, this depends on whether we are talking about anxiety disorders defined according to clinical guidelines or simply having many symptoms of anxiety. It is safe to say that both depression and anxiety are serious mental health problems in older adults, and that the reason depression is so prominent is because much less attention has been focused on anxiety. Nevertheless. it is estimated that 20 percent of elderly adults have "pathological" levels of anxiety and that it is even higher in very old adults (Raj, Corvea, & Dagon, 1993).

The major symptoms of **anxiety disorders** are feelings of fear, threat, and dread when no obvious danger is present. Sometimes the fear is an overreaction to a real danger, such as the fear of flying on an airplane or driving on an interstate highway. According to the DSM-IV, the most common anxiety disorders are (1) **panic disorder,** which involves recurring sudden episodes of intense apprehension, palpitations, shortness of breath, and chest pain; (2) **phobias,** which are fears and avoidance out of proportion to the danger; (3) **generalized anxiety disorder,** which entails chronic, persistent, and excessive anxiety and worry; and (4) **obsessive-compulsive disorders,** which involve guilt and anxiety over certain thoughts or impulses.

One type of anxiety disorder, phobias, don't decrease with age but occur with equal probability at any age. Most older adults with phobias have had them all their lives in some form or another, but in later years the most common form is agoraphobia, the fear of leaving one's home and going outdoors or out in public. In older adults this tends to be triggered by a specific event such as being mugged or experiencing a fall or other physical illness while away from home. As with younger adults, therapy for anxiety in older adults usually involves short-term therapy and/or antianxiety drugs that affect the neurotransmitter system of the brain.

One More Word About Depression and Anxiety

Over half of the people who suffer from depression also report significant anxiety, and this tendency does not change with age (Matt, Dean, Wang, & Wood, 1992). Furthermore, the tests designed to measure depression and the tests for anxiety have a lot of similar questions, both seem to have biological causes, and the same medications are used to treat both disorders (Alexopoulos, 1991). In recent genetic research, one gene has been identified that seems to cause both anxiety and depression. This **harm avoidance gene** is thought to determine the effectiveness of serotonin, a neurotransmitter in the brain. Researchers have found that 68 percent of the population has the active copy of this gene. Hamer and Copeland (1998) hypothesize that for these people, the gene interacts with the environment and under some circumstances produces either depression (when loss is actually experienced) or anxiety (when loss is only anticipated). Whether this is a cause for most depression and anxiety or only for some cases remains to be seen.

Summing Up Changes in Mental Health

So where does this leave us in our understanding of age changes (or continuities) in mental health over the adult years? We know that rates of mental disorders in general do not appear to change much over adulthood. At any given time, about one in five adults has some mental disorder. However, we do know that certain disorders occur at different rates across the life span. Two disorders common to older adults have been examined: depression and anxiety. Depression, as a clinical disorder, shows no change with age, but subclinical depression shows a U-shaped function, with higher rates in young adulthood and again in very old adulthood. Although depression can cause disability and physical decline (Mitchell, 1993), my own sense of the data is that this increase in depressed mood among the very old is in part because of the accumulation of physical limitations or infirmities that frequently occur in these years. We know, for example, that depressed mood is more likely among those elders who experience limitations in independent activities of daily living (IADLs) such as shopping or preparing meals (Lebowitz et al., 1997; Mitchell, Mathews, & Sesavage, 1993).

Anxiety is also a common psychiatric complaint of older adults, often accompanied by depression. Older adults have lower rates of anxiety than younger adults, but some types of anxiety, specifically agoraphobia, don't decline with age. My thinking is that some anxiety disorders, which have many physical symptoms such as decreased appetite or heart palpitations, are underreported in older adults because they are mistakenly thought to be part of normal aging. This is unfortunate in light of the success with which mental disorders can be treated. Depression and anxiety rank at the top of successfully treated mental disorders, and when they are recognized as secondary instead of primary aging, it can greatly enhance the quality of life for older adults and their families.

INDIVIDUAL DIFFERENCES IN HEALTH AND DISEASE

As usual, I have begun this chapter by giving you overall age-linked patterns. But as was true of the basic processes of physical aging, there are widespread individual differences in health and disease in adulthood.

Sex Differences

One fact apparent already in several of the tables and figures in this chapter is that women and men have different patterns of chronic problems and disability.

* Women die of basically the same diseases that men die of, but they do so at older ages.

* Women have more disability and more of almost every nonfatal chronic disease you can think of, and this is true beginning as early as midlife (Verbrugge, 1989) and in every country in which the pattern has been studied, including third world countries (Rahman, Strauss, Gertler, Ashley, & Fox, 1994). There are a few exceptions: Men have a higher incidence of hearing loss and visual impairment and more back problems. But women have higher rates of arthritis, disease of the skin, cataracts, gallstones, anemias, migraine headache, bladder infection, varicose veins, and sinusitis—to name only a few. (As a woman, I find this list depressing!) Women are more likely to seek medical treatment for their ailments (which may be one reason they live longer than men).

* Most types of mental/emotional disturbance are also more common in women, a pattern that is especially pronounced in the case of depression, which is roughly twice as common among women (Nolen-Hoeksema, 1987; Strickland, 1992). Exceptions are alcoholism and other substance abuse, criminal behavior, and suicide, which are found at higher rates among men at every age in this culture (Girard, 1993; Regier et al., 1988) and in other cultures that have data available (Butler et al., 1998).

CRITICAL THINKING

Before you read the alternative explanations offered for these sex differences, see how many different explanations you can think of. Physical differences? Cultural differences? What kinds of data would you need to check on some of your hypotheses?

Overall, what this means is that women have more "small" complaints—acute illnesses, or chronic disease—and they have them over more years. But they simply don't contract fatal diseases such as CHD or cancer until much later. Where might such sex differences come from? The explanations are partly biological, partly social. Most investigators agree that the differences in longevity and in resistance to major disease are primarily biological: Women have some built-in greater robustness, whether produced by a different genetic endowment which leads to slower physical aging, or by hormonal differences that give women early protection against some major fatal diseases, such as heart disease. There are also differences in exposure to hazardous environments (such as dangerous chemicals and noisy workplaces), although that difference is probably smaller in more recent cohorts as women have moved more into traditionally male occupations and workplaces have become safer for both genders.

Women's higher rates of nonfatal illnesses and of emotional disturbances are harder to explain. Hormone differences are an obvious possibility, although research on the link between hormone patterns and depression has not provided much support for this option (Nolen-Hoeksema, 1990). Women might also be more willing to talk about their symptoms and seek help. Other possibilities that have been suggested are that women's high rates of depression are results of having more stress due to multiple roles (Gutek, Searle, & Klepa, 1991), higher rates of poverty and victimization (Belle, 1990), and maladaptive ways of responding to life events (Nolen-Hoeksema, 1990). Clearly, what we have here is another set of puzzles waiting to be solved.

Social Class, Racial, and Ethnic Differences in Health

Given everything I have said so far, you will not be a bit surprised to learn that there are significant differences in the health patterns across adulthood for different social class groups or for various racial and ethnic groups. In addition to differences in life expectancy, which I've already mentioned, there are differences in the probability of chronic disease or disability. And there are differences among ethnic groups in risks for specific diseases.

Social Class Differences. The clearest data I know that show social class differences in health and disability over adulthood come from two large surveys of over 59,000 people in the United States analyzed by James House, along with Kessler and others (House,

Kessler, & Herzog, 1990). They looked at reports of chronic conditions and limitations in daily activities as a function of social class and age. The pattern of results, shown in Figure 4.7, is extremely clear. All groups show an increase with age in chronic conditions and limitations, but the increase is much earlier and steeper for the poor or the working class. Other research tells us that the same sharp differences exist for individual diseases as well, such as arthritis, hypertension, and some kinds of cancer (Adler et al., 1994). Equivalent social class differences in adult health, rate of disability, or longevity have been found in many other industrialized counties, such as Sweden (Thorslund & Lundberg, 1994) and England (Eames, Ben-Schlome, & Marmot, 1993), and they occur *within* ethnic groups

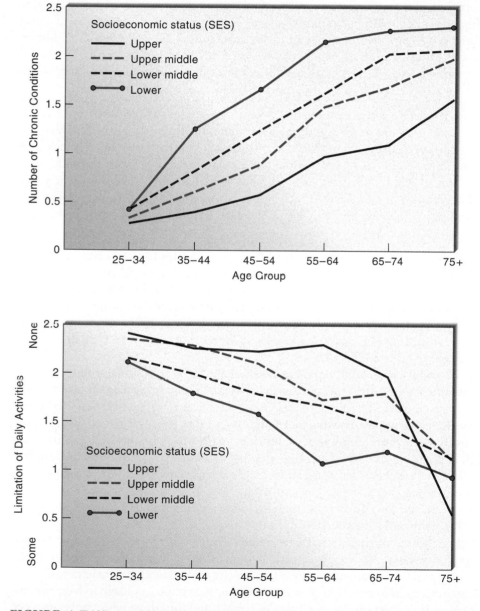

FIGURE 4.7 What could be plainer? Both chronic conditions (upper panel) and physical limitations (lower panel) show more rapid and extreme changes with age among the poor than among those adults who are economically or educationally better off.

Source: House, Kessler, & Herzog, 1990, Fig. 1, p. 396, and Fig. 3, p. 397.

in the United States as well as overall. That is, among African-Americans, or among Hispanics, or Asian-Americans, better educated adults or those with higher incomes have longer life expectancies and better health (Guralnik, Blazer, Fillenbaum, & Branch, 1993).

A substantial portion of such social class differences can be accounted for by variations in health habits. People with lower incomes and less education are more likely to smoke and experience far higher levels of stress. They also are more likely to lead sedentary lifestyles (U.S. Department of Health and Human Services, 1998). What other factors, other than overall stress, might account for the striking pattern shown in Figure 4.8? One likely candidate is access to health care. Adults with lower incomes are less able to afford medical care when they are ill, not to mention tests and screening that would lead to early detection of illnesses (Alaimo, Briefel, & Frongillo, & Olson, 1998). Another candidate is poor nutrition. The cumulative effect of medical neglect or undernutrition over the years of adulthood is likely to be shorter life expectancy and higher rates of both acute and chronic diseases, and higher rates of disability (Deeg, Kardaun, & Fozard, 1996). In addition, the less well educated adult may simply know less about good health practices, including good diet. However, as the average education and income of older adults are rising, we can expect an increase in health, since those are positively correlated (Posner, 1995).

Native Americans. Since 1940, the life expectancy rates for Native Americans have increased 40 percent—twice the rate of the general population in the United States—and is now only three years less than that of the Caucasian population (John, Blanchard, & Hennessey, 1997). However, they are more likely than other U.S. groups to suffer from diabetes, hypertension, and alcoholism, all potentially disabling. In addition, the prevalence of subclinical depression is greater in Native Americans, and, similar to the U.S. population as a whole, the rates for Native American women is significantly higher than rates for Native American males.

African-Americans. African-American adults have a shorter life expectancy and more chronic illnesses and disabilities than does the white population. They are more likely than are whites to suffer from certain specific diseases, such as hypertension, diabetes, arthritis, and many forms of cancer, including lung, breast, uterine, prostate, and stomach cancers (Chatters, 1991; Manton & Stallard, 1997; Ralston, 1997). African-Americans have a lower rate of osteoporosis than whites, resulting in a lower rate of disability from bone fractures in older adulthood.

Smith and Kington (1997) examined eight large-scale longitudinal studies and concluded that most of the differences in health between African-Americans and whites were due to socioeconomic factors. Some of the socioeconomic factors suggested that might contribute to decreased health are living in neighborhoods that are more dangerous and more distant from medical facilities and being restricted to jobs that are more hazardous, more stressful, and less apt to have health care benefits. Although these socioeconomic differences between races have decreased in recent decades, many older African-Americans spent most of their lives living in a society in which racial discrimination was not only the practice but was the law. There is no doubt that this continues to be a factor in their late-life health (Smith and Kington, 1997).

Although most of these differences can be accounted for by socioeconomic factors, a few specific diseases may be at least partially explained by genetic factors. For example, research suggests that a particular enzyme, if present in the blood, can help detoxify one of the carcinogens in nicotine. African-Americans appear to be less likely to have this enzyme, or have it in lower quantities (Blakeslee, 1994), and thus those who smoke are more likely to develop lung cancer. In addition, other research reports that African-Americans who smoke produce a higher level of another substance in their blood which may reflect enhanced effects of nicotine, making smoking both more dangerous and more addicting (Caraballo, et al., 1998).

Hispanic-Americans. In many respects, Hispanic adults in the United States have a rather good health picture. Among 65-year-olds, for example, Hispanics actually have a longer life expectancy than do Anglos, in part due to a significantly lower rate of major types of cancer and heart disease among both men and women (Markides et al., 1997). One possible explanation for this relatively good health picture for Hispanics is that the tight kin networks in this cultural group may provide an especially good buffer against the stresses of everyday life (P. Stanford & Du Bois, 1992). Other factors are a lower smoking rate than the general population and the **healthy immigrant effect**—those who come to the United States from other countries tend to be in better health than do those who were born here (Stephen, Foote, Hendershot, & Schoenborn, 1994).

Mexican-Americans have a rate of diabetes that is two to five times greater than that of non-Hispanics, and some genetic components are suggested because of their ancestral relationship with Native Americans, who also have significantly higher rates of diabetes. In contrast, Cuban-Americans do not share genes with Native Americans and have lower rates of diabetes (Rogers, 1991). Mexican-Americans have higher rates of Alzheimer's disease and other dementias than non-Hispanic whites (Tang et al., 1998) but lower rates of osteoporosis and resulting bone fractures (Markides & Black, 1996).

Much has been written about the tendency for Hispanic-Americans to underutilize the health care system, due to distrust of Anglo physicians, language difficulties, and cultural issues. It is interesting that Hispanic-Americans over the age of 65 years (whose costs are covered by Medicare) use health care services as much as non-Hispanic-Americans, suggesting that economics play a major role in health care use for this group.

Asian-Americans. The ethnic group within the U.S. population that seems to have the best health picture are Asian-Americans. Adults in these groups have longer life expectancies, although this is much less true of more recent Asian immigrant groups than for those more acculturated, well-educated groups such as Chinese-Americans and Japanese-Americans. What the specific disease risks may be in these groups is not well understood, in part because possible hereditary patterns are confounded with cultural variations. For example, in Japan and China and other Asian nations, rates of heart disease are typically very low; among Japanese-Americans and Chinese-Americans, heart disease risks rise as higher-fat Americanized diets, sedentary lifestyles, and cigarette smoking are adopted (Reed & Yano, 1997).

Personal Health Habits and Risk Behaviors

Most of the contributors to individual differences in health patterns I have been talking about so far—gender, race, ethnicity, social class, heredity—are factors over which you have little or no control. What you *can* control are your personal health habits. I have made this point several times already, but I want to emphasize it even more strongly here: Health habits play a major role in the rate with which you will experience the body changes of aging, the degree of good health you will have, and the length of your life. The evidence supporting such a statement comes from a variety of sources. You've already seen some of it in my earlier discussion of research on the risk factors for heart disease. The Framingham study, among others, shows that among those adults who appear to have some genetic risk for CHD, those who follow good health practices live longer, with fewer overt signs of disease.

A more striking, and more general, demonstration of the link between longevity and health practices comes from the Alameda County Study, a major longitudinal epidemiological study in one county in California (Belloc, 1973; Belloc and Breslow, 1972; Berkman and Breslow, 1983; Breslow & Breslow, 1993; G. A. Kaplan, 1992). The study began in 1965 with a random sample of all the residents of this county, a total of nearly 7000 adults. These subjects were then contacted again in 1974 and half of them again in 1983. Death records were monitored so that the time of death of each subject who died during the 18 years could be determined. At the outset, the researchers inquired about seven good health practices, listed in Table 4.7, each of which they thought might be crucial for long-term health and survival.

Five of these health practices—all but snacking and breakfast eating—turned out to predict rates of death over the years of the study. Furthermore, combining information about these five practices makes the prediction even more clear, as you can see in Figure 4.8, which shows the results for the first nine years of the study. In each age group, those men and women who had followed the most good health practices were least likely to die. Equally important, these researchers have found that the risk of later disability was only about half as high among those who had followed good health practices in 1965 as compared to those who had poor health habits (Breslow & Breslow, 1993; Strawbridge, Camacho, Cohen, & Kaplan, 1993).

The Alameda study is not the only one that points to these conclusions. For example, in the Duke longitudinal studies (Palmore, 1970), adults who exercised less, smoked more, and were overweight died earlier than one would predict from their age, gender, and race. In these same samples, poor health practices were also associated with more frequent illnesses. For instance, those adults who were relatively sedentary at the beginning of the study later had more illnesses that forced them to stay in bed, visited the doctor more, and rated their own health as worse than did originally active adults.

Perhaps unsurprisingly, it is the young who have the least healthy lifestyle. Data from the U.S. National Center for Health Statistics (U.S. Bureau of the Census, 1989b) show the highest rates of such poor health habits as poor exercise and nutrition practices, drinking to excess, and smoking among young adults, with health habits typically improving steadily with age. Two exceptions to this pattern are obesity, which is most common among those 45 to 64, and getting too little sleep (six hours or less), which is equally common at all ages.

Of course one of the reasons the young follow a riskier health path is that they have a difficult time seeing, or accepting, a link between their current behavior and such long-term outcomes as decreased life span, heart disease three decades later, or disability in old age. Human decision making is not completely rational. Among other things we tend to be more optimistic about our own situation than is warranted by the facts: We might assume that although other people become addicted, we can try some drug without be-

TABLE 4.7 **Good Health Practices Studied in the Alameda County Study**

1. Usually sleep seven or eight hours per night.
2. Eat breakfast almost every day.
3. Eat between meals once in a while, rarely, or never.
4. Weight for a man between 5% under and 20% over desirable weight for height. Weight for a woman not more than 10% over desirable weight for height.
5. Often or sometimes engage in active sports, swimming, or take long walks, or often garden, or do physical exercises.
6. Have no more than four drinks at a time.[a]
7. Never smoke cigarettes.

[a]Note that the listed good health practice with regard to alcohol is not that the person never drinks, but that the person does not drink to excess. In fact, a variety of information, including the data from the Alameda study, suggests that a moderate amount of alcohol intake, at the level of about one glass of wine per day, is associated with better health and longer life than is total abstention (Guralnik & Kaplan, 1989).

Source: Belloc & Breslow, 1972, p. 415. Reprinted by permission of Academic Press, San Diego, California, and the author.

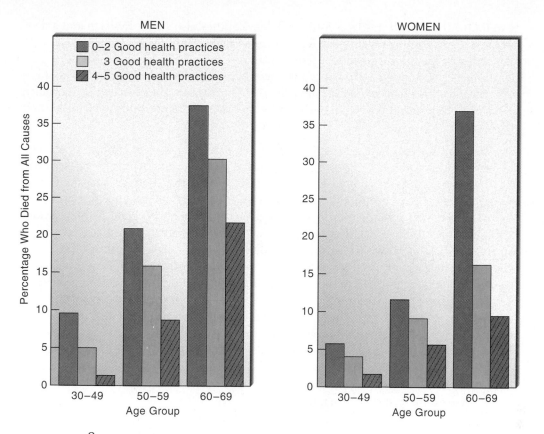

MEN WOMEN

■ 0–2 Good health practices
▨ 3 Good health practices
▨ 4–5 Good health practices

Percentage Who Died from All Causes

Age Group

FIGURE 4.8 The more good health practices a person followed in 1969, the less likely he or she was to die over the next nine years.

Source: Lisa F. Berkman and Lester Breslow, *Health and Ways of Living: The Alameda County Study*. Copyright © 1983 by Oxford University Press, Inc. Reprinted by permission.

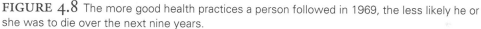

coming addicted, or that smoking won't affect us as it might others, or "it hasn't happened to me yet" (Jeffrey, 1989). We also tend to make decisions based on immediate rewards rather than on potential longer-term gains, so the immediate pleasure of overeating, alcohol, or smoking is likely to overwhelm any information we have about the long-term risks. As we get older, such optimism and such short-term hedonism may be more difficult to sustain as the poor health chickens come home to roost in the form of disease or disability. It becomes harder to deny the risks, and we change our behavior.

Public health information efforts have had some impact on this process. Nathan Maccoby and his colleagues (Maccoby, 1980), for example, have shown that intensive information campaigns in selected communities can lower heart attack incidence and risk in those communities by changing people's health habits—fewer eggs eaten per day, lower smoking rates, lower overall rates of cholesterol in the diet. What we do not know from these studies is whether the information campaigns were more successful with the middle-aged than with the young, a finding that would not surprise me in the least.

We also know that women follow better health practices than men do, a difference no doubt contributing to women's longer life spans. In an analysis of national data, William Rakowski (1988) finds that at all ages except middle age, women are not only more like-

CRITICAL THINKING

What rationalizations do you use to justify your own poor health practices?

ly to follow those good practices listed in Table 4.5, they also see a physician and a dentist more often, floss their teeth more regularly, and eat less red meat. Intriguingly, Rakowski found that in the middle-aged group in this survey (age 42 to 43 in his study) this gender difference disappeared. In that group it was education level and not gender that became the major predictor of good health habits, as if having seen their impending mortality, educated middle-aged men began to pay more attention to their health and changed their behavior.

Exercise: A Reprise. I talked at some length in Chapter 3 about the impact of exercise on overall rates of physical aging. I could repeat almost the same words here. Certainly, the conclusion is the same: Those adults who exercise regularly—both aerobic and weight strength—have better health. They have lower risk of heart disease and, perhaps more important for everyday life, lower rates of physical disability (S. N. Blair, Kohl, Gordon, & Paffenbarger, 1992; Deeg, Kardaun, & Fozard, 1996; Wagner, LaCroix, Buchner, & Larson, 1992). Contrariwise, longitudinal studies show that otherwise healthy older adults who *reduce* their rate of physical activity or exercise are more likely to develop disabilities in succeeding years compared to those who maintain their level of activity (Branch, 1985). Roberta Rikli and Sharman Busch (1986) conclude from their studies of physically active and inactive women that "a chronically active lifestyle plays an important part in preventing age-related declines in motor performance" (p. 649). The 65-year-old women in this study who had maintained a level of regular vigorous activity for at least the past 10 years had better reaction times, better flexibility, and better balance than did less active women of the same age. In fact, the scores of older active women were comparable to scores obtained by inactive women in their 20s.

What we do not yet know enough about is whether such benefits of exercise on health occur regardless of when one begins to exercise. We know that some physical characteristics, such as $VO_{2\,max}$, can be improved with exercise at any age, but whether that is true of health or disability more generally is not as clear. Probably the relationship is rather like what we see in the link between smoking and health: Not smoking at all is best; if you smoke, it is better to quit earlier in adulthood than later, but quitting is beneficial even

 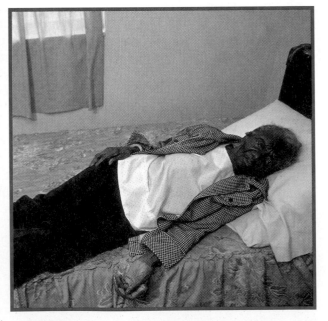

OLDER ADULTS WHO REMAIN PHYSICALLY ACTIVE enjoy better health than those the same age who are sedentary.

in later years. Similarly, maintaining fitness throughout adulthood by regular exercise is doubtless best, but improving your fitness at any age is likely to have a positive impact on your health, although the degree of benefit may well decrease with age.

Regrettably, the great majority of adults—young, middle-aged, and older—do not exercise sufficiently to acquire positive health or fitness benefits. Recent estimates are that less than 20 percent of Americans between 18 and 65 get enough exercise; among those over 65 the rates are even lower (E. McAuley, 1993). At the risk of sounding like a broken record, let me make the point again: This *is* something over which you have control, and the potential benefits are substantial.

Personality Differences and Health

One health/personality connection has been reported by Paul Costa and Robert McCrae (1980b), researchers whose work on the basic dimensions of personality I described in Chapter 2. They find that adults high in the personality dimension called **neuroticism** (see Table 2.3) complain more about their health than do those low in this dimension. They are also more likely to smoke (and have more trouble quitting) and to have drinking problems.

At one time it was thought that having a Type A personality, that is, being someone who is highly competitive, obsessed with time, and hostile, put one at higher risk for heart disease than having the more mellow Type B personality (M. Friedman & Rosenman, 1974; Rosenman & Friedman, 1983). More recently, it has been shown that only the hostility component of the type A personality is a good predictor of heart disease (Eysenck, 1990; Siegel, 1992).

Yet another link between personality and health is suggested by the work of David McClelland (1989), who studies human motivation. He has assembled impressive evidence for the existence of connections between specific motive patterns and particular illnesses. For example, men who show high levels of what he calls the **need for power** are more likely to be problem drinkers. They are also more susceptible to infectious diseases, apparently because their motive pattern leads them into a lifestyle with more chronic stress, which in turn has the effect of suppressing the immune system. In McClelland's studies, those adults with the best health were those with higher levels of what he calls **affiliative trust** (which enables a person to create cooperative, supportive, loving relationships) and a sense of **agency** (feeling as if you have some control over your life).

The importance for health of the latter quality, which Judith Rodin (1990) calls **perceived control,** has also emerged from a variety of other sources. The sense of control has been described in varying language, and with varying emphases, by several important theorists. Albert Bandura (1977; 1982; 1986; 1997) has written for over two decades about **self-efficacy,** which is a belief in one's ability to perform some action or to control one's behavior or environment. Such a belief is a product of one's entire history of experience with mastering tasks and overcoming obstacles.

Rotter (1966) expresses a similar idea with his concept of **locus of control.** He differentiates between **internal** and **external** orientations. Persons with internal orientation believe that things that happen to them have been caused by their own actions, and that they have some control over their lives. A person with an external locus of control believes that he or she is largely in the hands of fate or chance or the actions of others. There is some indication from studies in Finland that adults become somewhat more external in their orientation with age, since they feel less able to control health and their children as they get older (Nurmi, Pulliainen, & Salmela-Aro, 1992). But at any age there are wide individual variations in the tendency toward an internal or external sense of control.

Yet a third version of this same general idea comes from the work of Martin Seligman (1991), who differentiates between positions of **optimism** and **helplessness.** The person who feels helpless is pessimistic and believes that misfortune will last a long time, will undermine everything, and is his own fault. The optimist believes that setbacks are temporary and usually caused by circumstances. He is convinced that there is always some solution and that he will be able to work things out. Confronted by defeat, he sees it as a challenge and tries harder, whereas the helpless person gives up.

Research on the relationship between health and perceived control—whether measured as self-efficacy, internal locus of control, or optimism—shows clearly that those adults who feel least in control are more likely to become ill or depressed (Bandura, 1997; Seligman, 1991; Syme, 1990). One particularly clear demonstration of this comes from the Grant study of Harvard men. These men were interviewed first when they were about age 18, in 1938–1940. They were then reinterviewed repeatedly over the next 35 years. Researchers were able to use data from the age-25 interview to create a measure of each man's level of pessimism. They found that those who were most pessimistic at this age had significantly poorer health in their 40s and 50s (Peterson, Seligman, & Vaillant, 1988).

There is also evidence that adults who work at jobs in which they have high stress but little sense of personal control have unusually high rates of heart disease, a finding that has been replicated in studies in both the United States and Sweden (Syme, 1990). If you think about it, these are precisely the characteristics of many blue- or pink-collar jobs, while white-collar jobs typically offer more opportunity for individual control, a difference that may well contribute to the pattern you saw in Figure 4.7.

To make the causal link between a sense of personal control and good health even more persuasive, we actually have experimental evidence in this case, indicating that increasing a person's sense of control leads to some improvement in his or her health. For example, if you give older adults in nursing homes a chance to have control over even very minor aspects of their lives, such as whether they will have scrambled eggs or an omelet for breakfast, their chances of dying in the succeeding months declines compared to those of elders who have no such options (Rodin, 1986; Rodin & Langer, 1977). Indeed, one of the real benefits of exercise programs appears to be an increase in one's sense of personal control or self-efficacy, which in turn has beneficial effects on health over and above the physical exercise.

All of these findings point to potentially important links between personality and health. Personality apparently affects not only our health habits, and thus indirectly our current or later health, but may also have much more direct influences through impact on the immune system. And of all the personality characteristics mentioned, perhaps the most important is the sense of control or optimism, because this can be changed through specific choices or by deliberate social engineering.

REVIEW OF AGE PATTERNS OF HEALTH

As I did in the preceding chapter (and as I will do in each of the core chapters of the book), I want to summarize this mass of information in a table (Table 4.8).

Overall, most of us experience fairly robust health in the first decades of adulthood, although the early, nonsymptomatic stages of disease may be present even then. Measurable symptoms of such diseases, and loss of function or disability associated with those diseases, are likely to appear for at least some adults in their 50s and 60s, although among today's cohorts of adults, who are living into their late 70s, 80s, and 90s, many of the most negative health consequences are not experienced until past age 75. The good news in all of this fairly depressing stuff is that we each have some control over this process. Obviously, we cannot evade death; it comes to each of us. But there is a very good chance that we can improve not only our life expectancy but also the health we will experience during our lifetime. I know that it is difficult to adopt good health practices now when the payoff may be years away, especially when the "good health practices" involve denying yourself something pleasurable. But the data are clear.

TABLE 4.8 **Summary of Age Changes in Health and Illness**

Age 20–40	Age 40–65	Age 65–75	Age 75+
Lowest death rate; deaths mostly from accidents	Risk of death increases but is still low; most common causes of death are now heart disease and cancer.	Risk of death rises; heart disease becomes increasingly the most common form of death.	Risk of death at its highest; heart disease is largest risk, but both pneumonia and pulminary disease become much more common.
Acute illnesses most common; chronic illness least common	Medium risk for both chronic and acute illnesses.	Chronic problems become more common, but the majority of the young old have no known chronic ailment.	Some chronic problem is typical, as is some kind of disability.
Negligible incidence of any dementia	Still negligible risk of dementia of any type.	Risk of several forms of dementia begins to rise, but is probably not more than about 5–8% among th young old.	Risk of dementia rises considerably, to almost half of those over 85.
High risk for many forms of serious emotional disturbace; high risk of subclinical depression.	Risk for depression and other forms of emotional disturbance appears to be low in this age range.	Very low risk for all forms of emotional disturbance.	Low risk for all forms of emotional disturbance except subclinical depression, which appears to rise in this age range.
Poor health habits.	Slightly better health habits.	Probably best health habits.	Health habits probably somewhat less good,

SUMMARY

1. The risk of death rises with increasing age, and the causes of death change systematically with age. Among young adults, death is most likely to be the result of accidents. By midlife, heart disease and cancer are the largest causes of death.

2. The probability of acute (short-term) illness declines over adulthood, while the probability of chronic illness increases, particularly after midlife and for women.

3. Disabilities, including those that interfere with tasks of daily living, also increase with age. Roughly one-fifth to one-fourth of adults over age 65 report having some such disability.

4. Self-ratings of health change with age in a pattern consistent with the findings on disease and disability: Young adults are most likely to rate themselves as in good health or better; adults over 65 are the least likely to do so. Still, a full 39 percent of people over 65 rate their overall health as good or excellent.

5. On any given day, about 5 percent of adults over 65 are institutionalized or cared for in nursing homes or assisted living centers. The average duration of such a stay is shorter for men than for women. Such institutionalization is less common among Hispanic, African-American, and Asian-American elders than among Anglos.

6. Coronary heart disease (CHD) is the leading cause of death for both men and women in the United States and in other developed countries. It shows a geometric rise with age, with the most rapid increase beginning at about age 65.

7. Risk factors for CHD include high blood pressure, high cholesterol, obesity, low levels of exercise, a family history of heart disease, and smoking.

8. Cancer rises in frequency across adulthood at a fairly steady (not geometric) rate; among women it increases sharply in frequency, especially after menopause.

9. Alzheimer's disease, the most frequent type of dementia in adults, is increasing in incidence as the number of older adults in our population increases. Although there is no cure, it can be diagnosed with a high degree of accuracy and the course of decline can be predicted. Ten percent of people with dementia symptoms have conditions other than Alzheimer's disease that can be treated.

10. The rate of mental disorders across the age span is difficult to examine, but best estimates are that there are no age differences in overall mental health. Clinical depression rates do not change with age, but subclinical depression is higher in young adulthood and again in very old adulthood.

11. Suicide rises in old age, but only for white males. The reasons for this remains a mystery.

12. Anxiety does not increase with age, but due to the decrease in other disorders, it is one of the most common psychiatric complaints of the elderly. It often co-occurs with depression, and a gene has been identified that seems to cause both depression and anxiety, depending on the environmental conditions. This may explain only some cases of anxiety and depression.

13. Women and men have different patterns of health changes with age. Women have more chronic ailments, beginning at an earlier age, but contract terminal illnesses at a later age, which means that women spend more years of late adulthood living with chronic problems.

14. There is a strong relationship between social class and both longevity and health over adulthood. The poor and working class have more ailments and disabilities, and they have them at earlier ages. This appears to be due partly to variations in health habits and increased stress associated with poverty.

15. Among minority racial and ethnic groups in the United States, Asian-Americans have the best health. African-Americans have shorter life expectancy than whites and a higher rate of specific diseases; Hispanics have significantly lower rates of heart disease but suffer from other diseases at higher rates. Some of these differences appear to be linked to variations in health habits and social class; some appear to be genetic.

16. Health habits associated with lower risk of disease and greater longevity include not smoking, getting regular exercise, not drinking to excess, getting sufficient sleep, and maintaining proper weight.

17. Young adults as a group have poorer health habits than do older adults, particularly those over 65.

18. Personality may also influence both general susceptibility to disease and the specific disease from which you may suffer. Adults high in traits of hostility, depression, and neuroticism have poorer health histories; adults at any age who have a high sense of personal control or optimism are less likely to become ill.

KEY TERMS

mortality rate

morbidity

acute illnesses

chronic illnesses

activities of daily living
(ADLs)

instrumental activities of
daily living (IADLs)

aging in place

retirement communities

congregate living
facilities

assisted living facilities

continuing care
retirement community

coronary heart disease
(CHD)

atherosclerosis

mutations

Alzheimer's disease

dementia

beta-amyloid

depression

*Diagnostic and Statistical
Manual of Mental
Disorders,* 4th edition
(DSM-IV)

major depressive disorder

clinical depression

subclinical depression

anxiety disorders

panic disorder

phobias

generalized anxiety
disorder

obsessive-compulsive
disorders

harm avoidance gene

healthy immigrant effect

neuroticism

need for power

affiliative trust

agency

perceived control

self-efficacy

locus of control

internal locus of control

external locus of control

optimism

helplessness

SUGGESTED READINGS

Butler, R. N., Lewis, M. I., & Sunderland, T. (1998). *Aging and mental health: Positive psychosocial and biomedical approaches.* Boston: Allyn & Bacon.

Designed as a textbook or resource book for clinical psychologists, social workers, mental health counselors, and other professionals who work with older adults, this easy-to-understand book thoroughly explains issues that the clinician might face and a variety of answers, including therapy, medication, self-help groups, and information networks. It includes several valuable appendices with addresses of agencies, sample forms to use, and e-mail addresses of support groups.

Hamer, D., & Copeland, P. (1998). *Living with our genes: Why they matter more than you think.* New York: Doubleday.

Hammer is one of the world's leading behavioral geneticists. This book is informative, clearly written, and fun.

Nelson, J. L., & Nelson, H. L. (1996). *Alzheimer's: Answers to hard questions for families.* New York: Doubleday.

Experts on the ethics of health care write about moral issues faced by caregivers of family members with Alzheimer's disease. How to maintain parents' dignity, how to balance parents with job and children, how to respond to patients' requests for suicide assistance, how to resolve disagreements between family members, when to put parents in a nursing home—all are discussed sensitively and presented in the context of interviews with actual families that the authors counsel as researchers at the Hastings Center. The book includes a section on where caregivers can get help and information.

COGNITIVE
CHANGES

5

One of the most pervasive stereotypes about aging is that we all lose our cognitive abilities as we get old. The term *senile,* which the dictionary defines merely as "of or pertaining to old age," has acquired a common meaning of "mentally incompetent" or "forgetful." Most of us assume that as we age, we will begin to lose IQ points, forget things, and make foolish decisions.

But is all this really true? Yes and no. Yes, there is some decline or loss. But the size of the decline is often greatly exaggerated in our stereotypes about aging. Older scientists still do innovative and complex research; the oldest old can still comprehend complex articles in the newspaper, play chess, and do crossword puzzles. But there is, inescapably, some loss. It occurs later than you might think; it is smaller than you may have been led to believe; it affects different types of cognitive abilities differently; and there is a big variety in the ways it affects different people of the same age. But it occurs.

In exploring this literature, let me begin by looking at consistency and change the broadest measures of cognitive functioning—scores on IQ tests of various kinds—and then break that down into other types of cognitive skills, such as memory, problem solving, and creativity.

AGE CHANGES IN IQ DURING ADULTHOOD

Defining *intelligence* is one of the slipperier tasks in psychology. The typical definition goes something like this: **Intelligence** is "the aggregate or global capacity of the individual to act purposefully, to think rationally and to deal effectively with his environment" (Wechsler, 1939, p. 3).

Many psychologists assume that there is a central, general intellectual capacity, often called *g,* which influences the way we approach many different tasks (Jensen, 1998). The total score on an intelligence test (usually labeled **IQ,** which is short for *intelligence quotient)* is intended to describe this general capacity. As you doubtless know from previous psychology classes, the average IQ score is normally set at 100, with scores above 100 reflecting above-average performance and scores below 100 reflecting below-average performance. The question to be addressed here is whether *g,* as measured by IQ scores, remains constant with age or changes. And if it changes, does that change have a pattern?. Before I can answer that question, though, I need to set the stage a bit more by talking about what is meant by "consistency and change."

Meanings of Consistency and Change

In discussions of IQ and age, two types of consistency are relevant: correlational consistency and consistency in absolute level. According to Kagan (1980), a characteristic shows **correlational consistency** if individuals' scores on a measure of that characteristic retain the same relative position over time. For example, we would say that IQ is consistent in this sense if those adults who achieved the highest scores when they were 20 still have among the highest scores when they are 40 or 50, while those who originally had low scores still show low scores, even if the average score of the entire group has gone up or down.

Consistency in absolute level is achieved when individuals show minimal change in the absolute level of that quality over time. Physical qualities such as height show this kind of consistency in the early years of adulthood. We would say that IQ is consistent in this sense if the average IQ of a group of adults when they are 60 or 70 is the same as their average scores were when they were 20.

Notice that these two types of consistency are at least theoretically independent of one another. A characteristic could show both, or neither, or only one type. The scores of individuals may stay in the same relative positions while the group average score changes over time. Or the average scores of individuals may shift around quite a bit while the group average scores stay stable over time. As it happens, in the case of IQ scores over adulthood, it is the first of these combinations that actually occurs: There is correlational consistency but not consistency in absolute value.

Correlational Consistency in IQ Scores

A substantial number of longitudinal studies have been conducted in the United States and Europe that cover the years from youngest to oldest adulthood (Eichorn, Hunt, & Honzik, 1981; Hertzog & Schaie, 1986, 1988; Schaie, 1995; Steen & Djurfeldt, 1993). These studies tell us that IQ shows strong correlational consistency over the adult years. A typical finding, which I mentioned briefly in Chapter 1, is from the Berkeley Intergenerational Study (Eichorn et al., 1981). In this sample, there was a correlation of 0.83 for men and 0.77 for women between IQ scores at age 17 and those achieved by the same adults between ages 36 and 48. Over shorter time intervals the correlations are even higher. Christopher Hertzog and Warner Schaie, using data from the Seattle Longitudinal Study, have found that over seven-year intervals the correlations among IQ scores are very high, ranging from 0.89 to 0.96. Furthermore, they find the same high level of correlational consistency among those in their 60s and 70s as among those in their 30s and 40s (Hertzog & Schaie, 1986).

These are obviously very strong relationships. Still, there is some room for individual shifts within the range, especially over longer periods of time. In the Berkeley sample, for example, 11 percent of the subjects gained 13 or more IQ points over 20 to 30 years, while another 11 percent showed losses of 6 points or more. The latter group included a disproportionate number of heavy drinkers or those who had experienced some debilitative illness. Those with unusually large increases were likely to be married to someone with an IQ at least 10 points higher than their own IQ had been in late adolescence (Eichorn et al., 1981), a pattern also found among the subjects in the Seattle Longitudinal Study (Schaie, 1994).

Overall, then, IQ scores at the start of adulthood are highly predictive of IQ scores at later ages, although psychologically significant individual change can and does occur. What this does not tell us, though, is what happens to the average score as a group grows older.

Consistency in Absolute Level of IQ Scores

Most of the early information on consistency or change in adult intelligence came from early cross-sectional studies (1920s to 1950s), which seemed to show that declines in IQ began about age 20 and continued steadily thereafter. This depressing conclusion was widely reported and widely believed, but beginning in the second half of this century, longitudinal evidence began changing this, showing that adult intelligence was stable until at least age 50 (which was as far as the studies extended at that time). In the decades since then, we have learned a lot more about adult intelligence. Researchers have extended longitudinal studies to include the oldest old, they have begun to study cognitive processes other than overall IQ scores, they have invented new research designs that do away with some of the confounds of traditional methods, and they have suggested and adopted new conceptualizations of intelligence that might be more relevant to older adulthood (Woodruff-Pak, 1997).

One of the best known and most innovative research design is the sequential design that combines the best parts of the cross-sectional design with the best parts of the longitudinal design. This was devised by K. Warner Schaie and implemented in the Seattle Longitudinal Study (1983b, 1989a, 1993, 1994; Schaie & Hertzog, 1983). Schaie began with his dissertation study in 1956, a set of cross-sectional samples, seven years apart in age, ranging from age 25 to 67. A subset of subjects in each age group was then retested at seven-year intervals for the next 35 years. In 1963, another set of cross-sectional samples, covering the same age ranges, was also tested, and a subset of these was retested 7, 14, 21, and 28 years later, and so on.

The contrast between the longitudinal and cross-sectional analyses of IQ scores emerges very clearly from the results of this study, as you can see in Figure 5.1. The numbers in this figure are not traditional IQ scores with a mean of 100. Instead, Schaie calculated the mean of the IQ scores of all subjects on the first test that each had been given when they entered the study. This average score was then set (arbitrarily) at 50 points on a scale, with a standard deviation of 10. Thus two-thirds of all adults should fall between scores of 40 and 60 (one standard deviation on either side of the mean), and about 95 percent should fall between 30 and 70.

The lower line in Figure 5.1 represents the average scores of adults of each age in the cross-sectional samples tested in 1977. The upper line is Schaie's estimate of the longitudinal pattern of change, based on averaging the seven year longitudinal changes he had observed in several cohorts. When you compare these two lines in the figure, you can see

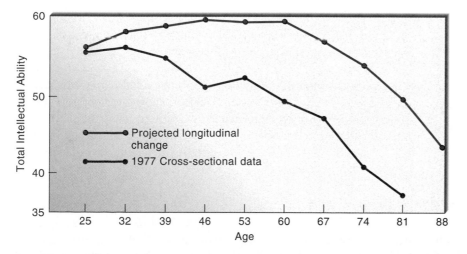

FIGURE 5.1 Age changes in total IQ based on cross-sectional comparisons and on longitudinal data. Cross-sectional comparisons clearly led to the erroneous conclusion that mental performance begins to decline at about age 40; longitudinal analyses show that IQ is maintained until at least 60.

Source: Data from Schaie, 1983b, Table 4.5, p. 89, and Table 4.9, p. 100.

that longitudinal and cross-sectional data yield very different answers to the question "does IQ decline with age in adulthood?" The cross-sectional evidence, of which the lower curve is highly typical, seems to show a beginning decline in IQ starting somewhere between age 32 and 39. The longitudinal information suggests a *rise* in IQ through middle adulthood and a decline beginning around 60. Only in the period from 67 to 74 do the total IQ scores in these samples drop below that seen at age 25.

The obvious explanation for the difference between the cross-sectional and longitudinal comparisons is that there are cohort effects at work here. As years of education and good health have increased in each successive cohort over the past century, average scores have generally gone up. Cross-sectional studies that compare IQ scores of people born decades apart are apt to show artificial drops in IQ with age because the older subjects not only show some age-related decline in IQ but also show the effects of poor health and education.

In the Seattle study, for example, Schaie has found that the scores of those born in the 1920s are roughly a half a standard deviation higher than those who were born in 1900. Despite these differences in the *absolute level* of scores, though, Schaie has found that the *shape* of the curves are very similar for all cohorts. Each successive generation appears to follow a pattern of maintenance of intellectual skill through early and middle adulthood, with a decline appearing only at age 65 or later. And since there was an increase in IQ scores from age 25 to about age 40, Schaie's subjects didn't go below their 25-year-old IQ until about the age of 70.

But what about **attrition?** You may recall from other discussions of longitudinal data that attrition is a big problem in these types of studies. People die, move away, become too disabled to participate any longer, especially at advanced ages. This might artificially raise the IQ scores at older ages because the ones who are left are healthier and more fit. In the Schaie studies, attrition effects have been noted and the analyses have been adjusted to minimize the confounding effect (Schaie, 1994).

One more statistical note: I have been talking about standard deviations and you probably know some long definition of this term. But in plain English, just how much intelligence are we talking about here? One standard deviation in IQ is 15 points. In

CRITICAL THINKING

Schaie has recently reported that current cohorts of older adults in his study appear to show a slower decline than was true for the earliest cohorts he studied (Schaie, 1993). How might you explain such a change?

Figure 5.1, the difference between the point on the vertical axis labeled 50 and the point labeled 40 is only 15 IQ points. If the subjects in this study began with an average IQ of 100, they increased to about 113 or so, stayed there until about 60, and then began to decline. But they were 70 when they crossed the 100 IQ line again on the way down, and still hadn't hit the 85 IQ line by age 88.

Since this pattern has also been found by other researchers (Sands, Terry, & Meredith, 1989; Siegler, 1983), there is good support for the optimistic view that general intellectual ability remains stable through most of adulthood. But now let's dissect intelligence a little and see what happens with age to some of the specific intellectual abilities that are considered components of IQ.

Age Changes in IQ Subtests

On standard IQ tests, the total score is the sum of a variety of subscores. For example, the Wechsler Adult Intelligence Scale (WAIS) is made up of subtests that measure verbal abilities (such as general knowledge, vocabulary, arithmetic reasoning) and performance abilities (such as puzzle assembly, block design, picture arrangement). The scores of each of these subtests are combined to produce a **verbal IQ** and a **performance IQ,** which in turn are combined to produce a single, **full-scale IQ.** Verbal IQ can be compared with performance IQ, and subtests can be grouped in a variety of other ways, depending on the researchers' interests. When comparing verbal and performance scores over age, verbal abilities generally show increases or stability through the adult age span, up to as late as the 70s, while performance abilities show much earlier decline (Busse & Maddox, 1985; Denney, 1982).

Some researchers (Cunningham & Owens, 1983; Jarvik & Bank, 1983; Jensen, 1993) emphasize the difference between **speeded tasks,** those subtests in which time is a factor, and **unspeeded tasks.** The general finding is that performance on speeded tests begins to decline earlier in the adult years than does performance on unspeeded tests. (This should come as no surprise because most verbal tasks are untimed, and most performance tasks are timed.)

A third distinction, between fluid and crystallized intelligence, was first proposed by Raymond Cattell and John Horn (Cattell, 1963; Horn, 1982) and has been widely influential among researchers studying adult cognition. **Crystallized intelligence** is heavily dependent on education and experience. It consists of the set of skills and bits of knowledge that we each learn as part of growing up in any given culture, such as verbal comprehension, vocabulary, the ability to evaluate experience, the ability to reason with real-life problems, and technical skills you may learn for your job or your life (balancing a checkbook, making change, finding the salad dressing in the grocery store). On standardized tests, crystallized abilities are usually measured by vocabulary and by verbal comprehension (e.g., reading a paragraph and then answering questions about it).

Fluid intelligence, in contrast, is thought to be a more "basic" set of abilities, not so dependent on specific education and more dependent on the efficient functioning of the central nervous system. A common measure of this is a "letter series test." You may be given a series of letters such as A C F J O and must figure out what letter should go next. This demands abstract reasoning rather than reasoning about known or everyday events. Most tests of memory are also part of fluid intelligence, as are many tests measuring response speed and those measuring more difficult or abstract kinds of mathematics. Horn has concluded that crystallized abilities generally continue to rise or show

THE ABILITY TO READ a road map is mostly dependent on what Horn calls crystallized intelligence. It requires specific map-reading experience and, once learned, is likely to be retained well into old age.

stability over adulthood (until age 70 or so, at least), while fluid abilities begin to decline much earlier, beginning perhaps at 35 or 40 (Horn & Donaldson, 1980; Horn & Hofer, 1992).

Whatever labels we apply to these two broad categories of intellectual tasks, it seems clear that abilities in one group (the unspeeded, verbal, crystallized tasks) are maintained into old age, whereas abilities in the other type of task (speeded, nonverbal, fluid) show signs of decline beginning in middle adulthood. This same idea is addressed a little differently in the Seattle Longitudinal Study data I discussed earlier. Instead of Wechsler subtests, Schaie (1983) used tests measuring mental abilities identified by Thurstone (1938) as being primary factors. These are **verbal meaning, spatial orientation, inductive reasoning, number,** and **word fluency.** Figure 5.2 shows the longitudinal gradients for the five factors. As you can see, there is a modest gain in all abilities from young adulthood to early middle age, but then declines begin in word fluency and number abilities, both of which are speeded nonverbal, fluid tasks. (But also notice that neither goes below the starting point until around age 53.) Around age 46, the remaining abilities stop increasing—verbal meaning, spatial orientation, and inductive reasoning—although none crosses below their starting point until much later (Shaie, 1994).

What can we say about intellectual abilities and age? It is certainly true that the stereotype of an older person who is mentally incompetent does not fit what we now know about primary aging. General intelligence, as measured by IQ tests, begins to decline around the age of 50 for some persons, but it is a small decline until the mid-70s. Furthermore, this change does not occur for all intellectual abilities. The group of abilities we label as speeded, performance, or fluid tasks are more likely to show decline, while

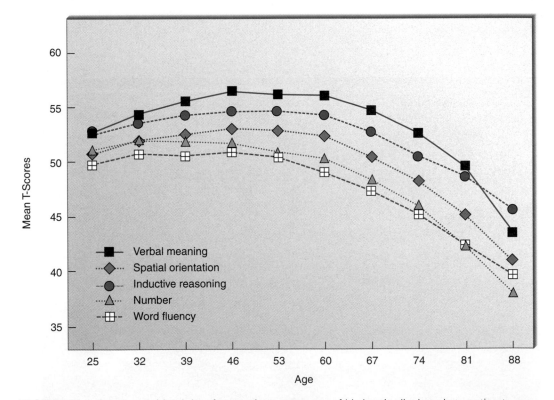

FIGURE 5.2 Schaie combined data from various segments of his longitudinal study to estimate age changes in five primary mental abilities from 25 to 88 years of age. These data show that substantial cognitive changes occur only late in life and tend to occur for abilities that were less central and less practiced.

the group of abilities we label as unspeeded, verbal, or crystallized tasks are less likely to decline. When abilities do decline in most older adults who are in good physical and psychological health, the amount of decline may be statistically significant, but not functionally significant.

Reversing Declines in Intellectual Abilities

Beginning in the 1970s, when it became apparent that intelligence did not drop off drastically with age, researchers began asking if anything could be done to reverse the moderate decline in IQ that the longitudinal studies were showing. The answer was, "yes." Different studies showed that physical exercise brought about significant improvement in intellectual performance (e.g., Powell, 1974), as did training subjects in the components specific to the task being tested (e.g., Labouvie-Vief & Gonda, 1976) and training in nonspecific aspects of the test such as willingness to guess when one is not sure of the correct answer (Birkhill & Schaie, 1975).

Schaie and Willis (1986) included a training study in one wave of their ongoing longitudinal study to determine whether training was effective for people who were already showing a decline or just for those who had not begun to decline yet. They gave five hours of training to 229 participants aged 64 to 94. About half of the participants had shown a decline over the last 14 years and about half had not. Some received training on spatial orientation and some on inductive reasoning, both abilities that tend to decline with age and are considered more resistant to intervention. When the results of the training were examined for those who had declined, it was found that about half had gained significantly and 40 percent had returned to their former level of performance. Of those who had not shown declines yet, one-third increased their abilities above their previous levels.

Seven years later, the same researchers retested 141 of these subjects (Schaie, 1994) and compared them to other subjects in the study who were the same age and had not received training. The group of trained subjects had declined from their previous levels, but they performed better than the controls, even though it had been seven years since their training. These subjects were then given an additional five hours of training, which raised their test scores again significantly but not to the level that it had seven years earlier.

These results, showing successful effects of training on declining intellectual abilities of older adults, have been replicated with another German sample (Baltes & Lindenberger, 1988; Baltes, Sowarka, & Kliegl, 1989) as well as with U.S. samples (Blackburn, Papalia-Finley, Foye, & Serlin, 1988; Hayslip, 1989). Researchers are now working to transfer these findings from the lab to real-life situations in which older adults can benefit from training that is offered as games and other enjoyable real-life activities (S. L. Willis, 1996).

CHANGES IN MEMORY

What I have been talking about so far are age changes on tests of intellectual ability, such as IQ tests or tests of specific intellectual abilities. Another aspect of cognition that is actively being studied is age changes in **memory,** the ability to retain or store information and retrieve it when needed. We are learning that this topic is more important to the aging adult himself or herself than are changes in IQ test numbers. Recent reports show that most adults over the age of 65 notice a decrease in their own memory abilities and express concern over this, associating it with illness, loss of independence, and their own mortality (R. S. Wilson, Bennett, & Swartzendruber, 1997). At the same time, clinical psychologists report an increase in the number of patients who show pathological levels of anxiety that their failing memory abilities are symptoms of Alzheimer's disease (Centofanti, 1998). The American Psychological Association task force on geropsychology has recommended that therapists and the public alike educate themselves about what constitutes memory changes in normal aging, and also about reversible causes of memory loss such as depression, lack of mental stimulation, and certain medications. So this is an important topic on several levels.

There is a vast amount of research touching on these questions, so you might suppose that the answers are clear-cut. But as is often true, the more deeply researchers have explored the question, the more we have discovered about the complexity of the process. In addition, we are hampered by the fact that the majority of research has been cross-sectional rather than longitudinal, often comparing only a group of 20-year-olds and a group of "old" adults, with little coverage of the ages of middle adulthood. Even worse, the 20-year-olds are nearly always college students, while most of the older adult subjects did not attend college.

Timothy Salthouse, one of the major figures in studies of memory change in adulthood, has shown that this method of choosing subjects clearly exacerbates the cohort problem and makes the age differences look much larger (Salthouse, Kausler, & Saults,1988). When he compared scores for young students, young nonstudents, and older adults he found that while both younger groups performed better than did the older adults, the students performed better than the young nonstudents on many tests. Keep these limitations and design flaws in mind as we go along.

Some Terms

Before I describe the findings, I need to define some terms. Several sets of words have been used to describe memory processes. One set of distinctions, still widely used, is among encoding, storage, and retrieval. **Encoding** refers to the processes by which information is committed to memory, which may include rehearsal, organizing the material into chunks, making mental pictures of it, or the like. **Storage** simply refers to what happens (if anything) to the memory over time, regardless of how it was encoded. **Retrieval** describes the processes by which you get information out of memory again when you need it. Of the several types of retrieval, **recognition** is easier than **recall.** (This is probably why multiple-choice questions are so much more popular among college students than fill-in-the-blank questions or the dreaded essay!)

CRITICAL
THINKING

Think about the way you go about studying for this class, and analyze it in terms of these various aspects of memory.

The distinctions are a bit like what you do when you put food in your refrigerator. Encoding is like what you do when you put food in the refrigerator in the first place. You organize all the vegetables together, all the cheese together, and put all the meat in a special drawer. Storage is what happens to the food over time if you don't eat it. Some of it just sits there, staying essentially the same, which is true of pasteurized process cheese food, which will last virtually forever. Some of it decays, such as the tomatoes in the bottom drawer, which grow green fur. Retrieval is the process of finding the stuff you want when you need it and taking it out of storage to use it.

A second way of describing the processes of memory focuses on the duration of the stored information. **Sensory memory** refers to information lasting a second or less, **short-term memory** lasts about 30 seconds, and **long-term memory** persists for periods from minutes to years (Salthouse, 1991). In this model, memory is seen in terms of a flow of information through the system. Think of what you do, for example, when you look up and then try to recall a phone number. When you first actually see the number you have a very brief visual impression. This is a sensory memory. If you do nothing more, you will not be able to recall the number even a second later. But if you pay attention to the number in some fashion, you transfer it to short-term memory. For example, if you say the number to yourself once, you can usually remember it long enough to dial without having to recheck the number. But short-term memory, too, decays. If I asked you to remember the number a few minutes later, you probably couldn't do so. You had put the number into short-term memory but not into long-term memory. Further processing is required to store something in long-term memory—more rehearsals, writing the number many times, or creating further associations, such as noting that the prefix is the same as some other number you know, or noting a pattern in the numbers. A perfect example: My mathematician husband pointed out to me that a number I call occasionally but had to look up each time, 256-4444, was easy to remember because 256 is the arithmetic result of 4 x 4 x 4 x 4. I have remembered this number easily ever since.

Obviously, these various ways of talking about memory are not mutually exclusive. All may be useful in understanding what happens to memory with age.

Evidence of Memory Changes

Whether we conclude that there is memory loss with age will depend very much on which of the several facets of the memory process we study.

Sensory Memory. You might think that sensory memory would get less efficient as you get older. But there is no evidence for a systematic decline in the ability to hold information for a fraction of a second in this sort of sensory memory. Of course, older adults have poorer vision and poorer hearing, so there are some things they simply do not perceive as well. But assuming that something (like a number in the phone book) has been perceived, there are only minor deficits in the memories of older adults compared to younger adults (Labouvie-Vief & Schell, 1982; Woodruff-Pak, 1997).

Short-Term memory. Memory span tasks that tap the ability to passively hold small amounts of information in memory for immediate recall show small but reliable age-related decrements (Craik & Jennings, 1992) until the late 70s or 80s, and then only modest declines (Johansson & Berg, 1989). In contrast, there are substantial decreases with age found in working memory tasks, those that involve holding information in short-term memory while performing an operation on it (Salthouse & Babcock, 1991; Wingfield, Stine, Lahar, & Aberdeen, 1988).

Both these points are nicely illustrated in a study by Robin West and Thomas Crook (1990) using a task much like the everyday task of recalling a phone number. Subjects sat in front of a computer screen, on which appeared a series of numbers, one at a time. Sometimes there were seven numbers in the series, sometimes 10 (the equivalent of a long-distance number). The subject said each number aloud as it appeared, and when the series of numbers was complete, had to dial the numbers on a pushbutton phone attached to the computer. Sometimes subjects got a busy signal when they dialed, and they had to dial again—a tougher test of short-term memory. Figure 5.3 shows the results.

You can see that in the least demanding situation—seven digits without a busy signal—there were essentially no age differences. But when the task was made more difficult in any way—by increasing the number of digits to 10, or by adding a busy signal—some pattern of decline with age appeared, with the largest age difference showing up in the most demanding condition. The effect of age is larger still if the person is asked to do anything with the information they are holding in short term memory—to rearrange it, or recall it in an order other than the one in which it was given, or repeat back only the words of a particular type—all tasks that involve working memory. Thus on simple short-term memory tasks, there is only a small age difference, but as soon as the task is made more complex in almost any way, older subjects are at a greater disadvantage (Salthouse, 1994; A. D. Smith, 1996).

Long-Term Memory. Still larger age differences appear when we look at long-term memory (Poon, 1985). Once you exceed the capacity of the short-term storage system, you must either transfer the information to long-term storage or you will forget it. In tasks measuring general long-term memory ability, most older adults run into difficulty. Perhaps most noticeably, retrieval becomes *slower* with age (Craik & Jennings, 1992; Madden, 1992). But

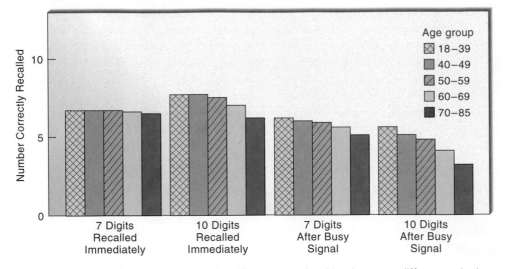

FIGURE 5.3 Results from West and Crook's cross-sectional study on age differences in the ability to recall telephone numbers, with and without a busy signal.

Source: Data from West & Crook, 1990, Table 3, p. 524.

more than just speed seems to be involved here. Older adults generally do about as well (although slower) as younger adults on tasks demanding recognition, but much less well on tasks demanding recall. If you give subjects a list of words to learn, for example, and ask them later whether particular words were on the list, older adults do quite well. But if you ask them to recall as many of the words as possible, they have more difficulty (Labouvie-Vief & Schell, 1982). So long-term memory becomes less accessible as we get older. Findings such as these reinforce the impression of many older adults that they often "know" things that they cannot bring to mind readily or quickly. If they are given a hint or are reminded of the item at a later time, the memory comes back.

Large decrements with age also occur in the encoding process. Older adults appear to use less efficient or less effective strategies for organizing new material for learning. For example, in the standard experimental procedure, subjects are given a list of words to learn. Several strategies have been shown to be effective memory aids on such a task. You can associate an image with each word, make up a sentence, or group the words into clusters that have some common element. Extensive research shows that older adults are much less likely to use strategies spontaneously, even if they are given unlimited time.

In one fairly typical study, Jan Rabinowitz (1989) compared 15 older (aged 61 to 74) and 15 younger (aged 18 to 25) adults on memory for such word lists. The two groups were matched on vocabulary knowledge and years of education. Rabinowitz asked each subject to learn and later recall four lists of 24 words each, two under standard conditions in which each word in the list was presented on a computer screen for 5 seconds, and two under unlimited study conditions in which the subjects controlled the speed of presentation, could take notes, and use any strategies they thought would help. You can see in Figure 5.4 that having extra study time helped both the younger and the older adults to remember more of the words, but it helped the younger adults proportionately *more.* The younger subjects in this study did not spend more time studying than did the elders, but they appeared to derive more benefit from the study time, presumably because they were better able to use the extra study time to mobilize various strategies for encoding the list of words—a conclusion bolstered by the fact that in this sample, those young subjects who took the longest times to study the words had the highest recall scores, but that was not true among the older subjects.

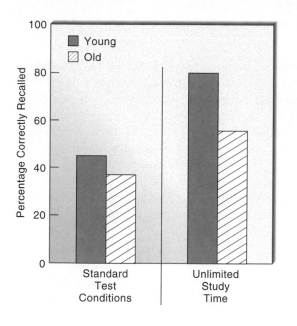

FIGURE 5.4 In Jan Rabinowitz's study, older adults had poorer recall of lists in both the standard condition, when a new word in the list was shown on the screen every 5 seconds, and with unlimited study time, when the subject controlled the rate of presentation.

Source: Data from Rabinowitz, 1989, Table 1, p. 379.

Reversing Declines in Memory Abilities. If memory ability declines with age because older people don't use strategies spontaneously when they process information, what happens if they are instructed to do so? This is the idea behind many memory training studies. For example, older adults have been successfully trained to remember names of people they have just met by using mental imagery to form associations between peoples' faces and their names (Yesavage, Lapp, & Sheikh, 1989). Bäckman and colleagues (Stigsdotter & Bäckman, 1989, 1993) trained older adults on encoding, attention, and relaxation in order to improve word recall. And Reinhold Kliegl and his colleagues (Kliegl, Smith, & Baltes, 1990) trained older adults to use the method of loci to remember words on a list by associating them with landmark buildings along a route in Berlin.

To answer the question about the efficacy of training: Yes, training improves declining memory function, but no, it doesn't do away with the decline completely. In none of these studies did the performance of older adults reach the level of performance of young adults, but all brought significant improvement over the subjects' earlier performances or over a control group of older adults who received no training.

Other memory researchers have focused on training older adults to use **external memory aids,** such as making lists, writing notes, using voice mail, placing items-to-be-remembered in obvious places, and using timers, voice mail, and hand-held audio recorders. In one such study, Orah Burack and Margie Lachman (1996) randomly assigned young and old adults to two groups—list-making and non-list-making—and gave them word recall and recognition tests. As expected, in the standard recall condition (non-list-makers), the older adults performed less well than the younger adults, but for the list-makers, there were no significant differences between the old and young groups. In addition, the older list-makers performed better than did the older non-list-makers.

In an interesting twist, the authors of this study added a condition in which some of the list-making subjects were told that they would be able to refer to their lists during the recall test, but were actually not allowed to use them. These subjects benefited as much from making the lists and not using them as the subjects who made the lists and did, suggesting that the activity of list making improves memory even when the list is not available at recall.

Studies such as these show that training on both internal and external memory aids can benefit older adults whose memories are not as sharp as they were in younger years.

They may not bring back 100 percent of earlier abilities, but intervention and improvement are possible.

Memory in Everyday Context. Most of the studies cited in this section have been done in laboratories and have involved artificial tasks. Some researchers have argued that the age differences found in memory ability may have more to do with older peoples' unwillingness to "play games" in the lab. In the 1990s, many memory researchers shifted away from lab studies and focused on studies of everyday memory. The goal was to find tasks that were **ecologically significant,** that is, relevant to daily living, meaningful to the subjects, and conducted in naturalistic settings instead of labs (Schaie & Willis, 1996). Using these goals, researchers found some tasks that older adults performed as well as younger adults. For example, older adults appear to be equally good at remembering experiences that were highly salient at the time, such as whether they voted in an election four years earlier (Hertzog and Rogers, 1989). In another study, no age differences were found between young, middle-aged, and old adults when they were asked to read a 200-word passage and summarize it in one sentence, to recall what the passage was about, and to complete a partial outline of the passage (Meyer & Rice, 1983).

CRITICAL THINKING

Before you read the next paragraph, think for a minute about how you might devise a test of memory that tapped "real life" or "everyday" memory.

However, most studies of everyday memory show significant age differences for most tasks, although those differences are reduced the closer the tasks are to real situations in which the older adults are likely to find themselves. For example, in one study (Crook & West, 1990), adults were introduced to four people and told to remember their names. There was no difference between the middle-aged and older adults on the task, but when the task was changed to require subjects to remember the names of 14 people—a situation that hardly qualifies as an everyday experience for an older adult—major age differences emerged .

In a similar study of everyday memory, Jan Sinnott (1986) tested a group of adults aged 23 to 93 who were part of the Baltimore Longitudinal Study. During the regular two-day testing session at the labs, each subject was asked to recall various bits of information about the labs themselves, about the daily routine, or about the other tests they had been given (e.g., When does the hospital cafeteria stop serving dinner?", "Describe one problem you worked on during the problem-solving test."). Some of these questions were highly salient for the subjects' daily life (such as the cafeteria serving times); others were not (such as what items had been on the table). Sinnott then called up each subject 7 to 10 days later, and again 18 to 21 *months* later, and asked the same questions. What she found was that the older adults did just as well at remembering the highly salient material, but much less well at the less salient information. Results like this suggest that what the older adult does is to focus their limited cognitive capacity on the crucial everyday stuff and ignore the rest. The younger adult, who may have quicker or more efficient cognitive processes, picks up a wider range of information.

It seems clear to me that although older adults often perform better on everyday memory tasks than on lab tasks, this artificiality of the lab situation is not the cause of age-related declines in memory. On most everyday tasks, such as remembering the main points of a story or a newspaper article, recalling movies, conversations, or recipes, recalling the information from a medicine label, remembering whether some action has been performed ("Did I turn off the stove before I left the house?"), or remembering to do something in the future, such as taking medication once a day, older adults recall less well than younger adults (Light, 1991; Maylor, 1993; Salthouse, 1991; Verhaeghen & Marcoen, 1993; Verhaeghen, Marcoen, & Goossens 1993). Even on highly familiar items crucial to everyday functioning in some occupation, such as the ability of pilots to recall instructions given to them by air-traffic controllers, there is evidence that older recreational pilots make more recall errors than do younger pilots (J. L. Taylor et al., 1994).

The weight of the accumulating evidence is quite clear: A decline with age in memory ability occurs on most everyday tasks as well as on traditional laboratory tasks. Such a decline is also found, particularly after 70, in the few longitudinal studies of memory (Arenberg, 1983; Hultsch, Herzog, Small, McDonald-Miszczak, & Dixon, 1992; Zelinski, Gilewski, & Schaie, 1993).

Preliminary Explanations. How do we account for these changes in memory? What underlying process might be involved? Some of the clearest evidence about the causes of age-related memory decline comes from a **meta-analysis** of 91 studies on cognitive processes in adulthood compiled by Paul Verhaeghen and Timothy Salthouse (1997). After combining the findings from all these studies, they conclude that age-related differences are present in many cognitive abilities, and that these differences are mediated by two major factors: speed of processing and working memory.

Speed of processing takes the major role underlying declines in cognitive abilities as we get older. This means that our birthdays are not as much an indication of our cognitive abilities as our processing speed is. And what determines processing speed? Attempts to locate the source of this loss have pointed to the central nervous system and not to more peripheral functions such as movement speed, sensory acuity, and speed of nerve conduction. Although there is slowing in all of these functions with age, it is not substantial enough to account for the large decline of perceptual speed and related cognitive declines. Instead, age-related changes in synaptic function (the time it takes for information to be transmitted across the gap between neurons) and functioning of the brain and brainstem, where sensory input and motor output are integrated, seem to be the best candidates for the underlying causes of much of the memory loss that occurs with age (Woodruff-Pak, 1997).

The second cause of intellectual decline in later adulthood is **working memory,** which is the mental skill used to hold information in short-term memory while some operation is performed on it, such as deciding if a word belongs to a certain category or making a visual image that will help you retrieve the information later. As you might imagine, decreased functioning in working memory can affect a variety of cognitive abilities, from short-term thought processes to encoding and retrieving information from long-term memory (Just & Carpenter, 1992). Neuropsychologists consider working memory to be the "blackboard of the mind" (Goldman-Rakic, 1992) and have shown in animal studies that it is a joint process of the prefrontal cortex and the hippocampus (Woodruff-Pak, 1997).

Lower speed of processing and decline in working memory ability seem to be the biggest factors in intellectual decline with age, but they don't tell the whole story. There appear to be other losses as well, such as a loss in the capacity to maintain attention, to inhibit extraneous stimuli, or to divide attention among several items. And I must add the familiar caveat that the meta-analysis by Verhaeghen and Salthouse was limited to cross-sectional studies. It will be interesting to see similar work done on longitudinal data when enough are available for large-scale analyses.

CHANGES IN PROBLEM-SOLVING ABILITY

Problem solving refers to the complex set of thought processes that you use to achieve a desired goal. They typically involve assessing the problem, defining the goal, generating possible ways to achieve the goal, and finally, deciding which possible way is the most feasible (Reese & Rodeheaver, 1985). If your car didn't start this morning and you still made it to your 10:00 psychology class, the process you went through is probably a good example of this very important cognitive ability. How does problem solving change over the course of adulthood?

Laboratory tasks of problem solving are varied, but a typical one requires the subject to figure out which combination of button pressings are needed to turn on a light. On such tasks younger adults are not only more likely to be successful, they also appear to use better strategies. As was true for memory tasks, this age difference is found even when the subjects are encouraged to take notes and keep track of each of the combinations they have already tried. Older adults in such studies take fewer and apparently less effective notes (Kluwe, 1986).

But is accurate button pushing really a problem that older adults would need to solve in their everyday lives? This issue was addressed in a study by Nancy Denney, who asked a group of over-65-year-olds to help her identify a set of real-life problems that older adults might typically encounter. Here's one of the problems on a topic suggested by the elders themselves: "Let's say that a 67-year-old man's doctor has told him to take it easy because of a heart condition. It's summertime and the man's yard needs to be mowed but the man cannot afford to pay someone to mow the lawn. What should he do?" (Denney & Pearce, 1989, p. 439).

Denney posed 10 problems identified in this way to adults of various ages from 20 to 79, scoring their answers according to the number of safe and effective solutions proposed.

CRITICAL THINKING

How many different solutions to this problem can you think of?

On this task, Denney has found the highest scores among those between 30 and 50, with those over 50 scoring the lowest (Denney & Pearce, 1989; Denney, Tozier, & Schlotthauer, 1992). This pattern of results held even when she controlled statistically for differences in educational levels among the various age groups. Other research suggests that older adults are as good or better at recognizing a good problem solution when they hear one (Light, 1992), but that they are less good at thinking up possible solutions, even when the problems to be solved are practical and relevant.

Although few in number, longitudinal studies suggest that the drop in problem-solving skill occurs later than age 50. For instance, data from the Baltimore Longitudinal Study point to age 70 as the age at which problem-solving ability begins to decline, a pattern that is highly consistent with Schaie's data on IQ and other general cognitive skills. But it seems clear that there is a decline. After reviewing the data, Rainer Kluwe (1986) concludes that in older adults, "the solution search, given well-defined problems, is not very well organized, it is inefficient, redundant, and finally not very successful" (p. 519). Some of this may reflect cohort differences, but it seems very unlikely that cohort differences can explain all of the changes in late adulthood.

Human Factors Research with Older Adults

In the past decade, cognitive psychologists who do **human factors research** have focused on how older adults actually solve everyday problems they encounter in their homes and around their neighborhoods. The goal of their research is not only to uncover problems but to help devise solutions. Studies in the United States and Germany have shown that older adults spend most of their time on seven activities, the instrumental activities of daily living (IADLs) discussed in Chapter 4. These include managing one's medication, finances, transportation, shopping, household maintenance, meals, and telephoning. The reason these activities take up so much time is because they become more and more complicated with age as physical and cognitive abilities decline. How to remain independent in the face of changing abilities is the major problem that older adults face every day (S. L. Willis, 1996).

Medication Nonadherence. In one series of studies, Denise Park and her colleagues tackled the problem of **medication nonadherence,** failure to take medication as prescribed by one's physician (Morrell, Park, & Poon, 1989; Park, 1992; Park & Kidder, 1995; Park, Morrell, Frieske, & Kincaid, 1992). Medication nonadherence is a considerable problem among older adults for several reasons. Older adults have many chronic health conditions, there are many drugs available to control these conditions, and many older adults have decreased memory function. This dangerous combination of factors results in high rates of admissions of older adults to hospital emergency rooms for either failing to take their medication or for inadvertently taking too much.

Park proposes a model to predict how well an older person will adhere to instructions about his or her medication. This model suggests three key factors: (1) how seriously ill the patient thinks that he or she is, (2) how well the patient functions cognitively, and (3) what external cues or strategies are available to help the patient take the medication as prescribed (Park & Jones, 1997). Why would a chronically ill person not take their illness seriously, especially when a remedy is available? Some people have the belief that chronic illness is part of old age and that nothing will really help. Others have their own cultural beliefs about the source of their illnesses and don't buy into the Western medical model at all. Still others take the medication for as long as they experience the symptoms, only to quit once they feel better. Clearly, if older people don't share their doctor's belief system or haven't been educated about their chronic conditions, attempts to bolster their cognitive abilities or to provide external memory aids won't do much good.

The patient's cognitive functioning includes understanding the physician's instructions, reading and comprehending the labels on prescription bottles, organizing the medication instructions into a daily plan that might include multiple doses and instructions for other medication, remembering the plan, and remembering to actually take the medication. Older people have problems on all of these aspects. For example, Park and her colleagues compared older and younger adults and found that older adults had more trouble comprehending information on the labels of their prescription containers, were less able to remember medication information over a period of time, and were less likely to comply with their doctors' instructions for taking the medication (Park & Jones, 1997).

One of the external aids that have been designed to help older adults solve the problem of nonadherence are new labels, shown in Figure 5.5, that communicate in

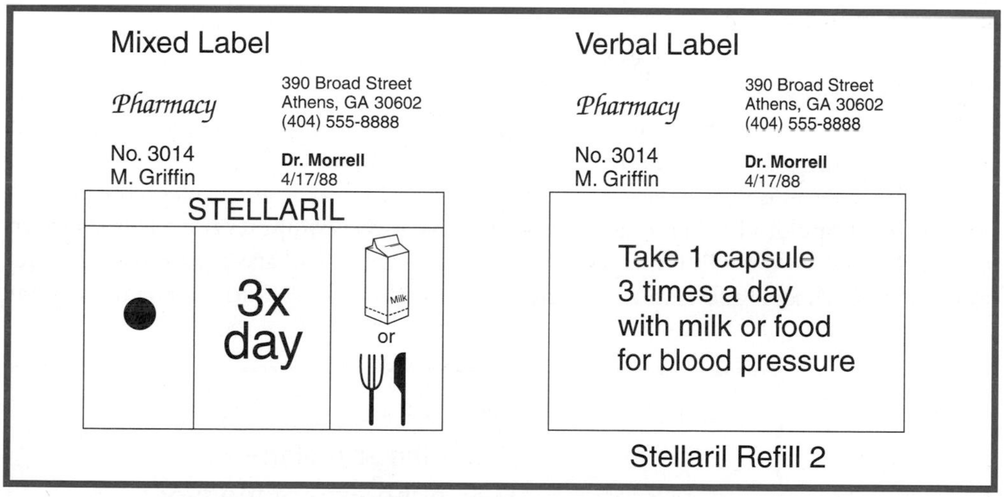

FIGURE 5.5 Examples of two prescription labels designed by Morrell, Park, & Poon (1988) that have well-structured instructions that do not require older patients to make inferences. Older people understood and remembered instructions better on these labels than on the actual labels used by pharmacies. (So did younger people.) And the verbal label was remembered better by older people than the mixed label.

Source: D. C. Park & T. R. Jones, 1997, Medication adherence and aging. In A. D. Fisk & W. A. Rogers (Eds.), *Handbook of human factors and the older adult.* San Diego, CA: Academic Press Figure 2, p. 277.

WHEN GIVEN AGE-APPROPRIATE INSTRUCTIONS, older adults can be capable and enthusiastic users of computers.

structions in a more understandable way (Morrell, Park, & Poon, 1988, 1989). Other aids include pills packaged in plastic blister packs on cards that contain the number of pills needed per day or provide other reminders (Wong & Norman, 1987), pill packets attached to calendars (Ascione & Shrimp, 1984), and plastic organizer boxes with separate compartments for each dose each day of the week (Park, Morrell, Frieske, Blackburn, & Birchmore, 1991).

Learning to Use Personal Computers. Another problem-solving dilemma faced by older adults is learning to use personal computers. Although this may sound like a trivial problem for older people, consider the many parts of our everyday lives that are enhanced by the use of personal computers, from communicating by e-mail, to ordering merchandise via the Internet, to finding information about health on Web pages. A few moments of thought should bring forth the realization that personal computers could be a solution to many problems that the elderly experience: for example, limited access to shopping and banking, social isolation, lack of transportation, difficulty hearing telephone conversations. The popular idea that older people are resistant to computer use has not proven to be true. When older adults are given access to computers and age-appropriate instructions, most are capable and enthusiastic users. Community centers and nursing homes that

10 Point	This is the size of the type.
11 Point	This is the size of the type.
12 Point	This is the size of the type.
14 Point	This is the size of the type.

FIGURE 5.6 Examples of type sizes. Research reviewed by Morrell and Echt (1997) shows that older readers prefer 14-point type and also demonstrated superior reading speed when text was printed with this size of type.

Source: Morrel & Echt, 1997, Fig. 2, p. 344.

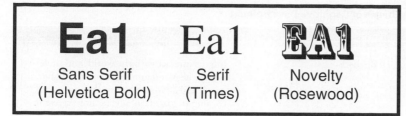

FIGURE 5.7 Examples of type faces. Sans serif typeface, above left, is recommended for older adults based on research reviewed by Morrell and Echt (1997). Sans serif refers to the lack of strokes at the end of some of the letters, as seen in the center example above. Novelty typeface, above right, is the least legible for older adults.

Source: Morrell & Echt, 1997, Fig. 1, p. 343.

have installed computers report that elderly residents who use them show increased feelings of accomplishment, self-confidence, autonomy, competency, self-esteem, and mastery (Eilers, 1989).

What are age-appropriate instructions for computer use? Robert Morrell and Katharina Echt (1997) have reviewed the research and have suggested the following: Instructional material should be written in large print at least 14 points in size (see Figure 5.6) using a sans serif typeface (see Figure 5.7); instruction should be paced slowly, with older learners paired with partners or in small groups (as opposed to individual instructions), and should follow a logical sequence, be broken down into small segments, and be reinforced with illustrations.

Studies such as these bring light to the nature of the age-related changes in cognitive processes that have been so well documented and give some assistance to older adults who are immersed in practical problem solving on a day-to-day basis.

CHANGES IN INTELLECTUAL STRUCTURE

All of the measures of intellectual ability I have talked about so far emerge from the tradition within psychology that defines intelligence in terms of *power* or *skill.* IQ tests are designed to tell us how well someone can do something, or how quickly. But there is another way to think about intellectual changes with age, typified by Jean Piaget's theory of cognitive development (1952; Piaget & Inhelder, 1969). Piaget was interested in changes in **cognitive structure** with age. What kind of logic does the young child use, and how does it change over the course of development? Piaget's work was focused almost exclusively on cognitive development in children, but his theory has influenced some of the thinking on cognition in adulthood and old age.

Piaget proposed that there are four major stages of cognitive development, sketched in Table 5.1. Shifts from one stage to the next occur gradually rather than suddenly, but each stage is thought to represent a general pattern of thinking. In Western cultures, virtually all adults think easily at the **concrete operational level;** perhaps half of adults think at the **formal operational level** at least some of the time. A number of theorists have argued that Piaget's model simply doesn't capture many of the kinds of thinking that adults are called upon to do. Perhaps, then, there are additional levels or new types of thinking that occur in adulthood. One such theorist is Gisela Labouvie-Vief (1980; 1990), who suggests that formal operations, with its emphasis on the exploration of all logical possibilities, is highly adaptive in early adulthood when the young person is exploring options, establishing identity. But adult responsibilities require reasoning that is tied to specific concrete contexts. Adult thought thus becomes *specialized* and *pragmatic.* The adult learns

TABLE 5.1 **Piaget's Stages of Cognitive Development**

Stage	Age	Description
Sensorimotor	Birth–2 years	Infants interact with the world, and understands the world around them, through senses and actions. Until at least age 1, according to Piaget, infants do not represent objects internally. They "know" objects only by what they can do with them or how they experience them directly.
Preoperational	2–6 years	Preoperational children are still tied to their own view ("egocentric" in Piaget's terms), but they can represent things internally, using words or images; they can engage in fantasy play; and they begin to be able to classify objects into groups. There is a primitive form of logic at this stage.
Concrete operational	6–12 years	The school-aged child moves into a kind of intellectual third gear, discovering an entire series of powerful mental actions, which Piaget calls *operations,* such as addition, subtraction, serial ordering, and the like. Children in this stage are capable of inductive logic (arriving at general principles by adding up specific experiences), and they are better able to understand others' points of view; but they are still tied to their own experience and cannot yet imagine things they have not known directly.
Formal operational	12 years and into adulthood	Formal operations represent intellectual high gear. Those teenagers and adults who achieve this level of thinking (and not all do) are capable of deductive logic ("if…then" reasoning, for example); can approach problems systematically, examining all possible combinations or operations; and can think about ideas as well as about objects. This is vastly more abstract than concrete operations, although concrete operations are sufficient for most everyday experiences.

how to solve the problems associated with the particular social roles he or she occupies or the particular job he or she holds, and discovers how to meet the specific difficulties or challenges. In the process, the deductive thoroughness of formal operations is traded off for **contextual validity.** In Labouvie-Vief's view, this trade-off does not reflect a regression or a loss, but a necessary structural change.

Labouvie-Vief (1990) has also emphasized a theme that is common to many of the newer structural ideas—that in adulthood we begin to turn away from the purely logical, the purely analytic approach, toward a more open, perhaps deeper mode of understanding that deals more in terms of myth and metaphor, paradox instead of certainty. Michael Basseches (1984, 1989) calls this new adult type of thinking **dialectical thought.** He suggests that while formal thought "involves the effort to find fundamental fixed realities—basic elements and immutable laws—[dialectical thought] attempts to describe fundamental processes of change and the dynamic relationships through which this change occurs" (1984, p. 24). Adults do not give up their ability to use formal reasoning, but they acquire a new ability to deal with those fuzzier problems that seem to make up the majority of the problems of adulthood—problems that do not have a single solution or in which some critical pieces of information may be missing. You might be able to make a decision about what kind of car to buy using formal, logical thought processes. But such forms of logic will not be as helpful in making a decision about whether to end a marriage, or whether to place your aging parent in a nursing home, or something apparently more straightforward, such as whether to take a new job in another city. Such problems demand a different kind of thinking: not a "higher" kind of thinking, but a different one.

Still a third model of "postformal" thinking comes from Patricia Arlin (1975, 1989, 1990). She refers to Piaget's formal operations stage as a stage of *problem solving* and argues that in adulthood there may be a further stage characterized by skill in *problem finding*. This new mode is helpful for problems that have no obvious solution or where there may be many possible solutions. It includes much of what others refer to as creativity. A person operating at this stage is able to generate many possible solutions to fuzzy problems or to see old problems in new ways. Arlin thinks that only a few adults actually achieve this level or stage of cognitive development, but that it represents a distinct fifth stage.

Wisdom. It is a popular notion that with age comes wisdom, and that this is a just compensation for losses that older people experience in other cognitive abilities. How true is this? Are there data to back this up? The answer to these questions is "we don't know" and "not much," respectively. Although there have been many theoretical papers published about the nature and acquisition of wisdom (Baltes, Smith, & Staudinger, 1992; Sternberg, 1990a), there have been few empirical studies done on the subject. In fact, there is little agreement about how to measure wisdom, in what behaviors wisdom would be displayed, and among which groups these behaviors would most likely be found (Schaie & Willis, 1996).

Paul Baltes and his colleagues (J. Smith and Baltes, 1990) have developed a definition of **wisdom** as an expert knowledge system about the pragmatics of life. They suggest five cognitive skills that are involved in wisdom: (1) *factual knowledge* about the present circumstances and the options available; (2) *procedural knowledge* about where to get information and how best to give advice; (3) *life-span contextualism* about the person's age and station in life; (4) *relativism* about the religious, spiritual, and cultural circumstances; and (5) *uncertainty* about the outcome and knowing that backup solutions may be necessary.

One recent empirical study by Francesca Happé and her colleagues (Happé, Winner, & Brownell, 1998) takes a little different tack by defining wisdom as an advanced ability to understand that each person has his or her own independent mental state and that behavior can be predicted and explained based on knowledge of those states. This ability, also known as **theory of mind,** has become a major research focus in developmental psychology during the past decade, although it has seldom been used to investigate adult cognition. The benefit of using this established concept to study wisdom is that the researchers can draw upon established definitions, measurement techniques, and a rich literature of previous research. The drawback is that it may not be a valid conceptual relationship.

In this experiment, a group of 19 older adults (61 to 80 years of age) and a group of 52 young adults (16 to 30 years of age) read two different types of short passages and answered questions about each passage immediately after reading it. The passages were either theory of mind stories (involving mental states such as making mistakes, telling white lies, bluffing) or control stories (not involving mental states such as people going to the hospital to get an x-ray after falling on the ice). To answer the questions correctly, subjects had to make inferences about the people in the story, but only the theory of mind stories

TABLE 5.2 **Results for Elderly and Young Groups by Story Condition**

Group	Theory of Mind Stories M	SD	Control Stories M	SD
Elderly (*n* = 19)	14.9**	1.2	12.4	2.2
Young (*n* = 67)	12.8	2.0	12.5	2.2

**Correlation significant at the 0.001 level.

Source: Adapted from Happé, Winner, & Brownell, 1998.

involved making inferences about their cognitive states or processes. Answers were scored for accuracy and completeness on a scale from 0 to 2, with 2 being the best. With eight stories in each group, the highest possible score was 16.

As you can see in Table 5.2, the older subjects scored significantly higher on the theory of mind stories than they did on the control stories. Older subjects also scored better on the theory of mind stories than did the young subjects, and the young subjects showed no differences in their answers to the theory of mind questions and the control questions. This study is a good demonstration that theory of mind ability is preserved in healthy older adults and superior when compared to both their own abilities on other types of cognitive tasks and the abilities of younger adults. This study documenting superior social reasoning by healthy older adults is the only study I have seen of this type and one of the few that looks at theory of mind in adults of different ages. Now whether this is wisdom, a component of wisdom, or an entirely different entity is another question. I would say that making valid inferences about other people's thoughts and feelings is a part of wisdom—an important part, but still just a part. Clearly, there is a lot more to find out.

CRITICAL THINKING

Suppose I were to argue, based on the data I've given you so far, that there ought to be an upper age limit for presidential candidates. Would you agree or disagree? Why?

CHANGES IN CREATIVITY AND PRODUCTIVITY

Although all of the changes I have been describing are of considerable interest, you may find the issues rather abstract. For many of us, the compelling question is not whether our reaction time slows by some fraction, but whether the cumulative changes in intellectual speed, power, or structure have any effect on our ability to do productive mental work as we get older. Do scientific breakthroughs—those rare, creative achievements—come mostly in early adulthood? Are older lawyers less effective advocates than younger ones? Do business executives have more difficulty solving problems later in life?

One of the most often cited studies on this topic was by Lehman (1953), who began by identifying major scientific breakthroughs and then asking how old each scientist had been at the time of the great discovery. He found that most of these discoveries were made by young adults, especially in science and mathematics. Einstein was 26 when he developed the special theory of relativity; the theory of natural selection was proposed by Darwin when he was 29.

But there is another way to ask the question that seems to me to be more relevant for those of us who are not in the same class as Einstein or Darwin: Over the adult life of the ordinary scientist or mathematician (or lawyer or businessperson or artist), does productivity, or quality of work, peak in the early years and then decline?

Dean Simonton (1991) approached the question by looking at the lifetime creativity and productivity of thousands of famous scientists from the nineteenth and earlier centuries. He identified the age at which each had done his or her first significant work, best or most famous work, and last work. The average age for the best work, in every discipline included in this unusual group, was about 40. But the curve was quite flat at the top. Most were still publishing significant work through their 40s and 50s. Simonton argues that the reason the best work is typically done at about age 40 is because that is the time when the largest quantity of work is done, and chance alone would suggest that the best work would be more likely at the time of peak productivity.

Studies of modern scientists show similar patterns (Simonton, 1989). For example, Karen Horner and her colleagues (Horner, Rushton, & Vernon, 1986) devised a cross-sequential study of the productivity of psychologists from four different cohorts: those born in 1909–1914, 1919–1924, 1929–1934, and 1939–1944. Horner examined the publication records of the more than 1000 academicians involved, with the results shown in Figure 5.8. Peak productivity occurred in midlife (35–44), but the major drop occurred only in the 65–74 period, which is postretirement age. And when you measure quality rather than mere quantity, such as by counting the number of times each paper is cited by peers, the quality remains high through the 50s and even into the 60s. Among creative artists, the quality of work may be maintained even longer. Simonton (1989) asked judges to rate the aesthetic qualities of the works of the 172 composers whose music is most often performed. Late-in-life works ("swan songs") were more likely than early works to be rated as masterpieces.

The conclusion here seems to be that high levels of creativity and effective problem solving can be maintained through middle adulthood, but there is likely to be a decline in both for many individuals past the age of 65 or 70. For those of you who thought people of 40 were intellectually over the hill, this may be a comforting conclusion.

SUMMARY OF AGE CHANGES IN INTELLECTUAL PERFORMANCE

I've given you myriad pieces of the puzzle. Now I need to try to create an overall picture, particularly in light of the long standing (and sometimes acrimonious) debate between those experts who have seen decline, and those who have seen maintenance and even improvement of intellectual abilities over the adult years. I think that we are reaching a point of empirical convergence in this debate, although there is still clearly a vast amount we do not yet understand. Here are the key points as I see them:

1. Most intellectual abilities are well maintained through early and middle adulthood, beginning to decline only in the 60s. The exceptions to this rule are some fluid abilities, especially those that require speed, which begin to decline earlier than this, and highly learned, well-rehearsed abilities such as vocabulary, which decline much later.

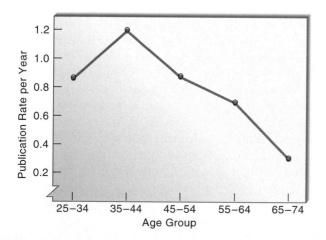

FIGURE 5.8 In this cross-sequential study, Horner and her colleagues examined the number of publications at each age for four cohorts of academic psychologists, born between 1909 and 1944.

Source: Horner, Rushton, & Vernon, 1986, Fig. 1, p. 321.

2. Although the declines are measurable (and statistically significant in the aggregate) in our 60s, they are initially small enough in most cases to have relatively little impact on our daily functioning. By our 70s and 80s, however, the declines have reached a sufficient magnitude that they may affect our ability to solve daily problems, to learn new things, to recall ordinary bits of information. Cognitive psychologists have found some training methods that seem to slow the age-related decline of cognitive abilities and even some that seem to bring improvement in functioning. In addition, external memory aids have been devised and human factors researchers are working on ways to improve products and instructions that will help older people perform their day-to-day activities despite decreased cognitive skills.

3. The most pervasive characteristic of this intellectual decline, and a major explanation of it, is a general slowing at the synaptic level, which affects virtually every type of intellectual activity. There is also a loss of working memory efficiency, although other factors, such as sensory, inhibition, and attention processes, are involved to a lesser extent.

4. Whether there are forms of intellectual activity unique to adulthood, such as practical or pragmatic intelligence, or wisdom, is simply not yet known.

5. All of the statements above are true only of the average. There are *wide* individual variations in timing and speed of intellectual decline—a subject I explore next in more depth.

INDIVIDUAL DIFFERENCES IN RATE OF COGNITIVE CHANGE IN ADULTHOOD

It would be difficult for me to exaggerate the extent of the individual variation in patterns of cognitive aging. For example, in the Seattle Longitudinal Study, although there were average declines on most measures in the 60s, at age 81 only about half of the individuals tested had shown a reliable decrement over the preceding seven-year period. The rest had maintained their level of skill, even in late old age (Schaie,1993).

You can get a further feeling for the variation from Figure 5.9, which shows scores on a vocabulary test for four different individuals from the Seattle study, each tested five times over 28 years (Schaie, 1989b). It does not take more than a glance at this figure to see that both the timing and the rapidity of the drop in vocabulary skill varied enormously.

Schaie doesn't tell us much about these individuals but he does give a few broad brush strokes. Subject A is a woman who has been a homemaker all her adult life; her husband is still alive and in good health. Subject B, in contrast, is a woman who worked as a teacher for a good portion of her life. After she turned 60, she divorced, retired, and began to experience significant health problems. Subject C is a man with a high school education who did clerical work most of his life. He showed essentially no change until his 70s, and again poor health may be implicated in this decline, since the final testing, at age 83, was only a year before his death. Finally, subject D is a man with a grade school education who had worked in a white-collar job. When he retired, his score on this test actually increased; it has gone down only at the latest assessment, at a time when he had recently become a widower and was experiencing health problems.

These brief profiles certainly point to health as a potentially major element in the individual differences equation. Other results from the Seattle study, as well as other longitudinal evidence, points to "exercise" —including mental activity of various kinds as well as physical exercise—as an important element as well.

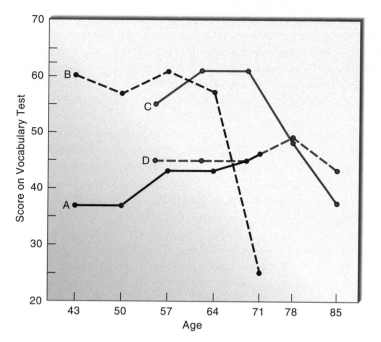

FIGURE 5.9 These four adults were all participants in the Seattle Longitudinal Study, and all had been tested five times, at seven-year intervals. There was obviously wide variation in the pattern of maintenance or decline of verbal abilities in this group.

Source: Schaie, 1989b, Figs. 5.13 and 5.14, pp. 82–83. Copyright 1989 by Springer Publishing Company, Inc. Used by permission of Springer Publishing Company, Inc., New York.

Health Effects

When I talk about the role of health in cognitive aging, there is a distinct echo from my earlier discussion of the link between health and physical aging. You'll remember from Chapter 3 that one of the key problems is to identify those aspects of physical change with age that are primary aging—inevitable in everyone—and those that are secondary, the results of disease. The same question returns here: How much of the average decline in mental abilities that I've been documenting is inevitable and linked to age, and how much is the result of disease?

The answer is similar, too: there is some of both. In general, unusually early or rapid decline in mental abilities is nearly always correlated with serious health problems. You can see an example of such a connection in Table 5.3, based on a survey of a representative

TABLE 5.3 **Relationship Between Self-Reported Health and Self-Reported Memory Problems (Percent)**

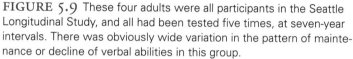

Self-Reported Health Health Compared to a Year Ago	Frequency of Trouble Remembering Things Compared to a Year Ago	
	More Often	**Same/Less Often**
Better	15.7	84.3
Same	13.1	86.9
Worse	42.9	57.1

Source: S. S. Cutler and Grams, 1988, Table 1, p. S85.

national sample of over 14,000 adults aged 55 and older. It's clear from the table that those adults who report that their health has worsened also report that their memory has worsened. But you can also see in the table that a health improvement wasn't associated with any improvement in memory. In general, within the range of fair to good health there was not a great deal of difference in reported memory problems. In other words, really poor health, or a recent rapid decline in health, seems to be associated with poorer mental performance.

Further support for this general conclusion comes from a 14-year longitudinal study of 90 of the parents of subjects who participated in the Berkeley studies. Dorothy Field and her colleagues (Field, Shaie, & Leino, 1988) found that knowing about a person's health in 1969, when the subjects were aged 59 to 79, did not predict that person's mental test scores 14 years later *except* for those at the extreme negative end of the distribution. Extremely poor health at the first test was associated with more mental decline over the 14 years. Other research confirms this and indicates that specific diseases, most notably Alzheimer's and cardiovascular disease, are also linked to earlier or more substantial cognitive declines (Schaie, 1983b; Schultz, Elias, Robbins, Streeten, & Blakeman, 1986).

At the same time, it is important to emphasize that the average decline in memory, in scores on speeded tests, and in problem-solving skills occurs even among adults who are free of apparent disease (Salthouse, 1991), just as primary physical aging occurs even among those who are otherwise healthy. Indeed, it seems very likely that this underlying primary physical aging is the *cause* of the basic changes in cognitive functioning that we see. Furthermore, variations in health within the normal range cannot account for variations in rate of cognitive loss or maintenance. To understand those variations, we will need to search further.

The Effects of Exercise

Another possible explanation of the wide individual differences in the pattern of cognitive aging may be mental or physical exercise, including not only aerobic exercise, but also taking classes, doing crossword puzzles, playing chess, reading the daily paper, or doing complex work. The basic hypothesis suggested by gerontologists and psychologists is that any intellectual ability that is used regularly will be maintained at a higher level, just as physically exercised bodies remain fitter. ("Use it or lose it" strikes again!). If that is true, individual adults who are more physically and intellectually active should show better maintenance of intellectual skill than should less active adults. Several strands of research support this hypothesis.

The Effects of Education. Education is the one factor that best predicts the rate of cognitive decline with age. All other things being equal, people with few years of formal education will show more cognitive decline as years go by than will their same-aged peers with more formal education. This evidence comes from the repeated finding that better educated adults not only perform intellectual tasks at a higher level but maintain their intellectual skill longer in old age (Jarvik & Bank, 1983; Palmore,1981; Schaie, 1983b), a pattern found in studies in Europe as well as the United States (Launer, Dinkgreve, Jonker, Hooijer, & Lindeboom, 1993).

There are several possible explanations of this correlation between education and maintenance of intellectual skill. The most obvious possibility is that it may not be education at all that is involved here, but underlying intellectual ability, leading both to more years of education and to better maintenance of intellectual skill in old age. A second explanation may lie in the fact that better educated people remain more intellectually active throughout their adult years. It may thus be the intellectual activity ("exercise" in the sense in which I have been using that term) that helps to maintain the mental skills.

The Effects of Intellectual Activity. Adults who read books, take classes, travel, attend cultural events, and participate in clubs or other groups seem to do better intellectually over time (Schaie, 1994). It is the more isolated and inactive adults (whatever their level of education) who show the most decline in IQ. In the Duke studies, for example (Busse & Wang, 1971), those adults who reported that they participated in many intellectual activities, which included reading, playing games, hobbies, and the like, actually showed a small but statistically significant *increase* in verbal skills over a six-year period, while those who were intellectually inactive showed a significant decline.

Cross-sectional studies show much the same thing. For example, Keith Stanovich and colleagues (Stanovich, West, & Harrison, 1995) compared the cognitive abilities of college students and older adults and then analyzed the difference in terms of how much reading the participants do. This is different than reading *ability* because some people who have high reading ability actually do little reading, and vice versa. Results showed that some cognitive abilities (crystallized, practiced skills such as cultural literacy and vocabulary) were better explained by how much a subject read than by how old the subject was, even when education level and general cognitive ability were controlled. This relationship was not evident for fluid, unpracticed skills such as working memory and syllogistic reasoning.

Arthur Shimamura and colleagues (Shimamura, Berry, Mangels, Rusting, & Jurica, 1995) demonstrated this point by testing the cognitive skills of a group of Princeton professors who were between 30 and 71 years of age and had between 21 and 22 years of education. Although the older professors showed lower scores on some types of cognitive abilities (reaction time, remembering word pairs), they did as well as the younger professors on a complex test of working memory that required them to discriminate between 16 different visual patterns over a period of time and also on a test of memory for written passages of different types. Since these abilities are known to decline with age in studies of standard groups of older adults, the authors offer two possible explanations: Mental activity reduces the changes in the brain that normally occur with age, or that the changes occur in everyone, but those who are mentally active are better able to compensate for some of those changes by using other abilities that have not declined.

In another study, researchers found that older adults who play bridge regularly have higher scores than those of nonbridge players on tests of memory and reasoning. The two groups did not differ in health, education, physical exercise levels, or life satisfaction, and they did not differ in their performance on other measures of cognitive functioning, such as reaction time or vocabulary size. Only on measures of those intellectual skills that might be sharpened by regular bridge playing did they show better scores (Clarkson-Smith & Hartley, 1990). Results such as these point to the possibility that there is no overall "intellectual fitness" that can be increased by any one of a variety of activities. Instead, each intellectual activity may require individual practice or rehearsal for maximum maintenance.

The Effects of Physical Exercise. The case for a causal link between physical exercise and intellectual skill is a bit stronger, although still not robust. The fundamental argument, of course, is that exercise helps to maintain cardiovascular (and possibly neural) fitness, which we know is linked to mental maintenance. And when researchers have compared mental performance scores for highly physically active and sedentary older adults, they have consistently found that the more active people have higher scores. For instance, Louise Clarkson-Smith and Alan Hartley (1989) compared 62 highly physically active and 62 inactive adults, all between the ages of 55 and 88. These active adults re-

CRITICAL THINKING

Can you think of an experimental design to test the proposition that mental activity sustains mental functioning in late adulthood? Do you think it would work simply to ask groups to read a newspaper every day, or to do a certain number of crossword puzzles daily? What might be the problems with research of this type?

ported an average of more than five hours of strenuous exercise or activity each week, including gardening and heavy housework as well as traditional aerobic exercise. In contrast, the low-activity group reported zero hours per week of such strenuous pastimes. The high-activity group scored consistently higher on tests of reasoning, short-term memory, and reaction time, and this was true even when the comparisons included only those subjects who were exceptionally healthy and when the two groups were matched for education.

A longitudinal study by Robert Rogers and his colleagues points us in the same direction (R. L. Rogers, Meyer, & Mortel, 1990). They followed a group of 85 men from age 65 to age 69. All had been in good health at the beginning of the study, and all were highly educated. During the four years of the study, some of these men chose to continue working, some retired but remained physically active, and some retired and adopted a sedentary lifestyle. When these three groups were compared at the end of the study on a battery of cognitive tests, the inactive group performed significantly worse, as you can see in Figure 5.10.

Of course (as many of you will have figured out yourselves), there is a difficulty built into these studies and the many others like them, despite the researchers' care in matching the active and inactive groups for education and health. These groups are self-selected rather than randomly assigned. The active group *chose* to be active, and it remains possible that those adults who are already functioning at higher intellectual levels are sim-

IT MAKES SENSE that the older adult in the photo on the left, who is still mentally active, will stay alert and have better mental functioning longer than the less active woman in the photo on the right. Longitudinal research supports this hypothesis, but of course it is possible that the causality is complex: Those adults who are initially more intellectually able are likely to remain mentally active longer and have generally had more education as well.

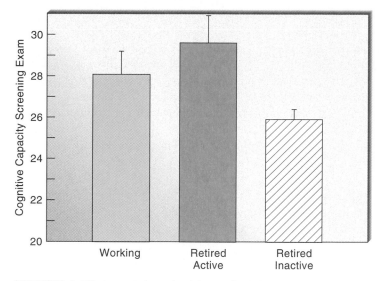

FIGURE 5.10 Among these healthy, well-educated men in their 60s, those who became physically inactive after retirement performed significantly worse on measures of cognitive functioning four years later.

Source: R. L. Rogers, J. S. Meyer, & K. F. Mortel, 1990, After reaching retirement age physical activity sustains cerebral perfusion and cognition, *Journal of the American Geriatric Society, 38,* 123–28. Figure 2, p. 126. Reprinted by permission of Williams & Wilkins.

ply more likely to choose to maintain their physical fitness. A better test would be an experiment in which healthy, sedentary adults are randomly assigned to exercise or nonexercise groups and then tested over a period of time.

Results from such experimental studies of exercise are highly mixed. Some find that the exercise group improves or maintains mental test scores better than the unexercising control group (e.g., Hawkins, Kramer, & Capaldi, 1992; R. D. Hill, Storandt, & Malley, 1993) while others do not (e.g., Buchner, Beresford, Larson, LaCroix, & Wigner, 1992; Emery & Gatz, 1990; Madden, Blumenthal, Allen, & Emery, 1989). There is some indication that positive effects of physical exercise on mental performance are more likely when the exercise program lasts for a longer period of time, such as a year or more, although there are not many data to rely on here (Buchner et al., 1992).

Environmental Complexity. A fourth piece of our puzzle comes from work of Melvin Kohn and Carmi Schooler (Kohn, 1978, 1980; Schooler, 1990), who have shown in a series of studies that the more complex the environment a person lives or works in, the greater the intellectual flexibility that person develops. In one study, they interviewed a group of men twice over a 10-year interval, assessing each subject's intellectual flexibility as well as the complexity of the work the man was then doing. Work complexity was measured by asking each subject to describe precisely what he did with written materials or data, what he did with his hands, and what he did with people. The complexity of each of these facets of each man's job was then rated.

Kohn and Schooler found that both intellectual flexibility and job complexity were highly stable over the 10-year period. A man who had been high in intellectual flexibility at the first interview was likely to be high at the second interview as well, and a man with a complex job at time 1 was likely to have a complex job 10 years later. But there were also some fascinating connections between the two measures.

First, greater intellectual flexibility led to higher job complexity. That is, men who were high in flexibility in 1964, when the first interview was completed, had more complex jobs 10 years later than did those men whose initial intellectual flexibility was lower. But second, those men who were employed at complex jobs became more intellectually flexible. So job complexity helped to *foster* intellectual flexibility, and greater intellectual flexibility then led to more complex jobs. In subsequent studies, Kohn and Schooler have found the same kinds of links for women, both those who work in the home and those who work outside the home (Schooler, 1990).

If we add these findings to what I have already said about individual differences in intellectual performance in adulthood, an intricate chain of influences is apparent. The starting points are a key part of the equation: Adults who begin with high levels of intellectual flexibility (or who are better educated or who have higher intellectual ability) are likely to end up in more complex, intellectually demanding jobs. They may continue their education in order to advance in those jobs. The complexity of the job, in turn, stimulates or maintains intellectual flexibility, so the adult reads more, discusses issues more, and thinks more about options and possibilities. Barring significant disease, these adults have a good chance of maintaining their intellectual power well into old age. In contrast, those who begin their adult years with lower levels of education or intellectual flexibility are funneled into less complex and demanding jobs. Such jobs do not provide much mental challenge, so there is little growth of mental flexibility or skill, and in later years, perhaps less maintenance of intellectual abilities.

At any point along the way, however, it looks as if the trajectory can be altered by increasing the complexity of one's overall environment, such as increasing physical or mental exercise, by moving into a more complex job, or by going back to school. I do not think that there is infinite flexibility here, nor that the "fall of the sands through the hourglass" can be halted or reversed simply by reading the newspaper every day, teaching yourself a foreign language, or memorizing telephone numbers. But there is at least suggestive evidence that all of these activities help to maintain intellectual abilities in the later years of adulthood.

REVIEW OF AGE PATTERNS AND A SEARCH FOR BALANCE

As in Chapter 4, I have summarized the various age changes in intellectual functioning in a table (Table 5.4). Although many of the losses in memory, problem solving, and other skills become functionally significant only in late adulthood, there is no gainsaying the existence of loss or decline, particularly a loss of basic speed, with all that entails. But what is the best way for us to talk and think about these changes? Paul Baltes, a key figure in research on aging, takes the position that we should by now be beyond the simple issue of "growth versus decline." Instead, he suggests that we ought to be talking about "potentials and limits" (Baltes, 1993).

Using a computer analogy, Baltes suggests that what he calls **cognitive mechanics,** the hardware of mental activity, declines or becomes less efficient with age, while **cognitive pragmatics,** the software of cognition, can be maintained or even improved throughout life. I am not sure I am entirely persuaded by the optimistic and positive picture that Baltes lays out. It is true that older adults can improve their functioning with training and can continue to learn new skills. But I believe that as the hardware becomes less efficient, it sets limits on the software as well. Still, Baltes's view gives us a needed balance with which to end this chapter. The process of cognitive aging is not or need not be entirely a story of losses. Plasticity—the capacity for new learning—remains.

CRITICAL THINKING

If you were asked to write a 25-word description of age changes in intellectual skill, what would you write? How positive or negative would your summary be? How confident do you feel in this summary statement?

TABLE 5.4 Summary of Age Changes in Intellectual Skills

Age 20–40	Age 40–65	Age 65–75	Age 75+
Peak intellecutal performance in both fluid and crystallized intelligence.	Maintenance of skill on measures of verbal, unspeeded, or crystallized intelligence; some decline of skill on measures of performance, speeded, or fluid IQ, although decline is not usually functionally significant in these years.	Among adults with major health problems, significant decline may be seen in these years, although usually not on measures of crystallized ability; on average, measurable and functionally significant decline occurs at about age 70.	Accelerating decline on most measures of cognitive skill, although there are many elders who show no decline or only very slight decline on measures of crystallized ability.
Optimum performance on memory tasks.	Reaction time declines gradually, which has some effect on memory skills, but not usually to a functionally significant degree.	Considerable slowing and less efficient memory processes notable in most adults in this age range.	Acceleration of memory problems, including loss of speed, with all that entails.
Peak performance on laboratory measures of problem solving.	Peak performance on real-life problem-solving tasks.	Decline in problem-solving skills on both laboratory and real-life problems.	Still further decline in problem-solving skills.
Peak in quantity of creative output.	Lessening of quantity of creative output, but no loss of quality.	Rapid decline in quantity; not clear if the quality declines, at least not in all areas.	Occasional examples of highly creative work still done in these years, such as among composers or artists.

SUMMARY

1. Correlational consistency of IQ is very high throughout adulthood. That is, a person's relative position in a group based on IQ score remains very much the same over time.

2. Cross-sectional comparisons of total IQ scores across the adult years show a decline beginning in the 30s or 40s; longitudinal studies show maintenance of IQ until approximately age 60, after which there is a decline.

3. Analyses of subscores of IQ tests suggest that performance on speeded, or nonverbal, or "fluid" tests declines earlier, perhaps as early as age 45 or 50, while performance on nonspeeded, verbal, "crystallized" tests show little decline until perhaps age 65 or 70. Training studies have demonstrated successful reversal of decline in some mental abilities.

4. Age changes in memory are observed in both short- and long-term memory, but are stronger in the latter. Both the encoding and retrieval processes become slower and less efficient. Older adults often do not use effective memory strategies, and although their performance improves with training, younger adults gain more from training.

5. Age differences in memory are found on most everyday tests of memory, as well as on standardized laboratory tasks.

6. The dominant explanation of these changes in memory emphasizes the role of a generalized slowing at the neural level. There may also be some loss of the capacity of working memory.

7. Problem-solving performance also shows changes in the 60s or 70s, with older adults using less effective strategies, even with familiar, real-life problems.

8. Human factors research has focused on the everyday problem solving of older adults with the goal of helping them maintain independent living. Some of the results are improved labels for prescriptions and better instructions for computer use.

9. New forms of logic or new ways of thinking about problems, including what we might call wisdom, may develop in adulthood, although the data on this point are limited.

10. Studies of real-life intellectual or artistic productivity suggest that quantity declines but quality does not, at least through the years of the normal working life.

11. In all the research, there are large individual differences in the timing and extent of intellectual maintenance or loss.

12. Markedly poor health is nearly always implicated in very early or very rapid declines in intellectual functioning. Within the more normal range of health the link is less clear.

13. Those adults who maintain higher levels of physical and mental activity (who "exercise" their minds) show slower rates of intellectual decline in old age. Since mentally active adults tend also to be better educated and higher in IQ in early adulthood, the causal links are not yet clear. Work complexity, however, appears to have a causal effect on intellectual flexibility.

KEY TERMS

intelligence	fluid intelligence	recall
g	crystallized intelligence	sensory memory
IQ	verbal meaning	short-term memory
correlational consistency	spatial orientation	long-term memory
consistency in absolute level	inductive reasoning	external memory aids
attrition	number	ecologically significant
verbal IQ	word fluency	meta-analysis
performance IQ	memory	speed of processing
full-scale IQ	encoding	working memory
speeded tasks	storage	problem solving
unspeeded tasks	retrieval	human factors research
	recognition	

medication nonadherence

cognitive structure

concrete operational
level

formal operational level

contextual validity

dialectical thought

wisdom

theory of mind

cognitive mechanics

cognitive pragmatics

SUGGESTED READINGS

Fisk, A. D., & Rogers, W. A. (Eds.). (1997). *Handbook of human factors and the older adult.* San Diego, CA: Academic Press.

> Collection of articles by cognitive psychologists on the topic of human factors research.

Gill, B. (1996). *Late bloomers.* New York: Artisan.

> Short biographies of 75 remarkable individuals whose greatest achievements were accomplished in the second half of their lives, including the painter Edward Hopper and the composer Charles Ives. Although this does not seem to be the typical pattern for group averages, it shows that there is a lot of variation in "blooming" time.

Leviton, R. (1995). *Brain builders! A lifelong guide to sharper thinking, better memory, and an age-proof mind.* Englewood Cliffs, NJ: Prentice Hall.

> Over 100 simple, effective techniques that people of all ages can use to retain and improve their intelligence, memories, and problem-solving skills. This book includes information on practically every cognitive aid that has ever been discussed—from yoga, to nutrition supplements, to study skills, to aroma therapy. The reader needs to pick and choose, but many proven methods are included and described in a very readable format.

or being more self-sufficient at midlife). The former involve changes in mastery or adaptation; the latter involve changes in status or meaning and are more profound and difficult.

Collectively, these social roles, in whatever combination or sequence, form a kind of lattice, a framework for the life structure each of us creates. Upon that lattice many specific shapes may be built, but the framework still sets certain limits or creates certain opportunities. So it is important for us to understand something about how those roles change with age and about the nature of the framework that accompanies each of the major social roles of adulthood.

It is also important to realize that the pattern of social roles is somewhat different for men and women—and this is still true in American society despite enormous changes in gender roles in the past few decades. **Gender roles** are culturally defined, and they shift as the culture shifts. But every society has *some* form of gender roles—some "job description" for men and women that includes expected behaviors and qualities. For example, in today's Western cultures, it is part of the female job description to provide aid to a frail, aging parent.

To understand the social role structure of adult life, then, we need to look at the age-linked social clock and at the varying gender roles within each period of adult life. I explore the personal relationships within those social and gender roles in Chapter 7, and then return to the description of adult roles patterns in Chapter 8, where the topic of work roles will be the central focus. Here let me begin with a brief look at what we know about gender roles and stereotypes in a general sense before looking at age changes in social roles.

GENDER ROLES AND STEREOTYPES IN ADULTHOOD

It is useful to distinguish between gender roles and **gender stereotypes.** The former describe what men and women actually do in a given culture in a given historical era; the latter refers to sets of shared, often quite inflexible beliefs about what men and women *ought* to do, how they *should* behave, what traits they *all* have, according to their gender. The presence of gender stereotypes is particularly evident when we make assumptions about the characteristics or behavior of an unknown person based solely on his or her gender. When we do this, we move from descriptions of what men and women typically do, to assumptions about what men and women *are* or are *supposed* to be. In the process we exaggerate both the similarities within each gender group and the differences between them.

Content of Gender Stereotypes

We know a good deal more about the content of the gender stereotypes than we do about actual gender roles, in part because the roles themselves are different among various subcultures and are changing rapidly while the stereotypes have remained remarkably stable over the past decades, even though things have changed immensely for women during that time. Gender stereotypes are also remarkably consistent across cultures.

The most comprehensive evidence comes from John Williams and Deborah Best (1990), who have looked at stereotypes in 25 different countries, including countries from every continent, both First World and Third World. In each country, college students were given a list of 300 adjectives (translated into the local language where necessary), and for each adjective the subject was to say whether it was more frequently associated with men, more frequently associated with women, or not differentially associated with either. The students were told that they were serving as reporters on their culture rather than expressing their own personal opinions.

Williams and Best found a striking degree of agreement across cultures. In at least 23 of the 25 countries, two-thirds or more of the respondents listed the following as male

CRITICAL
THINKING

What new roles have you acquired in the past five years or the past 10 years? What new demands did those roles make on you? What kind of changes did they require?

qualities: active, adventurous, aggressive, autocratic, courageous, daring, dominant, enterprising, forceful, independent, masculine, progressive, robust, rude, severe, stern, strong, unemotional, and wise. Similarly, the following qualities were a part of the female stereotype in 23 of the 25 countries: Affectionate, attractive, dependent, dreamy, emotional, fearful, feminine, sensitive, sentimental, softhearted, submissive, superstitious, and weak. In some countries rather different male and female stereotypes were obtained. For example, in Nigeria, students rated the adjectives *arrogant, lazy, robust,* and *rude* as being female qualities, even though these are typically male items in other cultures. Similarly, in Japan, *boastful, disorderly,* and *obnoxious* were associated with women, while in France *sympathetic* was associated with men. But these exceptions were quite rare. What is striking is how common the pattern is across cultures. The common male stereotype is centered around a set of qualities often labeled **instrumental,** including competence and agency, while the female stereotype centers around qualities of affiliation and expressiveness, often referred to as **communal** (Huyck, 1990; Turner & Turner, 1994).

Pervasive as these stereotypes are, it is important to realize that adults do not perceive them as entirely either/or propositions. In Williams and Best's study, the respondent was forced to place each item in one of three categories: male, female, or neutral. But when adults are asked to state a *probability* that men and women could have certain qualities, certain role behaviors, and certain physical characteristics, it becomes clear that the two stereotypes overlap more than the Williams and Best lists would suggest. Table 6.1 shows some results from Kay Deaux's (1984) research that illustrates the point.

If you look at the table carefully, though, you'll see that Deaux's subjects made sharper distinctions between male and female role behaviors than between male and female personality traits, a pattern Deaux has found in other studies as well (Kite, Deaux, & Miele, 1991). Personality traits overlap substantially, while role behaviors are seen as more separate. Even though the great majority of adult women are now employed for pay, the gender stereotype still contains the information that the man is the "financial provider" and the woman "cooks the meals" and "takes care of the children."

TABLE 6.1 **Gender Stereotypes: Probability That the Average Man or Woman Will Show a Particular Trait, Behavior, or Physical Characteristic, According to Adult Raters**

Characteristic	Judged Probability	
	Men	Women
Trait		
Independent	0.78	0.58
Competitive	0.82	0.64
Warm	0.66	0.77
Emotional	0.56	0.84
Role behaviors		
Financial provider	0.83	0.47
Takes initiative with opposite sex	0.82	0.54
Takes care of children	0.50	0.85
Cooks meals	0.42	0.83
Physical characteristics		
Muscular	0.64	0.36
Deep voice	0.73	0.30
Graceful	0.45	0.68
Small-boned	0.39	0.62

Source: Deaux, 1984. Reprinted by permission of the author.

Sources of Gender Stereotypes

Where might such stereotypes come from? One theory, the **social roles interpretation,** is that gender role stereotypes are the result of the division of labor within a culture (Eagly, 1987). According to this theory, everyone in the culture observes women carrying out communal roles, such as preparing food and taking care of the children, and men carrying out instrumental roles, such as providing and protecting the family. As a result, they expect themselves and others to be either communal or instrumental, depending on their gender, and they think of the skills that are required for these jobs as being "male" or "female," depending on who they see doing the jobs. Young girls are taught to be communal and young boys are taught to be instrumental.

In the **learning schema explanation** of gender stereotypes, the source is thought to be our own cognitive processes. Bem (1993) suggests that we are taught early to view the world and ourselves through gender schemas, or lenses, which are **gender polarized.** This means that we view the world in a distorted way by making artificial or exaggerated distinctions between what is considered male and what is considered female. Some people exaggerate these distinctions more than others and are considered to be **conventionally gendered.** In studies by Bem and others (Bem, 1981; Frable, 1989; Frable & Bem, 1985) participants who fit this category are more apt to avoid gender-inappropriate tasks, are better able to differentiate between people of their own gender than people of the opposite gender, cluster words according to masculine or feminine connotations, and accept gender stereotypes as real gender differences than do participants who are considered to be **nonconventionally gendered.**

In this theory, gender schemas, besides causing us to polarize gender differences, also cause us to be **androcentric.** This means that we not only see the world as being divided between male and female realms, we also have learned to value the male realm more than the female realm. Bem (1993) gives the example that many people, including psychologists, define the roles of a "mature, healthy adult" to include being a spouse or partner in a relationship, being a parent, and having a job. However, when asked about "women" who are married, have children, and work, these same people express concerns over the stress and strain that three roles would entail. In other words, there is a difference between a mature healthy *adult* and a mature health *woman,* with women being considered as less able to handle their expected roles. (As you will see in later parts of this chapter, these concerns about women's abilities to handle multiple roles are not well founded.)

The two theories above suggest that gender roles come from external sources, either based on divisions we observe in our culture or attitudes we are taught by parents, teachers, and the media. The third example is a theory from **evolutionary psychology.** This type of explanation holds that gender stereotypes come from within the individual and reflect actual behaviors that are programmed in the genes of the human species. Buss (1991) states that gender roles are psychological behaviors that evolved as solutions to problems our ancestors have faced over millions of years. Females and males are genetically predisposed to behave in different ways. Briefly, females who inherited genes for traits such as being nurturant and being attracted to males who are good providers were more successful in surviving and raising children (to pass along their successful genes). Males, on the other hand, survived and passed on their genes to the next generation if they were competitive and were attracted to females who looked fertile and behaved as though they would be faithful to them (Shackelford & Buss, 1997).

Although these three explanations of gender stereotypes are useful for understanding different viewpoints, it is not necessary to prove one or the other to be "right." Gender is one of the most complex topics in psychology, and we are not anywhere near a complete explanation for any of its manifestations in our lives.

C RITICAL
T HINKING

Do these theories make sense to you? Why or why not? Can you think of another explanation for the consistency of gender roles across cultures?

SOCIAL ROLES IN EARLY ADULTHOOD

Even in the midst of all the cultural changes in the United States and other Western countries over the past few decades—the huge increases in women's labor force participation, the percentages of infants born to unmarried mothers, the rise in cohabitation, the delaying of childbearing for many—it is still incontrovertibly true that more major social roles are acquired in the years of early adulthood than in any other period of adult life. Demographer Ronald Rindfuss (1991) refers to this as a time of **demographic density.** Figure 6.1 shows four separate patterns of change that peaks in early adulthood and then what they look like combined, illustrating the density of role changes clearly.

The *sequence* in which the various roles are taken up varies enormously. Some people complete school, get married, and then have a first child—the "traditional" sequence. Some give birth before they complete school and never marry; some marry before completing school, and so on. But it is still true that the great majority of adults take on most, if not all, of four major social roles in these early years: independent adult, spouse/partner, parent, and worker.

Leaving Home

For many, the first step in the process of role change in early adulthood is leaving home. In earlier cohorts in the United States, and still in many cultures around the world, the typical pattern was that young people remained at home until they married, which meant that independent adulthood and marriage occurred together. But in current cohorts of young people in many industrialized countries, these two role changes are much more often separated, with young people first moving out of their parents' home and living independently for some period of time and then moving in with a spouse or partner.

The most detailed analysis of leaving patterns come from Arland Thornton (Thornton, Young-Demarco, & Goldscheider, 1993), who has retrospective information on a group of 932 young people who were 23 in 1985. Each subject was asked to describe the entire sequence of living arrangements he or she had had since age 15. By age 23, only about a third of these young adults were still living at home. At 18 and 19, the most common nonparental living arrangement was "group quarters" of some kind, which includes dormitories or army barracks; at 20 and 21, living with housemates was common, and marriage began to account for a portion of the nonparental arrangement by age 21 or so. A few had had a child and lived separately as a single parent.

Other studies of the home-leaving process suggest that young people from single-parent homes are likely to move into independent living at somewhat earlier ages, while African-Americans move later. In particular, African-American women are much less likely to move into marriage, although they are just about as likely as are whites to move into other living arrangements away from the parental home (Buck & Scott, 1993). The parents' attitude or expectations also make some difference; those parents who expect their offspring to become independent at an early age generally have children who do indeed move out of the family home somewhat sooner (Goldscheider & Goldscheider, 1993).

In the last two decades researchers have noted an increase in the number of young adults who move *back* to their parents' homes after a period of independent living. William Aquilano (1996) examined data from a national study of over 13,000 households and found that 44 percent of young adults between 19 and 24 years of age had returned home to their parents after living apart for some time. This was more apt to happen to men than women, and most likely to happen within two years of leaving home for the first time. Furthermore, a quarter of these "returned" adult children left and returned a second time.

What all of this suggests is that the process of moving from childhood to independent adult status has become more complex, perhaps fuzzier than it used to be, with more intermediate steps, more transitional roles, and more choices for the individual young adult.

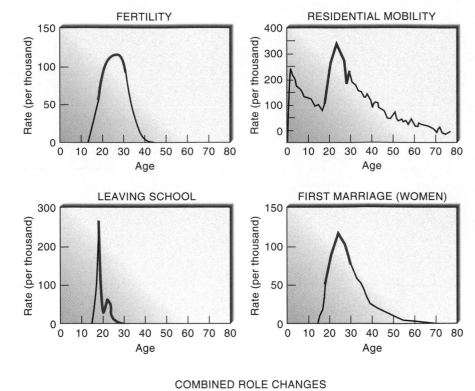

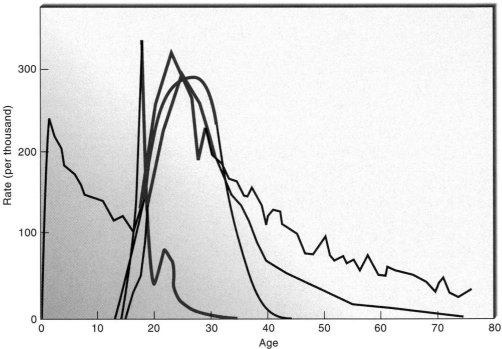

FIGURE 6.1 The pileup of role changes in early adulthood is clear in these data from Rindfuss's analysis. Each of four changes is shown individually in the top panels, and then combined in the lower figure.

Source: Rindfuss, 1991, Fertility and Residential Mobility panels from Fig. 1, p. 496, Leaving School and First Marriage panels from Fig. 2, p. 497, and a slightly adapted version of Fig. 3, p. 498.

Becoming a Spouse or Partner

Although marriage remains the traditional form of partnering in the United States and around the world, the proportion of people who marry is decreasing, while the age at which they marry is increasing. The proportion of adults 25 to 39 years of age who are single and have never married has doubled in the last two decades, and tripled for some age subgroups, while the age of first marriage has risen in that time about three years to 26.5 for men and 24.5 for women (R. L. Taylor, 1997).

Does this mean that young adults have changed, staying single longer and not forming relationships? The answer is no, because during the same time period, the proportion of young adults who are living together in unmarried relationships (or cohabiting) has increased. Thus the biggest change has not been in the number or timing of young adults' partnerships but in the *types* of partnerships that young adults form.

The number of unmarried couples living together in the United States has increased dramatically since the 1960s, as you can see from Figure 6.2. Although couples of all ages cohabit, about 40 percent of these couples are under 25, and for over 1 million of them, cohabitation is a kind of intermediate step in the process of acquiring the role of spouse. Kiernan and Estaugh (1993) have called these couples the "nubile cohabitants": youthful, never married, childless couples who seem to have simply taken their serious dating relationship "to the next level" and who may or may not decide to get married at some unspecified later date. Most of the couples who cohabit on the way to marriage are white, but African-American couples have a greater rate of cohabitation, with Hispanic couples being less likely to cohabit.

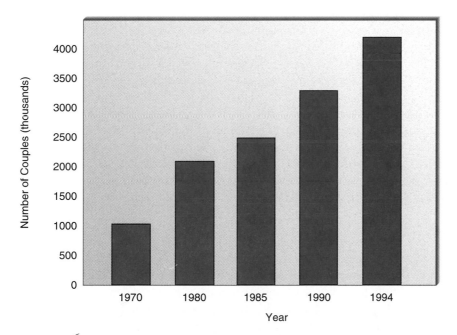

FIGURE 6.2 The number of unmarried U.S. couples of all ages living together has increased dramatically since 1970.

Source: U.S. Bureau of the Census, 1995.

Gender Roles Within Early Marriage/Partnership. Whether a young person cohabits first or moves directly into a marriage, it is clear that the acquisition of this new role brings profound changes to many aspects of the person's life. One of those major changes is in gender roles. Men's and women's roles are probably more egalitarian at the beginning of a marriage or partnership, before children are born, than at any time until late adulthood. But that does not mean that the traditional division of labor, so long a part of the gender roles in our culture, has no impact. It clearly does. Although researchers have found that men do more than their share to foster the relationship in the early stages (having the role of **relationship initiators**), women do more once they have settled into relationship routines (having the role of **relationship maintainers**). Does it work? Yes, the couples who have the most maintenance behaviors are also apt to report the most affection toward each other and the most satisfaction with their relationship (Winstead, Derlega, & Rose, 1997).

To add more support to this, Kirkpatrick and Davis (1992) investigated relationship success in people who fit gender stereotypes and those who did not. Men are stereotyped as avoiding serious relationships, and women are stereotyped as being anxious and preoccupied with relationships. If these are adaptive behaviors, there should be a difference in the relationship success of young adults who fit these stereotypes and those who do not. This is exactly what was found. Avoidant men and anxious women showed higher relationship stability than those who went against the stereotypes, anxious men and avoidant women. A caution is in order here, though, because relationship stability just means staying together, not necessarily being satisfied or happy in the relationship.

Household tasks also tend to divide along traditional gender lines, with women doing more of the cooking and cleaning, and men more of the grass cutting, household repairs, and auto maintenance. Even in this relatively egalitarian early period of marriage, wives still perform more total hours of household work than do their husbands, even when both are employed (Winstead et al., 1997).

Anthropologist David Gutmann points out that this division of labor in the man/woman relationship has an ancient (and honorable) history. In the days when tribal warfare was the rule, it was far more critical that the women be protected than the men. The women bore the children, cared for them in their dependent years, and thus bore the future of the tribe or group. So the women were literally placed "in the center." The men, with their greater physical strength, protected the borders and drove off invaders. Women were turned inward, men outward; women were in charge of care, men of protection.

Even though the need for physical protection from marauders is long gone, Gutmann argues that we still retain the sense that the woman's proper place in an intimate relationship or within the family is "at the center." She is the hearth, the heart; the man is the power, the strength. To be sure, there has been a great deal of change in this pattern in recent years. But the ancient history of men's and women's roles within relationships is not easy to abandon—as anyone who has attempted an egalitarian relationship can tell you.

Happiness and Health. A second effect of marriage is to bring an increase in happiness or well-being. The correlation is not huge, but it has been found again and again in different cohorts and different ethnic groups (Broman, 1988; Haring-Hildore, Stock, Okun, & Witter, 1985). There is also abundant evidence that, compared to single adults, married adults are physically healthier, live longer, and are less prone to depression and other forms of psychiatric disturbances (Gove, 1972; Hu & Goldman, 1990; D. G. Williams, 1988), a pattern that has been found in many developed countries.

Of course, such a difference could be the result of self-selection processes. If mentally and physically healthier adults are more likely to get married, the least healthy and poorest-functioning adults would be left in the "single" group. There is some indication that self-selection processes work in this way for men, but probably not for women. Since in this culture men tend to marry "down" the social class ladder and women tend to marry "up," unmarried women are likely to be relatively well educated, with above-average IQs and white-collar jobs, while unmarried men are likely to have more average IQs and to be less well educated.

An alternative explanation of the relationship between marriage and health focuses on the role of **social support,** defined as the combination of affect, affirmation, and aid that people receives from those around them (R. L. Kahn & Antonucci, 1980). We know that high levels of social support are associated with lower rates of physical disease and emotional disturbance (a relationship I discuss more fully in Chapter 11). Since getting married increases the available social support for most people, we should expect that married adults would be healthier than unmarried adults, which they are. We should also expect that married adults who have more supportive relationships with their spouses would have better mental health than those who receive less support, a pattern confirmed in a large study by Dorie G. Williams (1988).

Finally, if social support is the critical ingredient in making marriage a healthier state than singleness, we should expect quite high rates of physical and mental illness among divorced adults, who experience a marked loss in social support, and lower rates among those single adults who have an alternative source of social support. Researchers have found precisely these patterns. In general, rates of physical and mental illness are higher among the divorced than among the never married (Weingarten, 1985). And among single adults, they are lower for those who have some other (nonspouse) adult living with them, whether that second adult is a roommate, a parent, a grown child, or some other person (Anson, 1989).

The emotional and physical benefits of the spouse role, however, do not seem to be evenly divided between men and women. In the majority of studies, married men are found to have better physical and mental health than married women. Walter Gove (1972, 1979) suggested some years ago that this difference arises because the roles of husband and wife (in Western cultures, at least) are unequal in support, burdens, or gratification. For example, part of the wife's role is to provide nurturance and emotional support to all other family members, but the husband's role includes a lesser expectation of support toward the wife. In addition, the wife role is lower in status and higher in the number of unpleasant or routine jobs than is the husband role. Thus men find marriage to be a better buffer against the slings and arrows of normal life than do women.

CRITICAL THINKING

Do you think Gove is correct? Can you think of a way you might test this hypothesis?

Overall, given the existing role definitions of male and female roles and of spousal roles, the transition to marriage appears to be particularly beneficial for men: Married men show the lowest rates of illness or disturbances, while unmarried men (never married or divorced) show the highest. Married and unmarried women fall in between. But as role definitions change, these gender differences may change as well.

Becoming a Parent

The second major new role acquired by the great majority of us in the years of early adulthood is that of parent. Roughly 90 percent of adults in the United States will eventually become parents, most often in their 20s or 30s. For most of us, the arrival of the first child brings deep satisfaction, an enhanced feeling of self-worth, perhaps a sense of being grown up for the first time. In one early study, four-fifths of adults said that their lives had been changed for the better by the arrival of children (Hoffman & Manis, 1978). But the birth of the first child also involves a profound role change, often accompanied by considerable role strain.

Some Demographics. Just as marriage has been occurring later and later in the United States and other industrialized societies, so has the timing of the first birth been more and more delayed in recent years, especially compared to the pattern typical between

1945 and 1965, as is very clear from Figure 6.3. Many more women today are delaying their first child into their 30s, and the probability of a first birth by age 20 has dropped dramatically.

These overall trends seem very clear, but as usual with such sweeping generalizations, there are many exceptions. First, the pattern of delayed birth is far more true of white women than of African-American women (Chen, & Morgan, 1991). Second, it is important to emphasize that an increasing percentage of births (at least in the United States) are to women who have never been married. In 1990, 28 percent of all births in the United States (20 percent among whites and 65 percent among blacks) were to unmarried mothers, compared to 11 percent in 1970 (U.S. Bureau of the Census, 1993). Don't jump to the conclusion, by the way, that these are all or mostly unwed teenagers. Only a third of the births to unmarried mothers in present cohorts are to women 19 and younger.

These changes in the likelihood of marriage and the timing of birth are not just curiosities, of interest only to demographers. They have profound effects not only on society as a whole, but also on the pattern of adult life that a given person, or a given cohort, may expect to have. Never-married mothers and divorced mothers rearing their children alone face a variety of exceptional challenges, including considerably lower income and fewer job options. And those who delay childbearing change the timing of many subsequent life events.

For example, compare the experience of a woman born in the 1910–1919 cohort to one born between 1940 and 1949. Analyses by Arthur Norton (Norton & Miller, 1990) tell us that those born in the 1910 cohort had their last child, on average, when they were roughly 32, while those born in the 1940s had their last child at roughly age 27. Because the earlier cohort also had shorter life expectancies, these women experienced many fewer child-free years at the end of their lives than will be true for those born in 1940, who had their last children at much younger ages and could expect to live much longer.

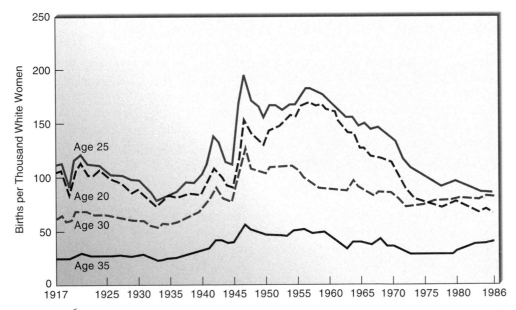

FIGURE 6.3 Number of white women, per thousand, who have given birth to at least one child at each of several ages over most of this century in the United States. It is clear that the period between 1945 and 1970, when first births occurred early, was actually *atypical*. The recent trend toward delayed childbearing returns birth patterns to something more like what was typical in the early part of this century.

Source: Chen & Morgan, 1991, Fig. 2, p. 516.

Many other changes in life patterns flow from the same shifts in the timing of marriage and childbearing. For example, women in the 1910–1919 cohort were much more likely to be widowed before their last child left home. Widowhood was thus a quite different state than it is likely to be today, when a woman is apt to be widowed 10 or 15 years after her last child has grown and moved away from home. In like manner, the pattern of delayed marriage and childbearing among today's young men and women will have predictable consequences for the timing and confluence of events downstream in their adult lives:

*   The departure of the last child from home will be delayed, thus reducing the number of postparental years in middle adulthood.

*   There will be an increased likelihood of experiencing a midlife squeeze in which financial and emotional demands from both children and aging parents will coincide.

*   Grandparenthood will come later, which may have implications for the style or quality of the relationship between grandparents and grandchildren.

The delay of marriage in the current cohort of young people has also had an impact on the family life-cycle experiences of their *parents'* cohort, since the nest is not emptying as fast as many parents had expected. Census Bureau statistics show that in 1992 roughly 20 percent of men and 15 percent of women aged 25 to 29 were still living with their parents. Twenty years earlier those numbers had been 10 percent and 5 percent respectively.

For me, two key points emerge from these analyses of secular trends. First, the timing of early family life-cycle events has a significant impact on the whole pattern of an adult's later life. Second, because the typical timing of such events changes from one cohort to the next, definitions of on-time or off-time are inevitably cohort specific. If your own timing matches that of your cohort, you will have lots of company in facing whatever stresses may be encountered as you move through the decades.

Gender Roles Among Couples with Children. After marriage, gender roles seem to move slightly in the direction of traditionalism. The effect of the birth of the first child is to accentuate this shift markedly. David Gutmann refers to this process as the **parental imperative** and argues that the pattern is wired in, or genetically programmed. Because human children are so vulnerable, parents *must* meet both the emotional and physical needs of the child, and it is very difficult for one person to do both. The woman bears the child and nurses it, so it is natural, Gutmann suggests, for the division of role responsibility to fall along the traditional lines. Here's one illustrative voice, that of a man named Joe: "The baby's coming was a good thing, because it drove home to me that I had to have a better job. And I knew I'd need an education to get one. I transferred to the evening shift so I could go to college during the day. The hours were hard, I was under a lot of pressure, and I missed my family, but it was something I had to do" (Daniels & Weingarten, 1988, p. 38). Thus Joe responds to the parental imperative by spending *less* time with his child, leaving his wife with the traditional task of child care. Whether Gutmann is correct about such a role division being genetically programmed or not is a matter of debate, but at an empirical level there is clear supportive evidence: Male and female roles do get more separate after the birth of the child.

Gutmann finds such a pattern in the several cultures he has studied, including the Navaho, the Mayan, and the Druze (Gutmann, 1975), and there have been similar findings in studies of U.S. families.

For example, Carolyn Cowan and her colleagues (Cowan, Cowan, Heming, & Miller, 1991) found that after the birth of a first child, a woman assumes more responsibility for both child care and household tasks than either partner had predicted before the child was born. And cross-sectional studies of the division of household tasks show that the largest gap in hours devoted to housework by husbands and wives occurs when children are young, a pattern vividly clear in Figure 6.4. The data in the figure are from the Panel Study on Income Dynamics (Rexroat & Shehan, 1987), which you may recall involves a group of over 5000 families studied over a period of several decades. Note that what is shown here reflects the division of labor among those couples in which both spouses work *full time*.

The data shown in the figure were collected in 1976, and you may think that things have changed a lot since then—that men are doing much more housework now, especially if their wives work. And they are; in particular, men with working wives are doing more *child care* now then they used to (Higgins, Duxbury, & Lee, 1994). But if you include all forms of housework—child care, cooking, cleaning, running errands, and so on—wives still do more than husbands do, even when both work full time. The typical statement is that women in such families do about twice as much household work as men do (S. L. Blair & Johnson, 1992), although a recent study in Canada, with data collected in the early 1990s, suggest that the difference may be smaller today (Higgins et al., 1994). The pattern of greater household work for women holds in stepfamilies as well as first marriages (Acock & Demo, 1994) and has been found in Anglo, black, and Hispanic families. Black and Hispanic men appear to spend more time in household labor than do Anglo men, but

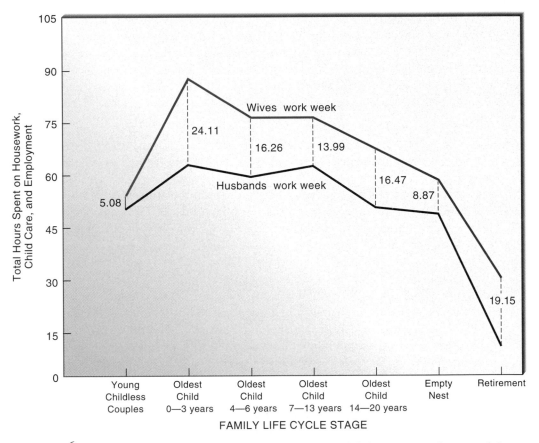

FIGURE 6.4 Even among couples in which both partners work full-time, women do more of the household work and child care, with the difference maximally large in the years immediately after the birth of the first child.

Source: C. Rexroat & C. Shehan, 1987. The family life cycle and spouse's time in housework, *Journal of Marriage and the Family, 49,* 737–750. Fig. 1, p. 746. Copyright 1987 by the National Council on Family Relations, 3989 Central Avenue NE, Suite 550, Minneapolis, MN 55421. Reprinted by permission.

the range of variation is not huge. Beth Shelton and Daphne John (1993), drawing on data from a very large U.S. national sample studied in 1987, report that 34 percent of household labor time is contributed by husbands among Anglo families, compared to 40 percent among black men and 36 percent among Hispanics.

Given my own belief in egalitarian gender roles (a belief I am sure is quite clear from what I have already written!), it is easy for me to give the impression that such an uneven division of household tasks is invariably a source of strain or difficulty. So let me offer a bit of balance here. Whether a wife, or a couple, finds a traditional division of labor to be a problem or not depends very much on their attitudes about gender roles in general. For example, one recent study suggests that middle-class dual-earner couples, many of whom hold relatively egalitarian views, experience higher levels of overall conflict when the wife thinks the husband is not doing his equal share of housework. But in working-class couples the lowest levels of marital conflict occurred when the division of labor was most traditional, with the wife doing the greater bulk of the housework (Perry-Jenkins & Folk, 1994). Findings like this remind us that in today's society, there are many different models of gender roles within marriage. What is important for the functioning of the marriage is the relationship between what type of gender role division a given couple believes ought to occur and what is actually occurring. Where the belief and the reality match reasonably well, the relationship benefits; when there is a poor match, there are more likely to be problems in the marriage (Gilbert, 1994).

Parenthood and Happiness. Unlike the transition to marriage, which seems to be accompanied by an increase in happiness, the new role of parent brings an initial decrease in happiness and marital satisfaction. You've seen one example of this pattern already in Figure 1.6, and you should go back and take another look at that figure. The general finding is of a curvilinear relationship between marital satisfaction and family stage, with the highest satisfaction being before the birth of the first child and after all the children have left home. In a review of all the research on this point, Norval Glenn (1990), concludes that this curvilinear pattern "is about as close to being certain as anything ever is in the social sciences" (p. 853).

For a change, we have longitudinal data as well as cross-sectional evidence to bolster the point. Table 6.2 shows one fairly typical set of findings from a study by Jay Belsky and his colleagues (Belsky, Lang, & Rovine, 1985). They studied a group of 61 young parents during pregnancy and then three and nine months after the birth of the baby. Each partner was asked a whole set of questions about the way his or her marriage relationship functioned, types of interactions with their spouse, and satisfaction with the relationship. For example, relationship conflict was measured by the responses to items such as: "How often do you and your partner argue?" An item such as "How much do you tell your part-

TABLE 6.2 **Changes in Marital Relationships Before and After the Birth of the First Child**

Measure of Marital Interaction	Time of Measurement		
	Pregnancy	3 Months After Birth	9 Months After Birth
Conflict	20.8	20.4	20.7
Relationship maintenance[a]	31.1	29.7	28.9
Satisfaction with relationship[a]	62.8	60.3	58.3
Expressions of love[a]	78.4	76.5	75.3
Expressions of ambivalence[a]	11.6	12.1	13.3

[a]These measures show statistically significant changes from before or after the birth of the infant.

Source: Belsky, Lang, & Rovine, 1985, Table 1, p. 859.

ner what you want or need from the relationship?" was a measure of relationship maintenance, while "love" was measured with such items as "To what extent do you have a sense of 'belonging' with your partner?" You can see that every one of these aspects of the relationship except conflict got worse after the birth of the child. Other longitudinal studies show very similar patterns (Roosa, 1988).

When an infant is added to the family system, the source of the difficulty seems to be the major increase in both **role conflict,** having two or more roles that are incompatible with each other, and **role strain,** not having the skills to fulfill all one's roles. Sociologists have argued, with considerable empirical support, that when you have too many roles, you don't fill *any* of them well (Rollins & Galligan, 1978).

Since the role of major caregiver and the role of spouse are at least partially in conflict, it should not be surprising that role conflict occurs. The new baby demands time, attention, and nurturance, leaving less of all of these for the spouse. There are not enough hours in the day for the same kinds of recreational activities, sex, or quiet companionship between husband and wife as there were before. There is also less time for friends, and less time for oneself. It is precisely this sense of not enough time, particularly affectionate or nurturant time with one's spouse, that marks this transition (Belsky, Spanier, & Rovine,1983; Myers-Walls, 1984).

For some parents there is also a sense of role strain, since caring for a child is a new and unfamiliar task. As you might expect, any factor that tends to increase the role conflict or strain is likely to make the marital satisfaction decline more. So, for example, couples that experience high levels of interference from their work, such as overtime demands or the need to bring work home, show more strain after the birth of a child than do couples with less work interference (Belsky et al., 1985). Whereas any factor that decreases role conflict, such as having sufficient financial resources to hire babysitters, will tend to reduce the impact of the child's birth on marital satisfaction or depression.

Before you feel persuaded that having children is a disaster, let me reiterate what I said at the outset: Despite the drop in happiness and marital satisfaction at this point in the family life cycle, having a child also brings profound satisfactions, including a greater sense of purpose, worth, or life meaning, a sense of being "grown up," and a shared joy between husband and wife.

Roles in Young Adulthood: A Summary Look

Go back and look again at Figure 6.1 in light of all that I have said since. For most of us, young adulthood is *full* of new roles, each of them complex, each of them demanding—and I haven't even begun to talk about the role of worker, which needs an entire chapter of its own (Chapter 8). Learning these roles is not simple, even when you try to ease into them more slowly through various semi-independent states such as cohabitation before marriage, or by delaying childbearing. Doing them all at once is positively daunting. All I can say is that it is a good thing that young adults are at their physical and mental peaks!

SOCIAL ROLES IN MIDDLE ADULTHOOD

A quite different picture holds in the years of middle adulthood. The same collection of central social roles are still present in most of our lives, but in the years between 40 and 65 they become less demanding, less confining. A few new roles are added, such as grandparent, or perhaps caregiver of an aging parent. But on the whole, the social clock simply ticks less loudly in this period as existing roles are redefined or renegotiated.

Naturally enough, there is a good deal of variability in the timing of these changes. Those adults who had their children in their 30s are obviously going to arrive at the postparental stage much later than those who had their children in their early 20s; some will divorce and remarry in middle age, beginning a second family or acquiring younger stepchildren. For them, middle adulthood involves a much more intense set of social roles. Similarly, when and whether one will take on the role of caregiver for an aging parent will obviously depend a great deal on the age and health of those parents. But despite these individual variations, the role changes of middle adulthood are nonetheless fundamentally driven by the basic biological rhythms of childbearing and child rearing. Women bear children in their 20s and 30s, so for the vast majority, the last child will leave home some time in the years of middle adulthood, and this change, perhaps more than any other, alters the middle adult's life pattern.

The Departure of the Children: The Empty Nest

Women now in their 40s and 50s in the United States had their last child, on average, when they were 26. If we assume that the last child will leave home when he or she is 25 or 26, the women in this current middle-aged cohort will be in their early 50s when the last child leaves. Because men marry at slightly older ages, the average middle-aged man today will be 55 or 56 when his last child departs for independent living.

CRITICAL THINKING

Because women can only bear children in early adulthood whereas men can father children in middle and old age, I could make an argument that the sequence and timing of women's social roles is more fixed, more shared, than is true for men. Would you buy this argument?

This stage is sometimes called *postparental,* as if the role of parent stopped when the last child walked out the door, suitcase in hand. Clearly, it does not. Adults who have reared children go on being a parent until they (or their children) die. They continue to give advice, provide financial assistance and instrumental help, babysit with grandchildren, and provide a center for the extended family. But on a day-to-day basis, the role of parent clearly changes, becoming far less demanding and less time consuming.

Folklore would have it that this "empty nest" stage is a particularly unpleasant and stressful period, especially for a woman, since she loses what may have been the most central role of her early and middle adulthood—that of full-time mother. As a result, she may lose a powerful sense of her own worth. Such a description may well be valid in some cultures and may have been accurate in earlier eras within our own culture, but it does not appear to be valid in today's society, at least not for the great majority of women.

Suicide rates do rise for women in middle age, but the rise occurs in the late 30s and early 40s, before the last child typically departs, and then drops after age 50, when the nest empties. Recall, too, that marital satisfaction typically goes up at this stage, while worries and anxieties go down (Antonucci, Tamir, & Dubnoff, 1980).

The same picture emerges when women have been asked directly about times of significant transitions in their lives. They are likely to list the departure of the children as a positive rather than a negative event. For example, Rochelle Harris and her colleagues (Harris, Ellicott, & Holmes, 1986) interviewed a group of 65 women between the ages of 45 and 60. Roughly half described a major transition at the time of "launching" the children from home, and another third described some kind of transition in the postparental period. But the majority of these were positive transitions, such as moving into a new job when the children left home or going back to college. When the transition was negative at this age, it was far more likely to be linked to dissatisfaction in the marriage relationship than with any sense of loss of the mothering role.

A little different view of the empty nest transition for parents is taken by Carol Ryff and her colleagues (Ryff, Schmutte, & Lee, 1996), who suggest that parents use their children's transition to adulthood as a time to evaluate their own accomplishments as parents. In a study of 215 midlife parents with adult children, they found that those who rated their children as successful (especially in personal and social adjustment), and believed that they were somewhat responsible for that success, showed better mental health and more positive perceptions of themselves at this transition point in their lives than did parents who did not share those beliefs.

Of course, we can't be sure that the experiences of these samples of parents reflect the story of the general population, but we can say that the findings from these studies are not consistent with the more pessimistic view of the empty nest stage that has been prevalent in both the popular and professional literature. Those women who do experience heightened distress at this role transition—and there clearly are some—appear to be primarily those who attempt to maintain their old homemaking/parenting role, especially those who do not work outside the home.

I am not trying to suggest here that for most adults the postparental period is a continuous idyll, devoid of problems, any more than the advent of children ushers in continuous difficulties. Rather, I am trying to suggest that as a general rule, filling more roles is more stressful and difficult than filling fewer. To be sure, multiple roles can also be a strength, since self-esteem or satisfaction can then have multiple sources. But there is no escaping the added conflicts and strains involved in multiple roles, perhaps particularly the role of parent. When this role is added in early adulthood, it brings inevitable new role conflicts or strains; when the role is partially shed at midlife, those conflicts and strains are reduced.

CRITICAL THINKING

If filling more roles is normally harder than filling fewer, should we expect that adults who fill the fewest roles are likely to be the happiest? Do you think that some minimum number of social roles is necessary for self-esteem or life satisfaction?

Gender Roles at Midlife

Much less clear is what happens to gender roles in middle adulthood. One influential voice has been that of David Gutmann, who proposed a major theory based on studies of many cultures (1987). Gutmann believes that a *crossover* of gender roles occurs in late midlife. Women take on more and more of the traditionally masculine qualities or role responsibilities, becoming more assertive, while men become more passive. Gutmann describes the change among men this way: "[M]en who were once adversarial, whether as warriors, slash-and-burn agriculturists, passionate pioneers, *politicos,* or trial lawyers, routinely become more pacific in later life; they turn to preserving life rather than killing, to maintaining social stability rather than fomenting ardent rebellion. In some cases, these transformations involve more than a drift away from flamboyant aggression, but an actual shift in gender distinctiveness, from univocal masculinity to sexual bimodality, or even implicit femininity" (1987, p. 94). In women, Gutmann thinks the transition is from an interior to an exterior focus, from nurturance to a kind of virility. In Native American cultures, for example, it is quite common to find that older women are allowed into tribal councils that would have been closed to them earlier. Older Iroquois women are said to become "manly hearted." And Japanese women over 60 appear to have far more freedom from social rules, including implicit permission to make bawdy jokes in mixed company. Similarly, Lebanese women become bawdier, more aggressive, and more controlling in late middle age.

There appears to be a kernel of truth in Gutmann's view of these changes, but more systematic studies suggest that it is better to describe the change as an *expansion* of gender roles rather than a crossing over. Gutmann's model implies that men and women trade places in some sense, and there is little evidence to support this (Huyck, 1994). But there is some sign of decreased gender stereotypes in middle age, at least among some groups. Perhaps because with the children gone from home, there is less pressure toward traditional role divisions, perhaps for other reasons associated with deeper personality changes (discussed in Chapter 9), both men and women at midlife can begin to express those unexpressed parts of themselves. For some men, this means an increased expression of compassion; for some women, this means increased assertiveness or autonomy.

For example, in their cross-sectional study of adults at various stages of the family life cycle, Sharon Nash and Shirley Feldman (1981) compared self-reported aspects of gender roles. They found that men in later stages of the family life cycle described themselves as more compassionate, women described themselves as more autonomous, but there was no crossing over. Each gender retained its own traditional qualities but added some qualities that would be attributed to the other gender in young adulthood. Similarly, in his longitudinal study of Harvard men, George Vaillant (1977) found that the men became more "feminine" in middle age: became more introspective, more concerned with feelings, more able to express emotions. But they did not thereby become less masculine. So Gutmann is probably correct that there is a shift in gender roles in this age period, but it is more a blurring than a crossing over.

Becoming a Grandparent

One of the roles that is typically added in middle adulthood is that of grandparent. About three-fourths of adults in the United States become grandparents before they are 65, and over half of women experience this event before the age of 54 (Marks, 1996), so this is clearly a midlife role for most of us. And with longevity increasing, most of today's adults will live long enough to see their grandchildren become adults (Cherlin & Furstenberg, 1986; Hagestad, 1988). As a personal example, I was 16 when the first of my grandparents died and in my late 40s when the fourth death occurred.

Most grandparents see or talk to their grandchildren regularly, often as frequently as every week or two, and most describe their relationships as warm and loving. At the same time, the role of grandparent has few fixed prescriptions. Unlike parenthood, which clearly involves full-time responsibility, there are many ways to be a grandparent. Which pattern a given adult follows will depend on the distance between grandparent and grandchild, economic resources, age, gender, ethnic group, and personal preferences.

Several studies suggest that both African-Americans and Hispanic grandparents describe closer and more frequent contact with their grandchildren than is true for Anglos (Bengtson, 1985; Kivett, 1991). And among all ethnic groups, the role of grandmother

THE GREAT MAJORITY OF ADULTS become grandparents. There are several distinct styles; this grandfather is most likely part of the largest group, labeled "companionate."

is likely to be both broader and more intimate than is true for grandfathers. In one study, Hagestad (1985) found that grandfathers gave advice, particularly about work or the world at large, and particularly to grandsons. Grandmothers gave advice about personal relationships as well.

But there are also style differences that cut across these ethnic and gender patterns. Andrew Cherlin and Frank Furstenberg (1986), who interviewed a nationally representative sample of over 500 grandparents, point to three basic styles:

1. **Remote grandparents.** This group, which represented 29 percent of the total sample, see their grandchildren relatively infrequently. The most common reason for such a remote relationship is physical distance, but it also occurs because some grandparents prefer a relationship that is more emotionally detached.

2. **Companionate grandparents.** The second type, the most common (55 percent), involves very warm, pleasurable relationships. Here is one voice: "When you have grandchildren, you have more love to spare. Because the discipline goes to the parents and whoever's in charge. But you just have extra love and you will tend to spoil them a little bit. And you know, you give" (p. 55). Yet the grandparents in this group also say that they are glad they no longer have the full-time responsibility; they are glad they can send the grandchildren home after a few hours.

3. **Involved grandparents.** The third and least common type (16 percent) includes grandparents who have a more intense involvement with the grandchild. Some see the child very frequently and have created an extremely close link. Others are heavily involved in the day-to-day care of the child, living in three-generation households and assuming much of the child care while the parent works, or caring for the grandchild during the day in their own home. Still others have full legal and emotional responsibility for the rearing of the grandchildren. The Census Bureau estimates that, in 1991, 3.3 million children in the United States lived in a household in which the grandparent was the head of the household (Saluter, 1992). In about one-fourth of those cases, the grandparent was the sole caregiver.

Within American society, this type of involved grandparent care is far more common among African-Americans than either Hispanic-Americans or Anglos. Twelve percent of African-American children in 1991 were being reared by or with a head-of-household grandparent, compared to 3.7 percent for Anglos and 5.6 percent for Hispanics. Full-time grandparent care is especially likely when the daughter is unmarried. In such cases, grandmothers frequently take on child-care responsibilities so that the daughter can continue in school or hold down a job. That such assistance is indeed helpful is indicated by the fact that teenage mothers who have such help from their own mothers do indeed complete more years of education and have more successful work careers in adulthood (R. J. Taylor, Chatters, Tucker, & Lewis, 1990).

Grandparents also assume an important role when parents divorce, especially maternal grandparents, who often provide financial and emotional support for their daughter and assume much of the parental role for their grandchildren. But such an intensive grandparent role involves a price for the grandparent, not only because it is off-time to be parenting in this way, but quite simply because it extends into middle adulthood the added demands of full-time parenthood. One grandmother with custody of her granddaughters said: "Before, I had all the freedom. I didn't need a baby sitter; I didn't need to check to see if I could go out of the house or when I had to be back or to make 9,000 arrangements to do anything.... She really thrives best on a routine, so that has definitely cut my leisure, plus the fact that babysitting's

CRITICAL THINKING

Which of these several types of relationship do you have, or did you have, with your own grandparents? Did you have different types of relationships with your various grandparents?

expensive" (Jendrek, 1993, p. 616). Other caregiving grandparents in this study talked about having less time for friendships, less time for their own marital relationship.

In Cherlin and Furstenberg's study, grandmothers more often fell into the companionate category, as did younger grandparents of both sexes. In contrast, grandparents over 65 are more likely to have a remote relationship, sometimes because their health is no longer good or because they find the heightened level of activity around young children to be more difficult to tolerate. Research is mixed about what effect grandparenthood has on the middle-aged adult. Some reports suggest that the role of grandparent is peripheral to the older person as a source of identity and satisfaction (Palmore, 1981), while others report that it is essential to the identity and well-being of the grandparent (Kivnick, 1982). With so many types of relationships and varieties of interactions, it is no wonder there is disagreement on this question. But with more and more grandparents in our population who are healthier and wealthier than ever before, certainly there is need for more research on how the Baby Boomers are approaching grandparenthood (Scott, 1997).

Caring for an Aging Parent

The other new role that *may* be added at midlife, and that *does* have a significant impact on life satisfaction, is that of caregiver for an aging parent. There is no doubt that the great majority of adults, in virtually every culture, feel a strong sense of filial responsibility. Should their parents need assistance, they will endeavor to provide it (Ogawa & Retherford, 1993; Wolfson, Handfield-Jones, Glass, McClaran, & Keyserlingk, 1993). But just how many adults actually take on this role is surprisingly unclear.

Part of the problem in determining the likelihood of this role is that the question is not often asked the right way around. Most often, researchers have begun by looking at older adults, asking whether they require assistance, and if so, who provides it. For example, we know that among the elderly in the United States who have at least one adult child, 18 percent actually live with one of those children (Crimmins & Ingegneri, 1990; Hoyert, 1991). But this does not tell us that 18 percent of middle-aged adults have a parent living with them. It also does not tell us how many daughters-in-law or sons-in-law have the parent of their spouse living with them.

Better—but still not great—information comes from a small number of studies in which middle-aged adults have been asked what kind of care they provide for their elderly parents or parents-in-law. One of the better studies of this type is by Glenna Spitze and John Logan (1990), who interviewed 1200 middle-aged men and women in upstate New York. Figure 6.5 shows the percentage who provided at least three hours a week of assis-

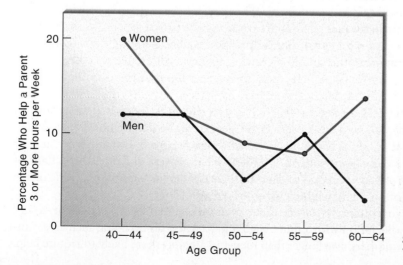

FIGURE 6.5 You may be surprised at how small the percentage is of middle-aged adults who provide care for an aging percent, although cross-sectional data like these cannot tell us what percentage of adults will ever have such a role.

Source: Data from Spitze & Logan, 1990, Table 2, p. 189.

tance to a parent. Overall, around 11 percent of these adults were providing assistance. You can see in the figure that the likelihood of providing care varied somewhat by age, with somewhat higher rates early in middle adulthood, largely because a greater percentage of adults in this age range still have living parents. Among those aged 60 to 64 in this study, only 8 percent had a parent still living, while among those 40 to 44, 55 percent still had at least one parent still alive.

Combining this information with evidence from similar research (Scharlach & Fredricksen, 1994), we can estimate that something between 10 and 15 percent of middle-aged adults are providing this level of regular care for an older parent at any given time.

Another way of looking at this is to ask what the probability is that a woman in middle adulthood will play the role of caregiver for an aging parent. In an elegant analysis, Christine Himes (1994) has estimated this lifetime probability, based on a large cross-sectional set of data. Using a very broad definition of caregiving, she calculates that among women now aged 45 to 49 who still have at least one living parent, roughly half will do some caregiving, about half of them before the age of 55. Furthermore, this number may well be higher in subsequent cohorts, as longevity increases, which means an increase in the number of frail elderly.

CRITICAL THINKING

See if you can design a study that would tell us what percentage of adults in today's cohorts are likely ever to fill the role of caregiver for an aging parent.

Who Provides Care? When an older parent does need care, who is most likely to provide it? The simplest answer is that women do—daughters and daughters-in-law—a point already somewhat evident in Figure 6.5. Women are two to four times as likely as are their brothers to provide assistance with daily tasks (G. R. Lee, Dwyer, & Coward, 1993; Dwyer & Coward, 1991). This difference is most often explained in terms of the woman's role as caregiver and **kinkeeper** within family relationships. Women are the ones who stay home from work to care for a sick child, stay in touch with relatives on both sides of the family, call their adult children, remember the birthdays and anniversaries (and select the gifts and plan the parties), write thank you letters for gifts, babysit with the grandchildren, and the like (A. J. Walker, 1992; E. M. Brody, Litvin, Albert, & Hoffman, 1994).

But although doubtless valid to at least some extent, this picture is too simple. When an older parent needs care, the child who is most likely to take on the role of caregiver, or who will assume the largest share of the responsibility, is the one who is not working, or not married, or who lives closest to the parent (J. E. Brody, 1994; Stoller, Forster, & Duniho, 1992). Among today's cohorts of middle-aged adults, this list of characteristics more often describes a daughter than a son, but when a son fits the description, such as an unmarried son, he is the one most likely to provide care. If more than one child is available as caregiver, there is often a division of responsibilities, with sons providing more financial assistance or instrumental support (mowing the lawn, repairs, perhaps shopping) and daughters more often providing help with actual activities of daily living.

To further complicate the simple picture, it makes a difference whether the frail elder is a mother or a father. Daughters are four times as likely as their brothers to help an older mother, but only 40 percent more likely than sons to help a frail father, as you can see in Figure 6.6 (G. R. Lee et al., 1993). The data shown in the figure come from an extremely large study, the National Long-Term Care Survey, which involved a nationally representative sample of adults 65 and older, all of whom reported difficulty with at least one ADL (activity or daily living) or IADL (independent activity of daily living). Each of the 4420 subjects involved was asked to describe what kind of assistance, if any, he or she received from each of his or her children over the age of 18.

This tendency for children to provide relatively more help to the same-sex parent means, again, that women will end up with a much higher probability of providing such care, simply because women (mothers) live longer than men and are thus more likely to require help.

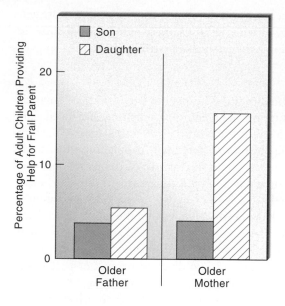

FIGURE 6.6 Daughters provide more care to frail parents than do sons, but the difference is far smaller when the recipient is an older father than when it is an older mother.

Source: Data from G. R. Lee, Dwyer, & Coward, 1993, Table 2, p. S12.

The Impact of Caregiving. In the past decade, there have been a great number of studies exploring the effect of such parent care on the lives of the caregivers. In most of these studies, the recipient of care has been diagnosed with some form of dementia, most often Alzheimer's disease. Because such people gradually lose their ability to perform the simplest of daily functions, they require a steadily increasing amount of care, and the demands on the caregiver can be very large indeed, up to and including constant supervision. When the middle-aged caregiver is also holding down a job, caring for a spouse, and assisting grown children and grandchildren, the impact can be substantial.

The cumulative evidence indicates that such caregivers are more depressed and have lower marital satisfaction than is true for matched comparison groups of similar age and social class (Hoyert & Seltzer, R. Schulz, Visintainer, & Williamson, 1990). There is also some indication that those who care for demented or frail elders are more often ill themselves, or that they have some reduced efficiency of immune system function (Dura & Kiecolt-Glaser, 1991; Hoyert & Seltzer, 1992; Kiecolt-Glaser, 1987). Collectively, these effects usually go by the name of **caregiver burden.**

We know much less about the amount of burden experienced by those who provide lower levels of assistance. On the face of it, there seems to be more than a few-order-of-magnitude differences between daily care of a demented elder and occasional lawn mowing or shopping assistance. In addition, it is clear that there are factors that can significantly mitigate the feeling of burden, even for those with major caregiving responsibilities. Those who have good support networks (including a supportive spouse) and other caregivers who can share the burden experience fewer negative consequences (E. M. Brody, Litvin, Albert, & Hoffman, 1992; R. Schulz & Williamson, 1991). However, factors such as one's perception of inadequacy as a caregiver can make the burden heavier. Elaine Brody (1985) has found that today's generation of caregivers have the false impression that they are doing less than their parents did in terms of care for aging parents. The truth is that fewer parents in past generations lived to be frail and disabled, and when they did, they didn't spend so many years needing care. Finally, the care they required was not as intense as today, and their caregivers were not so involved with multiple roles in their own lives.

In no way do I wish to understate the enormity of the task that may face some middle-aged adults who care for aging parents. The physical, financial, and emotional costs can be high. But let me say again that in today's cohorts, such a significant care burden is *not* a normative experience of middle age, at least in developed countries. The more general pattern is for the middle-aged adult to find herself in a kind of **generational squeeze,** providing some assistance both up and down the generations within the family.

The Generational Squeeze

In middle adulthood, the children may be out of the home, but they still need financial assistance, babysitting, and emotional support. The aging parents may not need daily care, but they need their adult children to advise them on their finances, help with shopping, or simply spend time with them. We don't know how many people in middle adulthood are in this squeeze, but we do know that about one-fourth of the people between 35 and 54 years of age have children at home *plus* a job *plus* a parent with limited health.

Several recent studies have examined the role of caregiver to one's elderly parent in relationship to other roles. Two theories have been suggested for the effect of multiple roles. One theory is that having multiple roles can exacerbate stress, and the other theory is that multiple roles will buffer stress. In one study, Stephens and Townsend (1997) interviewed 296 women who were primary caregivers to disabled parents or parents-in-law and were married, had jobs, and had children still living in the home. The results showed that women caregivers with multiple roles experienced more negative effects of caregiving if they also had stress in any of their other roles. Furthermore, women caregivers experienced a buffering effect from their role as an employee if they felt their job was rewarding. Clearly, the effect of multiple roles isn't a simple one of just having too many items on one's list of things to do. It also depends on what those roles are, what time of life they appear, and whether or not one perceives them as rewarding.

SOCIAL ROLES IN LATE ADULTHOOD

In young adulthood, we add key roles; in middle adulthood, we redefine those central roles; in late adulthood, we mostly shed social roles. The role of full-time worker is usually given up at retirement (which I discuss fully in Chapter 8); the role of spouse is given up at widowhood for a great many adults. Friends die or move away, children become more independent and involved with their own children, and positions in community organizations such as the Lions Club or the school board are turned over to younger adults.

Whether one sees this as loss or gain is a little like asking whether the water glass is half full or half empty. One influential "half-empty" view has been articulated by Irving Rosow (1985), who points out that we not only lose social roles in late life but that the roles that remain have less content. There is a social position or a label for the role, but there aren't as many duties or expectations as there were earlier in life. The older adult is still a parent, but the role of parent has fewer duties at this later time. This loss of role content can also be seen in many work or organizational roles. The university professor, for example, becomes an emeritus professor, a title with some honor but with essentially no obligations. Rosow says: "Although freedom from responsibility may sound heavenly to the young, it actually demands strong personal interests and motivation. In earlier periods, life is mainly structured by social duties. People's social positions and role obligations largely govern their general activities and time budgets. This is not true in old age for, *within objective constraints,* life is essentially shaped by individual choice and personal initiative" (1985, p. 72).

Other social scientists see the picture much more positively. Old age, especially for the young old, is a time of choice, a time when one's eccentricities can be given full rein, when a hobby can become a full-time interest with no negative consequences (J. Bond & Coleman, 1990). The weekend golfer can play every day; the baseball fan can watch every game on TV. Or one can take on a volunteer task, as older Americans have been doing in increasing numbers in recent years. In the most recent surveys, in 1989, 47 percent of adults between 65 and 74, and 32 percent of those 75 and older reported that they worked in some way to help others for no monetary pay—in their church or synagogue, for a charity, or for some other organization. Twenty years ago, only about one third of this many elders were volunteering their time (Chambré, 1993).

My own leanings are toward seeing the glass as half full. To assume that the absence of consuming work roles or family roles means that life has no meaning seems to me to be a very limited perspective. Yet objectively, Rosow is correct. The social roles of late adulthood are indeed far less constraining, far less prescriptive than at any other time of adulthood. This offers a challenge, or an opportunity, depending on one's point of view.

Living Alone

One of the new challenges that comes to many adults in their later years, especially to women, is that of learning to live alone, a change brought about by losing the role of spouse due to divorce or widowhood. Among adults over 75, roughly one-fourth of men and two-thirds of women fall into such a group. Adding the never-married into the equation means that among the old old and oldest old, only about 25 percent of women are still living with a husband, compared to about 65 percent of men. Figure 6.7, which shows where these many unmarried elders are living, makes it clear that about half of these single older adults live alone, although as I mentioned earlier, such a choice is less common among Hispanic-Americans, African-Americans, and Asian-Americans than among Anglos. In one recent study, Choi (1991) found that 73 percent of white widows over 65, but only 56 percent of nonwhite widows lived alone. Similar differences exist for single older men (Stinner, Byun, & Paita, 1990). In contrast, in Japan, only 7 percent of older adults live alone; over half live with a child (Tsuya & Martin, 1992). So there are clearly major cultural effects at work here.

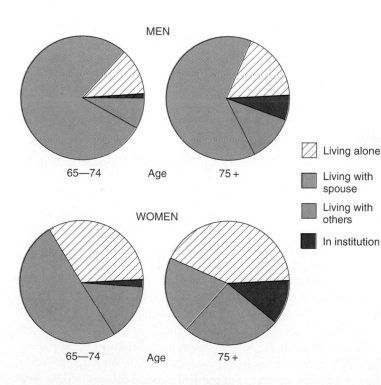

Living alone

Living with spouse

Living with others

In institution

FIGURE 6.7 One of the common role losses of old age is the loss of the role of spouse through widowhood or (less often in current cohorts) through divorce. This is especially true for older women, a great many of whom end up living alone in late old age.

Source: Brock, Guralnik, & Brody, 1990, Fig. 2, p. 8. Reprinted by permission of Academic Press, San Diego, CA, and the author.

In the United States and in other Western countries in which there is adequate financial support for older citizens, the great majority of older adults live alone by choice, not because there is no other alternative. Even when their health declines, older adults will persist in living alone as long as possible (Worobey & Angel, 1990). Health does make some difference, of course; those who have significant health problems are more likely to live with their children or with another relative than are those whose health is more robust (Choi, 1991).

Living alone is not only the preferred option for single adults, it also appears to be psychologically healthier than the alternative of living with a child, at least in American culture. For example, Alice and Lincoln Day have studied a nationally representative sample of white American women born between 1900 and 1910, who were between 77 and 87 when they were interviewed (Day & Day, 1993). Those who were living alone and those who lived with a husband were much more likely to report that they were contented. Because there is self-selection involved in comparisons of those living alone or living with relatives, it is difficult to be sure what is causing what in findings like these. Those who end up living with kin are likely to be poorest and least physically functional, both of which contribute to a lower sense of life satisfaction. But there are also some indications that living with kin itself has some negative effect on psychological well-being—a point I'll come back to in Chapter 7.

SOCIAL ROLES IN ATYPICAL FAMILIES

Except for a few paragraphs on the unmarried, everything I have said so far in this chapter describes the life patterns of adults who adopt the social roles of spouse (or long-term partner) and parent. But of course a great many adults do not follow such a pattern. Many never marry and an increasing number have no children. As one example, in 1980, 10.1 percent of women 40 to 44 had had no children; in 1992 the figure was 16.3 percent, including 11 percent of all married women in this age group (U.S. Bureau of the Census, 1993). And roughly half of those who marry in the United States today will eventually divorce, and of these, about 70 percent eventually remarry (Cherlin, 1992). The "traditional" family sequence involving a husband and wife, several children, and no divorce (the pattern upon which much of family sociology was based until quite recently) today represents a distinct minority of all adult lives. So I cannot leave this chapter without talking about the adult experiences of those whose social role experience in adulthood differs in significant ways from the nearly mythical norm: those who do not marry, those who do not have children, and those who divorce and remarry.

The Lifelong Singles

Singlehood is clearly increasing in the United States. One-fourth of all households today have only one person, and in nearly half these cases, the single householder is between the ages of 30 and 64. But of course this group is made up of many different subsets, including the divorced, the widowed, those who are unmarried but eager to find a partner, and those who are single by choice (Buunk & van Driel, 1989). It is estimated that somewhere between 3 and 5 percent of the elderly have been single all their lives, about half the rate of singlehood in many European countries (Newtson & Keith, 1997).

One point is quite clear: Lifelong single adults must cope with the fact that they are going against the grain of social expectations. Singlehood may be increasing, divorce may be nearly normative, but the social system is still organized around couples. In the terms I have been using in this chapter, the role of spouse or partner is still thought of as central to adult life. Those who lack this role are seen by many as deficient in some respect. One 44-year-old lifelong single man quoted in a newspaper article on singles (Nemy, 1991) said: "Whenever I go to a family wedding, I'm put with second cousins in their teens and early 20's. They never seat me with couples. I'm put at the children's table because I'm single. It's extremely insulting." Another, a woman in her early 30s, said: "If you're a woman over 30 and not married, people feel sorry for you rather than thinking you might have a fulfilling life. They think something must be wrong that you haven't married yet." In some respects, then, the lifelong single are treated by others as if they were not fully adult because they have not adopted a role that is central to adulthood.

Health of the older lifelong single adult has been the topic of a number of studies. Of the large group of older single adults (divorced, separated, widowed, and lifelong single) the lifelong single have the best health and the fewest disabilities. Furthermore, they report the most satisfaction with being single (Newtson & Keith, 1997). This certainly dispels the myth of fading spinsters and frail elderly bachelors.

Another challenge for the single adult is to create a supportive network, especially to find a confidant with whom life's problems may be discussed. This seems to be a special problem for divorced adults, especially divorced men, who relied on their former spouse to fill this role and now find themselves bereft. This group reports the highest levels of loneliness of any subgroup of singles, and as I described in some detail earlier in the chapter, the highest rate of depression and illness as well. But limited research on this subject suggests that those who have never married are *not* on average more lonely than are married adults (Cargan & Melko, 1982). The majority of the lifelong singles, recognizing the importance of a confidant, nurture such relationships and use them effectively.

As just one example: Robert Rubinstein and his colleagues describes the key relationships formed by 31 lifelong single women, all over 60. Twenty-nine of these 31 women said that enduring friendships had been highly significant parts of their lives. They often thought of these friends as "sisters." The majority of these women had also maintained very close relationships with their own parents and siblings, and many had special connections with nieces or nephews. About one-third had formed deep links to another family, feeling themselves "adopted into" some nonkin group. Each of these women had thus created, in some fashion, a set of roles or relationships that served many of the same emotional functions as a committed partnership or spousal relationship (Rubinstein, Alexander, Goodman, & Luborsky, 1991).

On the whole, we might think of singlehood as having something in common with the relative rolelessness of old age: It is a role with fewer daily demands and constraints. But that very freedom presents both a challenge and an opportunity.

The Childless

Having no children also changes the shape of adult life. The rhythm of the child's developmental timetable is simply not there to structure the adult's life experiences. Without the presence of children, for example, there is no dip in marital satisfaction in the 20s and 30s (Houseknecht, 1987; Ishii-Kuntz & Seccombe, 1989; Somers, 1993). Childless couples in this age range report higher satisfaction and more cohesion than do couples the same age with children.

In the postparental period, the picture is a little different. There is at least one study that shows marital satisfaction to be lower among the childless couples in their 50s and 60s than among couples the same age with children (Houseknecht & Macke, 1981). Thus childlessness seems to be associated with an essentially flat curve of marital satisfaction over age, in contrast to the U-shaped curve common among couples with children.

For women without children, another major difference is in the role of worker. Without children to care for, there is far less barrier to a woman's pursuit of a full-time career. Whether women who have made a commitment to a career choose not to have children, or whether those who do not have children subsequently make a stronger career commitment, is not completely clear. Some of both may well occur. What is clear is that childless women are more likely to work throughout their adult lives, to have somewhat higher-level jobs, and to earn more money (Hoffman & Manis, 1978; Houseknecht & Macke, 1987). Such work patterns are accompanied by a much higher investment in the work role among childless women.

For the childless couple, the absence of children also means that they will not experience a midlife generational squeeze, although the role of primary caregiver for an aging parent is *more* likely to fall to a childless adult (particularly a childless woman) than to her sister who has children.

One final interesting tidbit: We might expect that childless adults would lack adequate emotional support in later life, when aid from children appears to become so significant. Surprisingly, the research shows quite a different pattern. There are several studies that show that among postretirement adults, happiness or life satisfaction, loneliness or self-esteem, is unrelated to the amount of contact the adult has with children or grandchildren (G. R. Lee & Ellithorpe, 1982; G. R. Lee & Ishii-Kuntz, 1987; G. R. Lee & Sheehan, 1989; Seccombe, 1987). At this life stage, childless adults appear to be as happy as those with extended families, although this is more true of those who are childless by choice than for those who are childless by circumstance (Connidis & McMullin, 1993).

Two points stand out for me in this collection of findings. First, the research does not paint a picture of persisting sadness or distress among adults without children. On the contrary. Second, despite a more steady-state quality to the lives of childless adults during the early and middle adulthood periods, an argument can be made that in important respects the shape of adult role patterns is still highly similar. For the childless, as for those with children, early adulthood is the time when roles are added: spousal roles, work roles. Middle adulthood is the time when those roles go through systematic changes. For the childless adult there may be fewer such changes, but work roles do change in predictable ways (as I describe in Chapter 8), and marital relationships may also move through stages. Finally, late adulthood is a time when roles are shed, or when their substance declines, and that is just as true for the childless as for those with children. Thus it seems true that at the most fundamental level there is a common shape to the patterns of roles in adult lives.

Divorced Adults and Remarried Adults

I will be talking about the personal and emotional impact of divorce on adults in Chapter 11 when I discuss stresses of various kinds. Here I want to look only at the much narrower question of the impact of divorce or remarriage on social roles.

Of the 50 percent of today's young adults who will eventually divorce, approximately 70 percent will remarry, with an average unmarried interval of about three years (Bumpass, Sweet, & Martin, 1990). The rate of remarriage is highest among white men (about 75 percent) and lowest among African-American women (about 32 percent). Remarriage rates are also linked to age: The younger you are when you divorce and the fewer children you have, the greater the likelihood that you will remarry. And among all those who remarry, more than half will divorce a second time (Cherlin, 1992).

Although these patterns of marriage and remarriage produce an enormous array of family types, one of the really surprising facts is that divorce and remarriage patterns have a remarkably small effect on the *timing* of some of the important points in the family life cycle, such as a woman's age at the birth of her last child or the number of children she will eventually have. As an illustration, look at the findings in Figure 6.8, based on Arthur Norton's analysis of the experiences of the cohort of women born between 1940 and 1949 (R. Norton, 1983). Norton divided this cohort into subgroups based on the women's marital history, and then compared these subgroups on the timing of significant family life-cycle events. What I find surprising in these findings is that the total number of years in childbearing does not differ a great deal from one marital-status group to the next, ranging from 4.6 years for the group married and divorced once, to 6.7 years for the group married three times. Obviously, most women who remarry do not start over with a new

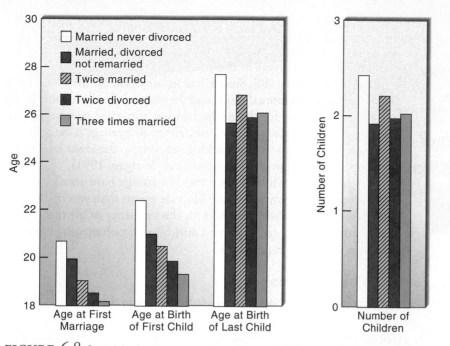

FIGURE 6.8 Surprisingly, there are only quite small differences in key family life-cycle events between women who have remained married and those who have been divorced and remarried. These numbers are for the cohort of women born between 1940 and 1949, but similar patterns hold for women born in earlier cohorts as well.

Source: Data from R. Norton, 1983, Tables 2, 3, 4, 5, and 6, pp. 269–270.

round of childbearing, which means that this aspect of family life cycle is not expanded a great deal because of divorce or remarriage.

At the same time, the years of child *rearing* may be increased for many divorced and remarried adults. This is especially true for men whose second marriage is to a woman much younger than themselves, who then have a second family, or who help to rear the new wife's young children. For some, this sequence of marriage and remarriage significantly shrinks or even eliminates any postparental years within middle adulthood. But for most, the effects of divorce on family life-cycle events seems to be smaller than you might suppose.

Nonetheless, it is clear that divorce brings with it a larger and more complex set of roles to fill. The single parent must now fill all of the adult family roles except spouse: breadwinner, emotional supporter, housekeeper, child-caregiver, activities director, chauffeur, and the rest.

With remarriage, another set of roles is added. Spousal roles once again enter the repertoire, along with that of ex-spouse, stepparent, or step-grandparent, and those charmingly ambiguous role relationships with the former spouse of one's spouse, and with the spouse's former in-laws who remain the grandparents of your new stepchildren. [If you think this sounds as if I am speaking from painful experience, you are quite correct! I have *two* sets of stepchildren, one set subsequently adopted, and the complexity is enough to make strong women (and men) weep.]

Such increases in the range of roles to fill can mean an increase in both role conflict and role strain. In the short run, the effect of such role overload is to lower the quality of all role performances and to lower marital satisfaction in remarried couples, which is doubtless why the divorce rate among remarried couples is higher in the first years after marriage than is true among first marriages (A. J. Cherlin, 1992).

Finally, there are large economic effects of divorce, especially for women, who typically experience a decline of 40 to 50 percent in their household income, a pattern that is clear in Figure 6.9. The data here come from an analysis by Pamela Smock (1993) of information from the National Longit___ ___ __ Youth, a sample that was studied repeated-ly between ____ the total family income in t____ ___ in the year after t____ not co-habiting. T____ only sure route back ____ vel of in-come tend____

Ove____ ler effects on the *tin____ ___* ___ ___ ___ might sup-pose, they____ ransitions, for the r____ ly, and for long-ter___

The Effect of Variati___

I've already talked somew____ ___ ___ ___ g of various role acquisitions such as ____ ____ations *with-in* a cohort. The most ge____ ____ e examples:

* Marrying and/or having a first child before the age of ___ ___ ___ __ are male or female, black or white, poor or middle class, is associated with (1) more children, more closely spaced together; (2) fewer years of education; (3) lower levels of oc-cupational success; (4) lower income; and (5) higher probability of divorce (Astone, 1993; Freeman & Rickels, 1993; Hofferth, 1987; Moore et al., 1993; Teti, Lamb, & Elster, 1987). These negative consequences are larger for those adults who were doing poorly in high school, or who come from families with low levels of education, and markedly larger for those who have several children while still teenagers.

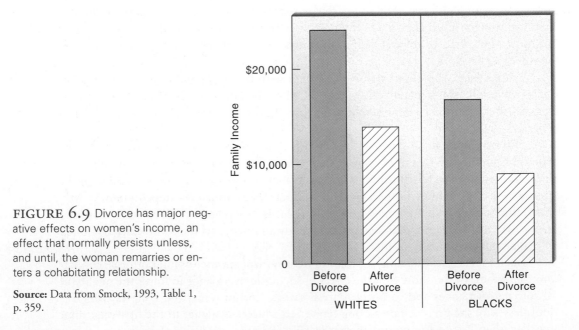

FIGURE 6.9 Divorce has major neg-ative effects on women's income, an effect that normally persists unless, and until, the woman remarries or en-ters a cohabiting relationship.

Source: Data from Smock, 1993, Table 1, p. 359.

* The sequence with which you add key roles has an effect as well. Dennis Hogan (1981), analyzing census data, finds the lowest divorce rates among men who followed the "normative" sequence of first finishing school, then finding a job, and then getting married. The highest divorce rates were for those who married first, even when that marriage was fairly late, and even among men with high levels of education.

* Parents whose children are still living at home at age 25 report higher levels of stress than do parents whose children left home at more normative times (Hagestad, 1986).

* Women who become grandmothers unusually early, such as in their late 20s or early 30s, report considerable discomfort with the role. "I'm too young to be a grandmother!" (Burton & Bengtson, 1985; Troll, 1985).

* Adults whose own parents die early, who thus find themselves "next in line" within the family lineage, often report a sense of dislocation and distress, over and above their feeling of grief at the death of the parent(s) (Hagestad, 1986).

I could give many more examples. The general point is not that some sequences, or some timing, are the ideal for all adults in all cultures, but rather that every culture, and every cohort within a culture, shares some set of expectations about the "normal" or "expected" pattern of adult life. We may not always be consciously aware of these expectations, but violating them involves some kind of price. Most generally, any time you experience some life event, acquire or lose some social role, at a time that is not typical for your generation, you are likely to experience heightened depression or distress (Hurwicz, Duryam, Boyd-Davis, Gatz, & Bengtson, 1992).

MATCH OR MISMATCH BETWEEN PERSONAL QUALITIES AND ROLE DEMANDS

So far I have been talking about the pattern and sequence of roles each of us is likely to fill over the years of adult life as if everyone reacted to these roles in the same way. But just as it is true that not everyone moves through the "typical" sequence of family life-cycle roles, it is also true that any given role will "fit" some people better than others.

The possible impact of a good or poor match between the roles one fills and one's own personal qualities is a much neglected area of research, so we do not have a great deal of evidence to work from. But the basic point seems to me to be so important for our understanding of the experience of individual adults that it is worth exploring.

The most complete and provocative study comes from Florine Livson, who has analyzed data from the Berkeley Intergenerational Studies (F. B. Livson, 1976, 1981). Livson has focused her attention on a group of men and women who, at age 50, were rated by the researchers as having particularly healthy and successful patterns of development: a high capacity for work and for satisfying interpersonal relationships, a realistic perception of themselves, and a sense of moral purpose. All of these adults had also been rated for overall emotional/mental health when they were about 40, so Livson was able to identify some who had been consistently healthy (the "stable" subjects), and some who had looked less integrated and healthy at 40 but looked good at 50 (the "improver" subjects).

When Livson then went back and looked at the information about each of these groups from earlier assessments in adolescence and young adulthood, she found that for both men and women, those who had shown a pattern of stable, positive emotional health were those whose personal qualities matched the gender and family roles prevailing for that cohort. The men were focused on work achievement and supporting their families; the women were focused on providing nurturance to their families and on an array of friendships. By temperament, these women appeared to be high in extraversion and low in neuroticism. They liked staying at home and raising a family, and even at midlife, when the children were gone, they were quite content with their lives. The improver men and women, in contrast, had tried to fit themselves into the prevailing gender roles but the match had never been good. These groups included women who had been more strongly intellectually oriented as teenagers (not so acceptable in this cohort as it is now), but who had married at the expected time and followed the usual pattern of the family life cycle. By age 40, they were unhappy, thin-skinned, and irritable. But by age 50, when they had reached the postparental stage, most had branched out into jobs or had returned to school.

Similarly, the improver men had been unconventional teenagers but had tried to fit themselves into the gray-flannel-suit male role expectations of their generation. They too, at 40, were unhappy, with their emotions under tight rein. But by 50, they had allowed their artistic interests and humor to bloom.

I think that the concept of match or mismatch between (cohort-specific) role demands and personal qualities points us in a very important direction in our thinking about the impact of roles on adult lives. It is far too simple to think of a role as something that "shapes" the adult who occupies it. Rather, we might think of a role as similar to a piece of clothing that one puts on: It is bound to fit some people better than others. So it is the interaction between the demands and the flexibility of the role on the one hand, and the adult's qualities on the other, that may be crucial in determining the effect of the role. Thinking of roles in this way obviously makes the job of describing adult development far more complicated. But in my view it also brings us closer to the reality of adult developmental patterns.

TABLE 6.3 **Summary of Age Changes in Social Roles over Adulthood**

Age 20–40	Age 40–65	Age 65+
Maximum gender role differentiation, particularly after the birth of the first child.	Some indication of greater androgyny, or some expansion of traditional gender roles.	Gender roles *may* become more similar, but evidence is mixed.
Role of spouse added for most adults.	Spousal role becomes more central, more satisfying, after the last child leaves home.	Spousal role is lost by the majority of older women in old age.
Role of parent added for most adults.	Significant change in parental role after last child leaves home, although significant assistance is still provided.	Role of parent changes as the direction of assistance is typically reversed.
Role of child to one's own parent continues, with young adults receiving more aid than they give.	Role of child to one's own parents shift toward more caregiving, less receiving of assistance; role is lost altogether when the last parent dies.	Role of child to one's own parent no longer exists for most in this age group.
Grandchild role continues but is not usually highly significant.	Role of grandparent added.	Grandparent role continues but becomes less central with increasing age.

AN AGE SUMMARY

As in earlier chapters, I have pulled together the various patterns of change with age in a summary table (Table 6.3) so that you can begin to build up composite pictures of the qualities and experiences of adults in different age groups. The key point to be reemphasized is the one with which I began the chapter: Despite all the variations in timing and sequence, the basic shape of the pattern of role accumulation and loss seems to me to be the same for virtually all adults. We add more roles in early adulthood than at any other age, redefine those roles in middle adulthood, and shed many of them in late adulthood. The specifics vary as a function of whether an adult marries, or has children, or divorces. But this basic shape, I think, characterizes the vast majority of adult lives.

SUMMARY

1. Despite increasing variation in the timing and sequence of family roles in current cohorts, it remains true that adult life is shaped by shared patterns of acquisition, redefinition, and relinquishment of major social roles.

2. Gender roles refer to the "job descriptions" for male and female behavior and qualities. Gender role stereotypes refer to the shared, excessively generalized, beliefs about what men and women should be like.

3. Gender stereotypes are strong and remarkably consistent across cultures. The male stereotype centers around qualities of competence and instrumentality; the female stereotype centers around qualities of affiliation and expressiveness.

4. More new roles are acquired in early adulthood than at any other time. For many in today's cohorts, there is a stage of independent living between "leaving home" and marriage or cohabitation.

5. Cohabitation has become another type of intermediate role for many adults, with marriage occurring at later ages.

6. Marriage is associated with an increase in happiness or life satisfaction, but also with a shift toward more traditional gender-role arrangements.

7. That shift is accentuated after the birth of the first child. Gutmann's concept of parental imperative suggests that such traditional role division is genetically programmed in the species.

8. Marital satisfaction, life satisfaction, and mental health all show some decline after the birth of the first child, as parents experience a rise in role conflict and role strain.

9. In middle adulthood, roles are less confining; they are reduced in complexity or redefined. Particularly important for this redefinition is the departure of the last child—the empty nest.

10. On average, marital satisfaction rises in middle adulthood, while depression and other signs of emotional distress are at low ebb.

11. The role of grandparent is added by most adults in their middle years. There are many styles of grandparenting, but the role is not always central to well-being for older adults.

12. A minority of middle-aged adults also take on a role as caregiver to an aging parent. For some, this role is all-consuming and burdensome; for others, it involves smaller time commitments.

13. Midlife can be described as the time of the generational squeeze, because those in this age range are likely to be called on to assist both their young adult children and their aging parents.

14. The most marked change in roles in late adulthood is a decline in the number of roles filled combined with a reduction in the prescriptiveness of the roles still occupied. This change may be perceived, or experienced, by some as greater freedom, by others as a loss.

15. Widowhood, more common for women than men, means a loss of the role of spouse and a period of living alone for a large fraction of older women.

16. The adult life pattern of lifelong single adults is somewhat different, but if the person has created a network of supportive relationships, long-term singleness is not linked to higher rates of distress or loneliness.

17. Childless adults do not experience the rhythm of role change that accompanies a child's development, but they nonetheless follow the basic pattern of adding roles in early adulthood, changing the basic roles in middle adulthood, and shedding roles in late adulthood.

18. Divorce and remarriage does not greatly alter the basic timing of many family life-cycle events (such as the timing of the last birth for women), but it does markedly increase the complexity of family roles to be filled. Divorce is also associated with significant economic decline for women.

19. Being off-time for your culture and your cohort is typically associated with increased stress or higher rates of specific problems, such as divorce.

20. In understanding the impact of gender roles and family roles on adult lives, it may also be helpful to examine the degree of match or mismatch between a person's personal qualities and the demands of the roles that she or he must fill. Where the match is poor, the adult may experience higher levels of stress and lower levels of physical and mental health.

KEY TERMS

social roles

gender roles

gender stereotypes

instrumental roles

communal roles

social roles interpretation (theory)

learning schema explanation

gender polarized

conventionally gendered

nonconventionally gendered

androcentric

evolutionary psychology

demographic density

relationship initiators

relationship maintainers

social support

prenatal imperative

role conflict

role strain

remote grandparents

companionate grandparents

involved grandparents

kinkeeper

caregiver burden

generational squeeze

SUGGESTED READINGS

Kornhaber, A. (1996). *Contemporary grandparenting.* Thousand Oaks, CA: Sage.

This book describes the findings of in-depth interviews with grandparents in Kornhaber's Grandparent Project. Many are raising grandchildren themselves, and others are vitally involved in the lives of their grandchildren, even when they are separated by great distances.

Lachman, M. E., & James, J. B. (1997). *Multiple paths of midlife development.* Chicago: University of Chicago Press.

This is a very unusual book in that it is totally about middle age, a very understudied time of the life span. It is also unusual because it includes a lot of longitudinal work. Various authors cover topics such as the self, gender identity, and multiple roles for women—all focused on midlife.

Turner, B. F., & Troll, L. E. (Eds.). (1994). *Women growing older. Psychological perspectives.* Thousand Oaks, CA: Sage.

This book is full of fascinating papers, several of which are relevant to the topics of this chapter, including one by Huyck on psychodynamic views of gender among older women, and one by Turner and Turner on gender stereotypes across age.

DEVELOPMENT
OF RELATIONSHIPS

Take a moment and think about some of the most joyous and some of the most painful moments in your life. Perhaps graduating from high school or college, getting promoted, or becoming a parent are on your list of joys. Your list of painful moments might include getting fired from your job or that day you got your first really bad grade in school. Certainly, many of life's highs and lows have to do with school or work experiences. But I will wager that most of the joys and pains you thought of first were connected to a few key relationships—with your parents, with your partner, with your friends. In particular, the processes of attachment and detachment, of creating and breaking bonds with others, lie at the heart of many of the turning points in our lives.

In Chapter 6 I talked about some of the key roles that involve family and relationships, focusing primarily on the form and timing of those roles. Here I want to look inside the roles, at the quality of the relationships themselves. Are there age-linked changes in the quality or quantity of relationships over adulthood? Are there typical changes in the number or type of friends we have over adulthood? Does the relationship between partners (spouses or lovers) go through predictable changes over time or over age? Do relationships with our parents, or our growing children, change in specific ways over the adult years?

THE UNDERLYING NATURE OF ADULT RELATIONSHIPS: SOME THEORY

If you think about your own relationships—with your parents, your friends, your partner/lover/spouse, your co-workers—it's clear immediately that these relationships are not all the same, either in intensity or in quality. But how can we describe those differences more precisely? What set of terms can we use to talk about the array of relationships we each create?

Theoretical interest in the qualities of adult relationships is relatively recent, so there are many new ideas, new concepts, and no clear agreement on the best framework. The disagreement is exacerbated by the fact that theorists have started from at least three different places: from studies of attachment, from analyses of love, and from research on social support systems.

Attachment

The concept of **attachment** has been used most commonly to describe the strong affectional bond formed by an infant to his or her major caregiver (Ainsworth, Blehar, Waters, & Wall, 1978; Bowlby, 1969, 1973, 1980, 1988a, 1988b). John Bowlby and Mary Ainsworth, two of the major theoretical figures in this area, have both made a clear distinction between the attachment itself, which is an invisible, underlying bond, and **attachment behaviors,** which are the ways in which an underlying attachment is expressed by the person. Since we cannot see the attachment, we have to infer it from behavior. In infants, we see it in their crying when their favored person leaves the room, in their clinging to the favored person when they are frightened, in their use of the favored person as a safe base for exploring some new situation. The three key underlying features are (1) association of the attachment figure with feelings of security, (2) an increased likelihood of attachment behavior when the child is under stress or threat, and (3) attempts to avoid, or to end, any separation from the attachment figure (Weiss, 1982).

In adults, of course, many of these specific attachment behaviors are no longer seen. Most adults do not burst into tears if their special person leaves the room; adults maintain contact in a much wider variety of ways than what we see in children, including the use of letters, phone calls, and fantasy and imagery. But if we allow for these changes in the *form* in which the attachment is expressed, it does appear that the concept of attachment is a useful way to think about many adult relationships, for several reasons.

First of all, we appear to form strong new attachments in adulthood, particularly to a spouse or partner, and we may maintain our attachment to our parents as well. As Weiss says, "In all these instances individuals display need for ready access to the attachment figure, desire for proximity to the attachment figure in situations of stress, heightened comfort and diminished anxiety when in the company of the attachment figure, and a marked increase in discomfort and anxiety on discovering the attachment figure to be inexplicably inaccessible" (1982, p. 173).

A personal experience brought this final point home to me very clearly. Several years ago I was separated from my husband under circumstances that made it impossible for me to contact him even by phone. Given the dictates of our separate careers, we have been apart many times. Separation itself is not anxiety provoking. But I found his inaccessibility quite surprisingly uncomfortable. I was plainly relieved when he was once again available, if only by phone.

Attachment theory may also be useful in helping us understand different types of attachment in adults. Attachment theorists have suggested that very young children can be classified according to their attachment behavior as exhibiting either *secure, anxious,* or *avoidant attachment.* More precisely, they proposed that each child creates an **internal working model** of attachment relations, and this internal model contains elements of security or insecurity. The internal model is a set of beliefs and assumptions about the nature of relationships, such as whether others will respond if you need them, whether others are trustworthy, and the like.

Mary Main and her colleagues (Main and Hesse, 1990; Main, Kaplan, & Cassidy, 1985) have extended this argument to adulthood, suggesting that each adult also has a basic internal working model of attachment, based on but not necessarily identical to the internal model created by the child in the early years of life. Main measures the adult's attachment model through an interview in which the subject is asked to talk about his or her childhood experiences and current relationship with his or her parents. Based on an analysis of this interview, Main identifies three types of adult attachment, as shown in Table 7.1.

Longitudinal research shows that an infant's attachment classification tends to remain stable into young adulthood (Waters, Merrick, Albersheim, & Treboux, 1995), and other studies show that an adult's attachment classification corresponds to their children's classification on infancy attachment measures (van IJzendoorn, 1995). Considered together, this evidence points to attachment as being a relatively enduring mental representation that is established in the early years and continues into adulthood, enabling the adult to establish a similar relationship with his or her own children.

TABLE 7.1 Types of Secure and Insecure Attachment Among Adults, Proposed by Mary Main

Secure/autonomous/balanced	These adult value attachment relations, view those relationships as having been influential in their current personalities. The subjects speak freely and coherently about their early experiences and have thought about what had motivated their parents' behavior.
Dismissing or detached	These adults minimize the importance or the effects of their early experience. They may idealize their parents, but have poor recall of their childhood, often denying negative experiences and emotions or calling them normal or typical. Their emphasis is on their own personal strengths.
Preoccupied or enmeshed	These adults often talk about inconsistent or role-reversed parenting. They may be confused about their experiences or about what had been expected of them. As adults, those in this group are still caught up in their family and in their relationships, either still struggling with anger or with the desire to please.

Source: Main & Hesse, 1990; Main, Kaplan, & Cassidy, 1985.

In an extension of attachment theory, several researchers have suggested that adult romantic relationship styles are reflections of attachment the adults had with their parents in childhood (Bartholomew, 1990; Hazan & Shaver, 1987). In one demonstration of this, Hazan and Shaver (1990) gave adults a questionnaire with three descriptions and asked them to select the one that best characterized the way they feel about romantic relationships. The three descriptions paralleled Ainsworth's three types of attachment in infants and are presented in Table 7.2. Initial findings were that the proportion of adults selecting each style are similar to the proportion of infants classified in each style (approximately 55 percent secure, 20 percent anxious, and 25 percent avoidant), which suggests that these styles in young adult romantic relationships reflect internal working models of attachment established in early childhood. Later research by others (Feeney & Noller, 1990; Mikulincer & Orbach, 1995) has confirmed these percentages, and a recent large-scale study by Shaver and colleagues (Mickelson, Kessler, & Shaver, 1997) shows that these proportions are similar in people who range in age from 15 to 54 years.

TABLE 7.2 Hazen and Shaver's Questionnaire on Adult Relationships Types[a]

Which of these three descriptions best characterize you?

1. I am somewhat uncomfortable being close to others; I find it difficult to trust them completely, difficult to allow myself to depend on them. I am nervous when anyone gets too close, and often, love partners want to be more intimate than I feel comfortable being.

2. I find that others are reluctant to get as close as I would like. I often worry that my partner doesn't really love me or won't want to stay with me. I want to get very close to my partner, and this sometimes scares people away.

3. I find it relatively easy to get close to others and I am comfortable depending on them. I don't often worry about being abandoned or about someone getting too close to me.

[a]The authors gave this questionnaire to young adults and found that most (55%) selected (3), which corresponds to Ainsworth's description of secure infants. About 25% selected (1), corresponding to avoidant infants, and 20% selected (2), corresponding to anxious infants.

Source: Hazan & Shaver (1990, p. 272).

Subsequent research showed that adults who classified themselves as secure according to the Hazan & Shaver questionnaire reported higher levels of satisfaction with their relationships than those who classified themselves in the anxious and avoidant categories (Brennan & Shaver, 1995). People showing anxious attachment were more obsessed with their relationships than were secure or avoidant people (Hazan & Shaver, 1987) and reported more frequent partners and more frequent breakups (Kirkpatrick & Davis, 1994). People showing avoidant attachment tended to react to stress in a relationship by withdrawing from their partners (Simpson, Rholes, & Nelligan, 1992). And what are people who show secure attachment like as relationship partners? This is summarized by Lilah Koski and Phillip Shaver (1997): "Secure adults communicate their feelings more accurately and sensitively than insecure adults, perceptively notice their partners' needs and feelings, respond more empathically, and express more optimism about the relationship" (p. 44).

An extension of Hazan and Shaver's model has been proposed that has four categories of attachment styles based on a person's model of the self and others (Bartholomew & Horowitz, 1991). Based on self-reported ratings of how much different statements describe their own attitudes toward relationships, people are classified as **secure** (having a positive model of both self and others), **dismissive** (having a positive model of self and a negative model of others), **preoccupied** (negative model of self and positive model of others), or **fearful** (negative model of both self and others). Using this relationship questionnaire with young adults, Bartholomew and Horowitz found that almost half rated themselves as being secure, while the other half were equally distributed among the remaining three categories.

Although attachment style is hypothesized by these researchers to be a stable, life-long phenomenon for most people, I am aware of only one study that has investigated this topic in older adulthood. Jeffrey Dean Webster (1997) recruited a group of 76 healthy older adults (mean age 68 years) through an ad in a Canadian newspaper directed at community-dwelling adults over the age of 50. Using the questionnaire devised by Bartholomew and Horowitz, Webster assessed the attachment styles of these participants and compared them with the young adults in the Bartholomew and Horowitz (1991) study. Results, as illustrated in Figure 7.1, show that the largest proportion of the older adults (52 percent) gave responses that assigned them to the dismissive category, compared to only 18 percent of the younger group. In contrast, only a third of the older group (33 percent) were classified as secure, compared to almost half of the younger group (47 percent). Webster suggested that the large proportion of dismissive relationship styles, which reflect a positive model of the self and a negative model of others, could be a coping skill that older

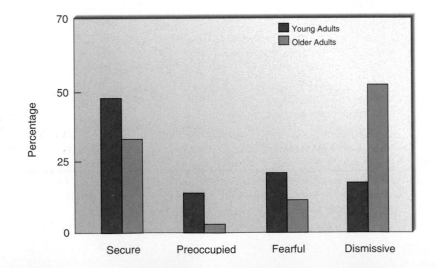

FIGURE 7.1 More young adults show secure attachment styles while older adults show dismissive attachment styles.

Source: Adapted from Webster, 1997.

people adopt as a reaction to the death of a spouse or other separation from partners. Over half of this sample were either widowed, divorced, or separated, and Webster's view of belief in one's own independence rather than the need for a partner as an adaptive move in late adulthood is a good one, especially when boosted by subsequent findings that the dismissive and secure participants scored higher than the preoccupied or fearful ones on a test of overall happiness.

As nicely as adult attachment research seems to tie together security in early childhood with relationship success in adulthood, there are some problems. The studies are all correlational, meaning that they have only established a relationship, not a cause. Although people who are secure as infants are also secure in adult relationships, multiple explanations are possible, and attachment theory is only one. Another reservation I have is that the responsive parent/secure child connection may be reflecting some shared emotional or behavioral traits that are genetic. Koski and Shaver (1997) have suggested large-scale behavior genetics studies of twins to investigate the contribution of genetics. It will be interesting to watch this very active program of research unfold.

Love

Although the topic of love may not seem to lend itself well to scientific scrutiny, it has become a topic of high interest for researchers during the last few decades. In fact, Michael Barnes and Robert Sternberg (1997) recently declared that theories about love had reached a "critical mass" and suggested arranging them in a hierarchy based on how they conceptualize love. (This is similar to the approach I described in Chapter 5 when I talked about the various approaches to the study of intelligence.)

The first type of theory according to Barnes and Sternberg (1997) includes those that view love as being a *single dimension,* a line that extends from one extreme to another and each person's experience of love can be plotted somewhere along that line. The most famous single-dimension theory of love is that of Freud (1952), who believed that love was **sexual desire.** According to Freud, everyone's experience of love can be expressed by how much or how little sexual desire they feel for the other person (whether they are consciously aware of it or not!). Zick Rubin (1973) theorized that love is a single dimension that ranges between liking and loving. **Liking** is defined as having feelings of respect and affection toward the other person, and **loving** is having feelings of caring and intimacy. According to Rubin, the distance between liking and loving contains all the possible feelings anyone would have toward a romantic partner, friend, or family member.

Other single-dimension theories suggest that love is measured by the amount of **limerance,** or acute longing, one feels for the other person (Tennov, 1979). According to this theory, extreme love means that you think about the other person all the time, even when you are trying to think of other things; you feel dependent on the other person and extremely emotionally attached; you feel exquisite pleasure when the other person seems to feel the same way. Your love for another person, using this theory, depends on how much they intrude on your daily thoughts and emotions.

Other theories, *multiple-factor theories,* propose that love is made up of several equally important factors. The love one person feels for another can be expressed in terms of how much of each factor they experience. Hatfield (1988) proposes that love is actually two feelings: passionate and companionate love. **Passionate love** is intense longing for the other person that can result in ecstasy if it is fulfilled or in despair if it is not. **Companionate love** is affection and familiarity. According to this theory, each person's love toward another person can be defined by the amount of passionate love and the amount of companionate love they experience.

Sternberg's (1986) multiple-factor theory of love is based on three primary components: (1) **intimacy,** which includes feelings that promote closeness and connectedness; (2) **passion,** which is a feeling of intense longing for union with the other person, including sexual union; and (3) **commitment** to a particular other, often over a long period of time. If these three components are combined in all possible ways, you end up with the subvarieties of love listed in Table 7.3. These eight combinations are theorized to cover the entire phenomenon of love.

Finally, a third type of theory, the *multiple-cluster theory*, posits that love is a set of a limitless number of feelings, thoughts, and behaviors that produce the overall effect known as love (Barnes & Sternberg, 1997). A good example of this theory is Berscheid's (1983) theory of emotion. She believes that love is a number of clusters or bonds that are interconnected and experienced as one overall feeling. In a relationship, each person participates in a chain of behaviors and expectations that are met by the other person's behaviors and expectations. The success of the relationship depends on the way the partners interact with and adjust to each other.

Which theory is right? Are more complex theories better than simple ones? Are the more recent theories better than old ones? Barnes and Sternberg (1997) suggest that the three types of theories—single factor, multiple factor, and multiple cluster—may be looking at the same thing at different levels. They suggest that instead of asking, "Which is right?" we should ask "How do they relate to each other?"

The Convoy Model

Another approach to relationships in adulthood comes from Toni Antonucci (1990, 1994a, 1994b; R. L. Kahn & Antonucci, 1980), who uses the term **convoy** to describe a network of social relationships that surround each of us through our adult lives. The purpose of this convoy is described by Antonucci and Akiyama (1997): "Convoy members protect and defend, aid, and socialize individuals as they move through life. Although not all relationships are long-term and significant, a sizable proportion of them are. These relationship fundamentally affect how the individual experiences the world. These relationships are assumed to be reciprocal and developmental. As the individual changes and develops

TABLE 7.3 **Eight Subvarieties of Love Suggested by Robert Sternberg**

Nonlove	When none of the three components of passion, commitment, and intimacy are present, there is no love. Most casual relationships are of this type.
Liking	Intimacy is present, but passion and commitment are not. Many enduring friendships have this quality.
Infatuation	Passion without intimacy or commitment.
Empty love	Commitment without passion or intimacy. May characterize some stagnant, long-term marriages or "friendships" that have gone on for years but have lost mutual involvement and mutual attraction.
Romantic love	Both passion and intimacy are present, but no commitment. May be characteristic of the early stages of a relationship.
Companionate love	Both intimacy and commitment are present, but passion is not. May describe long-term committed friendships, or relationships with parents or other kin, or with a partner with whom passion has waned.
Fatuous love	Passion and commitment, but no intimacy, as in a whirlwind courtship; the commitment is based on passion rather than on intimacy, although intimacy may come later.
Consummate love	All three components are present. The attainment of consummate love is no guarantee that it will last.

Source: Sternberg, 1987.

through time, the nature of expectations and exchanges is also likely to change" (p. 154). The nature of the convoy each of us creates is obviously affected by personal qualities, including, no doubt, the nature of the internal model of attachment we bring with us to the process, as well as our personality traits.

In their research using the convoy model, Antonucci and her colleagues use a mapping technique. They ask respondents to report on three levels of relationships and write the names of the people within three concentric circles (see Figure 7.2). The inner circle is for names of people who are so close and important to the respondent that he or she could hardly imagine life without them. The middle circle is for people who are also close, but not as close as those in the inner circle. And the outer circle is for names of people who are part of the respondent's personal network but not as close as the other two groups (Antonucci, 1986). This convoy map is useful for comparing the number of social relationships of various groups, (e.g., men and women or young people and old people) and also the closeness of the relationships.

In a typical study, Antonucci and Akiyama (1997) compared the convoy maps of men and women in two age groups, young middle age (35 to 49 years of age) and old middle age (50 to 65 years of age). They found that the younger group had more people in their convoys (approximately 22 compared to 18), and that the women had more people in their convoys than the men (approximately 22 to 18 again). Closer examination showed that all subjects had about the same number of people in their outer circles; the differences were in the inner two circles. There was also a difference in who was listed by the different age groups and genders. For example, the young middle-aged group mentioned their mothers in the inner circle and

CRITICAL THINKING

Try to diagram your own personal convoy on Antonucci's circles (Figure 7.2). After you read about Antonucci and Akiyama's (1997) findings, see how your convoy compares to others in your age and gender groups. How has your convoy changed with time?

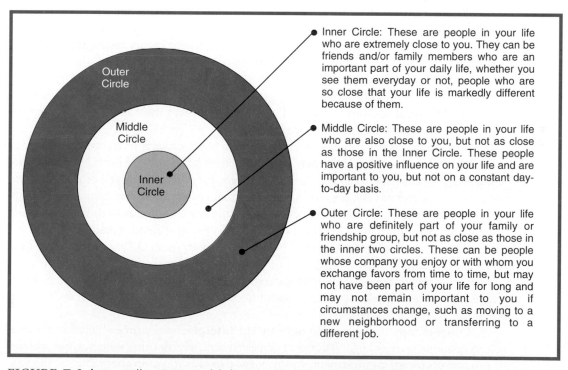

FIGURE 7.2 Antonucci's convoy model. Antonucci believes that each person's social network can be diagrammed by placing names of friends and family members in one of three concentric circles, according to degree of closeness.

the old middle-aged group did not (in fact, the older women mentioned their grand-daughters instead). This is obviously due to the fact that mothers of the older group had either died or were no longer able to continue a close relationship with their adult child.

An example of a gender difference was found in the inner circle of the younger middle-aged group, where women averaged one more person than the men did, and this turned out to be because women named sisters and men did not. Brothers for both groups were in the middle circle, but men also put sisters there, while women put sisters in the inner circle. Women in the older group had moved sisters out to the middle circle.

I find the image of a convoy, moving through time, highly evocative. New members are added to the convoy over time and others leave, but the core members tend to remain constant over long periods. What I want to focus on in this chapter are the relationships that are likely to be part of such a convoy for each of us: with a partner, with parents and other family members, and with friends. Let me begin with that relationship that is typically the most central of those relationships, the link with one's spouse or partner.

INTIMATE PARTNERSHIPS

I have quite purposely chosen to use the term *partnership* rather than *marriage* in this discussion, since I also want to include here both long-term committed homosexual relationships and unmarried but committed heterosexual relationships. Of course, the vast majority of the research has focused on marital relationships, which will make this discussion somewhat lopsided. However, limited recent research on cohabiting heterosexual and homosexual couples indicates that many of the same processes as are found in marriages occur in these other committed partnerships as well.

Choosing a Partner

The process of mate selection preoccupies most of us in our teens and 20s—the stage that Erikson calls *intimacy versus isolation*. For many adults the search for a partner becomes a preoccupation again after a divorce. At either time, we are searching for a partner with whom we hope to spend the rest of our lives. In attachment theory terms, we are searching for a "safe base" from which we may explore the world of adulthood.

Just what attracts one person to another? How does a couple move past passion or intimacy to commitment? Why do some early combinations break up, whereas others become stable? Social scientists have tried very hard to answer these questions, but despite the efforts, understanding still largely eludes us.

Proponents of **filter theories** describe mate selection as a series of steps that rule out more and more potential partners until only one is left (Cate & Lloyd, 1992). Bernard Murstein, for example (1970, 1976, 1986), suggests that when you meet a prospective partner, you first check for the degree of match on basic external characteristics, such as appearance, or manners, or apparent social class. If this first hurdle is passed, you then check for a match on attitudes and beliefs, such as politics, sex, or religion. Finally, if you are still interested in one another, the degree of role fit becomes an issue: Do your prospective partner's expectations fit with your needs or inclinations? Is there sexual compatibility, or agreement on gender roles? There is some support for filter theories of courtship, but it seems likely that all these factors are present from the beginning, rather than operating in sequence as Murstein suggests.

Other theorists have focused more on the **interpersonal process** between the couple. A relationship may begin because of perceived similarity or other matches, but whether it progresses toward commitment, in this view, depends more on the nature of the relationship that evolves (Cate & Lloyd, 1992; Surra, 1985; 1990). For example, several studies of couples who eventually marry indicate that there are distinct changes in facets of the relationship as the couple moves from casual dating to greater commitment to marriage

(Huston, Surra, Fitzgerald, & Cate, 1981). Feelings of belongingness and attachment (what Sternberg would call intimacy) increase over time, as do *maintenance behaviors,* such as disclosing feelings, trying to solve problems, and being willing to change in order to please the partner. Both ambivalence and conflict also increase early in relationships, with the peak just before a commitment to marriage is made, after which they decline. Ted Huston and his colleagues also found a gender difference in these patterns: Women appeared to be more cautious about forming an attachment or making a commitment, but once it was made, they took on more of the task of relationship maintenance, a standard female gender role task in this culture.

But not one of these approaches has really helped much to understand why it is that two people are drawn to one another and why some of those who are drawn form commitments and others do not. As Cate and Lloyd say: "Our knowledge of the mate-selection process is still quite rudimentary" (1992, p. 53). The one thing that is clear is that we chose our partners more on the basis of similarity than on any other single basis, a process that sociologists refer to as **homogamy** or assortive mating. We are far more likely to choose someone who is similar in age, social class background, race or ethnic group, religious preference or involvement, interests, attitudes, and temperament than someone who differs from us in these respects. A number of recent studies also indicates that we also tend to choose mates who have a similar type of internal working model of attachment. Securely attached young adults tend to choose securely attached mates, for example (Feeney & Noller, 1990; Senchak & Leonard, 1992).

The **exchange theory** of mate selection argues that each of us has some assets to offer a prospective partner and that in choosing, we try for the best exchange we can manage. According to this view, women often exchange their sexual and domestic services for the economic support offered by a man (Schoen & Wooldredge, 1989), which means that women are more likely to choose on the basis of the perceived stability or prospective earning power of a mate. Men, on the other hand, are more likely to focus on attractiveness.

One large national study supports this view (South, 1991). Over 2000 unmarried adults were asked how willing they would be, on a 7-point scale of willingness, to marry someone with various qualities, such as someone who was not good looking, someone younger, someone with less or more education than themselves, someone who earns more or less than themselves. You can see some of the results in Figure 7.3. Hispanic-American, African-American, and Anglo men were all less willing than were women of any ethnic group to marry someone who was not good looking, but more willing to marry someone with less education or less income. Women were more likely to want to marry someone older than themselves, or someone who had good earnings. In general, women appear to aim to marry "up" the socioeconomic ladder, while men are willing to marry "down" on any quality except attractiveness.

Marriage Versus Cohabitation

Once a commitment has been made, today's couples face another choice: marriage or **cohabitation,** which is living together in a committed relationship without marriage. In Chapter 6 you saw some of the evidence showing the rapid increase in cohabitation in the past few years. Here I want to focus on the question of the impact of cohabitation on the relationship itself.

Many couples who live together conceive of cohabitation as a final "filter," a sort of test run before marriage. Can we really get along together? Are we sexually compatible? In Sternberg's terms, it is a test of the commitment element of love. The assumption is that relationships that pass this test will end in marriage and that such marriages will be more satisfying and more durable. Interestingly, the great bulk of the evidence shows exactly the opposite.

Studies in the United States, Canada, and European countries such as Sweden all show that those who cohabit before marriage are *less* satisfied with their subsequent mar-

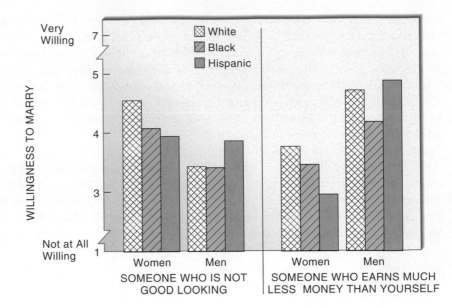

FIGURE 7.3 One model of mate selection focuses on the "exchange" of assets between prospective partners. These data from a national study provide some support. Men trade for attractiveness in a prospective mate; women trade for security.

Source: Data from South, 1991, Table 1, p. 932.

riages and *more* likely to divorce than are those who marry without cohabiting (Ferri & Smith, 1996; Hall & Zhao, 1995; Schoen, 1992). The most likely explanation of this surprising set of findings is not that cohabiting somehow spoils people for marriage but that adults who choose to live together before marriage are systematically different in key ways from those who reject such an option. DeMaris and Leslie (1984), for example, found that cohabitors are less traditional in gender roles, less likely to attend church, and less likely to agree that one should stick with a marriage no matter how bad it is, while noncohabitors are much more traditional in attitudes. Cohabitors also have been found to expect more from marriage and adapt less well to the traditional role expectations of marriage (S. Brown & Booth, 1996). Thus the difference in marital stability between co-habitors and noncohabitors is a matter of self-selection, not some causal processes attributable to cohabitation itself. Such an explanation is further strengthened by the finding that the negative correlates of cohabitation have become smaller and smaller in recent cohorts and have disappeared altogether in the cohort born between 1953 and 1957 (Schoen, 1992). Because cohabitation has become more and more common in these recent generations, self-selection is a less powerful factor, and the apparent negative effect vanishes.

Collectively, the data do not tell us that cohabitation somehow spoils people for later marriage. But neither do they suggest that cohabitation makes later marriage better, as most cohabitors believe.

CRITICAL THINKING

Do you think that any of this information about cohabitation would affect your own decision to cohabit or not to cohabit before marriage?

Creating a Relationship: The Role of Attachment

What is more important for the future of a partnership is the nature of the relationship the partners create together. And there is growing evidence that internal working models of attachment play a highly important role in shaping that relationship.

The basic argument is that each of us tends to recreate, in each significant relationship, the pattern we carry with us in our internal attachment model. This does *not* mean that the first attachment of infancy is simply carried forward in unchangeable form into adulthood. Main's research makes it clear that at least some adults who have secure adult attachment models had quite difficult and insecure childhoods. Through some process of internal analysis and self-understanding, these adults have been able to modify the original model. But whether an adult's internal model has been arrived at through such self-analysis or is carried forward relatively unchanged from early childhood, it is increasingly clear that each adult's internal model affects his or her expectations for his partner, his or her behavior toward the partner, and the stability of the relationship.

Adults with secure attachments, for example, are more likely to see their partner as friend as well as lover, are more trusting and less jealous, and are less anxious about whether their affection will be reciprocated (Hazan & Shaver, 1987; Simpson, 1990). In contrast, adults with a preoccupied attachment model are unsure of themselves, anxious about whether their feelings are returned, more jealous, and more preoccupied with their relationship, while those with dismissing or detached models are less trusting, more likely to avoid closeness, disclose less about themselves, provide less reassurance, and seek less support. They hold back from commitment, perhaps expecting rejection (Hazan & Shaver, 1990).

Just what role attachment models may play in relationship stability or satisfaction is not yet clear from the evidence we have. Some studies suggest that any pair including an insecurely attached person is likely to be less stable and satisfying than are pairs in which both partners are securely attached (Berman, Marcus, & Berman, 1994; Senchak & Leonard, 1992). But there is at least one longitudinal study, covering a period of four years, that indicates that only those pairs with an avoidant man or an ambivalent woman are less stable (Kirkpatrick & Hazan, 1994). It seems highly likely that there is some important link between these internal models and relationship process and success, but we don't yet understand precisely how it works.

Partnerships over Time

Actually, we need more longitudinal research of couple relationships from *any* theoretical framework. We know relatively little about what happens to the typical marriage or committed partnership over time. For example, is there some kind of systematic shift from one of Sternberg's categories of love to another? Do partnerships move from consummate to companionate love or even to empty love? We do know that marital satisfaction typically follows a curvilinear pattern across family life stages—a pattern you have seen several times already (recall Figure 1.6 and the discussion in Chapter 6). But such results only skim the surface.

The best way to delve deeper would be to study the same marriages over long periods of time, measuring the various aspects of the relationship, such as Sternberg's intimacy, passion, and commitment, at each of various time points. The only research I know of that approximates this design draws on data from the Berkeley Intergenerational Study. Sylvia Weishaus and Dorothy Field (1988) studied 17 couples, all parents of children who participated in the main study and all interviewed four different times, once in their young adulthood (1929), once in middle age (1946), once in young old age (1969) and once in old old age (1983). These 17 couples were the only pairs who had both survived that long and were still married to each other. The researchers found no common pattern of change or stability among these 17 marriages. The single most common pattern—found in seven of the couples—was the now-familiar curvilinear change, with high satisfaction in the early years, a drop in the middle years, and then a rise in later life. The descriptions of their marriages by these seven couples sound as if they moved through a time of "empty love" to a deeper attachment or to a companionate or consummate love in Sternberg's terms. They said things like, "our love has grown."

The remaining 10 pairs had had much more stable patterns: Five expressed high levels of satisfaction and positive emotion throughout the years (perhaps an example of consistently consummate love), three were largely neutral at every point (perhaps an example of empty love), and two were consistently negative.

Of course, we have no way of knowing whether these 17 couples are at all typical either of their cohort or of couples as a whole. Still, the study is intriguing, suggesting as it does the highly plausible hypothesis that there is not one but many different potential pathways through the marriage relationship. It is also plausible that the particular pathway one follows will depend a good deal on the kind of love or attachment that was present at the beginning.

In a 10-year longitudinal study of marriages, the Denver Family Project, Markman and colleagues (Lindahl, Malik, & Bradbury, 1997; Markman, 1981; Markman, Renick, Floyd, Stanley, & Clements, 1993) studied couples from before marriage until well into their first decade of marriage. For this group, marital satisfaction declined during the first three years but then leveled off and remained stable during the remainder of the first decade. Even though there were significant drops in marital satisfaction, most respondants expressed little distress about their relationships.

About 20 percent of the couples in the Denver Family Project divorced during the 10 years they were being studied. When Markman compared the data collected before marriage from the divorce group to that of the nondivorce group, some interesting differences emerged. Women in the divorce group had been younger at the time of marriage than those in the nondivorce group and showed a lack of problem-solving skills. Men in the divorce group expressed more negativity about the relationship than did those in the nondivorce group. And both men and women in the divorce group showed greater inability to acknowledge and accept their partner's expressed thoughts and feelings about the relationship.

The Denver Family Project also offered the participating couples marriage counseling, some of which was successful and some not. When the two types of outcomes were compared, several factors stood out that predicted poor chances of restoring the marriage. If the husband made comments to the wife that were insulting, hostile, and destructive; if the wife was unable (or unwilling) to contribute to solving their problems; if both spouses were insensitive to the emotional needs of the other. In other words, partners who are willing to listen and pay attention to each other, respond to each other's needs, and make attempts to find solutions to their problems have greater chances of successful marriages.

The only other longitudinal data we have come from short-term studies of the first year or two of marriage, such as the work of Ted Huston and his colleagues (Huston, McHale, & Crouter, 1986). They have documented some of the specific experiences that may contribute to the commonly reported drop in marital satisfaction after the honeymoon period is over. In this study of 168 couples, mostly young adults, all in their first marriages, each partner was interviewed at some length within the first three months of the marriage and then again after one year. In addition, in the weeks surrounding each of these time points, each couple was called nine times and asked to describe in detail what they had done over the previous 24 hours. Thus Huston has information not only about feelings and attitudes but about actual activities. He found that over the first year there was a decrease in satisfaction with both the quantity and the quality of interaction. These couples reported lower levels of love after one year, and that was true whether or not they had had a child. Furthermore, their activities had changed. In the early months they spent a lot more time in joint leisure activities; after one year, when they did things together it was more likely to be on "instrumental tasks" (grocery shopping, errands, housework, and the like). They also talked to each other less. Perhaps most important, the husbands and wives both described a sizable drop in the frequency with which the partner did pleasing things for them. Huston did not find any increase in negative interactions, but there was a sizable decline in positive interactions, a pattern you can see in the results I've shown in Figure 7.4. In Sternberg's terms, there was a decline in the intimacy aspect of love as well as in the passionate aspect—a combination that may lead directly toward an empty or devitalized marriage, at least for those couples who do not find ways to counteract the trend.

Signs that such a devitalization of marriage is quite common comes from one of my favorite cross-sectional studies. Clifford Swensen and his colleagues (Swensen, Eskew, & Kohlhepp, 1981) studied a sample of 776 adults that spanned the spectrum of family life-cycle stages. Each subject was asked to describe aspects of both loving and problematic marital interactions, from which Swensen developed two scales. A *love scale* describes the expressions of affection, self-disclosure, moral support and encouragement, material support, and toleration of the less pleasant aspects of the other person. A *marital problems scale* describes the degree of problems experienced in six areas: problem solving and decision making, child rearing and home labor, relationships with relatives and in-laws, personal care and appearance (does your partner leave more mess than you like? Has your partner gained too much weight? etc.), money management, and expressions of affection. You can see what happens to the scores on these two scales over the various family life-cycle stages in Figure 7.5. In this sample, expressions of love were lower with each succeeding age group, while problems peaked among those with young children. Swensen points out that although the older couples describe their marriages as satisfactory overall, these might nonetheless be described as **devitalized** or empty marriages, because the satisfaction is composed of both low problems *and* low expressions of love.

Joseph Veroff also found some evidence for such devitalization in his cross-sequential study (Veroff, Douvan, & Kulka, 1981), a study I have mentioned before. Recall that Veroff studied two sets of cross-sectional samples, one set in 1957 and one set in 1976. In both samples, the middle-aged and older adults reported both lower levels of problems and lower levels of physical affection in their marriages than did younger adults. But not everyone agrees that later-life marriages are devitalized. In a recent study in which middle-aged and older-aged couples were studied in detail, Robert Levenson and his colleagues (Levenson, Carstensen, & Gottman, 1993) found lower conflict but *higher* levels of reported pleasure among the couples in their 60s and 70s than among those in their 40s and 50s.

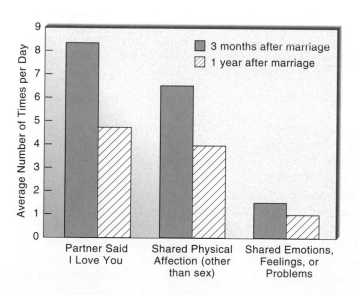

FIGURE 7.4 Most couples report that they become less satisfied with their marriages during the first year, whether they have children or not. They say fewer positive things to one another, express affection less often, and disclose their feelings less.

Source: Data from Huston, McHale, & Crouter, 1986, Table 7.4, p. 124.

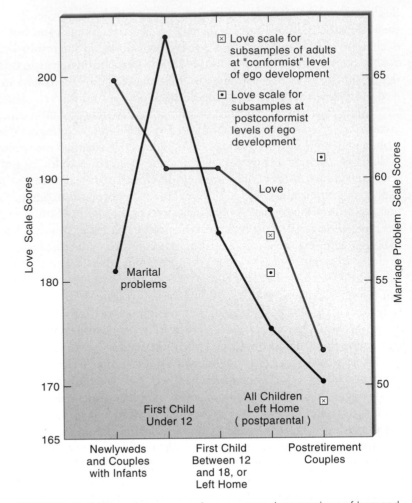

FIGURE 7.5 When these researchers measured expressions of love and marital problems in couples at various stages of the family life cycle, they found a pattern that helps to explain the typical curvilinear relationship between marital satisfaction and life stage. They also found that those older couples who scored at the postconformist level of ego functioning did *not* show the typical decline in expressions of love.

Source: C. H. Swensen, R. H. Eskew, & K. A. Kohlhepp, 1981, Stage of family life cycle, ego development, and the marriage relationship, *Journal of Marriage and the Family, 43,* 841–853. Fig. 1, p. 848, and data from Table 3, p. 849. Copyright 1981 by the National Council on Family Relations, 3989 Central Avenue, NE, Suite 550, Minneapolis, MN 55421. Reprinted by permission.

In attachment theory terms, it may be that one of the patterns of change in marriages over the adult years is a decline in frequency of certain classes of attachment behaviors, perhaps particularly in middle adulthood. The underlying attachment, however, certainly seems to persist, even in devitalized unions. Long-married older adults continue to turn to one another in times of stress and show marked distress at the death of the spouse—both signs of an enduring attachment. But attachment behaviors in the absence of stress may become less common, just as they do in children over the early years of life.

But while a pattern of declining and then rising satisfaction may describe the average pattern, it certainly does not describe changes in all relationships, as witness the five consistently positive long-term marriages in the Berkeley longitudinal study. Swensen and

NOT ALL long-time marriages are devitalized.

his colleagues give us a hint about one factor that may make a difference. For at least some of the two oldest groups of subjects shown in Figure 7.5, Swensen had obtained scores on Jane Loevinger's measure of ego development (see Table 2.2 for a review). He then divided the sample into those adults who scored at the conformist level and those who scored at the postconformist level, and looked again at the love scores. I've shown those scores in boxes in Figure 7.5. Among those in the postparental stage there was no difference in love scores between those at the conformist and those at the postconformist level. But among postretirement couples there was a very large difference, with the postconformist adults reporting much higher expressions of love in their relationship. Swensen says: "[P]ost-conformists are able to transcend role expectations and form relationships based more upon the reality of needs, feelings, wishes, and aspirations of the individuals. They are more capable of coping with conflict through discussion rather than avoidance, and so form relationships in which vitality, as measured by the expression of love, may increase over time" (Swensen et al., 1981, p. 850).

Further confirmation of this basic point comes from a study by Mark deTurck and Gerald Miller (1986), who measured the extent to which adults perceived their spouse as a unique human being as opposed to perceiving the spouse primarily in terms of the set of roles that he or she occupies. DeTurck and Miller did not use Loevinger's scale to measure this, but the parallel seems clear since perceiving and responding to others on the basis of unique individual characteristics is one of the features of the post-conformist stages. DeTurck and Miller found that marital satisfaction and cohesion were highest in those couples in which both persons perceived their mate in this more individualistic way and lowest in couples in which both responded primarily on the basis of roles.

Studies like this seem to me to be a major step forward. They tell us something about the kinds of individual skills or qualities that may promote or alter the commonly reported U-shaped pattern. But this research is only a bare beginning. We need to know a great deal more about the nature of changes in relationships over time and over age, not just in marital satisfaction, but in communication skills, values, empathy and humor. And we need to know far more about the links between the individual development of each partner and the quality of the relationship. To take just one example, I would like to know whether the often-reported rise in marital satisfaction in late middle age occurs in part because many more adults by that time have moved toward less stereotyped responses to the world in general. Could it also reflect increased gender role expansion? I not only want to understand the typical age-related patterns of change, I want to understand how those changes interact with the changes going on within each person in the partnership.

A Word of Caution. You've heard this song before, but let me sing it again: It is wise to remember that virtually all of the information we have on age-related patterns of marital interaction comes from *cross-sectional* comparisons. In this case, in addition to the usual problems of interpretation of developmental trends from cross-sectional data, there is another serious problem: Length of marriage, age, and stability of marriage are totally confounded in virtually every study. If we compare the marriages of adults in their 30s with marriages of adults in their 60s, the older group is not just older, they have also been married longer and their marriages have survived. Adults the same age who are divorced are simply not included in the study, nor have we studied groups of older couples who have been married only a short period of time. Longitudinal data can help sort out some of this problem but cannot solve all of it, since age and length of marriage are still going to be confounded in longitudinal designs. Thus we do not know whether the curvilinear pattern I have been talking about is related to age, or to length of marriage, or appears only in stable marriages. The fact that Huston finds a decline in affection over the first year of marriage, whether the couple has children or not, suggests that at least this first part of the curvilinear pattern is a real longitudinal change. But we need far more evidence of this kind.

CRITICAL THINKING

Think about how you might design a study that would get around some of the problems I've talked about here and that would add to our understanding of changes in marital relationships over time.

Good and Bad Marriages

A second window through which we can look at partnerships is through the study of good and bad or stable and unstable marriages. This very large body of research is largely *non*developmental. To my knowledge, no one has asked whether different elements contribute to marital breakdown or success at different points in the adult life cycle. But we may nonetheless glean some insights into the workings of this key relationship by a brief journey through this literature. I have summarized some of the main conclusions from this research in Table 7.4.

As you look at the items in this list, you may be struck by some of the same points that stood out for me as I read this literature. When a marriage begins, some couples have a lot of good things going for them. Others start out with a few strikes against them. In general, the more "resources" a couple has—such as more education, more communication skill or problem-solving ability, better physical and emotional health, more secure attachment models, and greater individual self-confidence—the better their chances of forming a satisfying intimate relationship. In the case of self-esteem, there are even some supportive longitudinal data. Using data from the Berkeley Intergenerational Study, Arlene Skolnick (1981) has compared the self-concepts at adolescence and early adulthood of three groups of middle-aged adults: happily married, unhappily married, and divorced. She found that those with satisfying marriages had had the highest self-esteem at both the earlier measurement points, in adolescence and early adulthood. Those with unsatisfying but enduring marriages had had the lowest self-esteem, with the divorced group falling in between. In the language of Erikson's theory, it looks like those young adults who have successfully completed the step of forming a clear (and positive) identity have a much better chance of creating a lasting and satisfying intimate partnership.

TABLE 7.4 Some Differences Between Satisfying or Lasting Marriages and Dissatisfying or Unstable Marriages

Personal Characteristics of People in More Successful Marriages

They married between ages 20 and 30.

They come from high-social-class families and have more education.

Their parents display(ed) lower levels of conflict in their own marriage and were somewhat less likely to have been divorced.

They have greater communication skills and greater cognitive complexity.

They are more likely to be highly involved in religion or to be of the same religious background.

They have higher levels of self-esteem.

They have better overall mental health, lower levels of depression, and lower levels of neuroticism.

They are more likely to have a secure internal working model of attachment.

Qualities of the Interaction of Couples in More Successful Marriages

They have high agreement on roles (including gender roles) and high satisfaction with the way the spouse is filling his or her roles.

They are roughly matched on levels of self-disclosure (high, medium, or low in both partners).

They have more positive than negative interactions. In particular, there is more reciprocation of negative behavior in dissatisfied or pre-divorce marriages.

They have lower levels of stereotyped or highly predictable behavior patterns; in dissatisfied couples, behavior patterns are more strongly routinized.

They have better conflict-resolution strategies, with low levels of both criticism and problem avoidance.

They are more symmetrical in their skill at reading each other's signals. In dissatisfied marriages, the husband appears to "read" the wife less well than she reads him.

They like each other and consider their spouse their best friend.

They spend more leisure time together.

Source Data from Cate & Lloyd (1992); Davidson, Balswick, & Halverson (1983); Filsinger & Thoma (1988); Gottman (1994a, 1994b); Halford, Hahlweg, & Dunne (1990); Heaton & Pratt (1990); M. S. Hill (1988); Kitson (1992); Kitson, Babri, & Roach (1985); J. H. Larson & Holman (1994); Schafer & Keith (1984); M. R. Wilson & Filsinger (1986).

Important as these initial skills are, though, they are clearly not the whole picture, nor even necessarily the most critical ingredient. Far more important is the pattern of interaction the partners create together. The most consistent interactional difference between happy and unhappy couples is simply the relative proportion of "nice" or "nasty" everyday encounters. John Gottman has shown very clearly that those couples who eventually divorce can be identified years ahead of time by looking at the pattern of these positive and negative exchanges. When negative items such as the ones Gottman singled out as being the "Four Horsemen of the Apocalypse"—criticism, contempt, defensiveness, and stonewalling—exceed the positive by too much, divorce becomes far more likely (Gottman, Katz, & Hooven,1997). As Gottman says: "One can think of each partner in a marriage as having a built-in meter that measures the totality of accumulated negativity in this interaction" (1994a, p. 333). Gottman proposes that once the level of this meter gets above some threshold, the partner's perception of the marriage "flips" from positive to negative. The accumulation of negativity may be gradual, but the *feeling*, the perception, switches rapidly, and the person then considers separation or divorce.

But Gottman is not proposing that all good marriages are alike and that all bad marriages are the same. His research suggests that there are three quite different types of stable or enduring marriages (Gottman, 1994b):

1. **Validating marriages.** In these marriages, disagreements rarely escalate. The partners listen, say "Mmm-hmm" or "I see" a lot, express mutual respect even when they disagree.

2. **Volatile marriages.** These couples squabble a lot, disagree, don't listen to each other very well when they argue. But they also laugh and show more affection than the average couple. They approach all their interactions with more passion, but the balance of positive and negative is in favor of positive.

3. **Avoidant marriages.** Gottman also calls this type *conflict minimizers.* These partners don't try to persuade each other, they simply agree to disagree, without apparent rancor. These marriages seem to be what is usually meant by "devitalized," although Gottman would argue that this is a quality present from the beginning of the marriage, not a stage all couples pass through over time.

Gottman suggests that there are also several types of unsuccessful marriages:

1. **Hostile/engaged marriages.** Like the volatile couples, these pairs argue often and hotly, but they do not have the balancing effect of the humor and affection.

2. **Hostile/detached marriages.** These couples fight regularly, but they rarely look at each other, the arguments tend to be brief, and there is also no balancing effect of affection or support.

In both unsuccessful types, the ratio of negative to positive encounters gets out of balance, and they spiral downward toward dissolution.

EVERY COUPLE FIGHTS at least once in a while. It is when the ratio of such angry exchanges compared to more positive expressions gets high that couples are likely to report serious dissatisfaction with their marriage.

Fortunately, these negative patterns are not unchangeable. Therapists who work with couples have found that marital satisfaction can be increased significantly by teaching couples how to solve conflicts, how to talk to one another, how to increase their positive interactions. So couples whose interactions have escalated toward discord can acquire new skills or relearn earlier patterns of interaction.

Homosexual Relationships

Accurate numbers are virtually impossible to obtain, but perhaps 4 to 6 percent of adults in the United States and other Western countries can be characterized as exclusively or typically homosexual (Gonsiorek & Weinrich, 1991). Long-lasting, committed relationships between same-sex partners have some fundamental differences from heterosexual partnerships because they are not supported by institutions such as religious groups and legal systems. In fact, relationships between same-sex partners is still illegal in some parts of the United States and openly condemned by some religious leaders. A good number of homosexual people prefer not to make their sexual orientation known, even to their families. Yet despite the difficulties and stress faced by gay and lesbian people, many manage to live in long-lasting, committed partnerships. Given these difficulties, it is interesting to learn what kinds of partnerships gay men and lesbians create and maintain. Are they similar to or different from what we see in heterosexual partnerships?

All summary statements I can make about gay relationships must be taken with great caution. A large percentage is hesitant to participate in research, so what we know about adult homosexuals and their relationships comes from studies of a subset, primarily those who are fairly well educated and those who are "out" about their homosexuality. Whether this subgroup is typical of the larger group of gay and lesbian people, we do not know.

A number of recurrent findings have emerged from this research, however, which I can summarize briefly. First, long-term committed relationships are very common among

IT IS ESTIMATED that about 70 percent of lesbian women live in committed, long-term relationships that tend to be highly egalitarian.

homosexuals, particularly among lesbians. Estimates vary, but perhaps 70 percent of lesbians are in committed relationships, in most cases living together. Among gay men, the percentages are somewhat lower, between 40 and 60 percent (Peplau, 1991). Among lesbians, monogamy within a long-term relationship is about as common as in heterosexual relationships (marriage or cohabitation), but monogamy is much less commonly a feature of gay male relationships. In one large national study, for example, sociologists Philip Blumstein and Pepper Schwartz (1983) found that 72 percent of lesbians in long-term relationships had been monogamous, compared to 79 percent of married women. In contrast, only 18 percent of gay men had been completely monogamous within their current relationship, compared to 74 percent of married men.

Second, homosexual relationships are, on the whole, more egalitarian than are heterosexual relationships, with less sharp role prescriptions (Kurdek, 1994). It is quite uncommon for homosexual couples to have one partner occupy a "male" role and the other a "female" role (Peplau, 1991). Instead, power and tasks are more equally divided. Again, however, this is more true of lesbian couples—among whom equality of roles is frequently a strong philosophical ideal—than for gay males. Among male homosexual couples, the man who earns the most money is likely to have greater power within the relationship (Blumstein & Schwartz, 1983). One gay male in the Blumstein and Schwartz study who was the more economically successful of the pair, said, for example: "I'd like him to come up with some ideas for free time together. But then he can't come up with ideas for free time that require spending money which he doesn't have. Like theater, plays, travel. If he made those decisions, he wouldn't have the money to do it.... So we do those things when I suggest it and feel like doing it" (p. 60).

Third, levels of satisfaction with their relationship are essentially the same among homosexual as among heterosexual couples. And satisfying and dissatisfying homosexual relationships differ in essentially the same ways as do relationships in equivalent groups of heterosexual couples (Peplau, 1991). Like marriages, gay relationships are more likely to persist and be satisfying if the two people express a strong sense of trust in each other, social support, and shared decision making (Kurdek, 1995).

The only longitudinal study of gay and lesbian couples that I am aware of was done by Lawrence Kurdek (1995), questioning 61 gay and 42 lesbian couples over a period of three years. Kurdek asked both partners to fill out questionnaires telling about their current relationship and their thoughts about what an ideal relationship would be by rating a set of statements on a scale from 1 to 9, depending on how much they agreed with each one. The statements were about **attachment** (doing things together as a couple), **autonomy** (acting independently), and **equality** (dealing with each other as equal partners). Over the three-year period, both the gay and lesbian couples reported decreased attachment, which is similar to findings of heterosexual couples. Kurdek explains that the need for togetherness decreases over time as a sense of trust and security intensify.

Couples also reported on their degree of commitment to each other, and this was used as a measure of relationship quality. What were the predictors that relationship quality would change from one year to the next? For both gay and lesbian couples, when statements about equality in the current relationship began to fall short of equality in the ideal relationship, it was reflected in lower levels of commitment to each other. Second, when statements about autonomy (being independent of one's partner) were rated higher than those about attachment (being together as a couple), commitment was also apt to decrease. In other words, this suggests that in gay and lesbian relationships, perceived equality needs to match ideal equality, and attachment needs to be greater than autonomy for the quality of the relationship to be maintained over time. Although this study suggests that gay and lesbian couples show many similarities in relationship maintenance over time, it would be interesting to see results from a group of heterosexual couples to see if the equality factor is as important in those relationships. To my knowledge, this has not been done.

Finally, at least one cross-sectional study shows that both gay and lesbian couples move through the same early stages of relationship described for married couples, with a drop in satisfaction in the early years (Kurdek & Schmitt, 1986).

In sum, homosexual relationships are far more like heterosexual relationships than they are different. Although long-term committed intimate pairings are less common among gay men than among other groups, when such commitments are made, they involve love and strong attachment. Many last a lifetime. Since homosexual relationships by definition involve two people who have both been socialized toward the *same* gender role, there are some differences in the dynamics of gay male and lesbian relationships. But the human urge to form one close, intimate, central attachment is evident in gay relationships as it is in heterosexual relationships.

RELATIONSHIPS WITH OTHER FAMILY MEMBERS

With so many adults living longer and with high divorce rates and remarriages, the term *family* these days may describe a far more complex set of relationships than was true even a few generations ago. At any one time, a family nearly always includes three generations, and many include four or even five.

With more generations, the sheer number of people with whom one is linked by family ties goes up, including not only children, grandchildren, and great-grandchildren, but their spouses and in-laws. When there have been divorces and remarriages, the combinations can become quite intricate. My own family may be an extreme example, but makes the point clearly: Three succeeding generations in my lineage have been divorced and remarried (both sets of grandparents, my parents, and my sister and myself), which creates patterns so complex that I have to draw genealogical charts to explain the relationships to others. There are stepgrandmothers, step-stepuncles, and many stepcousins. As Matilda Riley points out (1983), when the "family" is so broad, personal relationships within the family group cease to be based entirely on obligation or fixed kinship roles and become more and more determined by choice. One can pick and choose among the array of relatives those who might become part of one's own convoy. I have, for example, a very friendly relationship with one of my stepbrothers and his wife, as well as with the natural maternal grandmother of my two adopted children. (I know; it will take a brief pause for you to figure that one out.)

Research on family relationships in adulthood has not yet caught up to this complexity. Most research attention has been directed toward parent–child relationships, with less emphasis on sibling relationships or grandparent–grandchild links. There is essentially no information available on relationships between stepsiblings or even with in-laws (let alone former in-laws). Certainly, parent–child relationships are among the most enduring and the most central for many adult lives. In the future, though, I hope we will see explorations of a broader array of "family" connections and their effects on adult pathways.

General Patterns of Family Interactions

One of the consistent findings in research on family interactions in adulthood is the remarkable consistency with which nearly all of us maintain contact with our parents and siblings. Findings from a large study by Geoffrey Leigh (1982), while not new, are still representative. Leigh interviewed a total of about 1300 adults, spanning the full set of family life-cycle stages. Each adult reported how frequently he or she saw, spoke with, or wrote to parents, brothers and sisters, cousins, and grown children. Figure 7.6 shows the major findings for parents, siblings, and children. There is no real sign here of any variation in contacts with family members as a function of life-cycle stage except for a slight decline in frequent contact during the "new parent" stage. In this study, virtually all adults, whatever their age, reported at least some kind of contact with their parents at least monthly, and the majority also had regular contact with siblings.

Not surprisingly, the amount and type of contact is strongly affected by physical proximity. When parent and child live within one or two hours travel of one another, face-to-face contact is common; as distance increases, letters and phone calls become the most frequent form of communication (Dewit, Wister, & Burch, 1988; Moss, Moss & Moles, 1985). It is also clear that it is women who are the kinkeepers (Rosenthal, 1985); women make more of the phone calls, write more of the letters (to their in-laws as well as their own parents), and plan or encourage the visits.

There are also ethnic differences in family relationships among adults. Among Hispanic-Americans, especially Mexican-Americans, kin form a particularly central part of the relationship convoy. Whereas young adult Anglos often move away from family as part of a step toward independence, Hispanic-Americans are more likely to move *toward* kin (Vega, 1990). And among Hispanic-Americans, frequent visiting and kin contact—with siblings, cousins, aunts, and uncles as well as parents and children—is the rule rather than the exception. It is not enough to talk to your relatives; it is also necessary to see and touch them to maintain real contact (Keefe, 1984). Such a pattern seems to be more true of first-generation Hispanic-Americans, but second- and third-generation adults also appear to rely on kin more than is true for Anglos.

Extended family contact is also an important aspect of African-American adult life. In particular, multigenerational households are increasingly common in this group, very often consisting of three generations of women: a middle adult or young adult mother, a teenage or young adult daughter, and one or more grandchildren. One study suggests that six out of 10 black women now in their 40s lived in such a household at least for a

CRITICAL
THINKING

Think about your own family relationships for a moment. What life-cycle stage are you in? How has this affected the relationships you have with various family members? Do you think this will change in the future?

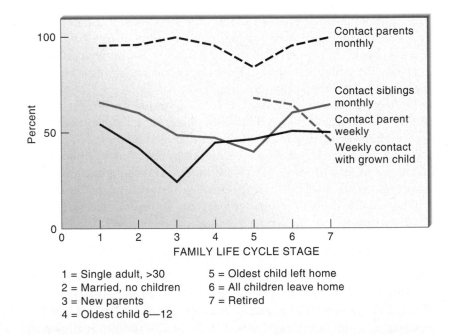

1 = Single adult, >30   5 = Oldest child left home
2 = Married, no children   6 = All children leave home
3 = New parents   7 = Retired
4 = Oldest child 6—12

FIGURE 7.6 Contact between adults and their parents, siblings, and grown children seems to remain remarkably high over adulthood, judging from these results from a 1976 survey.

Source: Data from Leigh, 1982, Table 2, p. 202.

period of time in young adulthood, compared to only 30 percent of Anglos (Beck & Beck, 1989). And even those who do not live in extended family groups have frequent contact with kin. Nearly two-fifths of African-American adults report that they have nearly daily contact with other family members, and many have important relationships with "fictive kin," neighbors or others with whom familylike bonds are created (R. S. Taylor, Chatters, & Jackson, 1993; R. S. Taylor, Chatters, Tucker, & Lewis, 1990).

Despite these variations, though, it is clear that for all ethnic groups, family relationships are a significant part of our lives throughout adulthood. What is the emotional quality of those relationships? Are they attachments or affiliations? Would we assign them to the inner, middle, or outer circles of our personal convoys? And when we make contact, what is the content of our interactions? Let me amplify.

Parent–Child Relationships

Attachments Between Adult Children and Their Parents. You'd think it would be fairly straightforward to figure out whether adult children are still attached to their parents. But it isn't. The answer obviously depends in part on how we define *attachment.* More important, it may depend on the age of the "adult children." In early adulthood, the young adult must transfer his or her most central attachment from the parent(s) to one or more peers. Robert Weiss puts it this way: "If children are eventually to form their own households, their bonds of attachment to the parents must become attenuated and eventually end. Otherwise, independent living would be emotionally troubling. The relinquishing of attachment to parents appears to be of central importance among the individuation-achieving processes of late adolescence and early adulthood" (1986, p. 100).

I do not agree with Weiss that the attachment to the parent is totally relinquished. It seems clear that at least *some* kind of attachment remains between adults and their parents. Not only do we typically maintain regular contact, we also show signs of deep grief and loss at the death of a parent. And in times of severe stress or need, most of us would be glad to have our parents on hand as support—all signs that an attachment is present. Yet Weiss is quite correct in pointing out that there has to be some pulling back from the central bond of childhood if there is going to be emotional room for a central attachment to a spouse or partner. Corinne Nydegger puts it nicely when she says that the task of the young adult "is to attain emotional emancipation from the parents, while remaining engaged as a son or daughter" (1991, p. 102).

Most young people manage this transition, gradually shifting their "proximity seeking," and "safe base" behaviors from parents to peers in late adolescence and early adulthood (Hazan, Hutt, Sturgeon, & Bricker, 1991). But an attachment to the parent remains, even while the attachment *behaviors* have changed. Indeed, four out of every five adults in a recent national sample said that their relationship with their parents is emotionally close (L. Lawton, Silverstein, & Bengston, 1994). Relationships with mothers are closer than those with fathers (Rossi, 1989); when the parents are divorced, the relationship tends to be less close, especially with a divorced father (Booth & Amato, 1994; Cooney, 1994). But even with these variations, it is still true that the parent–child relationship is affectionate and significant for people of all ages.

CRITICAL THINKING

Nearly all of you reading this will either be in the middle of this "distancing" stage or well past it. Do any of these descriptions capture the flavor of your own experience?

Attachments Between Parents and Their Adult Children. On the parents' side of the equation, the picture looks a little different. While the young adult is trying to negotiate a separation from the parent, the parent generation is trying to sustain a connection, not only because of their own bonds of nurturance and love for the child, but also because of what Vern Bengtson calls the **generational stake** the parent group has in the relationship. For the adult parents, their children and prospective (or actual) grandchildren represent continuity, even a kind of immortality.

Yet important as this relationship obviously is to the parents, it is not clear that it typically represents an attachment in the sense in which Ainsworth or Weiss have used that term. In particular, it is not clear that the presence of one's adult children brings with it that sense of security and comfort that is the central feature of an attachment. There is now abundant research evidence, for example, that among adults over 50, even among adults over 65 or 70, life satisfaction and happiness are simply *not* related to the amount of contact a person has with his or her grown children (G. R. Lee & Ishii-Kuntz, 1987; G. R. Lee & Sheehan, 1989; Markides & Krause, 1985; Mullins & Mushell, 1992; Seccombe, 1987). For example, in one study of over 1000 elders in Florida, all of whom were participating in a home-delivered meal program, the amount of loneliness older people reported was *un*related to how often they saw their children or how emotionally close they were to their children (Mullins & Mushell, 1992). Far more important was the presence or absence of a set of friends.

I have found such results surprising and thought at first that it might be a pattern unique to the dominant white American culture, within which independence is such a valued trait. But there is at least one study in which something similar has been observed among Mexican-American elders (Lawrence, Bennett, & Markides, 1992), a group for whom familial contact is a strong cultural value. Indeed in this study, those adults who had the most contact with their children had the highest levels of psychological distress, including depression. Even among those who were not physically dependent on their children, frequency of contact was not linked to satisfaction or to lower levels of depression. In all of these studies, the adults reported regular contact with children and grandchildren and said they enjoyed it. But family interaction was not necessary for, nor did it enhance, their sense of well-being.

Overall, this sounds more like what we might call an affiliative relationship than an attachment, although there are clearly many parent–child pairs with strong attachment-style bonds. When a strong attachment does exist—either from parent to child, or child to parent—it is more likely to involve a mother–daughter relationship than any other combination. But even mother–daughter relationships vary markedly. Two interesting studies by Linda Thompson and Alexis Walker (1984; A. J. Walker & Thompson, 1983) give us some insight into the elements in mother–daughter relationships that may affect attachment.

They have studied three-generational families of women, each with a grandmother, a middle-aged mother, and a college student granddaughter. In general, whenever the pattern of assistance or support in these pairs is uneven—such as when a middle-aged mother is providing high levels of assistance to her aging mother or to her college-aged daughter but is not receiving assistance in return—intimacy and attachment are lower. The best predictor of high attachment in these women was a high level of **reciprocal assistance** or contact. Findings from studies of middle-aged adults (primarily women) who take on major caregiving responsibilities for an elderly parent emphasize the same point: The affection and attachment to the parent *weakens* as the interaction becomes less and less reciprocal, or more and more a burden (Cicirelli, 1983). Since the probability of reciprocal relationships between parents and their grown children varies over their (and their children's) lifetimes, the attachment is also likely to strengthen and fade.

Influence Attempts Between Parents and Children. Parents and children not only provide affection and assistance to one another, they exercise **influence attempts** as they give each other advice, try to change each other's opinions, and attempt to influence each other's behavior. You may try to get your parent, or your child, to stop smoking or to eat more carrots or less fat. You may give advice about jobs or how to handle money, or try to persuade your parents or children to vote in a particular way. Advice and influence attempts, in fact, make up a large percentage of the interactions within families. Gunhild Hagestad (1984), who has done some of the most interesting research on family interactions, has interviewed three generations of adults in 150 families, asking each family member about the ways in which he or she had tried to influence the others, which other family members had tried to influence them, and how successful those influence attempts had been.

In these families, advice up the generational chain from middle-aged child to older parent dealt most often with health or with practical matters such as where to live, how to manage the household, money, and uses of time. Middle-aged adults also tried, but had less success, influencing their parents' attitudes on current social issues and on internal family dynamics. Older parents gave advice to their middle-aged children on subjects such as health, work, and finance. The youngest generation in these families tried to influence their own middle-aged parents as well, particularly regarding health, social attitudes, and the uses of free time. These younger adults helped their parents "keep up with the times."

Two other suggestive patterns emerged from Hagestad's research, both of which gave me food for thought about my own family and other families I know. She observed that in these three-generation families, parents were more likely to try to influence their children than the reverse, and this was true in both generational pairs (grandparents–parents, and parents–grown children). Interestingly, though, the influence attempts from children to parents were more likely to be successful. Only about a third of the advice or influence attempts from parents to children seemed to be effective, while about 70 percent of the influence attempts in the other direction found their mark. As parents, we don't seem to give up trying to influence our children, even when our children are in their

THESE FOUR GENERATIONS OF WOMEN in the same family are likely to have particularly strong bonds with one another. They probably also have a certain agenda of favorite conversational topics.

50s or 60s. But our children listen quite selectively! Perhaps in the process of emancipation from parents in the late teens or early 20s, most young adults learn to tune out many kinds of parental advice, and this pattern persists. But as our children become adults, we begin to tune them in, listening more openly to their suggestions.

Another of Hagestad's observations was that each family seemed to have a certain set of themes or topics that acted like a kind of glue, holding the family together. Different members in the same family tended to talk about the same things, describing the same types of advice or influence. Some families talked about their relationships and spent a lot of time giving each other advice about, or trying to change each other's behavior in those relationships. ("Don't you think you should write to your brother?"; "I wish you and Dad wouldn't argue so much about money.") Other families almost never talked about relationships, but talked instead about money, or jobs. Generational chains of men (grandfather, father, grown son) were more likely to focus their advice and influence on such practical matters, while generational chains of women spent more time on relationships, but each family also had a characteristic "agenda," and this agenda seemed to be a powerful force for cohesion across the generations. (On my mother's side of my own family, one of the common themes has been music, a passion shared in three generations. When we are together, we sing, which not only strengthens our bonds by creating mutual pleasure, it helps us avoid talking about all the subjects about which we disagree!)

All in all, family interactions have layers of subtlety and depth that researchers have only begun to plumb. Even those parent–child links that do not involve extremely strong emotional attachments are nonetheless characterized by strong patterns of habit, family tradition, assistance, and influence. The most complex positions in the family chain appear to be the ones in the middle—the generations that have both parents and grown children. Over a lifetime, each of us moves through these generational positions, acquiring new roles, and learning the changing "rules" of relationships at each step.

CRITICAL THINKING

What is the common agenda across generations in your own family? When the entire family gets together, what do you talk about? What subjects do you avoid? Do the men talk about different things from the women?

Relationships with Brothers and Sisters

The great majority of adults have at least one living sibling, and this relationship in adulthood is getting new research interest as the Baby Boomers get older. (One benchmark of the Baby Boom generation is that they will have more siblings than they have children.) Descriptions of sibling relationships in everyday conversation range from exceptional closeness, to mutual apathy, to enduring rivalry. While rivalry and apathy certainly both exist, the research suggests that at least moderate emotional closeness is the most common pattern (Cicirelli, 1982; Goetting, 1986). If you go back to Figure 7.5, you'll see that the majority of adults have fairly frequent contact with siblings. It is really quite rare for a person to lose contact completely with brothers and sisters.

But these relationships are rarely attachments in the sense in which Weiss uses that term earlier in this chapter. Facing a crisis or an important decision, few of us would turn first to a sibling for advice, and few siblings provide each other with financial or other assistance at any age. Victor Cicirelli, one of the key figures in research on siblings, suggests that there is a kind of "substitution hierarchy" when help is needed, with siblings quite low on the list, only called on when all other sources of support are unavailable (Cicirelli, Coward, & Dwyer, 1992).

Interestingly, though, there is growing evidence that sibling relationships become more significant in late life. Deborah Gold (1996) interviewed a group of older adults about their relationships with their sisters and brothers over the years they had been adults. The respondents were 65 years of age or older, had at least one living sibling, had been married at some point in their lives, had children, and were living independently in the community. Because some of the respondents had more than one sibling, 60 respondents gave information on 89 sibling dyads. The first question was whether they had changed in their closeness to each other over adulthood or whether they had stayed the same. Over one-third (35 percent) reported no change in relationship with their siblings over the course of their adult lives, but 46 percent reported growing closer over time and 18 percent reported growing more distant over time.

Gold asked about the effects of various life events during adulthood and how they might have contributed to the change in closeness between the sibling pairs. Figure 7.7 shows life events from early, middle, and late adulthood along with the magnitude and direction of change in closeness. As you can see, events in early adulthood, especially marriage and having children, seem to cause distancing between siblings. As one male respondant said about his relationship with his brother in early adulthood: "We had been close during our teen years, but the challenges of growing up—of becoming adults—interrupted our closeness. Instead of worrying just about ourselves and each other, we each had a job, a wife, and a family to worry about. We weren't as close any more, that's true, but we didn't hate each other either—we were running as fast as we could to keep up with things" (Gold, 1996, p. 240).

Beginning in middle adulthood, life events are characterized as bringing siblings closer together, especially the death of their second parent. A woman who was the oldest of three sisters said: "When Mom finally died after a long and difficult illness, I thought

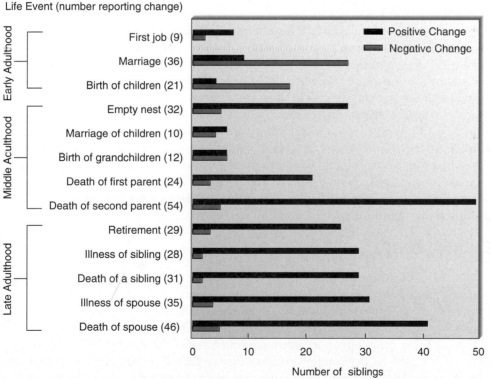

FIGURE 7.7 Older adults report that relationships with their siblings have become more positive as a result of life events that occurred in middle and later adulthood.

Source: Adapted from Gold, 1996.

it was up to me to try to stay close to my sisters. I was surprised—and pleased—when I realized that we all naturally looked to each other" (Gold, 1996, p. 238).

Late adulthood also brings life events conducive to increased closeness between siblings. Retirement brings more free time to spend together and can reunite siblings whose jobs required them to live far apart. Loss of spouse or illness brings siblings to help "fill in the blanks." Finally, some siblings end up being the only surviving members of their family of origin and the only ones to share the memories. One woman respondent talked about her relationship with her sister, her last remaining sibling of nine: "We call every other day… sometimes every day. There is no one else left. We are the family survivors, and that has made us very close" (Gold, 1996, p. 241).

To be fair, 18 percent of the respondents reported becoming more emotionally distant to their siblings with time. Some went through the typical distancing in early adulthood and never got back together; others had anticipated that life events would bring renewed closeness and were disappointed that they did not, especially when they had anticipated more help during bad times such as widowhood or illness.

What type of sibling relationship is the most successful? It probably won't surprise you to learn that sisters are the key. Cicirelli (1989) found that among a group of elderly men and women, those who described themselves as close to a sister had the lowest levels of depression. Those with poor relationships with their sister(s) had the highest levels of depression, while the quality of relationships with brothers was unrelated to depression. Similarly, Shirley O'Bryant (1988) found that among recently widowed women, those who had a sister nearby adjusted far better to widowhood than did those lacking such sisterly support. The availability of brothers had no such beneficial effect, and neither did contact with children—yet another example to reinforce the point I made earlier. Once again, then, it is women—mothers, wives, sisters—who are the kinkeepers, who provide the nurturance and emotional support.

Culture obviously plays a part here. In the United States, close sibling relationships are more common in some subgroups, such as Italian-Americans or African-Americans (Gold, 1990; C. L. Johnson, 1982). Cicirelli also points out that in industrialized countries, sibling relationships are largely "discretionary." There are no formal role obligations between siblings; instead, we choose the form of relationship we will have. But in many nonindustrialized cultures, such as some South Pacific or Asian cultures, sibling relationships, especially brother–sister relationships, are more likely to be obligatory, with quite intricate patterns of interaction prescribed over the life span (Cicirelli, 1994). The brother may play a role in arranging his sister's marriage or may manage his sister's dowry. In such cultures, solidarity among siblings is highly valued. Thus we should not conclude that sibling relationships are "normally" less important; how they are defined is strongly affected by cultural role definitions.

FRIENDSHIPS

If you made a list of the significant people in your life, the list might well include your parents, your children, your brothers and sisters, or your boss or a significant co-worker. For most of us, the list would also include a number of friends. When Toni Antonucci and Hiroko Akiyama (1987) asked a nationally representative sample of 718 adults aged 50 to 95 to describe their convoy, as described earlier in this chapter, by listing the 10 people they felt closest to, beginning with those they could not imagine living without, and moving outward to those who were important but not quite that close, the majority of those listed were family members, but nearly a fifth were friends, as you can see in Figure 7.8. In this study, friends did not very often appear in the "inner circle" of closest relationships, but they nonetheless made up an important segment, a segment that seems to have a significant role in our adult lives.

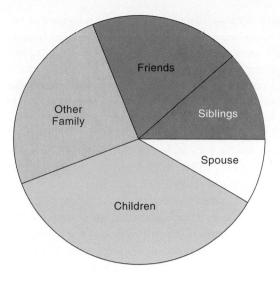

FIGURE 7.8 Answers older adults gave when Antonucci asked them to list the 10 people closest to them. Family choices, collectively, represented roughly eight out of 10 choices, with friends filling the remaining two positions.

Source: Data from Antonucci & Akiyama, 1987, Table 2, p. 524.

What Is a Friend?

But how shall we define friendship? Psychologists and sociologists who have studied friendship in adulthood have used many different definitions, which makes it extremely difficult to add up the findings. If you think about your own friendships for even a moment it will be clear that they run the gamut from close confidants to rather casual pals with whom you share particular activities. John Reisman (1981) divides this continuum into two parts, which he calls **associative friendships** and **reciprocal friendships.** The latter may be similar to what sociologists call an *affiliative* relationship, while the former may reflect any one of a number of different types of relationship: collaboration, help-obtaining, or some other. In a few cases, friendships may reflect genuine attachments: that friend's presence gives you a sense of security and comfort; his or her absence leaves you with a feeling of loss or emptiness.

The stronger, more intimate, reciprocal friendships involve mutual feelings of affection, loyalty, and emotional disclosure. Such friends seek each other out, desiring and enjoying one another's company. In a talk on friendship I once gave to a group of middle-aged professionals, I suggested two somewhat homelier "tests" of a genuinely intimate friendship: A good friend is one who does not "keep score" of who owes whom a favor or time, and a good friend is someone you are always glad to see, no matter what the circumstances—your hair in curlers, or while sick with the flu, or when the baby has just spit up all over your shirt.

In a great deal of the research on friendship in adulthood such a distinction between casual and reciprocal friendships has not been maintained. Most often, subjects have merely been asked to say how many friends they had, without being told just how "friend" should be defined. This makes it *very* hard to add up the evidence into any kind of coherent picture. Yet despite this serious limitation, and despite the usual scarcity of longitudinal information, there are still some interesting patterns.

Choosing Your Friends

Many of the same processes that affect the choice of partner seem to affect the choice of friends. Most generally, we choose people as friends whom we see as like ourselves: in age, in gender, in social class or education, in interests or attitudes, in family life-cycle stage (Dickens & Perlman, 1981; J. E. Norris & Rubin, 1984). This does not mean that all of your friends are your own age or your gender. Perhaps 30 to 40 percent of adults have cross-gender friendships; older adults (more than younger adults) are also likely to have friends from generations other than their own. Still, similarity is a powerful first filter. Propinquity is also part of the equation. Our friends come from among those who live near us, such as those who live on the same floor in a dorm or those who live on the same block or in the same neighborhood as your family home. In middle adulthood, we choose friends from among work colleagues—who share both similarity and frequency of contact—and from those involved in some other mutual activity, such as a church choir, a book group, a bowling league, or the equivalent. In late adulthood, many friendships are of long standing, but new friends may be chosen from among those in a new neighborhood, or who share some activity.

CRITICAL THINKING

Think about each of your friends. Where did you meet? By what process did your relationship move from acquaintanceship to friendship? Was the process the same in each case, or did it vary from one friend to the next?

Past the point of first acquaintance, the crucial ingredient for the shift from acquaintance to friendship is the willingness of the other person to be open about feelings. Particularly in the early stages of friendship, and particularly for women, such intimacy is a key ingredient.

Friendship Patterns over Adulthood

There is little really good information about whether the number of friends, or the style of friendship, changes over the years of adulthood. Most researchers and theorists assume that young adults have more friends and that friendships decline, beginning perhaps in the 20s, as the number of other social roles pile up and time for friendships declines. But because there is such a wide variability in the definitions of *friendship* used in various studies, it has not been possible to demonstrate such a hypothesized developmental pattern clearly (Blieszner & Adams, 1992). Still, I'm inclined to hang onto this model of friendship over the adult years. It makes sense to me theoretically and practically. And there are several interesting bits of evidence that support it.

For example, in one small study, Mary Levitt and her associates (Levitt, Weber, & Guacci, 1993) interviewed 53 three-generation families of women, some of them Anglos, some of them Hispanic-Americans. Each woman was asked to describe her close relationships, following the same basic system that Antonucci used (recall Figure 7.8), except that Levitt did not put an upper limit on the number of convoy members who could be listed. Figure 7.9 shows the proportion of those listed who were close family, other family, and friends, for each of the three generations for each of the two cultures.

What impresses me about these results, despite the small size of the sample, is their consistency: Friends formed a smaller portion of the convoy with each successively older generation in both cultural groups. And although these are still cross-sectional comparisons, the fact that these are three-generation lineages in the same families makes age comparisons somewhat more reasonable.

We also have a small piece of longitudinal data from the now-familiar Berkeley Intergenerational Studies. Laura Carstensen analyzed information from the files for 50 subjects who had been studied repeatedly from adolescence through age 50 (1992)—the same sample you saw in Figure 1.3, by the way. Among other things, she rated the relationship that each subject described with a best friend: the frequency of their interaction, their reported closeness, and their reported satisfaction with this relationship. Carstensen found that the frequency of interaction with a best friend dropped between age 17 and age 50, while closeness rose very slightly.

Carstensen's general model, which she calls **socioemotional selectivity theory,** is that over adulthood, we each selectively reduce our social interactions, narrowing our focus to fewer relationships in an effort to maximize social and emotional gains and minimize social and emotional risks. But at the same time, she argues, the retained relationships be-

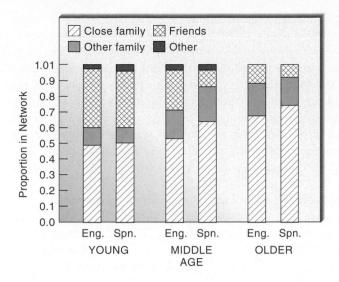

FIGURE 7.9 Three-generation lineages of women, some English-speaking Anglos and some Spanish-speaking Hispanics, were asked to list their close relationships. Here you see that the proportion that were friends declined with age.

Source: Levitt, Weber, & Guacci, 1993, Fig. 1, p. 325.

come more close. So we have fewer friendships, but the ones we have are more intimate; we may see our friends less often, but the relationships become deeper over time.

Such a view is consistent with what we know about loneliness over the life span. Despite the apparent contraction of the personal network with increasing age, fewer older than younger people describe themselves as lonely (Peplau, Bikson, Rook, & Goodchilds, 1982). As Peplau and Perlman define it, loneliness arises when there is a discrepancy between the amount of social contact you *want* and the amount you have. So although older adults have a smaller set of friends and kin with whom they interact, they apparently either want less or are more satisfied with the interactions they do have.

If I put Carstensen's model together with some of the other theoretical models and data I have given you in this chapter, I would summarize it this way: In early adulthood, we make many friends and have a wide circle of acquaintances. We seek out and establish many affiliative bonds. Within a few years, however, most young people's attention shifts from affiliative to attachment bonds—they begin to seek out that one person who might be a life partner and to focus on deepening their relationships with a few close friends who will become part of their relationship convoy.

The convoy is not totally static, of course. Membership changes over the years, with friends lost or gained, parents lost to death, losses or gains from marriage or divorce. But most of us have some continuing members of this group who follow us through life. In the middle years of adulthood, although friends may be added or lost, the focus seems to be on maintaining the relationships with core members of the convoy. In late old age, our convoys begin to shrink again, as spouses and old friends die, which makes the remaining relationships, including those with still-living friends, all that much more important. Among widows, for example, relationships with friends become especially central to a sense of well-being—a point I've made before (e.g. S. K. Gallagher & Ferstel, 1993).

Some Individual Differences in Friendship Patterns

This general developmental picture differs in important ways, though, for several subgroups of adults. Most notably, there are consistent gender differences in friendship patterns observed in both childhood and adulthood.

Gender Differences. In this culture, men generally have larger social networks (counting both associative and reciprocal friendships), but women's friendships are more intimate, involving more mutual self-disclosure and more exchange of emotional support. When men interact, they are more likely to compete, less likely to support or agree with one another (Dindia & Allen, 1992; Ginsberg & Gottman, 1986; Reisman, 1981). Writing about children's relationships as well as adults' (1990), Eleanor Maccoby describes the female pattern as an **enabling style.** Enabling includes all the activities that tend to keep an interaction going and to foster intimacy, including supporting the partner, agreeing, and making suggestions. E. E. Maccoby labels the male pattern a **restrictive style.** "A restrictive style is one that tends to derail the interaction or bring it to an end" (1990, p. 517), including contradicting, interrupting, boasting, or other types of self-display. These two different styles are found in pairs as young as preschool age, and at every age thereafter. Among adults, women disclose more, talk more, describe a greater intimacy; men are more likely to do things together rather than talk; they are task-oriented rather than relationship-oriented.

One of my favorite quotes, from a 38-year-old male executive interviewed by Robert Bell (1981), illustrates the difference in self-disclosure clearly: "I have three close friends I have known since we were boys and they live here in the city. There are some things I wouldn't tell them. For example, I wouldn't tell them much about my work because we have always been highly competitive. I certainly wouldn't tell them about my feelings of any uncertainties with life or various things I do. And I wouldn't talk about any problems I have with my wife or in fact anything about my marriage and sex life. But other than that I would tell them anything. [After a brief pause he laughed and said:] That doesn't leave a hell of a lot, does it?" (pp. 81–82).

Whether one sees the female pattern or the male pattern as "better" or "worse" obviously depends on one's gender and point of view. Theorists continue to argue the point (Antonucci, 1994a). Most research shows men to be less satisfied with their friendships than women are (although they are equally satisfied with their family relationships), and women clearly gain in quite specific ways from the buffering effect of their social network. But there are also gains for men from their style of relationship. Women's style, for example, sometimes has the effect of burdening them too much with emotional obligations, while men are more able to focus on their work (Antonucci, 1994a). Setting aside these value judgments, the important point remains: men and women, boys and girls, appear to create different kinds of relationships and this difference permeates our culture.

Social Class Differences. Friendships in adults also differ by social class. In general, working-class adults (and most of this research is on men) appear to have fewer close friends than do middle-class adults (Bell, 1981; Farrell & Rosenberg, 1981). In contrast, kin relationships (parents, children, siblings, etc.) seem to be closer in working-class families than in the middle class (Dickens & Perlman, 1981). In other words, the total size of the social network may be about the same for adults from different social strata, but the network is composed differently. Just what the causes or consequences of such differences in network compositions may be for adult development I do not know. But such a difference is definitely worth further study.

REVIEW OF RELATIONSHIPS IN ADULTHOOD

Table 7.5 summarizes the myriad age-linked patterns in relationships I have talked about so far. Some of these are curvilinear patterns, some reflect increases, and some reflect declines in relationships. On the face of it, there seems very little consistency. Erikson's theory, however, may help to make sense of these patterns.

In the very early years of adulthood, perhaps 18 to 25, it looks as if virtually all relationships are highly significant. This is the period that Erikson describes as the stage of intimacy versus isolation, and that label seems to capture the flavor well. Adults in their early 20s are searching for and forming intimate partnerships and typically are highly satisfied with their marriages. They also have large networks of friends, creating that convoy of relationships that will travel with them through the years. But a sense of isolation is also

TABLE 7.5 **Summary of Age Changes in Relationships**

Age 20–40	Age 40–65	Age 65–75	Age 75+
Marital satisfaction peaks early in this period, immediately following marriage; marital problems are high, as are expressions of affection.	Marital satisfaction usually remains low until the postparental period, when it usually rises; relationships include fewer problems, but possibly also fewer expressions of affection.	Marital satisfaction is at a level similar to what is seen in early adulthood, although the components of that satisfaction may be different. Marital problems typically low.	Marital relationship remains central for those who have not been widowed; satisfaction is high, and time spent with spouse is strongly linked to overall life satisfaction.
After a period of "emancipation" from central attachment to the parent, a new form of relationship, close and enduring, is usually forged with parents. Women's relationship with their mothers is typically the strongest bond.	Relationship with parents remains a strong element in the personal convoy for most adults, although the form of the relationship changes as the parent ages.	Contact with parents ends when parents die; contact with children continues and is satisfying but does not contribute to, nor is it critical for, life satisfaction.	Contact with children may increase as need for assistance increases, but the amount of contact with children is not linked to overall life satisfaction or degree of loneliness.
Contact with siblings is relatively high and steady, but few sibling relationships are in the form of attachments.	Contact with siblings remains steady.	Some indication that sibling relationships become more significant in later years.	Some indication of even closer relationships with surviving siblings.
Friendships may be most numerous at this age, forming a larger percentage of the relationship convoy.	Friendships may be fewer in number but more intimate.	Possibly further decline in the number, but a deepening of quality, of friendship relationships.	Perhaps the number of friends in the core convoy is lower, but friends are highly significant sources of social and emotional support in late adulthood.

common. More young adults report feelings of loneliness than is true for any other age group. In other words, relationships *matter* very much at this age, and any lack in relationships is felt keenly.

In the years from 25 to 40, the period Erikson calls *generativity versus stagnation,* two things seem to happen. First, even though marital satisfaction is often at its lowest point, the partnership relationship is nonetheless clearly the key relationship of these years. Relationships with one's parents, with siblings, and with friends seem to be at a lower ebb. Energy is devoted to the immediate family and to work. The convoy is still there, but adults in their 30s spend little energy expanding or working on that convoy.

From 45 to 65, as the adult moves into Erikson's period of *integrity versus despair,* the quality of relationships once again seems to become an issue. Marital relationships seem to improve for many couples, perhaps as a result of new attention devoted to the interactions. Friendships, too, may become somewhat more intimate, although not more frequent. These are also the years in which many adults find themselves the "sandwich" generation in their own family lineage and have heightened family responsibilities both upward and downward in the genealogical chain.

Finally, in the years past retirement, the convoy continues to shrink in size, but is highly valued. Partnership relationships remain central for those who have not been widowed or divorced; relationships with friends and siblings appear to be of increasing importance. Contacts with family are typically numerous but become *less* central for the older adult's psychological well-being.

Beyond this Eriksonian description of the age changes in relationships, I want to emphasize several points. First, the changes in our relationships over time occur not just because time passes but because we engage in active renegotiation. This renegotiation process is clearest in the case of the relationship with one's parents, but occurs in other relationships as well, such as those with children, siblings, grandparents, partner, in-laws, and many others. In the parent–adult child relationship, the young adult first must negotiate a separation from her parents, staking out her own territory (literally as well as figuratively). Gunhild Hagestad (1979) talks about the **demilitarized zones** that are often created in this process: "silent mutually understood pacts regarding what not to talk about" (p. 30). Or there may be no taboo subjects, but there may be boundaries past which neither parents nor young adult offspring dare to go (Greene & Boxer, 1986). In later years, many of these DMZs disappear and the boundaries become much more permeable. And still later, as the older generation requires more and more assistance, there may be new terms to be negotiated.

CRITICAL THINKING

Does this resonate for you? What are the taboos, or the boundaries, in your relationship with your own parents? How have they changed over time?

Second, the **reciprocity** of any given relationship seems to be a key feature, affecting a person's sense of satisfaction with that relationship or with life in general. If you receive more than you can give, or give much more than you receive, you are likely to be less satisfied with a relationship. And when an ongoing relationship shifts from being reciprocal to being less so, adults report that they become less satisfied, less emotionally supported by that relationship. This may help to explain why relationships with friends and siblings become more central to life satisfaction in old age, since relationships with peers are far more likely to be reciprocal than are those with one's children.

Finally, each of us brings to our adult relationships our own internal working model of attachments and interactions. It is becoming increasingly clear that these models, which have their roots in early childhood experiences, are carried into adult life and affect our relationships not only with our children but with other adults. The general point, well worth repeating, is that in our central convoy relationships, we each tend to recreate the patterns from our family of origin, as we understood them and translated them into our internal working models. In yet another remarkable analysis of the Berkeley Intergenerational Study subjects, Glen Elder and his colleagues (Elder, Caspi, & Downey, 1986), give us a glimpse of how this process works longitudinally. Those subjects who described their own parents as most irritable and unstable were much more likely to have unstable marriages and to be less affectionate and more hostile toward their own children. Their own children, in turn, were more likely to show problem behavior and higher rates of divorce in their own marriages. Doubtless secure attachments, too, are transmitted from one generation to the next.

Each of us, then, begins adulthood not only with some amount of the specific skills needed to form and maintain relationships; we also begin adulthood with deeply embedded expectations about patterns of interaction. These internal models affect our choices of partners and friends as well as the quality of the relationships we create. These models can be changed, of course. A *healing relationship*—to use a phrase George Vaillant introduced to describe some of the men he followed in the Grant study—can alter an insecure model. Growing personal maturity can lead to the self-awareness needed to alter the patterns. But lacking such intervention or personal effort, the basic template will remain, shaping our relationships throughout our adult life.

Summary

1. The term *attachment* has been used to describe relationships between adults as well as between infants and caregivers. The key feature of an attachment is a sense of security, safety, or comfort in the presence of the other and a sense of loss when apart.

2. Love is conceptualized in a variety of ways including single dimensions, multiple dimensions, and multiple clusters. Theorists may be describing the same relationships at different levels.

3. The relationship with an intimate partner is typically the most central relationship in adulthood. The process of partner selection is poorly understood but is influenced initially by perceived similarity, and by propinquity, as well as by internal models of attachment.

4. Cohabitation before marriage among young adults does not appear to improve the quality or durability of later marriage relationships; if anything, it is associated with lower rates of later marital satisfaction.

5. In the year following a marriage, most couples show a decline in the overt expression of affection and agreement. Marital satisfaction then typically remains low until the postparental years. But not all couples follow such a pattern; some show consistent satisfaction, others consistent dissatisfaction or neutrality.

6. Some partnerships, in middle and old age, can be described as "devitalized," with low levels of expression of affection but also low levels of reported problems. This pattern may be more common among those who do not progress past the conformist stage of ego development.

7. Satisfying and unsatisfying marriages differ on a number of key dimensions, with the key ingredient the relative frequency of positive versus negative interactions.

8. Not all stable partnerships show precisely the same type of interaction. Validating, volatile, and avoidant relationships may all be stable, while unstable marriages all involve more negative/hostile interactions than positive/supportive ones.

9. Long-term partnerships are also common in homosexual couples, especially in lesbian pairs. Such partnerships appear to be more egalitarian in role allocation and power than are heterosexual partnerships.

10. Interactions with parents and siblings occur at high and relatively constant levels throughout adulthood. Nearly all adults have at least some contact with their parents at least once a month. Some studies show increased closeness with siblings in middle and late adulthood.

11. For a young adult to achieve independence, the initially strong attachment to his or her parents must be attenuated, although some level of attachment typically remains throughout adult life. Stronger attachments to parents are common for daughters and for unmarried adults.

12. One repeated finding is that in late adulthood contact with children, while common and reported as pleasant, is unrelated to the elder's sense of life satisfaction or well-being.

13. Parents and children try to influence each other. More influence attempts are directed from parents to children than the reverse, but influence is more successful from adult child to parent.

14. Although relatively constant over the life span, relationships with siblings appear to be strongest in late adulthood. Changes in sibling relationships seems to be related to life events, with events occurring later in life (death of parents, retirement) making siblings closer than events occurring in early adulthood.

15. In contrast, friendships appear to be quite central in early adulthood and perhaps again in middle age and beyond; friends may become less numerous over the adult years (although that is not fully clear), but they appear to become deeper and more intimate.

16. Women's friendships are typically more intimate than are men's, and working-class adults typically have fewer friends than do middle-class adults.

17. These patterns of relationships can be partially understood by using the framework of Erikson's theory of developmental stages.

18. The concept of internal working models of relationships may also be helpful in understanding the ways in which each adult recreates the patterns of relationship that he or she understood to exist in his or her own family of origin.

KEY TERMS

attachment

attachment behaviors

internal working model

secure attachment

dismissive attachment

preoccupied attachment

fearful attachment

sexual desire

liking

loving

limerance

passionate love

companionate love

intimacy

passion

commitment

convoy

filter theories

interpersonal processes

homogamy

exchange theory

cohabitation

devitalized marriages

validating marriages

volatile marriages

avoidant marriages

hostile/engaged marriages

hostile/detached marriages

autonomy

equality

generational stake

reciprocal assistance

influence attempts

associative friendships

reciprocal friendships

socioemotional selectivity theory

enabling style

restrictive style

demilitarized zones (DMZs)

reciprocity

SUGGESTED READINGS

Blieszner, R., & Adams, R. G. (1992). *Adult friendship*. Newbury Park, CA: Sage.

One of a series of very helpful small books published by Sage that explore aspects of personal relationships. This volume summarizes all the current research.

Cate, R. M., & Lloyd, S. A. (1992). *Courtship.* Newbury Park, CA: Sage.

Another in the Sage series. This one offers a good review of what we know (and don't know) about the courtship process.

Gottman, J. M. (1994). *Why marriages succeed or fail.* New York: Simon & Schuster.

An absolutely wonderful book, aimed at a lay audience, written by one of the most thorough and thoughtful researchers to study marriage success and failure. The book is full of examples from actual marital interactions as well as quizzes you can take to identify your own style and specific suggestions about how to improve your own partnership. I highly recommend this book for everyone in a relationship or contemplating one.

Hargrave, T. D., & Hanna, S. M. (1997). *The aging family: New visions in theory, practice, and reality.* New York: Brunner/Mazel.

Researchers and theoreticians from various fields write chapters about family interactions and how they change as family members age. It includes how roles change within the family, marriages in middle and late adulthood, dealing with unfulfilled dreams at the end of life, and other timely topics.

Karen, R. (1994). *Becoming attached.* New York: Warner Books.

Another wonderful new book written for the general reader. An understandable, beautifully written explication of current theories and research about attachment. Most of the emphasis is on childhood, but there is a section on adult attachment as well.

Sternberg, R., & Hojjat, M. (1997). *Satisfaction in close relationships.* New York: Guilford Press.

Instead of writing about length of relationships, this group of experts writes about the *quality* of marriage and other romantic partnerships, how to measure it, and how it changes over the life course.

Troll, L. E. (1994). Family connectedness of old women: Attachments in later life. In B. F. Turner & L. E. Troll (Eds.), *Women growing older: Psychological perspectives* (pp. 169–201). Thousand Oaks, CA: Sage.

The title of this paper is somewhat misleading; it deals with attachments and connections across the entire life span, exploring many of the ramifications of the concept of attachment as it applies to adult relationships.

WORK
AND WORK ROLES
IN ADULTHOOD

8

"I'm probably the youngest general foreman in the plant, yes, sir. I'm in the chassis line right now. There's 372 people working for us, hourly. And thirteen foremen. I'm the lead general foreman" (Terkel, 1972, p. 249). The speaker, Wheeler Stanley, was just 30 when Studs Terkel talked to him in 1972. Stanley had started at a Ford plant when he was 20, fresh out of the paratroopers. His goal in life was to be a "utility man"—the man in the plant who can do all the assembly-line tasks, and spot-relieves other workers. "I thought that was the greatest thing in the world. When the production manager asked me would I consider training for a foreman's job, boy! my sights left utility. I worked on all the assembly lines. I spent eighteen months on the line, made foreman, and eighteen months later I made general foreman" (p. 250). Now Wheeler Stanley's goal is to be superintendent, and then maybe production manager. He likes his work, likes the company, but hopes his son will do something better.

Ray Wax has had a very different working life. He sold cakes in an outdoor market when he was 12, caddied at a golf course at 14, and as an adult tried a whole range of jobs, all at least partially successful. He exported cars to South America, speculated in land, built houses, built and ran a hotel, and now in his 50s is a stock broker. The restlessness that has been part of his work life all along is once again visible. "I can't say what I'm doing has any value. This doesn't make me too happy.... When I built the houses, I hired a bricklayer, I hired the roofer, I determined who put the goddamned thing together. And when I handed somebody a key, the house was whole. I made it happen. I can't do that in the market. I'm just being manipulated... " (Terkel, 1972, pp. 446–447).

Not everyone gets promoted or shifts from job to job. Dolores Dante has been a waitress for 23 years, working in the same restaurant. She started working when her marriage broke up and she had three young children to support. Waitressing was a way to make good money from tips without a lot of training or schooling. She has stayed with it because she's very good at it and enjoys it. "When somebody says to me, 'You're great, how come you're *just* a waitress?' *Just* a waitress.... It makes me irate. I don't feel lowly at all. I myself feel sure. I don't want to change the job. I love it" (Terkel, 1972, p. 391). But it's tiring work. Her feet hurt, she aches, she doesn't eat right, and at the end of a day's shift, at 2:00 A.M., she's drained and nerve-racked. But she wouldn't want to give up working. "I won't give up this job as long as I'm able to do it. I feel out of contact if I just sit at home" (p. 395).

Sigmund Freud was reportedly once asked to define *maturity*. His answer was that maturity was determined by one's capacity for work and love. I would probably add a few things to that list, but no one would argue about

WORK OUTSIDE THE HOME has always been central to men's lives; in recent years it has also become central for women. Most of you in today's cohorts will spend 30 to 40 years of your adult life working.

CRITICAL THINKING

How would you define maturity?

Would you agree with Freud?

What else might you put on the list?

the centrality of both love and work in adult life. I talked about love in Chapter 7; now I will talk about work.

For Wheeler Stanley, Ray Wax, and Dolores Dante, as for most of us, work is one of the most time-consuming, significant, identity-defining aspects of adult life. An occupation, a "career," probably consumes a third to a half of a man's waking hours over a period of 40 years, not counting the time spent lying awake at night worrying about the report you're supposed to write, or the promotion you didn't get, or the hours getting to and from work, or taking special classes.

Women have not typically spent as many years focused on a career, but that situation has been changing rapidly. In 1996 in the United States, 69.3 percent of all women between 25 and 65 were in the labor force. As you can see in Figure 8.1, this number has increased dramatically in the past 50 years (Johnson, 1998). Current projections are that U.S. women born in 1980 will spend an average of 29.4 years working outside the home, compared to an average of only 12.1 years of work for those in my generation, born in 1940 (Spenner, 1988). In contrast, in 1996, almost 90 percent of all working age men were in the labor force.

I do not mean to imply by this that childrearing or homemaking (or unpaid volunteer work) are not "work." They are. I have talked about these roles and their effect on adults in Chapter 6, and I'll turn later in this chapter to the question of combining work and family roles. But here I want to focus on paid employment, on "jobs" or "careers."

It will not surprise you to hear that most of what we know about work and its effects over adulthood comes from studies of men. Even our knowledge of men's work patterns is drawn primarily from studies of middle-class occupations: business executives, lawyers, doctors, professors. We know a bit about men like Wheeler Stanley, who is in a

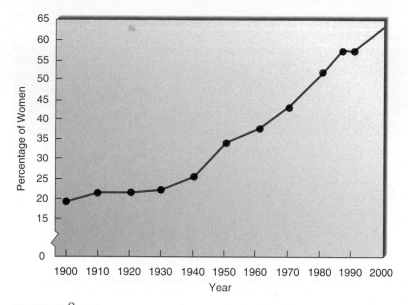

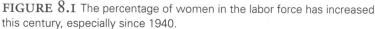

FIGURE 8.1 The percentage of women in the labor force has increased this century, especially since 1940.

Source: Johnson, 1998, p. 66.

job with a clear "career ladder," a sequence of steps or promotions from entry-level jobs on up. But we know almost nothing about the Dolores Dantes of the world: the waitresses, garbage collectors, meter readers, artists, flight attendants, and many others who work at jobs that don't have steps or clear promotion sequences or who have little chance for advancement. What we know, then, is incomplete, but nonetheless fascinating.

PATTERNS OF WORK FOR MEN AND WOMEN

One way to look at work lives over adulthood is simply to count how many people have worked continuously throughout their adult lives compared to those who have had periods of time that they were not working. This is relatively easy using large, existing databases of longitudinal studies, and gives us an idea of the **work patterns** that typified the adult lives of those participants.

One of the most obvious findings in these reports is the difference in work patterns between men and women. The majority of men work continuously from early adulthood until retirement. If there is a break in a man's work history, it is most likely to happen only once, such as when he goes back to school, changes careers, or is temporarily unemployed (Corcoran, 1978)

In contrast, women tend to move in and out of the workforce over their adult years. One particularly helpful analysis comes from the Panel Study of Income Dynamics. Phyllis Moen (1985) has looked at the work patterns of 3586 women included in this sample, all of whom had been interviewed repeatedly between 1972 and 1976. Because these are longitudinal data, Moen has been able to track each woman's movement in and out of the workforce over the five-year period. Table 8.1 shows the work patterns for women who were at various stages of the family life cycle at the beginning and end of the five-year study period. The data show quite clearly that the majority of women moved out of the labor force when they had young children. They also show that many women

TABLE 8.1 **Percentage of Women with Various Work Patterns in the Panel Study of Income Dynamics Between 1972 and 1977**

Work Pattern	No Child Any Year[a]	Family Status During Five-Year Study		
		First Child Born After Year 1	At Least One Preschool Child Throughout the Five Years	Preschool Child at Year 1; School-Aged in Year 5
No paid work in any year	0.8	12.8	27.5	23.4
Part time, all years	0.9	1.1	2.9	2.5
Full time, all years	54.4	20.7	10.6	23.4
Part time and full time	31.2	13.3	7.8	5.7
No work and part-time work	1.6	4.6	19.1	19.8
No work and full-time work	5.9	27.9	17.4	11.8
No work, part-time, and full-time work	5.2	19.6	14.7	10.5

[a]To make the comparison more comparable, this subgroup contains only women who were less than 38 and thus still potentially in their childbearing years.

Source: Adapted from Moen, 1985, Table 4.3, p. 132.

in these cohorts used part-time work as an intermediate step, especially when their children were young.

Moen's study is extremely helpful, but it doesn't tell us about the full sweep of women's work patterns over 30 or 40 years. Annemette Sørensen's (1983) research helps to fill the gap, although her subjects represent an older cohort, those who graduated from high school in 1958. She has examined the employment history of a group of over 3500 of these women, all graduates of Wisconsin high schools, all married at least once, who gave retrospective reports of their work and family histories in 1975, when they were in their middle to late 30s. Approximately one-fourth of these women had worked continuously. Twenty percent had left the work force after their first child was born and went back to work after the last child was born; another 18 percent left after the first birth and had not returned to work as of the 1975 interview.

There is a surprising degree of unanimity in these findings: While the percentage of women who work at least *some* time has risen dramatically, along with the percentage of women working at any given time, only 20 to 25 percent of women appear to work *continuously* through their adult lives. Such continuous work patterns are more common in some subgroups of women than others: among black women (Corcoran, 1978), those in nontraditional or "masculine" jobs (E. L. Betz, 1984), those who are philosophically committed to the idea of women's work (Greenstein, 1986), those whose husbands strongly approve of the woman's employment (Moen, 1985), those with strong commitments to work or career (E. L. Betz, 1984; Rexroat, 1985), and the unmarried or those with no children (Sørensen, 1983).

For the majority of women in the United States, however, some form of interrupted pattern appears to be the norm. Of course it is possible, even likely, that the percentage of women who have worked continuously is higher among women now in their late 30s or early 40s than it was in the preceding cohort, and that it will be higher still among those who are now in their early 20s. But here is one fragment of data that suggests otherwise: Francine Blau and Marianne Ferber (1991) asked a group of 1988 college business school seniors what their expectations were for their future earnings, work plans, and family plans. The 227 young women who responded, all part of today's cohort of 20-somethings, expected to work full time for 29.1 years, compared to 37.7 years for their male classmates, and they anticipated working part time for 6.2 years. To be sure, these young women anticipated working more years than their own mothers had worked, and they may well work more (or fewer) years than they now expect. But it is interesting that even in this highly educated group of current young women, most of whom have a strong commitment to a career, the average expectation includes some time out to bear and rear children. So although the cultural climate has changed drastically with regard to women's work patterns, it has not changed totally and is unlikely to do so.

Impact of Different Work Patterns on Women's Lives

Does it make a difference which work pattern a woman follows? Well, if work achievement is one of your goals, continuous work patterns appear to be most successful. Van Velsor and O'Rand (1984), for example, have examined work success in a large seven-year longitudinal study of a national sample of women, all of whom were between age 30 and 44 at the start of the study. In this group, the women who had worked continuously had the highest salaries, a finding confirmed by other researchers (E. L. Betz, 1984). In other words, the best way to succeed in the world of work is to follow an essentially "male pattern" of continuous work and high work commitment.

For those women who do *not* work continuously, two strategies seem to be associated with higher earnings: (1) remaining in the same field or along the same career path rather than switching from one type of job to another each time you return to the labor force (Van Velsor & O'Rand, 1984) and (2) returning to the labor force regularly rather than remaining out of work for one long period and then going back to work after all the children are gone from home (Gwartney-Gibbs, 1988). Even when the total months or years of nonwork is the same, women who have had several short bursts of work in the midst of a nonwork period do better economically in the long run than do those who are unemployed continuously for one stretch. The most likely explanation is that women in the first groups have repeatedly regained or updated their work skills. The use of part-time work as an in-between step, as many women in Moen's study had clearly done (Table 8.1), thus appears to be a highly rational strategy for many women *if* work success or higher earnings are among their goals or needs.

All of this research no doubt makes clear something you already knew: The trade-offs are extremely difficult to judge, the decisions hard to make.

Sᴛᴀɢᴇꜱ ᴏꜰ ᴡᴏʀᴋ ʟɪᴠᴇꜱ

The second way of looking at the role of work in organizing the lives of adults is to see if different work patterns occur at different ages. Some theorists have suggested developmental sequence that occur over the adult years from early adulthood until retirement. These theories have been based almost exclusively on interviews with men, but recently studies of women have been added, giving us at least *some* information about similarities and differences in the work lives of adults of both genders.

Stages of Men's Work Lives

Donald Super, a major figure in the study of career development in adulthood, suggests that it is helpful to divide a continuous career into a set of stages, each with its own character (1957, 1971, 1986). These stages are similar to the ones Levinson described in his theory of men's lives you may recall from Chapter 2.

Age 15 to 25. Super referred to this as the **trial stage** and said that during this time the young man must decide on a job or career, searching for a fit between his interests and personality and the jobs available. Young men particularly value jobs that are intrinsically interesting and challenging; neither salary nor job security is as critical in the job choice at this stage as is challenge. There is some trial and error involved in the entire process. Jobs may be tried and rejected and new jobs tried. Perhaps because many jobs available to young men are relatively low in challenge, and because many young men have not yet found the right fit, job changes are at their peak during this period.

Levinson (1978, 1986) referred to this time of a young man's life as the **early adult transition.** You may remember from Chapter 2 that he argues that a relationship with a **mentor** may be an especially important aspect of this phase of the work career. A mentor can provide support and information that is vital in professional growth and advancement (Chao & Gardner, 1992). And a mentor not only teaches the young man the job and smoothes the way to advancement, he can also provide a key transitional relationship in the young worker's shift from dependence on parents to complete independence.

Interestingly, in Levinson's own research, relatively few men described having mentors. In contrast, several studies of business executives suggest that having a mentor is a fairly common experience for young men. In one study, 83 percent of 140 male and female middle- and upper-level executives in a variety of business firms said that they had mentors, although only 43 percent listed their mentor as one of the most significant helpers in their career (G. L. Shapiro & Farrow, 1988). Furthermore, within such organizations, it appears that having a mentor is related to success for the junior worker. Protégés are more likely to be promoted, get larger raises, and have more opportunities within a company, law firm, or other group than is true of young workers who have no mentor (Dreher & Ash, 1990; Fagenson, 1989). But whether this advantage arises from the mentoring process itself is not so clear, for the obvious reason that those who are selected as protégés are likely to be the more strongly motivated or best skilled among the younger workers (Fagenson, 1992).

Levinson suggests that this stage also has another key feature, the creation of **the dream.** Young scientists dream of winning the Nobel prize; Wheeler Stanley dreamed early on of being a "utility man" and later modified his dream to being a production manager. During the trial stage, according to Levinson, each young man takes his first steps toward a private fantasy of eventual success.

CRITICAL THINKING

How could we find out more about mentors and being mentored? What kind of study or studies could you do that would clarify the significance of the role of mentor to young adults' work careers or to their psychological development?

Age 25 to 45. In the next stage, which Super called the **establishment** or **stabilization stage,** the man strives hard to fulfill the Dream. In the early years of this period the striving often pays off with promotion or improvement; toward the end of this period there is a substantial slowing of progress, but job satisfaction is higher because the work is more complex and interesting.

Levinson called this stage **early adulthood,** a time of peak physical, mental, and emotional functioning but also a time of peak stress and contradictions. During the early part of this stage, a man makes some key choices about his career and family. Midway through this stage Levinson argues that men undergo the **age-30 transition,** when they reappraise the choices they made and make some adjustments in their lives, either making up for development left undone in earlier stages or preparing for stages yet to come. During the second half of this stage, Levinson believes that the man becomes more comfortable in his career and family choices and prepares to move from being a junior member of the adult world to being a senior member.

Age 45 to 60. During the early part of this stage, which Super called the **maintenance stage,** a change seems to take place. Satisfaction and personal power is high, but there is some contradiction. By then, most men have gone as far as they will go in their work; promotion or other advancement after midlife is quite unusual. Tamir says of this rather odd combination of midlife work characteristics: "[I]t is likely that job satisfaction and clout are expressed by [men at midlife] for one of two reasons; (1) success and status actually have reached a satisfying peak by middle age or (2) at middle age the man becomes resigned to the fact that further advancement is unlikely and therefore needs both to convince himself of current satisfaction and to convince himself and others that he indeed has achieved high status at work" (1982, pp. 95).

Some men have come close to their dream and are satisfied; others realize that they will not achieve their dream, but they handle this disappointment by changing the way the game is played, by changing their expectations or values. Tamir's own analyses provide further evidence for just such an internal shift, as you can see in Table 8.2. For men under the age of 40 in this nationally representative sample, job satisfaction was quite strongly related to overall life satisfaction, to a sense of zest for life, and to self-esteem; for men at midlife there was *no* such relationship. To put it another way, for a young man, being successful at his job is one of the key elements in self-esteem or overall satisfaction. For a middle-aged man it is not, despite the fact that this is the time in his life when a man is likely to be maximally successful and to have the greatest clout in his work.

Other research also points to redefinition of work values at midlife, along with a deemphasis on the centrality of work for self-esteem or life satisfaction. For example, in an analysis of information from the middle-age interviews with middle-aged men in the Berkeley longitudinal sample, John Clausen (1981) found that men younger than 45 valued their jobs primarily in terms of the intrinsic interest of the job and whether the job used their skills; men older than 45 evaluated their jobs by these same standards but *also* judged their jobs in terms of income, job convenience, and job security—all extrinsic factors that seem to be less important to younger workers. What we see in this midlife work stage is a "disengagement from work as a source of personal fulfillment, or at minimum a reconsideration of the place work has in one's life. Perhaps this is due to the fact that nearly all that is attainable has been reached by middle age and the challenge of work has diminished. Other sources of fulfillment now must be sought to take its place" (Tamir, 1982, p. 95).

Levinson called this stage **middle adulthood** and although the men in his study had not yet reached this age, he hypothesized that it is a time of mature creativity and responsibility for a man, not only for his own work but often for the work of others. They are full-fledged senior members of the adult world. Some men experience an age-50 transition, similar to the age-30 transition. These are usually men who have not made significant developmental changes in the first part of this stage or who have made inappropriate changes.

TABLE 8.2 **Relationship Between Job Satisfaction and Other Aspects of Life Satisfaction for Men of Various Age Groups in Tamir's Cross-Sectional Study**

Correlation Between Job Satisfaction and:	Age Group	
	Young (25–39)	Middle Aged (40–49)
Overall life satisfaction	0.31**	0.04
Zest[a]	0.43**	0.09
Self-esteem	0.26**	-0.02

**Correlation is significant at the 0.001 level, which means that if there were really no link between the two variables, such a correlation could occur by chance only once in every 1000 samples of this size.

[a] These correlations are for college-educated men only.

Source: Data from Tamir, 1982, Tables 4.14, 4.15, and 4.16, pp. 91 and 92.

Age 60 and Beyond. This stage is called **adjustment to retirement** by Super and **late adulthood** by Levinson. It is the final stage and involves the transition to retirement, a subject I'll explore in detail later in the chapter.

It is important to note once again that although I have given approximate ages for each of the four stages, it is probably time-in-job rather than age that is the more critical variable. Despite Levinson's insistence that the steps are strongly age-linked, the research findings simply don't fit that model terribly well. New workers in any field, whatever their age, have certain characteristics in common. A man coming to a new career at 40 will go through a trial period and a period of stabilization before reaching a maintenance/reassessment stage. This is an important point, because such late entry is, in fact, common for women, even in today's cohorts. So let me turn to what we know about women's work patterns.

Stages of Women's Work Lives

As I mentioned before, the major theorists of work lives have focused almost entirely on men's lives. One exception is a recently published study Daniel Levinson conducted in which he and his colleagues interviewed 30 career women born between 1936 and 1947, questioning them in depth when they were around the age of 45 about their early career aspirations, their families' attitudes toward their career, their experiences in the workplace, and their decisions concerning family and work (Levinson, 1996). Half of the women (the business group) were working in corporate or financial careers at the time of the interviews (1980 to 1982), and half (the academic group) were faculty members at universities. This allowed Levinson to compare this group to the men he had studied previously and on whom he had based his developmental theory of adulthood, and also compare the two types of career paths the women had chosen.

One caveat is in order before I present this material: This is only one study, and the findings probably reflect heavily on that particular cohort (the daughters of *The Feminine Mystique,* as Levinson describes them, referring to the influential book of that era by Betty Friedan). Despite these limitations, there are some aspects that apply to women in any era. Levinson found that the career women he studied fell into the same developmental stages as men do, and these are generally the same as Super's stages described in the section above. However, the *content* of those stages differed somewhat.

Age 17 to 23: Transition to Early Adulthood. All 30 career women in Levinson's study attended college away from home, and an important task during this time was to select a major. This choice turned out to be a compromise between their parents' expectations and their own desires to be independent. None of the 30 women selected traditionally female majors such as nursing or education, and none selected traditionally male majors such as science or engineering. Most selected "neutral" majors such as social sciences, arts, and humanities, or marginally "male" majors such as economics and business administration. Although most adults in their lives during this time were professors, only a few of the young women were in mentor–protégé relationships during college, and only one of the 30 reported having conceptualized the dream during this time.

The women in this study were ill prepared for college and being away from home. Only one-fourth of them recalled their freshman year as being a positive experience, but they all remained in school and most reported their later years of college being more positive. It seems that the young women in this study had dual tasks during this stage—making decisions for their future careers and trying to find a way to attain independence from their family while retaining ties with them. It seems apparent that compared to men in this stage, the future career plans of the young women suffered. If this is truly the time of life that the idealistic work self is formed, it didn't happen for 29 of these 30 women.

Age 22 to 45: Early Adulthood, The women in Levinson's study entered this stage of work life with their undergraduate educations completed but little concept of what they would do next. During the first half of this stage, the women could be classified into three groups. One-third were on a well-defined career path; they knew what they wanted and had either entered graduate school or career-track jobs that would help them reach that goal. One-third were on a well-defined career path but would change it later to become either the academic or business women they were when Levinson interviewed them. (For example, one future academician was teaching high school, although she later returned to graduate school and became a professor.) The remaining one-third were not on a well-defined career path at all. Instead, they were working in entry-level, dead-end jobs such as executive assistants or secretaries at large publishing houses in New York City. These were truly "women's jobs" because no man with comparable educations would take them. However, the women believed that these were their best chances to get noticed, and perhaps this was true considering the open discrimination against hiring women in the 1950s and 1960s. However, all the women at this stage had jobs and were part of the adult world.

By this time about one-third of the women, mostly those in the academic jobs, had mentors at work. Almost all the mentors were men, probably due to the scarcity of women in senior positions. This was helpful in some ways but also brought problems. The mentors found it difficult to establish traditional mentor–protégé relationships with young women due to social constraints. For this reason, perhaps, none of the mentors were able to help their protégés articulate their dream. They also found it difficult to envision a young woman as being their professional equal in the future, much less someone who might surpass them.

About half of the women were married when they entered this stage, most of them in the academic group. Interestingly, many reported that their marriages had a component of a mentor–protégé relationship to them. The husbands were often ahead of them in a similar field, such as being an assistant professor or a senior graduate student. The husbands believed in their wives' careers and supported their nontraditional choices, such as postponing parenthood until their careers were established. These marriages simplified the lives of the young women in several ways. They sanctioned the romantic relationships they were having and satisfied their parents' admonitions to find a good husband. They took the young women out of the dating scene and made their social lives more predictable. And the mentoring relationship gave them someone close to them who supported both their independence and their decisions to be more than traditional homemakers.

Levinson believes that there is a shift in the middle of this stage, at the age of 25 for these women, when people reevaluate their careers and make whatever changes they may need to get back on the right path. In this group of women, the remaining single women either decided at 25 to get married or gave themselves permission to remain single. Twelve of the married women decided around the age of 25 to have their first child. Although the marriages and births occurred over the next few years, the decisions were made at 25, and for Levinson, demonstrate the 25-year shift. Also at this time, most single women became more interested in marriage and family; most married women became more interested in their careers.

By the end of this stage, all 15 academic women and nine of the 15 businesswomen were making progress on their career paths. The businesswomen had left their entry-level jobs and either had begun to advance in those companies or changed to other companies that were less prestigious but had more opportunity for advancement. The remaining three women were making plans to leave their jobs and either become full-time homemakers or work in less demanding jobs.

Nine of the academic women and five of the businesswomen had children. All 30 women in this study had entered the work world planning to leave for a few years when their children were young, but at the end of this stage, those who had children were questioning this idea. They wanted to continue their professional development and their personal growth. The biggest concern of these women was how to combine career and family.

The conflict these women experienced during this stage in trying to fulfill both work roles and family roles is different than what men experience at comparable ages. The women in this study walked a tightrope of trying to be successful career women and successful family women. They entered relationships that would be conducive to their careers and postponed parenthood until they had established themselves in a career track of some kind. Once there, they had to balance between responsibilities toward work and home. To further complicate things, they were not particularly welcome in the careers they chose and they had to blaze the trail themselves. It will be interesting to see studies dealing with the work lives of today's working women, the "granddaughters of *The Feminine Mystique.*"

CHOOSING AN OCCUPATION

Choosing an occupation is not simply one big decision. For most of us it is a series of minidecisions made over a period of time: deciding what to study in school, picking summer jobs, choosing a first job after high school or college, leaving one job to take a similar one with another company, or shifting to another occupation altogether. Few adults stay in the same job throughout a lifetime. Donald Super found that of a group of 100 men studied longitudinally from high school to their mid-30s, 30 percent had shifted from one field of work to another (1985). Robert Havighurst (1982) estimates that as many as 10 percent of men over 40 make radical shifts in careers, a figure that is likely to increase in today's job market, with technology changing so quickly and retraining for new jobs becoming so common. Nonetheless, the initial choice is a significant one, and that first choice is influenced by many factors, including gender, race, intelligence, personality, family background, and education.

The Effects of Gender

Despite enormous changes in the work roles and opportunities available to women, it is still true in the United States (and in other developed countries) that there is a very high degree of occupational gender segregation (Reskin, 1993). There are more job categories dominated by males, and these jobs are typically higher in both status and income than are traditional women's jobs. Most of the jobs held predominantly by women are **pink-collar jobs** such as secretarial and clerical jobs, retail sales position's, and service jobs (Donelson, 1999). They are low in status and pay, offer few benefits, and give little chance for advancement. Another category of jobs that are filled predominantly by women is **semiprofessional jobs** such as nursing, social work, teaching, and library work. These jobs require college degrees but have relatively low pay and little chance for advancement (N. E. Betz & Fitzgerald, 1987).

CRITICAL THINKING

As you think about your own career choices, how conscious are you of these gender designations for various jobs? Do they affect your thinking, however subtly?

Figure 8.2, based on data from Teresa Amott and Julie Matthaei (1991), gives you one kind of look at this difference, comparing women from various U.S. ethnic groups with the pattern for European-American men. You can see that Asian-American women, along with European-American women, have moved more into the traditionally male higher-level jobs than is true of either Chicanas or African-American women. But in every one of these ethnic groups of women, lower-level jobs dominate.

In addition, one obvious fact needs to be discussed here, and that is that women earn significantly less than men do. In the United States the ratio of female to male earnings is about 0.75 today, a figure that is also typical for both industrialized

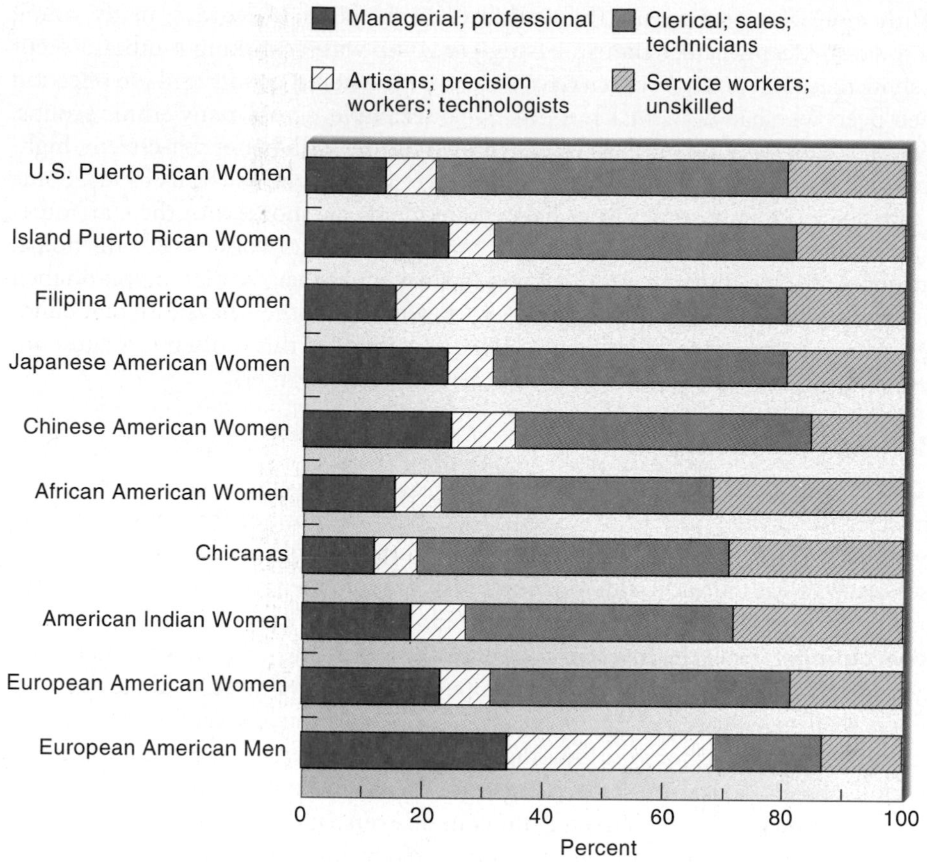
Managerial; professional
Clerical; sales; technicians
Artisans; precision workers; technologists
Service workers; unskilled
U.S. Puerto Rican Women
Island Puerto Rican Women
Filipina American Women
Japanese American Women
Chinese American Women
African American Women
Chicanas
American Indian Women
European American Women
European American Men
0
20
40
60
80
100
Percent

FIGURE 8.2 The difference in the status of men's and women's jobs is clear in this analysis, as is the fact that, among women, some groups have higher-status jobs than do others. Asian-Americans, a group with a strong cultural emphasis on the role of education in achieving higher status, have done particularly well.

Source: Amott & Mattaei, 1991, Fig. 10-1, p. 347.

and developing countries around the world. In the United States, African-American women earn less than African-American men, Hispanic-American women earn less than Hispanic-American men, and disabled women earn more than disabled men (Donelson, 1999). The hopeful news is that the earning gap is not as large among younger men and women as it is among middle-aged men and women, suggesting that the future will bring more equal wages.

Family Influences

Families also affect occupational choice in at least two ways. First, families can have a profound effect on educational attainment. Middle-class parents are far more likely than working-class parents to encourage their children to attend college and to provide financial support for such further education. This is not just an ability difference in disguise, either. Even when you compare groups of high school students who are matched in terms of grades or test scores, it is still true that the students from middle-class families are more likely to go on to further education and better-paying, higher-prestigious jobs. And young people from working-class families which also put a strong emphasis on academic and professional achievement are also likely to move up into middle-class jobs (Gustafson & Magnusson, 1991).

With more women entering the workforce in the last few decades, many young women today are facing career choices having grown up with a working mother. Recent studies show that these young women have different ideas about gender and job selection than their peers who had homemaker mothers. For example, across many ethnic groups, young women with working mothers face their own futures with better self-esteem, higher educational goals, and aspirations toward more prestigious careers (Beal, 1994). Some of this difference certainly comes from having a resident role model, but there are other differences in these families than the simple fact that the mothers work outside the home. Women who work have different attitudes, personalities, and behaviors that impact on their children (and so do their husbands). Families with working mothers have different child-rearing practices and different division of chores. The result of this is often more responsibilities and independence for the children, especially the daughters.

The Role of Personality

A third significant influence on occupational choices is the young person's personality. The chief figure in the study of personality/occupational connections has been J. L. Holland (1973; 1992). His basic argument has been that people tend to choose, and to be most satisfied with and successful in jobs that have requirements or features that match the person's own personality. More specifically, Holland proposed six basic personality types: **conventional, realistic, investigative, artistic, social,** and **enterprising.** Each personality type has a corresponding work environment, which I've listed in Table 8.3.

These six personality types can be measured using any one of several tests on which you are asked to say whether you like, dislike, or are indifferent to a whole range of jobs, school subjects, activities, amusements, situations, and types of people. Scores on each of the six dimensions are derived from your answers, and these scores then can be used not only by researchers who might be interested in the effects of matched or mismatched personality and careers, but by counselors who use the scores to advise you on suitable occupations.

Holland also proposed that these six types were related to each other in quite specific ways, as shown in the hexagon in Figure 8.3. He argued that the types closer to each other on this hexagon are more like each other and that those adults whose personality profile is such that they are high in adjacent areas on the hexagon should have more stable job histories than those whose personality or interests are all over the map.

Research in non-Western as well as Western cultures, and among Hispanics, African-Americans, Native Americans, and whites in the United States, has generally supported Holland's contention that choice of careers is affected by personality type (Eberhardt & Muchinsky, 1984; S. B. Kahn, Alvi, Shaukat, Hussain, & Baig, 1990; Meier, 1991; Tracey & Rounds, 1993). Among both men and women, for example, ministers score highest on the social scale, car salespersons on the enterprising scale, and engineers and doctors score highest on the investigative scale (Benninger & Walsh, 1980; Walsh, Horton, & Gaffey, 1977).

Once the career choice is made, the degree of match between personality and job qualities is also predictive of the person's satisfaction with his or her job. The correlation between the two is not large. Combining the results of 41 separate studies, Assouline and Meir (1987) report an average correlation of 0.20 between job satisfaction and broad measures of match between personality and occupation. The correlation is considerably stronger (0.42), if a narrower measure of match is used, such as by looking at subspecialties within occupations. Among physicians, for example, surgery and pediatrics are very different in job qualities and may attract, and satisfy, adults with quite different personalities. However, Holland seems to have been wrong in his hypothesis that job *success* is linked to the degree of match. Adults can and do succeed at jobs that match their own skills or qualities poorly. But they are more satisfied with jobs that offer a good fit.

TABLE 8.3 **John Holland's Six Personality Types and Six Work Environment Types**

Type	Personality	Work Environment
Realistic	Aggressive, masculine, physically strong, low in verbal or interpersonal skills. Prefer mechanical activities and tool use, choosing jobs such as mechanic or electrician or surveyor.	Explicit, ordered, or systematic manipulation of tools or machines or objects or animals.
Investigative	Thinking, organizing, planning, particularly abstract thinking. These people like ambiguous, challenging tasks but are generally low in social skills. They are often scientists or engineers.	Creative investigation or observation of physical, biological, or cultural phenomena.
Artistic	Asocial, preference for unstructured, highly individual activity.	Ambiguous, free, unsystematized activities to produce art or performance.
Social	Similar to extraverts (see Chapter 2). Humanistic, sociable, need attention. Avoid intellectual activity, dislike highly ordered activity. Prefer to work with people.	Training, caring for, enlightening of, informing, or serving others.
Enterprising	Highly verbal and dominating; like organizing and directing others; persuasive, high in leadership.	Manipulation of others, such as in sales of all types.
Conventional	Prefer structured activities and subordinate role; like clear guidelines; see themselves as accurate and precise.	Systematic, ordered, precise manipulation of data, such as keeping records, filing, bookkeeping, organizing written material, following a plan.

Source: Holland, 1973.

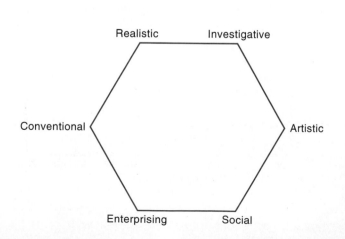

FIGURE 8.3 Holland's model of his six work/personality types. Traits that are close together on the hexagon are thought to be more closely related.

Source: Adapted from Holland, 1992, Fig. 3.

GENERAL AGE TRENDS IN WORK EXPERIENCE

Research by sociologists and industrial psychologists show several well-replicated patterns of change in work-related attitudes and behaviors over the adult years, most of which appear to hold for women as well as for men (Rhodes, 1983).

Job Satisfaction

The facet of work life that has been most frequently studied is overall job satisfaction. Cross-sectional comparisons show a consistent and clear pattern: Work satisfaction increases quite steadily throughout the work life, from age 20 to at least age 60, for both college-educated and non-college-educated adults. Figure 8.4 shows some fairly typical findings from Norvall Glenn and Charles Weaver's (1985) analysis of the combined results of a series of annual surveys between 1972 and 1982, each involving a representative national U.S. sample of roughly 800. Each respondent was asked to rate her or his overall satisfaction with work on a four-point scale that ranged from very dissatisfied to very satisfied. For the data in Figure 8.4, a "very satisfied" reply was assigned a score of 3, a "very dissatisfied" reply was given a score of 0.

It seems clear from the figure both that the average level of satisfaction was quite high and that older workers reported higher satisfaction than did younger ones. Still, these are cross-sectional data. Is it possible that this is all just a cohort effect? Maybe current younger cohorts will continue to be less satisfied throughout their working lives; maybe current older cohorts were more satisfied at every age. We do not have longitudinal evidence to allow us to sort this out, but Glenn and Weaver's data do allow a time-sequential analysis. Since they have new samples for each year over a 10-year period, we can look at each cohort as it moves through that 10-year interval. It is not the same *people* being measured at each time point, but it is a sample from the same *cohort*. Figure 8.5 shows what happens when we look at this set of findings in this fashion.

Each line in this figure represents workers from a single birth cohort measured at two time points 10 years apart. So, for example, the left-hand lines represent samples of women

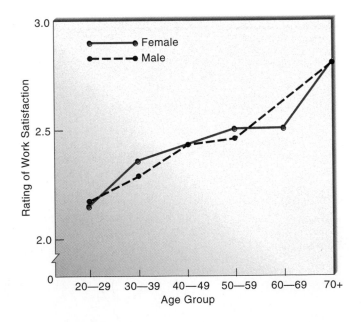

FIGURE 8.4 These cross-sectional data, averaged over separate samples interviewed each year from 1972 to 1982, show a clear rise in work satisfaction with age for both men and women in the United States.

Source: Data from Glenn & Weaver, 1985, Table 1, p. 92.

and men born between 1943 and 1952 (the early part of the Baby Boom generation), who were 20 to 29 in 1972 and 30 to 39 in 1982; the pair of lines on the far right represent samples born between 1913 and 1922 who were aged 50 to 59 at the first assessment and 60 to 69 at the second. You can see that while the overall pattern is similar to what appeared in Figure 8.4, there are also some signs of cohort effects. In particular, those who were aged 30 to 39 at the time of the first testing (who were thus born between 1933 and 1942) consistently reported more positive attitudes toward their work than did the youngest cohort. One possible explanation of this apparent peculiarity is that the 1933 to 1942 birth cohort was particularly small, so these adults have had fewer competitors for available jobs. The Baby Boomers, in contrast, are part of a very large cohort, with greater competitiveness and fewer job choices available to them. Even with this cohort variation, however, it is still true that seven of the eight lines in this figure move upward, indicating that for each cohort, work satisfaction was higher at older ages than at younger ages.

Why would work satisfaction rise with age? In part, this pattern seems to be explained by time-in-job rather than age itself (Bedeian, Ferris, & Kacmar, 1992). Older workers have typically been in their job longer, which usually means that they have reached a level with more intrinsically challenging or interesting jobs, better pay, more job security, and more authority. This is an important point to keep in mind, because as people change jobs more, as women move in and out of the labor market, many people will not accumulate large amounts of time-in-job, so may not experience the rise in satisfaction that is normally correlated with age. Similarly, when women move into the job market for the first time in their 30s or 40s, they may experience the peak of job satisfaction in their 50s rather than in their 40s. (This may be a cause for the research findings that women who don't begin to work until after their children are older keep working after traditional retirement age, as I will discuss a little later in this chapter.)

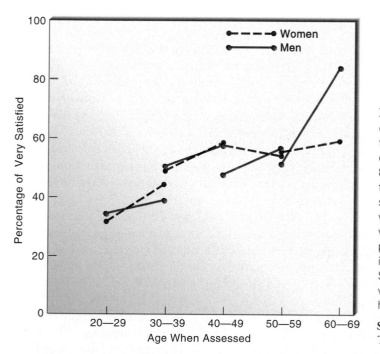

FIGURE 8.5 Glenn and Weaver's cross-sequential analysis of work satisfaction can take us a step beyond the cross-sectional information in Figure 8.4. Each line in this figure represents the percentage *from a given cohort,* sampled in 1972 and again in 1982, who said they were "very satisfied" with their work. It is not the same people at both time points for each line, but it is a sample from the same cohort. Seven of the eight lines show a rise with age, although there are clearly cohort differences at work as well.

Source: Data from Glenn & Weaver, 1985, Table 3, p. 95.

Still, time-in-job cannot account for all of what we see in Figures 8.4 and 8.5. There are also **"young" jobs** and **"old" jobs.** Young people are much more likely to hold physically difficult, dirty, or less complex and less interesting jobs (Spenner, 1988). Some of this may naturally reflect inexperience, but some of it may simply reflect the fact that young adults are physically hardier.

There is undoubtedly some **selective attrition** operating here, too. Workers who really dislike some line of work don't stay in it. Older workers in any given occupation are thus likely to be people who sought out or chose to stay in that line of work because it gives them a good match to their personality or their interests (A. T. White & Spector, 1987).

CRITICAL THINKING

Can you think of any other explanations for the rise in job satisfaction with age?

Job Commitment

Researchers have also observed an increase with age in commitment to or involvement with work. Over time, workers become more and more committed to their specific job or their specific employer, and more involved with the work itself (Rhodes, 1983). Men in their 40s and 50s are less likely to change jobs than are younger men (although this pattern may not hold in current cohorts); they see their current job as something they are likely to keep on doing until retirement; they show lower levels of avoidable absenteeism (Martocchio, 1989). All of these are indications of greater commitment to the job. Older men, in other words, take their work more seriously and find things about it that they like. Younger men are still experimenting, still searching for the right job or occupation, so they may be focused more on what is *wrong* with the current job than what is right about it.

Job Performance

Most research concludes that job performance does not appear to change with age, that older workers are as good as younger workers by most measures (McEvoy & Cascio, 1989; Warr, 1994). This is a little surprising because we also know that there *are* age-related declines in some general abilities that are central to many jobs, such as reaction time, sensory abilities, physical strength and dexterity, cognitive flexibility, and so on. Timothy Salthouse and Todd Maurer (1996) examined this paradox and suggested several explanations. First was methodological problems with the studies that find no relationship between job performance and age. There are not that many studies and not that many participants in them. Considering that the major finding is "no relationship," only the largest differences would be detected with such a small sample. In other words, there may be age-related changes in job performance, but a large sample of participants would be necessary to show them statistically. Another methodological problem is that few of the studies had participants over the age of 40—hardly the age at which age-related declines would be evident. In addition, older workers who have declined in job performance might have left the job, leaving only those older workers who had not declined, a familiar situation you probably recognize as selective attrition.

Aside from methodological problems, how else might we explain the discrepancy between finding a decline in ability with age versus no decline in job performance with age? Salthouse and Maurer suggest that job performance is made up of two factors: general ability and job experience. Although general ability may decline with age, job experience increases, perhaps enough to compensate for the decline and give us the research results of no decline in overall job performance with age.

An example of this ability/experience trade-off is demonstrated in a study of typing ability among women who ranged in age from 19 to 72 years (Salthouse, 1984). Two tasks were used, one that measured reaction time and one that measured typing speed. Not surprisingly, speed of reaction decreased with age; older women took more time to react to visual stimuli. However, typing speed was the same regardless of age. How did this happen? Evidently, the older women relied on their *increased* job experience to compensate for their *decreased* general ability. As they typed one word, they read the next few words and were ready to type those words sooner than their younger colleagues who processed the words one at a time.

Although the relationship between age and job performance has been studied for over a century, we still have a lot of questions. Does the ability/experience trade-off continue into very old age? Is this true for all workers, or are there considerable individual differences? And is it true for all types of jobs? Are there other factors that should be considered, such as personality types or job satisfaction?

Answers to these questions are becoming increasingly important as more older workers who are healthier and have more useful years ahead of them than any generation before also have more options about whether to remain on the job, change jobs, or retire. It is also an important concern for employers who are faced with decisions about an aging work force (Schaie, 1994). I look forward to more research evidence in the near future.

Career Advancement

A quite different way of looking at overall work experience over time is to focus on the career advancement of individual adults in particular occupations. The metaphor of a **career ladder** is a pervasive one. Most of us think of our adult work life in terms of a series of definable steps, or rungs on a ladder. In the academic world this is very clear: from instructor to assistant professor to associate professor to full professor. In the Ford assembly plant where Wheeler Stanley worked, there was an equally clear ladder: from assembly-line worker, to foreman, to general foreman, to superintendent, to predelivery manager, to production manager, and on up the line. Clearly, not all occupations have such sharply defined promotion steps. But most jobs have at least some hierarchy.

Just how does one move up this ladder or through this sequence? Are the steps equidistant? Can you skip steps? Does everyone move along them at the same rate? Answering such questions requires either retrospective reports from individuals about their work history or, preferably, longitudinal data. As usual, there is only a small amount of evidence that fits this prescription. A particularly helpful study is James Rosenbaum's (1984) analysis of the work histories of a group of 671 adults who entered a large company (called ABCO by Rosenbaum) between 1960 and 1962 and were still employed by the company in 1975. Since company policy specified that all workers should enter the company at the submanagement level, Rosenbaum was able to trace career paths for a large group of individuals who had begun at roughly the same point. A second helpful study is a 20-year study of AT&T managers (Bray & Howard, 1983). The AT&T researchers have focused less on sequences of individual career moves and more on factors that affected career success, but the results are illuminating nonetheless.

Several generalizations are possible from these and equivalent studies. First, a college education makes a very large difference in the pathway an individual worker follows. Even with measures of intellectual ability held constant, a college degree is associated with earlier and more career advancements.

Second, those who are promoted early go further. Sample results from Rosenbaum's study in Table 8.4 illustrate this. Eighty-three percent of those workers who received their first promotion (to foreman) within three years of joining the company had moved up to at least the first level of management within 13 years, but only 33 percent of those who took that first step to foreman at a later time made it to the management level. College-educated workers were more likely to be promoted early, so these are not independent bits of information. But even among those who did not go to college, early promotion was associated with greater overall advancement.

TABLE 8.4 **Relationship Between Earliness of First Promotion and Achievement of Middle-Level Management in Managers in the ABCO Company**

Period During Which Worker Received First Promotion	Eventually Promoted to at Least Lower Management			
	Yes	No	Total	Percent
During the first three years	56	11	67	83
Later than first three years	42	86	128	33

Source: Adapted from Rosenbaum, 1984, Table 2.4, p. 56. Reprinted by permission of Academic Press, San Diego, California, and the author.

A related finding is that most work advancement occurs early in adult life (or perhaps early in a career). By age 40 or 45, most adults have gone as far as they will go on their career ladder. Again, data from Rosenbaum's study of ABCO employees, in Figure 8.6, are illustrative. For this cross-sectional analysis Rosenbaum used data for all the workers in this company in the period from 1962 to 1965. Workers at the nonmanagement level had a very low probability of promotion after the age of 45; for promotion to foreman the pattern is even more striking. There was a high probability of promotion until about age 30 or 35, and then a very sharp drop. This general pattern has also been found in other occupations, such as in Kenneth Spenner's analysis of career moves among

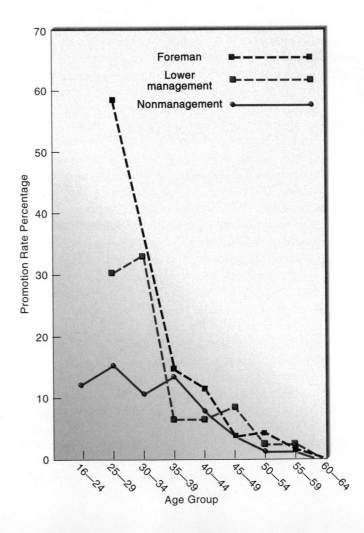

FIGURE 8.6 Results from Rosenbaum's study of a large corporation show that promotions come early in workers' careers. Promotions are comparatively rare past about age 40, in part because the number of positions decreases at each successively higher level.

Source: Rosenbaum, 1984, Fig. 3.1, p. 80. Reprinted by permission of Academic Press, San Diego, California, and the author.

accountants (Spenner, 1988), so it appears not to be unique to ABCO, or to business career ladders, although all of these studies have focused on adults who entered some occupation in their 20s and remained in it throughout their 20s, 30s, and 40s. We do not know if the same pattern would hold for adults who changed jobs or occupations.

Rosenbaum uses the metaphor of a **tournament** to describe the process of career advancement. Career paths are marked by decision points at which you either "win" (get promoted, get a raise, receive a bonus or new responsibility) or "lose" (are considered for but fail to receive a promotion, a raise, or increased responsibility). If you win, you are still in the tournament until the next decision point, and so on until you lose and thus remain at whatever level you had reached.

This metaphor describes the data reasonably well but needs several supplements. First, it seems to make a difference just what sort of new responsibilities or skills the worker is given at the next-higher level of the system. In the AT&T studies, for example, the degree of challenge of the person's job had a significant impact on later advancement: Workers at any given level who had more challenging jobs were more likely to be promoted later (Bray & Howard, 1983). Given Kohn and Schooler's work on the impact of work complexity on intellectual flexibility (which you may remember from Chapter 5), this link makes very good sense. A complex job increases your intellectual flexibility, which in turn makes you a better prospect for further advancement. Since most promotions move a worker into more complex and challenging jobs, promotions themselves will tend to increase a worker's skills and capacities. The "fast track," then, is not just a reflection of entering skills; it *creates* skills.

The tournament model also needs to be modified to take account of the fact that "losing" does not put you totally out of the game, particularly at early steps in the career. Many people make slower or later progress in their careers; a few fail many times and then succeed spectacularly. Sports metaphors are risky; life is not really much like a tournament. But the metaphor does capture some of the features of career mobility patterns in at least some occupations. What it fails to show is that there are many games in this system. If a worker "loses" in one profession, or with one company, he or she can try another. And that is precisely what most people do, especially during their 20s and early 30s, when the steps up the career ladder are mostly taken.

THE EFFECTS OF WORK ON MEN AND WOMEN

I have been focusing so far on work itself and its role in adult lives. But an equally important issue for a developmental psychologist interested in adults is the effect of work on other facets of adult functioning or development. Very little of the research on this topic is really developmental in nature. Researchers have not asked, for example, whether certain kinds of work have more or less impact on personality change or growth at different points in the adult years. But there are several sets of studies that yield some interesting fragments.

Effects for Men

I've already given you one set of relevant data in Table 8.2. Tamir obviously found that for men under the age of 40, those who were satisfied with their work were also likely to be more satisfied with their lives as a whole. Averaging across many studies and across all ages, Marianne Tait and her colleagues (Tait, Padgett, & Baldwin, 1989) find a correlation of 0.31 between work- and life-satisfaction among men. This is not an overwhelmingly large correlation, but the result is found consistently: On average, men who like their work like their lives better.

The picture is different, though, if we look at *success* in work instead of work satisfaction. I can find little evidence that men who are more successful in their careers are a great deal happier or better adjusted than those who are less successful. In the most interesting study in this area, the 20-year longitudinal study of AT&T managers, Bray and Howard (1983) found that the men who had moved farthest up the corporate ladder at midlife were more satisfied with their *jobs* than were the less successful men, but they were *not* happier or better adjusted overall, nor did they have higher marital satisfaction. Like the AT&T studies, the Berkeley Intergenerational Study, suggests that successful men and well-adjusted men are distinctly different types. The most successful were most cognitively astute, less nurturant and deferential, and more aggressive than the best adjusted. The best adjusted were less cynical, more religious, less selfish, and had steadier temperaments.

CRITICAL THINKING

Does it surprise you that men who are very successful in their work are not more satisfied with their lives overall? What kind of psychological processes do you think might be at work here?

The causality seems to run both ways. Some of these differences were already present at the beginning of the men's careers and influenced the men's work commitment and behavior. But to some extent, success and strong work commitment bring about changes in personality or values, just as Kohn and Schooler have shown that intellectual flexibility increases with high levels of work complexity. The moral seems to be that work success (or lack of it) does have an effect on men, but the effect is not primarily on overall happiness or life satisfaction.

Effects for Women

For women, as for men, satisfaction with work is moderately associated with life satisfaction. In Tait's combined analysis of many studies, the average correlation for women was 0.22. But if only those studies reported after 1974 are included, the correlation is the same as that found for men: 0.31. This pattern of results suggests that as more women have worked, the quality of their work experience has begun to make more difference in their overall life satisfaction, although that conclusion can obviously be only tentative, since we are working with correlational data here.

Most of the research on the impact of work on women's lives, however, has been focused not on the effects of variations in work experience but on the effects of *work itself*. That is, the question has been whether women who work *at all* are better off or worse off psychologically or physically than women who do not work. Research comparing the life satisfaction of working women and homemakers is highly inconsistent, in part because of the rapid changes in women's work roles in recent years. Most current research shows that working women are slightly more satisfied with their lives and have somewhat better mental and physical health than housewives (N. E. Betz & Fitzgerald, 1987), although this difference is less clear for working-class women than for the middle class. Several longitudinal studies of older cohorts of women, however, do not show this general positive effect of work. For example, Janice Stroud's analysis (1981) of the work histories of the women in the Berkeley Intergenerational Study showed no overall benefit in life satisfaction for the working women. Among college-educated women, those who had been homemakers for all their adult lives had the highest morale and self-esteem at midlife, followed closely by those with a strong commitment to work. The lowest levels of esteem and morale occurred among women who had had uneven or interrupted work histories and who had had only a moderate level of work commitment. Similar results have emerged from the Terman longitudinal study of gifted men and women (Willemsen, 1980).

It appears that in the generations of women born from 1900 to about 1930, high life satisfaction could be found either through commitment to family or through commitment to work. Subsequent generations have increasingly tried to combine the two, assuming that women, like men, need to mature in both "love and work." Studies of these more recent cohorts do show higher morale, life satisfaction, and self-esteem for women who work than for those who do not. But the effect is not a large one, nor is it shared by all subgroups of women. Whether a woman finds that work helps to foster higher self-esteem or greater life satisfaction appears to depend at least in part on the way in which she combines work and family roles, a subject to which I now turn.

COMBINING WORK AND FAMILY ROLES

In Chapter 7 and so far in this chapter I have talked largely about family roles and work roles as if they were quite separate. Yet for the great majority of adults today, these two sets of roles are inextricably intertwined. To try to understand the linkages, we need to look at the connections from both directions: the effect of family roles on work experiences, and the effect of work on family.

The Impact of Family Roles on Work Experiences

Although men with young children have traditionally worked outside the home, it is a relatively new experience for women. Figure 8.7 gives an idea of how women's roles have changed in the last two decades. The proportion of women in the workforce with preschool children has increased from 39 percent to over 60 percent, and those with school-aged children has increased from 55 percent to 77 percent. These numbers translate into major changes in the roles of many men and women and also changes in the lives of their children. As the workforce consists more and more of mothers with preschool and school-aged children, are these women's work roles affected by their multiple roles? Do family roles have different effects on women's work lives than they do on men's? Does a male worker with a two-year-old child at home differ on the job from a woman with a two-year-old child at home? Not surprisingly, the answer is "yes."

Not only do employed women actually do more of the hours of family work, as you've already seen in Chapter 6 (recall Figure 6.4), there is also a difference in the way that men and women experience the intersection of these two sets of roles. One suggestion has been that the boundaries between work and family are more permeable for women than for men (Crouter, 1984; J. Pleck, 1977). For a woman, family roles spill over more into her work life, not only in the sense that she is much more likely to leave the work-

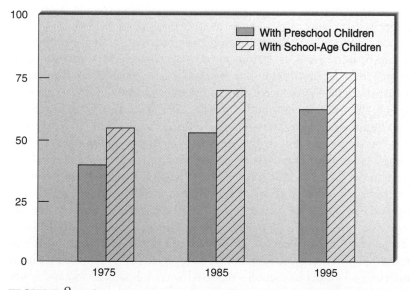

FIGURE 8.7 Over the past two decades the proportion of women in the workforce who have children has increased steadily.

Source: U.S. Bureau of Labor Statistics data as presented in R. J. Alsop, 1998, p. 316.

For Better or For Worse®   **by Lynn Johnston**

force entirely when her children are young but in the sense that she is more likely to stay home with a sick child or be the one to rearrange her schedule so that she can go to a teacher's conference or a PTA meeting.

Working women also clearly feel greater role conflict and strain between the two roles than do their husbands. A lovely anecdotal illustration comes from Anne Seiden (1980): "A distinguished woman professional, about to give a scientific paper, suddenly is distracted as she sits on the podium by the thought, "Oh, my God, I forgot to buy toilet paper." [These researchers] did not find male professionals of similar rank who as often felt a sense of personal responsibility for remembering, scheduling, and orchestrating the purchase and maintenance of routine or unusual domestic supplies" (p. 171).

Less anecdotal evidence comes from a Canadian study by Christopher Higgins (Higgins, Duxbury, & Lee, 1994). Between 1990 and 1992, Higgins asked 3616 fathers and mothers of preschool, school-aged, and adolescent children to indicate how much they agreed or disagreed with a set of statements describing possible role overload or role interference between family and work. For example, the item "I feel I have more to do than I can comfortably handle" was included in the role overload scale, while "Family life interferes with work" was one item on the family-to-work interference scale. Two things are clear in the results, shown in Figure 8.8: Women report more overload and more family interference with work, but women experience less and less overload or interference as their children get older. For men, in contrast, the age of the children has little effect on their experience of role overload.

Still, although men experience lower levels of role overload or strain, there are nonetheless important links between work and family roles for them. I mentioned in Chapter 6 that married men are healthier and more satisfied with their lives than single men. It is also true that as a general rule married men are more successful in their jobs than are men who remain single (Aldous, Osmond, & Hicks, 1979). Some of this difference may be self-selection: Healthier and brighter men may simply be more likely to marry. But some of the difference undoubtedly reflects the impact of family life on the men. The responsibility of earning a living for his family motivates the man to strive (the "parental imperative" that Gutmann describes), and the assistance of a wife who provides emotional and logistical support frees the man to devote more attention to his work.

If the latter argument holds, we ought to find that the most successful men are those with wives who do not work, who thus can devote more time and attention to supporting their husbands in their careers. There are several bits of data to support this hypothesis. As one example: In a large national survey completed in 1977 (Stanley, Hunt, & Hunt, 1986), men in dual-earner households reported lower job satisfaction and lower overall life satisfaction than did men who were the single earners, and this was even more true at higher status levels and when the wife was strongly committed to her career. Of course, this may have changed since 1977, but perhaps not. In role-theory terms, a man

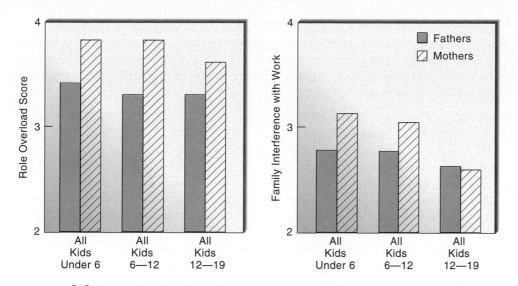

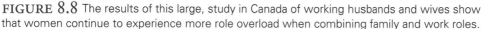

FIGURE 8.8 The results of this large, study in Canada of working husbands and wives show that women continue to experience more role overload when combining family and work roles.

Source: Data from Higgins, Duxbury, & Lee, 1994, Table 4, p. 148.

can most readily fulfill the demands of his work role when he has low conflict or strain between work and family roles. Since in a two-earner household the man's family roles become more demanding, two-job or two-career family patterns may exact a career price for men, even while they add career success for women. On the other side of the coin, there are some men in two-career couples who report feeling greater freedom in their career choices because they do not have the same pressure to be the sole breadwinner (Gilbert, 1985).

Another sort of family–work interaction for men is suggested by evidence that men are more likely than women to carry emotional strain or bad moods from family interactions into the workplace. In one study in which husbands and wives kept diaries over a period of a month and a half (Bolger, DeLongis, Kessler, & Wethington, 1989), men more often than women reported that an argument at home was followed by higher rates of argument with co-workers or supervisors at work the next day. The research base is very thin, so we do not know whether this is broadly true, but it raises the highly important point—that family life is highly *important* for men. Joseph Pleck, who has been studying men's roles for many years, says: "What is perhaps most surprising is that the view that men are obsessed by their work and oblivious to their families has persisted so long in spite of the fact that the available data have almost always disconfirmed it" (1985, p. 134). In the same vein, Robert Weiss (1990) concludes that for most men, including men who are highly work committed and successful in their careers, family is far more important than work for a man's overall life satisfaction. Work is fundamental to a man's sense of who he is and his sense of worth; but family is where he is rooted, where he finds his emotional support. The marital role is central to a man's mental and physical health (Barnett, Marshall, & Pleck, 1992). So it is perhaps not surprising that men carry emotional distress from the family into the workplace, even though they do not experience the same degree of role strain or overload as do women.

CRITICAL THINKING

Let me offer a hypothesis: A man who has a close friend/confidant in addition to his wife would be less likely to carry anger or distress from home into the workplace than would a man whose only confidant is his wife. Do you agree? How could we test this hypothesis?

The Impact of Work on Family Roles

When we turn the question around and ask about the impact of work on family life, we again have different types of information for men and for women. For men, we have two sources: studies of the impact of unemployment and a set of research findings on the effect of job quality on family interactions.

Men's Unemployment. When a man is laid off from his job, he is likely to show an increase in depression, anxiety, and risk of physical illness in the months after the job loss, a set of results found in studies in European countries as well as the United States (Kessler, Turner, & House, 1988; Liem & Liem, 1988; Price, 1992; Warr, Jackson, & Banks, 1988). There are also clear stresses on the unemployed man's family, including a higher risk of divorce, physical abuse, and child neglect. Even when these very serious negative consequences do not occur, there is typically a loss of marital satisfaction, apparently caused by a sharp increase in hostile and negative behavior by the now-unemployed husband (Conger et al., 1990; Crouter & McHale, 1993). Given what I've already said about the impact of negative interactions on marital quality, it isn't surprising that marital satisfaction drops under such circumstances. These negative effects can be ameliorated if the unemployed man receives emotional support from his wife, and they are worsened if the wife engages in "undermining" behavior, including criticism or devaluing of the husband, again as one would expect from Gottman's analyses of marital interactions (Vinokur & van Ryn, 1993). These changes largely disappear when the man returns to work, but during the period of unemployment, the effects are substantial, illustrating strongly the importance of work for a man's sense of self-esteem.

The Effect of Job Quality on Family Life. We have several pieces of information about the links between the quality of a man's work and his family life. For one thing, we know that women's marital satisfaction is higher if their husbands are successful at work, although wives of men who are *highly*-committed to work have somewhat lower marital satisfaction (Aldous et al., 1979), presumably because such men simply have less time or energy for their family lives.

But success is not the only aspect of a man's work that seems to make a difference. There is also evidence from Kohn and Schooler's research on the substantive complexity of work that men in less complex jobs, particularly jobs that are embedded in authoritarian hierarchies, become less flexible in their thinking and bring that lack of flexibility home with them. Such men are more likely to emphasize obedience and discipline with their children, while men in more complex or less authoritarian jobs are likely to encourage greater autonomy and flexibility (Kohn, 1980; Kohn & Schooler, 1983). These same patterns also seem to hold for mothers; those in jobs high in complexity also provide more cognitive stimulation and emotional warmth to their children (Menaghan, 1991; Parcel & Menaghan, 1994).

Conflict and long hours at work also have an impact on family life. In the Bolger diary study (1989), for example, arguments at work were likely to be followed by arguments with the spouse at home that evening. And when the man came home overly tired from work, the wives in this study reported that they picked up more of the slack at home. The reverse pattern occurred less often—the husband picking up the slack when the wife had had an especially hard day.

When we turn to studies of the impact of women's work on family life, the nature of the data changes. The most common emphasis has not been so much on the quality of the woman's work experience as on simply on whether or not she works. There are hundreds of studies comparing family lives for working and nonworking wives or mothers. Let me try to summarize the findings by focusing on three issues: how the wife's employment affects the way decisions are made in the family, the way household labor is allocated, and the sense of overall marital satisfaction.

Effect of Wife's Work on Decision Making and Power. Most (but not all) of the research on two-worker couples suggests that in such families the wife has more power than in families in which the husband is the only wage earner. Compared to housewives, employed women have more say in important family decisions and more control of finances (Spitze, 1988). The general rule is that whoever earns the money has the largest say in how it is spent. When both partners earn money, there is greater equality in decision making, and the more equal the earnings, the more equal the power (Steil, 1994).

Effect of Women's Work on Division of Family Labor. You've already seen in Chapter 7 that women do more household work, including both child care and housework, than their spouses do, whether or not the woman works full time. But there is no doubt about the fact that men with employed wives do *more* household work than do those with homemaker wives, and that this is even more true of current young adults than it was in previous generations (e.g., S. L. Blair & Johnson, 1992; Shelton, 1990). That said, it is also the case that the increase is not huge. In Blair's study (1992), based on interviews with a sample of married women interviewed in 1988, nonemployed women reported that their husbands did an average of 12.23 hours of household labor each week compared to 15.28 hours reported by employed wives. Children pick up some of the rest of the slack, but the biggest change is that in dual-earner households, a lot of household work is simply not done, or not done as thoroughly.

Those of you committed to the idea of egalitarian family life may find these various findings somewhat depressing. In reply, let me offer two potentially comforting points. First, there is now good evidence that the best predictor of a husband's involvement in housework and child care in two-worker households is his own gender role ideology. Men with more egalitarian attitudes provide more household help (Perry-Jenkins & Crouter, 1990; Schwartz, 1994). If such egalitarian ideology becomes more prevalent, we may well begin to see a change in the average data as well.

Second, it is easy to blame men for the lack of a greater shift toward equality of household labor in two-worker households, but it's not so clear that this is either fair or correct. There is also some resistance on the part of women to having their husbands take on more family/household responsibilities. One woman, whose husband was very involved in their care of their infant, said: "I love seeing the closeness between him and the baby, especially since I didn't have that with my father, but if he does well at his work *and* his relationship with the baby, what's my special contribution?" (Cowan & Cowan, 1987, p. 168) To the extent that a woman derives an important part of her sense of identity from her role as wife and mother, she may be reluctant to give up her central responsibility for home care.

Effect of Wives' Work on Marital Satisfaction and Stability. Given what I've said so far, you might expect that husbands of working wives would be less satisfied with their marriages. These men have lost some power in the relationship and they are expected to provide more assistance around the house and with the children. And I've already reported that men with working wives have somewhat lower satisfaction with their work. So it is perhaps surprising to find that in studies, men whose wives work are neither more nor less satisfied with their lives or their marriages than are men whose wives are housewives (Spitze, 1988; Vannoy & Philliber, 1992). Studies in the 1960s, when women's employment was much less common, typically did show that men with working wives were less satisfied with their marriages. Today, it is only in selected subgroups that we see lower satisfaction or more distress among men whose wives work: among high-income or professional men, and among men whose wives have salaries competitive with their own (Cotton & McKenna, 1988). Divorce rates are also higher among couples in which the woman earns more than half of the family income (Greenstein, 1990). Overall, though, what matters more than the wife's employment status are the gender-role attitudes of the husband and the wife's perception of his gender-role attitudes. When the man holds, or his wife perceives that he holds, traditional gender-role attitudes, marital satisfaction is lower. This is especially true if the wife works and if her earnings are especially high. And if the wife competes directly with her husband, marital satisfaction is low (Vannoy & Philliber, 1992). Clearly, today's couples must adapt to a rapidly changing cultural environment. Those who have held to more traditional views seem to be experiencing more strain than are those who have moved with the cultural shift.

Coping with Conflict and Strain

There is no perfect way to eliminate all the overload and role conflict that come from attempting to combine two paid jobs with complex family roles. But there are some strategies that help, so let me offer a bit of advice. I've phrased these suggestions as if they were aimed only at women, simply because it is women who experience the greatest sense of strain or overload. But men could profit from the same advice.

1. *Improve management skills, especially time management.* These are skills that can be learned, so it may be worth your while to take a class in time management, offered through many community colleges and elsewhere.

2. *Redefine or restructure the family roles.* In several older studies, Douglas Hall (1972, 1975) found that women who find ways to distribute tasks to other family members, or simply give up doing some tasks, experience less stress. The living room rug does not have to be vacuumed every day, men *can* clean toilets, teenage children can cook. And of course, given enough economic support, help can be hired. Clearly, a great many working women have chosen this route, because we can see in the data that the total hours spent on household work by working women is a good deal less than full-time homemakers devote to the task.

3. *Redefine your concept of what you ought to be.* Gender role definitions are not written on stone tablets for all eternity. Each of us learned those gender-role job descriptions as children and teenagers, and they are strongly ingrained. But it is possible to change the way one thinks about family roles and work roles. Women who undertake this kind of cognitive restructuring report lower levels of role conflict (Elman & Gilbert, 1984).

One strategy that does *not* help is simply trying harder to do it all. Superwomen report high levels of strain. But those who become skillful in using any or all of the three more helpful strategies are able to reduce their role conflict and achieve a reasonable balance of work and family life. Still, the balance is quite fragile, easily disrupted by unexpected demands such as a child's illness, or a car breakdown, or any of the myriad other small crises of everyday life. The simple fact is that there is no way to combine these roles that will completely eliminate the conflict or the strain—for either husband or wife. That may sound discouraging, but it is realistic.

RETIREMENT

I have talked so far about working and its effects. But what about the cessation of work at the time of retirement? What effect does it have on adult lives? Two distinctly different images of retirement are part of our cultural lore. On the one hand there is the vision of rest and relaxation, time at last to do as you please, release from the daily grind. Move to the Sunbelt and sit in the sun; get up at noon if you feel like it; stay up and watch late-night TV without worrying if that will make you too tired the next day; have time at last for your hobby or to donate hours to your favorite charity. The other vision of retirement is nicely captured by some comments I read several years ago in a one-page reprint making the rounds among faculty in my husband's department. "There is no way to describe adequately" it said, "the letdown many people feel when they retire from a responsible executive post." It went on to predict that retirees would undertake a desperate and doomed search for other sources of meaning and satisfaction, followed by depression and illness.

Which of these visions is valid? Does retirement bring large increases in satisfaction or happiness, or does it bring illness, depression, loss of a sense of self-worth, or something in between? In general, research on retirement supports the sunnier of these two visions.

CRITICAL THINKING

When you think of retirement, which of these two visions do you have? Where do you think your ideas about retirement come from?

Preparation for Retirement

Retirement is not something that just happens to us on some random date. Barring an unexpected illness, disability, or job layoff, the vast majority of adults who retire do so after some period of planning and expectation. Adults prepare for retirement in various ways, beginning perhaps as early as 15 or 20 years before the anticipated time of retirement (L. Evans, Ekerdt, & Bossé, 82, 1985). They talk with their spouse, with relatives and friends, read articles, do some financial planning, begin an IRA account. These activities seem to increase fairly steadily as the expected retirement date draws closer.

Such preparatory activities are not equally likely in all middle-aged workers, however. In a panel study of 2000 men in the Boston area, Linda Evans and her colleagues, found that men over 45 were more likely to report retirement-planning behavior if they were looking forward to retiring, if they enjoyed hobbies and pastimes, thought their pensions would be adequate, were dissatisfied with their jobs, or had a good friend who had retired. Those who dreaded retirement did the least preparation, but even in this group, those closest to retirement age showed more preparation than did those more distant from it.

The Timing of Retirement

Just as planning varies, so does the actual timing of retirement. What you may not realize, though, is that the typical age of retirement, in the United States and in most industrialized countries, is much closer to 60 than 65. As recently as 1970 in the United States, 65 was the most common retirement age for men, which may be why so many of us still think of 65 as "retirement age." But over the past several decades, people have begun to retire at younger and younger ages. In many countries, 60 is now the official age at which workers can begin receiving pensions; in many others, 65 is the age at which a full pension may be received, but reduced pensions may be drawn at earlier ages (Inkeles & Usui, 1989), as is true in the United States.

In part because of these various early pension benefits, the age of retirement has dropped rapidly in many countries. Some European countries, concerned about a reduced labor force, are trying to reverse this trend by gradually raising the age of eligibility for public pensions. A similar change has been proposed in the United States, and such public policy changes may affect individual retirement decisions in the future. But at this moment in the United States, the single most common age for men to retire is 62, and more than half retire *before* age 65 (Leonesio, 1993).

Less is known about women's retirement patterns, but Figure 8.9 shows the proportion of middle-aged men and women in the labor force compared to the number of older men and women currently working full time. If you compare the midlife group to the U.S Bureau of Labor statistics of 90 percent of working-age men and 70 percent of working-age women who have full-time jobs, you can see the result of early retirement. And if you look at the older group, you can see an even greater reduction

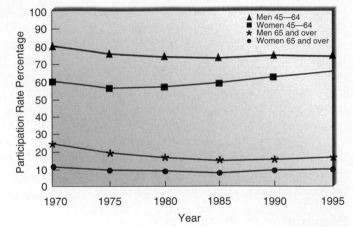

FIGURE 8.9 Percentage of older men and women who still hold full-time jobs compared to midlife men and women. Numbers have declined over the last two decades except for midlife women, whose proportion has increased.

Source: U.S. Bureau of the Census, 1996.

in full-time employment. Comparing the numbers over time. the increase in midlife women's work is very apparent—it is the only proportion that has actually increased since the 1970s.

Reasons for Retirement

Our knowledge about how people choose when (or whether) to retire has been greatly augmented by a remarkable analysis by Erdman Palmore and his colleagues of a group of seven large longitudinal studies of adults before, during, and after retirement (Palmore, Burchett, Fillenbaum, George, & Wallman, 1985). Included in this set of studies is not only the now-familiar Duke Longitudinal Studies of Aging and the Panel Study of Income Dynamics, but major studies by the Department of Labor (the National Longitudinal Surveys), Social Security Administration (the Retirement History Study), and several others. In all, over 7000 adults of retirement age participated in these studies, each interviewed at least twice, typically three or four times over a period of 6 to 10 years. The evidence from all of these studies, taken together, points to a few key factors that influence retirement decisions.

Health. One of the strongest predictors of the timing of retirement is health. Those in poor health are likely to retire earlier than those in good health. Among workers between the ages of 60 and 67, poor health lowers the average age of retirement from one to three years (Sammartino, 1987). This is true for Hispanics and African-Americans as well as Anglos (E. P. Stanford, Happersett, Morton, Molgaard, & Peddecord, 1991), and the same pattern is found in many other industrialized countries as well (McDonald & Wanner, 1990), although it has not been found in one study in China (Hayward & Want, 1993). Among men who retire later, however, such as those who retire at 65 or later, health plays less of a role in the decision to retire, presumably because most such adults are in reasonably good health. Thus to a significant degree people retire early because they are no longer able to work, or are unable to work to their previous levels of proficiency.

Age. A second factor is obviously age itself. For any given cohort in any given culture there is a certain normative time to retire. Each of us is aware of those norms and the norms tend to push us toward common retirement ages. Mandatory retirement ages also have an influence, although the big majority of older adults report that they retired not because they were forced to but because they chose to.

Having Children Still at Home. Whatever the adult's age, those with children still at home are much less likely to retire. Men with late-life children tend to stay in the workforce until their children are launched, even if this takes them past the normative retirement age.

Pension Programs. Not surprisingly, availability of adequate financial support during retirement makes a big difference in individual decisions, both for early and for normative retirements. Those who belong to a private pension program (who will thus have income in addition to Social Security) retire earlier than do those who lack this economic support during retirement.

The effect of health and pension systems often work in the opposite direction, because many working-class adults can expect little retirement income except Social Security, which would push them to wait until the official pensionable age to retire. But many such adults are also in poorer health, which would push them toward earlier retirement. Of the two, poor health seems to be the stronger influence, because working-class adults typically retire *earlier* than do middle- and upper-class workers. But there is a significant minority of working-class adults, including many minority adults, who continue working as long as they are physically able to do so in order to supplement Social Security.

At the other end of the economic scale, health and pension benefits work against each other in the opposite way. Such adults are, on average, in better health and can expect better pensions. They also have more interesting jobs, and these three factors together usually mean that these workers retire somewhat later than average.

Work Characteristics. The self-employed and the highly work-committed retire later than do those who work for others or who are less committed to their work, a pattern that suggests the not-surprising conclusion that men who find greater gratification in their jobs are more likely to continue working past the normative retirement age. In an interesting supplementary analysis of the results of the National Longitudinal Survey sample, Mark Hayward and Melissa Hardy (1985) have found that men in more substantively complex jobs retire later. For this group, only ill health or a particularly good pension program are significant pushes toward retirement. Among those in less complex jobs it is the timing of availability of pensions that is a key ingredient. Thus men with low-level repetitive jobs are highly likely to retire as soon as they are eligible for private pensions; those in more challenging jobs are likely to put off retirement until either pushed by ill health or attracted by some special financial inducement.

Women and Retirement

As you probably noticed, most of the information we have on retirement is based on studies of the work lives of men. There are several reasons for this. One is that most men have always worked outside the home for pay, whereas women have only recently entered the workforce in large numbers. Second, women who have worked outside the home often have had the types of jobs that don't have official "retirement" (or pensions or investment benefits). And third, researchers have been more concerned with men's experience at retirement because it was thought to be such a traumatic transition for them, and that women had less of their self-concept and identity tied up in their jobs. In the last decade or so, women have been included in retirement research, and an interesting, if sometimes gloomy, picture is emerging.

First, women are not as likely to plan for retirement as men are. They do not attend retirement seminars offered by their employers, they do not seek out information on their retirement benefits, and they do not make financial plans for their retirement years. Many depend on their husbands to "take care of things," but not even those who are recently divorced or widowed make the effort to prepare for retirement that their male co-workers do. This is especially alarming when you consider that women usually have fewer years on the job, lower pay, and jobs that are less likely to have good pensions (Carp, 1997).

Women retire earlier than men do and for different reasons. Whereas men retire for work-related reasons, women retire for family-related reasons. One of the most frequently reported reasons for a woman's retirement is because her husband has retired, but this companionable-sounding statistic can be misleading. Many of these wives report that they feel pressured by their husbands to retire before they are ready to leave their jobs (Szinovacz, 1991). If a woman has worked during her child-rearing years, she is more apt to retire early; if she has only begun to work after her children were grown, she is more apt to retire late (Henretta, O'Rand, & Chan, 1993).

Women's adjustment to retirement depend on their preretirement work status. Professional women who were happy in their careers are also happier in their retirement than women with lower-status jobs or women who were not happy in their careers (Richardson & Kilty, 1991). In an interesting study by Adelman (1993), older women were asked to categorize themselves as being retirees, homemakers, or retirees *and* homemakers. Those who claimed the dual roles showed higher self-esteem and lower depression than those who claimed either single role.

Retirement may soon be one of the longest periods of life for women—spanning approximately one-third of their years. It is important for women to make a smooth transition to retirement and to adjust to this new stage of life. Many times women go through this transition alone; about 35 percent of women retire as widows (compared to 10 percent of men). In addition, about 10 percent of women have never married, and a growing number of divorced women reach retirement age without remarrying. Studies of single women in retirement communities show that groups of retired women form book clubs, travel, and do volunteer work together; in other words, they continue to rely on the social convoys they have carried with them throughout their lives—family members, friends, and former co-workers (Carp, 1997).

The Decision Not to Retire

The great majority of retirees have no desire to begin work again. When asked what they would do if they were offered a job in their geographical area, only 5 percent of a nationally representative sample of men aged 69 to 84 said they would take the job (Parnes & Sommers, 1994). Most say they have "had it" with work, or that their health would not permit it. But there are, nonetheless, a significant number of adults who do continue working past the normative retirement ages. This subgroup actually includes two types of people: (1) those who never retire from their previous line of work but continue to work at their normal occupation until they die, such as college professors who become emeritus professors and maintain an active research life into their 70s and 80s, or legislators such as the late Congressman Claude Pepper of Florida, champion of causes of the elderly, and (2) those who retire from their regular occupation but then take what is sometimes called a **bridge job:** a new type of

SOME PEOPLE NEVER RETIRE. Dr. Michael E. DeBakey, at age 91, is currently working with NASA to develop a self-contained, miniaturized heart.

job, often part time, often in a totally new line of work. An analysis of the data from the Retirement History Study (Quinn & Burkhauser, 1990) suggests that as many as 20 percent of current American workers continue working past the typical retirement following one or the other of these two patterns. Four to five percent continue working full time, even into their 70s and 80s (Herzog, House, & Morgan, 1991; Parnes & Sommers, 1994). Such people are often described as having "shunned" retirement.

We know almost nothing about women who choose not to retire, but we do know something about men who shun retirement. Some of them are men with very low education, poor retirement benefits, and thus very low incomes. These men continue working out of economic necessity. Another fraction of the retirement shunners are highly educated, healthy, highly work-committed professionals, many of them with wives who are also still working (Parnes & Sommers, 1994). Many of them have been highly work committed all their adult lives. For example, men in the National Longitudinal Surveys sample, a group that has been studied over 25 years, were asked in their 50s whether they would continue working if they suddenly found themselves with enough money to live comfortably. Those who said they would continue working no matter what are much more likely to shun retirement and to be still working in their 70s and 80s (Parnes & Sommers, 1994). These are men with a strong work commitment and a distaste for retirement. For them, work continues to provide more satisfaction than they expect retirement to offer.

The Effects of Retirement

Once an adult has retired, what happens? Does life change totally? Does health decline? The striking fact is that for most adults retirement itself has remarkably few effects on income, health, activity, or attitudes.

Effects on Income. What I'm going to say here is quite culture-specific, because I'm going to focus almost entirely on retired adults in the United States. Because pension programs differ so widely from one country to another, it is not possible to draw a general picture that will be valid for other cultures, although I'll try to give you a bit of cultural context where I can.

Many younger people believe that retirees live on Social Security payments. In actuality, only 16 percent are in this category, as you can see in Figure 8.10. About two-thirds

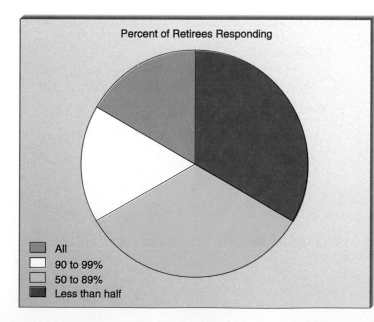

FIGURE 8.10 What percent of your income comes from Social Security? Over two-thirds of Americans over 65 report that the majority of their retirement income comes from Social Security.

Source: Adapted from Social Security Administration, 1997.

report that they receive most of their income from Social Security. This leaves a third that receive most of their income from other sources, which can be other pensions offered through an employer or the military, earnings from continued work, income from savings or other assets, and—for those below the poverty line—public assistance.

This doesn't tell us how the incomes of retired adults compare to their *preretirement* incomes. In fact, data from the combined longitudinal studies (Palmore et al., 1985) suggests that income typically drops about 25 percent upon retirement. But this number is misleading and gloomy. Many retirees own their homes free-and-clear and thus no longer have to make mortgage payments; their children are launched; they are eligible for Medicare and thus have potentially lower payments for health care; they are also entitled to many special senior citizen benefits. When you include all these factors in the calculation, you find that on average, adults in the United States, Australia, and most European countries have incomes that are 85 to 100 percent of preretirement levels (Smeeding, 1990). In the United States, incomes for some older adults actually *increase* after retirement, because the combination of Social Security and SSI is greater than they earned in their working years (Palmore et al., 1985).

This upbeat report of the economic status of American elderly is possible primarily because of improvements in Social Security benefits in the United States over the past several decades. Indeed, the financial position of America's elderly has improved more than that of any other age group in recent years. In 1966, 28.5 percent of those over 65 were living below the poverty line. In 1996, that number was 10.8 percent. Figure 8.11 shows the change in the proportion of older people living in poverty over the last three decades compared to the same changes for children. As you can see, a greater proportion of children live in poverty today in the United States than do older adults (U.S. Bureau of the Census, 1997).

But just as the figures on the drop in income with retirement are misleadingly pessimistic, the figures on the rate of poverty for retired persons are misleadingly optimistic. While the number living below the official poverty line has indeed dropped, there is still a large percentage in a category Smeeding calls "tweeners," those whose incomes are between the poverty level and double the poverty level. Roughly one-fifth of all older cou-

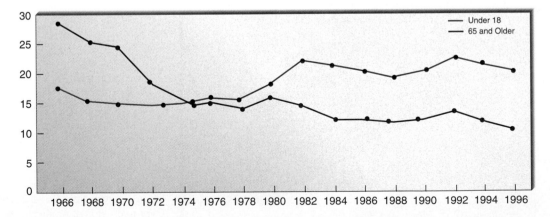

FIGURE 8.11 In the three decades from 1966 to 1996, the poverty rate for adults over 65 has dropped while the rate for children has risen.

Source: Adapted from U.S. Bureau of the Census data as presented in R. J. Alsop, 1998, p. 316.

ples, and two-fifths of single older adults are in this category (Smeeding, 1990). And because these adults are ineligible for many special programs designed to provide support for the poor, they are in many ways the worst off financially of any subset of the elderly.

Poverty is also not equally distributed across ethnic groups or gender. Older women are about twice as likely to be poor as are older men, and African-American and Hispanic elderly are considerably more likely to be poor than are Anglos. The respective percentages living below the poverty line for the three groups in 1991 were 33.8, 20.8, and 10.3 (U.S. Bureau of the Census, 1993). Combining these two factors, we find that the group most likely to be poor are African-American women, among whom as many as 70 percent live in poverty. Finally, because women live longer than men do, which means there are many more older women than men, we find that roughly two-thirds of all the elderly poor are women.

This **gendering of poverty,** in which we find a larger proportion of women than men among the poor, especially among older adults, has many causes. One obvious cause is that so many older women are widowed. In the United States, the Social Security rules are such that a widow is entitled to *either* her own Social Security payments or 100 percent of her husband's Social Security entitlement, whichever is higher. That may seem like a good deal, but in fact it results in a substantial drop in *household* income. When the husband was still alive, both spouses received pension support; when he dies, only the woman receives income, and the widow's total income will be somewhere between half and two-thirds the previous household income. This drops a great many women into poverty (Burkhauser, Duncan, & Hauser, 1994).

But it is too simple to attribute older women's greater likelihood of poverty simply to widowhood or living alone. The gendering of poverty in old age flows from a whole string of differences in adult life experiences for men and women who are now in late life. Current cohorts of older women were much less likely to work, less likely to be involved in private pension plans even if they did work, and worked at lower wages than did their male peers, all of which affect their incomes at retirement (Hardy & Hazelrigg, 1993). Add to this the facts I've already presented about women's reluctance to make financial plans for retirement (Carp, 1997). Some of these differences still exist for younger cohorts, and will thus continue to contribute to gender differences in economic conditions in old age for today's younger cohorts. But the differences are likely to shrink at least somewhat in later generations.

Many of the statistics I've given you are quite discouraging and give a very negative impression of the financial status of the elderly. But let us not lose sight of two bits of information I gave you at the beginning of this section: on average, the effective income of older adults declines only slightly at the time of retirement, and elderly in the United States are better off financially now than ever in the past.

Effects on Residence. Another effect of retirement for many adults is an increase in choices about where to live. When you are no longer tied to your job, you can choose to live nearer to one of your children or move south for sunnier weather. Many of you may have the notion, as did I, that such a move is common among older adults. Somewhat to my surprise, I find that it is not. Some adults do indeed take advantage of their greater freedom in this way, because there is a small burst of residential moves right around retirement age. But this burst only brings the rate of moves to about 1 percent a year (Longino, 1990). There is another burst of moves roughly 10 years later, beginning at about age 75.

Charles Longino (D. J. Jackson, Longino, Zimmerman, & Bradsher, 1991; Litwak & Longino, 1987; Longino, Jackson, Zimmerman, & Bradsher, 1991), who has been a diligent investigator of residential moves among the elderly, proposes that there are three types of moves. The **amenity move** is the one that typically occurs right around the time of retirement. It is most often in a direction *away* from the older person's children, frequently to a warmer climate—Florida, California, and Arizona being the most popular destinations in the United States. In Canada, amenity moves are most often westward, particularly to British Columbia; in Britain, the equivalent move is to the seaside.

Retirees who make such amenity moves are likely to be still married, relatively healthy, and have adequate or good retirement income. Most report higher levels of life satisfaction or morale after such a move, although there are some who move back to their home base because they find themselves too isolated from kin. These days, a growing number of older adults split the difference with a pattern of **seasonal migration,** spending winter months in sunnier areas and summer months at home, nearer to family. One survey of older residents of upstate New York found that 14 percent had spent at least part of the winter in another state, usually in the Sun Belt (Krout, 1983).

Longino labels the second type of move **kinship migration.** It occurs when the older adult—most often a widow living alone—has developed a sufficient level of chronic disability that she is having serious difficulty managing an independent household. When a move of this type occurs, it is nearly always a shift to be closer to a daughter or son or some other relative who can provide regular assistance. Finally, for some there is a third type of migration in late adulthood, which Longino labels **institutional migration,** to nursing home care, a type of move I have talked about earlier.

Of course, very few older adults actually move three times. Longino's point is that these are three very different kinds of moves, made by quite different subsets of the population of elderly and at different time points in the years of late adulthood. Amenity moves are usually early, kinship moves are likely to be mid- to late-old age, while institutional moves are clearly late in life. Only the first of these reflects the increase in choices and options that may open up during the retirement years.

Effects on Physical Health. There is a pervasive belief that retirement can somehow cause a decline in one's health; this is simply not true. Although retirement and poor health may be related, it is because they both tend to occur more often in older adults than younger ones. If anything, poor health *causes* retirement, not vice versa. The best conclusion I can draw from a number of studies is that retirement has little effect one way or the other on health. People who are in good health at retirement age show the same level of illness over the following years whether they retire or keep on working (Palmore et al., 1985).

Effects on Attitudes and Mental Health. Similarly, the bulk of the evidence suggests that retirement has little or no effect on life satisfaction or a person's subjective sense of well-being. Those longitudinal studies that included such measures show little difference between preretirement and postretirement, and there is little indication of any increase in depression after retirement (Palmore et al., 1985).

The inescapable conclusion is that for the great majority of adults, retirement is simply not a stressful life event. One set of data that makes this point particularly clearly comes from a longitudinal study of some 1500 men (Bossé, Aldwin, Levenson, & Workman-Daniels, 1991). At one point in the study, the men were asked to rate the relative stressfulness of 31 life events, including such things as divorce, institutionalization of a parent, a child's divorce, a move to a less desirable residence, death of a friend, and so on. In this list, retirement was rated next to last in stressfulness. The only thing rated as less stressful than retirement was the retirement of the spouse. Of those in this study who had retired in the preceding year, 7 out of 10 said they found retirement low in stress. Indeed, those men still working were almost twice as likely to list work problems as were retired men to list retirement problems.

When the subjects in this study did indicate that they had had some problems with retirement, poor health and poor family finances were the most common causes. In general, those who describe most problems with retirement are those who had the least control over the process, such as those forced into retirement by mandatory retirement plans when they would have preferred to continue working, or those who are pushed into retirement by ill health (Floyd et al., 1992; Herzog, House, & Morgan, 1991).

If we look at an even broader pattern, what predicts life satisfaction in later adulthood is not whether a person has retired or not but whether he or she was satisfied with life in earlier adulthood. We take ourselves with us through the years; grumpy, negative young people tend to be grumpy, negative old people, and cheerful, positive young adults are usually cheerful and positive in retirement as well. The consistency in this is quite striking and provides very good support for consistency theories of adulthood. Work does shape our daily lives for upward of 40 years of our adulthood; but our happiness or unhappiness with life, our growth or stagnation, seems less a function of the specifics of the work experience than it is a function of the attitudes and qualities we bring to the process.

Furthermore, retirement itself is unstressful because it is a *scheduled* change rather than an unscheduled one. As Leonard Pearlin has reminded us repeatedly, it is the unscheduled life changes that are associated with major negative consequences. Since most of us can prepare for retirement and plan its timing, for most of us it is a highly scheduled and nonstressful event.

REVIEW OF WORK ROLES IN ADULTHOOD

As before, I have summarized the age-related changes described in this chapter in a table (Table 8.5). The pattern here is strongly reminiscent of the pattern of family and gender-role changes I talked about in Chapter 6. Early adulthood is marked by the acquisition

TABLE 8.5 **Summary of Age Changes in Work Roles**

Age 20–40	Age 40–65	Age 65+
Trial stage of career, with first choice of occupation, influenced by personal qualities, formation of a dream, and the finding of a mentor. Establishment stage, with maximum career steps, focus on succeeding in the chosen job or career.	Maintenance stage of career, during which there are few additional upward career steps; may take the role of mentor; may redefine the importance of work in the overall life scheme.	Retirement for most workers, accompanied by some reduction in income but no marked reduction in health or satisfaction.
Job satisfaction is typically low at the beginning of these years and rises steadily.	Job satisfaction maximally high in these years, as is job involvement. Job performance does not decline.	
For women, this period typically includes an "in and out" phase, in which the woman moves in and out of the labor force, often several times.	For those women who work, this is a more stable work period, with continuous work patterns more common than at earlier ages. Some women enter the workforce for the first time in these years. Women who work in these years are generally more satisfied with their lives than are women who do not work.	

and mastery of new work roles. A job must be found, and after each promotion or job change, the new job must be learned. In middle adulthood, in contrast, there are few totally new work roles but the existing roles undergo redefinition. Emphases change, work values change, the relative importance of work changes. And in late adulthood work roles are lost, just as is true of many family roles.

Each of these tasks—acquisition of roles, redefinition of roles, and loss of roles—has its own set of issues, problems, and stresses. Different adults are likely to find particular periods difficult or easy, depending on their temperament or circumstances. So for some, the heavy dosage of role acquisition in early adulthood may be particularly stressful, especially if many complex roles must be mastered simultaneously. For others, the redefinitions at midlife are more stressful, perhaps particularly for those who are low in openness to experience or who lack the cognitive skill or intellectual flexibility to reassess or redefine. For a few, the loss of roles in late life is most difficult. Thus, while we can identify a general pattern of role change over adulthood that seems to be common for the vast majority of adults, in many cultures, the experience of that pattern will vary markedly from one person to another.

Summary

1. Most men follow a pattern of continuous work through adulthood. In contrast, roughly one-fourth of women have worked continuously, another 50 percent have moved in and out of the workforce, depending on family responsibilities, and the remainder have remained at home full time.

2. Women who work continually have higher salaries than those of women who interrupted their careers. Among women who interrupt their careers, those who did it later had higher salaries than those who did it earlier.

3. Men's work lives can be divided into stages. In the early 20s the young man selects an occupation through trial and error; he may also form a dream and find a mentor. From the late 20s to the mid-40s, he learns his craft, striving for whatever success he can achieve. In the late 40s to retirement, men come to terms with their level of success and may reduce the emphasis they place on work success as a mark of personal value. These stages are given various labels by various theorists.

4. At least one theorist has studied the early stages of women's work lives and found that they are generally the same as men's, but there are a few exceptions. In the early 20s, women choose a career path, but few find a mentor or establish a dream. From the late 20s to early 40s, women establish themselves in their careers, but also grapple with issues of career versus family.

5. Occupational choices are affected by gender, family background, and personality.

6. Traditional "men's jobs" are more varied and higher in status than traditional "women's jobs." Traditional female jobs offer lower pay, fewer benefits, and little chance for advancement.

7. Families affect job choice by influencing educational attainment, especially for daughters of working mothers, providing role models and instilling responsibility and independence.

8. Adults also tend to select occupations whose demands match their own personality characteristics or values. Six personality/job types have been suggested by Holland: realistic, investigative, social, conventional, enterprising, and artistic.

9. Cross-sectional research generally shows job satisfaction and job commitment to be lower among young workers, higher among older workers. Some cohort effect seems to influence this pattern, but genuine age effects remain.

10. Early research that shows little relationship between job performance and age has been questioned for methodological reasons. Current thinking is that as specific abilities decline with age, experience increases enough to help compensate for the decline.

11. Individual movement up a career ladder is facilitated by higher education and by early promotion. Most adults achieve whatever upward movement they are likely to experience within the first 15 to 20 years in an occupation.

12. Men who are satisfied with their work generally report higher life satisfaction in general, although work success is not similarly linked to life satisfaction or better adjustment. For women, having a job is generally associated with higher life satisfaction than is full-time homemaking.

13. When both husband and wife work, role conflict and role strain increase, especially for women. In two-job families, compared to one-job families, women have more power, remain responsible for homemaking tasks and child rearing, but spend fewer hours actually doing housework.

14. Marital satisfaction is unrelated to wives' employment, except in select subgroups. Lower satisfaction is found among men with high income or those with wives who are very highly work committed or earn salaries competitive with those of their husbands.

15. Among adults in the United States and most other industrialized countries, retirement has been occurring at earlier and earlier ages; 60 or 62 is now modal.

16. Most men begin to prepare mentally and emotionally for their retirement some years before retirement age. Compared to those who retire later, those who retire early tend to be in poorer health, are lower in social class, are less committed to their work, and have adequate pension programs.

17. Recent research on women's retirement transition shows that there are some gender differences. Women are not as apt to plan for retirement or seek information about pensions. They retire for family reasons, sometimes against their own wishes. Many women go through the transition to retirement alone and most make good adjustments to this stage which can now comprise a third of their lives.

18. The impact of retirement on individual income is a mixed story. On average, U.S. elders are better off financially than ever before, but a significant fraction of older women (especially minority women) live at or near poverty.

19. Several different types of residential moves occur in the retirement period. A minority make an amenity move, often soon after retirement; later, kinship migration is more likely, when the elder moves nearer a child or other relative; in late old age, a move to an institution occurs for some.

20. Neither health nor life satisfaction show any consistent change—negative or positive—as a result of retirement. Indeed, there is little sign that retirement is a stressful life change for the great majority.

KEY TERMS

work patterns

trial stage

early adult transition

mentor

the dream

establishment or
   stabilization stage

early adulthood stage

age-30 transition

maintenance stage

middle adulthood

adjustment to retirement

late adulthood

pink-collar jobs

semiprofessional jobs

conventional personality
   type

realistic personality type

investigative personality
   type

artistic personality type

social personality type

enterprising personality
   type

"young" jobs

"old" jobs

selective attrition

career ladder

tournament

bridge job

gendering of poverty

amenity move

seasonal migration

kinship migration

institutional migration

SUGGESTED READINGS

Fisk, A. D., & Rogers, W. A. (1997). *Handbook of human factors and the older adult.* San
   Diego, CA: Academic Press.

This is a collection of articles by researchers who have applied psychology to practical problems facing older adults both at home and in the workplace.

Levinson, J. (1996). *The seasons of a woman's life.* New York: Ballantine.

This is the full report of a study Levinson did in the 1980s, interviewing 45 women
in depth about their careers and family transitions over the years of early adulthood
through middle age. He compares the women who were homemakers and career
women, and then compares the women with similar men he interviewed as the basis
for his earlier book, *The Seasons of a Man's Life.*

Posner, R. A. (1996). *Aging and old age.* Chicago: University of Chicago Press.

This book, written by a noted economist (who is also a federal judge and senior citizen himself), applies economic theories to several aspects of aging, such as retirement, age discrimination, euthanasia, rate of voter turnout and jury participation,
and mental competence. It is clearly written for the noneconomist and gives a new
way of looking at some familiar topics.

Quadagno, J., & Hardy, M. (1996). Work and retirement. In R. H. Binstock & L. K.
   George (Eds.), *Handbook of aging and the social sciences (4th ed.).* San Diego, CA:
   Academic Press.

This is a very interesting discussion of how the transformation to retirement has
changed over the past century. This article gives some valuable insight about why people today retire when they do and may give younger readers some predictions about
their own futures.

Terkel, S. (1972). *Working.* New York: Avon.

If you want to know what work feels like to Americans across an enormous range of occupations, read Studs Terkel's fascinating book.

Weiss, R. S. (1990). *Staying the course: The emotional and social lives of men who do well at work.* New York: Free Press.

The men described in this book are a particular subset, those who have achieved well in demanding careers. This book is fascinating whether you aim to be such a man or know someone who fits this description.

CHANGES

IN PERSONALITY
AND MOTIVES

One of the remarkable things about our sense of self over the years of adult life is that we simultaneously see ourselves as staying the same and as changing. The sense of sameness is easy to identify. Think about yourself when you were 18 or 20, and then think about yourself as you are now and see if that isn't true. (Of course, this will not be so helpful an exercise if you are now only 20, but bear with me.) Your sense of who you are is composed in large part of a set of traits or qualities that are the same over time.

There are dozens of ways in which I am the same person I was at 20. I was then, and still am, talkative, assertive, friendly, definite, uncoordinated, somewhat rigid (my family might argue that the term *somewhat* is a slight understatement!), well organized, unorthodox, and strongly solitary. I liked things to be predictable when I was 20 and still do. Time by myself was something I greatly valued as a child, as a young adult, and now. It is no accident that I have chosen an occupation that lets me work alone, nor that I make my living with words. It is also no accident that I have ended up on the board or as the manager of virtually every organization I have ever joined, nor that when I wanted to get in better physical shape I chose running rather than a team sport, aerobics classes, or a competitive sport such as tennis.

A particularly wonderful example of consistency comes from David McClelland (1981), a Harvard psychologist who has been one of the major figures in personality research. McClelland describes his encounters over a 25-year period with a man originally known as Richard Alpert, a man I also knew briefly when he was a visiting professor at Stanford and I was a graduate student. In the early 1960s, Richard Alpert was a professor at Harvard, very verbal, charming, and successful. He could hold classes or audiences spellbound. McClelland, who was Alpert's colleague at Harvard, also describes him as having been ambitious, interested in influencing others, and with a strong need for power, accompanied—so McClelland reports—by guilt about wanting such power. Then, when he was a young faculty member at Harvard, Alpert got involved with Timothy Leary, another Harvard professor who was experimenting with LSD and who advised young people of that time to "turn on, tune in, and drop out." Alpert did all three. He left Harvard, drifted about for a few years, then went to India for some years, where he stayed at the ashram (study center) of a guru. Eventually, Alpert came back to the United States with a new name—Ram Dass—and a new philosophy. McClelland says:

> When I first saw Ram Dass again in the early 1970s he seemed like a completely transformed person. His appearance was totally different from what it had been. He was wearing long Indian style clothes with beads around his neck; he was nearly bald but had grown a

CRITICAL THINKING

How would you describe your own enduring qualities?

long bushy beard. He had given away all his possessions, refusing his father's inheritance, carried no money on his person, and for a time lived as a nomad in a van which was all he had in the world. He had given up drugs, abandoned his career as a psychologist, no longer wanted even to save the world and talked all the time as if he were "nobody special," although previously it had been clear to himself and others that he was somebody special… yet after spending some time with him, I found myself saying over and over again "It's the same old Dick,"… He was still very intelligent… he was still verbally fluent… and he was still charming…. At a somewhat less obvious level, Alpert was very much involved in high drama, just as he had always been…. I would certainly conclude that he continues to have a strong interest in power…. Furthermore he still feels guilty about being so interested in power. (1981, pp. 89–91)

Several years ago I had a chance to hear Alpert/Ram Dass speak and came away with the same impression, both from watching him and from listening to his words. In some ways he was still the same man I knew 30 years ago. He still held the audience spellbound, he still had a wonderful self-deprecating form of humor, he still seemed pleased to be admired—although now he was aware of this and made fun of himself. He said quite explicitly that the same neuroses, the same foibles are still there. In some sense they define him. That's who Dick Alpert (or Ram Dass) is.

Yet in the midst of all this continuity, all this sameness, there is clearly change as well. I am not the same as I was at 20, just as Dick Alpert is not. He has lost the restlessness of mind and body that I remember and now radiates an inner quiet and calm. At 55, I am still comparatively rigid, but I am a lot *less* rigid than I was at 20, a lot more forgiving, more able to laugh at myself, less intense, more confident, less anxious—or perhaps more accurately, anxious about fewer things.

In this chapter I want to explore both parts of this system, both the consistencies and the changes. What aspects of personality tend to stay the same, and why? What kinds of changes do we see, and can those changes be thought of as growth or inner development, as Loevinger or Erikson might say, or are they more in the way of adjustments to changing circumstances, as Levinson suggests?

ALMOST 40 YEARS separate these two photos—of me, as you may have guessed. I was 7 in the picture on the left, 44 on the right. The differences are obvious. In the more recent picture I have more wrinkles, white hair, am fully grown. But I still feel like the same person in many respects, despite the maturing.

CONSISTENCY IN PERSONALITY ACROSS ADULTHOOD

What Kind of Consistency Are We Talking About?

Go back and look at the definitions of consistency at the beginning of Chapter 5. Nearly all of the research on consistency I'm going to talk about here belongs in the category of **correlational consistency.** Just as was true of those studying consistency in IQ, psychologists studying consistency of personality are most often asking whether each individual's relative position on some constant measure has remained the same over time. Typically, the researcher uses the same personality-measuring procedure at two or more times several years apart, and looks at the correlation between the two sets of scores.

Researchers are interested in both **personality traits,** which are relatively enduring ways of thinking, feeling, and acting, and **personality trait structures,** which refers to the relatively small number of factors that represent the basic dimensions of personality. One of the primary measures of personality they use has been a procedure called a **Q-sort** (Block, 1971), a technique that is unusual enough to require some elaboration.

A Q-sort consists of a large number of cards, each containing words or phrases that might describe a person's personality traits, such as "socially poised," "feels guilty," or "satisfied with self." A highly skilled rater, using all the information available about a subject, including interview responses, observations by other psychologists, and test scores, sorts the many cards into nine separate piles, with those containing statements that seem to be most true of the subject placed in pile 9 and those least true of the subject placed in pile 1. The sorting is restricted in one additional way: The number of items that can be placed in each pile is specified ahead of time, forcing the rater to create a normal distribution of items in the nine piles. Piles 9 and 1 are each allowed only a few statements, piles 2 and 8 can have a few more, but the bulk of the statements must be placed in the middle piles. For each subject, each item in the set is then assigned a score that corresponds to the pile in which it was placed. Clusters of traits, such as those that may reflect extraversion, openness, or some other basic structure, can then be summed and those scores compared from one time point to the next to give a measure of consistency.

For the subjects in the Berkeley studies, five separate Q-sorts have been completed for each subject, each by a different rater, each based on information at a single age. It is important to understand that given this type of measurement, change or continuity from one age to the next represents change or consistency in *intraindividual* patterns. We are asking whether the internal structure or distribution of qualities has remained the same or changed. A Q-sort is also a measure of trait consistency (or change), since the rater is searching for underlying traits, not surface behavior. Quite different behaviors at each age might lead a rater to decide to place a particular item in pile 8 or 9 for that individual. Of course, it is still possible to examine these types of consistency using correlation coefficients since we can correlate each subject's cluster scores from one age to the next, much as we would correlate scores on some standardized test.

Evidence for Consistency in Personality

The strongest evidence for consistency of personality in adulthood comes from the work of Paul Costa and Robert McCrae (1980a; 1984; 1994; McCrae & Costa, 1997, 1987; McCrae & John, 1992), who identified five major dimensions of personality that have come to be accepted by most personality researchers and known as the **big five.** The dimensions of this five-factor model, described in Table 9.1, are **neuroticism, extraversion, openness, agreeableness,** and **conscientiousness.** Research shows that each of these five is stable over relatively long periods of adulthood. In their Baltimore Longitudinal

Study of Aging, men and women who ranged in age from 21 to 76 at the time of first testing were retested six years later (Costa & McCrae, 1988). Personality consistency was then examined by correlating the scores on these two sets of tests. Other researchers have studied adults over even longer periods, such as a group of college women studied over 16 years by Helson and Moane (1987) and a group of men studied over 30 years by Finn (1986). The general finding is that over short periods, such as the six-year interval in the Costa and McCrae study, stability on these five personality dimensions is very high. Over longer periods, the stability is lower but still considerable. Table 9.2 will give you some actual numbers to go with those generalizations. It shows the correlations between the scores on the first and second tests in Costa and McCrae's six-year follow-up, as well as the median correlation found over several different longitudinal studies, including both Helson and Moane, and Finn.

Similarly, Norma Haan's analysis of data from the Berkeley study shows quite strong consistency on Q-sort clusters over periods of 10 to 15 years, but less consistency over the full span of adulthood (Haan, Millsap, & Hartka, 1986). The Q-sort clusters Haan studied are not the same as the "big five" personality dimensions identified by Costa and McCrae, and of course the method of measurement being used is different in the two cases. But the underlying pattern of results is similar: There is a strong base of personality consistency that runs throughout adulthood. Yet strong as this consistency may be, there is nonetheless room for change—either individual change or shared developmental change of one type or another. Costa and McCrae estimate that about three-fifths of the variations in underlying personality trait structure is stable over the full life span.

Interestingly, there is some indication that these personality qualities are *least* stable in early adulthood and then become more consistent in the middle and late years. In virtually all the longitudinal studies represented in Table 9.2, as well as in the Berkeley data reported by Haan, the years of the 20s show the least individual consistency in personality, as if the final personality were not yet formed at this age (Costa & McCrae, 1994). Thus six-year or 10-year longitudinal consistency scores, such as those shown in Table 9.2, are lower for the period from 20 to 27 or 30 than from 30 to 40. Still, even in these years the basic five personality dispositions are at least moderately consistent, leading

TABLE 9.I **The Big Five Personality Dimensions**

Dimension	Definition	Characteristics
Neuroticism	Emotional instability vs. stability	Anxiety, hostility, self-consciousness, self-pity, tension, touchiness, worry, depression, impulsiveness
Extraversion	Sociability vs. introversion	Assertiveness, warmth, gregariousness, activity, excitement-seeking, energetic, enthusiastic, optimistic
Openness	Curiosity and interest in variety vs. preference for sameness	Openness to fantasy, aesthetics, feelings, actions, ideas, values
Agreeableness	Compliance and cooperativeness vs. suspicion	Trust, altruism, modesty, tendermindedness, straightforwardness; also appreciative, forgiving, generous, kind, sympathetic
Conscientiousness	Discipline and organization vs. lack of seriousness	Competence, order, dutifulness, achievement, striving, self-discipline, deliberation, efficiency, reliability, responsibleness, thoroughness

Source: Adapted from McCrae & John, 1992, Table 1, pp. 176–177.

TABLE 9.2 **Correlations Between Measures of the Big Five Personality Dimensions over Periods of Years**

Trait	Correlation over six Years from Costa and McCrae	Median Correlation from [a] All Studies
Neuroticism	0.83	0.64
Extraversion	0.82	0.64
Openness	0.83	0.64
Agreeableness	0.63	0.64
Conscientiousness	0.79	0.67

[a]For neuroticism and extraversion, six longitudinal studies are included; for conscientiousness, five studies, and for openness and agreeableness, four studies.

Source: Adapted from Costa & McCrae, 1994, Table 1, p. 32.

Costa and McCrae to conclude that "[w]e now know that in many fundamental ways, adults remain the same over periods of many years and that their adaptation to life is profoundly shaped by their personality. People surely grow and change, but they do so on the foundation of enduring dispositions" (1994, pp. 35–36). Thus we take *ourselves* along on our journey through life. Recall, for example, that adults high in neuroticism are consistently less satisfied with their lives, while those high in extraversion are consistently *more* satisfied (Costa & McCrae, 1984; McCrae & Costa, 1990). Those who are high in openness are more likely to make midcareer shifts in their jobs (McCrae & Costa, 1985). These enduring structures provide a kind of basic disposition, or perhaps we could say a strong *flavor,* that can affect the entire trajectory of each adult's life.

Explaining Personality Consistency

Where might such personality consistency come from? If you think back to the discussion of continuity in Chapter 1, you'll realize immediately that the two obvious possibilities are that old familiar dichotomy: heredity and environment.

Genetic Influences on Personality Consistency. Angleitner, Riemann, & Strelau (1995) studied nearly 1000 pairs of adult twins in Germany and Poland to investigate the heritability of the five-factor model of personality. Each participant completed a self-report questionnaire, and then the twins' scores were correlated with their co-twins' scores. As you can see in Table 9.3, the identical twin pairs, who share the same genetic make-

CRITICAL THINKING

Can you think of other examples of ways in which any of these five basic personality traits might influence the pattern of an adult's life?

TABLE 9.3 **Self-Report and Peer Ratings of Five Personality Trait Structures for Identical and Fraternal Twins**

Personality Trait Structure	Correlation from Self-Report Ratings		Correlation from Peer Ratings	
	Identical	Fraternal	Identical	Fraternal
Neuroticism	0.56	0.28	0.40	0.17
Extraversion	0.53	0.13	0.43	0.03
Openness	0.42	0.19	0.32	0.18
Agreeableness	0.54	0.18	0.43	0.18
Conscientiousness	0.54	0.35	0.48	0.31

Source: Angleitner, Riemann, & Strelau, 1995. Cited in Plomin, DeFries, McClearn, & Rutter, 1997.

up, had significantly higher correlations than the fraternal twin pairs, who share only about 50 percent of their genes, suggesting that all five of these personality trait structures are moderately influenced by genetics.

In a novel twist, these experimenters also gave questionnaires to two friends of each twin and asked them to respond about the twin's personality, providing a more objective rating than the self-reports. The two friends agreed with each other "substantially" (the correlation coefficient was 0.63), and the mean of their scores agreed with the twins' self-reports "moderately" (the correlation coefficient was 0.55). This gives a little more weight to self-report tests of personality. The results of the peer ratings are also shown in Table 9.3.

Behavior geneticists estimate that between 30 and 50 percent of the variation in personality, as measured by the typical self-report instruments used in these studies, can be accounted for by genetic differences (Loehlin, 1992; Plomin, DeFries, McClearn, & Rutter, 1997). This is lower than the estimated heritability for intelligence, but still substantial.

More evidence that personality has a substantial genetic component comes from a recent study by Robert McCrae and Paul Costa (1997), in which they compared the personality trait structure of over 7000 individuals in seven language groups: American English, German, Portuguese, Hebrew, Chinese, Korean, and Japanese. These language groups represent five distinct families of language and also a variety of cultures, political systems, social norms, attitudes, values, and economic structures. In addition, the samples varied in age, gender, education, and socioeconomic levels.

Researchers administered a standardized personality test to the participants in their native languages. Respondents were given 240 statements and asked to indicate how much they agreed or disagreed with each. Analyses showed that people in all five language groups gave responses that could be grouped into five clusters of items that had been identified as belonging to the major personality trait structures. In other words, regardless of language group or any of the other variables in this study, people from all over the world seem to fall into the same basic personality categories. A Chinese person whose responses show a high level of anxiety and anger (indicators of a neurotic personality) will also tend to give responses that indicate high levels of self-consciousness, depression, impulsiveness, and vulnerability—as will Germans and Japanese.

Costa and McCrae claim that these results clearly show that the five-factor structure of personality transcends language and strongly suggest that it may be universal. Our personalities do not seem to be rooted in our language, our political system, or any of the other environmental conditions included in this study. Although this stops short of providing conclusive evidence for genetic roots, it does support this interpretation.

Environmental Influences on Personality Consistency. Important as the genetic influence on personality may be, it is clearly not the only force moving us toward consistency. Avshalom Caspi, Daryl Bem, and Glen Elder (1989), whose ideas you also encountered briefly in Chapter 1, describe two ways in which the environment also has a profound effect, which they call cumulative continuity and interactional continuity. **Cumulative continuity** refers to the fact that our actions produce results; those results then accumulate over time, moving us along specific trajectories. Once on a particular trajectory, we tend to stay on it, which produces continuity. There is a good deal of choice involved in all of this: We each choose environments that fit our own particular characteristics and avoid those that demand things we think we cannot deliver, just as I avoid learning how to play tennis because I assume I could not ever perform skillfully, or a shy person avoids applying for a job that would require outgoing interactions.

But cumulative continuity is not all a product of conscious (or even unconscious) choice. There are also consequences for our actions that accumulate and tend to keep us in a particular pattern over time. Among other things, we learn specific strategies, specific patterns of interaction that work for us. Faced with new situations, we first try what we already know. If that works, we seek no further (Atchley, 1989).

Interactional continuity refers to the patterns of interaction between any person and those around him or her that tend to reinforce habitual personality qualities. Workers high in neuroticism are likely to have difficulty getting along with bosses or co-workers. They may lose their jobs more often, or quit more often, because of their personalities. But this merely reinforces neuroticism and maintains the basic pattern. We also tend to set things up so that our expectations will be confirmed. There is research with children, for example, that shows that highly aggressive boys expect more hostility from others than do less aggressive boys. When such a boy behaves aggressively, he does in fact elicit hostility, thus confirming his expectations. In the same way, the research on the processes of partner choice, which I discussed in Chapter 7, suggests that adults choose partners who will likely confirm their preexisting secure or insecure internal model of attachment. In these ways, preexisting patterns are strengthened and continuity is reinforced.

Both of these types of continuity are illustrated by Caspi and Elder's own research, which you have already encountered in Chapters 1 and 2. Recall that they found that among the subjects in the Berkeley studies, those who began adulthood with high levels of either ill-temper or shyness had different life histories than those who were less extreme on these dimensions. Ill-tempered men did indeed end up at lower occupational levels than did less ill-tempered men, and ill-tempered women were more likely to divorce and to be critical and angry with their own children.

Ravenna Helson has also provided evidence illustrating the impact of cumulative continuity, particularly the process of self-selection into different environments, from her 31-year study of a group of women who were part of the 1958 and 1960 graduating classes at Mills College, a women's college in California. In one analysis, Helson and Moane (1984) divided the group into those who had followed a "feminine social clock" (marrying and having their first child before 28 and never being highly committed to a career) and those who had followed a "masculine social clock" (marrying late, or not marrying at all, with a strong commitment to work.) Those women who most consistently followed the masculine social clock had already been distinctly different from their peers in their early 20s. They were more dominant, more sociable, had the greatest self-acceptance, independence, empathy, and "social presence." In contrast, those women who most closely followed the feminine social clock were described, at 20, as seeking to follow the social norms. These young women had been quite well adjusted and content with themselves but perceived that achievement could best be reached through conforming. Each group chose a life path that would tend to reinforce their preexisting qualities and thus to strengthen the very personality consistency illustrated in Table 9.2.

In the face of such powerful forces moving each of us toward consistency, it is impressive that there is also significant change in personality over the years of adulthood. Not only do individuals shift somewhat from one relative position to another on measures of personality, but adults show at least some *shared* patterns of personality change over the years.

It is important for me to reiterate what I said in Chapter 5: It is logically quite possible to have *both* a high level of individual correlational consistency in personality *and* shared changes in the level of some personality trait. For example, there could be a general shift toward greater independence over the adult years, which would be a shared change, even while it could still be true that the most independent 20-year-olds were highly likely still to be the most independent 50-year-olds. What I've just been describing is all the evidence for individual consistency; what I want to turn to now is the question of shared change.

CRITICAL
THINKING

This is such an important point that you should stop for a moment and make sure that you fully understand. *Both* **individual consistency and collective change can exist simultaneously, even on the same measures.**

CHANGES IN PERSONALITY OVER ADULTHOOD

First of all, why should we expect personality to change in any systematic way over adult life? David Buss (1994) offers the clearest argument. He suggests that personality changes "when different adaptive problems are encountered over time" (p. 42). Insofar as the years of adulthood involve shared changes in adaptive problems—and I think they do, as I have argued in earlier chapters—there should be a push toward common pathways of personality change. But just what might those common pathways be?

Stronger folk than I have quailed in the face of the task of summarizing the evidence on personality changes in adulthood. You have already seen that many different measures of personality have been used in different studies, which already creates problems for any kind of summing up of the results. Furthermore, despite the fact that there are a number of theories of personality change in adulthood (many of which you met in Chapter 2), most of the research has been essentially atheoretical, so the measures chosen are frequently ill-adapted to exploring specific theoretical ideas. Add to that the usual difficulty of combining longitudinal and cross-sectional findings in a coherent fashion and you have a situation rather like trying to put together a jigsaw puzzle only to find that you have pieces from three or four different puzzles, none of which add up to a complete picture. The task is easier now than it was a few years ago since more longitudinal evidence is now available, but it is still formidable.

In trying to create some order out of this chaos, rather than simply list the various findings and risk leaving you with no sense of the patterns that may be there, I am going to err in the direction of oversimplification and focus on what I see as common threads.

One more caveat before we move on: I have said this before, but need to reemphasize the fact that virtually all the evidence we have comes from studies of adults reared in the United States during a particular time in history. We do have some cross-cultural evidence, but any statements I may make about general developmental patterns of change in personality should be taken with a good deal of caution until we have comparable findings from longitudinal studies in other cultures and a wider range of cohorts within this culture.

Changes from Early to Middle Adulthood

A case can be made for three different clusters of shared changes in personality between early adulthood and midlife: (1) An increase in confidence/self-esteem/independence/achievement striving; (2) a greater openness to self, particularly to previously unexpressed parts of the self; and (3) an increase in overall maturity, including maturity of defense mechanisms.

Increases in Confidence/Self-Esteem/Independence/Achievement.
I am including a lot of seemingly disparate things in this cluster, but I think there is an underlying theme that links the separate items in this list. The biggest shift in personality in the years from 20 to 45 seems to be a kind of **individuation.** The young adult seems to move from a more dependent reliance on others (such as parents) toward an independent definition of the self, from an emphasis on doing for others to an emphasis on defining the self. One might also summarize this shift as an increase in what David Bakan (1966) has called an **agentic orientation,** or an emphasis on achieving, doing, succeeding, and making one's mark in the world. Evidence for this shift comes from a number of excellent longitudinal and sequential studies, covering several different cohorts. Let me give some examples.

Norma Haan's analysis of the Q-sort scores on the Berkeley subjects gives us one long-term look at changes in this area of personality. Figure 9.1 shows the scores on two relevant clusters, one describing self-confidence versus a sense of being victimized and the other describing assertiveness versus submissiveness. You can see that for both measures

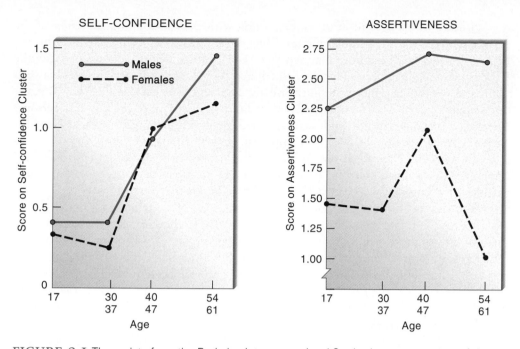

FIGURE 9.1 These data from the Berkeley Intergenerational Study show two aspects of the general increase from early to middle adulthood in confidence/self-esteem. For both men and women in this study, self-confidence and assertiveness become more prominent parts of their personalities at midlife, with particularly clear increases in the 30s and early 40s. Two sets of ages are given, by the way, because two different samples were followed, one at ages 17, 30, 40, and 54 and the other at ages 17, 37, 47, and 61.

Source: N. Haan, R. Millsap, & E. Hartka, 1986, As time goes by: Change and stability in personality over fifty years, *Psychology and Aging, 1,* 220–232. Figs. 1 and 2, p. 228. Copyright 1986 by the American Psychological Association. Adapted by permission.

there was a general rise to midlife, with some indication that the rise was more rapid in the 30s and early 40s than in the 20s.

Results of Helson's longitudinal study of the Mills College women (Helson, Mitchell, & Moan, 1984; Helson & Moane, 1987; Helson & Stewart, 1994; Wink & Helson, 1993) strengthens this picture. She and her colleagues assessed these women once at age 21 and then again at ages 27, 43, and 52. They found relatively few shared changes between 21 and 27, a time when personality appears to be more in flux, but many and significant changes between age 27 and midlife. In their report of the results up to age 43, Helson and Moane (1987) note that the women increased particularly in dominance and independence. In Wink and Helson's analysis of the results up to age 52 (1993)—an analysis that, unfortunately, uses a different set of personality measures and scores than does their earlier report—they find increases between age 27 and 52 in **competence** (becoming more organized, thorough, practical, and clear thinking), in **affiliation** (becoming more sociable, understanding, cheerful, and affectionate), and in **self-confidence,** along with a substantial decrease in **succorance** (caring for others).

It is worth noting that many of the individual items that make up these clusters, such as dominance and independence, also showed some individual stability over these same years. So we are seeing both continuity and change in the same sample, on the same measures of personality, just as we do in the Berkeley sample. That is, those women who were higher in dominance than their peers when they were 21 or 27 were still likely to be higher than their peers at 43 or 52, but the entire group has increased in dominance over those same years.

Studies of changes in motives, beginning with Bray and Howard's study of the AT&T managers, paint a similar picture (Bray & Howard, 1983). The 422 men included in this study had been born between 1927 and 1936, a cohort that falls between the Berkeley and Mills subjects. They had all entered AT&T as low-level managers between 1956 and 1960 (when they were in their early 20s), and were then studied for 20 years. Each subject completed a standardized personality assessment called the Edwards Personal Preference Schedule (EPPS), and each was rated by observers on scales such as Need for Superior Approval and Need for Peer Approval. Bray and Howard found that there was a decline over the 20 years in several measures of dependency, including both Need for Superior Approval and Need for Peer Approval and a clear increase in something called the Need for Autonomy, a change I have shown in Figure 9.2.

You can see in the figure that the pattern of change was the same for both college-educated and non-college-educated men. Furthermore, to check to see if such an increase in autonomy with age was unique to the original cohort, in 1977 Bray and Howard also tested a new group of young managers (including both men and women) whose scores on this measure are also shown in Figure 9.2. This 1977 cohort, born in roughly 1952, scored at the same approximate levels as had young managers in 1956, a finding that lends support to the assumption that this is an age-related or developmental change and not merely a pattern characteristic of a single cohort.

Changes on other measures included in the Bray and Howard study provide additional insights into the nature of this increased push toward independence and away from dependence. "The men showed a decline in motivation to make and enjoy friends, to understand others' motives or feelings, and to conform to authority and regulations" (1983, p. 293). Overall, Bray and Howard suggest that these men have become "harder" over the 20-year period.

This increase in autonomy is replicated in yet another longitudinal study in which (happily) the same personality measurement was used. David Stevens and Caroll Truss (1985) tested three groups of adults in 1978: (1) a group of 40-year-olds who had first taken the EPPS as college students in the late 1950s, (2) a group of 30-year-olds who had

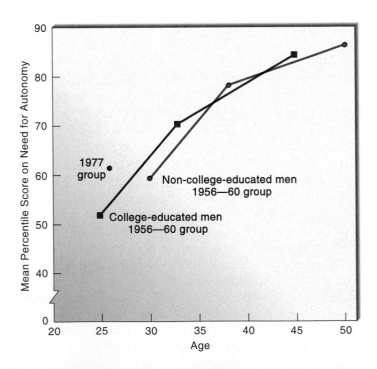

FIGURE 9.2 In the AT&T managers studied by Bray and Howard, the need for autonomy rose from early to middle adulthood, in both college-educated and non-college-educated groups. Twenty years later, another group of young managers reported a level of need for autonomy similar to that of the young managers in 1956 to 1960, which tells us that this pattern is not characteristic of just a single cohort.

Source: Adapted from Bray & Howard, 1983, Fig. 8.5.

first taken the EPPS as college students in 1965, and (3) a group of mid-1980s college students, aged about 20. Like Bray and Howard, they found that both the male and female subjects in their samples had increased in autonomy between ages 20 and 40, and that the 20-year-olds in 1978 had low autonomy scores, just as did the 1977 cohort in the Bray and Howard study. Stevens and Truss also found that scores on achievement increased in early adulthood, as did a measure of dominance.

Collectively, these various results seem to me to point to a basic shift in personality in early adult life—a shift toward greater autonomy, greater achievement striving, greater self-confidence, greater personal assertiveness. That these same general changes are found by researchers using widely different research designs and widely different measures of personality only strengthens the general point.

Increased Openness to Self. A second cluster of changes seems best described as increased **psychological openness.** Middle-aged adults seem more willing to acknowledge and explore the previously unexpressed parts of themselves, to acknowledge inconsistencies, to examine their assumptions critically. Research touching on this aspect of change is much scarcer, so I can be less confident about this shift. But there are at least fragments.

One piece of information comes from the Berkeley study. In her 1981 analysis, Norma Haan (1981) looked at age changes on a cluster of Q-sort items she referred to as "openness to self," which included high placement of such items as "insightful," "introspective," and "think unconventionally," and low placement of items such as "conventional" or "self-defensive." She found that the scores on this cluster rose from early to middle adulthood, with a particularly clear increase in the late 30s and early 40s.

Another fragment comes from Helson's Mills College study. She found that when the women were in their 40s, they were much more likely than they were when in their 20s to say spontaneously that they were discovering new parts of themselves or that they had an intense interest in their inner life (Helson & Moane, 1987).

The hypothesized **gender-role crossover** at midlife, which Gutmann observed in a number of other cultures, might also be thought of as an example of increased openness to the expression of previously un- or underexpressed parts of the self. To the extent that a woman has focused in early adulthood on traditional feminine qualities such as nurturance or affiliation, or a man on traditional masculine qualities, any exploration or increased expression of the less expressed qualities would look like a blending or even a crossing over of gender roles. As I pointed out in Chapter 6, there is little evidence for an actual crossover, but there are signs of increased androgyny at midlife; men and women become more like one another in personality.

For example, in the Mills College study, Helson and her colleagues collected data at ages 27 and 52 not only from the women graduates but also from their male partners. Because many of the women had divorced and remarried, it was often not the *same* partners at the two times, which complicates the methodological problem a lot. Fortunately, the pattern of results is essentially the same whether one looks only at the 21 pairs who had remained together or at the entire sample. Figure 9.3 shows the results for the 21 constant pairs on three measures. Both men and women showed increases in competence and self-confidence and decreases in succorance over these years, but on all three measures men and women were more like one another at midlife than in early adulthood. Similarly, Norma Haan found that in the Berkeley sample, women became more masculine and men more feminine at midlife.

Yet the research results do not all conform to this pattern. In a cross-sectional study, Marjorie Lowenthal and her colleagues (Lowenthal, Thurnher, & Chiriboga, 1975) found that masculinity was higher for women at midlife than at any other age but did not find a parallel peak

CRITICAL THINKING

No one of these studies fully explores the quality of greater psychological openness. See if you can think of some type of study that would address this hypothesis more fully.

FIGURE 9.3 Between ages 27 and 52, these Mills College women and their partners not only increased in self-rated competence and self-confidence and decreased in succorance, they became more like one another on these traits at midlife.

Source: Data from Wink & Helson, 1993, Table 2, p. 601.

in femininity for men. And Carol Erdwins and her colleagues (Erdwins, Tyler, & Mellinger, 1983) found that the highest masculinity scores in their study were recorded by a group of college-aged women and the lowest by a group of older homemakers (aged 40 to 75).

One possible explanation for these diverse findings is that the trend toward androgyny at age 40 or 50 is evident particularly in those cohorts born around the 1920s who reached midlife at the time the women's movement was beginning to be strongly felt. For these adults, one could argue that a shift toward expressiveness in men and assertiveness in women reflects social changes and not shared developmental processes. Yet I think even such a cohort difference is consistent with my more basic point that at midlife adults become more open to exploring and expressing whatever aspects of themselves have been less expressed previously. The particular facets of personality that have been less expressed will change from one cohort to the next, from one person to the next, and from one culture to the next, depending on gender roles, the particular pathway chosen in early adult life, and the temperament or personality with which one begins adulthood. For each person, then, as well as each generation and each culture, the specific manifestations of "increased openness to self" at midlife will differ, even while this basic developmental change may be shared by many adults.

Intriguing as these bits of evidence may be, I cannot leave this discussion without pointing out a strong piece of counterevidence. In his cross-sequential Seattle study, Schaie (1983b) has found a fairly steady increase with age in personal rigidity as measured by a standardized test (the rigidity scale of the California Psychological Inventory). Helson has observed a similar increase: The Mills College women described themselves as less flexible at 43 than they had at 27. It is hard to reconcile "increased openness" with "decreased flexibility," although Helson and Moane found signs of both in the same subjects (1987). The resolution of this apparent paradox will have to await further research.

Increases in Maturity. The third shift in personality that seems to occur between early and middle adulthood is an increase in what one might call **maturity,** as expressed in a variety of ways. In a very large cross-sectional study, Costa and McCrae found that compared to people in their 30s or older, college students were higher in impulsiveness, vulnerability, anxiety, and depression, and lower in self-discipline and trust (Costa & McCrae, 1994). These authors conclude that "both cross-sectional and longitudinal studies might be interpreted as showing an increase in maturity in the decade of the 20s" (p. 34).

A similar argument is put forward by Vaillant (1977), who proposes that there is a shift between early and middle adulthood toward greater use of mature defense mechanisms. One could argue that this shift is just another facet of increased openness to self, since more mature defense mechanisms generally involve less self-deception, more conscious awareness of one's anxieties and fears. But I list this separately because of the theoretical importance placed on this change by Vaillant and others.

Vaillant's own data provide one set of supportive evidence for such a change. He has drawn upon data from the Grant Study, which included 268 men originally studied when they were Harvard sophomores between 1936 and 1942 (and who were thus born between approximately 1917 and 1922). The men chosen were all thought to be relatively "healthy" and successful as undergraduates, so the sample includes few men who had any serious emotional problems. The men later completed questionnaires annually or biennially and were interviewed at length in 1950–1952. Vaillant then interviewed a subsample of 100 men 30 years after they had entered the study, when the men were then in their late 40s or early 50s. The analysis of changes in defense mechanisms was based on scores given by judges who read transcripts of interviews and responses to open-ended questions on the questionnaires. As you can see in Figure 9.4, Vaillant found that there was a shift with increasing age toward more mature defenses and away from immature defenses.

Such a change has been replicated by several other longitudinal investigations, including Haan's assessments of the Berkeley subjects, Helson's study of the Mills College women, and an analysis by Hart (1992) of information about a group of men who had been studied from adolescence into their late 30s. Haan (1976) reports decreases with age in self-defensiveness, fantasizing, and projection. Similarly, Helson reports that between ages 21 and 43, and again between ages 43 and 52, the women in this study increased in

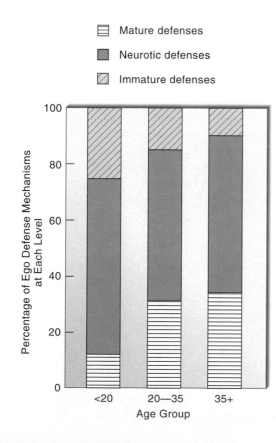

FIGURE 9.4 These scores on the three categories of defense mechanisms come from analyses made by Vaillant of the interviews and questionnaires of 100 men in the Grant study who had been followed from college age to age 50. Immature defenses declined, and mature defenses increased over these years.

Source: From George E. Vaillant, *Adaptation to life.* Copyright 1977 by George E. Vaillant. By permission of Little, Brown and Company.

such **coping skills** as objectivity and intellectuality and decreased in the use of denial and primitive defenses (Helson & Moane, 1987; Helson & Wink, 1992). Hart, too, finds steady decreases in the 20s and 30s in the use of immature defenses such as regression, projection, or denial, and increases in the use of logical analysis and in tolerance of ambiguity. Thus we have four quite different studies reporting similar declines in immature defensive patterns between early adulthood and midlife. Both men and women show this change, and it occurs in adults born in several different cohorts, all of which makes it appear that this is a fairly basic developmental process.

Adding Up the Personality Changes from Early Adulthood to Midlife. Taken together these three changes describe a basic shift from a position of conformity to parental or societal expectations toward an exploration of the limits of the self. We see increasing insistence on independence or autonomy, increasing emphasis on personal achievement, and increasing self-confidence. To accomplish this change, an adult must become more open to himself or herself, must shift from repression and denial to less distorting defenses such as suppression. The middle-aged adult thus typically has a more complex personality, is more individual, and is perhaps more hard-edged.

Changes from Middle to Late Adulthood

From midlife to old age, if there is any common change, it seems to involve a softening of those hard edges a shift away from the intense preoccupation with individuation and autonomy. What is much less clear is just what the older adult's personality is shifting *toward*. We have much less evidence to work with here, especially less longitudinal evidence, and the findings are less consistent. One possibility is that with increasing age there is simply more and more variability in pathways, so that there is no common set of changes but only individual patterns of coping. Alternatively, we may simply have failed to find the right model for describing or understanding personality change in later life. Let me give you a sampling of the findings and the possible explanations.

Reductions in Achievement/Autonomous Orientation. One possibility is that between middle and old age there is a decline in the emphasis on autonomy and achievement that seems to be one hallmark of the middle years. Evidence pointing in this direction comes from the Berkeley Intergenerational Study. If you go back and look at Figure 9.1, you'll see that self-confidence continued to rise into the 60s, but that assertiveness, especially among the women in this sample, dropped after midlife. Haan has found similar peaks at midlife for a cluster she calls **cognitively committed,** as you can see in Figure 9.5. This cluster seems to tap aspects of both openness and achievement/independence. It includes high placement of such descriptors as "wide interests," "ambitious," "introspective," "values intellect," and "values independence" and low placement of items such as "conventional" and "submissive." The very clear rise from early to middle adulthood for both men and women on this cluster reinforces the points I have already made about that period. But note that as with assertiveness, there is decline in the centrality of these qualities after midlife.

CRITICAL THINKING

Does it make sense to you that such a decline in the intensity of achievement or independence is part of the process of preparation for retirement? How could you test such a hypothesis?

There is also some cross-sectional evidence that points in a similar direction. In a large study in Germany, Jochen Brandtstädter (Brandtstädter & Baltes-Götz, 1990; Brandtstädter & Greve, 1994) has tested several thousand adults across the full range of adult life. Among the measures he has used is one assessing what he calls **tenacious goal pursuit,** and another called **flexible goal adjustment.** A person high in the former quality would be likely to agree with such statements as: "The harder a goal is to achieve, the more desirable it often appears to me. Even if everything seems hopeless, I still look for a way to master the situation" (p. 216). Adults high in flexible goal adjustment would be

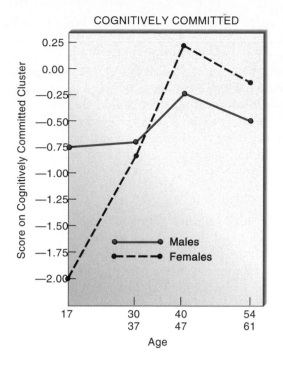

FIGURE 9.5 Signs of the reduction in centrality of autonomy and assertiveness come from these data from the Berkeley studies. Those who scored high on the cluster Haan calls cognitively committed were ambitious and introspective, valued intellect and independence, and were low in conventionality and submissiveness. These qualities peaked in midlife and then declined.

Source: N. Haan, R. Millsap, & E. Hartka, 1986, As time goes by: Change and stability in personality over fifty years, *Psychology and Aging, 1,* 220–232. Fig. 3, p. 229. Copyright 1986 by the American Psychological Association. Adapted by permission.

likely to agree with such statements as: "In general, I'm not upset very long about an opportunity passed up I can adapt quite easily to changes in a situation I usually recognize quite easily my own limitations" (pp. 215–216).

You can see in Figure 9.6 that tenacious goal pursuit drops from about age 50 onward, while flexible goal adjustment rises at the same time.

Brandtstädter and Greve (1994) make the point that such greater flexibility in setting goals and lessening of tenacity are reasonable, adaptive responses to the increasing number of physical, social, and psychological losses that are an inevitable part of aging. We know that despite such losses, older adults do *not* report lower levels of well-being or

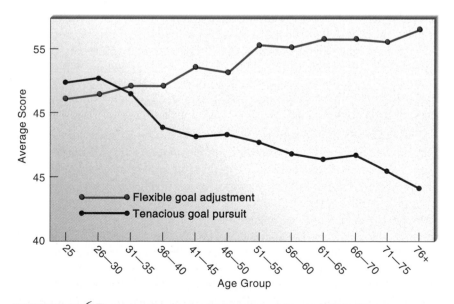

FIGURE 9.6 These results, from a large cross-sectional study in Germany, suggest a kind of "mellowing" of personality in the later years of life.

Source: Brandtstädter & Greve, 1994, Fig. 3, p. 67.

self-esteem and are not more often depressed. Such a positive attitude and positive view of the self can only be sustained in later life, Brandtstädter maintains, by means of just the sort of increased flexibility of goals that is reflected in Figure 9.6.

In a somewhat similar fashion, Carol Ryff (1982; Ryff & Baltes, 1976) suggests that there is a shift in values between middle age and old age from what she calls instrumental values to terminal values. **Instrumental values** relate to desirable modes of conduct *(being* something), such as "ambitious," "capable," or "courageous." **Terminal values** describe desirable end states of existence *(having* something), such as a sense of accomplishment, freedom, or happiness. In both her studies, Ryff found that women in their 40s and 50s were more likely to select instrumental values, while women in their 60s and 70s were more likely to select terminal values. However, Ryff found no such difference in men.

Collectively (although not uniformly), this evidence points to a peak in instrumentality or agentic orientation at midlife, with a sort of mellowing thereafter. The older adult appears to be less intense, less tenacious, more focused on having-what-you-have and being-who-you-are and less on gaining or achieving. As Helson puts it, the 52-year-olds in the Mills College study said that they were "happier with what I have and less worried about what I won't get" (Helson, 1993, p. 203).

Increased Concern for Others. There is also limited evidence for a shift away from pre-occupation with the self and toward concern for others. One bit of information comes from Schaie's major cross-sequential study. Schaie's central concern has been changes in intelligence, as you'll recall from Chapter 5. But Schaie also included some measures of personality in this study, including one he calls **humanitarian concern.** Scores on this measure declined slightly between early and middle adulthood, and then rose steadily from middle to late adulthood. This pattern was found in two separate cross-sectional comparisons and over a seven-year longitudinal interval (Schaie & Parham, 1976).

Consistent with this finding is the fact that older adults are also more generous in contributing to worthy causes, although here the evidence is entirely cross-sectional. In one experiment, female researchers (Midlarsky & Hannah, 1989) solicited donations for a charity devoted to the welfare of infants with birth defects. Half the time the solicitor was visibly pregnant, half the time she was not. Adults of all ages were more likely to contribute if the solicitor was pregnant, but proportionately more older than younger adults donated under either condition. And when the researchers adjusted for the incomes of the contributors, they found that older adults also gave proportionately more. A 1988 national survey by the Gallup organization (Hodgkinson, Weitzman, & Gallup, 1988) shows the same trend: The percentage of household income donated to charity increases steadily with age. Figure 9.7 shows the results from both studies, so you can see the strong similarity in the shape of the curves.

Naturally, we need to be cautious in interpreting such findings. First and most obviously, except for the Schaie seven-year longitudinal follow-up, we are looking at entirely cross-sectional comparisons. We can't be sure whether this apparent age-linked pattern reflects some underlying developmental change or whether it reflects changes in society such that current older adults are more likely to have grown up placing a high value on generosity or some other cohort-related explanation.

Counterevidence comes from a study by Carol Ryff (1989), who interviewed middle-aged and older adults at length about their current life, their past life experiences and their ideas about what made up a good life. *Both* age groups emphasized an orientation toward others, including being a compassionate, caring person and having good relationships, as being central to their sense of well-being. At the same time, Ryff found that the middle-aged (but not the older), subjects emphasized self-confidence, self-acceptance, and self-knowledge as important aspects of their sense of well-being. So in this study there

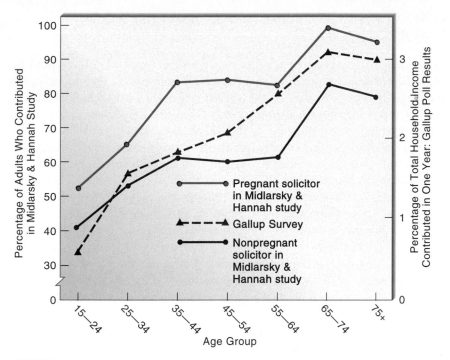

FIGURE 9.7 Two quite different cross-sectional studies show that financial generosity is higher among older adults in the United States than among the middle-aged or young.

Source: Data from Midlarsky & Hannah, 1989, Table 1, p. 349; Hodgkinson, Weitzman, and Gallus, reported in the U.S. Bureau of the Census, 1989a, Table 615, p. 371.

was a difference between the two age groups that is consistent with the peaking of achievement/confidence qualities in midlife, but there is little indication here that older adults place more value on compassion or caring for others than do the middle-aged.

Given this mixture of findings, the best I can say is that the jury is still out on the hypothesis that in later adulthood there is a shift toward greater concern for others.

Increase in Interiority. Similarly, the jury is still out on a proposal by Bernice Neugarten, one of the influential figures in gerontology, that there is a shift in old age toward what she calls **interiority.** She proposes that older adults are less focused on trying to change the world, less "outer directed," more focused on interior processes. In support of this hypothesis is the finding from several cross-sectional studies that introversion increases slightly over the adult years (Costa et al., 1986; Leon, Gillum, Gillum, & George, 1979). On the other side of the scale is once again research by Ryff (1984; Ryff & Heincke, 1983). She asked young, middle-aged, and old adults to describe their current selves and to describe themselves as they had been at earlier points. She could find no age differences at all on her measures of interiority, either in the subjects' descriptions of their current selves or in their recollections of themselves at earlier ages.

Summing Up Personality Changes in Late Life. You can see that the set of information we have about personality changes in later life do not add up to some tidy statement. The best I can do at the moment is to provide a kind of "flavor" of the shift that seems to occur—from striving to accepting, from ingesting to digesting, from active to somewhat more passive, from exploration to observation. No one of these contrasts is quite right, but collectively they give you some feel for a shift that has been far harder to grasp or describe than has the set of changes from early to middle adulthood.

EXPLAINING THE CHANGES IN PERSONALITY OVER ADULTHOOD

What I have said so far about these personality changes is, as I warned you it would be, an oversimplification. Even so, you can see that there is far from perfect agreement on just what sort of changes may be occurring. And I have simply glossed over the set of studies, both cross-sectional and longitudinal, all using standardized pencil-and paper-instruments as assessments of personality, that show *no* age differences in personality at all. Schaie and Parham, for example (1976) found no differences on 18 of the 19 measures they used; only the measure of humanitarian concern showed changes with age. Similarly, Ilene Siegler and her co-workers (Siegler, George, & Okun, 1979) found no changes in personality on a measure called the Cattell 16 Personality Factor test over the eight years of the Duke Longitudinal Studies. These adults were 46 to 69 at the start of the study, 54 to 77 at the end, so the relevant age range is certainly being sampled. Similarly, except for the period of moderate personality flux between age 20 and 30, Costa and McCrae (1994) have found little sign of any shared patterns of personality change in the adult years.

To make sense out of all this, we have to do two things: First, we must account for the apparent fact that personality is both stable and changing, and second, we have to explain or try to understand the changes that do appear to occur.

The first task is not so difficult; we need only propose, as have a number of writers, such as Dan McAdams (1994), that personality is made up of several layers or levels. The first level is made up of what McAdams calls *dispositional traits,* such as the five factors of personality identified by Costa and McCrae. These dimensions have a strong genetic base and tend to be highly stable over the adult years. At the second level, however, change can and does occur, both individually and in ways that are shared within a cohort or culture. Included here are motivations, desires, strategies for achieving goals, defense mechanisms, and coping styles. Both of these levels are aspects of personality, but one remains quite constant while the other may shift. Naturally, these two levels are linked to one another in each of us; our enduring traits flavor our experiences, affecting our choices and motives. But it seems to me quite reasonable to think of these as separable aspects of personality.

The second task—to account for the pattern of results on personality change—is much more difficult. How can one explain both the patterns that do seem to exist as well as the obvious inconsistencies in the data? Three types of explanation are available: First, I can appeal to methodological differences or flaws in the various studies; second, I can examine the potential impact of role changes on personality; and third, I can go back to the theories I described in Chapter 2 and see if any of them does a decent job of encompassing the various research findings.

Methodological Explanations

Types of Measurement. As I look over the array of evidence, I note that those studies showing no change with age and those reporting the most discrepant findings are typically those in which personality has been measured with standardized pencil-and-paper tests. By and large, these standardized instruments appear to be measuring the unchanging aspect of personality, those "dispositional traits" that Costa and McCrae have identified and that McAdams describes as the first level of personality. The fact that studies using such instruments find little change with age need not be taken as evidence that personality does not change over time, only that this particular layer or level of personality changes little.

In contrast, studies in which researchers have derived scores from open-ended written comments, or from extensive interviews, have generally shown systematic and reasonably consistent age effects. Measurement strategies of this type seem more likely to tap that second level of personality in which change occurs. Furthermore, most of these smaller longitudinal studies have attempted to delve both deeply and broadly, using many different types of measures. In this way, the researchers hope to capture changes in structure or pattern rather than simply changes in level in one or more specific trait. The Q-sort data, for example, tell us something about changes in structure of personality, as may Vaillant's analysis of changes in defense mechanisms. My preference for these more depth-oriented studies is obviously a matter of taste. Other psychologists may wish to place much greater weight on those studies in which reliable, standardized instruments were used and may thus conclude that there is little evidence for personality change in adulthood. But the two approaches can be reconciled using McAdams' concept of levels of personality.

Cohort Differences. The other obvious methodological point is one that has surely occurred to you. The differences between one study and the next, and the reported age differences themselves, may reflect cohort differences rather than shared developmental patterns. Even longitudinal data won't let us escape this problem, as you'll recall from Chapter 1: Each longitudinal study normally includes adults from only one cohort. So whatever "developmental" change they appear to show may reflect, instead, historical factors that influenced that cohort at particular ages.

A good example comes from the Mills College study. Helson and her colleagues have data on the *parents* of a subsample of their subjects, data collected when the daughters were college seniors and the parents were in their late 40s or early 50s. Thirty years later, Helson obtained similar data from the daughters and the daughters' partners, when they were in their early 50s. This enables Helson to compare two different cohorts at middle age: the women who graduated from college in about 1960, born about 1938 or 1939, and their mothers and fathers, born in about 1915. Figure 9.8 shows the scores of these two cohorts on the personality cluster Helson calls **competence.** The Mills women themselves, as well as their partners, show the now-familiar increase in their sense of competence from their late 20s to their early 50s. The fathers of the Mills women similarly were high in this quality at midlife. But the mothers had not shown such a high sense of competence when they had been in midlife. Of course, we do not have data on these mothers when they were 22 or 27; it could be that their sense of competence was even lower then than it was at 50. But the more likely possibility is that the substantial rise in midlife

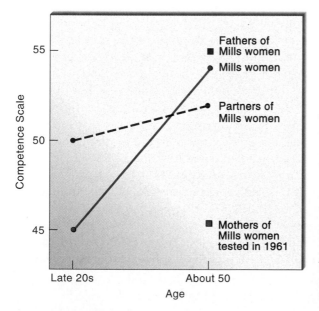

FIGURE 9.8 A cohort effect is the likeliest explanation of these results. The mothers of the Mills College women in Helson's study did not show the same high level on the competence cluster at midlife (in 1961) as did their daughters at age 52 (in 1990).

Source: R. Helson & A. Stewart, 1994, Personality change in adulthood. In T. F. Hetherton & J. L. Weinberger (Eds.), *Can personality change?* Fig. 2, p. 214. Copyright 1994 by the American Psychological Association. Original data from Wink & Helson, 1993.

in a sense of competence that we see in the Mills classes of 1958 and 1960 occurred at least in part because these women's adult lives were shaped by the power of the women's movement in the United States, a force that was particularly dominant in the 1970s and 1980s—a pattern I know well, as this is precisely my own cohort.

CRITICAL THINKING

Are you persuaded by my arguments? Why or why not?

I cannot reject such explanations out of hand, but I think a good case can be made for the more general validity of at least some of the changes I have described. My argument rests on several points: First, at least one of the changes I am suggesting—the greater "openness to self"—is an attempt to get *behind* cohort differences to a deeper level of change. The specific manifestations of such a greater openness will necessarily vary from one cohort to the next, but the underlying change would still be present. Second, we now have a number of longitudinal studies involving cohorts born over nearly a 40-year period, including both men and women, both working class and middle class. Samples of adults from each of these cohorts have shown similar changes.

This is not to say that some specific findings may not be particularly vulnerable to a cohort-differences explanation. The age difference in generosity is one obvious example. But I am not persuaded that cohort differences can explain away the full pattern of findings I have described to you.

Role Changes as Explanation of Personality Changes

If, then, we assume that there are some real age changes in personality left to account for, what are the alternative explanations? The most obvious possibility is that the horse pulling this particular cart is the set of changes in gender, work, and family roles I described in Chapters 6 and 8. Avshalom Caspi and Glen Elder say: "Successful transitions to age-graded roles are the core developmental tasks faced by the individual across the life course. The corresponding agenda for personality psychology is to examine how individuals confront, adapt, and make adjustments to age-graded roles and transitions" (1988, pp. 120–121).

Several lines of argument can be mustered in support of role changes as the driving force in personality change in adulthood. First, there are some obvious parallels between the overall shape of the pattern of role acquisitions that I talked about in Chapters 6 and 8, and the shape of changes in personality that I have been discussing here. In early adulthood we must learn and combine a series of hugely complex roles: adult gender roles, worker, spouse, parent. We try to fit ourselves into those roles, to conform to their demands. At this early point, the emphasis is less on individuality or personal achievement and more on adapting to external expectations. The power of that external set of definitions seems to wane as we learn the roles themselves and discover the flexibilities in them, the ways we can bend the rules to fit our own situations. By our 30s, certainly by our early 40s, our own individuality is more dominant, hence the shift on measures of personality toward greater individual achievement motivation, greater independence and autonomy, greater emphasis on personal mastery. One woman of 41, an interior designer interviewed by Amia Lieblich (1986), put it this way: "I never did anything that wasn't the thing to do. I feel I have not developed due to the limitations… which I have accepted for myself—female limitations, personal limitations, and being married limitations. Now, I will take the freedom to pursue whatever job I want to pursue, and if we can set it up being married, fine, and if I can't set it up being married, also fine" (p. 307). As the roles are learned, and as the demands of the various roles of early adulthood diminish, there is simply more room for individuality.

If this argument is valid, we ought to find that the types of changes in personality I have been describing are linked to role transitions or role statuses and not to age. Several sources of data point to just such a conclusion.

One interesting bit of evidence comes from a study by Rochelle Harris, Abbie Ellicott, and David Holmes (1986) of 60 women, aged 36 to 60, each of whom provided detailed retrospective descriptions of their lives, their feelings, their inner experiences, over the period from their early 30s to the present. Raters then searched the transcripts for evidence of major personal transitions—major changes in life structure in Levinson's terms. Eighty percent of the women reported at least one such transition, nearly always linked to some particular shift in the family life cycle rather than to age. Table 9.4 summarizes the results.

What is especially interesting here is not only that these transitions were linked to role changes, but that the content of the transitions at the launching and postparental stages sounds so much like the personality changes at midlife I have already described. Since, on average, these two life-cycle stages are likely to occur roughly at midlife, these findings suggest that for women at least, the shift toward greater individuality, greater assertiveness, greater achievement orientation may be caused by changes in family roles that accompany grown children's departure from home.

Another way to separate out the effects of age and role changes as they affect personality is to look at groups of adults of roughly the same age who occupy different roles, such as women who work outside the home and those who do not. In one set of studies of this type, Carol Erdwins (Erdwins & Mellinger, 1984; Erdwins, Tyler, & Mellinger, 1983) found that a woman's employment status is a better predictor of personality or motivation than is age. Full-time homemakers in these studies had higher affiliation motives than did married or single working women, regardless of age. The working women of all ages tended to be higher on self-acceptance, autonomy, and achievement via independence.

Strong evidence in support of this point comes from the Mills College study. In one analysis, Helson and Picano (1990) divided the total sample into four groups of women who varied in the role pattern they had followed in early adulthood: "homemakers," who had married and not worked between age 21 and 43; "neotraditionals," who had married, had children, and also worked at least some years in their 20s and 30s; "divorced mothers," who had married, divorced, and worked; and "nonmothers," all of whom had had

TABLE 9.4 **Link Between Family Life-Cycle States and Personal Transitions in Harris, Ellicott, and Holmes' Study of Middle-Aged Women**

	Percentage of Women Who Described a Major Personal Transition During That Phase	Reported Content of the Transition
Newborns/preschooler	28	Reduced personal life satisfaction; reduced number of friendships
Launching period	48	End of period of increased introspection; inner change; increased assertiveness
Postparental phase	33	General personality change; ending period of stability; increased introspection; increased assertiveness

Source: R. L. Harris, Ellicott, & Holmes, 1986.

paying jobs. Figure 9.9 shows the scores of these four groups of women on a personality cluster called **independence.** The three groups whose members had had paid employment in the years of early adulthood all showed substantial increases on this measure, whereas homemakers did not.

Helson has also explored the impact on personality of other differences in roles or life experiences such as divorce. She compared the personality patterns of two groups of women who had both followed a feminine social clock: those who were later divorced, and those who stayed in unrewarding marriages. Women in the former group appeared to have been pushed into a new personality organization by the divorce. They increased in self-control and in psychological mindedness (a tendency to introspect and analyze their own and others' behavior) after the divorce. The women who stuck with bad marriages—who remained in the same basic roles, ungratifying as they might have been—showed a loss of poise, confidence, empathy, sociability, and sense of well-being over time.

Have I convinced you? Certainly, all of this evidence makes a strong case for the primary causal effect of role changes and role sequences in shaping the personality changes we see over the adult years. But there is another side to the argument, too.

First of all, it is clear that roles alone do not impose personality patterns on adults. The very fact that there is strong consistency in personality in at least some traits tells us that much. Furthermore, I already pointed out that one reason for such consistency is that people *choose* roles and role patterns that fit with their existing personality. Recall, for example, the finding from Helson's study of the Mills women (Helson et al., 1984) that those who followed the feminine social clock differed in initial personality from those who followed a more masculine social clock. The latter group, at 21, was more domi-

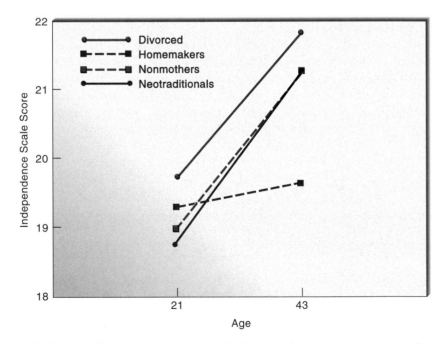

FIGURE 9.9 These results from the Mills College study point to the power of roles in shaping personality change or continuity.

Source: R. Helson & A. Stewart, 1994, Personality change in adulthood. In T. F. Hetherton & J. L. Weinberger (Eds.), *Can personality change?* Figure 3, p. 216. Copyright 1994 by the American Psychological Association. Original data from Helson & Picano, 1990.

nant, independent, and sociable. Taken in this light, Carol Erdwin's research does not necessarily prove that the working role pushes women toward greater assertiveness; equally likely is that more assertive women choose to work. If the latter is true, we are left with no obvious explanation for the average rise in assertiveness and autonomy with age among women (or men).

Similarly, if it is the reduction in the potency or demand of the various key social roles that allows the flowering of individuality in midlife, why isn't there still further flowering of the same kind of independence/autonomy/achievement orientation in late life when social roles become markedly less prominent? What role change produces the *decline* in autonomy and assertiveness after midlife? One might appeal to work roles, and the loss of work roles at retirement, as key ingredients in this second change, but it is difficult to account for the findings from the Berkeley study in that way since the women in the cohorts included in this study mostly did not work outside the home and certainly experienced no "peak" of work accomplishment at midlife. Yet they, too, showed a drop in assertiveness and cognitive commitment after middle age.

Even more striking are the results of a second study by Harris and Holmes and their co-workers (Reinke, Holmes, & Harris, 1985) of a group of women aged 30 to 45. Detailed retrospective interviews with these women revealed that in this group, unlike the older women in the parallel Harris, Ellicott, and Holmes study I described earlier, it was age and not family life-cycle stage that predicted personal transitions. Seventy-eight percent of these women reported a transition between the ages of 27 and 30. Such a transition was more common among those women who worked outside the home than among those who did not, but was equally common among those with and without children and did not vary as a function of the age of the children. "For many women this time of life [age 30] was characterized by disruption of one's previous sense of self, altering one's aims and seeking something for self, and finally the emergence of increased feelings of personal competence and confidence" (p. 1359).

This basic finding of a widely shared transition at roughly age 30 is replicated in an analysis by Priscilla Roberts and Peter Newton (1987) of the lives of 39 women who had been interviewed in depth as part of several unpublished smaller studies. Of those women who were over 30 at the time of the interview, all but one described a major transition between 27 and 32, typically characterized as a process of "individuation."

Of course, these findings do not tell us that there is something inherent in being biologically 30 that causes a change in personality. It may well be that in our society at this time in history, age 30 has been invested with a particular kind of social significance that causes adults to rethink their priorities at that age. We may perceive that "over 30" is a different state, even a different role, than "under 30." In that sense these two studies might be seen as consistent with a role-change explanation of personality change. Yet it is still true that in these two studies, family role changes in these young adult women were not associated with changes in personality, whereas age was.

If I take all this evidence together, there seems little doubt that differences in role patterns, in the specific sequence and timing of the sequence of role changes, have an impact on personality and motivation. Most adults enter several **role streams** in their early 20s and are carried along those streams for at least the next 30 or 40 years. The fact that many of us are in the same streams means that there are likely to be shared changes in personality or motives roughly correlated with age. All of this is important. But I am not convinced that it is the whole story. There seem to me to be deeper changes going on, changes that may be triggered by role changes for some adults or may trigger role changes in others. It is just such deeper change that is hypothesized by various theories of personality development.

Theoretical Explanations

There are three theorists whose ideas we need to take a look at: Erikson, Maslow, and Loevinger. Two you have met before; one (Maslow) I have not yet described.

Erikson's Theory of Identity Development. Certainly, the most familiar theory of adult personality change is Erik Erikson's. You will remember that he proposes three basic stages in adulthood: **intimacy versus isolation** in the early years of adulthood, **generativity versus stagnation** in the middle years, and **ego integrity versus despair** in late life. Erikson suggests that the central issues of each of these stages are brought to the fore by essentially universal experiences of adulthood: the need to create a lasting central relationship with a mate, the need to bear and rear children and to take one's place in—and make one's mark on—adult society, and the need to come to terms with one's own mortality.

If you think about the various patterns of personality change in adult life that I've been describing, you'll see that there is at least a rough correspondence between those changes and Erikson's three stages. At the very least, there is some sign that three basic steps or stages may be involved, one in early adulthood, one in middle adulthood, and one in late life. But it is not as clear to me that the specifics of Erikson's stages, particularly his stage of generativity, are a very good match to the data. As I pointed out in Chapter 2, Erikson does talk about generativity not just in terms of bearing and rearing children but also of generating ideas or products. But the quality of "passing on the flame," a quality that is central to the stage of generativity, does not seem to me to be quite the same as the intensification of individuality at midlife that is most consistently shown in the research findings. Generativity, as Erikson has described it, has an outward-directed quality that is quite opposite to what we see in studies of early and middle adult life. On the other hand, Erikson's description of the final stage of ego integrity seems to capture many of the contradictions in the findings; both interiority or increased concern for others can be encompassed in the concept of integrity.

Maslow's Hierarchy of Needs. A quite different approach comes from Abraham Maslow (1968, 1970a, 1970b, 1971), a psychologist who traces his theoretical roots to Freud and other psychoanalytic thinkers and who has offered some highly original insights. Maslow's most central concern has been with the development of motives or needs, which he divides into two main groups: deficiency motives and being motives. **Deficiency motives** (also called D-motives) involve instincts or drives to correct imbalance or to maintain physical or emotional homeostasis, such as getting enough to eat, satisfying thirst, or obtaining enough love and respect from others. Deficiency motives are found in all animals. **Being motives** (also called B-motives), in contrast, are distinctly human. Maslow argues that humans have unique desires to discover and understand, to give love to others, and to push for the optimum fulfillment of their inner potentials.

In general, the satisfaction of deficiency motives prevents illness, or cures illness, or recreates homeostasis (inner balance). In contrast, the satisfaction of being motives produces positive health. The distinction is like the "difference between fending off threat or attack, and positive triumph and achievement" (Maslow, 1968, p. 32). But being motives are quite fragile and do not typically emerge until well into adulthood, and then only under supportive circumstances. Maslow's widely quoted needs hierarchy (shown in Figure 9.10) reflects this aspect of his thinking. The lowest four levels all describe different deficiency needs, while only the highest level, the need for **self-actualization,** is a being motive. Further, Maslow proposes that these five levels emerge sequentially in development and tend to dominate the system from the bottom up. That is, if you are starving, the physiological needs dominate. If you are being physically battered, the safety needs dominate. The need for self-actualization emerges only when all four types of deficiency needs are largely satisfied.

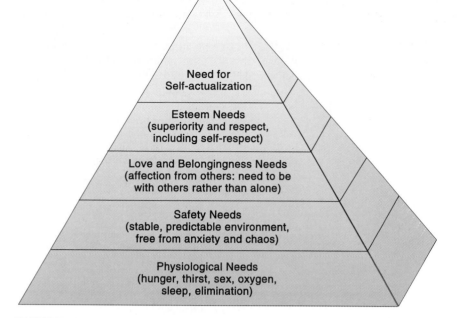

**Need for
Self-actualization**

**Esteem Needs
(superiority and respect,
including self-respect)**

**Love and Belongingness Needs
(affection from others: need to be
with others rather than alone)**

**Safety Needs
(stable, predictable environment,
free from anxiety and chaos)**

**Physiological Needs
(hunger, thirst, sex, oxygen,
sleep, elimination)**

FIGURE 9.IO Maslow's needs hierarchy. Maslow proposed that these needs dominate the system from the bottom up, with higher-level needs becoming prominent only later in life and only when (or if) the lower needs are largely satisfied.

Source: Maslow, 1968, 1970a.

To understand Maslow's theory you need to have a fuller sense of his concept of self-actualization and of the self-actualizing person. His interest was in positive health, in genuine growth, not simply in the avoidance of illness or the creation of stability. So he sought to understand the personalities and characteristics of those few adults who seem to have risen to the top of the needs hierarchy and achieved significant levels of self-understanding and expression, people such as Eleanor Roosevelt, Albert Schweitzer, Albert Einstein, and Thomas Jefferson. Some of the key characteristics of self-actualized people, as Maslow saw them, are listed in Table 9.5.

As you read this list, you may wonder whether anyone—short of sainthood—is really like this! In fact, Maslow thought that complete self-actualization was quite rare and likely to occur only quite late in life. But he believed that as they move into their middle years, many adults may come to display at least a few of these characteristics, gradually adding more and more as lower-level needs are satisfied and as the need for self-actualization comes to dominate the motive system. Yet those adults whose environments or relationships do not adequately satisfy their lower-level needs rarely experience the press of the need for self-actualization and may show few of these qualities.

Maslow's theory of motives has had little scientific testing, in part because it was not stated with great precision, and he developed no methods of assessing the dominance of the various motives he proposed. The theory has nonetheless been widely influential, perhaps because there is a certain ring of truth to it—a ring of truth reinforced by the correspondences between the sequence of motives Maslow proposes and the research findings I have described in this chapter. Collectively, these findings could be interpreted as show-

CRITICAL THINKING

Do you personally know anyone who seems to have many of these qualities of a self-actualized person? Do you see these qualities as admirable? Are they qualities you would like to develop yourself? Why or why not?

TABLE 9.5 **Some of the Characteristics of the Self-Actualizing Person, As Proposed by Maslow**

Accurate perception of reality	These people are relatively free of delusion and sees others and the environment clearly.
Acceptance of self and others	These people are more tolerant of both themselves and others, accepting frailty as well as strength, generally lacking shame or anxiety about themselves.
Spontaneity and self-knowledge	These individuals are quite "natural," perhaps even eccentric in their behavior and lifestyle, since they are not constrained by fear of what others will think of them. They know themselves well and follow that understanding.
Problem centering	Despite their high level of self-knowledge, self-actualizing persons are typically not very introspective or "self-centered." Rather, they are typically involved in external problems and may have a consuming mission in life involving wide philosophical or ethical issues.
Freshness of appreciation and richness of emotional response	Self-actualizers live rich emotional lives and have the capacity to "see" things freshly, to experience again and again the wonder and joy of existence or the intensity of pain.
Peak experiences	Experiences of perfection or a momentary loss of the sense of separate self, a submersion in a sense of unity. It may occur during sex, during creativity, in profound insight such as a scientific discovery, or in meditation or prayer.
Social interest	Self-actualizing persons have deep sympathy and compassion for their fellow beings and a strong desire to help others.
Deep, loving personal relationships	Personal relationships with spouse and close friends tend to be extremely deep and not motivated by deficiency love needs. Sex is seen as meaningless without love; they are attracted to others who display goodness and considerateness.
Need for privacy	Paradoxically, self-actualizing adults also have stronger-than-normal needs for time alone, for solitude. There is a kind of emotional detachment that characterizes these individuals, even while their relationships are extremely loving.
Creativity	Every self-actualizing person Maslow studied displayed some unusual form of creativity, whether artistic or otherwise.
Sense of humor	These adults dislike humor that involves making fun of others. Their humor may take the form of anecdotes, but does not involve sarcasm.

Source: Adapted from Maslow, 1968.

ing that love and belongingness needs dominate in early adulthood, esteem needs dominate up to and through midlife, and self-actualizing needs become prominent for at least some adults in late life. On the whole I think that describing the personality changes that seem to occur in one's 30s and 40s in terms of dominance of esteem needs comes closer to the mark than describing them in terms of increased generativity.

Even better, in my view, is Loevinger's theory.

Loevinger's Stages of Ego Development. Go back and look at Table 2.2, which summarizes Jane Loevinger's proposed stages. She argues that each of these stages involves a basic structural change, a fundamental shift in the way the person experiences and understands his or her relationships and the world. Unlike Erikson, who thought that all adults eventually face all the key developmental dilemmas whether or not they have worked out the earlier ones successfully, Loevinger does not assume that all adults move through the sequence of stages that she describes. What she proposes instead is that *if* a person's personality changes, it will change in a particular sequence, moving from dominance by social roles and conventionality to increasing individuality and autonomy and then toward increasing awareness of inner complexities.

In early adulthood, most adults are in the **conformist stage,** characterized by an external definition of what is good or right and a desire to live up to the expectations of the group to which one belongs. Note that Loevinger is not saying that all conformist behavior is the *same.* Rather, she is saying that each of us goes through a period in which we understand ourselves and experience ourselves in relation to group norms. If all your peers are going to college and then combining work and motherhood, that may be the norm to which you conform. But if your peers (and parents) value the role of full-time homemaker, you will be likely to follow that path and derive your values and your motives from that role pattern.

Some adults remain in this conformist pattern for all of their lives. But others, because the roles do not fit, or because some kind of trauma shatters the system, or because of some inner push toward greater self-understanding, gradually move away from this external definition of self toward what Loevinger calls the **conscientious stage** and **individualistic stage.** Adults who make this transition struggle to find some internal definition, to discover who they are and what they can do independent of others' expectations and definitions. In the process, adults often become focused on success or on striving, because these are ways of asserting and exploring their own individuality. At this stage, being uncomfortable with the dependence involved, many adults also show some turning away from relationships.

Daniel Levinson (1978) used the term **detribalization** to describe this same underlying shift from external to internal definition of the self. At midlife, he said, the adult "becomes more critical of the tribe—the particular groups, institutions and traditions that have the greatest significance for him, the social matrix to which he is most attached. He is less dependent upon tribal rewards, more questioning of tribal values, more able to look at life from a universalistic perspective" (p. 242). The 41-year-old designer I quoted a few pages ago is describing a kind of detribalization when she talks about rejecting the limitations of her earlier life and striking out for the job she really wants.

Loevinger proposes that there are still further stages, such as the **autonomous stage,** in which some adults reach a degree of security and comfort in their own independence/autonomy that allows them to turn outward, toward helping others, toward "humanitarian concern."

To me, this theoretical model comes closer than any of the others to encompassing the various research findings I have described. In particular, the transition from conformist to conscientious or individualistic stages sounds very like the basic shift toward greater individuality, autonomy, and self-confidence that seems to occur between early and middle adulthood. The hints of greater openness to inner feelings and more mature defense mechanisms would also be consistent with the shift that Loevinger describes.

Depending on the role patterns they have chosen or have been thrust into, men and women may display this change quite differently. Individuality for the man or the woman who has initially conformed to a traditional masculine social clock may be expressed in high achievement strivings or a motive for power; for women who began by conforming to a more traditional female role sequence, midlife individuality may be expressed in changing patterns of interaction within the family, such as reduced nurturance or in reduced reliance on friendships. A woman need not abandon her family roles to become more individualistic, but she may redefine them.

In later life, too, we find some confirmation for Loevinger's model in the signs of a move away from this heightened individuality and toward a broader set of concerns. These patterns make at least some sense if we think of the midlife period, when the conscientious stage and the individualistic level are likely to be achieved, as one in which the person attempts to *do* things, to have an effect on the world, be it in work or in family life. For those who make the transition to the autonomous stage, the later life period is more focused on *being,* on acceptance of the self, on what Erikson calls ego integrity.

Since Loevinger does not think that all adults move completely through this sequence of stages, relatively few adults will reach the level of an autonomous ego structure. In this theory, age is only a very rough correlate of the kind of personality and motivational changes Loevinger is describing. Given that assumption, the older the group studied, the more variability there should be in the stages or levels represented in the sample. Thus while the transition from conformist to individualistic stages should be fairly widespread, the later shift toward autonomy should be much more difficult to detect. The lack of consistency in the results for older adults is thus to be expected. Whether a particular pattern is found or not will depend very heavily on the particular subjects studied.

Loevinger's theory can also help us to understand some of the processes of self-selection of roles and pathways. As one example, Helson (Helson et al., 1984) offers the hypothesis that those women in her study who followed the traditional masculine social clock were already, at 20, beyond the conformist stage. Those women who chose to follow the more traditional feminine social clock, in contrast, appeared to be very much in the conformist stage and tended to remain there unless forced out of that position by some major life change such as divorce.

I do not want to suggest that every piece of evidence on personality change and continuity in adulthood can be fitted tidily under the umbrella of this or any other single theory. There remain some glaring contradictions, most notably the increase in personal rigidity with age that Schaie found for both men and women (Schaie, 1983b). Erikson, Maslow, and Loevinger would all probably predict the opposite, at least for some older adults. However, I am suggesting that theories such as Loevinger's may provide some insight into the underlying pattern of personality change that lies behind the surface diversity. Changes in family roles or gender roles or work roles, major life changes such as divorce or the death of a spouse, can all be catalysts for change. But what theory can suggest to us is the *direction* or *sequence* that such change is likely to follow.

I am also suggesting that it would be extremely fruitful if theoretical models like these were more often used as a basis for research designs. Simply using a standardized pencil-and-paper test of personality on adults of varying ages, without taking varying role patterns or personality structure into consideration, is not going to lead to much insight. We might, as one example, look at the later-life personality changes in adults who are at varying stages at midlife. Do middle-aged adults at the conformist stage have different experiences of later life than those at the conscientious or individualist stages? We might also ask what sorts of life experiences are likely to trigger a transition to a new stage. Are normative role transitions enough? Or does it take some more dramatic or traumatic event to stimulate a change? Perhaps the sort of mismatch between personality and role demands that Florine Livson studied in the Berkeley subjects (and that I described in Chapter 6) is enough to trigger change. Certainly, in Livson's study those who experienced such a mismatch not only went through a time of upheaval, they seemed to come out on the other side with a different structuring of personality.

I could multiply these examples at length but I hope the basic point is clear: In the study of personality, as in many other areas of the study of adult development, we need a better marriage between theory and research if we are to understand the basic processes.

TABLE 9.6 **Summary of Age Changes in Personality and Motivation**

Age 20–40	Age 40–65	Age 65+[a]
Over these years, an increase from low to higher levels of autonomy, achievement orientation, independence, self-confidence, cognitive commitment, assertiveness.	Peak levels of assertiveness, cognitive commitment, achievement, autonomy reached in midlife, after which a decline begins in these traits.	Perhaps declines in assertiveness, cognitive commitment, achievement, autonomy, etc. from the midlife peak.
Increase from low to higher levels of openness to self.	High levels of openness to self.	No evidence on whether such openness remains or increases in later years.
High levels of immature and low levels of mature defenses.	Increase in mature defenses, decrease in immature defenses.	No evidence on whether there is continued increase in maturity of defenses, although such an increase would be suggested by theory.
Low levels of humanitarian concern; lower levels of generosity toward others.	Medium levels of humanitarian concern and generosity, although peak in volunteering time for charity.	Highest levels of humanitarian concern and generosity.
Lowest levels of personal rigidity.	Medium levels of rigidity.	Highest levels of personal rigidity.

[a]Because we have essentially no information on personality change *within* late adulthood, I have not subdivided this period into young old and old old.

Review of Age Changes in Personality and Motivation

As usual, I've summarized the age changes in a table (Table 9.6). It is clear from the table that in early adulthood, age is a fairly decent predictor of the personality changes we see, perhaps because the timing of major role changes is more widely shared in early adulthood than later, or simply because many more adults make the basic transition from conformist to individualist perspectives than is true for later transitions. Whatever the reason, there are far fewer widely shared changes in personality past midlife.

One of the possible changes in old age, to which I have given little attention in this chapter, is an increased emphasis on issues of meaning. Do adults in their later years become sufficiently freed of the constraints of individual roles or circumstances to allow them to become concerned with wider-reaching metaphysical issues, with the nature of personal integration (as Erikson suggests) or the meaning of life? It is precisely to this question of the development of meaning over the adult years that Chapter 10 is addressed. So read on.

Summary

1. As we move through adulthood each of us has both a sense of self-continuity and a sense of personal change. We both stay the same and develop.

2. Virtually all the information we have about consistency in personality or motives concerns correlational consistency, although there is also limited evidence about both pattern and trait consistency.

3. There is strong evidence for stability of personality over the years of adulthood for all five of the "big five" personality trait structures.

4. At least some of the observed personality consistency appears to have a genetic basis.

5. Consistency is also fostered by the fact that the consequences of individual actions accumulate over time and by the fact that each adult tends to choose situations and create patterns of interaction that will tend to support his or her existing qualities.

6. Personality change over the adult years has also been demonstrated, although both the amount and the nature of the change seem clearer in early than in late adulthood.

7. Between early adulthood and middle life adults show three types of changes: (a) an increase in a cluster of behaviors related to individuality, including achievement strivings, autonomy, independence, confidence and self-esteem; (b) an increase in openness to self; and (c) an increase in maturity. Of these three, the evidence is clearest for the first, least clear for the second.

8. Evidence demonstrating these changes comes from several longitudinal studies describing adults from several different cohorts, so there is some reason to have confidence in the generality of the findings—at least for this culture.

9. Between midlife and old age the changes in personality are less clear. There are signs that individuality peaks in midlife and declines thereafter, and some indications that older adults may be more altruistic, more concerned for others. Paradoxically, there are also signs of greater interiority.

10. Several explanations of these patterns of change in personality are available. They may be due to methodological problems with the research, such as imprecision of measures based on interviews or cohort differences.

11. Personality change may also be caused (and explained) by changes in family, work, and gender roles. Some research suggests that personality differences are more strongly related to variations in role occupancy than they are to age, although the reverse has also been found. The shift from the primacy of roles in early adulthood to a midlife state in which roles are both looser and better learned is certainly consistent with the observed changes in personality, although which is cause and which is effect is not clear.

12. Some explanation of the changes observed may also be found in theory, particularly Jane Loevinger's model of personality change. In her terms, the changes involve a fairly widespread shift from a conformist to an individualistic model between early and middle adulthood, followed by a much-less-common shift to an autonomous stage in later life.

KEY TERMS

correlational consistency	agreeableness	affiliation
personality traits	conscientiousness	self-confidence
personality trait structures	cumulative continuity	succorance
Q-sort	interactional continuity	psychological openness
neuroticism	individuation	gender-role crossover
extraversion	agentic orientation	maturity
openness	competence	coping skills

cognitively committed

tenacious goal pursuit

flexible goal adjustment

instrumental values

terminal values

humanitarian concern

interiority

competence

independence

role streams

intimacy versus isolation

generativity versus
   stagnation

ego integrity versus
   despair

deficiency motives

being motives

self-actualization

conformist stage

conscientious stage

individualistic stage

detribalization

autonomous stage

SUGGESTED READINGS

Bender, S. (1989). *Plain and simple. A woman's journey to the Amish.* San Francisco: Harper & Row.

I found this book deeply touching, not only as a highly personal description of one person's struggle with the transition from an individualistic to a more integrated perspective, but in its descriptions of life in an Amish family. The book is like its title: plain and simple—short, clear, highly provocative.

Helson, R. (1997). The self in middle age. In M. E. Lachman & J. B. James (Eds.), *Multiple paths of midlife development* (pp. 21–43). Chicago: University of Chicago Press.

This is a very nice chapter that presents the "change" side of the change versus stability argument, and centers its focus on middle age, an oft-neglected part of the life span.

Hetherton, T. F., & Weinberger, J. L. (Eds.). (1994). *Can personality change?* Washington, DC: American Psychological Association.

This book will give you a very rich look at the various theories and data about personality stability and change. Included here is a very good recent paper by Costa and McCrae stating the case for personality consistency, and one by Helson and Stewart stating the case for personality change.

Hulbert, K. D., & Schuster, D. T. (Eds.). (1993). *Women's lives through time: Educated American women of the twentieth century.* San Francisco: Jossey-Bass.

The papers in this book each describe a longitudinal study of American college women, varying from the classes of 1930 up to groups graduating in the 1970s and 1980s. The emphasis is on the impact of women's role changes in this century on the choices and early adult life patterns of women. Not all of these studies included measures of personality, so some of this material is more relevant to Chapter 7 than to Chapter 10, but all of it is interesting.

Kogan, N. (1990). Personality and aging. In J. E. Birren & K. W. Schaie (Eds.), *Handbook of the psychology of aging* (3rd ed., pp. 330–346). San Diego, CA: Academic Press.

This brief review of the research on personality change and continuity over adulthood covers many of the same points I have made in this chapter, albeit in more technical language.

Schaie, K. W. (1983). *Longitudinal studies of adult psychological development.* New York: Guilford Press.

Included in this book are reports of many of the most complete and interesting longitudinal studies covering intellectual and personality change in adulthood. Schaie's own study is described here, as is the AT&T study, the Duke study, and several others.

THE GROWTH
OF MEANING

WHY A CHAPTER ON THE GROWTH OF MEANING?

In Chapter 9 I talked about changes in personality and self-actualization, which is certainly one aspect of inner development or growth in adulthood. But there is another aspect to inner development—perhaps more speculative, but certainly no less vital to most of us—that touches on questions of meaning, of purpose, of human potential. As we move through adulthood, do we interpret our experiences differently? Do we attach different meanings, understand our world in new ways? Do we become wiser, or less worldly, or perhaps more spiritual?

Certainly, a link between advancing age and increasing wisdom has been part of the folk tradition in virtually every culture in the world, as evidenced by fairy tales, myths, and religious teachings (Chinen, 1987; Clayton & Birren, 1980). Wisdom, in such sources, has been understood to mean not only an increased storehouse of worldly knowledge and experience, as discussed in Chapter 5, but also a different perspective on life, different values, a different world view, often described in terms of some kind of self-transcendence. What I am interested in knowing is whether such changes in world view or meaning, such potential for self-transcendence, is part of—or a potential part of—the normal process of adult development.

You may well think that the answers to such questions lie in the province of religion, not psychology. Despite the increasing numbers of psychologists interested in the psychology of religion, in wisdom, and in adults' ideas of life's meaning (Frankl, 1984; Koplowitz, 1990; Levin, 1994a; Palus, 1993; Reker, 1991; Reker & Wong, 1988; Sinnott, 1994; Sternberg, 1990b), you are not likely to find any discussion of this subject in any other textbook on adult development. So perhaps my first task here is to explain to you why I think this is important. Why talk about meanings? There are three reasons.

It Is the Meaning We Attach, Not the Experience, That Matters

Most fundamentally, psychologists have come to understand that individual experiences do not affect us in some automatic way; rather, it is the way we interpret an experience, the meaning we give it, that is really critical. A fairly trivial personal example may make the point:

In my late 40s, after a 25-year hiatus, I began taking singing lessons again. Over the many years when I sang mostly at campfires, accompanying myself on a guitar, I got away with pitching songs in a range that was easy and comfortable for my very low voice. But when I started singing once more with a good choir, I discovered that the regular alto register took me up into the twilight zone of my vocal range. So I went to a voice teacher to see if she could help me learn how to sing those higher notes again. Since the whole purpose of the lessons was for me to learn to sing those high notes, we spent a lot of time on it, and a lot of the time the noises coming out of my mouth were less than attractive.

The objective fact, then, is that I had technical difficulties singing notes in a particular range. But it is not that fact that is most significant to me; rather, it is the *meaning* I attached to those difficulties that is critical. There are obviously several different possibilities. I could have perceived them purely as technical problems. That's the meaning my voice teacher would have liked me to attach to the situation. Or I could have concluded that those notes just aren't "in there" and stop worrying about it. But as you can probably guess by now, neither of those is the meaning I attached to this experience. Instead, I experienced this difficulty as a personal failure. I felt that I ought to be able to conquer this problem easily, that once my teacher had explained the problem to me I should have been able to soar to the note and sound like a gorgeous opera singer. When I couldn't do that, I was incredibly frustrated.

My distress arose not from the objective situation but from my interpretation—from the meaning I attached to the event. Furthermore, the meanings I give to events are not random. There are certain basic assumptions I make about the world and my place in it, about myself and my capacities, that affect my interpretations of many experiences. Such a system of meanings is sometimes referred to as a **world view** or an **internal model.** I've touched on other aspects of this same point in earlier chapters without labeling it in quite this way. For example, we can think of an "internal working model" of attachment relationships as a meaning system. If my internal model includes the assumption that "people are basically helpful and trustworthy," that assumption is clearly going to affect not only the experiences I will seek out, but my interpretation of those experiences. I will see helpfulness and trustworthiness where another person, with a different internal model, might see manipulativeness or self-interest. The objective experiences each of us has are thus filtered through various internal models, various meaning systems. I would argue that the ultimate consequence of any given experience is largely (if not wholly) determined by the meaning we attach and not the experience itself.

CRITICAL THINKING

Can you think of a similar example in your own life? Suppose that you do badly on a test in some class. How would your meaning system affect your interpretation of such an event?

To the extent that this is true, then, it is obviously important for us to try to understand the meaning systems that adults create.

Adults Say That Meaning Is Important to Them

A second reason for exploring this rather slippery area is that if you ask adults what issues are of central concern to them, questions of meaning loom large in the answers. For example, Milton Yinger (1977) asked a group of college students in Japan, Korea, Thailand, New Zealand, and Australia the following question: "What do you consider the one most fundamental or important issue for the human race; that is, what do you see as the basic and permanent question for mankind, the question of which all others are only parts?" Sixty percent of the answers touched on some aspect of life's meaning as being the fundamental question for the human race: What is the meaning of suffering or injustice? What is the purpose of existence?

This theme finds echoes in the writings of many clinicians and theorists. Erich Fromm listed the need for meaning as one of the five central existential needs of human beings; Victor Frankl (1984) argues that the "will to meaning" is a central human motive. James Fowler, a theologian and developmental psychologist, has made a similar point: "One characteristic all human beings have in common is that we can't live without some sense that life is meaningful" (1983, p. 58). Thus not only do we interpret our experiences and in this way "make meaning," it may also be true that the need or motive to create *meaningfulness* may be a central one in adult (and perhaps children's) lives.

Furthermore, there is now a growing body of evidence that adults who seek quite explicitly for meaning systems through regular religious/spiritual observances, whether organized or private, are healthier and live longer than adults who have less religious/spiritual involvement (Levin, 1994b). And adults who report greater sense of mission and direction, a stronger sense of the purpose of their lives, also remain healthier in the face of stress than do those whose sense of personal meaning is less clear (Reker & Butler, 1990). Given evidence of this type, it seems clear that meaning systems are important aspects of adult lives.

Meaning Systems May Change with Age

Finally, there is a developmental argument as well: There are a number of theories and at least some data (consistent with the message from myths and fairy tales) pointing to the possibility that there may be shared or potential changes in our meaning systems as we move through the adult years, just as there may be shared changes in personality. In fact, the personality changes I talked about in Chapter 9 may be embedded in a broader shift in meaning systems. If so, it is obviously important for us to try to understand meaning systems and their potential developmental changes.

HOW CAN WE STUDY POSSIBLE AGE CHANGES IN MEANING SYSTEMS?

Assuming that I have persuaded you that this subject is worth exploring, we then come to the equally sticky/tricky question of method. How do we explore something so apparently fuzzy? One way, of course, is to look for some outward sign of adults' search for meaning systems. Since one of the key functions of religion is to provide answers to fundamental questions about the meaning and purpose of life and about human beings' relationship to the universe, one obvious place to look would be at adults' involvement with religious observances of various kinds. Are there particular points in adulthood when people become more, or less, involved in religious practices such as church attendance? Does prayer (or meditation, or equivalent) play a larger role in life at some ages than at others? One group of researchers has pursued this line, and I'll look at this evidence in a moment.

Many theologians and developmental psychologists, however, have been dissatisfied with this approach. Involvement in organized religious activities may or may not change with age, but in any case such change or stability does not tell us about any changes in the *purpose* of religion in adults' lives or about adults' more basic meaning systems. To understand these, we need to go beyond or behind observable behavior and ask people about their lives and their understanding of their own lives. Gary Reker has pioneered the use of standardized questionnaire techniques to study meaning systems (Reker, 1991), a strategy that makes larger-scale studies more feasible. Others have used primarily open-ended interview techniques, a procedure that may yield considerable depth but that leaves the researcher with the task of categorizing or analyzing the answers, looking for some kind of orderliness. Personality researchers have used such open-ended techniques for many years, often very fruitfully, as you have seen in the results of many of the personality studies I talked about in Chapter 9. In studies of meaning, such a research method has been used not only by Lawrence Kohlberg and his many colleagues in their studies of the development of moral reasoning, but by Fowler in his studies of faith development and Robert Kegan (1982) in his exploration of "the evolving self." With the striking exception of research on moral reasoning, which is extensive, the amount of empirical evidence from either research strategy is distinctly limited, but the alternative methods are at least familiar.

More controversial is the use of individual case studies drawn from biographies or autobiographies: personal reports by well-known adults (politicians, saints, philosophers, mystics) about the steps and processes of their own inner development. Collections of such independent reports have been analyzed, perhaps most impressively by William James (a distinguished early American psychologist) in his book *The Varieties of Religious Experience* (1902/1958) and by Evelyn Underhill (1911/1961), in her book *Mysticism.*

Even detailed analyses of such personal reports do not fit with our usual concept of "scientific evidence." Only those few adults who have chosen to write about their inner "journey" can be included—hardly a random sample. Still, information from such sources has had a powerful effect on theories of potential changes in meaning systems. At the least, they tell us something about what *may* be possible, or about the qualities, meaning systems, or capacities of a few extraordinary adults who appear to have plumbed the depths of the human spirit. Yet even if we accept such descriptions as valid reports of inner processes, it is a very large leap to apply the described steps or processes to the potential experiences of ordinary folks. I am going to take that leap in this chapter. You will have to judge for yourself whether it is justified.

A CAVEAT

I need to make one further preparatory point: It is surely obvious (but nonetheless worth stating explicitly) that I bring my own meaning system to this discussion. Of course, that statement is true about this entire book (or anyone else's book). I cannot report "objectively." Inevitably, I select, place emphasis, integrate information in a way that is influenced by my basic biases, my assumptions about human nature. Such bias, although always present, is less troublesome in areas in which there is an extensive body of empirical evidence,

CRITICAL THINKING

Do you share this bias? If so, where do you think your "world view" came from? If not, what alternative assumption do you make?

such as in the study of physical or mental development. But it becomes far more troublesome when I talk about the development of ideas about life's meaning itself. So let me at least make my biases clear.

I approach this subject with a strong hypothesis that there are "higher" levels of human potential than most of us have yet reached, whether that is expressed as the potential for wisdom, in Maslow's terms as self-actualization, in Loevinger's concept of the integrated personality, or in Fowler's concept of universalizing faith. When I describe the various models of the development of meaning systems, I am inevitably filtering the theories and the evidence through this hypothesis. There is no way I can avoid this, any more than you can avoid filtering this chapter through your own assumptions, your own meaning system. Keep it in mind as you read further.

RELIGIOUS PARTICIPATION OVER ADULTHOOD

Let us begin at the level of overt behavior, with research on religious participation. Most of the data are cross-sectional, as usual, but there are at least a few longitudinal studies of older adults. The findings can be summarized quite briefly.

Cross-sectional studies show a slight increase in church or synagogue attendance with age. National census data from 1991, for example, show that 60 percent of 18 to 29 year-olds were church or synagogue members, compared to 67 percent of those aged 30 to 49 and 76 percent of those over 50 (U.S. Bureau of the Census, 1993). Religious involvement (including attendance at religious services, regular prayer, reading religious books or magazines, and the like) is higher among blacks than among whites in the United States, and generally higher among women than men (Levin, Taylor, & Chatters, 1994), but religious involvement increases with age in all these groups. Some typical data from an analysis of a nationally representative black sample, by Linda Chatters and Robert Taylor (1989), shown in Figure 10.1, will show you what the age pattern looks like. These results are based on a five-point scale on which a 5 meant the respondent reported attending a religious service daily and a 1 indicated attendance less than once a year. Church attendance obviously rises steadily until late life, with a drop only after age 75.

Such a drop in church attendance in old age has been replicated in other research, including longitudinal studies. For example, participants in one of the Duke longitudinal studies, who were age 60 to 90 at the start of the study, collectively showed a decline in religious participation over the next 14 years (Blazer & Palmore, 1976). It would be a mistake, however, to interpret this late-life drop in church participation as a sign of decreased interest in religion. Rather, it seems to reflect decreased mobility or energy. On measures of other types of personal religious practices, such as private prayer, reading religious books, or listening to or watching religious programs, there is essentially no decline in old age (Ainlay & Smith, 1984; Hunsberger, 1985; Levin & Taylor, 1993).

Overall, then, there is some hint here of an increase in religious participation in middle and old age. We can't be entirely sure of this because we have no longitudinal evidence covering the years of early and middle adulthood, but we can find some supportive evidence in the finding that as adults age, they become more concerned with issues of personal morality or spirituality. The longitudinally observed increase with age in "humanitarian concern" that I reported in Chapter 9 (Schaie & Parham, 1976) is one example of such a change.

Additional evidence consistent with this trend comes from two cross-sectional studies. Savage and his colleagues (Savage, Gaber, Britton, Bolton, & Cooper, 1977), in their study of a large group of elderly adults in Britain, found that the older the person, the more likely she was to select items that reflected moral qualities as key elements in her self-concept (e.g., "I am an honest person.") Similarly, Veroff and his colleagues (Veroff, Douvan, & Kulka, 1981), in their time-sequential study of national samples in 1957 and 1976, found that at both times, older adults were more likely than younger ones to use moral or virtuous qualities as self-descriptions (e.g., "I lead a clean life," or "I'm unselfish"). Veroff et al. conclude: "It is as though older people refocus identity from interpersonal relationships

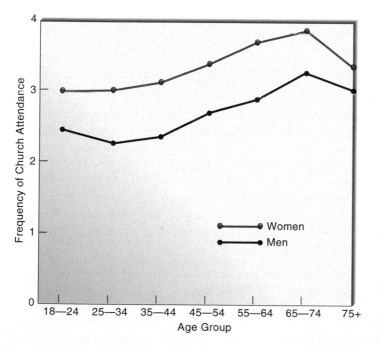

FIGURE 10.1 These cross-sectional data are from a nationally representative sample of African-Americans. Subjects were asked how often they attend some kind of formal religious service and given a five-point scale on which to answer. A 5 indicated daily attendance, a 4 indicated at least weekly attendance, and so on. Church attendance was higher among the middle-aged and older adults but dropped off past age 75—a pattern found in other studies as well.

Source: Chatters & Taylor, 1989, Table 1, p. S186.

to broader social concerns. Older people indicate less need of social acceptance, and they less often feel inadequate in social roles. While we can interpret this as a diminishing energy for role performance and interpersonal relationships, we can also think of these results as reflecting the fact that older people are more at peace with themselves and more invested in moral and spiritual values" (pp. 378–379).

These findings are suggestive, especially those from Veroff's studies of values, but to my taste they do not go deeply enough. They tell us little about possible changes in the role of religion in adults' lives as they age, or about other changes in meaning systems that may be taking place. To explore this, we need to look at some broader theory and data.

THE DEVELOPMENT OF MEANING SYSTEMS OVER ADULTHOOD

For several reasons, I want to start this exploration with a look at Lawrence Kohlberg's theory of the development of moral reasoning—reasoning about what is right and wrong and how to judge the rightness or wrongness of an act. Although the questions Kohlberg has addressed touch on only a corner of the subject I am examining, his basic theoretical model has been the foundation of much of the current thinking about adults' evolving world views or meaning systems. Kohlberg's theory has also been tested extensively with empirical research and has been accepted widely among developmental psychologists, so it provides a relatively noncontroversial jumping-off point.

Kohlberg's Theory of the Development of Moral Reasoning

Faced with conflict between different values, on what basis does a child or an adult decide what is morally right or wrong, fair or just? Kohlberg argued, as an extension of Piaget's theory of cognitive development, that children and adults move through a sequence of stages in their moral reasoning, each stage growing out of, but superseding, the one that came before. In this view, each stage reflects a meaning system or model, an internally consistent and pervasive set of assumptions about what is right and wrong and how it should be judged in others (Colby, Kohlberg, Gibbs, & Lieberman, 1983; Kohlberg, 1964, 1973, 1976, 1981, 1984; Kohlberg & Kramer, 1969).

Kohlberg made an important distinction between the form of thinking (what one thinks) and the content of thinking (why they think a certain way). The issue is not whether the child or adult thinks, for example, that lying is wrong, but *why* they think it is wrong. Kohlberg searched for developmental changes in the form of thinking about moral questions, just as Piaget searched for developmental changes in broader forms of logic (recall Table 5.1).

The Measurement Procedure. Kohlberg assessed a person's level or stage of moral reasoning by means of a "moral judgment interview" in which the subject is asked to respond to a series of hypothetical moral dilemmas. In each dilemma, two different potential principles are in conflict. For example, in the now-famous Heinz dilemma (presented in Table 10.1), the subject must grapple with the question of whether a man named Heinz ought to steal a drug to save his dying wife if the only druggist who can provide the drug is demanding a higher price than Heinz can pay. In this instance, the conflicting principles are the value of preserving life and the value of respecting property and upholding the law.

The Stages. Based on many subjects' responses to such dilemmas, Kohlberg concluded that there were three basic levels of moral reasoning, each of which could be divided further into two stages, resulting in six stages in all, summarized in Table 10.1.

The **preconventional level** is typical of most children under age 9, but is also found in some adolescents and in some criminal offenders. At both stages at this level the child

TABLE IO.I Kohlberg's Stages of Moral Development

Kohlberg's theory of moral development was based on responses about moral dilemmas. This story of Heinz is the best known of these moral dilemmas:

In Europe a woman was near death from a special kind of cancer. There was one drug that doctors thought might save her. It was a form of radium that a druggist in the same town had recently discovered. The drug was expensive to make, but the druggist was charging $2000, or 10 times the cost of the drug, for a small (possibly lifesaving) dose. Heinz, the sick woman's husband, borrowed all the money he could, about $1000, or half of what he needed. He told the druggist that his wife was dying and asked him to sell the drug cheaper or to let him pay later. The druggist replied, "No, I discovered the drug, and I'm going to make money from it." Heinz then became desperate and broke into the store to steal the drug for his wife. Should Heinz have done that?

The following responses are examples of people operating in different stages of moral development:

Level I: Preconventional morality

Stage 1: Punishment-and-obedience orientation

Yes, Heinz should take the drug. *Why?* Because if he lets his wife die, he could be responsible for it and get into trouble.

> No, Heinz should not take the drug. *Why?* Because it is stealing. It doesn't belong to him and he can get arrested and punished..

Stage 2: Naive hedonism

Yes, Heinz should take the drug. *Why?* Because he really isn't hurting the druggist and he wants to help his wife. Maybe he can pay him later.

> No, Heinz shouldn't take the drug. *Why?* The druggist is in business to make money. That's his job. He needs to make a profit.

Level 2: Conventional morality

Stage 3: Good boy or good girl orientation

Yes, Heinz should take the drug. *Why?* Because he is being a good husband and saving his wife's life. He would be wrong if he didn't save her.

> No,. Heinz should not take the drug. *Why?* Because he tried to buy it and he couldn't, so it's not his fault if his wife dies. He did his best.

Stage 4: Social-Order-Maintaining Morality

Yes, Heinz should take the drug. *Why?* Because the druggist is wrong to be interested only in profits. But Heinz also must pay for the drug later and maybe confess that he took it. It's still wrong to steal.

> No. Heinz should not take the drug. *Why?* Because even though it is natural to want to save your wife, you still need to obey the law. You can't just ignore it because of special circumstances.

Level 3: Postconventional (or principled) morality

Stage 5: Social contract orientation

Yes, Heinz should take the drug. *Why?* Although the law says he shouldn't, if you consider the whole picture, it would be reasonable for anyone in his situation to take the drug.

> No, Heinz should not take the drug. *Why?* Although some good would come from him taking the drug, it still wouldn't justify violating the consensus of how people have agreed to live together. The ends don't justify the means.

Stage 6: Individual principles of conscience orientation

Yes, Heinz should take the drug. *Why?* When a person is faced with two conflicting principles, they need to judge which is higher and obey it. Human life is higher than possession.

> No, Heinz should not take the drug. *Why?* Heinz needs to decide between his emotion and the law—both are "right" in a way, but he needs to decide what an ideally just person would do, and that would be not to steal the drug.

Source: After Kohlberg, 1976, 1984.

sees rules as something outside himself or herself. In Stage 1, the **punishment-and-obedience orientation,** what is right is what is rewarded or what is not punished; in Stage 2, right is defined in terms of what brings pleasure or serves one's own needs, or what is negotiated with others. So at this stage children insist that rules of games must be followed precisely, and that fairness is a crucial value for any kind of human interaction. (Parents who have elementary school–aged children will recognize this stage immediately; children in this stage of moral reasoning make a big point about fairness in the family and "That's not fair!" becomes a commonly heard cry.) Stage 2 is sometimes described as **naive hedonism,** a phrase that also captures some of the flavor of this stage.

At the **conventional level,** which is characteristic of most adolescents and most adults in our culture, the person internalizes the rules and expectations of her family or peer group (at Stage 3) or of society (at Stage 4). In early presentations of the stages, Stage 3 is sometimes called the **good boy or good girl orientation,** while Stage 4 is sometimes labeled as the **social-order-maintaining morality.**

The **postconventional level,** which is found in only a minority of adults, involves a search for the underlying reasons behind society's rules. At Stage 5, which Kohlberg calls the **social contract orientation,** laws and regulations are seen as important ways of ensuring fairness, but they are not perceived as immutable, nor do they necessarily perfectly reflect more fundamental moral principles. Since laws and contracts are usually in accord with such underlying principles, obeying society's laws is reasonable nearly all the time. But when those underlying principles or reasons are at variance with some specific social custom or rule, the Stage 5 adult argues on the basis of the fundamental principle, even if it means disobeying or disagreeing with a law. Civil rights protesters in the early 1960s, for example, typically supported their civil disobedience with Stage 5 reasoning. Stage 6, known as the **individual principles of conscience orientation,** is simply a further extension of this same pattern, with the person searching for and then living in a way that is consistent with the deepest set of moral principles possible.

Another way to look at the shifts from preconventional, to conventional, to postconventional levels of reasoning is as a **process of decentering,** a term Piaget used to describe cognitive development more generally. At the preconventional level, the children's reference points are themselves—the consequences of their own actions, the rewards they may gain. At the conventional level, the reference point has moved outward away from the center of the self to the family or society. Finally, at the postconventional level the adult searches for a still broader reference point, some set of underlying principles that lie behind or beyond social systems. Such a movement outward from the self is one of the constant themes in writings on the growth or development of meaning systems in adult life.

CRITICAL THINKING

As a way to try to make these stages more real, see if you can imagine a society in which everyone reasoned at Kohlberg's Stage 3; now how about a society in which everyone reasoned at Stage 5? How might these two societies differ from one another?

Kohlberg argued that these forms of moral reasoning emerge in a fixed sequence and that the stages are hierarchically organized. That is, each new stage grows from and eventually replaces the one before it, and each successive stage is more differentiated and integrated than the last. Of course, during the transition from one stage to the next, a person will use reasoning reflecting at more than one stage, but eventually, according to this argument, the lower levels of reasoning will drop out and be replaced by the more complex, more integrated system of reasoning. This is the strictest form of a stage theory. In contrast, Erikson's stages are sequential but not hierarchically organized. That is, in Erikson's system each new stage ushers in a new set of issues, but the old issues do not vanish and there is no assumption that the new stage involves some new internal model, some integration and reorganization of an old way of thinking.

The Data. Only longitudinal data can tell us whether Kohlberg's model is valid. If he is correct, not only should children and adults move from one step to the next in the order he proposes, they should not show regression to earlier stages. Kohlberg and his colleagues tested these hypotheses in three samples, all interviewed repeatedly, each time asked to discuss a series of moral dilemmas: (1) 84 boys from the Chicago area first interviewed when they were between 10 and 16 in 1956, some of whom were reinterviewed up to five more times (the final interview was in 1976–1977, when they were in their 30s) (Colby et al., 1983); (2) a group of 23 boys and young men in Turkey (some from a rural village and some from large cities), followed over periods of up to 10 years into early adulthood (Nisan & Kohlberg, 1982); and (3) sixty-four male and female subjects from kibbutzim in Israel (intentional collective communities), who were first tested as teenagers and then retested once or twice over total periods of up to 10 years (Snarey, Reimer, & Kohlberg, 1985).

Figure 10.2 gives two kinds of information about the findings from these three studies. In the top half of the figure are total "moral maturity scores" derived from the interview. These scores reflect each subject's stage of moral reasoning and can range from 100 to 500. As you can see, in all three studies the average score went up steadily with age, although there are some interesting cultural differences in speed of movement through the stages. In the bottom half of the figure are the percentages of answers to the moral dilem-

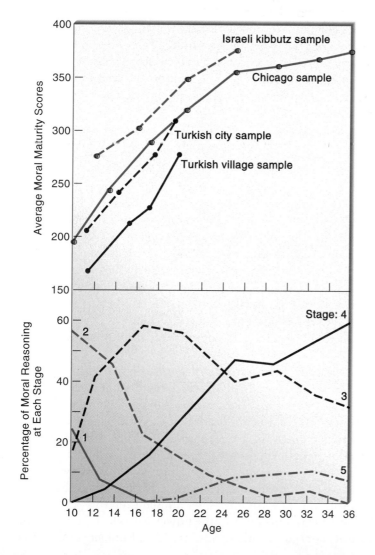

FIGURE 10.2 The upper half of this figure shows moral maturity scores, which reflect level of reasoning on Kohlberg's moral dilemmas. Included are findings from teenagers and young adults in three countries. As you can see, overall scores go up as age increases. The lower half of the figure shows the percentages of answers to moral dilemmas among subjects in the Chicago study rated at each stage of reasoning at each age in the longitudinal study. It is clear that preconventional reasoning drops while conventional reasoning rises in adolescence and early adulthood. Principled reasoning, however, is relatively rare, even in adulthood.

Sources: Data from Colby, Kohlberg, Gibbs, & Lieberman, 1983; Nisan & Kohlberg, 1982; Snarey, Reimer, & Kohlberg, 1985. Colby et al. © The Society for Research in Child Development, Inc., and the author.

mas that reflected each stage of moral reasoning for subjects at each age. These data are for the Chicago sample only, since that sample has been studied over the longest period of time. As we would expect, the number of Stage 1 responses drops out quite early, while conventional morality (Stages 3 and 4) rises rapidly in the teenage years and remains high in adulthood. Only a very small percentage of answers, even of those in their 30s, show Stage 5 reasoning (postconventional reasoning), and none show Stage 6 reasoning.

Both analyses show the stages to be strongly sequential. Such a sequential pattern is also supported by the fact that in none of these three studies was there a single subject who skipped a stage, and only about 5 percent showed regressions—a percentage that would be consistent with scoring errors. Each subject also showed a good deal of internal consistency at any one testing, using similar logic in analyzing each of several quite different moral problems. These same patterns have also been found in both shorter-term longitudinal studies (L. J. Walker, 1989) and in studies using a questionnaire method of measuring moral judgment rather than the more open-ended interview (Rest, Davison, & Robbins, 1978; Rest & Thoma, 1985).

Unfortunately, no equivalent longitudinal data exist for any adults past midlife. Cross-sectional results (Lonky, Kaus, & Roodin, 1984; Pratt, Golding, & Hunter, 1983) show no age differences in overall level of moral judgment between young, middle-aged, and older adults. Such findings might be taken to mean that the level of reasoning achieved in early adulthood remains relatively stable throughout adulthood. But the longitudinal data do not support such an assertion, at least not through the middle 30s. Among Kohlberg's sample were quite a few people who shifted from Stage 3 to Stage 4 while in their 20s, and a few who moved to Stage 5 while in their 30s. At least some adults may thus continue to develop through Kohlberg's stages throughout adulthood. The only way to know this for sure will be to assess moral reasoning longitudinally over the full years of adult life.

Stage 6, and the Possibility of Stage 7. In his early work Kohlberg suggested that a fair number of college students reached Stage 6. In his later writings, however, he changed his mind and concluded that this universalistic stage is extremely uncommon (Colby & Kohlberg, 1987). The longitudinal data suggest that Stage 5 may be the typical "endpoint" of the developmental progression. Adults who reach Stage 5 (about 15 percent of those in their 30s in Kohlberg's samples) do indeed operate on some broad, general principles. What they lack, however, is "that which is critical for our theoretical notion of Stage 6, namely, the organization of moral judgment around a clearly formulated moral principle of justice and respect for persons that provides a rationale for the primacy of this principle" (Kohlberg, 1984, p. 271). In other words, at Stage 5 one develops some broad principles that go beyond (or "behind") the social system; at Stage 6, the rare person develops a still broader and more general ethical system in which such basic principles are embedded. Among those who Kohlberg lists as apparent Stage 6 thinkers are Martin Luther King and Gandhi.

Kohlberg also speculated about the existence of a still higher stage, Stage 7 (Kohlberg, 1973; Kohlberg, Levine, & Hewer, 1983), which he thought might emerge only toward the end of life, after an adult has spent some years living within a principled moral system. It is the confrontation of one's own death that can bring about this transition. As they ask the fundamental questions, "Why live?" and "How to face death?", some people transcend the type of logical analysis that typifies all the earlier forms of moral reasoning and arrive at a still deeper or broader decentering. As Vivian Clayton and James Birren (1980) describe it: "The individual shifts from seeing himself as the center of the universe to identifying with the universe and seeing himself from this perspective. What results is that the individual senses the unity of the universe in which he is but one element..... [it is a] nondualistic, nonegoistic orientation" (p. 122). Kohlberg himself put it this way: "Generally speaking, a Stage 7 response to ethical and religious problems is based on constructing a sense of identity or unity with being, with life, or with God" (Kohlberg et al., 1983).

Evaluation and Comment. The body of evidence that has accumulated concerning the development of moral reasoning provides strong support for several aspects of Kohlberg's theory:

1. There do appear to be stages that children and adults move through in developing concepts of fairness and morality.

2. At least up to Stage 5, those stages appear to meet the tests of a hierarchical stage system: They occur in fixed order, each emerging from and replacing the one that preceded it, and forming a structural whole.

3. The stage sequence appears to be universal. The specific *content* of moral decisions may differ from one culture to the next, but the overall form of logic seems to move through the same steps in every culture in which this has been studied— a list that includes 27 different countries, Western and non-Western, industrialized and nonindustrialized (Snarey, 1985).

4. The stages have some relevance for real life as well. As one example, Edward Lonky and his colleagues (Lonky, Kaus, & Roodin, 1984) have found that adults who reason at the principled level are more able than are those at the conventional level to deal positively and constructively with significant losses in their lives, such as the death of a family member or the breakup of a relationship.

At the same time, a number of critics have pointed out that Kohlberg's theory is relatively narrow, focusing almost exclusively on the development of concepts of justice or fairness. Other aspects of moral/ethical reasoning, other facets of meaning systems, are omitted.

The most eloquent of the critics has been Carol Gilligan (1982; Gilligan & Wiggins, 1987). She argues that Kohlberg was interested in concepts of justice and not concepts of care, so his theory and research largely ignore an ethical/moral system based on caring for others, on responsibility, on altruism or compassion. In particular, Gilligan proposes that women more often than men approach moral and ethical dilemmas from the point of view of responsibilities and caring, searching not for the "just" solution, but for the solution that best deals with the social relationships involved. She argues that men, more often than women, use a morality of justice.

This aspect of Gilligan's argument has not been strongly supported by research findings. In studies in which boys and girls have been compared on stage of moral reasoning using Kohlberg's revised scoring system, no gender differences are typically found (Smetana, Killen, & Turiel, 1991; L. J. Walker, de Vries, & Trevethan, 1987), although several studies of adults do show the difference that Gilligan hypothesizes (Lyons, 1983). What is clear from the research to date is that girls and women can and do use moral reasoning based on principles of justice when they are presented with dilemmas in which that is a central issue. Nonetheless, Gilligan's more basic point seems clearly valid: Kohlberg's approach does focus only on a narrow range of aspects of moral judgment or meaning. Despite this narrowness, however, it is possible to take the basic structure and assumptions of Kohlberg's theory and build on it to explore not only ethics based on relationships and caring, such as Gilligan has described, but also religious beliefs and more general facets of personal meaning systems, as James Fowler has done in his theory of faith development.

CRITICAL THINKING

Suppose for the moment that Gilligan is right, that adult women more often make judgments from an ethic of caring, whereas men more often judge from an ethic of justice. How might such a difference affect communication between men and women?

Fowler's Theory of Faith Development

In talking about stages of faith development, James Fowler (1981; 1983) goes beyond questions of moral reasoning to search for the emergence of each person's world view or model of his or her relationship to others and to the universe. He uses the word **faith** to describe such a personal model—a somewhat confusing usage since the word *faith* more commonly refers to any specific set of religious beliefs. In the language I have been using in this chapter, Fowler's model might be called a theory of the development of meaning systems, but I will use his own term—faith—to be true to the original formulation.

In Fowler's view, each of us has a faith whether or not we belong to a particular church or organization. Moral reasoning is only a *part* (perhaps quite a small part) of faith. Faith is broader. In my terms it is a set of assumptions or understandings, often so basic that they are not articulated, about the nature of our connections with others and with the world in which we live. At any point in our lives, he argues, each of us has a "master story" which is "the answer you give to the questions of what life is about, or who's really in charge here, or how do I live to make my life a worthy, good one. It's a stance you take toward life" (Fowler, 1983, p. 60).

Like Kohlberg, Fowler is interested not in the specific content of one's faith but in the structure or form of that faith. A Christian, a Hindu, a Jew, or an atheist could all have faiths that are structurally similar, even while they differ sharply in content. Thus when Fowler talks about the development of faith, he is not talking about specific religious beliefs or about conversions from one religion to another. He is searching for the underlying *structure* or logic that is common to many different specific beliefs or creeds.

And like Kohlberg, Fowler hypothesizes that each of us develops through a shared series of faith structures (or world views, broad internal working models, meaning systems, or whatever we might choose to call them) over the course of childhood and adulthood. Two of the six stages he proposes occur primarily in childhood, and I won't describe them here; the remaining four can be found among adults.

The Stages of Faith. The first of the adult forms of faith, which Fowler calls **synthetic-conventional faith,** normally appears first in adolescence and then continues well into early adulthood for most of us. Like Kohlberg's level of conventional morality, conventional faith is rooted in the implicit assumption that authority is to be found outside oneself. Although the teenager does go through a process of creating a new identity, a process that normally includes reexamination of old beliefs, this process still goes on against the backdrop of the basic external-authority assumption. The young person chooses some set of specific beliefs from among those that are "out there."

Many adults remain within this form of faith/meaning throughout their lives, defining themselves and interpreting their experiences within the meaning system of a group or specific set of beliefs. Let me give you two concrete examples from Fowler's own interviews that may make the point clearer. Mr. D., a 63-year-old retired teamster, talked about his beliefs this way: "My views are quite the same as those of any teamster, or any working man.... I'm not now a religious man, never was, and never will be. Religion is just a lot of nonsense as I see it. As I see it, we are born, we live here, we die, and that's it. Religion gives people something to believe in, that there's something more, because they want there to be something more, but there isn't. So… you see, I'd rather put some money down on the bar and buy myself a drink, rather than put that same money into a collection plate!" (Fowler, 1981, pp. 165–166). Mr. D. is rejecting formal religion, but there is still an external authority here—working men or other teamsters. In fact he defines himself as "one of the boys."

In contrast, the external authority for Mrs. H. is very definitely a specific set of religious beliefs. A 61-year-old southern woman who grew up on a tenant farm, at the time Fowler interviewed her she had recently rededicated herself to the Baptist church after many years away from church activity. At one point she said: "I feel very sad and ashamed for the way I have wasted my life. I do know that God has forgiven me for every wrong that I've done, and that He loves me. I feel very close to God most of the time, now that I am active in the work of the church again. Of course there are times that I don't feel as close to Him as I'd like to, but I know that I am the one who moves away, not He. I've learned that we all have so much to be thankful for, if we only stop and count our blessings" (Fowler, 1981, p. 172).

It is precisely this reliance on external authority that changes when an adult moves to the next proposed stage, which Fowler calls **individuative-reflective faith.** "For a genuine move to Stage 4 to occur there must be an interruption of reliance on external sources of authority… there must be a relocation of authority within the self" (Fowler, 1981, p. 179). In making this shift, many adults first reject or move away from the faith community to which they had belonged. Often, there is also a rejection of ritual or myth and an embracing of science or rationality. But the transition can occur without such rejections. The key is that the person not only reexamines old assumptions but takes responsibility in a new way.

It is hard to convey just how profound a change this is. The metaphor I have found most helpful is one I have adapted from mythologist Joseph Campbell's writings (1986). It is as if in the stage of conventional faith we experience ourselves as like the moon, illuminated by *reflected* light. We are not ourselves the source of light (or knowledge) but are created by outside forces. In the stage of individuative faith we experience ourselves as like the sun, radiating light of our own. We are no longer defined by the groups to which we belong; rather, we choose the groups, the relationships, based on our self-chosen beliefs or values. Thus even if the specific beliefs we choose at this point are the same ones with which we have grown up, the underlying meaning system is changed.

Rebecca, a woman in her mid-30s interviewed by Robert Kegan in another context, seems clearly to have made this transition:

> I know I have very defined boundaries and I protect them very carefully. I won't give up the slightest control. In any relationship I decide who gets in, how far, and when. What am I afraid of? I used to think I was afraid people would find out who I really was and then not like me. But I don't think that's it anymore. What I feel now is— "that's me. That's mine. It's what makes me. And I'm powerful. It's my negative side, maybe, but it's also my positive stuff—and there's a lot of that. What it is is me, it's my self—and if I let people in maybe they'll take it, maybe they'll use it—and I'll be gone."… This "self," if I had to represent it I think of two things: either a steel rod that runs through everything, a kind of solid fiber, or sort of like a ball at the center that is all together. (Kegan, 1982, pp. 240–241)

The next stage in Fowler's model, **conjunctive faith,** requires an opening outward from the self-preoccupation of the individuative level. There is an openness here to paradox, a moving away from fixed truth toward a search for balance, not only of self and other but of mind and emotion, of rationality and ritual. The person who lives within this meaning system, which is not typically found before midlife, accepts that there are many truths, that others' beliefs, others' ideas, may be true for them—a point of view that not only brings far greater tolerance toward others but also very commonly brings the person to an interest in service or commitment to the welfare of others.

Here's one illustrative voice, that of Miss T., a 78-year-old woman who had been variously a Unitarian, a Quaker, and a follower of Krishnamurti and other Eastern teachers. When asked if there were beliefs and values everyone should hold she said:

> If somebody asked me that and gave me just two minutes to answer it, I know what I'd say. It's a line from George Fox, the founder of Quakerism. It's old-fashioned

English and it seems to me to have the entire program of anybody's life. Its a revolution, it's an enormous comfort, it's a peace maker. The line is: "There is that of God in every man." Now, you can start thinking about it. You can see that if you really did believe that, how it would change your relationships with people. It's far-reaching. It applies nationally and individually and class-wise; it reaches the whole. To anyone that I loved dearly I would say, "Put that in your little invisible locket and keep it forever." (Fowler, 1981, p. 194)

Other statements by Miss T. make it clear that the content of her faith at this point involves a kind of return to some of the elements of her earlier religious teachings, but she has reframed it, casting it in language that has meaning to her now and that focuses on finding fulfillment in service to others—all of which are significant elements of conjunctive faith.

The final proposed stage in Fowler's system he calls **universalizing faith.** Like Kohlberg's Stage 6, reaching this stage is a relatively rare achievement, but Fowler argues that it is the next logical step. To some extent it involves a step beyond individuality. In the stage of conjunctive faith the person may be "open" and "integrated" but is still struggling with the paradox of searching for universality while attempting to preserve individuality. In the stage of universalizing faith the person *lives* the principles, the imperatives, of absolute love and justice. Because such people live their lives based on such basic outward-oriented principles, they are heedless of their own self-preservation, much as Mother Theresa continued caring for the dying up until the end of her own life. They may even be seen by others as subversive to the structures of society or traditional religion, since they do not begin with the assumption that society or religion is necessarily correct in its institutions or customs. So Mahatma Gandhi, who based his later life on the basic principle that injustice should be eradicated from the world, was profoundly disruptive of the established social order.

Some Basic Points About Fowler's Stages. Some key points need emphasis. First, like Kohlberg, Fowler assumes that these stages occur in a sequence but that the sequence is only very roughly associated with age, especially in adulthood. Some adults remain within the same meaning system, the same faith structure, their entire lives, others make one or more transitions in their understandings of themselves and their relationships with others.

Second, Fowler nonetheless contends that each stage has its "proper time" of ascendancy in a person's lifetime, a period at which that particular form of faith is most consistent with the demands of life. Most typically, Stage 3 (conventional faith) is in its ascendance in adolescence or early adulthood, Stage 4 (individuative-reflective faith) in the years of the late 20s and 30s, while a transition to Stage 5 (conjunctive faith), if it occurs at all, may occur at approximately midlife. Finally, Stage 6, if one can reach it, would be the optimal form of faith in old age, when issues of integrity and meaning become still more dominant. Each stage, at its optimum time, has the "potential for wholeness, grace and integrity and or strengths sufficient for either life's blows or blessings" (Fowler, 1981, p. 274). But remaining at a particular stage of faith past the "proper" time or age may bring problems. This is a potentially testable assertion but one that has not yet been studied systematically.

Third, Fowler conceives of each stage as wider or more encompassing than the one that preceded it. And this greater breadth helps to foster both a greater capacity for a sense of sureness and serenity and a greater capacity for intimacy—with the self as well as with others.

Research Findings. No longitudinal data have yet been collected to test the sequential aspect of Fowler's theory. However, Fowler has reported some cross-sectional data that show the incidence of the stages of faith at each of several ages (see Figure

10.3). The data included in this figure came from several different studies in both the United States and Canada, all of which involved extensive open-ended interviews with teenagers and adults. The assignment of an overall stage of faith was based on raters reading the entire interview.

Since these are cross-sectional rather than longitudinal data, they do not tell us whether each person has moved through the proposed stages in the sequence Fowler describes. But the findings fit the theory reasonably well. Stage 3 (conventional) faith is most common in the teenage years, Stage 4 (individuative) peaks among those in their 20s, while Stage 5 (conjunctive faith) really emerges only in the 30s. Only one adult interviewed in any of these studies was placed at Stage 6, and he was a man in his 60s. Thus the stages appear to emerge in the order, and at the approximate ages, that Fowler suggests. Further, these data are consistent with the idea that not all adults continue to shift from one stage to the next. Among adults of 30 or older, Stages 3 and 4 are as common as Stage 5 faith.

Another study that offers consistent evidence comes from Gary Reker, who has developed a very similar model of the emergence of meaning systems over the years of adulthood. Reker (1991) argues that an adult can find meaning in life through any of a variety of sources, such as leisure activities, personal relationships, personal achievement, traditions and culture, altruism or service to others, or enduring values and ideals. Reker suggests that these various sources of meaning can be organized into four levels, beginning with "self-preoccupation," in which meaning is found primarily through financial security or meeting basic needs, to "individualism," in which meaning is found in personal

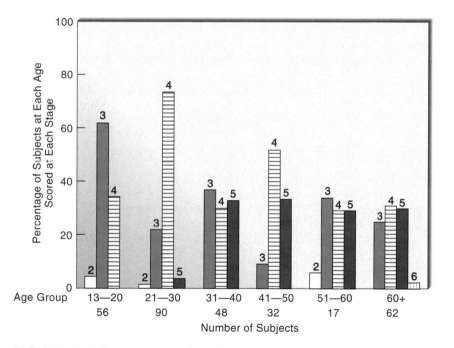

FIGURE 10.3 Cross-sectional information about stages of faith from studies in several cities. Fowler scores interview responses in half steps. To simplify, I have combined each half step with the stage above it. The findings suggest that Stage 3 is modal in the teenage years, with Stage 4 emerging strongly in the 20s. Stage 5 does not appear frequently until the 30s, all of which is consistent with Fowler's theory.

Source: Adapted from Fowler, 1981, Table B.3, p. 318.

growth or achievement, or through creative and leisure activities, to "collectivism," which includes meaning from traditions and culture and from societal causes, to "self-transcendence," in which meaning is found through enduring values and ideals, religious activities, and altruism.

In one cross-sectional study of 360 adults, Reker has found age differences in these four levels. The subjects were asked to rate on a seven-point scale how meaningful each of these areas were to them—leisure, personal achievement, and so on. He found that there were no differences between young (aged 18 to 29) and middle-aged (aged 30 to 59) adults as to the importance they placed on any of these dimensions, but both groups differed from the older adults (aged 60+) in this study in a number of ways. Older adults placed significantly more emphasis on both "collectivism" and "self-transcendent" meaning and less on personal achievement, which is part of "individualism." Figure 10.4 shows part of these results.

Reker's work does not provide a direct test of Fowler's model, but it is consistent with the basic idea that there may be systematic changes over the years of adulthood in the framework that adults use for defining themselves and finding meaning in their lives.

A Preliminary Assessment. Theories like Fowler's, and research like Reker's, supplement our thinking about adulthood in important ways, if only to help us focus on the importance of meaning systems and their possible sequential change with age. But it is still very early days in our empirical exploration of this and related theories. The greatest immediate need is for good longitudinal data, perhaps initially covering the years that are thought to be transitional for many adults, but ultimately for the entire adult age range.

INTEGRATING MEANING AND PERSONALITY: A PRELIMINARY THEORETICAL SYNTHESIS

No doubt some of the parallels between these several theories and those I discussed in Chapters 2 and 9 have already struck you. The surface similarities are obvious, as you can see in Table 10.2.

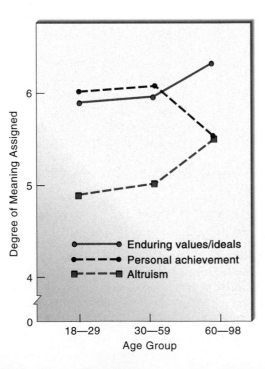

FIGURE 10.4 Adults were asked how meaningful each of 13 different areas of their lives are—such as financial security, personal growth, and traditions and culture. Age differences on three of these areas are shown here.

Source: Data from Reker, 1991, Table 6.

* Loevinger's conformist stage certainly sounds a great deal like both Kohlberg's conventional morality and Fowler's conventional faith. There seems to be agreement that in adolescence and early adulthood, people tend to be focused on adapting to the demands of the roles and relationships society imposes on them and assume that the source of authority is external.

* Loevinger's conscientious/individualistic stages sound a great deal like Maslow's layer of esteem needs, Kohlberg's early principled reasoning, and Fowler's individuative faith. All four theorists agree that the next step involves a shift in the central source of meaning or self-definition from external to internal, accompanied by a preoccupation with the self and one's own abilities, skills, and potentials.

* Loevinger's autonomous stage and Fowler's conjunctive faith are also similar, possibly related to self-actualization needs as described by Maslow. All speak of a shift away from self-preoccupation toward a search for balance, a shift toward greater tolerance toward both self and others.

* Finally, there seems to be agreement about some still-higher stage that involves some form of self-transcendence: Kohlberg's Stage 7, Fowler's stage of universalizing faith, Maslow's peak experiences.

Of course, we are not dealing with four independent visions here. These theorists all know of each other's work, have been influenced by each other's ideas. This is particularly true in the case of Fowler and Kohlberg, since Fowler's theory is quite explicitly an extension of Kohlberg's model. So the fact that they all seem to agree does not mean that we have uncovered "truth" here. However, my confidence in the validity of the basic sequence all these theorists describe is bolstered by three additional arguments:

First, although they have influenced one another, there are still three quite distinct theoretical heritages involved. Kohlberg's (and Fowler's) work is rooted in Piaget's theory and in studies of normal children's thinking; Loevinger's work is rooted in Freud's theory and in clinical assessments of children and adults, including those with emotional disturbances; Maslow's theory, although influenced by psychoanalytic thought, is based primarily on his own observations of a small number of highly unusual "self-actualized" adults. The fact that one can arrive at such similar views of the sequence of emergence of meaning systems from such different roots makes the convergence more impressive.

Second, in the case of both Kohlberg's and Loevinger's models, we have reasonably strong supporting empirical evidence, especially concerning the first step in

TABLE 10.2 **Synthesis and Summary of Stages of Personality, Moral, and Faith Development**

General Stage	Loevinger's Ego Development Stages	Maslow's Needs Hierarchy	Kohlberg's Stages of Moral Development	Fowler's Stages of Faith
Conformist or culture-bound self	Conformist; self-aware	Belongingness and love needs	Conventional morality	Synthetic-conventional
Individuality	Conscientious; individualistic	Self-esteem needs	First stage of principled morality (Stage 5)	Individuative
Integration	Autonomous and integrated	Self-actualized	Stage 6: universal ethical principles	Conjunctive
Self-transcendence	—	Some peak experiences	Stage 7: ethics based on unity	Universalizing

the commonly proposed adult sequence, of a move from conforming/conventional to individualistic. Transitions beyond that are simply much less well studied, in part because longitudinal studies have not yet followed adults past early midlife, perhaps in part because the later transitions are simply less common. Still, this is not all totally speculative stuff. We can anchor at least part of the commonly proposed basic sequence in hard data.

Finally, this basic model seems plausible to me because the sequence makes sense in terms of a still more encompassing developmental concept proposed by Robert Kegan (1982).

Kegan's Synthesizing Idea

Kegan proposes that each of us has two enormously powerful and equal desires or motives built in. On the one hand, we deeply desire to be **connected,** to be joined, to be integrated with others. On the other hand, we desire equally to be **independent,** differentiated from others. No accommodation between these two is really in balance, so whatever "evolutionary truce" (as Kegan calls each stage) we arrive at, it will lean further toward one than toward the other. Eventually, the unmet need becomes so strong that we are forced to change the system, to change our understanding. In the end, what this creates is a fundamental alternation, a moving back and forth of the pendulum, between perspectives or meaning systems centered around inclusion or union, and perspectives centered around independence or separateness.

The child begins life in a symbiotic relationship with the mother or mother figure, so the pendulum begins on the side of connection and union; by age 2 the child has pulled away and seeks independence, a separate identity. The conformist or conventional meaning system that we see in adolescence and early adulthood (if not later) is a move back toward connection, toward the group, while the transition to the individualistic meaning system is a return to separation and independence. The term *detribalization* that Levinson uses to describe one facet of the midlife transition fits nicely with Kegan's basic model. In shifting the source of authority from external sources to one's own resources, there is at least initially a pushing away of the tribe and all its rituals and rules.

If the model is correct, the step after this ought to be another return toward connection, which seems to me to be precisely what most of the theorists I have described have proposed. As I see it, most of them talk about two substeps in this shift of the pendulum, with Fowler's conjunctive faith or Kohlberg's Stage 6 being intermediate steps on the way toward the more complete position of union or community represented by universalizing faith or Kohlberg's Stage 7.

Although I have talked here as if the process were one of a pendulum moving back and forth, clearly Kegan is not proposing that movement is simply back and forth in a single groove. Instead, the process is more like that of a spiral in which each shift to the other "side" of the polarity is at a more integrated level than the one before.

If such a basic alternation, such a spiral movement, really does form the underlying rhythm of development, why should we assume that it stops even at so lofty a point as Kohlberg's Stage 7? When I first understood this aspect of Kegan's theory, I had one of those startling *ah ha!* experiences when I realized that the descriptions of the stages of the mystical "journey" given by Evelyn Underhill and by William James could be linked seamlessly with the sequence Kegan was describing.

I am well aware that describing such mystical experiences here will seem to some to be going very far afield, perhaps totally outside the realm of psychology. But to me the risk is worth it, not only because in

CRITICAL THINKING

Can you identify these two competing desires or motives in yourself? Does it seem reasonable to think of your own life in terms of alternating periods in which first one, then the other, of these desires dominated?

this way perhaps I can make a case for my own basic assumption regarding the immense potential of the individual human spirit, but also because the pattern that emerges fits so remarkably well with Kegan's model.

Stages of Mystical Experience

The stages I am describing here are those suggested by Evelyn Underhill (1911/1961) in her book *Mysticism,* based on her reading of autobiographies and biographies and other writings of the lives of hundreds of people from every religious tradition, all of whom described some form of **mysticism,** or self-transcendent experience. Not everyone described every one of the steps or stages listed, but Underhill reports that there was a remarkable degree of unanimity about the basic process, despite huge differences in historical period and religious background.

Step 1 in this process, which Underhill calls **awakening,** seems to me to correspond to the usual endpoint in theories such as Kohlberg's or Fowler's. It involves at least a brief self-transcendent experience, such as the peak experiences that Maslow describes. In Kegan's model, this step is clearly represented on the "union" end of the polarity; it is an awakening to the possibility of stepping outside one's own perspective and understanding the world from a point of deep connection.

Step 2, which Underhill calls **purification,** is clearly a move back toward separateness. The person, having "seen" himself or herself from a broader perspective, also sees all his or her own imperfections, fruitless endeavors, and flaws. As St. Teresa of Avila, one of the great mystics of the Christian tradition puts it: "In a room bathed in sunlight not a cobweb can remain hidden" (1562/1960, p. 181). To understand and eliminate those flaws, those cobwebs, the person must turn inward again. At this stage many people are strongly focused on self-discipline, including special spiritual disciplines such as regular prayer or meditation, fasting, or the like.

Step 3 clearly moves us back toward union. Underhill calls this the stage of **illumination.** It involves a much deeper, more prolonged awareness of light, or greater reality, or God, and may in fact encompass some of what Kohlberg refers to as Stage 7. In Plato's metaphor of the cave, this is the step in which the individual, after realizing that the figures on the wall of the cave are only shadows, and after struggling to find the mouth of the cave, finally steps outside into the sun. This is accompanied by deep joy.

But even this illumination is not the end of the journey. Underhill finds two other steps described by many mystics that appear to lie beyond. The first of these, often called the dark night of the soul, involves a still further turn inward, back toward separateness. At the stage of illumination, the person still feels some personal satisfaction, some personal pleasure or joy in having achieved illumination. According to mystics who have described these later stages, if one is to achieve ultimate union, even this personal pleasure must be abandoned. And the process of abandonment requires a turning back to the self, to awareness of, and exploration of, all the remaining ways in which the separate self has survived. Only then can the person achieve the endpoint, that of union—with God, with reality, with beauty, with the ultimate—however this may be described within a particular religious tradition.

I cannot say, of course, whether this sequence, this spiral of inner human progress, reflects the inevitable or ultimate path for us all. I can say only that the developmental analyses of stages of morality, or stages of faith or personality that have been offered by many psychologists, for which we have at least some preliminary supporting evidence, appear to form a connected whole with the descriptions of stages of mystical illumination. At the very least, we know that a pathway similar to this has been trod by a long series of remarkable individuals, whose descriptions of their inner journeys bear striking similarities. There may be many other paths or journeys. But the reflections of these remarkable few point the way toward the possibility of a far vaster potential of the human spirit than is apparent to most of us in our daily humdrum lives.

THE PROCESS OF TRANSITION

Coming down a bit from these lofty levels but still assuming for the moment that there *is* some basic rhythm, some developmental sequence, in the forms of meaning we create, let me turn to the question that may be of special personal importance: What is the process by which **transitions** or transformations from one stage to the next take place? What triggers them? What are the common features of transitions? How are they traversed?

Most developmental psychologists who propose stages of adult development have focused more on the stages than on the transition process. But there are some common themes in the ways that transitions are described.

A number of theorists have described transitions in parallel terms, with each shift from one "level" or "stage" to the next seen as a kind of death and rebirth—a death of the earlier sense of self, of the earlier faith, of the earlier equilibrium (W. James, 1902/1958; D. Johnson, 1983; Kegan, 1980). The process typically involves first some glimpses or precursors or premonitions of another stage or view, which are then followed by a period (which may be brief or prolonged) in which the person struggles to deal with these two "selves" within. Sometimes the process is aborted and the person returns to the earlier equilibrium. Sometimes the person moves instead toward a new understanding, a new equilibrium. There is, as William Bridges (1980) puts it simply and clearly, first an ending, then a middle, and then a beginning.

The middle part of this process, when the old meaning system has been partially given up but a new equilibrium has not yet been reached, is often experienced as profoundly dislocating. Sentences such as "I am beside myself" or "I was out of my mind" may be used (Kegan, 1980). And like the transitions I described in Chapter 9, the process of equilibration may be accompanied by an increase in physical or psychological symptoms of various kinds, including depression.

Kegan perhaps best summarizes the potential pain of the process: "Development is costly—for everyone, the developing person and those around him or her. Growth involves a separation from an old system of meaning. In practical terms this can involve both the agony of felt meaninglessness and the repudiation of commitments and investment. . . Developmental theory gives us a way of thinking about such pain that does not pathologize it" (1980, p. 439). Such transitions may emerge slowly or may occur rapidly; they may be the result of self-chosen activities, such as therapy or exercise, the happenstances of ordinary life, or from unexpected experiences. In Table 10.3 I have suggested some of the stimulants for such transitions, organized around what appear to be the three most frequent adult transitions: (1) from conformity to individuality, (2) from individuality to integration or conjunctive faith, and (3) from integration to self-transcendence. I offer this list quite tentatively. We clearly lack the longitudinal evidence that might allow us to say more fully what experiences may or may not stimulate a transition.

You can see in the table that I am suggesting that somewhat different experiences may be involved in each of these three transitions. Attending college or moving away from home into a quite different community seem to be particularly influential in promoting aspects of the transition to individuality. For example, in longitudinal studies, both Kohlberg (1973) and Rest and Thoma (1985) have found a correlation between the amount of college education completed and the level of moral reasoning. Principled reasoning was found only in those who had attended at least some college. This transition, then, seems to be precipitated by exposure to other assumptions, other faiths, other perspectives. Such a confrontation can produce disequilibrium, which may be dealt with by searching for a new, independent, self-chosen model.

CRITICAL THINKING

Think about the last point in your life you would label as a "transition." Did it follow the pattern Bridges suggests: having an ending, a middle, and then a beginning?

TABLE IO.3 **Transitions from One Stage to Another: Some Possible Triggering Situations of Experiences That May Assist in Passing Through a Transition**

Specific Transition	Intentional Activities That May Foster That Transition	Unintentional or Circumstantial Events That May Foster That Transition
From conformist to individualistic	Therapy; reading about other religions or faiths	Attending college; leaving home for other reasons, such as job or marriage; usual failures or reversals while "following the rules"; development of personal or professional skills
From individualistic to integrated	Therapy; introspection; short-term programs to heighten self-awareness (e.g., Gestalt workshops)	Illness or prolonged pain; death in the family or prolonged crisis; peak experiences
From integrated to self-transcendent	Meditation or prayer; various forms of yoga; self-disciplines	Near-death experience; transcendent experiences such as peak or immediate mystical experiences

I have also suggested that therapy may play some role in triggering or assisting with either of the first two transitions. In fact, helping a client to achieve full integration is the highest goal of many humanistically oriented therapies, such as those based on the work of Carl Rogers or Fritz Perls. But my hypothesis is that traditional forms of therapy do little to assist the transition from integrated person to a level of self-transcendence. This transition, I think, requires or is assisted by a different form of active process, such as meditation or other forms of yoga or systematic prayer (LeShan, 1966).

Both painful experiences and transcendent ones can also be the occasion for a new transition. The death of a child or of a parent may reawaken our concern with ultimate questions of life and death. A failed marriage or discouragement at work may lead to questioning or to a loss of the sense of stability of one's present model. Peak experiences, too, by giving glimpses of something not readily comprehensible within a current view, may create a disequilibrium. Most adults who have had a "near death experience," for example, report that their lives are never again the same. Many change jobs or devote their lives to service in one way or another. Other forms of peak experiences or religious "rebirth" may have the same effect.

I have been consistently using the word *may* in the last few paragraphs to convey the fact that such life changes do not invariably result in significant reflection or decentering. In an argument reminiscent of the concept of scheduled and unscheduled changes, Patricia Gurin and Orville Brim (1984) have offered an interesting hypothesis to explain such differences in the impact of major life changes. In essence, they argue that widely shared, age-linked changes are not likely to trigger significant reassessments of the sense of self precisely because expected changes are interpreted differently than are unexpected ones. Shared changes are most often attributed to causes outside oneself, for which one is not personally responsible. In contrast, unique or off-time life changes are more likely to lead to significant inner reappraisals precisely because it is difficult to attribute such experiences to outward causes. If everyone at your job has been laid off because the company has gone out of business during a recession, you need not reassess your own sense of self worth. But if you are the only one fired during a time of expanding economy, it is much more difficult to maintain your sense of worth.

Some shared experiences, such as college, may commonly trigger reappraisals or restructuring of personality, moral judgment, or faith. But most age-graded experiences can be absorbed fairly readily into existing systems. It may then be the unique or mistimed experiences that are particularly significant for changes in meaning systems. This hypothesis remains to be tested but raises some intriguing issues.

COMMENTARY AND CONCLUSIONS

For me, one of the striking things about the information I have presented in this chapter is that it is possible to find such similar descriptions emerging from such different traditions. But let me say again that the fact that there is a great deal of apparent unanimity in the theoretical (and personal) descriptions of development of moral judgment, meaning systems, motive hierarchies, and spiritual evolution does not make this shared view true.

It does seem fair to say that most adults are engaged in some process of creating or searching for meaning in their lives. But this is not necessarily—perhaps not commonly—a conscious, deliberate process. Some adults appear to engage in a conscious search, and their descriptions of the process are remarkably similar. But as I pointed out earlier, this may or may not mean that such a search, or even a nonconscious, or nonintentional, sequence of faiths, is a "natural" or essential part of adult development.

Furthermore, it is important to realize that all of what I have said and all of what these various theorists have said is based on a single metaphor of development, the metaphor of "life as a journey" (a kind of Pilgrim's Progress). We imagine the adult trudging up some hill or along some road, passing through steps or stages as he or she moves along. Implicit in this metaphor is the concept of a goal, an endpoint or *telos* (a Greek word from which our word *teleological* comes, meaning having purpose or moving toward a goal). This is a journey *going somewhere*. And if the purpose of the journey is thought of as "growth" or "evolution," we must have some concept of "highest growth."

The linearity and teleology of this journey metaphor may well limit our thinking about changes in adult meaning systems. Sam Keen (1983) suggests several other ways in which we might think of the process, two of which I find particularly appealing:

1. "When we think of this eternal dimension of our being, the circle is more appropriate than the line. If life is a journey, then, it is not a pilgrimage but an odyssey in which one leaves and returns home again" (p. 31). Each step may be a circling back, a remembering of the "still point" within (to use poet T. S. Eliot's phrase). Progressively, we understand or "know" ourselves and our world differently with each movement of the circle, but there is no necessary endpoint.

2. We could also think of the entire process as "musical themes that weave together to form a symphony; the themes that are central to each stage are anticipated in the previous stage and remain as resonant subthemes in subsequent stages" (p. 32). Still another possible metaphor is that of life as a tapestry, in which one weaves many colors. A person who creates many different meaning systems or faiths may thus be weaving a tapestry with more colors, but it may be no more beautiful or pleasing than a tapestry woven intricately of fewer colors.

The basic point I am trying to make here is a simple one, although often hard to absorb thoroughly: Our theories are based in part on metaphors. We begin our search for understanding of adult development with such a metaphor and it colors all of what we choose to examine and all of what we see. The journey metaphor has dominated most of the current thinking, but it is not the only way to think about the process.

If we are to understand this process further, if we are to choose among these several metaphors, what we need is a great deal more empirical information to answer questions such as the following. First, is there a longitudinal progression through Fowler's stages of faith or through equivalent sequences proposed by others, such as Loevinger's stages of ego development? I pointed out in Chapter 9 that Loevinger's theory is at least roughly consistent with some of the evidence from existing longitudinal studies. But more direct tests are needed.

Second, what are the connections, if any, between movement through the several sequences described by the various theorists? If we measure a given person's moral reasoning, his stage of ego development in Loevinger's model, and his type of faith, will that person be at the same stage in all three? And when a person shifts in one area, does he shift across the board? Alternatively, might integration occur only at the final steps, at the level of what Loevinger calls the integrated person? Just as was proposed in the timing models I described in Chapter 2, each sequence may develop somewhat independently. Disequilibrium may be created when two or more sequences are significantly out of synchrony, thus triggering further moves toward overall integration.

THE METAPHOR of the journey, often depicted as a movement up an apparently endless flight of stairs, is at the root of many theories of adult personality or meaning development. But the journey metaphor is not the only one we might adopt and may be misleading in its strong emphasis on both linearity and on a clear goal.

We do not yet have the evidence that would allow us to choose among these alternatives, but several existing studies point to at least some consistency across the sequences. For example, measures of Loevinger's ego development and moral reasoning are typically found to be correlated moderately, in the range of $r = 0.50$ (Loevinger, 1984; Sullivan, McCullough, & Stager, 1970), although several studies of adults in their 20s show much lower correlations (Commons et al., 1989; King, Kitchener, Wood, & Davison, 1989). Similarly, Leean (1985) reports a moderate relationship between scores on a measure of stage of faith development and on a measure of extent of completion of Erikson's stages. Data from still another study suggest a link between postconventional or principled moral reasoning (Level 3 in Kohlberg's system) and "openness to experience," which we might take as an aspect of the shift to individualistic/integrated stages (Lonky et al., 1984). But these are merely the first whiffs of evidence. Much more is needed.

Third, assuming that longitudinal data confirm that there are stages of meaning making, we need to know what prompts a shift from one to the next. What supports a transition? What retards it? Finally, we need to know more about a possible connection between stages of faith (or models of meaning, or constructions of the self) and a sense of well-being, or greater physical health, or greater peace of mind. Reker's study suggests such a link; he found a small but significant correlation between the extent to which subjects placed emphasis on "self-transcendent" meaning and their degree of psychological well-being. My own further hypothesis is that adults might experience greater happiness or satisfaction with their lives when they exist within a meaning system that lies at the "union" end of the dichotomy than when they are embedded in any of the more self-oriented stages. To check this hypothesis, is it not enough to look at changes with age in life satisfaction (although that is interesting for other reasons). Rather, one must measure stages of faith or stages of ego development (preferably longitudinally) and examine life satisfaction at the same time.

No longitudinal study fits this bill, but one cross-sectional study goes part way. Costa and McCrae (1983) measured ego development stages using Loevinger's Sentence Completion Test, assessed extraversion and neuroticism, and asked each of nearly 1000 men about his feeling of well-being. Among these men aged 35 to 85, the researchers found no overall correlation between ego development and a sense of well-being, but they did not check for the possibility of alternating higher and lower levels of well-being.

Answers to some of these questions may be forthcoming in the next decades, as researchers devise better ways to measure and explore these elusive dimensions of adult lives. For now, much of what I have said in this chapter remains tantalizing and intriguing speculation—but speculation that nonetheless points toward the potential for wisdom, compassion, even illumination within each adult.

SUMMARY

1. In addition to studying inner development by examining personality change over adulthood, we can also ask about changes in meaning systems, faith, or spirituality.

2. It is important to study personal meaning systems for several reasons, including the impact of any given experience is mediated by the meaning we attach to it; adults place the search for meaning high in their list of life goals; some aspects of meaning systems, particularly religious/spiritual involvement, are linked to health, longevity, and psychological well-being.

3. Changes in formal religious participation with age may be one way to assess changes in meaning systems or values. Church attendance appears to rise steadily through adult life, with a decline only in late old age. That late-life decline is, however, compensated by an increase in private religious practices, suggesting that the overall increase in religiosity with age continues throughout adulthood.

4. Theories of the development of systems of meaning have been strongly influenced by Kohlberg's theory of the development of moral reasoning. Kohlberg describes three sequentially achieved levels of moral reasoning, with two stages at each level. Level 1 is preconventional reasoning, in which right is understood as that which brings pleasure or approval. Level 2 is conventional reasoning, in which right or justice is defined by the rules or mores of the family, and later of society. Level 3 is postconventional or principled reasoning, in which right or justice is defined by appeal to a set of principles that lie behind social customs or laws.

5. Kohlberg also proposes a final stage, Stage 7, which involves a form of self-transcendence, a sense of unity with being or life.

6. Longitudinal data show that teenagers and young adults do move through these stages, without skipping, and with little indication of regression. In adults, conventional reasoning is most common. The sequence has been found in every culture studied thus far.

7. Fowler's theory of faith development is broader in concept than Kohlberg's model, encompassing the ways in which adults explain to themselves the purpose of life. Fowler proposes six stages, of which the final four are characteristic of adulthood: synthetic-conventional, marked by external sources of authority; individuative-reflective, in which the source of authority is seen as within the self; conjunctive, which involves an integration of mind and emotion; and universalizing, which goes beyond individuality to a sense of universal connectedness.

8. Cross-sectional data are consistent with Fowler's theory, with Stages 3, 4, and 5 first found at approximately the points in adult life that he proposes. Among adults, however, Stages 3, 4, and 5 are all about equally common.

9. Integration of Kohlberg's and Fowler's theories with those of Loevinger and Maslow suggests a common set of stages, moving first from conformity to external authority and external self-definition toward individuation and then toward universalizing or self-transcendent meaning systems.

10. This sequence can be understood in terms of Kegan's proposal that the underlying rhythm of development is a basic alternation between the motive for union and the motive for separateness or individuality.

11. Descriptions by mystics of the stages of inner illumination appear to follow the same underlying rhythm.

12. Transitions from one stage to the next in this progression are frequently experienced in terms of loss or "death" of the old self or the old view. Transitions may thus be profoundly dislocating.

13. Transitions may be triggered by unique life changes, by suffering, by peak experiences, by intentionally pursued self-knowledge, or by self-disciplines.

14. To move beyond the speculative aspect of these theories, additional longitudinal and cross-sectional data will be required.

KEY TERMS

world view

internal model

preconventional level

punishment-and-
obedience orientation

naive hedonism

conventional level

good boy or good girl
orientation

social-order-maintaining
morality

postconventional (or
principled) level

social contract
orientation

individual principles of
conscience orientation

process of decentering

faith

synthetic-conventional
faith

individuative-reflective
faith

conjunctive faith

universalizing faith

connection

independence

mysticism

awakening

purification

illumination

dark night of the soul

unity

transitions

SUGGESTED READINGS

Given my obvious interest in this area, you will not be surprised that I have a long list of
books to recommend to you. Any of these would be provocative.

Birren, J. E., & Feldman, L. (1997). *Where to go from here: Discovering your own life's wisdom in the second half of your life.* New York: Simon & Schuster.

> James Birren is a pioneer in the field of successful aging and most familiar for his
> scholarly writing. But in this book he introduces his technique of guided autobiog-
> raphy to help older adults take stock of their past and find meaning in their future.

Fowler, J. (1981). *Stages of faith.* New York: Harper & Row.

> You may find the case material he gives as fascinating as the theory.

Frankl, V. E. (1984). *Man's search for meaning* (3rd ed). New York: Simon & Schuster.

> Frankl is a psychiatrist who came to the conclusion that an understanding of a pa-
> tient's model of meaning was the key to any successful therapy. The roots of this con-
> clusion came from his own experience in a concentration camp. He describes both
> in this book.

James, W. (1902). *The varieties of religious experience.* New York: Mentor. (Mentor edition
published 1958)

> I find this a delightful book, remarkably free of the convoluted style that otherwise
> seems to be common in this area.

Kegan, R. (1982). *The evolving self.* Cambridge, MA: Harvard University Press.

> Kegan, too, has been influenced by Kohlberg. You may find the case material par-
> ticularly interesting in this book.

Levin, J. S. (1994). Investigating the epidemiological effects of religious experience.
Findings, explanations, and barriers. In J. S. Levin (Ed.), *Religion in aging and health*
(pp. 3–17). Thousand Oaks, CA: Sage.

A very interesting paper reviewing not only what we know about the relationship between religious participation and health, but also considering some of the alternative explanations for this link as well as the various reasons why social scientists have so long shied away from exploring these questions.

St. Theresa of Avila (1577). *Interior castle* (E. Allison Peers, Trans.) Garden City, NY: Image Books. (Image Books edition published 1960)

Many experts consider St. Theresa's several descriptions of her inner spiritual journey to be the most complete and comprehensible available. I found it astonishing: delightfully written, provocative, and stimulating.

Underhill, E. (1911). *Mysticism.* New York: E.P. Dutton. (Dutton edition published 1961)

This book is a scholarly tour de force. Underhill has combined and distilled the essence of the reports of hundreds of mystics and other religious teachers, from all religious traditions, into a single coherent account. Her style is clear and straightforward.

DEALING WITH THE STRESSES OF ADULT LIFE

CHAPTER 11

There may be a few exceptionally lucky people in this world who rarely face crises, upheavals, or loss. But most of us encounter these experiences regularly. I consider my own adult years to have been comparatively crisis free, but in the 35 years since I turned 20, I have gone through the usual failed love affairs, a divorce, 16 moves, seven or eight job changes, several minor car accidents, assorted small surgeries and the usual collection of illnesses, and the death of a close friend and of two grandparents. I have also twice been the victim of a crime. Most people have doubtless had to cope with far more.

As I have pointed out all along, some crises and upheavals are predictable and are quite widely shared by adults as they move through the various normative roles and stages. But many experiences, or their timing, are unique to each individual. If we are to understand the various pathways through adulthood that a person may take, we need to look at the effect of such stresses on adults. We also need to look at those qualities of adults, or their environments, that may soften or shorten the effect of stress.

Fortunately, the study of stress has been a hot research topic for some years, so there is an extensive literature, and I have discussed some of the new findings in Chapter 4. Less fortunately, very little of the research is developmental in conception or design. Nonetheless, some extremely interesting concepts and provocative findings have emerged that expand our understanding of the ways that adults cope with life experiences.

DEFINITIONS OF STRESS

Let me begin by defining the term *stress*. Writing a definition would be a simple task if there were agreement among stress researchers. But at this stage there are still at least three types of definitions, each associated with a different body of theory and research: response-oriented theories, stimulus-oriented theories, and interactionist theories.

Response-Oriented Theories

The founder of modern stress research, Hans Selye (1936; 1976; 1982), defines stress as "the nonspecific (that is, common) result of any demand upon the body, be the effect mental or somatic" (1982, p. 7). That is, stress is the body's *response* to demand. The more demands there are on a person—demands from roles, from environmental hazards such as heat or noise, from time pressures, and so on—the stronger the stress response.

According to Selye, the body's stress reaction occurs in three stages, which he calls collectively the **general adaptation syndrome** (GAS). First comes the **alarm reaction,** which has two phases. In the **shock phase** there is an initial, immediate effect of some noxious stimulus on the body's tissues, marked by such indicators as a drop in both body temperature and blood pressure. Then there is a **countershock phase** in which some kind of physiological defenses are mounted. The adrenal cortex enlarges and secretes higher levels of hormones, and the body temperature and blood pressure move back toward normal levels. If the stressor continues, these alarm reactions fade and are replaced by a stage that Selye calls **resistance,** in which the body strives to achieve normality, or homeostasis. One particularly notable physical change in this stage is the shrinkage of the thymus gland, which is important because the thymus is centrally involved in immune responses. Thus in this phase the person is able to control the initial alarm reaction to the stressor but does so in a way that lowers resistance to other stressors or stimuli. If the stressor continues long enough (and many chronic stressors do continue over very long periods of time), the somewhat fragile adaptation of the resistance phase breaks down and the person reaches the stage of **exhaustion,** when some of the alarm-stage responses reappear. If the stressor is severe enough, exhaustion is accompanied by physical illness or even death.

Furthermore, Selye specifically postulates that the return to "rest" after the stressor has stopped and the GAS is terminated is never complete. One *almost* gets back to the old level but not quite. The process we call aging may thus simply be the accumulation of the effects of many GASs, each leaving a residue of effects on the hormone system, the cardiovascular system, the immune system.

Selye's definition of stress has prompted a great deal of useful research, primarily by physicians and physiologists who have attempted to identify the specific physiological patterns that are part of the stress response or GAS. In particular, the very exciting new research on the impact of stress on the immune system owes much to Selye's work. But I suspect that Selye's definition of *stress* does not match your own everyday use of the word. Normally, when we say "Joan has been under a lot of stress lately," or "I must have gotten this cold because I'm really stressed out," we are referring not to our body's reaction to an external event, but to the external event itself—to the outside stimulus and not the inner response. This is the approach taken by the next set of theorists.

Stimulus-Oriented Theories

Some psychologists define stress in terms of the degree of environmental demand the person is experiencing. For a researcher using such a definition of stress, the task is to specify just what classes of events are stressful and what the effects of that stress may be on the individual.

A number of different lists of stresses have been developed, one of the earliest and most widely used of which is the **Social Readjustment Rating Scale** developed by Thomas Holmes and Richard Rahe (1967). It consists of the 42 **life-change events** listed in Table 11.1. The basic idea is that any change, be it positive or negative, requires adaptation. The more changes, the more the adaptation. Because some life changes are more profound or severe than others, Holmes and Rahe assigned different numbers of points to each life change to reflect the degree of adaptation it appeared to require. A subject's score on this instrument is thus the sum of the points for all the changes that he or she checks off as having occurred during the past six to 12 months. Holmes and Rahe hypothesized that the higher the score, the greater the likelihood that the person would become physically ill or emotionally disturbed within the next year. In particular, a score over 200 predicts a moderate crisis, and 300 predicts a major crisis and sharply increased chance of a stress-induced illness.

There is a great deal of research evidence supporting Holmes and Rahe's original hypothesis (which I'll describe shortly). At the same time, serious questions have been raised about this definition of stress and this method of measurement (G. W. Brown, 1989; L.

TABLE II.I **Life-Change Events Included in the Holmes and Rahe Social Readjustment Rating
Scale**

Life Event	Points Assigned
1. Death of a spouse	100
2. Divorce	73
3. Marital separation from mate	65
4. Detention in jail or other institution	63
5. Death of a close family member	63
6. Major personal injury or illness	53
7. Marriage	50
8. Being fired at work	47
9. Marital reconciliation with mate	45
10. Retirement from work	45
11. Major change in the health or behavior of a family member	44
12. Pregnancy	40
13. Sexual difficulties	39
14. Gaining a new family member (e.g., through birth, adoption, elder moving in, etc.)	39
15. Major business readjustment (e.g., merger, reorganization, bankruptcy, etc.)	39
16. Major change in financial state (a lot worse off or a lot better off than usual)	38
17. Death of a close friend	37
18. Changing to a different line of work	36
19. Major change in the number of arguments with spouse (more of less)	35
20. Taking out a mortgage or loan for a major purchase	31
21. Foreclosure on a mortgage or loan	30
22. Major change in responsibilities at work (e.g., promotion, demotion, lateral transfer)	29
23. Son or daughter leaving home	29
24. Trouble with in-laws	29
25. Outstanding personal achievement	28
26. Wife beginning or ceasing work outside the home	26
27. Beginning or ceasing formal schooling	26
28. Major change in living conditions (e.g., building a new home, remodeling, deterioration of home or neighborhood)	25
29. Revision of personal habits (dress, manners, associations, etc.)	24
30. Trouble with the boss	23
31. Major change in working hours or conditions	20
32. Change in residence	20
33. Change to a new school	20
34. Major change in usual type and/or amount of recreation	19
35. Major change in church activities (e.g., a lot more or a lot less than usual)	19
36. Major change in social activities (e.g., clubs, dancing, movies, visiting, etc.)	18
37. Taking out a mortgage or loan for a lesser purchase (e.g., for a car, TV set, freezer, etc.)	17
38. Major change in sleeping habits (a lot more or a lot less sleep, or change in part of day when asleep)	16
39. Major change in number of family get-togethers (e.g., a lot more or a lot less than usual)	15
40. Major change in eating habits (a lot more or a lot less food intake, or very different meal hours or surroundings)	15
41. Vacation	13
42. Christmas	12
43. Minor violations of the law (e.g., traffic tickets, jaywalking, disturbing the peace, etc.)	11

Source: Reprinted with permission from T. S. Holmes and T. H. Holmes, Short term intrusions into life-style routine. *Journal of Psychosomatic Research,* 14, 121–132. Copyright 1970, Pergamon Press, Ltd.
(Original publication of the Social Readjustment Rating Scale appeared in the *Journal of Psychosomatic Research, 11,* 1967, pp. 213–218. Copyright 1967, Pergamon Press, Ltd.)

H. Cohen, 1988b). First of all, it is not so obvious that all kinds of life change are equivalent in their stress-producing effects. Are positive life changes and negative life changes really equally stressful? And even among life changes that may be classed as negative, are there some subvarieties that are more stress-producing or more likely to lead to illness than others? And what about events that can be positive in one situation (pregnancy to a long-married couple who have been trying to conceive for a few years) and negative in another (pregnancy to an unmarried teenage girl)?

With these questions in mind, several researchers have suggested subcategories of life changes or stress experiences that may prove to be more helpful predictors of illness than the original Holmes and Rahe list. For example, Pearlin (1980; 1982b) makes a distinction between **chronic life strains** and life changes. And as you will remember from earlier chapters, he distinguishes between **scheduled life changes** and **unscheduled life changes**.

Richard Lazarus and his colleagues (Lazarus & Folkman, 1984) similarly suggest that we will better understand the links between stress and illness if we count not just major life changes, but also **daily hassles** and **daily uplifts**. Hassles, which may be transient or chronic, include such familiar experiences as misplacing your keys, having to fill out forms, finding you've gained a pound when you step on the scales in the morning, or getting caught in a traffic jam on your way to an important meeting. Uplifts may include laughter, pleasant times with your family, or other joyous or satisfying moments. Some research has shown that hassles are better predictors than major life events of anxiety, depression, and other psychological symptoms (Kanner, Coyne, Schaefer, & Lazarus, 1981). In fact, Lazarus argues that the reason the large events affect our mental and physical health is that they produce so many little hassles. There is some evidence for this in at least one study by Pillow, Zautra, and Sandler (1996), who found that people who have recently experienced a traumatic event have more hassles than people who have not had recent trauma.

Another question raised about defining stress only in terms of major life changes is whether there are cultural differences in the way that people experience stress? What is stressful in the United States might not be in another culture. For example, one recent study in China indicates that the single most common stressful event in that culture was being "misunderstood or berated" (Zheng & Lin, 1994)—a stress that does not appear on the Holmes and Rahe list at all. Chinese women also reported high rates of problems with their mothers-in-law, and both these types of stress were strongly linked to well-being among the Chinese subjects.

Furthermore, even within a given culture, different individuals may interpret the same event differently. For an actor whose work pattern involves regular layoffs, losing a job may not have the same stressful effect as it would for a blue-collar worker who has had the same job for 25 years. Arguments like these have led many investigators to the conclusion that the crucial factor is likely to be the person's subjective interpretation (which Lazarus calls an **appraisal**) of an event, not the objective event itself. In the terms I used in chapter 10, perhaps it is the *meaning* we assign to some event itself, rather than the event, that determines both our psychological and physiological reactions to it (G. W. Brown, 1989). Questions of this kind have led to a third, interactionist, view of stress.

Interactionist Approaches

Interactionist definitions of stress focus on the person's perception of an event, or on the extent to which some experience exceeds a person's ability to adapt. For example, stress may be defined as "a (perceived) imbalance between demand and response capability, under conditions where failure to meet demand has important (perceived) consequences" (McGrath,

1970, p. 20), or as "a particular relationship between the person and the environment that is appraised by the person as taxing or exceeding his or her resources and endangering his or her well-being" (Lazarus & Folkman, 1984, p. 19).

Looked at this way, stress is neither located solely in the environment nor in the body; rather, the physiological GAS is mediated by the person's perception or appraisal of a situation. Thus when a person says "I'm really under stress," this is not an objective statement about some amount of external pressure but a statement about that person's sense of strain or difficulty in coping with the pressures that he or she experiences. Only when a person feels unable to cope with a demand would we expect some potential stressor to trigger the general adaptation syndrome and thus be related to disease or emotional disturbance. Exactly the same environmental event might therefore be "stressful" to one person and not to another.

What do you mean when you say "I'm really stressed?" Which of these various models of stress best fits your everyday use of the term?

A Combined View

My own leanings are toward an interactionist approach, but I would add still further elements, such as a person's temporary or long-term vulnerability (such as might accompany a lack of social supports), and the repertoire of coping skills that he or she can bring to the situation. Figure 11.1 shows this system schematically.

Note that age does not appear in this figure, but age or developmental stage might affect the stress response system at any one of several points. Adults of different ages may be exposed to different types or number of potentially stressful experiences. Or, as they move through the life span, their meaning systems may change, so that they interpret, or appraise, life changes differently. Adults may become more skilled at coping with the stressful experiences they encounter as they get older. Most of the research I'll be talking about is not cast in such a developmental framework, but there are at least some bits and pieces that I will weave into the discussion as we move along.

Let me begin the exploration of the elements in this system by looking at the most studied portion of the figure, the link between potentially stressful experiences and illness.

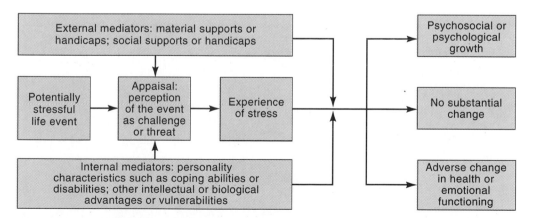

FIGURE II.I First approximation of a model describing the link between stress and adverse or positive changes during adulthood. Whether or not some potentially stressful life event, such as a major life change or an accumulation of daily hassles, will lead to illness depends on how a person perceives the event, whether that person has adequate support to help meet the stress, and the specific coping strategies the person uses.

Source: Adapted and modified from a similar model by Dohrenwend & Dohrenwend, 1980, Fig. 1.1, p. 2.

EFFECTS OF STRESSFUL EXPERIENCES ON ADULT FUNCTIONING

Physical Illness

The research examining the links between stress and disease has involved a variety of measures of stress, ranging from lists of potentially stressful life events, such as the one in Table 11.1, to much more elaborate interviews in which the person's own interpretation of the event is measured as well. But the common finding is quite clear: The more stress a person has encountered within the past six to 12 months, whether measured in number life changes, hassles versus uplifts, or the like, the greater the likelihood of physical illness. This does not mean that if you have a score above 300 on the Holmes and Rahe scale, you will automatically get sick. It does mean that the risk of illness rises. Similarly, among people who have already contracted some specified disease, such as cancer, high levels of life changes or experience of stress are linked to poorer prognosis. Let me give you some specific examples:

* In a Swedish study, Rosengren, Orth-Gomér, Wedel, and Wilhelmsen (1993) interviewed a large group of 50-year-old men (all born in 1933). At the first interview, each man was asked whether each of 10 major negative life events had occurred in his life in the past year (e.g., death of family member, divorce or separation, loss of job, forced job change, etc.). Rosengren and her colleagues then looked at rates of death for the men over the succeeding seven years. Figure 11.2 shows the main result: a remarkably consistent relationship between risk of death and number of negative life changes experienced.

* A German study shows that among women interviewed before surgery for suspicious breast lumps, those later diagnosed with malignancies describe four times as many severe life events in the preceding eight years as did those whose lumps were later diagnosed as benign (Geyer, 1993).

* An experimental study in which volunteers were given nasal drops containing cold viruses (S. Cohen, Tyrrell, & Smith, 1991, 1993) provides the most powerful

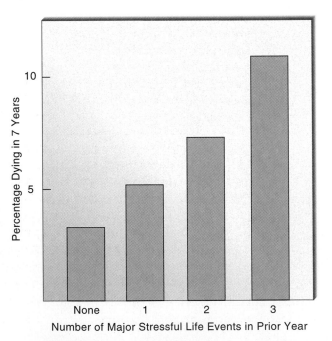

FIGURE 11.2 In this longitudinal study in Sweden, the risk of a middle-aged man's dying over a seven-year period was clearly linked to the number of stressful life events he had experienced immediately prior to the seven-year period.

Source: Data from Rosengren, Orth-Gomér, Wedel, & Wilhelmsen, 1993, Table 1, p. 1103.

evidence yet: The higher the subject's reported level of stress, whether measured by negative life-change events, perceived stress level, or negative feelings, the higher the likelihood that the subject would actually become infected with a cold. Figure 11.3 shows the main result—a remarkably clear relationship between the "dose" of stress and the likelihood of disease.

* Jane Leserman and her colleagues (1997) have some of the only longitudinal evidence that links stress and depressive symptoms with reduced immune function in gay men with positive HIV diagnoses. As part of the Coping in Health and Illness Project at the University of North Carolina at Chapel Hill, Leserman interviewed 66 men who had been diagnosed with the HIV virus but had no symptoms of AIDS. These men were interviewed again at six-month intervals for two years, examining the amount of non-disease-related stress in their lives and also monitoring their immune function. Those with the most stress at any six-month interval showed a reduction of immune system functioning (a reduced number of natural killer cells and one type of T-cell).

* Women who have been diagnosed with breast cancer showed higher levels of immune system functioning when they participated in a support group that included stress reduction exercises and techniques to better cope with social and emotional stress in their lives (Andersen et. al., 1998).

* Kiecolt-Glaser and colleagues (1993) have shown that newlywed couples who displayed high levels of negative or hostile behaviors in a 30-minute discussion of marital problems showed more immunological decrements over the following 24 hours compared to those whose interactions had been more neutral. At the same time, there is evidence that small *pleasurable* events, such as getting together with friends, enhance immune system functioning over the succeeding several days (Goleman, 1994).

Despite the consistency of these findings, the size of the effect is nonetheless fairly small. In addition, a great many people who experience stress of one kind or another do not get sick as a result, and many who get sick have no clear history of stress. (For example, take another look at Figure 11.3: More than one-fourth of those with the lowest lev-

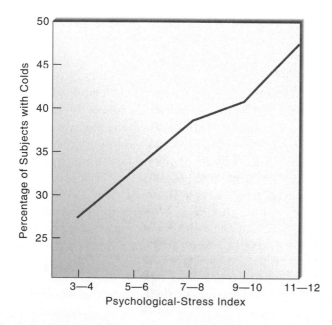

FIGURE 11.3 All the 394 subjects in this study were deliberately exposed to cold viruses, but the likelihood that the subjects would actually develop a cold was strongly linked to the amount of negative life change or other stress in their lives.

Source: Adapted from S. Cohen, Tyrrell, & Smith, 1991, Figure 1, p. 609. Reprinted by permission of the *New England Journal of Medicine*, vol. 325, 1991, pp. 606–612.

els of stress nonetheless caught the cold.) The correlation between subjects' scores on the Holmes and Rahe scale and illness, for instance, is typically only around 0.30. When the measure of stress takes the subject's perception of stress into account, or focuses primarily on negative life changes, the link is normally stronger, but still far from perfect. People obviously get sick, or have accidents, for a whole lot of reasons other than stress. Still, it is clear that stress plays a significant role in the process.

Emotional Disturbances

A similar picture emerges when we look at the relationship between life change and emotional disturbance. There is a link, but the size of the effect is relatively small. As Lieberman and Peskin say, "most people do not become mentally ill even when terrible things happen to them" (Lieberman & Peskin, 1992, p. 128). Still, stress appears to play a role, particularly in the onset of depression and anxiety.

One way that stress can be implicated in mental disorders is illustrated by a set of studies in the search for a gene for mood disorders. Studies with twins (Kendler et al., 1992a, 1992b) have shown that the personality trait of **harm avoidance** has an extremely high **heritability rating** (99 percent). For every identical twin who shows this trait, there is a 99 percent chance that his or her twin pair will also show this trait. The manifestations of harm avoidance are anxiety, depression, or both anxiety and depression. The surprise occurred four years later when this gene was located and found to be dominant, appearing in about two-thirds of the population (Lesch et al., 1996). So the big question is: Why aren't more of us depressed and/or anxious? One possible answer is that perhaps more than one gene is involved. Another possible answer is that the environment is as important as the gene in determining emotional well-being. Perhaps those who have the gene in question *and* high levels of stress are more apt to have emotional difficulties. Furthermore, *type* of stress seems to determine which of the symptoms will be experienced. Dean Hamer and Peter Copeland (1998) suggest that people who have the dominant form of the gene *and* have stress in their lives about future events will have symptoms of anxiety; people with the dominant form of the gene *and* stress about events that have already occurred will have symptoms of depression.

These studies and hypotheses are very new on the drawing board of genetics and are probably only preliminary steps to more research, but they suggest a good model of how stress can affect to emotional well-being.

CRITICAL THINKING

Think about your own most recent experience of stress over future events or stress over events that have already occurred. Does your experience match what Hamer and Copeland are suggesting?

Possible Positive Effects of Stress

In Chinese, the characters that form the word *crisis* mean both danger and opportunity (Levinson, 1990). Mindful of this point, perhaps we ought to look to see whether crisis also has a less negative side. Indeed, many theories of adult development have as one of their cornerstone concepts the notion that stress or crisis can be transformative rather than (or in addition to) being disruptive. Erikson's theory has some of this element, as does Carl Jung's. Morton Lieberman and Harvey Peskin (1992) suggest several examples: "[T]he envy of youth in middle age may mobilize untapped resources of caring... ; the keener awareness of death in middle age may permit a more equanimous attitude toward one's mortality, a lessening of strivings for perfection, and a new realization of creative potential... ; the death of a loved parent may help free the survivor to become more his or her own person" (p. 132).

Whether some kind of stress or crisis is *required* for growth is another matter, although some such link makes a certain amount of sense. Just as it is pain that usually tells us that something is wrong with our physical body, so unhappiness or anguish may be necessary to get our attention, to tell us that we need to change in some way. Marriages may become deeper and more intimate if the couple has been through difficult times and learned how to communicate better; early widowhood may force a young woman to develop her own skills in a way she would not have done otherwise.

There is not a great deal of evidence on this point, but there are at least a few fragments. For example, Haan reports that those subjects in the Berkeley Intergenerational Studies who had been hospitalized or physically ill more often over their adult lives were later rated as more empathic and more tolerant of ambiguity than were those who had been physically healthier (Haan, 1982). In a cross-sequential study of four groups—high school seniors, newlyweds, middle-aged parents, and retired adults—David Chiriboga (1984; Chiriboga & Cutler, 1980) found that among the among the retired men, changes in political or religious beliefs, in hobbies, and in anticipation of impending stress were associated with *lower* levels of reported emotional problems.

Because there is so little information on this point, I need to be careful about placing too much emphasis on these specific results. But the possibility obviously fits with the general view of personality and inner change I have proposed in the preceding two chapters. Under some circumstances or for some people, major stresses or life changes may be the stimulus or the occasion for reassessment and transformation, and thus for growth.

Developmental Differences in Stress Experiences and in Response to Stress

When age differences in life-change events or stress experiences have been examined, the consistent finding is that older adults experience fewer major life changes than do younger adults, a finding that won't be surprising to you, given what you have already seen in Figure 6.1 about the piling up of major role shifts in early adulthood (Murrell, Norris, & Grote, 1988). Chiriboga's studies showed that the number of life changes reported by adults decreases significantly with age; the older you are, the fewer life changes you are likely to have to deal with.

What is not so clear is whether there is any change with age in the meaning or appraisal that adults give to life changes. Research findings have been mixed. We do know that there is a causal link between a high level of life change and poor health outcomes among older adults, just as there is among the young. So we can't conclude that older adults are immune to the stress-producing effects of life changes even if they are able to interpret them differently or take them less seriously. The jury is still out on this set of questions.

A Quick Summary

To summarize all of this, we have evidence that the absolute incidence of life changes appears to be higher in early adulthood than in later adulthood, and that adults of differing ages encounter different sets of life changes as they move through the normative series of role acquisitions and losses. But at every age, high levels of life change, particularly major life changes that involve emotional losses or losses of relationships, are linked to higher rates of physical illness and emotional disturbances such as depression and anxiety. Daily hassles, too, accumulate and increase the risk of both physical and emotional illness.

RESISTANCE RESOURCES

This summary leaves a great many questions unanswered. In particular, it does not explain why it is that different adults, faced with the same life change or potential stressor, do not all respond in the same way. One possible answer is genetic variation, but there are many environmental influences also. To understand such individual variations, we must turn our attention to those personal and social resources that may buffer a person from the potential impact of stress. Such resources may be collectively called **resistance resources**. Central among these are the availability of social support, a sense of personal control, and individual coping responses.

Social Support

In Chapter 7 I gave an initial definition of **social support** as the receipt of affect, affirmation, and aid from others. But how should we measure such support? In many early studies, it was measured only by such objective criteria as marital status and frequency of reported contact with friends and relatives. Recent studies suggest that subjective measures may be more powerful. A person's *perception* of the adequacy of his or her social contacts and emotional support is more strongly related to physical and emotional health than are most objective measures (Feld & George, 1994), just as subjective measures of stress have turned out to be more powerful predictors than mere listings of life change events. It is not the actual amount of contact with others that is important, but how that contact is understood or interpreted. Barbara Sarason and her colleagues (Sarason, Sarason, & Pierce, 1990) take this a step further. They propose a specific link between attachment and the sense of support, suggesting that the tendency to perceive support as being "out there" and "sufficient" is related to the security of a person's basic attachment. The more secure the attachment, the greater our "sense of social support" is likely to be.

However it is measured, it is clear that adults with adequate social support have lower risk of disease, death, and depression than do adults with weaker social networks or less supportive relationships (Berkman, 1985; S. Cohen, 1991; Uchino, Cacioppo, & Kiecolt-Glaser, 1996). One particularly clear demonstration of this relationship comes from the Alameda County study, a longitudinal epidemiological study I talked about in Chapter 4. Recall that they began in 1965 with a random sample of all the residents of this California county, a total of nearly 7000 adults. These subjects were then contacted again in 1974. In one analysis, Berkman looked at the relationship between the frequency of reported contact with friends and relatives and the risk of death over the first nine years of the study, with the results shown in Figure 11.4.

Similar patterns have been found in other countries, including Sweden (Orth-Gomér, Rosengren, & Wilhelmsen, 1993) and Japan (Sugisawa, Liang, & Liu, 1994), so this link between social contact and physical hardiness is not restricted to the United States, or even to Western cultures. Of course, it is possible that social support is not the crucial variable here. Perhaps people with low social support are different in other ways that are significant for health, such as health habits or social class. Berkman (1985) checked out these possibilities in the Alameda data and found that the link between support and risk of death persisted even when initial physical health status, social class, smoking, alcohol consumption, level of physical activity, weight, race, and life satisfaction were taken into account.

The Buffering Effect of Social Support. This beneficial effect of social support is even clearer when a person is under high stress. That is, the negative effect of stress on health and happiness is smaller for those who have adequate social support than for those whose social support is weak. This pattern of results is usually described as the **buffering effect of social support** (S. Cohen & Wills, 1985). It may not be a coincidence that many of the top-rated life changes on the Holmes and Rahe list involve a loss of social support (divorce, separation, death of a loved one, even loss of a job).

Research has shown that women who fill multiple roles of parent, wife, worker, and caregiver of elderly parents suffer greater effects of stress when they don't have adequate social support in their own lives (Stephens, Franks, & Townsend, 1994). Such a buffering effect of social support is not limited to women. For instance, in a short-term longitudinal study of men who had been laid off from work because their companies had gone

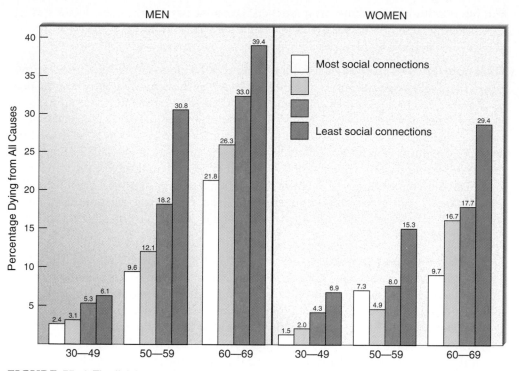

FIGURE II.4 The link between social support and risk of death is clear in these results from the Alameda County Study.

Source: Lisa F. Berkman and Lester Breslow, *Health and ways of living: The Alameda County Study,* Fig. 4-3, p. 130. Copyright © 1983 by Oxford University Press, Inc. Reprinted by permission.

out of business, Kasl and Cobb (1982) found that those men who felt that they had adequate social support from their wives and friends showed fewer physical and emotional symptoms than did those men with lower levels of perceived support.

Social support also reduces the negative impact of stressful experiences among the elderly. Neal Krause has shown this particularly nicely in an elegant series of studies of a random community survey of more than 300 older adults in Galveston, Texas. In one analysis, Krause (1987a) has shown that chronic financial strain significantly increases the chances that these elderly adults will report depressive symptoms, but this effect is considerably weaker among those with adequate social support, particularly if they received adequate informational support. Krause proposes (Krause & Borawski-Clark, 1994) that social support has a beneficial effect in part because it bolsters feelings of control and self-worth and that this is especially true if the stress is occurring in some area of your life that threatens an important role.

Finally, an already classic study by Spiegel, Bloom, Kramer, and Gottheil (1989) shows that *adding* social support can have beneficial physical effects. Spiegel randomly assigned women with advanced breast cancer to either a group that met weekly to provide support to one another or to a control group that received no such group support. The women with the added social support lived an average of 18 months longer than did the controls. Furthermore, there is preliminary evidence that such added social support has the effect of strengthening the immune system, which in turn is linked to longer survival times (B. L. Andersen, Kiecolt-Glaser, & Glaser, 1994).

These studies and others like them certainly confirm the commonsense assumption that having supportive relationships helps you ride out the various storms of life. But the buffering effects of social support are not nearly so straightforward or so general as these findings may lead you to think. As researchers have gone beyond the mere demonstration of a buffering effect, they have discovered some complexities. Let me suggest a number of refinements to the basic buffering hypothesis.

The Importance of Intimacy. First, for a buffering effect to exist, the most critical property of social relationships appear to be their **intimacy**, or the comfort and trust of the people involved to confide in each other and share their innermost thoughts and feelings. Even very small networks can be helpful if the relationships are intimate. The smallest number of intimate relationships that seems to be absolutely necessary is one. To be sure, the majority of adults have at least one confidant. In one large survey of over 4000 adults, Gary Lee (1988) found that 85 percent of the women and 70 percent of the men reported having at least one confidant. So the majority of adults (at least in this culture) are at least minimally buffered against the most serious effects of stress. But there is a significant minority who do not have a confidant and who may thus be particularly vulnerable to the negative effects of stressful life experiences.

The Match Between the Source of Support and the Type of Stress. Second, as Morton Lieberman points out, "it is not the total amount of help that is salient, but rather the fit between a particular kind of problem and the help provider" (1982, p. 771). Different types of crises may require different forms or sources of support. The source of support that is most often critical is that of a spouse or lover (Ducharme, 1994). For example, women who are pregnant or have just given birth to their first child suffer fewer physical and emotional problems if they have their husband's support. Other sources of support, such as from close friends or other family members, apparently do not do the trick or do not work as well (Lieberman, 1982). The relationship with spouse or lover is not invariably the most helpful. For a life change such as widowhood (which I'll talk about in detail shortly), where it is precisely the *loss* of that central intimate source of social sup-

IF YOU ARE FACING a life crisis of some kind, having at least one good friend or confidant you can talk to like this seems to be critical in helping you weather the storm without too much ill-effect.

port that must be dealt with, the source of support associated with the greatest buffering effect appeared in one study to be the widowed person's parents or other widowed friends (Bankoff, 1983), especially during the early phases of mourning.

Morton Lieberman has taken this argument a step further by suggesting that "It may very well be that when the salient support person is available but does not provide needed [support], substitution becomes almost impossible; this may not be the case when the critical relationship no longer exists" (1982, p. 773). In Bankoff's study of widows, for example, those widows who had the most difficult time were those whose parents were still alive but not providing help and emotional support. For these women, substitute support from friends did not appear to have a buffering effect. But those widows whose parents were deceased appeared to be able to use the support of widowed friends as a replacement. Similarly, one might guess that in Lieberman's study of women who have just given birth, the greatest risk of physical and emotional difficulties would be among those women whose husbands or lovers failed to provide the level of support the woman expected or wanted.

Lee's study of confidants, although not specifically focused on the buffering impact of social support, is nonetheless consistent with Lieberman's hypothesis as well. He found that adults whose single most important confidant was their spouse had much higher marital satisfaction than did those whose spouse was not listed as a confidant. More surprising is the fact that adults who had a close confidant *other than* the spouse actually reported lower marital satisfaction than did those who had no confidant at all.

The Role of Expectation. I find Lieberman's hypothesis especially intriguing because it once again points to the importance of interpretation or meaning as a key variable. It begins to look as if the causal ingredient in the buffering effect of social support is the individual's *perception* that his or her support network is sufficient to aid in critical ways (S. Cohen & Wills, 1985). Feeling let down by a key person alters that perception of support adequacy and limits or eliminates the buffering effect, even for a person with an extensive network.

Krause has been able to show this causal connection unusually clearly in his study of older adults in Galveston. Not only did he find that subjects' satisfaction with their level of social support was a better predictor of health than was the objective amount of support (Krause, 1987c), but when he traced the sequence over an 18-month period he found that a decline in an adult's sense of satisfaction with his social support was likely to be followed by an increase in depressive symptoms, rather than the other way around (Krause, Liang, & Yatomi, 1989).

Some Negative Effects of Social Networks. Lest I give the impression that there is nothing but sweetness and light in the world of social relationships, let me hasten to add that there are costs associated with social networks. Network systems are generally reciprocal. Not only do you receive support, you give it as well. And as I pointed out in Chapters 6 and 7, there are particular points in the life cycle when the giving side of the equation seems to be more heavily weighted than the receiving side, which may increase stress and daily hassles.

Everyday social interactions can also be a significant source of hassles. Most of us have at least some regular interactions with people we do not like or who irritate us to distraction: your co-worker, whose desk is constantly messy; your neighbor, who stops by for a chat every time you have settled down for an hour of pleasant solitude; your mother, who invariably tells you how to rearrange your living room furniture each time she comes to visit. When these negative social interactions involve anger, dislike, criticism, or under-

CRITICAL
THINKING

Imagine yourself having an auto accident or having a fight with your spouse/boyfriend/girlfriend. Who would be the first person you would turn to in each case? Are the two different? Why or why not? And if the first person you turned to was unwilling or unable to help you, is there a reasonable substitute?

mining, especially when such negative feelings come from those who are central to a person's social convoy, they have a substantial negative effect on an adult's overall feeling of well-being (Antonucci, 1994b; Vinokur & van Ryn, 1993).

CRITICAL THINKING

See if you can convert all this information into advice for the giving of social support to others. Are there any rules you can devise? Or does it depend totally on the specific situation?

Social support can also operate in a negative way when it is "too much of a good thing." Indeed, the relationship between total amount of social support and stress buffering may be curvilinear rather than linear. Either too much, or too little, is associated with poorer outcomes. Antonucci, (1994b), for example, finds that among women, those who have the largest number of people in the inner circle of their convoy describe themselves as *less* happy than do those who have medium numbers. Krause (1987c) makes a similar argument. He suggests that social support operates to buffer a person from the effects of life change by increasing the adult's sense of personal control over his or her own life. But when you are facing a crisis and your myriad friends and relations are hovering over you in an effort to be maximally supportive, you may feel less in control, and thus ultimately less able to deal with the crisis, than if they had backed off a little or if there had been fewer of them.

Age Differences in the Effects of Social Support. As far as I know, no researcher has looked specifically for a possible relationship between age and the buffering effect of social support. The research I've already described, of course, shows that it is possible to find examples of such buffering in each age group, but there is much that has not been explored. For example, we do not know whether some age groups are more skillful in using their social networks than are others, or whether definitions of the adequacy of support may change with age. Our developmental information is limited to comparisons of the properties of networks of adults of different ages, much of which I have already described in Chapters 6 and 7.

The one change in the functioning of social networks that does appear to occur in the later years of adulthood is a reduction in the amount of support *given*. Once an adult leaves the years of the "sandwich generation," when maximum help is given in both directions in the generational chain, there is a gradual drop in the amount of help or other social support given to the members of one's network. This may imply a decline in the amount of reciprocal interactions that occur between family members or with friends. Since most adults report preferring reciprocal relationships, there may develop some reluctance to call on the assistance of the network in times of stress, which might result in some loss of the buffering effect of the support system. But such a possibility has not been tested empirically.

A Sense of Personal Control

Another major buffer against the impact of stress is a sense of personal control, a concept I talked about at some length in Chapter 4. You'll recall that whether we measure such a sense of personal control by assessing **internal versus external locus of control** or **optimism versus helplessness,** those who have a stronger sense of control are less likely to become physically ill or depressed. Such a sense of control also serves as a buffer against stress, in much the same way that social support acts as a buffer. That is, among people facing some major life change or chronic stress, those who approach the problem with a strong sense of self-efficacy or optimism are less likely to develop physical or emotional symptoms, or recover more quickly from physical problems. For a sample of men who had undergone coronary bypass surgery, Michael Scheier, Chuck Carver, and their colleagues (Scheier et al., 1989) found that those with a more optimistic attitude, measured before the surgery, recovered more rapidly in the six months after surgery: they returned more quickly to their presurgery pattern of life. Clearly, then, a sense of personal control is a significant resistance resource in the face of stress.

Coping Behaviors

The third piece of the puzzle in understanding the effects of stress are the specific coping behaviors we each use when faced with some problem. Suppose that you have been working to get into a particular graduate program and you find out that you weren't accepted. Or suppose that your apartment was damaged by a fire and most of your belongings were lost. How do you cope with these stresses? **Coping** is a very broad and fuzzy word to describe all the things you might think, feel, and do in response to such events in an effort to handle the stress, and might include any of the following, adapted from Folkman and Lazarus's Ways of Coping Questionnaire (Lazarus, 1993, p. 237):

* *Confrontive coping* (e.g., "I expressed anger to the person who caused the problem.")
* *Distancing* (e.g., "I made light of the situation; I refused to get too serious about it.")
* *Self-controlling* (e.g., "I tried to keep my feelings to myself," or "I kept others from knowing how bad things were.")
* *Seeking social support* (e.g., "I talked to someone to find out more about the situation.")
* *Accepting responsibility* (e.g., "I criticized or lectured myself," or "I realized I brought the problem on myself.")
* *Escape-avoidance* (e.g., "I hoped a miracle would happen," or "I avoided being with people in general.")
* *Planful problem solving* (e.g., "I made a plan of action and I followed it.")
* *Positive reappraisal* (e.g., "I came out of the experience better than when I went in," or "I found new faith.")

Many theorists and investigators have tried to organize this array of coping strategies into useful subcategories. One way to cut the pie is to divide coping responses into acting, thinking, and feeling, usually called **problem-focused** (doing things), **appraisal-focused** (thinking, planning, analyzing), and **emotion-focused** coping (Billings & Moos, 1981; Moos & Billings, 1982). Lazarus argues that which type of coping a person may use in a given situation is strongly dependent on the stress or problem being faced. When people perceive that their problem is not amenable to change, such as a diagnosis of metastatic cancer, emotion-focused coping predominates. But when people think that their problem can be altered, problem-focused coping is much more likely. Thus any one of the many types of coping may be suitable and helpful in some circumstances, and indeed Lazarus finds that most people use the full array of coping strategies at various times and in varying situations.

Another way to organize the universe of coping strategies is to divide them into **approach coping** and **avoidance coping.** Either approach or avoidance might involve acting, thinking, or feeling. For example, taking it out on other people, repressing thoughts about a problem, or keeping feelings to one's self would all be forms of avoidance coping (C. J. Holahan & Moos, 1990; Moos, 1988). This division, unlike the previous one, carries a value judgment: The basic hypothesis, supported now by a variety of studies, is that approach coping is generally more beneficial than avoidance coping. For example, in several longitudinal studies, C. J. Holahan and Moos (1986, 1987, 1990) have found that among adults who face high levels of stress, those who use more avoidance coping strategies are more likely to experience depression or physical illness than are those who use more approach coping. Similarly, in a study of a large number of adults with AIDS, Fleishman and Fogel (1994) find that those who use more approach and less avoidance coping are less depressed after one year.

But, as you might guess, the picture is not quite as clear as this might suggest. There are some situations in which avoidant strategies seem to be more functional. In particular, when there is nothing that can be done about some problem, denial or other avoidant forms of coping may actually be quite effective ways to handle the problem. For example, if a person is given a diagnosis of some treatable disease, then going to the library to read everything you can find about the disease is a useful strategy, linked to better outcomes. But if an untreatable disease is diagnosed, such an active search for information is actually counterproductive, raising arousal and increasing blood pressure (Davey, Tallis, & Hodgson, 1993).

In a similar vein, Lazarus points to evidence that in responding to a heart attack, denial seems to be a helpful strategy during the postattack period when the patient is still in the hospital. But denial is counterproductive at the time of the attack itself (because it leads to delays in getting medical care), as well as in the time after discharge from the hospital.

Thus while it is roughly true that approach strategies are more likely to eliminate or alleviate the worst effects of stress, the best coping strategies will vary from one kind of stress situation to the next. Those adults who have a large repertoire of coping strategies are likely to be most successful in buffering themselves from the worst effects of potentially stressful life changes or daily hassles.

CRITICAL THINKING

What connection do you see, if any, between approach and avoidant coping and Vaillant's categorization of mature and immature defense mechanisms?

Age or Developmental Differences in Personality or Coping Strategies. As usual, most of the research I have just described has not been cast in a developmental framework. But there is now a growing, if confusing, body of research exploring age differences in coping strategies. Some researchers have found absolutely no age differences at all, including Robert McCrae (1989) in a seven-year longitudinal study of a sample of nearly 200 adults of various ages. He found simply no sign of systematic change, at least over this period of years, in the types of coping that people used.

Several other longitudinal studies, however, do point to some changes in coping styles. Recall from Chapter 10 that Vaillant's data from the Grant study as well as Haan's analyses of the Berkeley data, show a decline with age in various forms of immature defense mechanisms, including denial and repression, a pattern also found in some more recent cross-sectional studies (Feifel & Strack, 1989).

Several cross-sectional studies using Lazarus's measure of coping styles (Folkman, Lazarus, Pinley, & Novacek, 1987; Irion & Blanchard-Fields, 1987) also point to systematic age changes in types of coping. Both sets of researchers found that young and middle-aged adults, compared to adults over 65, reported using more active, problem-focused interpersonal forms of coping, such as confrontive coping, planful problem solving, and seeking social support. Adults over 65 reported that they used more passive, internal, emotion-focused forms of coping, such as positive reappraisal and accepting responsibility. Thus the younger adults are using more problem-focused strategies, while the older adults are using more emotion-focused and appraisal-focused strategies, a pattern that is generally consistent with the decline with age in "tenacious goal pursuit" and the increase in "flexible goal adjustment" Brandtstädter has observed and that I discussed in Chapter 9 (recall Figure 9.6) (Brandtstädter & Renner, 1992).

These are not longitudinal findings, so we don't know if these results reflect only cohort differences, or whether there are real age-linked changes at work here. We also don't know whether any changes with age we may detect reflect fundamental psychological shifts toward a more inward-turned, or more adaptive approach, or whether they simply reflect a different set of stresses that the older adult is likely to face. For example, older adults are more likely to have to deal with health problems that are simply less amenable to the more active forms of "approach" coping, whereas the crises facing younger adults may be more suitably handled with highly active coping strategies. For now, we have to be content with the fragments of information we have available.

Other Resistance Resources

Social support, a sense of personal control, and good coping strategies are not the only resistance resources that make a difference in adults' responses to stress. A decent income helps as well, as does good health and vitality. Specific beliefs may also help a person cope with major life changes. For instance, any source of hope may be helpful, be it a belief in God, or in justice, or simply in the efficacy of a particular doctor, a particular program, a new diet, or whatever. Personal skills may also have an effect. An adult with a wide range of occupational skills may face divorce or relocation more easily; an adult with good social skills, including those skills that allow one to relate easily and well to others and to form close relationships, may be able to form new networks if old ones are disrupted. All of these additional resources may affect the range of coping strategies or options that are available to the individual in the face of some stress, as well as affecting the person's choice among the options that are available.

RESPONDING TO STRESS: AN OVERVIEW

All of these pieces can be put together, at least in a preliminary way, using the model I proposed in Figure 11.1. Stressful stimuli are most likely to result in illness or depression (or other adverse change) if a person appraises the potential stressor as a threat, has a low level of social support, particularly if he or she lacks a close confidant appropriate for that stress and fails to apply suitable coping strategies. The opposite set of conditions *may* lead to a higher chance of growth or maturing in the face of stress.

To make all this more real to you, let me explore at least briefly the impact of a few particularly critical or interesting life changes or stress experiences, in this case widowhood, divorce, and relocation in old age.

APPLICATION OF THE BASIC PRINCIPLES

Widowhood

In 1992, there were roughly 14 million adults in the United States who had lost a spouse by death, most commonly when they were in middle or late adulthood. Of these, over 11 million were women. Over half of all women over 65 in the United States today are widowed, compared to only about 12 percent of men. Because of this sex difference in frequency, most of the research on widowhood describes the adaptation of women. When researchers have studied both men and women, however, the pattern of response to bereavement seems to be very similar. So for the following discussion, unless I say otherwise, assume that the findings hold for both sexes, and that when I use the word *widow,* I mean either gender.

The death of a spouse is itself a huge life change, and it triggers a whole string of other changes. It involves not only the loss of a relationship but also the loss of the support and assistance of the spouse and loss of the role of spouse itself. Justine Ball (1976–1977) describes one widow as saying that she "felt she had no name or label now. She was not a 'wife' or 'housewife' and with no job, it gave her no concept of who she was" (p. 329). For a man, or for a woman who has been employed regularly or who has some other source of identity, the loss of identity may be less severe, but the loss of support from the spouse is still substantial, perhaps particularly for men, since they are less likely to have other close, supportive relationships outside their marriage.

Given the size of this life change/stress, we would certainly expect increases in rates of disease, death, and depression among widows—which is generally what the research shows. Large epidemiological studies in many countries show that in the year following the spouse's death, rates of death and disease among widows rise slightly (Reich, Zautra, & Guarnaccia, 1989; W. Stroebe & Stroebe, 1993). For example, in an enormous study in Finland, Kaprio and Koskenvuo (cited in W. Stroebe & Stroebe, 1986) examined the mortality rates for a group of 95,647 widowed persons over the five years following the spouse's death. They found that compared to the population at large, death rates among widows rose during the first six months after bereavement, after which the mortality risk returned to normal. We also know that immune system function declines in the first few months after a spouse's death, which doubtless contributes to the slightly higher rate of physical illness found among recent widows (Gallagher-Thompson, Futterman, Farberow, Thompson, & Peterson, 1993; Irwin & Pike, 1993).

A very similar pattern is found for depression, which typically rises in the first six months after the spouse's death. For example, in one longitudinal study, Fran Norris and Stanley Murrell (1990) repeatedly interviewed a sample of 3000 adults, all age 55 or older at the beginning of the study. Forty-eight of these adults were widowed during the 2-1/2 years of the study, which allowed Norris and Murrell to look at depression and health status before and immediately after bereavement. They found no differences between the widowed and nonwidowed on physical health, but did find a rise in depression immediately following the loss, a set of results you can see in Figure 11.5. For comparison purposes, I have also included scores for a group of subjects who had experienced the death of a child or a parent in the same period, to illustrate the larger effect of widowhood.

In this sample, the widowed had already been slightly (but not statistically significantly) more depressed before the spouse's death, presumably because at least some were already aware of the spouse's illness. But depression rose sharply in the first six months after bereavement and then dropped again by the end of one year. Other research confirms that the first six months are the most critical; most find that within 18 months after bereavement there is no residual effect on physical or mental health (McCrae & Costa, 1988).

Age Differences. These immediate negative effects appear to be greater for younger widowed men and women than for widowed adults in their 60s, 70s, and 80s (Balkwell, 1985; Ball, 1976–1977; Wortman, Silver, & Kessler, 1993), although there is also some

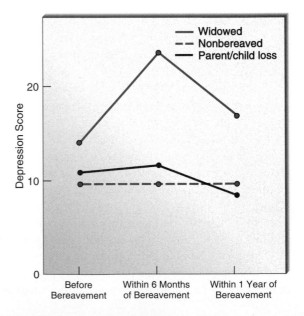

FIGURE II.5 Among widows, but not among those who had experienced the death of a parent or child, there was a significant increase in depression in the six months after bereavement.

Source: Data from F. H. Norris & Murrell, 1990, Table 1, p. 432.

indication that younger widows may bounce back somewhat more quickly than do older widows (Sanders, 1993). This pattern of findings fits quite nicely into Pearlin's model of the effect of scheduled and unscheduled changes. The death of a spouse is rarely "scheduled," but for those over 65 or so, such a death is not altogether unanticipated. In contrast, having your spouse die when you are in your 30s or 40s is clearly unscheduled or off-time. Pearlin's general hypothesis would lead us to expect that such early widowhood should be associated with greater experience of stress and heightened physical and emotional effects, which is just what the research shows.

Gender Differences. One of the prevalent assumptions about widowhood is that men handle it less well than women do. Current research offers some support for this assumption, although not in all areas. Epidemiological studies show quite convincingly that the risk of death from either natural causes or suicide in the months immediately following widowhood is significantly greater for men than for women (M. S. Stroebe & Stroebe, 1993), even when higher male death rates at most ages are taken into account. Thus men's physical health appears to be more affected by this particular stress than is women's.

The results for emotional health are not so clear. Some investigators find no differences; a few find that widowed women are more likely to suffer depression than are widowed men. The preponderance of the evidence, however, points to a somewhat more negative effect for men (Sanders, 1993). Camille Wortman and her colleagues (1993) suggest that part of the reason for the disparity of results is that men and women experience different kinds of stress following the death of a spouse. For women, the greatest source of vulnerability (at least in this culture) is from increased financial strain; for men, vulnerability arises more from loss of social support. As you already know, men's social support networks are typically less extensive and less intimate than are women's. In particular, men are more likely to have only a single confidant, their wife. When she dies, they are left without that key element of the social network.

Social Networks, Personality, and Coping Skills. Such a gender difference is part of a more general pattern: Those widows who show the fewest physical and emotional symptoms following bereavement are those with the most supportive social networks.

One of the best illustrations of this effect comes from a longitudinal sample studied by Evelyn Goldberg (Goldberg, Comstock, & Harlow, 1988). Goldberg and her colleagues interviewed a group of over 1000 women, all of whom had been between 62 and 72 in 1975. Of these, 150 were widowed in the several succeeding years, and Goldberg was able to interview them within six months of bereavement (a design very similar to the Norris and Murrell study you saw in Figure 11.5). Twenty five of these widows reported needing help for an emotional problem during the postwidowhood months, and Goldberg could go back and see how those 25 women had initially differed from those who did not have significant emotional problems after widowhood. You can see in Figure 11.6 that among the widows, those who had had fewer friends, smaller networks, and less closeness to their children before being widowed were more likely to have significant problems adjusting to widowhood. In a similar longitudinal study, Feld and George (1994) found that the likelihood that a widowed older adult would be hospitalized in the two years following bereavement was highest among those lacking close friends or who perceived that their social support was inadequate.

But as I pointed out earlier, not all elements in a social support network are interchangeable. Recall Bankoff's study (1983), which showed that the most buffering relationships were with the widow's parents or with widowed friends. Contact with children, interestingly enough, seems to provide less buffering against the negative effect of bereavement than does contact with friends. In several classic studies of widows, Helena Lopata, (1973, 1979; Lopata, Heinemann, & Baum, 1982) does find that widowed

Number of friends
before widowhood

Total size of social
network before
widowhood

Closeness to
children before
widowhood

Percentage Needing Help for an
Emotional Problem After Widowhood

FIGURE 11.6 Among this group of widows who had been studied both before and after widowhood, those who had more friends, larger social networks, and closer relationships with their children before they were widowed were less likely to report a significant emotional problem after they were widowed.

Source: Data from Goldberg, Comstock, & Harlow, 1988, Table 1, p. S207.

CRITICAL THINKING

See if you can generate some hypotheses about links between various types of coping strategies and response to widowhood. How might you test those hypotheses?

women with children report less loneliness than do widows without children, but there is no indication that widows with children show lower rates of disease or depression than do widows without children.

The role of enduring personality characteristics in a person's adjustment to bereavement has been (surprisingly) less often studied. But there is a bit of information. In one study in Germany, Wolfgang and Margaret Stroebe (1993) found that widows and widowers who were low in neuroticism had lower levels of illness and depression following bereavement than did those high in neuroticism. But they found essentially no link between internal/external locus of control beliefs and response to widowhood.

Studies like these take us a few steps closer to understanding what it is that makes one widow come apart at the seams and another cope fairly readily with the loss. But we clearly need to know a great deal more.

Divorce

In Chapter 6 I talked about what may happen to family roles after a divorce, but I sidestepped the question that I want to address now: the impact of divorce on a person's functioning. Like widowhood, divorce is linked to increases in both physical and mental illnesses. Recently separated or divorced adults have more automobile accidents, are more likely to commit suicide (a finding replicated in many countries), lose more days at work because of illness, and are more likely to become depressed (Menaghan & Lieberman, 1986; Stack, 1992a; 1992b; Stack & Wasserman, 1993). They also report greater loneliness and strong feelings of failure and loss of self-esteem (Chase-Lansdale & Hetherington, 1990).

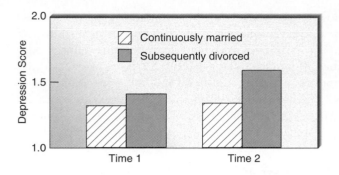

FIGURE 11.7 A rise in depression following divorce is a common finding. In this case, the evidence is longitudinal.

Source: Data from Menaghan & Lieberman, 1986, Table 1, p. 323.

The impact of divorce on depression is nicely illustrated by Elizabeth Menaghan and Morton Lieberman's panel study (1986) of a group of Chicago adults first interviewed in 1972 and reinterviewed four years later. Seven hundred fifty-eight of the subjects were married to the same spouse at both times, while 32 had been married at the first interview but were subsequently divorced. The married and the subsequently divorced had *not* differed significantly on a measure of depression when they were first interviewed, but the divorced were significantly more depressed after the divorce, a pattern you can see in Figure 11.7.

As is true of widowhood, the period of maximum upheaval seems to last about two years, with the first six to 12 months being the worst time (Chase-Lansdale & Hetherington, 1990; Kitson, 1992). Mavis Hetherington has provided us with an in-depth look at this period in a longitudinal study of a group of divorcing adults over the two years following the decree (Hetherington & Camera, 1984; Hetherington, Cox, & Cox, 1978). In those months, daily routines became chaotic, with meals taken at irregular hours. Discipline of the children became erratic as well. The men in the study, most of whom had moved out of the family house, often felt rootless and without a clear identity. The divorced women felt unattractive and helpless. Both often felt isolated from their still-married friends. Divorce also causes financial upheaval, although (as you have seen in Chapter 6) more for women than for men.

Over the long term, results are more varied. Some adults appear to grow from the experience and show better psychological functioning five or 10 years later than they had shown before the divorce. Others seem to be worse off psychologically, even a decade later (Wallerstein, 1986). There are a few indications that those who remarry are generally better off psychologically than those who remain single, which is consistent with the more general finding that a stable partnership is linked to better mental and physical health. Yet for the many who divorce a second time (perhaps 40 percent of remarriages), the negative consequences appear to be even greater (Spanier & Furstenberg, 1987).

Explaining the Negative Effect of Divorce. Obviously, there are several possible explanations for these heightened levels of sickness, death, and disaster among the divorced. One possibility, usually called the **selectivity theory,** is that people who eventually get divorced were less stable to begin with. No doubt that is at least partially true. In one five-year longitudinal study, for example, Erbes and Hedderson (1984) found that on a measure of psychological well-being, those men who eventually divorced had had lower scores as many as five years before the divorce than had continuously married men.

But selectivity does not seem to account for all of the results, including the findings from Menaghan and Lieberman's Chicago study shown in Figure 11.7. Selectivity also cannot readily account for heightened rates of illness, death, and emotional disturbance in widowed persons. Doubtless, a bidirectional effect is at work. Initial instability or unhappiness may increase the likelihood of divorce or other life changes. But the life change itself also increases the risk of later disease or disturbance.

Age Differences in Effects of Divorce. In the United States today, roughly half of all divorces occur within the first seven years of marriage, which means that most divorces occur in early adulthood. Three-fourths of those receiving a divorce in this country today are under the age of 40 (Uhlenberg, Cooney, & Boyd, 1990). So to the extent that this is a "scheduled" life event, it is normative in early adulthood and not in late adulthood—at least in present cohorts. Thus if Pearlin's model is correct, in contrast to the pattern for widowhood, we ought to find that *older* divorcing persons have a more difficult time adjusting to this life change than do younger adults, which is precisely what researchers have found (Bloom, White, & Asher, 1979).

Gender Differences in the Stressfulness of Divorce. The differences in men's and women's responses to divorce are much less clear. Women certainly suffer far greater economic upheaval and more often have to deal with the complexities and stresses of single-parenting. But there are hints that divorcing men may have slightly higher levels of emotional and health problems than do women. More divorced men end up as inpatients in psychiatric hospitals than do divorced women, for example (Bloom et al., 1979), despite the fact that in the population at large there are more women psychiatric patients than men. Yet not every study shows such a pattern (Doherty, Su, & Needle, 1989; Kitson, 1992). Once again, the jury is still out.

Social Support and Coping Strategies in Divorce. The one clear finding is that for *both* men and women, adequate emotional and social support from friends, kin, and new intimate relationships helps to speed the process of recovery (Hetherington & Camera, 1984). However, to the extent that men's friendships and kin relationships are less intimate, and thus possibly less supportive, men may have fewer social resources on which to draw.

At the same time, there are a few signs that social support after a divorce, as in other areas of life, is not necessarily an unmitigated blessing. For example, in her several studies, Gay Kitson (1992) has found that the lowest levels of distress were reported by those divorced adults who received services of various kinds (babysitting, being driven places, invitations to events, and the like), or those who had received financial assistance. But when these forms of assistance were combined with unsolicited advice or guidance from friends or relatives, the effects were sometimes negative. It's a point worth remembering when dealing with friends or family members who have recently divorced.

Other than social support, those personal qualities that appear to assist an adult in dealing effectively with the crisis of divorce are readily predictable from what I have already said about personality and coping strategies. Divorced adults who have higher self-esteem, stronger feelings of internal control, are open-minded and tolerant of change and show better or more rapid adjustment to the divorce (Hetherington & Camera, 1984). They are likely not only to weather the immediate crisis of the divorce without major symptoms, but may also show real personal growth in the process.

Relocation in Old Age

The third life change I want to talk about is relocation in old age, including any of the three types of postretirement moves I talked about in Chapter 8: **amenity move, kinship migration,** and **institutional migration.** What is the psychological and health impact of such life changes? Several conclusions emerge from the research.

First, a critical variable is whether the individual elder has a sense of control over the move. Those older adults who choose to move or who have some clear control over their move or their destination typically show *increases* in morale or life satisfaction and little sign of increased physical disease or other symptoms. Thus nearly all amenity moves, and the great majority of kinship moves, are linked to positive outcomes.

THESE RETIRED FOLKS are probably among the minority who have made what Charles Longino calls an "amenity" move—a move to a sunnier climate or to a special retirement location.

It is the *involuntary* moves, forced on the older person by family members due to declining health or lack of support services, such as moves to a nursing home, that are likely to cause the greatest stress—at least as indicated by rises in death and disease rates. On average, involuntarily relocated elderly adults show increases in death rates compared to roughly equivalent groups who have remained at home—although such comparisons are fraught with methodological difficulties (Fields, 1992).

Similarly, on average, those elders who are in settings that allow them some control over their everyday life do better than those who are less in control (Fields, 1992; M. P. Lawton, 1990). But these average statements mask some important variations in experience. What appears to be critical is the degree of "fit" between the personal qualities of the elder and the qualities of the institution. This conclusion emerges particularly from a set of studies of institutionalized older adults by Morton Lieberman and Sheldon Tobin (1983). In one of these studies, they looked at outcomes for a group of adults who had voluntarily moved into nursing homes. One year later, about half had adapted well and showed no negative effects; the other half showed marked physical or psychological deterioration, or had died. When Lieberman and Tobin compared these two groups, they found that the flourishing group were much more likely to be in institutions whose organization and style matched the elder's own personal qualities well.

CRITICAL THINKING

Can you figure out what the methodological problems would be in this case? Why is it so hard to tease out the unique effect of institutionalization per se from all the other variables involved?

This conclusion is confirmed in a recent study of over 1000 nursing home residents in Canada (O'Connor & Vallerand, 1994). The investigators found that the psychological adjustment of the residents was higher when there was a match between the degree of choice and control offered by the home and the degree to which each resident's motivation was **self-determined,** which in this case means something roughly analogous to Rotter's concept of internal locus of control. Thus residents who were strongly self-determined in their motives did better in an institution in which they had some element of choice and personal control. But residents with less self-determined styles did better in institutions with clear structure and rules.

An elder's adaptation to an institutional move is also affected by the personal resources that he or she can bring to the situation. Lieberman and Tobin's studies suggest that those older adults whose intellectual abilities, health, and energy level are above some threshold level are likely to adapt successfully to an institutional move. But those who fall below the threshold in any area are at greater risk. These same factors, of course, are significant elements for older adults who do *not* move; those whose intellectual abilities or health are lower at any given time are likely to decline more rapidly or to die over the subsequent year or two. So institutionalization is not the sole culprit here. Still, it appears that these least well-functioning elders are most negatively affected by the move to an institution, and often decline more rapidly in such a setting than they might have done had they remained at home.

At the same time, I should point out that a move to an institution is often most needed by precisely these same impaired elderly, because they can no longer receive the care they require at home. In such cases, a move to an institution may be the best choice, even when the move is involuntary or resisted: a difficult choice, and one that will be faced by increasing numbers of elders and their families as the number of frail elders continues to rise.

Summary

1. Stress is defined in at least three ways: as a physical response to demand; as an external stimulus, such as a life change or hassle that demands adaptation; or as the result of interaction between a demanding environmental event and the person's coping capacity.

2. Response-oriented approaches are typified by Selye's description of the general adaptation syndrome, which includes stages of alarm, resistance, and exhaustion.

3. Stimulus-oriented approaches have commonly involved measurement of the number of major or minor life changes experienced by a person in a given space of time. Current measures typically distinguish between positive and negative events.

4. Interactionist views of stress emphasize not only the demands of the environment and the body's response to that demand, but in predicting the consequences of such stress, these views stress the person's interpretation of the event and the availability of such resistance resources as social support or a repertoire of coping responses.

5. A small but consistently observed increase in the risk of disease or emotional disturbance has been found associated with heightened levels of life changes or hassles. Undesirable life changes, particularly those involved in a loss of a relationship, appear to be especially likely to be linked to increased risk of disease. This effect has been linked to lowered immune system functioning in several studies.

6. Life changes may also be associated with some positive outcomes, such as personal growth, although this is much less well established.

7. Older adults experience fewer major life changes and fewer daily hassles than do younger adults, but some specific life changes are more common in late life, including (of course) retirement, illness, and loss of spouse and friends to death.

8. The effects of stress may be buffered by any of several resistance resources, including social support, certain personality patterns, and certain coping strategies.

9. Studies of social support in stressful conditions suggest that the intimacy of the relationships within a social network is a key variable. Adults with emotionally supportive, intimate relationships are less likely to respond to stress with illness than are adults without such support.

10. The optimal supportive relationship may vary from one type of life change to another, with the central relationship with spouse or partner most often the key source of support.

11. Social networks can also have some negative effects, since their maintenance may increase daily hassles, and they may include genuinely negative interactions.

12. Also important in mitigating the effect of stress is a sense of personal control, which may be defined or measured in a variety of ways, as self-efficacy, as an internal locus of control, or as optimism.

13. Of the many varieties of coping strategies in the face of life changes or hassles, those described as "approach" are generally (though not uniformly) more effective than those described as "avoidance."

14. Other resistance resources include adequate income, health or vitality, and a generally positive outlook on life.

15. These general principles can be applied to responses to such specific major life changes as widowhood, divorce, and relocation in old age.

16. Widowhood is associated with heightened rates of illness, depression, suicide, mortality from other causes, and auto accidents. The disease and death effects are somewhat larger for men; there may also be an equivalent gender difference in depression or other emotional responses to widowhood, but this is less consistently found.

17. Divorce similarly is associated with heightened rates of depression and illness, with the effects most noticeable in the first year.

18. Divorce has a greater negative impact on older adults, while the effects of widowhood are generally larger for any adult widowed early in life or unexpectedly. This pattern of results supports Pearlin's hypothesis that "scheduled" or predictable life changes are less stressful.

19. Relocation in old age has relatively little negative effect if the move is voluntary. An involuntary move may also have little or no negative effect if the move is to a setting or institution in which the person has some personal autonomy or control, or to an institution that matches the person's personal motives or style. Involuntary moves to nonmatching institutions are the only ones consistently associated with increased levels of mortality or illness.

20. Overall, in the face of some kind of potentially stressful experience, illness or emotional disturbance is most likely if the person appraises the experience as a threat, has a low level of social support, lacks options or control, and lacks suitable coping strategies.

KEY TERMS

general adaptation
  syndrome (GAS)

alarm reaction

shock phase

countershock phase

resistance

exhaustion

Social Readjustment
  Rating Scale

life-change events

chronic life strains

scheduled life changes

unscheduled life changes

daily hassles

daily uplifts

appraisal

interactionist definitions

harm avoidance

heritability rating

resistance resources

buffering effect of social
  support

intimacy

locus of control

optimism

helplessness

coping

problem-focused coping

appraisal-focused coping

emotion-focused coping

approach coping

avoidance coping

selectivity theory

amenity move

kinship migration

institutional migration

self-determined
  motivation

SUGGESTED READINGS

Chiriboga, D. A. (1997). Crisis, challenge, and stability in the middle years. In M. E. Lachman & J. B. James (Eds.)., *Multiple pathways of midlife development* (pp. 293–322). Chicago: University of Chicago Press.

Chiriboga writes about his concepts of micro, mezzo, and macro stressors, and how they describe the findings of the longitudinal normative transitions study he has been affiliated with for a number of years. This is especially interesting because it shows that stress can initiate personal growth and change at many points across the life span.

George, L. (1996). Social factors and illness. In R. H. Binstock & L. K. George (Eds.). *Handbook of aging and the social sciences (4th ed.,* pp. 229–252). San Diego, CA: Academic Press.

This chapter provides a thorough review of research and includes factors that are implicated in health outcomes as well as social buffering. There is also a good section on methodological considerations.

Stroebe, M. S., Stroebe, W., & Hansson, R. O. (Eds.). (1993). *Handbook of bereavement: Theory, research, and intervention.* Cambridge, England: Cambridge University Press.

This is a wonderful collection of papers, including contributions by most of the major figures in this area.

The bookstores are full of stress management books and self-help books that apply to various stressful events in one's life. If you are facing a crisis of some type, there are good books on coping with divorce, bereavement, retirement, and losing one's job. The best general book I have read lately is:

LoVerde, M. (1998). *Stop screaming at the microwave: How to connect your disconnected life.* New York: Fireside Books.

Dr. LoVerde is a former medical school professor who also has a working husband and three children. Her book is a combination of research findings, humor at her own experiences, and stories from people she has met on the lecture circuit. Part of the book tells about coping with stress and part tells about increasing your social support relationships.

THEMES OF ADULT DEVELOPMENT: AN OVERVIEW

CHAPTER 12

For most of this book I have been describing age differences, or age changes, in each of a series of domains: physical functioning and health, mental functioning, roles, relationships, and so on. I've tried to point out some of the connections among these many different developmental tracks as I've gone along, but despite my best efforts I'm sure that by now you have a rather fragmented view of adulthood. So now I need to put the adult back together by looking at the ways in which all the various threads come together in each age period.

In most of the earlier chapters I summarized the major trends and age changes in a table, so one way to give you a look at the whole picture is to combine them all into a single giant table such as Table 12.1. You'll see that in this megatable I have subdivided early adulthood as well as late adulthood, in order to highlight several key points about age patterns.

Also note that the table describes the "average" or typical sequence of events for an adult who follows the culturally defined sequence of roles at the modal ages. I'll have a lot more to say about individual pathways in the final chapter (Chapter 14). For now, though, it is important to think about the typical or average. The normative pattern is clearly to marry in one's early 20s and begin having children before 25. The children then typically leave home by the time one is about 50. Each row of the table represents a highly condensed version of one facet of change we might see over the lifetime of a person who follows such a modal pattern.

Of the seven rows in the table, four seem to me to describe genuinely maturational or developmental sequences. Clearly, the physical and mental changes summarized in the first two rows are strongly related to highly pre-

TABLE 12.1 Summary of Changes in Eight Different Domains of Adult Functioning

	Young Adulthood, 18–25	Early Adulthood, 25–40	Middle Adulthood, 40–65	Late Adulthood (Young Old), 65–75	Late, Late Adulthood (Old Old), 75+
Physical change	Peak functioning in most physical skills; maximum health; optimum childbearing period.	Still good physical functioning and health in most areas; health habits established now create pattern of later risks.	Beginning signs of physical decline in some areas (e.g., strength, elasticity, height, cardiovascular functioning).	Physical decline more noticeable, but rate of decline is still relatively slow; reaction time slows.	Acceleration of rate of physical and health decline.

TABLE 12.1 **Summary of Changes in Eight Different Domains of Adult Functioning (continued)**

	Young Adulthood, 18–25	Early Adulthood, 25–40	Middle Adulthood, 40–65	Late Adulthood (Young Old), 65–75	Late, Late Adulthood (Old Old), 75+
Cognitive change	Cognitive skill high on most measures; peak synaptic speed.	Peak period of cognitive skill on most measures at about age 30.	Some signs of loss of cognitive skill on fluid, timed, unexercised skills; little functional loss.	Small declines for virtually all adults on crystalized and exercised skills; larger losses on fluid skills, but rate of loss is still slow for most.	Acceleration in the rate of cognitive decline, particularly in memory.
Family and gender roles	Major role acquisition; marriage and family formation, clear separation of male and female roles.	Family roles strongly dominant, with continued differentiation of gender roles.	Launch children; postparental phase; for some, added role of care of elderly parents.	Grandparent role; significantly less dominance of family and gender roles.	Family roles now relatively unimportant.
Relationships	Maximum emphasis on forming friendships and partnership; usually high marital satisfaction until birth of first child.	Lower marital satisfaction; fewer new friends; continued contact with family members.	Increased marital satisfaction; perhaps more intimate friendship relationships.	High marital satisfaction for those not widowed; friendships and sibling relationships may become more intimate. Relationships with children frequent but not central to well-being.	Majority are widowed; friends and siblings remain important.
Work roles	Choose career, often several job changes; lower job satisfaction.	Rising work satisfaction; major emphasis on work or career success; most career progress.	Plateau of career steps but high work satisfaction on average.	Retirement for vast majority.	Work roles unimportant for virtually all.
Personality and meaning	Task of intimacy; typically conformist level of personality or meaning.	Increasing individuality (e.g., increasing self-confidence, independence, autonomy). Task of generativity.	Some sign of a softening of the individuality of the earlier period; fewer immature defenses; possibly autonomous level.	Task of ego integrity; perhaps more interiority; a few may reach integrated level.	Continuation of previous pattern.
Major tasks	Separate from family; form partnership; begin family; find job; create individual life pattern.	Rear family; establish personal work/family pattern; strive for success.	Launch family; redefine life goals; achieve individuality; care for aging parent.	Cope with retirement; cope with declining body and mind; redefine life goals and sense of self.	Possibly reminiscence to come to terms with one's own life and with death; cope with illness or disability.

dictable and widely shared physical processes. While the *rate* of change is affected by lifestyle and habits, the sequences appear to be maturational. More tentatively, I have argued that the sequences of change in personality and in systems of meaning may also be "developmental" in the sense in which I have used that term throughout the book. These are not strongly age-linked changes, but there is at least some evidence that they are sequential and *not* merely a function of particular or culture-specific changes in roles or life experiences. The remaining four rows, describing roles, tasks, and relationships, seem to describe sequences that are common insofar as they are shared by many adults in a given cohort in a given culture. If the timing or the sequence of those roles or tasks changes in any particular culture, however, the pattern described in the table changes as well.

A second way to look at the table is to read down the columns rather than across the rows. This gives some sense of the various patterns that may occur simultaneously, the meshing of the several "gears" in Perun and Bielby's timing model I described in Chapter 2 (recall Figure 2.3). Let me look at each of these periods in a bit more depth.

CRITICAL THINKING

Before you read further, consider which period of adult life you would describe as, overall, the most rewarding. Why that particular period more than any other? As you read the rest of the chapter, see if your view changes.

YOUNG ADULTHOOD: FROM 18 TO 25

These days we are so indoctrinated with the idea of a "midlife crisis" that we may well assume that midlife is the time of greatest changes and potential for greatest stress, but a good case can be made that it is young adulthood and not middle age that holds the honor as the period of adult life with the most changes. Consider the following: Between 18 and 25 young adults:

* Complete the major part of their education, which requires intensive learning and remembering

* Must separate from their parents, establishing an independent existence

* Typically add more major roles than at any other time in their lives: a work role, marriage, typically parenthood

* Change jobs more frequently and move more frequently than any other age group, producing higher total numbers of "life changes" than at any other time in life

* Are likely to have the dirtiest, least interesting, least challenging jobs, and to like their jobs less well than any other age group

The results of such high level of change and stress are apparent. Recall, for example, that rates of self-reported loneliness are higher among adults in this age range than in any other group, and depression is more likely in this period than at any other period except (possibly) late, late adulthood.

Fortunately, young adults have a number of striking assets to help them deal with these high levels of demand. Most obviously, these years are the ones in which body and mind are at their peak. Neurological speed is at maximum, so physical and mental reaction time is swift; new information is learned easily and recalled easily; the immune system is at its efficient best so that one recovers quickly from disease or injury; the cardiovascular system is similarly at its peak, so that sports can be played with speed and endurance. One feels immortal.

Young adults also deal with the changes by creating a network of friendships and other close relationships—part of what Erikson talks about as the task of intimacy. Friendships seem to be not only numerous but particularly important in these years; loneliness is high in these years precisely because relationships are felt to be so important.

When one's relationships do not meet those high expectations, one is more vulnerable, more likely to feel alone than is true at other ages, when the quality of relationships may not be so central.

Perhaps because the role demands are so powerful, the young adult's sense of himself or herself, the meaning system with which he or she interprets all these experiences, seems to be dominated by rules, by conformity, by a sense that authority is external to the self. We think of these years as a time when the young person is becoming independent, but in becoming independent of their parents, most young adults are not becoming individualized in the sense in which I used that term in Chapters 9 and 10. Most are still locked into a conformist view, seeing things in black-and-white terms, looking to outside authority to tell them the rules. If midlife is a time of **detribalization** (to use Levinson's term), these earliest adulthood years are a time of maximal **tribalization.** We define ourselves by our tribe and our place in that tribe.

Roger Gould, whose theory of adult development I mentioned very briefly in Chapter 2, has put it slightly differently. He has talked about a series of assumptions or myths that are the basis for our existence at each of a series of ages or stages. In this early adult period, so Gould argues, one of the key assumptions is that "rewards will come automatically if we do what we're supposed to do. . . . We expect that if we do our part, life will pay off accordingly. Our dreams will come true. People will respond to us the way loving and decent people ought to respond; fair play is guaranteed, and we will be compensated for our efforts" (1978, p. 59). From society's point of view this is a highly adaptive world view since it keeps young people in the mold, nose to the grindstone. From the person's perspective, too, a conformist inner model can be highly adaptive (perhaps especially for those young people whose temperament or personal qualities happen to match the then-current cultural expectations). Hard work *is* frequently rewarded; finding a mate and beginning a family in one's early 20s *is* associated with maximum marital stability over the long haul and has the advantages of being on-time rather than off-time. Such a conformist or conventional world view is also adaptive precisely because this is a time in life when external role demands are so intense. The biological clock may be largely inaudible at this age, but the *social clock* is ticking very loudly indeed.

In the next period, from 25 to 40, the social clock remains louder than the biological clock (with the obvious exception of the childbearing clock for women), but most adults begin to respond to the social demands in new ways.

CRITICAL THINKING

Think about yourself at 20 or 25. Did you (do you) share the basic assumption that Gould is describing? Did you (do you) have some deep-seated belief that if you just follow(ed) the rules, you'd be rewarded? If you are older than 25, ask yourself whether you still believe this, and if not, when the change occurred and why.

EARLY ADULTHOOD: FROM 25 TO 40

Like the young adulthood period I have just been describing, the years from 25 to 40 are blessed with peak or near-peak physical and mental functioning. You have enough energy for a 50- or 60-hour workweek or for keeping track of several small children, or both. Among the several age strata in the U.S. culture, these years of early adulthood are also afforded the highest social status, as Figure 12.1 shows.

The data in this figure are from a study by Paul Baker (1985), who asked adults (aged 17 to 35) to read a series of 28 profiles of fictional individuals who varied in age and gender and to rate each for overall status on a seven-point scale where a rating of 7 reflected status "far above average." The 28 profiles were created to span 14 different age levels from age 5 to age 90, with a male and a female profile written for each of the 14 ages. Each was intended to reflect the normative features of a person of that age and gender. You can see in the figure that there was a sharp increase in perceived status between 25 and 30, and that the peak status for both men and women was between 30 and 40.

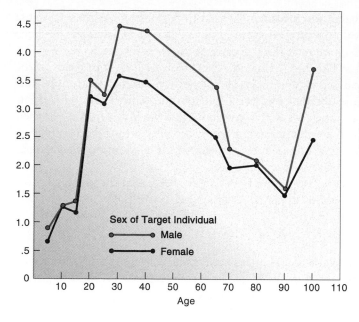

FIGURE 12.1 Ratings of the overall social status of adults of various ages in this study by Baker suggest that (in Western culture at least) status is at its peak in the years between 30 and 40.

Source: Baker, 1985, Fig. 1, p. 507.

There are some flaws in this study, among them the fact that the people doing the ratings were all relatively young. Baker found that the pattern of ratings was not affected by the age of the person doing the rating, but it is of course possible that middle-aged or older raters would rate the later periods of life as having higher status than young adulthood. The study would also have been better if there had been several different profiles for each age/gender combination so that age and the specific features of the profile were not confounded, but the findings are interesting nonetheless and match other data on the status of different age groups.

Perhaps it is the "generative" quality of this age period that leads to such a high level of status. It is the time that Levinson describes as "settling down," in both work and family life. In our early 20s most of us choose the role niches we will fill—the particular job, the particular spouse or partner, the number and timing of children. In our late 20s and our 30s we set to work to fulfill the demands of those role niches, to achieve our dream. In the work domain, this is the time when most adults experience their greatest or most rapid advancement. In family life, it is the time when children are borne and reared.

But it is also a time when the conformist or conventional world view begins to give way to a more individualistic approach. We can see this in all the personality changes I chronicled in Chapter 9, including increases in independence and autonomy.

This change seems to come about for several reasons. Among other things, we discover that following the rules doesn't always lead to reward, a realization that causes us to question the system itself. Neither marriage nor having children, for example, leads to unmitigated bliss, as evidenced by the well-replicated drop in marital satisfaction after the birth of the first child and during the period when the children are young. For those who married in their early or middle 20s, that drop in satisfaction occurs in their late 20s and 30s, contributing to a kind of disillusionment with the entire role system. A second reason for the change in perspective, I think, is that this is the time in which we develop really individual skills. In conforming to the external role demand that we find work and pursue it, we also discover our own talents and capacities, a discovery that helps to turn our focus inward. We become more aware of our own individuality, more aware of the parts of ourselves that existing roles do not allow us to express. This change is reflected in the growing self-confidence noted by many researchers, as well as by the greater "openness to self" described by Norma Haan and others.

But while this individualization process begins in our 30s, it is nonetheless true that this period of early adulthood, like the period from 18 to 25, is dominated by the social clock. In our 30s we may chafe more at the strictures of the roles in which we find ourselves; we may be less and less likely to define ourselves solely or largely in terms of the roles we occupy, but the role demands are still extremely powerful in this period. This fact tends to make the lives of those in early adulthood more like one another than will be true at any later point. To be sure, some adults do not follow the normative pattern, and their lives are less predictable. But the vast majority of adults do enter into the broad river of family and work roles in their 20s and are moved along with the common flow as their children grow older and their work status progresses.

One of the key changes as we move into middle adult life is that the power of those roles declines; the social clock begins to be less audible, less compelling.

MIDDLE ADULTHOOD: FROM 40 TO 65

Although the change is usually gradual rather than abrupt, the period of middle adulthood is really quite distinctly different from the years that have come before. As Elizabeth Barrett Browning said in another context, "Let me count the ways:"

The Biological Clock

Most obviously, the biological clock begins to be audible, since it is during these years that the first signs of physical aging become apparent—the changes in the eyes that mean most adults require glasses for reading, loss of elasticity in the skin that makes wrinkles more noticeable, the diminished reproductive capacity, most noticeable for women but present for men as well, the heightened risk for major diseases such as heart disease or cancer, the slight but measurable slowing in reaction time or foot speed, perhaps some slowing in the speed of bringing names or other information out of long-term memory.

The early stages of this physical aging process normally don't involve much functional loss. Mental skills may be a trifle slower but not enough slower that you can't do your job or teach yourself something new such as using a computer. Achieving and maintaining fitness may take more work, but it's still quite possible. If you've been out of shape, you can even improve significantly, running faster or doing more pushups than you could when you were 30. But as you move through these years toward retirement age, the signs of aging become more and more apparent and less and less easy to ignore.

David Karp (1988) has documented this growing awareness of physical aging in a series of interviews with 72 men and women between the ages of 50 and 60. This is not a representative sample; all these adults are white, all are in professional occupations. Karp's study doesn't tell us whether working-class men and women, or minority adults, would respond in the same way. Still, he has given us an in-depth look at the experience of a few. He says, "The fact of aging seems to be one of life's great surprises, a surprise that is most fully sprung in the fifties" (1988, p. 729).

The reminders are both external and internal. The body itself sends you some messages. As one of Karp's subjects said: "I do not see the signs of old age, but I can see some of the clues. I have arthritis. You can't deny that. To me that's kind of old age. I've been running for 20 years and I didn't run last year. My arthritis caught up with me and a couple of other things like that. So, I see myself fitting it [age], but I'm only on the threshold of what I would call becoming old" (p. 730). And our culture sends messages as well. When I turned 50 I received in the mail an invitation to join the American Association of Retired Persons. "Hey," I said, "I'm not retired! I'm not old enough to belong to AARP!" But I am. Their membership begins at 50. And one of Karp's subjects told of hearing an insurance salesman on television inquiring, "'Do you know someone between 50 and 80 years old?' His response was, 'My God, he's talking about me'" (p. 729).

There are also generational reminders, such as the increasing infirmity or death of one's elderly parents, or seeing one's children entering their late 20s or 30s. One professor who was part of Karp's study said: "More recently, I would say in the last five years… when I meet the parents of students, it occurs to me that not only am I old enough to be their father, but I'm half way on the way to being their grandfather" (p. 732). My father expressed an equivalent realization, albeit one stage later. On hearing that he was about to become a great-grandfather, he said, "I don't mind so much being a great-grandfather; what I mind is being the father of a grandmother!"

The Social Clock

At the same time, the social clock becomes much less significant. To a considerable degree, of course, this is the result of the fact that by middle adulthood many of us have completed at least some of the key roles, as I described in Chapter 6 in some detail. If you had your children in your 20s, then by your late 40s or early 50s they are likely to be launched. And in your work life you are likely to have reached the highest level that you will achieve, you know the role well, and the drive to achieve may peak and then decline.

But the softening or weakening of the social clock is also the result of the detribalization process that Levinson talks about, perhaps part of a deeper shift in personality or meaning systems toward a more individualistic view. The greater openness to self that emerges at this time includes an openness to unexpressed parts of the self, parts that are likely to be outside the prescriptions of the roles. The change is thus both external and internal.

If you think about the relationship of these two clocks over the years of adulthood, you might visualize them something like the pattern in Figure 12.2. The specific point of crossover of these two chronologies is obviously going to differ from one adult to another, but it is most likely to occur some time in this middle-adulthood period.

Work and Marital Satisfaction. One of the ironies is that the decline in the centrality of work and relationship roles in midlife is often accompanied by greater satisfaction with both work and relationships. You'll recall from Chapters 7 and 8 that both marital and work

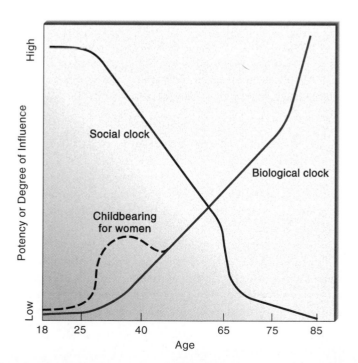

FIGURE 12.2 One way to think about the different phases or stages of adulthood is in terms of the relative potency or importance of the biological and social clocks. Except for the issue of childbearing for women, the biological clock is relatively unimportant until some time in midlife, after which it becomes increasingly important. The social clock follows an opposite pattern.

satisfaction rise in these years of middle adulthood. As always, there are undoubtedly many reasons for the rise, including the fact that the actual work one is doing in these years is likely to be objectively more interesting than was true in one's 20s or even 30s, and that once the children are grown and gone, one of the major strains on a marriage declines. But the improvement in satisfaction with both work and relationships may also be a reflection of the inner shift of perspective I have been talking about. Adults who experience the world from a more individualist or conscientious perspective take responsibility for their own actions, so they may find ways to make their work and relationships more pleasant. Or they may choose to change work or partners.

The Sense of Choice. It is precisely this sense of choice that seems to me to be a key aspect of this age period. There are certainly still roles to be filled; one does not stop being a parent just because the children have been launched; one still has work roles to fill, relationships with one's own parents, with friends, with the community. But adults in middle life have more choices about how they will fill those roles, both because the roles of this age themselves have more leeway and because we now perceive roles differently, as being less compellingly prescriptive.

Variability. A related phenomenon is the increased variability of pathways that we see in midlife. In early adulthood, because of the power of the various roles and of our attitude toward them, there is a certain lockstep quality to development. Certainly there are variations; I've talked about a lot of them. But if you followed the norm, or close to the norm, in your early adult life, the next 20 years are reasonably predictable.

CRITICAL THINKING

Before you read what I have to say about the midlife crisis, think about your own exposure to this concept. Before you read this book, did you simply assume that a midlife crisis was a normal, even an inevitable part of aging? Where did such a belief come from? Books? Movies?

In an inner sense, too, there are signs that there is more commonality of psychological functioning in early adulthood than there is later. In Loevinger's terms, for example, virtually everyone reaches the conformist stage; many reach the individualist stage, but fewer and fewer will be found achieving each subsequent stage. In old age, physical aging will again impose some uniformity, but in personality and meaning systems the diversity should be even greater.

Research support for such greater variability in midlife and in late adulthood has been accumulating in recent years (Christensen et al., 1994; Dannefer, 1988). One example: Norma Haan (1981) has found that the range of scores on the dimension of "openness to self" in the Berkeley longitudinal sample was significantly larger at midlife than it had been when the subjects had been in their teens, 20s, or 30s. That is, not only did the average score on this dimension go up, the diversity also rose.

Is This Picture Too Rosy? The picture I've been painting is pretty rosy, isn't it? In midlife we have more choices, our work and marital satisfaction is likely to rise and there is a likelihood of some inner growth or transformation as well. To be sure, there is also the growing awareness of physical aging, but for most of us such an awareness is not dominant. We still feel pretty fit and capable. It sounds as if these years, when neither the biological nor the social clock is deafening us with its sound, are the best of all worlds.

But isn't this also the time when the infamous midlife crisis is supposed to hit? In this more negative view of midlife, "midlife men [are seen] as anxious, conflicted, and going through a crisis. The women are menopausal, fretful, and depressed" (S. Hunter & Sundel, 1989, p. 13). Can these two views be reconciled? I've been sidestepping the question of whether there really is a midlife crisis for most of this book; now I need to face it more squarely.

Midlife Crisis: Fact or Myth?

The notion that a personal or emotional crisis at midlife is an integral part of adult experience has been fed by characterizations in novels, plays, and films as well as by such popular books as *Passages* (Sheehy, 1974) and *New Passages* (Sheehy, 1996). The existence of some kind of crisis at this time of life is also part of several theories you have become familiar with already, including most notably Levinson's.

You'll remember from Chapter 2 that Levinson argues that coping with the constellation of developmental tasks that confront us at midlife, including acceptance of death and mortality, recognition of biological limitations and health risks, restructuring of gender identity and self-concept, reorientation to work, career, creativity, and achievement, and reassessment of primary relationships, guarantees some kind of significant reassessment and change of basic life structure in the early 40s, typically accompanied by depression, distress, and upheaval.

But is it really true? I realize that the concept of a midlife crisis has become so widely accepted that to raise doubts about it will align me against a good deal of popular culture. But doubts I do have.

Transition Versus Crisis. To make any sense out of the evidence and theory in this area, I must first distinguish between a transition and a crisis. Levinson, as well as other theorists, proposes that adult life is made up of a series of *transitions,* times when existing life structures are reassessed and may be altered. A transition may be very gradual and smooth, or it might be a **crisis,** when the demands of some transition overwhelm the individual's social support system and internal resources. With this distinction in mind, we have to ask two questions about midlife: (1) Do *all* adults (or even *most* adults) experience a transition of some kind at midlife? (2) Is this particular transition likely to be experienced as a crisis, especially in comparison to other transitions in adult life?

Transition at Midlife? No researcher has yet developed a real measure of transitions, so it is difficult to answer this first question cleanly. But there is widespread agreement among researchers who study midlife that this is a period of significant transition, in roles as well as in inner perspectives (W. Gallagher, 1993). The timing of such transitions is quite variable, however, depending on the timing of various role changes, on the longevity of each adult's parents, or on such unexpected events as unemployment or divorce. Thus, contrary to Levinson's model, there is no single age in the middle years that is the designated time of transition.

Is It a Crisis? Where opinions differ is on whether these transitions normally involve crisis. In one recent book on *Midlife Myths* (S. Hunter & Sundel, 1989), two respected researchers reading the same evidence came to opposite conclusions. David Chiriboga concludes that "there is mounting evidence from research studies that serious midlife problems are actually experienced by only 2 to 5 percent of middle-agers" (1989, p. 117), while Lois Tamir not only argues that there is a significant transition at this age but that the transition is marked with "deep-seated self-doubts or confusion" (1989, p. 161).

My own reading of this set of evidence leads me to the conclusion that Chiriboga's summary is the correct one. Clearly, there are some adults who experience this transition as a crisis; it may even be possible that this particular transition is more likely to be crisislike than are other adult transitions. But there is little evidence to suggest that crisis is a common feature of midlife.

Much of the evidence against the existence of a widespread midlife crisis seems to me to be compelling. For example, Costa & McCrae (1980a; McCrae & Costa, 1984) developed a midlife crisis scale which included items about a sense of inner turmoil, a sense of failing power, marital dissatisfaction, or job dissatisfaction. When they then used this scale in a cross-sectional study of over 500 men aged 35 to 70, they could find no age at which scores were particularly high. Some men at each age reported feelings of crisis. Farrell and Rosenberg (1981), whose study of friendship patterns in men I mentioned in an earlier chapter, similarly found no age difference on a scale measuring midlife crisis, nor did Pearlin (1975) find a piling up of depression or anxiety at midlife in his cross-sectional study of life stresses. Epidemiological studies also do not show any clear rise or peak in midlife for such likely signs of crisis as divorce, alcoholism, or depression (S. Hunter & Sundel, 1989). As an example, go back and look at Figure 5.6 again: In this major study, serious depressions were more common in the period from 25 to 44 than in the 45 to 64 period (Regier et al., 1988).

Of course, all of this is cross-sectional evidence. Studies such as Costa & McCrae's may tell us that there is no specific age at which some kind of upheaval is common, but they don't tell us whether each person, as he or she passes through the decades of midlife, is likely to have an upheaval at *some* time. Since the span of years we are calling "midlife" is fairly broad, it might still be that some kind of a crisis is common between 40 and 60, but that it happens at different times for different adults, depending on the timing of particular kinds of life changes, such as the topping out of one's career or the children leaving home.

Such a possibility is strengthened by the retrospective studies of Rochelle Harris and her colleagues (Harris, Ellicott, & Holmes, 1986) that I described in Chapter 9. You may remember that they studied a group of women aged 45, 50, 55, and 60, asking each to talk in detail about the years of her adult life. Their descriptions were then rated for the presence of transitions. Eighty percent of the 64 women in this study reported at least one such transition between the ages of 36 and 60, but the transitions were linked not to age but to some change in family life-cycle status. Not all these transitions were crisislike; many involved uplifting feelings rather than depressions. But the findings at least raise the possibility that crises might be common but simply not detected by our usual cross-sectional techniques of study.

Longitudinal evidence is obviously the best antidote to this problem. Yet here, too, there is little support for the expectation of widespread midlife crises. For instance, in her analysis of the subjects in the Berkeley and Oakland longitudinal studies, Norma Haan (1981) found no indication of a widespread upheaval in midlife. Those who experience a genuine upheaval at this period of life, and perhaps 5 percent of the population do, are likely to be those who experienced upheavals at other times as well. That is, "having a crisis" is, to some extent, aspect of personality rather than a characteristic of an age period.

However, there is one subgroup for whom a crisislike experience may well be more common in midlife: white professional or middle-class males. It is precisely this group that Tamir has studied, so perhaps it is not surprising that she concludes that a midlife crisis is widespread. In a cross-sectional study of a national sample of roughly 1000 men aged 25 to 69, Tamir (1982) found that among college-educated men, the period from age 45 to 49 was characterized by lower levels of zest, more "psychological immobilization," drinking problems, and more turning to prescription drugs to relieve nervous tension than any other age period. You'll also recall from Chapter 4 (Figure 4.6) that suicide rates among white men begin to rise in midlife, although they continue to rise for this subgroup well into old age, which does not suggest some uniquely crisislike feature of midlife.

It may well be that for well-educated, successful men in this culture and in current cohorts, the period of midlife is particularly stressful, perhaps because members of this group have had more extravagant dreams and thus have more adjustments to make to the realities of their accomplishments. But the bulk of the evidence suggests, instead, that the great majority of midlife adults manage the transitions of this period in a gradual, gentle process rather than through upheaval and crisis (W. Gallagher, 1993). The cultural myth of the inevitable midlife crisis is just that, a myth.

In many ways the "young old" are more like the middle-aged than they are like the old old. So why make a division at age 65?

From a physical point of view there is nothing notable about age 65 that would suggest that some new stage or phase has begun. Certainly, some adults in this age range experience significant disease or chronic disability. But the norm is rather that small—albeit noticeable—physical changes or declines continue to accumulate at roughly the same rate as was true in one's middle years. Hearing loss is now more likely to become a problem, as is arthritis; one is likely to have an increased sense of being a bit slower. But for most adults (in Western countries at least) the rate of physical or mental change does not appear to accelerate in these years. What makes this 10-year period unique is the rapid drop in role demands that accompanies retirement, a drop that once again changes the balance between what I have been calling the social clock and the biological clock, as I have tried to suggest in Figure 12.2.

There is certainly little evidence that this change is marked by any kind of crisis. As I pointed out in Chapter 8, research on retirement shows no increase in illness or depression or other distress that can be linked causally to the retirement itself. For those who retire *because* of ill health, the picture is rather different; for this subgroup retirement is linked with further declines in health and perhaps depression. But for the majority, and with the notable exception of the continuing rise in suicide among white males, every indication is that mental health is as good—or perhaps better—in this age group than at younger ages.

What does mark this change is the loss of the work role, which is of course accompanied by a continuing decline in the centrality of other roles as well. Spousal roles continue, of course, for those whose spouse is still living; there is still some parental role, although that too is less demanding and less clearly defined; the role of friend and of brother or sister to one's aging siblings may actually become more central. But even more than was true in middle life, these roles are full of choices.

Edwin Shneidman (1989), writing about the decade of one's 70s, puts it this way: "Consider that when one is a septuagenarian, one's parents are gone, children are grown, mandatory work is done; health is not too bad, and responsibilities are relatively light, with time, at long last, for focus on the self. These can be sunset years, golden years, an Indian Summer, a period of relatively mild weather for both soma and psyche in the late autumn or early winter of life, a decade of greater independence and increased opportunities for further self-development" (p. 684). But what is it that adults in this period of early old age, of "Indian Summer," choose to do with their lives? Do they remain active and involved, or do they begin to withdraw, to turn inward toward self-development or reminiscence? If there has been controversy about this age period, it has centered on some variant of this question. The issue is usually framed in the terms of the theory of *disengagement* in old age.

Disengagement in Old Age: Another Myth?

The term **disengagement** was first proposed by Cumming and Henry (1961) to describe what they saw as a key psychological process in old age. As restated by Cumming (1975), this process was seen as having three features or aspects: (1) Adults' social "life space" shrinks with age, a change especially noticeable in the period from 65 on when we interact with fewer and fewer others, and fill fewer and fewer roles as we move through old age; (2) in the roles and relationships that remain, the aging person becomes more individualized, less governed by the rules and norms; and (3) the aging person anticipates this set of changes and actively embraces them, disengaging more and more from roles and relationships.

Few would disagree with the first two of these points. In old age, most adults do show a decline in the number of social activities they engage in, they occupy fewer roles, and those roles have fewer clear prescriptions. Older adults participate in fewer clubs or organizations, go to church less often, see friends less often. This has been found in both longitudinal studies, such as the Duke studies of aging (Palmore, 1981) and in cross-sectional ones (D. L. Morgan, 1988), so the pattern seems well established.

But the third of Cumming and Henry's points about disengagement is in considerable dispute. They argued that disengagement is not only natural but optimally healthy in old age, so that those who show such disengagement the most are going to be the happiest and least disturbed. And this is simply not shown by the research. There is no indication that those who show the greatest decline in social activity (who "disengage" the most) are happier or healthier. On the contrary, the common finding is that the *least* disengaged adults report slightly greater satisfaction with themselves or their lives, are healthiest, and have the highest morale (Adelmann, 1994; Bryant & Rakowski, 1992; C. K. Holahan, 1988; Palmore, 1981). The effect is not large, but the direction of the effect is consistently positive: More social involvement is linked to better outcomes.

The picture is not totally one-sided. On the other side of the ledger is a significant body of work pointing to the conclusion that solitude is quite a comfortable state for many older adults. Note, for example, the finding I reported to you in Chapter 7, that among all age groups loneliness is least common among the elderly. Indeed, some older adults clearly find considerable satisfaction in an independent, socially isolated (highly disengaged) life pattern. For example, in a study of some of the parents of the subjects in the Berkeley longitudinal studies, Maas and Kuypers (1974) describe a group of satisfied older men they call "hobbyists," whose lives revolved around a solitary hobby such as woodworking or birdwatching. Similarly, in studies in England, Savage and his colleagues (Savage, Gaber, Britton, Bolton, & Cooper, 1977) found some introverted, socially isolated elderly adults who seemed largely content with their lives. Clearly, then, it is possible to choose and to find contentment in a largely disengaged lifestyle in these older years. What these data do not say, however, is that such disengagement is *necessary* for mental health. On the contrary, most of the evidence says exactly the opposite: For most older adults, social involvement is both a sign of, and probably a cause of, higher levels of satisfaction. Those who do not have satisfactory contact with others, particularly with friends, are typically less satisfied with their lives.

So while our lives become less ruled by roles in this decade of the young old, we still maintain, even need, social contact with others.

CRITICAL THINKING

There is a tricky methodological problem in testing disengagement theory. If we find that the most active adults are the most happy with their lives (i.e., if there is a positive correlation between activity and happiness), that could be because happiness leads to social involvement, rather than the reverse. What kind of research design might we use to get around this problem?

LATE, LATE ADULTHOOD: FROM 75 UNTIL DEATH

The fastest-growing segment of the U.S. population is the group of elderly adults Bernice Neugarten calls the "old old," those over 75. As life expectancy increases, more and more of us are living well past the fabled "four score and ten" years. And as health has improved, it is not until these years of late late adulthood that the processes of physical and mental aging really accelerate. It is at this point that the "functional reserve" of many physical systems is likely to fall below the level required for everyday activities (Pendergast, Fisher, & Calkins, 1993), creating a new level of dependence or disability.

I do not want to make too big a deal about the age of 75. The demarcation point between the period of the young old and that of the old old is more a function of health than it is of age. Some adults may be frail at 60; others may still be robust and active at

EVEN AMONG THOSE NEUGARTEN would call the old old, there is a great deal of variability in physical function (or dysfunction) and in living circumstances. Still, there is no escaping the fact that in this age range, the biological clock becomes a potent factor in everyone's lives.

85. But if you look at the norms, as I have been doing in this chapter, it appears that age 75 is roughly where the shift takes place, at least in today's cohorts in the United States and other industrialized countries.

Our knowledge of the old old is not extensive; only in relatively recent years have there been large numbers of such adults; only quite recently has the Census Bureau begun to divide some of its statistics for the elderly into decades rather than merely lumping all those over age 65 into a single category. But we do have some information that points to a qualitative change that takes place at roughly this time.

Go back and look again at Figure 5.1, for example. You'll see that the acceleration in the decline in total mental ability scores starts at about 70 or 75. There is decline before that, but the rate of decline increases in the old old. And as one moves into the 80s and beyond, the incidence of physical and mental frailty rises rapidly (Guralnik & Simonsick, 1993). For example, census data tell us that over half of those over 85 have a disability that would make it impossible for them to use public transportation; many more have more limited disabilities (Longino, 1988).

As a result of the loss or reduction of mobility that now becomes common, elders in the years after 75 also show some further "disengagement" socially. You'll remember from Chapter 10, for example, that church attendance drops at about 75 not because elders are less religious but because getting to church becomes more of a strain. Since widowhood is also the norm in these years, those old old who still live independently are spending more time alone, although it would be a mistake to describe them as socially isolated. Most maintain regular, if reduced, contact with their children, with other family members, and with friends. They may go to fewer club meetings or other group gatherings, but they keep in touch. These changes appear to be part of a more general adaptive process.

Reserve Capacity and Adapting to Old Age. Paul and Margaret Baltes (1990a) have suggested that one of the key features of these later years of adulthood is that the person operates much closer to the edge of reserve capacity than is the case for younger or middle-aged adults. To cope with this fact, and with the fact of various physical declines, one must use a process that the Balteses call **selective optimization with compensation** (1990a, p. 21). There are three elements:

1. **Selection.** The older adult restricts the range of activities or arenas in which he or she will operate, concentrating energy and time on those needs or demands that are truly central. Thus an older adult may choose to serve on only one committee instead of three, or choose to spend time only with good friends, rather than continuing a more general level of social activity.

2. **Optimization.** The older adult can enrich and augment his or her reserves by learning new strategies and keeping old skills well practiced, such as by reading the paper regularly, keeping up some level of fitness, or eating a good diet.

3. **Compensation.** Where the first two strategies are not sufficient, the older adult compensates for losses in many ways, such as wearing glasses or a hearing aid, driving at off-peak times or not driving at night, writing more lists rather than relying on internal memory.

The very fact that such compensation, optimization, and selection are necessary in late late adulthood is a crucial point. Reserve capacities *are* reduced. But it is also crucial to realize that many adults in this age group can and do compensate and adjust their lives to their changing physical circumstances.

Life Review. Finally, let me say just a word about another process that *may* be involved in the process of adaptation in late life. If you think back to Erikson's theory, you'll recall that the stage he proposes for late adulthood is **ego integrity versus despair.** One of

Erikson's notions was that to achieve integrity, older adults must think back over their lives and try to come to terms with whom they had been and who they now are.

Some years ago, Robert Butler (1963) expanded on this idea of Erikson's. Butler proposed that in old age, all of us go through a process he called a **life review,** in which there is a "progressive return to consciousness of past experience, and particularly, the resurgence of unresolved conflicts." Butler argued that in this final stage of life, as preparation for our now clearly impending death, we engage in an analytic and evaluative review of our earlier life. Further, Butler argued that such a review is a necessary part of achieving ego integrity in late life.

This has been an attractive hypothesis. Clinicians who work with the elderly have devised life review interventions for use with older adults. Noted gerontologist James Birren recommends that older adults form **autobiography groups** and discuss various stages and turning points in their lives in order to determine how to best spend their remaining years of life (Birren & Feldman, 1997). And indeed, there are several studies that show that a process of structured reminiscence may increase life satisfaction or self-esteem among older adults (Haight, 1988, 1992). However, the research evidence is generally weak and not uniformly supportive of Butler's ideas. A number of investigators have found no beneficial effects of a life review process (Stevens-Ratchford, 1993; Wallace, 1992). More significantly, we do not know if reminiscence is actually more common in the elderly than among the middle-aged or any other age group. At this point we are left with many unanswered questions: Is some form of reminiscence really more common among the elderly than at other ages? How much do the elderly vary in the amount of reminiscence they engage in? How much of reminiscence is really integrative or evaluative rather than merely story telling for amusement or information? Is reminiscence a necessary ingredient in achieving some form of integration in late life?

On the whole, I think there is good reason to doubt the validity of Butler's hypothesis that life review is a necessary part of old old age. At the same time, it is clear that some kind of preparation for death is an inevitable, even central part of life in these last years. Although death certainly comes to some adults in their 30s, 40s, 50s, or 60s, most younger adults can continue to push the idea of death away: That's something for later. But in the years past 75, the imminence of death is inescapable and must be faced by each of us.

SUMMARY

1. It is useful to look at the various ways in which the several threads of development interact in each of the major periods of adulthood.

2. The years from 18 to 25 appear to have the highest levels of stress but also the greatest physical and mental assets. This period is also marked by the domination of the demands of various roles, which the young person typically experiences from a "conformist" perspective.

3. In the years from 25 to 40 the "social clock" continues to dominate, but there is increasing individualization both in day-to-day lives and in inner perspectives. These years also appear to have the highest status within our culture.

4. In middle adulthood, from 40 to 65, the social clock becomes less compelling while the biological clock begins to have a greater impact, as the first clear signs of physical aging appear. Social roles become less dominant not only because many young-adult roles are well learned or even largely fulfilled, but also because the middle-aged adult perceives the roles differently, experiencing the world from a more individualist perspective.

5. Work and marital satisfaction are typically at high points in the midlife decades, as is a sense of choice. Variability in pathways or characteristics appears to increase as well.

6. Midlife is commonly a time of transition, but such transitions are rarely crisislike.

7. Adults between 65 and 75 are often referred to as the "young old." Although physical and mental aging continues in this age range, the rate does not normally accelerate and most adults in this age range are still independent and relatively fit. Because of retirement from work, however, the social clock becomes even less significant.

8. Some aspects of disengagement theory's description of these years have been supported: There is a reduction in the total number of social contacts of adults past age 65. But there is no indication that disengagement is central to mental health. If anything, the reverse is true.

9. Those past 75 are often called the "old old." It is in these years that the rate of physical and mental aging accelerates, especially after age 80 or 85, so that frailty becomes more common, disabilities more limiting.

10. Reminiscence or life review in these later years may aid some older adults to reassess and integrate the meaning of their lives, but this hypothesis remains to be adequately tested.

KEY TERMS

detribalization

tribalization

transition

crisis

disengagement

selective optimization with compensation

selection

optimization

compensation

ego integrity versus despair

life review

autobiography groups

SUGGESTED READINGS

Gallagher, W. (1993). Midlife myths. *Atlantic Monthly,* May, pp. 51–68.

> This is a particularly good article summarizing in a very readable way much of the scientific information about midlife, including the topics of midlife crisis and menopause. A very upbeat description of the midlife years.

Hunter, S. & Sundel, M. (Eds.). (1989). *Midlife myths: Issues, findings, and practice implications.* Newbury Park, CA: Sage.

> If you want to look at the alternative views of midlife crisis, this is a good recent source. Compare Tamir's paper with the one by Chiriboga. This book also has other useful chapters about the period of midlife, many written by authors whose names will be familiar from the pages of this book.

Karp, D. A. (1988). A decade of reminders: Changing age consciousness between fifty and sixty years old. *The Gerontologist, 28,* 727–738.

Although Karp's sample is certainly not random nor representative, this is one of the few papers in which the actual voices of a particular age group can be heard, in this case adults between 50 and 60. The article is both absorbing and thought-provoking (perhaps particularly for me, since I am now in this decade!)

Lachman, M. E., & James, J. B. (1997). *Multiple paths of midlife development.* Chicago: University of Chicago Press.

This is a collection of articles about midlife development of the self, social relationships, health, and work—all based on longitudinal data.

Sarton, M. (1993). *Encore: Journal of the 80th year.* New York: W.W. Norton.

May Sarton has written several journals of individual years of her life, all of which I have found fascinating. In this journal she writes about a period when she was recovering from a stroke, so it is relevant for the issue of frailty and infirmity in old age.

THE FINAL STAGE: DEATH AND DYING

CHAPTER 13

I n Chapter 12 I talked about the various phases or stages of adult life, but there remains one stage left to discuss, the period of dying and death. In exploring this difficult subject, it is not enough merely to describe the last months or days of life. We have to start earlier. Just as we prepare mentally and physically for earlier stages of adulthood, such as by planning for retirement or by reassessing our priorities and choices periodically, so do we prepare for our own death in various ways over many years. Each adult has attitudes about death, fears of death, and makes preparations for death long before the final confrontation with dying. So let me begin the story by looking at these attitudes, fears, and preparations over the adult years.

THE MEANINGS OF DEATH

"The one invariant of the meaning of death for both the individual and society is that death matters. And so does the process of dying. The event of death and the process of dying have immense impact on individuals and on the community, whether judged by emotional feelings, social relationships, spiritual well-being, financial stresses, or changes in daily living" (Kalish, 1985, p. 149). Understandings of death change over the life span. Preschool children, for example, typically believe that death can be reversed, that dead persons still feel or breathe, and that death can be avoided by some people, such as those who are clever or lucky, or perhaps their own family (Lansdown & Benjamin, 1985; Speece & Brent, 1984, 1992). At about school age, children begin to understand both the permanence and the universality of death.

In adulthood, the concept of death goes well beyond the simple understanding of inevitability and universality. Most broadly, death has important social meaning. The death of any one person changes the roles and relationships of everyone else in that family. When an elder dies, everyone else in that particular lineage moves up one step in the generational system. If a middle-aged person dies, it may dislocate that same generational system because there may now be no one in the "sandwich generation" to take on tasks of elder care. Beyond the family, death also affects other roles, such as by making room for younger adults to take on significant tasks. Retirement serves some of the same functions because the older adult "steps aside" for the younger. But death brings many permanent changes in social systems.

Kalish (1985) suggests four other meanings that death may have for adults, typically mixed in any person's meaning system.

Death as an Organizer of Time. Death defines the endpoint of one's life, so the concept of "time until death" may be an important one for a person trying to organize his or her life. In fact, Bernice Neugarten (1968, 1977) suggests that one of the key changes in thinking in middle age is a switch in the way one marks one's own lifetime, from time since birth to time until death. Her interviews with middle-aged adults frequently yielded statements like the following: "Before I was 35, the future just stretched forth. There would be time to do and see and carry out all the plans I had…. Now I keep thinking will I have time enough to finish off some of the things I want to do?" (Neugarten, 1970, p. 78) Such a change in time perspective, accompanied by a greater awareness of (and worry about) death, does not occur at midlife for every adult. Nor do all older adults think of their lives in terms of time until death. In one study of elderly adults, for example, Pat Keith (1981–1982) found that only about half of her sample of 568 72- to 99-year-olds seemed to think about or precisely define "time remaining." But such a recognition of time remaining may be a useful (perhaps even a necessary) aspect of coming to terms with one's own death. In Keith's study, those adults who did talk about time remaining also had more favorable attitudes toward and less fear of death. Other research confirms this pattern: Older adults who continue to be preoccupied with the past, who avoid thinking about the future, are more likely to be fearful or anxious about death than are those who face the future (and their own deaths) more fully (Pollack, 1979–1980).

Death as Punishment. Children are quite likely to think of death as punishment for being bad—a kind of ultimate Stage 1 moral reasoning. But this view and its reverse (that long life is the reward for being good) are still common in adults. For example, Kalish and Reynolds (1976) found that 36 percent of adults in their study agreed with the statement that "most people who live to be 90 years old or older must have been morally good people." Such a view is strengthened by religious teachings that emphasize a link between sin and death.

Death as Transition. Death involves *some* kind of transition, from life to some sort of life after death, or from life to nothingness. In one study, Daniel Klenow and Robert Bolin (1989–1990) found that 70 percent of adults in a nationally representative U.S. sample reported believing in life after death. Women were more likely to believe in an afterlife than were men, and Protestants and Catholics were much more likely than Jews to have such a belief, but there was no significant age difference. Adults in their 20s were just as likely to believe in life after death as were those older than 60.

Death as Loss. Perhaps most pervasively, death is seen by most of us as a loss—loss of the ability to complete projects or carry out plans, loss of one's body, loss of experiencing, of taste, smell, and touch, loss of relationships with people. No more hot fudge sundaes, no more delight in the reds and golds of autumn leaves making a pattern on the ground, no more caresses or kisses, no more Bach chorales, no more trips to exotic new places. Of course, some of these losses may occur during a person's lifetime. A loss of hearing will already cut out the Bach chorales; widowhood may deprive an adult of caresses. But death guarantees all of these losses.

Unlike beliefs in an afterlife, in this domain there are age differences. In particular, the specific losses that adults associate with death appear to change as they move through the adult years. Young adults are more concerned about loss of opportunity to experience things and about the loss of family relationships; older adults may be more concerned with the loss of time to complete some inner work. These differences are reflected in the results of a study by Richard Kalish (Kalish & Reynolds, 1976). He interviewed a group of roughly 400 adults, equally divided among African-Americans, Japanese-Americans, Mexican-Americans, and Anglo-Americans. Among many other questions, he asked the following: "If you were told that you had a terminal disease and six months to live, how would you want to spend your time until you died?"

CRITICAL THINKING

Think about your own answer to this question before you read any further.

TABLE 13.1 Answers to Survey Question "What Would You Do If You Knew You Were to Die in Six Months?"

	Age Group		
	29–39	40–59	60+
Make a marked change in lifestyle (e.g., travel, sex, experiences)	24	15	9
Center on inner life (read, contemplate, pray)	14	14	37
Focus concern on others, be with loved ones	29	25	12
Attempt to complete projects, tie up loose ends	11	10	3
No change in lifestyle	17	29	31
Other	5	6	8

ªPercent of subjects in a Los Angeles study who gave these types of answers.

Source: Kalish & Reynolds, 1976, p. 205. Reprinted by permission of University of Southern California Press.

There were relatively few ethnic group differences, except that Mexican-Americans were much more likely to say that they would increase the time they spent with family members. Age differences were more striking, as you can see in Table 13.1. Younger adults were clearly more likely to plan to spend time either experiencing things or on relationships, while older adults much more often said they would read, contemplate, or pray—more evidence, perhaps, for the greater "spiritual" preoccupation in later life that I suggested in Chapter 10.

FEAR AND ANXIETY ABOUT DEATH

The view of death as loss is strongly linked to the most studied aspect of death attitudes, namely the fear of or anxiety about death. If we fear death, it is in part the losses of experience, sensation, and relationships that we fear. Fear of death may also include fear of the pain or suffering or indignity that may be involved in the process of death itself, fear that one will not be able to cope well with such pain or suffering, fear of whatever punishment may come after death, and a fundamental fear of loss of the self.

The most common method of measuring fear of death is with some form of questionnaire. For example, David Lester asks subjects to indicate, on a five-point scale, how disturbed or anxious they are made by many aspects of death or dying, such things as the "shortness of life" or "never thinking or experiencing anything again" or "your lack of control over the process of dying" (Lester, 1990). James Thorson and F. C. Powell, in a similar measure, include questions such as "I fear dying a painful death," or "coffins make me anxious," or "I am worried about what happens to us after we die" (Thorson & Powell, 1992).

Age Differences in Fear of Death

On measures such as these, researchers have quite consistently found that middle-aged adults show the greatest fear, and older adults the least, with young adults falling somewhere in between (Gesser, Wong, & Reker, 1987–1988; Riley & Foner, 1968; Thorson & Powell, 1992). Older adults are more anxious about the process of *dying* but have less fear of death itself.

The shift in fear of death between middle age and old age is particularly clear in a well-designed study by Vern Bengtson and his colleagues (Bengtson, Cuellar, & Ragan, 1977). Bengtson's sample, all

CRITICAL THINKING

Before you read further, consider how you would explain this pattern of results. Why might the peak of fear of death be among the middle aged?

between 45 and 74 years of age, was selected to be representative of adults in the Los Angeles area and included approximately equal numbers of whites, blacks, and Mexican-Americans. The measure of fear of death was quite simple (perhaps too much so, in fact). He asked each subject "How afraid are you of death? Would you say you are: not at all afraid?/somewhat afraid?/or very afraid?" Only 37 percent said that they were either somewhat or very afraid, but these were mostly the middle-aged subjects, as you can see in Figure 13.1. The fact that the shape of the curve is so strikingly similar for all three ethnic groups makes the results even more persuasive.

Bengtson's study only tells us that fear of death is higher in middle age than in old age; since he did not include adults younger than 45, we can't tell whether fear of death is lower or higher among those in early adulthood. But a more recent study by Gina Gesser and her associates (Gesser et al., 1987–1988) fills in the gap, showing precisely the same curvilinear relationship of age and fear of death as Riley had found several decades before. Gesser found the highest levels of fear of death and of the dying process among middle-aged subjects, the lowest levels among those over 60, with intermediate levels among young adults. In this study, the over-60 group also showed more acceptance of death, agreeing with such statements as "I look forward to a life after death," or "I would neither fear death nor welcome it."

Collectively, these results are consistent with the suggestion made by Levinson (based on both Jung's theories and the work of psychoanalyst Elliott Jaques (1965) that one of the central tasks of midlife is to come to terms with the inevitability of death. The greater awareness of body changes and aging that is part of this period, coupled perhaps with the death of one's own parents, combine to break down the defenses we have all erected against the knowledge of and fear of death. In particular, the death of one's parents may be especially shocking and disturbing, not only because of the specific loss to be mourned but because you must now face the realization that you are now the oldest generation in the

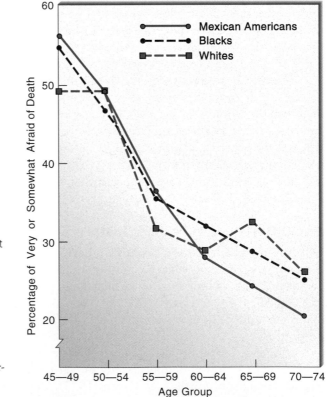

FIGURE 13.1 The remarkable similarity that these three different groups show in the patterns of age change in overt fear of death lends credence to the view that older adults are less consciously fearful of death than are middle-aged adults.

Source: Bengtson, Cuellar, & Ragan, 1977, Figure 1, p. 80. Reprinted by permission of *Journal of Gerontology, 32* (1), 76–88.

family lineage and thus "next in line" for death. So in midlife we become more aware of the fear, more preoccupied with death and its imminence. In these years, many adults grope toward new ways of thinking about death, eventually accepting it in a different way, so that the fear recedes in old age.

This does not mean that older adults are unconcerned with death. On the contrary, they are more likely to talk about it and think about it than are younger adults (Kalish, 1985). But while death is highly *salient* to the elderly, it is apparently not as *frightening* as it was in midlife.

Other Predictors of Fear of Death

Age is not the only element in fear of death. Several other personal qualities, familiar from my discussions of resistance resources and personality in earlier chapters, appear to be related to conscious fearfulness. First, **religiosity,** or the degree of religious feeling, seems to make some difference. In general, adults who describe themselves as deeply religious or who go to church regularly are less afraid of death than are those who describe themselves as less religious or who participate less regularly in religious activities (Kalish, 1985; Thorson & Powell, 1990). In some instances, however, researchers have found a curvilinear relationship, with both those who are deeply religious and those who are deeply irreligious describing less fear of death. Thus the most fearful may be those who are uncertain about, or uncommitted to, any religious or philosophical tradition.

Individual temperament or personality is another variable in the fear-of-death equation. The trait of extraversion is not consistently related to fear of death, but **neuroticism** is. A typical finding is Patricia Frazier and Deborah Foss-Goodman's (1988–1989) reported correlation of 0.41 between a measure of neuroticism and a measure of anxiety about death in a group of college students. Since neuroticism is generally characterized by greater fear or negative attitudes toward many aspects of life, we can see that fear of death is, to at least some extent, a reflection of a more general trait.

More interesting, I think, is the link between fear of death and a sense of **personal competence** or self-worth. Several facets of this domain have been studied. Adults who feel they have achieved the goals they set out to achieve, or who think of themselves as not too discrepant from the person they wanted to be, are less fearful of death than are those who are disappointed in themselves (Neimeyer & Chapman, 1980–1981). Adults who feel that their life has some purpose or meaning also appear to be less fearful of death (Durlak, 1972), as do those who feel some sense of personal competence (Pollack, 1979–1980).

Such findings suggest at least the possibility that those adults who have successfully completed the major tasks of adult life, who have adequately fulfilled the demands of the roles they occupied, who developed inwardly are able to face death with greater equanimity. Those adults who have not been able to resolve the various tasks and dilemmas of adulthood face their late adult years more fearfully, more anxiously, even with what Erikson describes as despair. Fear of death may be merely one facet of such despair.

In some sense, then, all of adult life is a process of moving toward death. Adults' attitudes toward death, and their approaches to it, are influenced by many of the same qualities that affect the way they approach other life changes or dilemmas.

PREPARATION FOR DEATH

Preparation for death occurs on other levels as well. At a practical level, for example, a person can make out a will or obtain life insurance. Such preparations become more common with increasing age, especially in late middle age and thereafter. For example, 61 percent of men in the United States between ages 18 and 24 have life insurance compared, to 86 percent of men between 55 and 64 (U.S. Bureau of the Census, 1989). Far fewer people prepare for death by making out a will; only about 30 percent of adults in

ONE WAY THAT ADULTS PREPARE for death is by buying life insurance, although this action is more common among middle-aged and older adults. This young man is somewhat unusual to be taking this step so early in his life.

the United States have done so. But it is still true that older adults are more likely than younger ones to have taken this step. Similarly, older adults are more likely to have made arrangements for their own funeral or burial.

At a somewhat deeper level, adults may prepare for death through some process of reminiscence, such as the life review Butler suggested or an autobiography. As you know from Chapter 12, we have little evidence that older adults typically or necessarily go through such a review process. But for some, such a review may be an important aspect of "writing the final chapter" or legitimizing one's life in some fashion (Birren & Feldman, 1997). For instance, in their 80s, two of my four grandparents wrote autobiographies for circulation within the family. I found the documents fascinating not only because they told me more than I had known about my grandparents' lives and about family history, but also because of the self-justification and self-explanations they contain. I know of no research that would tell me how common such explicit review may be, but such acts may form an important part of the preparation for death for at least some elders.

THE PROCESS OF DYING

Elizabeth Kübler-Ross (1969) created a model of coming to terms with death based on her work with terminally ill adults and children. In her early writings, she proposed that those who know they are dying move through a series of steps or stages before they accept this knowledge. This model of stages of dying has had many critics; even Kübler-Ross herself, in her later writings, no longer argues that dying moves through clear or sequential stages (Kübler-Ross, 1974). Instead, she now talks of emotional tasks rather than stages. But because her original ideas have been immensely influential and her terminology is still widely used, you need to have at least some familiarity with these concepts.

Kübler-Ross's Stages of Dying

After watching and listening to many patients, Kübler-Ross suggested that the process of dying involves five steps or stages, occurring in a particular order:

1. **Denial.** When confronted with a terminal diagnosis, the first reaction most patients report is some form of "No, not me!" "It must be a mistake." "The lab reports must have been mixed up." "I don't feel that sick, so it can't be true." "I'll get another doctor's opinion." All these are forms of denial, which Kübler-Ross argues is a valuable, constructive first defense. It gives the patient a period of time in which to marshal other strategies of coping with the shock. Some patients, of course, continue to use denial right up to the end. But for most, according to Kübler-Ross, the extreme versions of denial fade within a short time and are replaced by anger.

2. **Anger.** The classic second reaction, so Kübler-Ross argues, is "Why me?" The patient resents those who are healthy and becomes angry at whatever fate put her in this position. This may be reflected in angry outbursts at nurses, family members, doctors—anyone within reach. In part, this anger may be a response not just to the verdict of death, but also to the typically dependent and helpless position of a patient.

3. **Bargaining.** At some point, Kübler-Ross saw anger being replaced by a new kind of defense. The patient now tries to "make a deal" with doctors, nurses, with God. "If I do what I'm told and don't yell at everyone, then I'll be able to live till Christmas." Kübler-Ross (1969) describes one woman with terminal cancer who wanted to live long enough to attend the wedding of her oldest, favorite son. With help from the hospital staff she learned how to use self-hypnosis to control her pain for short periods and was able to attend the wedding. As Kübler-Ross reports, "I will never forget the moment when she returned to the hospital. She looked tired and somewhat exhausted and—before I could say hello—said, 'Now don't forget I have another son!'" (1969, p. 83).

4. **Depression.** Bargaining only works for so long, however, and as disease processes continue and the signs of the body's decline become more obvious, patients typically become depressed. This is a kind of mourning—for the loss of relationships as well as of one's own life. Often, the dying person sinks into a sort of despair, which may last for a prolonged period. But Kübler-Ross argues that this depression is part of the preparation for the final step, acceptance. The dying person must grieve for, and then give up, all the things of the world. Only then can acceptance of death occur.

5. **Acceptance.** The final step, according to this theory, is a quiet understanding, a readiness for death. The patient is no longer depressed, but may be quiet, even serene. In a widely quoted passage, author Stewart Alsop, who was dying of leukemia, described his own acceptance: "A dying man needs to die as a sleepy man needs to sleep, and there comes a time when it is wrong, as well as useless, to resist" (1973, p. 299).

Kübler-Ross thought that a current of hope ran through all of these stages. Patients hope for a new form of therapy, a new drug, a miraculous cure. And patients hope that they can die "well," without too much pain and with some acceptance.

An Assessment of Kübler-Ross's Stages

Kübler-Ross's description has been (and still is) enormously influential. She has provided a common language for those who work with dying patients, and her highly compassionate descriptions have, without doubt, sensitized health care workers and families to the complexities of the process of dying. There are moments when what the patient needs is cheering up and moments when he needs simply to be listened to; there are times to hold his or her hand quietly and times to provide encouragement or hope. Many new care programs that arrange for terminally ill patients, such as the hospice programs I'll describe in a moment, are clearly outgrowths of this greater sensitivity to the dying process. These are all worthwhile changes. But Kübler-Ross's basic thesis, that the dying process necessarily passes through these specific five stages, in this specific order, has been widely criticized, for several good reasons.

Methodological Problems. Kübler-Ross's hypothesized sequence was initially based on clinical observation of perhaps 200 patients, and she does not provide information about how frequently she talked to or spent time with them, or over how long a period they continued to be assessed. She also did not report the ages of the patients she studied, although it is clear that many were middle-aged or young adults, for whom a terminal illness was obviously off-time. Nearly all were apparently cancer patients. Would the same processes hold for those dying of other diseases, diseases in which it is much less common to have a specific diagnosis or a short-term prognosis? Thus Kübler-Ross's observations might be correct, but only for a small subset of dying persons.

Culture Specificity. A related question has to do with whether reactions to dying are culture-specific or universal. Kübler-Ross wrote as if the five stages of dying were universal human processes. But most social scientists would now agree that reactions to dying are strongly culturally conditioned. In some Native American cultures, tradition calls for death to be faced and accepted with composure. Because it is part of nature's cycle, it is not to be feared or fought (DeSpelder & Strickland, 1983). In such a culture, would we expect to find stages of denial, anger, and depression?

As another example, in Mexican culture, death is seen as a mirror of the person's life. Thus your death, your way of dying, tells much about what kind of person you have been. And unlike the dominant U.S. culture, in which death is feared and thoughts of it repressed, in Mexican culture death is discussed frequently, even celebrated in a national feast day, the Day of the Dead (DeSpelder & Strickland, 1983). It seems inescapable that such cultural variations will affect a person's reaction to his or her own impending death.

CRITICAL THINKING

Think for a minute about the extent to which your own ideas about death and dying have been influenced by the culture or subculture in which you were reared.

Are There Stages at All? The most potent criticism, however, centers on the issue of stages. Many clinicians and researchers who have attempted to study the process systematically have not found that all dying patients exhibit these five emotions at all, let alone in a specific order. Of the five, only some type of depression seems to be a common thread among Western patients, and there is little indication that acceptance or disengagement is a common endpoint of the process (Baugher, Burger, Smith, & Wallston, 1989–1990). Some patients display such acceptance, whereas others remain as active and engaged as possible right up to the end. Edwin Shneidman (1980, 1983), a major theorist and clinician in the field of **thanatology**, (the study of dying), puts it this way: "I reject the notion that human beings, as they die, are somehow marched in lock step through a series of stages of the dying process. On the contrary, in working with dying persons, I see a wide panoply of human feelings and emotions, of various human needs, and a broad selection of psychological defenses and maneuvers—a few of these in some people, dozens in others—experienced in an impressive variety of ways" (1980, p. 110).

Instead of stages, Shneidman suggests that we think of the dying process as having many **themes,** common elements that can appear, disappear, and reappear in the process of dealing with death in any one patient: terror ("I was really frightened"), pervasive uncertainty ("If there is a God..."), fantasies of being rescued ("Somebody... that maybe could perform this miracle"), incredulity ("It's so far fetched, so unreal... it is a senseless death"), feelings of unfairness, a concern with reputation after death, the fight against pain, and so on.

Thus, instead of each person following a series of five fixed stages, each person moves back and forth, in and out of a complex set of emotions and defenses. Kübler-Ross herself would now agree with this view. In one later writing (1974) she says: "Most of my patients have exhibited two or three stages simultaneously and these do not always occur in the same order" (pp. 25–26). Given this variability, the term *stage* does not seem to be an appropriate label for these several themes. Certainly, those who work with the dying should not expect a tidy sequence of emotions.

Farewells

One aspect of the process of dying that is not reflected in Kübler-Ross stages or in most research on dying but which is clearly a significant feature for the dying person and his or her family is the process of saying farewell. A study in Australia by Allan Kellehear and Terry Lewin (1988–1989) gives us a first exploration of such goodbyes. They interviewed 90 terminally ill cancer patients, all of whom had been told they were within a year of their death, and a smaller group of 10 patients who were in hospice care and thought to be within three months of death. Most had known they had cancer for over a year before the interview but had only recently been given a specific short-term prognosis. Each subject was asked whether he had already said some goodbyes or intended future farewells to family or friends, and if so, when and under what circumstances. The minority (19 of the 100) said they did not plan any farewells at all. The rest had either already begun to say goodbye (22) or planned their farewells for the final days of their lives—deathbed goodbyes, if you will.

The early farewells had often been in the form of a letter or a gift, such as giving money to a child or grandchild, or passing on personal treasures to a member of the family who might especially cherish them. One woman made dolls that she gave to friends, relatives, and hospital staff. Another knit a set of baby clothes to give to each of her daughters for the child that neither daughter had yet had.

More commonly, both planned and completed farewells were in the form of conversations. One subject asked her brother to come for a visit so that she could see and talk to him one last time; others arranged with friends for one last get together, saying goodbye quite explicitly on these occasions. Those who anticipated saying farewell only in the last hours of their conscious life imagined these occasions to be times when loving words would be spoken or a goodbye look would be exchanged.

All such farewells, whether spoken or not, can be thought of as forms of gifts. By saying goodbye to someone, the dying person signals that that person matters enough to them to warrant such a farewell. They also serve to make the death real, to force the imminent death out of the realm of denial into acceptance by others as well as by the dying person. And finally, as Kellehear and Lewin point out, farewells may make the dying itself easier, especially if they are completed before the final moments of life. They may make it easier for the dying person to disengage, to reach a point of acceptance.

Individual Adaptations to Dying

The process of dying varies hugely from one person to the next, not only in the emotions expressed (or not expressed), but also in the physical process. Some experience a long, slow decline; others die instantly, with no "stages" or phases at all. Some experience great pain; others little or none. Similarly, the way each person handles the process also varies. Some fight hard against dying; others appear to accept it early in the process and struggle no further. Some remain calm; others fall into deep depression. The question that researchers have begun to ask is whether such variations in the emotional response to impending or probable death have any effect at all on the physical process of dying.

I should say at the outset that virtually all of the research we have on individual variations or adaptations to dying involve studies of patients with terminal cancer. Not only is cancer a clear diagnosis, many forms of it also progress quite rapidly, and the patient not only knows that he or she is terminally ill but roughly how long he or she has to live. Some other diseases, such as AIDS, have these same features, but most other diseases do not. Most particularly, heart disease, which is also a leading cause of death in middle and old age in industrialized countries, may exist for a long period, the patient may or may not know that he has significant heart disease, and the prognosis is highly variable. We simply do not know whether any of the conclusions drawn from studies of cancer patients can be applied to adults dying less rapidly or less predictably. Still, the research is quite fascinating.

The most influential single study in this area has been the work of Steven Greer and his colleagues (S. Greer, 1991; S. Greer, Morris, & Pettingale, 1979; Pettingale, Morris, Greer, & Haybittle, 1985). They have followed a group of 62 women diagnosed in the 1970s with early stages of breast cancer. Three months after the original diagnosis, each woman was interviewed at some length and her reaction to the diagnosis and to her treatment was classed in one of five groups:

1. *Positive avoidance* (denial): rejection of evidence about diagnosis; insistence that surgery was just precautionary.

2. *Fighting spirit:* an optimistic attitude, accompanied by a search for more information about the disease. They often see their disease as a challenge and plan to fight it with every method available.

3. *Stoic acceptance* (fatalism): acknowledgment of the diagnosis but without seeking any further information; ignoring the diagnosis and carrying on their normal life as much as possible.

4. *Helplessness/hopelessness:* overwhelmed by diagnosis; see themselves as dying or gravely ill; devoid of hope.

5. *Anxious preoccupation* (originally included in the helplessness group but separated out later): includes those whose response to the diagnosis was strong and persistent anxiety. If they seek information, they interpret it pessimistically; they monitor their body sensations carefully, interpreting each ache or pain as a possible recurrence.

Greer then checked on the survival rates of these five groups after 5, 10, and 15 years. Table 13.2 shows the 15-year results. Only 35 percent of those whose initial reaction had been either denial or fighting spirit had died of cancer 15 years later, compared to 76 percent of those whose initial reaction had been stoic acceptance, anxious preoccu-

TABLE 13.2 **Differences in 15-Year Outcomes Among Women Cancer Patients with Differing Psychological Responses to the Initial Diagnosis**

Psychological Response Three Months After Surgery	Outcome 15 Years Later			
	Alive and Well	Died of Cancer	Died of Other Causes	Total
Positive avoidance	5	5	0	10
Fighting spirit	4	2	4	10
Stoical acceptance	6	24	3	33
Anxious preoccupation	0	3	0	3
Hopelessness	1	5	0	6
	16	39	7	62

Source: Adapted from S. Greer, 1991, Table 1, p. 45.

pation, or helplessness/hopelessness. Because the five groups had not differed initially in the stage of their disease or in treatment, these results support the hypothesis that psychological response contribute to disease progress, just as coping strategies more generally affect the likelihood of disease in the first place.

Similar results have emerged from studies of patients with melanoma (a deadly form of skin cancer) as well as other cancers (Temoshok, 1987) and from several recent studies of AIDS patients (Reed, Kemeny, Taylor, Wang, & Visscher, 1994; Solano et al., 1993). [You'll also recall from Chapter 11 that Scheier and Carver's study of optimism and pessimism among coronary heart bypass patients (Scheier et al., 1989) is consistent with the same point.] In general, those who report less hostility, more stoic acceptance, more helplessness, and who fail to express negative feelings die *sooner* (O'Leary, 1990). Those who struggle the most, who fight the hardest, who express their anger and hostility openly, and who also find some sources of joy in their lives, live longer. In some ways, the data suggest that "good patients"—those who are obedient and not too questioning, who don't yell at their doctors or make life difficult for those around them—are in fact likely to die sooner. Difficult patients, who question and challenge those around them, last longer.

CRITICAL
THINKING

How many different explanations can you think of to account for a possible link between psychological processes and survival time?

Furthermore, there are now a few studies linking these psychological differences to immune system functioning. A particular subset of immune cells thought to be an important defense against cancer cells, called NK cells, have been found to occur at lower rates among those patients who report *less* distress and who seem better adjusted to their illness (O'Leary, 1990). And among AIDS patients, one study shows that T-cell counts declined more rapidly among those who respond to their disease with repression (similar to the stoic acceptance or helplessness groups in the Greer study), while those showing fighting spirit had a slower loss of T cells (Solano et al., 1993).

Despite the growing body of results of this type, two important cautions are nonetheless in order before we leap to the conclusion that a fighting spirit is the optimum response to any disease. First, there are some careful studies in which no link has been found between depression/stoic acceptance/helplessness and more rapid death from cancer (Cassileth, Walsh, & Lusk, 1988; Richardson, Zarnegar, Bisno, & Levine, 1990). Second, it is not clear that the same psychological response is necessarily optimum for every form of disease. Consider heart disease, for example. There is a certain irony in the fact that many of the qualities that appear to be optimal among cancer patients could be considered as reflections of a **type A personality** (or perhaps A-). Because the anger and hostility components of the type A personality are considered a *risk* factor for heart disease, it is not so obvious that a "fighting spirit" response which includes those components would necessarily be desirable.

One of the major difficulties in all this research is that investigators have used widely differing measures of psychological functioning. Greer and his colleagues have found quite consistent results with their category system; others, using standardized measures of depression or hopelessness, have not necessarily found the same patterns. My own reading of the evidence is that there is indeed some link between psychological responses to stress (including a fatal diagnosis) and prognosis, but that we have not yet zeroed in on just what psychological processes may be critical for which disease. Fortunately, this is an area in which a great deal of research is under way, giving some hope that clearer answers may emerge before long.

The Role of Social Support. Another important ingredient in a person's response to imminent death is the amount of social support that he or she may have available. Those with positive and supportive relationships describe lower levels of pain and less depression during their final months of illness (Carey, 1974; Hinton, 1975). High levels of social support are also linked to longer survival times. For example, heart attack patients who live alone are more likely to have a second attack than are those who live with someone else (Case, Moss, Case, McDermott, & Eberly, 1992), and those with significant levels of atherosclerosis live longer if they have a confidant than if they do not (D. R. Williams, 1992). The latter study involved a sample of African-Americans, suggesting that the connection is not unique to Anglo culture.

Furthermore, you know from Chapter 11 that this link between social support and length of survival has also been found in *experimental* studies, such as Spiegel's study of cancer patients assigned to participate in a support group or to be in a control group without added social support. Recall that Spiegel found that the average length of survival was twice as long for those in the support group as for those in the control group (36.6 vs. 18.9 months). Thus, just as social support helps to buffer children and adults from some of the negative effects of many kinds of nonlethal stress, so it seems to perform a similar function for those facing death.

WHERE DEATH OCCURS

In the United States and other industrialized countries today, the great majority of adults die in hospitals rather than at home or even in nursing homes. The exact pattern naturally varies a great deal, as a function of such factors as age or type of disease. Among the old old, for example, death in a nursing home is quite common. Among younger adults, in contrast, hospital death is the norm. Similarly, adults with known progressive diseases, such as cancer or AIDS, are typically in and out of the hospital for months or years before death; at the other end of the continuum are many who are hospitalized with an acute problem, such as a heart attack or pneumonia, and die within a short space of time, having had no prior hospitalization. In between fall those who may have experienced several different types of care in the last weeks or months, including hospitalization, home health care, and nursing home care. Despite such diversity, it is still true that the majority of deaths, particularly among the elderly, are preceded by some weeks of hospitalization (Merrill & Mor, 1993; E. Shapiro, 1983).

In recent years, however, an alternative form of terminal care has become prominent: **hospice care.** The hospice movement was given a good deal of boost by Kübler-Ross's writings because she emphasized the importance of a "good death," a "death with dignity," in which the patient and the patient's family have more control over the entire process. Many health care professionals, particularly in England and the United States, began to suggest that such a good death could be better achieved if the dying person were at home or in a homelike setting in which contact with family and other friends would be part of the daily experience.

Hospice care emerged in England in the late 1960s and in the United States in the early 1970s (Mor, 1987). By 1982, the idea had gained so much support in the United States that Congress was persuaded to add hospice care to the list of benefits paid for by Medicare. Today there are more than 1500 hospice programs in the United States, serving thousands of terminally ill patients and their families.

The philosophy that underlies this alternative setting or approach to the dying patient has several aspects (Bass, 1985):

1. Death should be viewed as a normal, inevitable part of life, not to be avoided but to be faced and accepted.

2. That the patient and the family should prepare for the death by examining their feelings, by planning for their later life.

3. That the family should be involved in the care to as full an extent as possible, so that each family member can come to some resolution of his or her relationship with the dying person.

4. Control over the care and the care-receiving setting should belong to the patient and family.

5. Medical care provided should be palliative rather than curative. Pain should be alleviated and comfort maximized, but a minimum of invasive or life-prolonging measures should be undertaken.

Three somewhat different types of programs following these general guidelines have been developed. The most common types of hospice programs are home-based programs, in which there is one central family caregiver—most frequently the spouse—who provides hour-to-hour care for the dying person with the support and assistance of specially trained nurses or other staff who visit regularly, provide medical services as needed, and help the family deal psychologically with the impending death. A second type is a special hospice center in which a small number of patients in the last stages of a terminal disease are cared for in as homelike a setting as possible. Finally, there are hospital-based hospice programs that provide palliative care following the basic hospice philosophy, with daily involvement of family members in the patient's care, but within a hospital setting.

Two major studies comparing hospice care with traditional hospital care have recently been completed, so we are now in a position to say at least something about the relative merits of these two approaches to dying and death. The National Hospice Study, headed by David Greer and Vincent Mor (Greer et al., 1986; Mor, Greer, & Kastenbaum, 1988), analyzed the experiences of 1754 terminally ill cancer patients treated in 40 different hospices and 14 conventional hospital settings. Half the hospice programs studied were home-

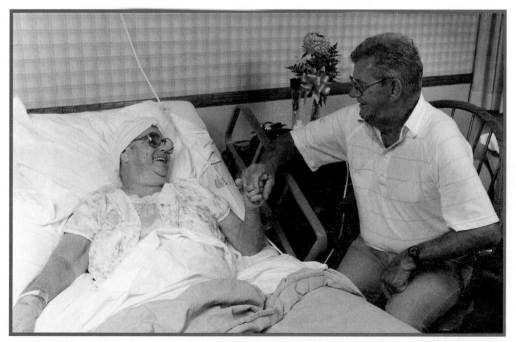

HOSPICE CARE, either in a special hospice unit in a hospital or at home as shown here, has become a widely available alternative in recent years. The emphasis is on palliative care rather than on prolonging life, but also on helping each dying person (and his/her family) to cope with the dying process with as much grace and dignity as possible.

based, half were hospital-based. The researchers examined not only the quality of life, as reported by the patient and the central caregiver, but also the patient's reported pain and satisfaction with the care received. Each of these measures was obtained several times over the weeks preceding death. It is a remarkable study, but because the individual patients *chose* which form of care they received, there remains the possibility that any observed differences are the result of self-selection rather than effects of the type of care.

The second major study, by Robert Kane and his colleagues (Kane, Klein, Bernstein, Rothenberg, & Wales, 1985; Kane, Wales, Bernstein, Leibowitz, & Kaplan, 1984), solved this problem by assigning dying patients randomly to either hospice or regular hospital care. The hospice care was a combination of home- and hospital-based; many of the hospice patients remained at home when possible but were in the hospital's hospice unit at other times. The drawback in this study is that only one specific hospice program and one specific traditional hospital program are being compared. Still, if the results from the two studies are consistent with one another, we can have some confidence in the conclusions.

As it happens, there is a fair degree of agreement in the findings. Both studies found *no* differences between hospice and regular hospital care in the patient's reported pain, in the patient's day-to-day functioning, or in length of patient survival. But they did find differences in the reported satisfaction with the care received. In Kane's study, the patients in hospice were consistently more satisfied with the quality of care they received and with their own involvement in that care. The caregivers in Kane's hospice program were also more satisfied with their own involvement in the patient's care than was true for family members of patients in standard care. The National Hospice Study did not show any difference in patients' reported satisfaction with care, but the family caregivers of patients in *hospital-based* hospice programs were more satisfied with the patient's care. Kane also found that anxiety was lower among the family caregivers in the hospice group, a finding not matched in the National Hospice Study.

Overall, then, the differences between hospice and regular hospital care appear to be small. When there is a difference, it is not in physical measures such as pain or length of survival, but in social/emotional measures. On some of these measures but by no means on all, hospice patients and their families are slightly more satisfied. Still, hospice care is not an option to be undertaken lightly. The burden of care is enormous and may require skills that the caregivers do not have. In the National Hospice Study, those caregivers involved in the family-based programs did report a significantly greater feeling of burden. In another study, Bass (1985) has found that some families that initially chose hospice care later placed their dying relative in a hospital setting because they could no longer cope. But as with renewed health care options at the beginning of life, including the return of midwifery and home delivery, it seems to me to be a very good thing that in many communities today, dying adults and their families have some choices about where and how the process of dying will occur. Since that sort of choice and control is one of the coping strategies that seems most effective in helping adults deal with other life crises, it is likely to have the same beneficial effect in the case of the ultimate life change—death.

CRITICAL THINKING

Given what you have just read, do you think you would choose hospice care for yourself or urge it for someone you love? Why or why not?

AFTER DEATH: RITUALS AND GRIEVING

Whether a death is sudden or prolonged, anticipated or unexpected, it leaves survivors who must somehow come to terms with the death and eventually pick up the pieces of their lives. I talked a bit about widowhood in Chapter 11 as part of the discussion of the impact of several major life changes. But my emphasis there was primarily on the epidemiological effects—the rate of illness, emotional disturbance, or premature death among the survivors. Let me turn here to a more general discussion of the process of grieving itself.

Ritual Mourning: Funerals and Ceremonies

Every culture has some set of rituals associated with death. Far from being empty gestures, these rituals have clear and important functions. As Marshall and Levy put it: "Rituals provide a... means through which societies simultaneously seek to control the disruptiveness of death and to make it meaningful.... The funeral exists as a formal means to accomplish the work of completing a biography, managing grief, and building new social relationships after the death" (1990, pp. 246, 253).

One way in which rituals accomplish these goals is by giving the bereaved person(s) a specific *role* to play. Like all roles, this one includes expected and prohibited or discouraged behaviors. The content of these roles differs markedly from one culture to the next, but the clarity of the role in most cases provides a shape to the days or weeks immediately following the death of a loved person. (I have an unreasoning bias, by the way, against the phrase "loved one," which sounds to me like unctuous, funeral director language.) In our culture, the rituals prescribe what one should wear, who should be notified, who should be fed, what demeanor one should show, and far more. Depending on one's religious background, one may need to arrange to sit shiva, or gather friends and family for a wake, or arrange a memorial service. One may be expected to respond stoically or to wail and tear one's hair. But whatever the social rules, there is a role to be filled that provides shape to the first numbing hours and days.

At the same time, the rituals provide less central but significant roles for friends, most particularly that of support-giver. Friends and family may bring food to the home of the bereaved person, for example, or drop in to offer help, or send letters of condolence. Death rituals may also bring family members together as no other occasion (except a family wedding) is likely to do. I was particularly struck by this at the funeral of my father's mother, who died about nine years ago. Among those who came to the memorial service were several cousins I had not seen for at least 30 years. Not only was I quite unprepared for the strong sense of family connection I felt for and with these strangers, I found myself greatly drawn to one of the cousins I barely knew. We have since created a warm friendship that I expect to last for the rest of our lives. In this way death rituals can strengthen family ties, clarify the new lines of influence or authority within a family, pass on the flame in some way to the next generation.

Rituals surrounding death can also help to give some meaning to the death itself by emphasizing the meaning of the life of the person who has died. It is not accidental that most death rituals include testimonials, biographies, witnessing. By telling the story of the person's life, by describing that life's value and meaning, the death can be accepted more readily. In a sense, a funeral is often like a "life review" and serves for the living some of the same purpose that Butler thought it served for the elderly person approaching death. And of course, ceremonies can also provide meaning by placing the death in a larger philosophical or religious context. In this way, mourning rituals can give some answers to that inevitable question, "Why?"

FUNERAL RITUALS, such as this one, may sometimes seem overly elaborate or emotionally draining for the remaining family members and friends, but they serve important functions.

The Process of Grieving

But when the funeral or memorial service is over, what do you do then? How does a person handle the grief of this kind of loss, whether it be of a spouse, a parent, a child, a friend, a lover? Research and theory on the process of grieving has been dominated by two approaches. The older approach, still highly influential, describes grieving in terms of stages, similar in many ways to Kübler-Ross's stage theory of dying. More recently, a "revisionist" approach has emerged, primarily from the work of Camille Wortman and Roxane Cohen Silver (1989, 1990, 1992, Wortman, Silver, & Kessler, 1993). Their research has persuaded them that grief is a much more variable process than stage theories would suggest and that we would do better to think of it in the same way that we think of other responses to stress: as affected by personality and by coping strategies. Let's take a brief look at each of these approaches.

Stages of Grief. John Bowlby, whose work on attachment you already encountered, is one of the central figures here as well. He described four phases of grieving (1980), listed in Table 13.3. In the first period of **numbness,** or shock, people say things like "I can't keep my mind on anything for very long," or "I'm afraid I'm losing my mind. I can't seem to think clearly" (Sanders, 1989, p. 47, 48).

In the second stage, Bowlby thought this shock gives way to **yearning,** a pattern Bowlby thought had some of the elements of what we see when a young child is temporarily separated from his mother. In the young child, such searching is a sign of a powerful attachment, so it is not surprising that we should see it in adults permanently separated from some object of strong attachment. But this second stage or phase also commonly includes some anger, so you hear people say things like "His doctors didn't try hard enough," or "His boss should have known better than to ask him to work so hard."

In the third stage, **disorganization and despair,** restlessness disappears and there is instead a great lethargy, often considerable depression, very like the stage of depression Kübler-Ross describes. A 45-year-old woman whose child had just died said: "I can't understand the way I feel. Up to now, I had been feeling restless. I couldn't sleep. I paced and ranted. Now, I have an opposite reaction. I sleep a lot. I feel fatigued and worn out. I don't even want to see the friends who have kept me going. I sit and stare, too exhausted to move.... Just when I thought I should be feeling better, I am feeling worse" (Sanders, 1989, p. 73).

TABLE 13.3 **Stages of Grief as Proposed by Bowlby**

Proposed Stage	Description
Numbness	Disbelief, confusion, restlessness, feelings of unreality. Normally lasts only the first few days.
Yearning	The bereaved person may actively seek the lost one, searching or wandering as if searching. Also a time full of anxiety and guilt, fear and frustration, often with many tears or poor sleeping.
Disorganization and despair	Searching stops, and the loss is accepted, but with acceptance comes depression or a sense of helplessness. There is often great fatigue accompanying this phrase.
Reorganization	This is the time when the person again takes control of his or her life. Some forgetting occurs, energy is renewed, there is some sense of hope, and depression declines.

Source: Adapted from Bowlby, 1980.

Finally, Bowlby argued that a time of **reorganization** comes. The person takes up his usual activities, finds new relationships. This is equivalent to the stage of acceptance in Kübler-Ross's system, although in the case of grief there is less an element of resignation than there is constructive and active restructuring of one's life.

Bowlby argued that these stages are not confined to the grief that an adult shows on the death of a spouse or partner. They should characterize any loss of someone to whom a person has a strong attachment. So the loss of a partner, a child, or a parent is likely to trigger the emotions that Bowlby is describing, whereas the loss of a good friend, a sibling, or a cousin, with whom we are not likely to have such a deep attachment, is less likely to trigger the full array of grieving responses (Murrell & Himmelfarb, 1989).

But whether these grieving responses invariably or even regularly occur in a sequence is not as clear from the research. Herman Feifel states the counterargument:

> We are discovering that just as there are multitudinous ways of living, there are numerous ways of dying and grieving.... The hard data do not support the existence of any procrustean stages or schedules that characterize terminal illness or mourning. This does not mean that, for example, Kübler-Ross's "stages of dying" and Bowlby's "phases of mourning" cannot provide us with implications and insights into the dynamics and process of dying and grief, but they are very far from being inexorable hoops through which most terminally ill individuals and mourners inevitably pass. We should beware of promulgating a coercive orthodoxy of how to die or mourn. (1990, p. 540)

Some would argue that it would be better to think in terms of themes or aspects rather than stages, such as themes of anger, guilt, depression, anxiety and restlessness, and preoccupation with the image of the deceased. One way to reconcile these several views would be to think of each of these themes as having a likely trajectory, such as the pattern suggested in Figure 13.2 by Selby Jacobs and his colleagues (Jacobs et al., 1987–1988). Jacobs is not arguing that every person follows exactly this pattern, for different individuals these features may follow longer or shorter courses at higher or lower levels. The argument is rather that in the first few days or weeks, numbness is likely to be the dominant theme, with separation anxiety or awareness of loss becoming dominant somewhat later, followed by despair and depression, producing a stagelike sequence, even though each theme may be present to some extent in each phase.

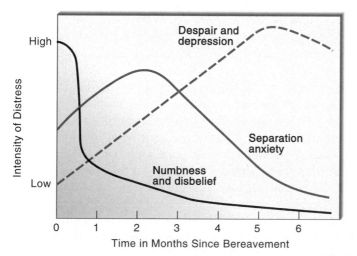

FIGURE 13.2 This model of the possible course of grieving takes us a step beyond simpler stage concepts. At any one time, several themes may be present, but each theme may still be likely to dominate at a particular time, thus producing a stagelike sequence in many people.

Source: Jacobs et al., 1987–1988, Fig. 1, p. 43.

Wortman and Silver's Ideas. Wortman and Silver begin by noting that Bowlby's descriptions of grieving have been highly informative and helpful, sensitizing theorists and practitioners to the variety of responses to grief that we may see. But like Feifel, they note that there is little or no support for the *stagelike* aspect of Bowlby's theory. Further, Wortman and Silver dispute two points about the traditional view of grieving: that distress is an inevitable response to loss, and that *failure* to experience distress is a sign that the person has not grieved "properly." The psychoanalytic view, represented in Bowlby's approach and dominant for many decades, holds that lack of overt distress must indicate significant repression or denial of painful feelings. Ultimately, according to this view, such denial or repression will have negative consequences. Bowlby argued that those who express their pain, who "allow themselves to grieve," are behaving in an ultimately healthy way.

If this formulation is correct, we should find that those widows or other grieving persons who show the *most* distress immediately after the death should have the best long-term adjustment, while those who show the least immediate distress should display some kind of residual problem later. But the data do not support this expectation. On the contrary, those who show the highest levels of distress immediately following a loss are typically the ones who are still depressed several years later, while those who show little distress immediately show no signs of delayed problems.

Wortman and Silver (1990) conclude that there are at least four distinct patterns of grieving:

* **Normal grieving:** relatively high distress immediately following the loss, with relatively rapid recovery
* **Chronic grieving:** continuing high distress over several years
* **Delayed grieving:** little distress in the first few months, but high levels of distress at a later point
* **Absent grieving:** no notable level of distress either immediately or later

Contrary to the predictions of stage theories of grief, it turns out that the pattern of absent grief is remarkably common. In Wortman and Silver's own first study (Wortman & Silver, 1990), 26 percent of bereaved subjects showed essentially no distress either immediately after the death or several years later, a pattern confirmed in other research (L. H. Levy, Martinkowski, & Derby, 1994). In all of these studies, the least common pattern is delayed grief. Only 1 to 5 percent of adults show such a response to loss, while as many as a third show chronic grief. Thus there is little support for either aspect of the traditional view: High levels of distress are neither an inevitable nor a necessary aspect of the grieving process. Many adults seem to handle the death of a spouse, a child, or a parent without significant dislocation, although *on average* it remains true that widowed or other bereaved persons are higher in depression, lower in life satisfaction, and at greater risk for illness than are the nonbereaved.

As yet, we know relatively little about the characteristics of people who react to bereavement in these quite different ways. Wortman and Silver's research (Wortman et al., 1993) gives us several hints. In their studies, those widows who had had the *best* marriages were the ones who showed the most persistent grief reactions. More surprisingly, they found that those widows who had had the *strongest* sense of personal control, self-esteem, or mastery prior to the spouse's death had the *most* difficulty, as if the loss of the spouse had undermined this very sense of control. Research in Germany by Wolfgang and Margaret Stroebe (1993), which I mentioned in Chapter 11, suggests another factor that may be important: *neuroticism.* In their study, those widows who were high in the personality trait of neuroticism before bereavement showed stronger and more persistent negative effects.

These are interesting findings, especially because some of them run against the grain of other research on coping with stress. It may well be that the death of a person to whom one is strongly attached is simply a different order of magnitude of stressful event, one for which many of the typical "rules" do not apply. Similarly, although a strong sense of personal control may be a very helpful quality for many kinds of stresses, it may be detrimental when the person faces a crisis in which no control is possible. It will be interesting to see, in the coming years, whether further research confirms these initial findings.

Wortman and Silver's views seem to me to be an important modification of the standard view of grief. Not only do they cause us to rethink old assumptions (always a valuable process in science), but they also point the way to potentially better understanding of individual variations in grief pathways. There are also obvious practical implications flowing from this perspective. To the extent that our cultural norm for grieving includes the expectations of heightened distress, "working through" the grief, and then getting on with your life, any bereaved person who does not follow this pattern is likely to be perceived as deviant. In particular, the person who shows little despair or depression may be accused of "not dealing" with his or her grief or of not having loved the deceased person. Of course, it *is* possible that such lower levels of distress are indicative of weaker attachments, but we have as yet little evidence to confirm (or reject) such a hypothesis. Meanwhile, Wortman and Silver's arguments should serve to make each of us more sensitive to the unique process of grieving that we may see in friends or family members.

Those who seem deeply distressed or despairing may benefit from some kind of support group or therapy; certainly, they are not likely to find it helpful or sensitive for you to urge them to get "back in the swim" right away. Those who express little obvious distress, on the other hand, may not be repressing but may be coping in other ways. They may not take kindly to your suggestion that they should "get it all out" or to "be sure to take time to grieve." As usual, the best way to be helpful to a person dealing with such a loss is to be highly attentive to the signals you are receiving, rather than imposing your own ideas of what is normal or expected.

Finally, let us not lose sight of the fact that loss can also lead to growth. Indeed, the majority of widows say not only that they have changed as a result of their husband's death, but that the change is in the direction of greater independence, greater skill (Wortman & Silver, 1990). Like all crises, all major life changes, bereavement can be an opportunity as well as, or instead of, a disabling experience. Which way we respond is likely to depend very heavily on the patterns we have established from early childhood: our temperament or personality, our internal working models of attachment and self, our intellectual skills, and the social network we have created.

LIVING AND DYING: A FINAL WORD

If it is true that we die as we have lived, then it is also true that to some extent we live as we die. Our understanding of death and its meaning, our attitude toward the inevitability of death, the way in which we come to terms with that inevitability, affects not only the way we die, but the way we choose to live our lives throughout adulthood. David Steindl-Rast, a Benedictine monk, makes this point: "Death… is an event that puts the whole meaning of life into question. We may be occupied with purposeful activities, with getting tasks accomplished, works completed, and then along comes the phenomenon of death—whether it is our final death or one of those many deaths through which we go day by day. And death confronts us with the fact that purpose is not enough. We live by meaning" (Steindl-Rast, 1977, p. 22).

An awareness of death is thus not something we can put off until, one day, we hear a diagnosis of our own impending death. It can, instead, help to define and give meaning to daily life.

SUMMARY

1. Four different aspects to the meaning of death have been identified: death as an organizer of time, death as punishment, death as transition, and death as loss.

2. Anxiety or fear of death seems to peak in midlife. Younger adults are still partially convinced of their own immortality, and older adults have to some degree accepted the inevitability.

3. Adults who are more afraid of death are also likely to be higher in neuroticism and to have lower opinions of their own competence or worth. Higher fear is also associated with uncertain positions on religious questions, while those with very high or no religious commitment are typically lower in fear of death.

4. Preparations for death include wills and insurance (more common among older adults) and may include a process of reminiscence or life review, although this possibility is in considerable dispute.

5. Immediately prior to death, there are also signs of "terminal" changes in intellectual performance and emotional response. Adults within a year of death show declining intellectual performance, declining memory, reduced emotional complexity and introspectiveness, and a more passive, accepting self-concept.

6. Kübler-Ross proposes five stages in the actual dying process: denial, anger, bargaining, depression, and acceptance. Research does not support the contention that all dying persons show all these emotions, in this or any other order. The process of dying is more individual, more varied, less sequential than Kübler-Ross proposed.

7. Many people, when they know they are dying specifically plan for farewells to those they love, often through gifts or personal conversations.

8. Individual variations in adaptation to dying are parallel, to at least some degree, to individual variations in handling other life dilemmas or changes. Limited research evidence suggests that those who respond to a terminal diagnosis with a "fighting spirit" rather than stoic acceptance are likely to survive longer.

9. Where a death occurs may also have an impact on the degree of acceptance and comfort the person experiences. Hospice care is a relatively new form of care in which the dying person is largely cared for by family members (often at home) and controls major decisions about care.

10. Research comparing hospice with normal hospital care shows few differences except that hospice patients and their family caregivers are slightly more satisfied with the quality of care.

11. Those left to mourn after a death are helped by clear rituals associated with death, which provide roles for the bereaved and for friends and may give a sense of transcendent meaning to the death.

12. Once past the rituals, the grieving person is thought to move through a complex grief process. Stage theorists propose four main stages: shock or numbness, awareness of loss or yearning, conservation-withdrawal or despair, and finally, healing or reorganization.

13. Newer research, however, does not support the stagelikeness of the process. Some adults appear to adjust rapidly to bereavement, with little evident despair; others show high levels of disorganization and despair for many years, with little evidence of healing.

KEY TERMS

religiosity	depression	yearning
extraversion	acceptance	disorganization and despair
neuroticism	thanatology	reorganization
personal competence	themes	normal grieving
denial	type A personality	chronic grieving
anger	hospice care	delayed grieving
bargaining	numbness	absent grieving

SUGGESTED READINGS

Alsop, S. (1973). *Stay of execution: A sort of memoir.* New York: Lippincott.

This book is a very personal, moving, and informative description of one man's journey from the beginning of his illness with leukemia until his death.

Brooks, A. M. (1985). *The grieving time: A year's account of recovery from loss.* Garden City, NY: Dial Press.

This is a brief, touching book describing one woman's grieving for her husband. Her experience followed Bowlby's stages rather nicely, so this is an example of a "normal" grieving process in Wortman and Silver's terms.

Feifel, H. (1990). Psychology and death: Meaningful rediscovery. *American Psychologist, 45,* 537–543.

This article presents a good, brief review of many current themes in psychologists' current research on death and dying, along with an exploration of why it has taken so long for psychologists to begin to study this important subject.

Kübler-Ross, E. (1969). *On death and dying.* New York: Macmillan.

This was the original major book by Kübler-Ross that significantly changed the way that many physicians and other health professionals viewed the dying process. It is full of case material and reflects very well Kübler-Ross's great skill as a listener and clinician.

Lyell, R. (1980). *Middle age, old age: Short stories, poems, plays, and essays on aging.* New York: Harcourt Brace Jovanovich.

This anthology includes several stories about death and dying, from many perspectives. Bunin's "The gentleman from San Francisco," Tolstoy's "The death of Ivan Ilych," and Dylan Thomas's "Do not go gentle into that good night" all touch on attitudes toward death.

Sanders, C. M. (1989). *Grief: The mourning after.* New York: Wiley-Interscience.

This book will give you a good, nontechnical look at the "traditional" view of the grieving process, including five proposed stages that follow Bowlby's model quite closely. The book has lots of examples from the reactions of real-life people and some practical advice about intervention strategies.

Schreiber, L. (1990). *Midstream.* New York: Viking.

Stewart Alsop's book gives a firsthand account of the time leading up to death; Le Anne Schreiber—a sportswriter of some renown—gives an equally moving secondhand account, in this instance the death of her mother from cancer, detailing both her own feelings and reactions and those of other family members.

THE SUCCESSFUL JOURNEY:
PATHWAYS, TRAJECTORIES, AND GULLIES

CHAPTER

14

Barbara grew up in a middle-class white family in the south during the 50s, attending segregated schools and being encouraged to find a nice professional man, marry, and settle down to raise children. She married young, and moved to a college town where she worked to put her husband through school, participated in peace marches and voter registration drives, and had three children. After a long stint as a stay-at-home mom, she enrolled in community college, taking classes between carpool duties and Little League games. She spent time as a volunteer tutor at her children's schools, a city library board member, and after a divorce, a single parent. By the time the children were ready for college, she had a master's degree in developmental psychology and a new husband who was a college professor. Since there was no Ph.D. program nearby, she taught classes at local colleges and worked as a researcher on various projects. She wrote a textbook on child development, magazine articles on parenting, and a book about discipline for parents of toddlers. But something was missing, so Barbara decided to get a Ph.D. Her husband took a leave of absence from his job and they moved to another state so that she could take coursework for a year as a 50-year-old graduate student. Then they moved back home and she worked on her dissertation for two years. Finally, with her three grown children, her six grandchildren, her parents, three sisters, and a very proud husband all looking on, she put on a cap and gown and received her Ph.D. hood. She is currently teaching developmental psychology courses at a local university and working on the revision of a college textbook (this one).

This story describes a much different journey through adulthood than my story in Chapter 1. Barbara and I grew up a decade apart and in different parts of the country. I focused on career in my early years and Barbara on family. I adopted two children in my mid-30s and Barbara gave birth to three children before her mid-20s. Now I am ready to wind down my writing career, but Barbara is going full throttle. My sights are set on more time for volunteer work, while Barbara has "been there, done that" years ago when her children were young. But despite our diverse paths, both of us experience great feelings of life satisfaction and I believe it is fair to say that we are good models of "successful aging."

Throughout this book, I have been talking about the ways in which people's lives move in similar ways through the years of adulthood—the common changes of body, mind, and personality, and the common challenges of marriage, child rearing, work demands, and relationships. Such a normative approach to understanding the adult years has its uses. It tells us something about the average or expected pathways. It also underlines the fact that the very perception that there is a common or modal pattern affects our expectations, goals, and aspirations: For there to be off-time events, there have to be some shared concepts of on-time.

But the normative approach, however helpful, cannot give us a full description or explanation of adult life. To understand the process of adult development and change, we also have to understand the ways in which lives are likely to differ, the variations in their reactions to the stresses and challenges they will encounter, and in the eventual satisfaction or inner growth they may achieve. To put it another way, if we are to comprehend adult lives, we need to understand not only the lawfulness and order that makes us the same, but also the rules or laws that underlie the enormous diversity.

Reaching such understanding is as immense a task as the diversity is great. But let me offer two approaches, beginning with an exploration of the growing literature touching on variations in what has come to be called **successful aging** (Baltes & Baltes, 1990b; Maciel, Heckhausen, & Baltes, 1994; Rowe & Kahn, 1998) and concluding with my own attempt at a model of both normative and individual aging.

Variations in Successful Adult Development

Overall Life Satisfaction

In their long-standing effort to understand why some adults are happier or more satisfied with themselves than are others, psychologists and sociologists have devised dozens of measures of happiness, well-being, or life satisfaction (Diener, 1984). Some have used only a single question, such as "Taking all things together, how would you say things are these days—would you say you are very happy, pretty happy, or not too happy?" (A. Campbell, 1981). Among researchers who use more than one question to tap life satisfaction, Bradburn's (1969) approach is one of the most widely used. Bradburn argued that overall life satisfaction reflects the combination of positive and negative feelings. His scale includes a set of items about negative emotions (loneliness, depression, boredom, restlessness, or being upset with criticism) and a set about positive emotions (feeling on top of the world, excited or interested in something, pleased with an accomplishment, pride). The resultant sum of the positive and negative feelings Bradburn calls **affect balance.** The various measures of life satisfactions capture somewhat different facets of well-being or happiness, but all these measures normally correlate quite highly with one another, suggesting that there a single dimension is being tapped by all.

Age and Life Satisfaction. Interestingly, age seems to have very little systematic relationship to the level of reported well-being (Palmore, 1981; Stock, Okun, Haring, & Witter, 1983). Happily, we have longitudinal as well as cross-sectional data to draw on here. In the Duke Longitudinal Studies, for example, Palmore found no change in overall life satisfaction over a six-year period among adults originally aged 47 to 68. Paul Costa and his colleagues (Costa et al., 1987) have found the same thing in a much larger, nine-year longitudinal study of a nationally representative sample of nearly 5000 adults originally aged 25 to 65. The age groups did not differ in average level of satisfaction, and there was no significant change in satisfaction with age.

Yet age is not irrelevant in our understanding of life satisfaction. Costa's study, along with other evidence, suggests that while the overall score is about the same across age, younger adults may experience both positive and negative feelings more strongly (higher highs and lower lows) than do older adults. Furthermore, the ingredients that make up life satisfaction change somewhat with age, a pattern that makes perfectly good sense given the descriptions of the various age periods I have given in Chapter 12. Health, for example, is a more significant predictor of life satisfaction or happiness among older adults than it is among the young or the middle aged (Bearon, 1989), and income is a less significant predictor among young adults than among either middle-aged or older adults

(George, Okun, & Landerman, 1985). Still, these age variations seem insignificant beside the overall consistency in life satisfaction with age. On average, older adults are as satisfied with themselves and their lives as are younger or middle-aged adults. To understand happiness or well-being, then, we will have to go beyond age as a benchmark and look at both demographic and personal differences.

Demographic and Personal Differences in Life Satisfaction. Table 14.1 summarizes the major findings on the connections between life satisfaction and various demographic and personal characteristics. Let me comment on a few of the especially interesting or significant patterns.

Perceived Differences and Perceived Adequacy. One of the recurrent themes evident in the table is that in many areas it is not absolute differences that matter but the adult's *perception* of some quality or characteristic, yet another illustration of the point I made in Chapter 10 when talking about meaning systems (Rudinger & Thomae, 1990). For

CRITICAL THINKING

Does it surprise you that there are no age differences in average level of life satisfaction? Given the increased health problems and other declines or losses in old age, why wouldn't you expect older adults to be less satisfied?

TABLE 14.1 **Factors Associated with Life Satisfaction Among Adults**

Demographic Factors	
Income/social class	Those with higher income are more likely to be satisfied with their lives, even when you hold other factors, such as health, constant.
Education	A very weak relationship: Higher-educated adults are only slightly more satisfied.
Gender	There is essentially no difference, even among older adults, among whom women experience more aches and pains.
Employment	Employed adults are more satisfied than unemployed, even when income is matched.
Marital status	Married adults are more satisfied.
Race/ethnicity	There is no general tendency for Africa-Americans, Hispanics, or other minority groups to have lower (or higher) life satisfaction beyond the effects of social class and income. Thus in this case there is no "double jeopardy."
Personal Qualities	
Personality	Adults low in neuroticism, and those high in extraversion, are more satisfied.
Sense of control	The greater the sense of control, the higher the life satisfaction.
Social interaction	Those with more contact with others, especially more intimate contact, and those more satisfied with their level of contact, have higher life satisfaction in general.
Health	Those adults with better self-perceived health are more satisfied than those who perceive themselves as ill or disabled; especially true in late adulthood.
Religion	Those who describe themselves as religious, or who say that religion is important in their lives, are more satisfied.
Negative life events	The more negative life changes that an adult has recently experienced, the lower the life satisfaction.

Source: Data from Antonucci, 1991; Diener, 1984; George, 1990; Gibson, 1986; Koenig, Kvale, & Ferrell, 1988; Markides & Mindel, 1987; Murrell & Norris, 1991; Willits & Crider, 1988.

example, an adult's perception of his or her own health is a better predictor of life satisfaction than is a doctor's objective health rating (Diener, 1984; Palmore, 1981), and it is the perceived adequacy of social interactions and not absolute quantity that is most strongly related to happiness (George, 1990; Gibson, 1986).

Something similar seems to operate in the relationship between income and life satisfaction. Although it is true that on average, those with higher income are more satisfied, the relationship is actually more relative than absolute. That is, if you have more money than others with whom you compare yourself, you are likely to be slightly happier than are those who are lower on the comparative totem pole. But if everyone in your comparison group experiences a rise in income at the same time you do, your level of life satisfaction or happiness doesn't go up, even though you can now afford things you couldn't afford before (Diener, 1984).

The general lack of age differences in happiness is further evidence for the same point. Middle-aged adults generally have higher incomes than younger adults or than they themselves had when they were younger, yet middle-aged adults are not on average more satisfied with their lives than are young adults. This makes sense if we assume that an adult's primary comparison group is his or her own cohort. Since the whole cohort has risen in income between the ages of 20 and 45, there is no overall increase in happiness. Only those adults who gained comparatively more than their cohort are likely to be more satisfied with their lives. Conversely, those who gained less than the typical amount are likely to be less satisfied.

Using a similar idea, we can perhaps understand why it is that life satisfaction does not decline in old age, despite the obvious losses in many domains. Because one's peers are also all aging, a person's *comparative* status remains roughly the same. We'd expect to find that those elders whose health or physical status has declined more than average would have lower satisfaction, and that is just what we find. Furthermore, older adults appear to lower their standards or their level of expectation (Brandtstädter & Greve, 1994; Brandtstädter & Rothermund, 1994). For example, when an older adult describes himself as being in "good health," he is unlikely to mean precisely the same thing that he meant when he was 25. His standard of "good health" has been adjusted to match the realities of his current situation. In this way, by no longer aiming toward goals that are now unreachable, older adults redefine success and failure and change the comparative base. They are therefore able to maintain their self-image as an effective, functioning person, and thus to remain satisfied with their lives, despite their awareness of losses or growing incapacities.

Personality. Among the most interesting effects listed in Table 14.1 are those connecting personality or temperament with life satisfaction. I have mentioned this connection in earlier chapters, but let me provide some research results to bolster the point.

Costa and McCrae have found such relationships both concurrently and predictively in longitudinal studies of men (Costa & McCrae, 1980b; Costa, McCrae, & Norris, 1981). Those men who score higher on measures of extraversion, and lower on measures of neuroticism, described themselves as happier at first testing, and still described themselves as happier 10 to 17 years later when happiness was again measured. Some sample findings from these studies are given in Table 14.2, a pattern of findings replicated in a six-year longitudinal study in Australia (Heady & Wearing, 1989).

None of the correlations in these studies is particularly large; clearly many other factors affect life satisfaction. But these studies do suggest that it may be possible to make some prediction of happiness in middle or old age from knowing something of the personality or temperament of young adults. In particular, any temperamental or personality qualities that make it easier for a person to form satisfying and supportive relationships appear to be especially good predictors of long-term life satisfaction. This conclusion is

TABLE 14.2 **Relationship Among Extraversion, Neuroticism, and Life Satisfaction**

	Correlation with Neuroticism	Correlation with Extraversion
Concurrent Relationships		
Scores on the Bradburn affect balance scale		
Positive affect	−0.10*	0.25*
Negative affect	0.34*	−0.12*
Affect balance	−0.27*	0.25*
Predictive (Longitudinal Relationships		
Scores on the Bradburn affect balance scale 10 years after neuroticism and extraversion were measured		
Positive affect	−0.08	0.23*
Negative affect	0.39*	0.03
Affect balance	−0.30*	0.14*
Scores on a single measure of life satisfaction 10–17 years after neuroticism and extraversion were measured		
Life satisfaction score	−0.08	0.35*

Note: Correlations marked with an asterisk are statistically significant at the 0.05 level or better.

Source: Data from Costa & McCrae, 1980b, Table 4, p. 674 and from text; Costa, McCrae, & Norris, 1981, Table 3, p. 81.

further supported by the repeated finding that the life satisfaction of socially isolated adults can be increased by providing them with training that increases their social skills (Fordyce, 1977). We cannot rule out the possibility that the causal chain runs the other way as well: Being happy with yourself and your life may help you to relate more positively to the people around you. But the preponderance of evidence points to the opposite effect—that positive social interactions, perhaps especially close relationships, contribute strongly to happiness and life satisfaction.

A Sense of Control. A third thread that runs through a number of the items in Table 14.1 is the sense of personal control. We can think of this either as something similar to a general personality trait, or as a quality of individual life circumstances, but the results are similar in both cases. Those adults who normally feel that they are in charge of their own lives and responsible for their own decisions are generally happier than those who feel that their lives are controlled by others or by fate or chance. Furthermore, adults whose real-life circumstances are such that they feel that they *have* some choices and options are generally happier than those who perceive themselves as being trapped in circumstances they cannot control (Diener, 1984). And when life circumstances change so that a person feels that she or he has *lost* control, the effect appears to be particularly detrimental. For example, financial strain among the elderly appears to be linked to overall life satisfaction or depression primarily through the loss of any sense of control over one's life, a link found in studies in both Japan and the United States (Krause, Jay, & Liang, 1991).

A similar conclusion emerges from studies on the impact of life changes. Even life events that seem objectively highly stressful may have little negative effect on life satisfaction

CRITICAL THINKING

Before you read this next section, see if you can make a prediction about which of the many variables listed in Table 14.1 is likely to be the most potent single predictor of life satisfaction.

if a person feels that he or she has some choice. So *involuntary* retirement or *involuntary* institutionalization have negative effects, whereas planned and chosen retirement or a planned move to a nursing home generally do not.

Relative Importance of Predictors of Happiness. The list in Table 14.1 is informative but it doesn't tell you how these different variables might be weighted. Which factors are the most important? Do they simply add up, or do they interact? The one thing that is clear is that there is no one element in adult life that guarantees high life satisfaction for everyone who possesses it, nor any one experience or quality that leads automatically to unhappiness. Happiness seems to be made up of a great many small things that are probably weighted differently by each person. Even combining the four key demographic variables (income, gender, education, and marital status) we can account for no more than about 10 percent of the variation in happiness (Diener, 1984). Health and personality each account for no more than a similar 5 to 10 percent.

Nonetheless, there is one predictor that is more potent than all the others: the person's reported happiness in marriage or family relationships. In several national surveys, the correlations between satisfaction with marriage or family life and overall life satisfaction are in the range 0.40 to 0.45, which means that perhaps as much as 15 to 20 percent of the variation in happiness is attributable to this feature of adult life (A. Campbell, 1981; Glenn & Weaver, 1981). It is not a magic happiness pill; the correlation is far from perfect. But satisfaction with one's relationships is a better predictor of overall life satisfaction than either demographic factors or satisfaction with such other key aspects of adult life as one's work. This is even true among highly educated men, among whom work commitment is typically very high.

In his autobiography, former Chrysler chairman Lee Iacocca made this point clearly: "Yes, I've had a wonderful and successful career. But next to my family, it really hasn't mattered at all" (1984, p. 289). Robert Sears often heard similar comments from the 60- to 70-year-old men he interviewed as part of Terman's 50-year longitudinal study of a group of intellectually gifted persons (1977). Sears reported that of six areas studied (family, occupation, friends, culture, service, and joy), "family experience was reported retrospectively to have been the one most important for securing satisfaction" (pp. 125–126).

Since the amount of social contact is also related to happiness, it appears likely that the size and variety of your social network, as well as the quality of social support available in your key intimate relationships, not only affects your ability to handle stress or life change, but also strongly affects your ongoing level of life satisfaction or happiness.

Other Measures of Life Success

The degree of happiness an adult experiences may be one measure of "success" in the adult years. But there are other ways of defining successful adulthood that rely more on professional assessments of a person's psychological health or on objective measures of life success. Two approaches, both involving analyses of rich longitudinal data, are particularly interesting.

Researchers working with the Berkeley longitudinal data have developed a measure of ideal adult adjustment or "psychological health" based on the Q-sort of personality I described in Chapter 9. In this research, psychotherapists and theorists agreed on the pattern of qualities of an optimally healthy person, which included the "capacity for work and for satisfying interpersonal relationships, a sense of moral purpose, and a realistic perception of self and society" (Peskin & Livson, 1981, p. 156). According to this view, ideally, healthy adults are high in warmth, compassion, dependability and responsibility, insight, productivity, candor, and calmness. They value their own independence and autonomy as well as intellectual skill, and behave in a sympathetic and considerate manner, consistent with their own personal standards and ethics.

Each subject in the study was then compared to this "ideal" profile, and each adult was given a score on psychological health. When this measure was correlated with the subjects' reported satisfaction with work, with family life, and with the closeness or affection in marriage, they found that adults who are rated by observers as having more "healthy" qualities also described themselves as more satisfied with their lives.

George Vaillant has approached the definition of successful aging somewhat differently in his studies of the Harvard men included in the Grant study. He has searched for a set of reasonably objective criteria reflecting what he calls *psychosocial adjustment,* and then has asked what factors in the men's childhood or in their adult lives are predictive of good or poor psychosocial adjustment (Vaillant, 1974, 1975; Vaillant & Vaillant, 1990).

You'll remember from earlier chapters that the Grant study men were evaluated and assessed in college and then regularly thereafter, with in-depth assessments at age 45 to 50 and again most recently at roughly age 63. Unfortunately, Vaillant has *not* used the same criteria to judge psychosocial adjustment in the men at each age, although the basic strategy has been the same. When the men were 45 to 50, their interview and questionnaire information was evaluated against a 32-point adult adjustment scale; at age 63, only nine items were used to measure adjustment, all of which are listed in Table 14.3, along with a selection of the items from the longer midlife scale.

You'll see from the table that the midlife scale is phrased in terms of *maladjustment,* whereas the 63-year-old scale is turned around and phrased positively, but in both cases a high score indicates that the man was *less* well adjusted. In both scales, following Freud's lead, Vaillant has included items that touch on successful or unsuccessful "working and loving," as well as items that describe medical or psychiatric problems. Like the Berkeley researchers, he has found that this relatively objective assessment is correlated with other measures of adult success, including both a measure of maturity of defense mechanisms and life satisfaction (Vaillant & Vaillant, 1990).

TABLE 14.3 **Vaillant's Psychosocial Adjustment Scales**

Selected Items from the Midlife Psychosocial Adjustment Scale (All Scored Yes or No)	Full set of Items in Age 63 Psychological Adjustment Scale
No steady advance in career	Continued employment (1 = full, 3 = retired)
Earned income less than $20,000 (in 1970)	Sustained job success (1 = yes, 2 = no)
No public service besides job	Job or retirement satisfaction (1 = clear satisfaction, 3 = clear dissatisfaction)
Lacks 10-year stable marriage	
No pleasant contact with parents or siblings	3+ weeks of vacation (1 = yes, 2 = no)
No objective evidence of friends	Few psychiatric visits (1 = 0, 3 = >10)
No pastimes with nonfamily members	Little tranquilizer use (1 = 5 days use per year, 3 = 30 days use per year)
Stints vacation	Fewer than 5 sick days per year (1 = yes, 2 = no)
No clear enjoyment of job	
Heavy use of drugs or alcohol	Marital satisfaction (1 = clear satisfaction, 3 = clear dissatisfaction)
Psychiatric diagnosis	Recreation with others (1 = yes, 2 = no)
More than 10 psychiatric visits	
2 or more sick leave days/year	
Often seeks medical attention	

Source: Data from Vaillant, 1975, Table 1, p. 422; Vaillant & Vaillant, 1990, Table 1, p. 32.

Despite their quite different strategies for measuring successful aging, the findings from the Berkeley and the Grant studies are reasonably consistent, and lead to some intriguing suggestions about the ingredients of a healthy or successful adult life. Both studies show that the most successful and well-adjusted middle-aged adults were those that grew up in warm, supportive, intellectually stimulating families. In the Berkeley study, N. Livson and Peskin (1981; Peskin & Livson, 1981) found that those who were higher in psychological health at age 30 or 40 grew up with parents who were rated as more open minded, more intellectually competent, with good marital relationships. Their mothers were warmer, more giving and nondefensive, more pleasant and poised. Similarly, Vaillant found that the men who were rated as having the best adjustment at midlife had come from warmer families and had better relationships with both their fathers and mothers in childhood than had the least well-adjusted men (Vaillant, 1974).

Both studies also show that well-adjusted or successful middle-aged adults began adulthood with more personal resources, including better rated psychological and physical health at college age, a practical, well-organized approach in college (Vaillant, 1974) and greater intellectual competence (N. Livson & Peskin, 1981). Both of these sets of findings are pretty much what we might expect. To put it most baldly and simply: Those who age well are those who start out well. To be sure, none of the correlations is terribly large, so even among the midlife subjects there were some who began with two strikes against them who nonetheless looked healthy and successful at 45 or 50, and some who started out with many advantages who did not turn out well. But in general, these findings point to a kind of consistency.

Yet when Vaillant looked at his subjects again when they were at retirement age, a very different picture appeared (Vaillant & Vaillant, 1990). Among these 173 men, *no* measure of early family environment remained a significant predictor of psychosocial adjustment at 63, nor did any measure of early-adult intellectual competence. Those who turned out to be "successful" 63-year-olds had been rated as slightly more personally "integrated" when they were in college, and they had had slightly better relationships with their siblings. But other than that, there were simply no childhood or early adulthood characteristics that distinguished between those who had turned out well and those who had turned out less well.

What does predict health and adjustment at age 63 among these men is health and adjustment at midlife. The least successful 63-year-olds were those who had used mood-altering drugs at midlife (primarily prescribed drugs intended to deal with depression or anxiety), abused alcohol or smoked heavily, and who used mostly immature defense mechanisms in their 30s and 40s.

Obviously, these findings come from only a single study, including only men, and only very well-educated professional men at that. So we shouldn't make too many huge theoretical leaps from this empirical platform. Still, the pattern of results suggests one (or both) of two possibilities:

1. It may be that each era in adult life simply calls for different skills and qualities, so that what predicts success or healthy adjustment at one age is simply not the same as what predicts it at another age. As one example, college-age intellectual competence may be a better predictor of psychosocial health at midlife simply because at midlife an adult is still in the midst of his most productive working years, when intellectual skill is more central. By retirement age, this may not be so critical an ingredient.

2. Alternatively, we might think of a successful adult life not as something foreordained from one's childhood or one's early adult qualities, but rather as something created out of the resources and opportunities available over the course of the decades. Those who start out with certain familial and personal advantages have a greater chance of encountering still further advantages, but it is what one does

with the experiences—stressful as well as constructive—that determines the long-term success or psychosocial health one achieves. The choices we make in early adulthood help to shape the people we become at midlife; those midlife qualities in turn help to shape the kind of older people we become—a process I might describe as *cumulative continuity*. Early childhood environment or personal qualities such as personality or intellectual competence are not unimportant, but by age 65 their influence is indirect rather than direct.

It seems likely to me that both of these options are at least partially true, but it is the second possibility that I find especially compelling. It helps to make sense out of a series of other facts and findings.

One relevant fragment comes from yet another longitudinal study in which George Vaillant has been involved, in this case of a group of 343 Boston men, all white, and nearly all from lower-class or working-class families. As teenagers, these men had been part of a nondelinquent comparison group in a major study of delinquency originated by Sheldon and Eleanor Glueck (1950, 1968). They had been interviewed at length when they were junior high school age and were then reinterviewed by the Gluecks when they were 25, and 31, and by Vaillant and his colleagues when they were in their late 40s. In one particular analysis by the Vaillant group (Snarey, Don, Kuehns, Hauser, & Vaillant, 1987) the researchers looked at the outcomes for those men

CRITICAL
THINKING

See if you can translate this view of adult development into advice for the young adult.

who had not had children at the normative time to see how the men had handled this childlessness. Of this group of childless men, those independently rated at age 47 as clearly "generative" in Erikson's sense were those who were likely to have responded by finding someone else's child to parent, such as by adopting a child or joining an organization such as Big Brothers or becoming an active uncle. Those childless men who were rated as clearly not generative at 47 were much less likely to have adopted a child; if they had chosen a substitute it was more likely a pet. Among the childless men, the generative and the nongenerative had not differed at the beginning of adult life in either social class or level of industry, so the eventual differences in psychosocial maturity do not seem to be the result of differences that existed at age 20. Rather, they seem to be a result of the way the man responded to or coped with an unexpected or nonnormative event in early adult life.

Another type of finding that fits into the same overall picture is one I talked about in Chapter 9 in discussing the consistency of personality over the adult years. You may remember that when researchers have measured personality characteristics several times in the same persons, they find that the correlations between such measurements at adjacent ages, even ages a decade or two apart, are reasonably robust. But when continuity is examined over longer periods, such as 40 or 50 years, the correlations drop to a much more modest level.

The entire process reminds me a bit of predicting the weather. To predict tomorrow's weather your best bet is to predict that it will be just like today. You will be right more than half the time. But predicting next week's weather is more difficult, and next month's is virtually unknown. Each day is linked to the day before and the day after, and all are part of a long causal chain of influences, but the weather today is only very indirectly related to the weather six months ago or to what will happen six months from now.

The central point for me is that there are many pathways through adulthood. The pathway each of us follows is affected by the departure point, but it is the choices we make as we go along, and our ability to learn from the experiences that confront us, that shapes the people we become 50 or 60 years later. If we are going to understand the journey of adulthood, we need a model that will allow us to make some order out of the diversity of lifetimes that results from such choices and such learning or lack of it. So as a final step in the synthesis I have been attempting in this final chapter, let me try my hand at such a more general model.

A MODEL OF ADULT GROWTH AND DEVELOPMENT: TRAJECTORIES AND PATHWAYS

Let me offer a set of four propositions. The first takes us back to many of the points I made earlier in this chapter as I summarized the information we have on normative or common pathways:

> **Proposition 1:** There are shared, basic sequential physical and psychological developments occurring during adulthood, roughly (but not precisely) age-linked.

Whatever other processes may influence adult life, it is clear that the entire journey is occurring along a road that has certain common features. The body and the mind change in predictable ways with age. These changes, in turn, affect the way adults define themselves and the way they experience the world around them. As I said in Chapter 12, I also place the sequence of changes in self-definitions or meaning systems outlined by Loevinger, Fowler, and others in this same category. The difference is that unlike physical and mental changes, the process of ego development or spiritual change is not an inevitable accompaniment of aging, but a *possibility* or potentiality.

Within the general confines of these basic processes and sequences of development, however, there are many individual pathways—many possible sequences of roles and relationships, many different levels of growth or life satisfaction or "success." Which brings me to the second major proposition:

> **Proposition 2:** Each adult's development occurs primarily within a specific pathway or trajectory, strongly influenced by the starting conditions of education, family background, ethnicity, intelligence, and personality.

I can best depict this individuality by borrowing Waddington's (1957) image of the **epigenetic landscape,** a variation of which is shown in Figure 14.1. Waddington introduced this idea in a discussion of the strongly "canalized" development of the infant years, but the same general concept can serve for a discussion of adulthood. Like Figure 14.1, the original Waddington image was of a mountain down which ran a series of gullies. In my version of this metaphor, the bottom of the mountain represents old age while the top of the mountain represents early adulthood. In our adult years, each of us must somehow make our way down this mountain. Since we are all going down the same mountain (following the same basic "rules" of physical, mental, and spiritual development), all journeys will have some features in common. But this metaphor also allows for wide variations in the specific events and outcomes of the journey.

Imagine a marble placed in one of the "gullies" at the top of the mountain. The particular pathway it follows to the bottom of the mountain will be heavily influenced by the gully in which it starts. If I also assume that the main pathways are deeper than the side tracks, then shifting from the track in which one starts is less probable than continuing along the same track. Nonetheless, the presence of choice points or junctions makes it possible for marbles starting in the same gully to end up in widely varying places at the bottom of the mountain. From any given starting point, some pathways and some outcomes are much more likely than others. But many possible pathways diverge from any one gully.

I am aware that the mountain metaphor has at least one major drawback: It implies that our progress through adulthood is nothing but a downhill slide involving only decline or loss. Some readers of earlier editions of this book have objected to the metaphor for this reason and because it fails to convey the possibility of growth or development

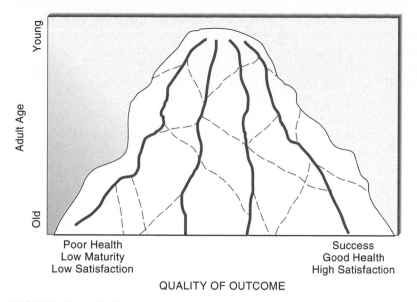

FIGURE 14.1 The image of a mountain with gullies running down it is one way to depict the alternative pathways through adulthood. The journey down the mountain (from youth to old age) can begin in any one of many tracks. As the adult moves down the track, he or she experiences periods of stability as well as transition points or disequilibria, during which the person may shift from one track to another.

that I have been emphasizing throughout these last few chapters. I have chosen to continue to use the image, nonetheless, because it is the only metaphor I can think of that conveys the *momentum* that is created by the sequence of choices we make in early adulthood and as we move through our adult years. So bear with me.

This model or metaphor certainly fits with the general findings from Vaillant's long-term study of the Grant study men. The gully one starts in certainly does have an effect on where you are likely to be on the mountain at midlife. But the eventual ending point is much more strongly linked to where you were at midlife than where you started out. One might even depict this using the mountain-and-gully model by showing the main gullies becoming deeper and deeper (harder to get out of) as they move down the mountain.

The model also fits with another finding I mentioned in Chapter 12, that there is an increase in variability of scores on various measures of health, mental skill, personality, and attitudes with increasing age. In early adulthood, the various alternative gullies are more like each other (closer together) than is true 40 or 60 years later.

Still another feature implicit in Figure 14.1 as I have drawn it is significant enough to state as a separate proposition:

CRITICAL THINKING

Can you think of another metaphor that would work better—that would convey the momentum but not imply only "decline"?

> **Proposition 3:** Each pathway is made up of a series of alternating episodes of stable life structure and disequilibrium.

In the mountain-and-gully metaphor, the stable life structures are reflected in the long, straight stretches between junction points; the junctions represent the disequilibria.

This aspect of the model is obviously borrowed from Levinson's theory of adult personality development. Like Levinson, I conceive of each stable life structure as a balance achieved by a person among the collection of role demands that she is then facing, given the skills and temperamental qualities at her command. This balance is normally reflected in a stable externally observable life pattern: getting up at a particular time every day to get the kids off to school, going off to your job, doing the grocery shopping on Saturday, having dinner with your mother every Sunday, going out to dinner with your spouse every Valentine's day, or whatever. It is also reflected in the quality and specific features of relationships and in the meaning system through which we filter all these experiences. These patterns are not totally fixed, of course. We all make small adjustments regularly, as demands or opportunities change. But there do appear to be times in each adult's life when a temporary balance is achieved.

The Relationship of Stable Periods and Age. These alternating periods of stability and disequilibrium or transition appear to be *related* to age. I've suggested such a rough age linkage in Figure 14.1 by showing more choice points at some levels of the mountain than at others. But I think this age linkage is much more approximate, much less stage-like, than Levinson originally proposed. The evidence I have described throughout the book does not conform terribly well to the strict age grading of stability and transition that Levinson suggests, although there are hints that a fairly common transition may exist at roughly age 30, at least in this culture in current cohorts.

But even if Levinson is wrong about the universality of the specific ages for transitions, it still seems to me to be true that the content of the stable structures at each approximate age, and the issues dealt with during each transition, are somewhat predictable. After all, we are going down/along the same mountain. There is a set of tasks or issues that confront most adults in a particular sequence as they age, as I outlined in Table 12.1. In early adulthood this includes separating from one's family of origin, creating a stable central partnership, bearing and beginning to rear children, and establishing satisfying work.

In middle adulthood the tasks include launching one's children into independence, caring for aging parents, redefining parental and spousal roles, exploring one's own inner nature, and coming to terms with the body's aging and with the death of one's parents. An adult who follows the modal "social clock" will thus be likely to encounter transitions at particular ages and to deal with shared issues at each transition (George, 1993). But I am not persuaded that there is only one order, or only one set of ages, at which those tasks are or can be confronted. In this respect the mountain-and-gully model is misleading since it does not convey the variability in *timing* of major choice points that clearly does exist, such as what happens when an adult does not marry, does not have children until his or her 30s or 40s, or becomes physically disabled or widowed or ill in his early adult years, or the like. But whatever the variations in timing, it still appears to me to be valid to describe adult life as alternating between periods of stability and transition.

Turning Points. The periods of disequilibrium, which we might think of as turning points in individual lives, may be triggered by any one or more of a whole series of events. There is no way to depict these in the mountain-and-gully model, so I have to turn to a more common kind of two-dimensional diagram, the (very complicated!) flowchart or path diagram shown in Figure 14.2. The major sources of disequilibrium, listed on the left-hand side of this figure, are the following:

1. *Role changes,* such as marriage, the birth of a child, the departure of the last child from home, retirement, changes in jobs, and so on.
2. *Asynchrony of timing* in the several different dimensions of adult change or growth. This is part of Perun and Bielby's timing model of development, which I

MAJOR SOURCES OF
DISEQUILIBRIUM

FACTORS OR QUALITIES
AFFECTING THE RESOLUTION
OF DISEQUILIBRIUM

QUALITY OF
RESOLUTION

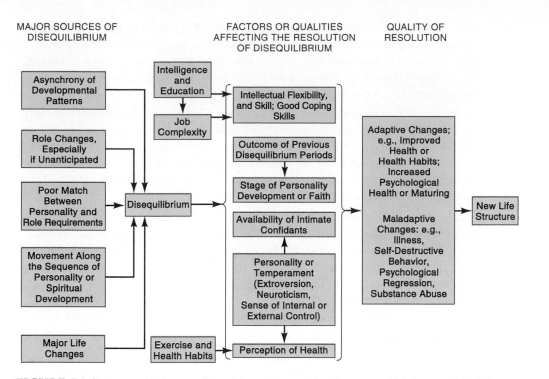

FIGURE 14.2 I know this is complicated, but take a crack at it anyway. This is a model of disequilibrium and its resolution. I am suggesting that such a process occurs repeatedly during adulthood, with the effects of these transitions accumulating over time. Each such transition affects the pathway (the gully) along which the adult then moves.

talked about in Chapter 2. When physical development, or mental development, or role patterns are "out of synch," there is tension or disequilibrium in the system. Being significantly off-time in any one dimension of adulthood automatically creates such asynchrony and is thus associated with higher rates of stress. Having a first child in your late 30s is not only a role change, it is also an asynchronous role change, which should increase the likelihood of a major disequilibrium, just as will the failure to have children at all, such as among the childless men in the Glueck/Vaillant study of working-class men that I mentioned a few pages ago. The general rule, as I have indicated before, is that on-time role changes seldom trigger major crises or self-reexamination precisely because they are shared with one's peers. The person can easily explain both the change and the strain it may cause as originating "outside" himself or herself. Nonnormative changes, by contrast, are difficult to explain away except with reference to one's own choices or failures or successes. These more individual experiences, then, are far more likely than the normative ones to bring about reassessment or redefinition of the self, of values, of systems of meaning.

3. *Lack of match* between the demands of a particular set of roles and an adult's own temperament or personality. This is, in some sense, another kind of asynchrony. The study by Florine Livson of the several pathways to high-level health in middle age that I described in Chapter 6 is one example of matching or nonmatching patterns. As you'll recall, Livson found that those adults who looked psychologically healthy at 50 but had shown signs of distress or disturbance at 40 were likely to be those whose qualities as teenagers didn't match the then-prevalent gender roles. The less social and more intellectual young women in this group tried to fit

into a mold of full-time homemaking and found it distressing; the more creative and emotional men tried to fit into the mold of the gray-flannel-suit society and were disturbed at 40. Both groups went through a process in their 40s of freeing themselves of the constraints of those early, ill-fitting roles, and emerged at 50 looking very much put together.

4. *Major life changes or major chronic stresses,* particularly losses in relationships, such as the death of a close family member or friend, or the loss of a friendship or love relationship. While unanticipated or off-time changes may be the most difficult in most instances, even some anticipated changes that involve such relationship losses, such as the death of your parents when you are in your 40s or 50s, still call for significant reassessment and reorganization.

5. Finally, disequilibrium can be triggered by a *change in inner psychological tasks,* such as any movement along the dimension described by Erikson or Levinson, or by Fowler's stages of faith. Such inner changes typically occur in *response to* the disequilibrium-causing agents I have just described. But once begun, a transition such as from conformist to conscientious ego structure, or from individuative to conjunctive faith, carries its own disequilibrium. Any new stable life structure that emerges at the end of the disequilibrium period must be built on the new sense of self, or faith, that has evolved.

Whether a person will experience such a disequilibrium period as a crisis or merely as a rather transitory phase seems to depend on at least two things: the number of different sources of disequilibrium, and the person's own personality and coping skills. When there is a pileup of disequilibrium-producing events within a narrow span of years, such as changes in roles, major relationship losses, and asynchronous physical changes, anyone is likely to experience a major transition. But the tendency to respond to this as a crisis may also reflect relatively high levels of neuroticism, low levels of extraversion, or the lack of effective coping skills.

In the model I am proposing here, it is our response to these disequilibrium periods that determines our particular pathway down the mountain, which leads me to the fourth basic proposition:

> **Proposition 4:** The outcome of a period of disequilibrium maybe either positive (psychological growth, maturity, improved health, etc.), neutral, or negative (regression or immaturity, ill health).

Which kind of outcome occurs at any choice point—which channel one follows—is determined or affected by a wide range of variables, which I have sketched in the middle of Figure 14.2. *Intellectual flexibility* or skill seems to be a particularly critical ingredient in leading to the "higher" stages of maturity and growth that Vaillant or Loevinger describe. An adult's intellectual flexibility, in turn, is influenced by the complexity of the environments in which he or she lives, particularly the complexity of job [either a job outside the home, or even the complexity of housework (Schooler, 1984)]. Janet Giele puts it well: "It is the degree of social complexity on the job or in other aspects of everyday life that appears critical. Those who must learn a great deal and adapt to many different roles seem to be the most concerned with trying to evolve an abstract self, conscience, or life structure that can integrate all these discrete events. By contrast, those with a simple job, limited by meager education and narrow contacts, are less apt to experience aging as a process that enhances autonomy or elaborates one's mental powers" (1982, p. 8).

And, of course, job complexity is itself partially determined by the level of original education each adult has attained. So well-educated adults are more likely to find complex jobs and are thus more likely to maintain or increase their intellectual flexibility. Linkages such as these help to create the pattern of predictability we see between early adulthood and midlife, but since none of these relationships is anywhere near a perfect correlation, there is a good deal of room for shifts from one gully to another. Some blue-collar jobs, for example, are quite complex, while some white-collar jobs are not, and such variations may tend to push people out of the groove in which they started.

Underlying temperamental tendencies are another key ingredient. Adults who are high in what Costa and McCrae call neuroticism appear to be more likely to respond to disequilibrium by increases in substance abuse, illness, depression, or regressive patterns of defense. Adults with less neurotic or more extraverted temperament, in contrast, respond to disequilibrium by reaching out to others, by searching for constructive solutions.

The availability of close supportive confidants is also a significant factor, clearly not independent of temperament. Adults who lack close friends or the supportive intimacy of a good marriage are more likely to have serious physical ailments in midlife, or to have significant emotional disturbances, to drink or use drugs, and to use more immature forms of defense (Vaillant, 1977). Such friendless or lonely adults do more often come from unloving and unsupportive families, but even such a poor early environment can be overcome more readily if the adult manages to form at least one close, intimate relationship. Vaillant describes several men in the Grant study who had grown up in unloving or highly stressful families, who were withdrawn or even fairly neurotic as college students, who nonetheless went on to become "successful" and emotionally mature adults. One of the common ingredients in the lives of these men, especially compared to those with similar backgrounds who had poorer outcomes, was the presence of a "healing" relationship with a spouse. Similarly, David Quinton and his colleagues have looked at the adult lives of several groups of young people in England, some of whom had had teenage histories of delinquency (Quinton, Pickles, Maughan, & Rutter, 1993). Quinton finds that the likelihood that the young adult will show a continuation of problem behavior (such as criminality) is far lower when the person finds a nondeviant, supportive partner than when the problem teen later joins up with a nonsupportive or problem partner. Thus early maladaptive behavior can be redirected, or "healed," through an appropriately supportive partner relationship.

Health may also make some difference in the way an adult responds to a period of disequilibrium. Poor health reduces options; it also reduces your level of energy, which affects the range of coping strategies open to you or the eventual life structures you can create.

Cumulative Effects of Transitions. As a final point, I would argue that the effects of these several disequilibrium periods are cumulative, a process that Gunhild Hagestad and Bernice Neugarten (1985) describe as the "transition domino effect." Such a cumulative effect of earlier stages or transitions is a key element in Erikson's theory

CHOOSING TO GET MORE EDUCATION, as these adults are doing, may often be an adaptive response to a current problem or task. It is also likely to increase the range of resources the individual has available when facing subsequent tasks. Thus, the choices we make at each point along the way have repercussions for later turning points as well.

of development, as you'll recall from Chapter 2. Unresolved conflicts and dilemmas remain as unfinished business, as excess emotional baggage that makes each succeeding stage more difficult to resolve successfully. Vaillant and others who have studied adults from childhood through midlife have found some support for this notion. Men in the Grant study who could reasonably be described as having failed to develop trust in their early childhood did have many more difficulties in the first few decades of adulthood. They were more pessimistic, self-doubting, passive, and dependent as adults and showed many more maladaptive or unsuccessful outcomes compared to those with more trusting childhoods.

CRITICAL THINKING

What other examples of off-time events can you think of that would have the same kind of lifetime effect?

Other forms of cumulative effect operate as well. One major off-time experience early in life, for example, may trigger a whole series of subsequent off-time or stressful experiences. The most obvious example is the impact of adolescent parenthood, which often leads to early school departure, which in turn affects the complexity of the job one is likely to find, which affects intellectual flexibility, and so on through the years.

Another form of cumulative effect occurs when a person's response to an early disequilibrium alters the choices he or she has available at later forks in the road. For example, in the face of some transition period, perhaps particularly a transition at midlife, an adult might begin a regular exercise program. This decision not only changes his or her life structure, but is also likely to increase the person's actual health or perception of health. Such an adult thus faces the next transition with the resource of better health, perhaps more vitality. For another adult, one of the resolutions of a prior disequilibrium point might be a change to a more complex job, or a return to school. Such a change not only alters the life structure, it also increases the adult's intellectual flexibility, which in turn affects the range of cognitive coping skills in the person's repertoire. The next transition might thus be faced more adaptively. We can see just such cumulative effects in the results of the Grant study. Those men who responded to early adulthood transitions and challenges by drinking more or with prolonged depression reduced their overall coping abilities; they got off track and stayed off track.

NOT ALL RESOLUTIONS of transitions or disequilibrium periods are adaptive or positive. Some, like increasing alcohol or drug use, may temporarily ease the pain or help repress the problem, but they leave the adult less able to cope with both current and future tasks.

Adaptive or Maladaptive Outcomes Versus Happiness. It is important for me to emphasize that the range of possible outcomes I have labeled *adaptive* and *maladaptive* changes are not identical to happiness and unhappiness. Maladaptive changes such as illness, substance abuse, suicide attempts, or depression obviously are correlated with unhappiness. But such adaptive changes as improved health habits, increased social activity, or movement along the sequence of stages of ego or spiritual development are not uniformly associated with *increases* in happiness. McCrae and Costa, for example (1983), did not find that adults who were at the conscientious or higher levels of ego development reported any higher life satisfaction than did adults at the conformist stage. Thus profound changes can result from a disequilibrium period without such changes being reflected in alterations of overall happiness or life satisfaction. Instead, a change in ego development stage may alter the criteria of happiness a person applies to his or her life. As McCrae and Costa say: "We suggest that the quality and quantity of happiness do not vary with levels of maturity, but that the circumstances that occasion happiness or unhappiness, the criteria of satisfaction or dissatisfaction with life, may vary with ego level. The needs and concerns, aspirations and irrations of more mature individuals will doubtless be different—more subtle, more individualistic, less egocentric. The less psychologically mature person may evaluate his or her life in terms of money, status, and sex; the more mature, in terms of achievement, altruism, and love" (1983, p. 247). Maturing clearly does not automatically make an adult happy, as demonstrated by (among other things) the lack of correlation between age and happiness. Maturing and other adaptive changes alter the agenda, and thus alter the life structures we create and the way we evaluate those life structures.

A LAST LOOK AT THE MODEL

I am sure it is clear to you already that the model I have sketched in this chapter, complex as it is, is nonetheless too simplistic. It is doubtless also too culture-specific, although I have tried to state the elements of the model broadly enough to encompass patterns in other cultures. It may also be quite wrong in a number of respects. Among other things, I have assumed throughout this discussion that something like Loevinger's sequence of ego development stages actually exists, and that all adults mature in this pattern if they mature at all. But as you know from Chapters 9 and 10, that assumption is based on slim evidence.

Despite these obvious limitations, however, the model may give you some sense of the rules or laws that seem to govern the richness and variety of adult lives. In the midst of a bewildering array of adult patterns there does appear to be order, but the order is not so much in fixed, age-related sequences of events as in *process*. To understand adult development it is useful to uncover the ways in which all pathways, all gullies, are alike. But it is equally important to understand those factors and processes that affect the choices an adult will have and the way he or she will respond to those choices. Perhaps the most remarkable thing about this journey is that with all its potential pitfalls and dilemmas, most adults pass through it with reasonable happiness and satisfaction, acquiring a modicum of wisdom along the way. May you enjoy your own journey.

SUMMARY

1. To understand the journey of adulthood we need to go beyond the normative approach followed in Chapters 12 and 13 and look for some kind of orderliness in the enormous variability of individual life patterns.

2. One strategy has been to study "successful aging," with success most often defined in terms of life satisfaction. Average levels of life satisfaction do not change significantly with age, although the ingredients may differ from one age period to the next.

3. Life satisfaction is related to several demographic and personal qualities: More highly satisfied adults are likely to have relatively higher income than their peers, to be slightly better educated, to be employed, and married. They are more likely to be extraverted, to be low in neuroticism, and to have a sense of personal control.

4. Perceived adequacy of health and social relationships are also predictors of life satisfaction, again illustrating the central importance of the meaning attached to experiences rather than the experiences themselves.

5. The largest single predictor of life satisfaction appears to be the perceived quality of social relationships, especially family relationships. But no one predictor accounts for a very large percentage of the variation in satisfaction among adults. Individual happiness is composed of many ingredients, many of them highly individual.

6. Other measures of successful aging include subjective ratings of psychological health by experts, or combinations of objective criteria such as success in "work and love."

7. Studies using such measures suggest that family background and early-adulthood resources are predictive of midlife psychological health or success, but that such early-life experiences are not related to later-life health or success. Such late-life success is much more strongly related to midlife qualities or skills, suggesting a kind of "cumulative continuity" of life pathways.

8. A preliminary model of adult development includes the metaphor of a mountain with gullies running down it. Each adult, with his or her own combination of beginning characteristics, moves down the mountain (through adulthood) in a particular gully, somewhat resistant to change.

9. Each pathway can also be thought of as being made up of alternating periods of stable life structures and disequilibrium periods. During the disequilibria, the adult may shift to another track or gully, or continue along the same pathway.

10. In any one culture, the stable periods are age-linked because they are largely defined by the set of family and work roles assumed by adults of particular ages.

11. Disequilibrium may be triggered by role changes, by asynchrony in timing of the several aspects of development, by a lack of match between a person's characteristics and particular role demands, by unanticipated life changes or stress, and by psychological growth such as movement to a new level in Loevinger's stages of ego development.

12. Whether the outcome of a period of disequilibrium will be positive/adaptive, negative/maladaptive, or neutral will depend on the person's intellectual flexibility and coping resources, underlying temperamental qualities, availability of close, supportive confidants, physical health, and the outcomes of previous disequilibrium periods.

KEY TERMS

successful aging

affect balance

epigentic landscape

SUGGESTED READINGS

Atkinson, R. (1989). *The long gray line.* Boston: Houghton Mifflin.

> This book presents the story of 20 years of the lives of the group of young men who formed the class of 1966 at West Point. Only selected men are highlighted in this story, but you can still get some sense of the kinds of pivotal experiences that shaped individual lives, the role of marriage in the lives of the men, and the interplay of personality and life demands. Fascinating reading.

Bateson, M. C. (1989). *Composing a life.* New York: Atlantic Monthly Press.

> Mary Catherine Bateson, daughter of Margaret Mead and Gregory Bateson, writes about her own life and that of four other women, exploring many of the very same questions of continuity and change that I have examined in this chapter and in this book. Once again, this is fascinating reading.

Clausen, J. A. (1993). *American lives: Looking back at the children of the great depression.* New York: Free Press.

> This is the most recent description of the results of the Berkeley Longitudinal Study, a group of people who have been followed from childhood into old age. The most recent contact was when they were in their 60s and 70s. The book is full of fascinating case material, following individual lives over many decades.

Vaillant, G. E. (1977). *Adaption to life.* Boston: Little Brown.

> I have recommended this book before, so you may already have dipped into it. I recommend it again here because it is one of the really good descriptions of actual lives over time, although it includes information on these men only up to about age 50; the 63-year-old interviews that Vaillant has now completed are too recent for the findings to have been part of this book.

GLOSSARY

absent grieving According to Wortman and Silverman, a type of grieving that involves no notable distress either immediately after a loss or later.

acceptance In Kübler-Ross's theory of coping with one's impending death, the last of five stages, which involves a lifting of depression and serene understanding of one's impending death.

accommodate In vision, the ability of the lens of the eye to change shape and focus on near objects or small print.

activities of daily living (ADL) Phrase used to describe a set of basic self-care activities, including bathing, toileting, self-feeding, walking a short distance, and dressing. Degree of disability is often measured in terms of inability to perform one or more of these activities.

acute illnesses Short-term, often severe illness.

adjustment to retirement According to Super, the final stage of a person's work life.

adulthood Arbitrarily defined here as the period from age 18 to death.

affect General term used by psychologists to mean roughly "emotion" but used more specifically here as a defining attribute of social support.

affiliation Being sociable, understanding, cheerful, and affectionate.

affiliative trust According to McClelland, a motive pattern that predicts good health.

affirmation A defining attribute of social support suggested by Kahn and Antonucci, it includes expressions of agreement or acknowledgment.

age-30 transition In Levinson's theory, the phase of reflection and reorientation that follows the novice phase of the 20s; leads to the culminating phase known as "settling down."

ageism Term used most generally to refer to any prejudice or discrimination against or in favor of a particular age group. More frequently refers to prejudice against older adults.

agency A sense of control over one's life that is predictive of good health.

age norms Set of expectations for the behavior of individuals of any given age group, such as teenagers or the elderly. Such norms are specific to a given culture or subculture and may change from one cohort to another.

agentic orientation In young adulthood, the development of an emphasis on achieving, doing, succeeding, and making one's own mark in the world.

age strata Layers or groupings by age within any given society. Individuals in each age stratum are expected to occupy certain roles and have certain privileges.

aging Passage of years in a person's life—without any connotation of loss or deterioration.

aging in place The goal for older adults to remain in their own homes as long as possible as they grow older.

agreeableness According to Costa and McCrae's Big Five personality dimensions, the extent to which a person is compliant and cooperative.

aid A defining attribute of social support suggested by Kahn and Antonucci, it includes direct physical, financial, or informational assistance.

alarm reaction In Selye's general adaptation syndrome (GAS), the first of three stages of stress reaction in which a noxious stimulus is perceived and physiological defenses are mounted.

Alzheimer's disease One of several causes of senile dementia, characterized by loss of brain weight and tangling of neurofibers of the brain, and resulting in gradual and permanent loss of memory and other cognitive functions.

amenity move Type of residence change that occurs typically around the time of retirement, often to a warmer climate and away from family members.

androcentric Having a world view that is gender polarized and believing that the male pole is superior.

androgyny Combination of high levels of both feminine and masculine traits and qualities.

anger In Kübler-Ross's theory of coping with one's impending death, the second of five stages, which involves negative emotional feelings toward various targets of blame for their impending death.

antibodies Proteins produced by the immune system that react to foreign organisms such as viruses.

antioxidants Vitamins and minerals that can prevent the formation of free radicals within cells.

antistage theories Theories pertaining to the belief that changes in a person's abilities or psychological structures over time are not sequential, qualitative, or systematic. *Contrast with* Stage theories.

anxiety disorders Feelings of fear, threat, and dread when no obvious danger is present.

anxious attachment In adulthood, relationship style characterized by obsession with relationships, frequent partners, and frequent breakups.

appraisal According to Lazarus, a person's subjective interpretation of an event, which is a better predictor of stress than an objective evaluation.

appraisal-focused coping Category of ways to handle stress that involve thinking, planning, and analyzing.

approach coping Category of ways to handle stress that involve taking measures to stop the stress. *Contrast with* Avoidance coping.

artistic personality type According to Holland, workers who are high in individualism, low in structure and sociability, and work best in the arts.

assisted living facilities Residential complexes for older adults in which care is available up to 24 hours a day.

associative friendship The less intimate form of friendship proposed by Reisman, characterized by some shared activity or interest.

asynchrony Not occurring at the same time or at the same rate.

atherosclerosis Gradual blockage of the coronary arteries with fibrous and calcified tissue.

attachment Particularly deep affective bond between any two people, characterized by, among other things, an enhanced sense of security when in the presence of the attachment figure.

attachment behaviors Outward expressions of an underlying attachment, such as smiling, trying to be near, writing letters to, hugging, and so on. Specific attachment behaviors displayed change over the life cycle.

attrition In longitudinal studies, the loss of subjects over time due to various causes, such as death, illness, loss of interest, or moving.

autobiography groups According to Birren, a group of older people who discuss various turning points and stages of their lives in order to learn how best to spend their last years.

autonomous stage Next-to-highest stage proposed by Loevinger, characterized by the capacity to acknowledge and deal with inner conflict.

autonomy In relationships, partners acting and thinking independently.

avoidance coping Category of ways to handle stress that involve taking measures to better protect oneself against the stress. *Contrast with* Approach coping.

avoidant attachment In adulthood, relationship style characterized by emotional withdrawal from partner as primary reaction to relationship stress.

avoidant marriages Long-lasting marriages in which the partners don't argue, but have agreed to disagree with no apparent rancor.

awakening According to Underhill's writings about mysticism, the first of five steps toward mystical experiences, which involves a realization of the possibility of stepping outside one's own perspective and understanding the world from a point of deep connection.

balance Ability to perform physical actions with stability.

bargaining In Kübler-Ross's theory of coping with one's impending death, the third of five stages, which involves attempts to make deals with physicians, nurses, and even God in order to escape their impending death.

b cells Cells produced in the bone marrow that make antibodies as part of the immune system function.

behavioral genetics Study of the genetic basis of behavior, such as intelligence or personality. One major technique is the comparison of degree of similarity of identical and fraternal twins.

being motives According to Maslow, unique human desires to discover and understand, to give love to others, to push for optimum fulfillment of inner potentials. *Contrast with* Deficiency motives.

beta-amyloid Dense protein found in brain tissue of Alzheimer's patients.

biological clock Theoretical internal mechanism that is responsible for time-dependent aspects of development.

bridge job Job taken by a person who is close to retirement that typically involves less stress and responsibility.

buffering effect of social support Finding that negative health effects of stress are smaller among people who have supportive friends and family members.

career consolidation Stage suggested by Vaillant as an addition to Erikson's stages of adulthood, said to occur in one's early 30s, when attention is focused on work success and achievement.

career ladder Concept of one's career as a set of steps or rungs of a ladder.

cataracts Condition common to older people marked by a gradual clouding of the lens of the eye.

change Term used in this book to describe some pattern of variation with age when it is not clear that that pattern reflects primary aging or development.

chronic grieving According to Wortman and Silverman, a type of grieving which involves high distress that continues for several years.

chronic illnesses Long-term, lingering illness.

chronic life strains According to Pearlin, sources of stress that are continuous and unavoidable. *Contrast with* Life changes.

climacteric General term used to describe the period (for both men and women) in which reproductive capacity is gradually lost during adulthood. Menopause is another word to describe the climacteric in women.

clinical depression Alternative term for major depressive disorder.

cognitively committed According to Haan, cluster of personality traits that peak at midlife and involve independence, achievement, and openness.

cognitive mechanics According to Baltes, using a computer analogy, the hardware of mental activities. *Contrast with* Cognitive pragmatics.

cognitive pragmatics According to Baltes, using a computer analogy, the software of mental activities. *Contrast with* Cognitive mechanics.

cognitive structure According to Piaget, theoretical parts of the brain that grow as new knowledge and abilities are acquired.

cohabitation Living together in a committed, sexual relationship without marriage.

cohort Group of individuals born at approximately the same time who share the same pattern of historical experiences in childhood and adulthood.

cohort effect Differences between groups of people of different ages that is due to the historical circumstances of their lives rather than to aging or other developmental processes.

cohort-sequential design Type of sequential research design, it involves two or more consecutive longitudinal studies.

commitment According to Sternberg, feelings of being connected emotionally to another person over a long period of time.

communal roles Social roles based on qualities that are passive, nurturing, and emotional.

companionate grandparents Grandparents who have warm, loving relationships with their grandchildren but do not take on day-to-day responsibility for them.

companionate love According to Hatfield, the affection and familiarity that one feels toward another person.

compensation According to Baltes, one of three elements of selective optimization with compensation in which the older person finds ways to make up for energy and skills that are missing and cannot be brought back with practice.

competence Being organized, thorough, practical, and clear thinking; according to Helson, cluster of personality traits that involve feelings of being capable and qualified.

concrete operational level According to Piaget, the third of four stages of cognitive development featuring logical, but not abstract, thought.

conformist stage Stage proposed by Loevinger in her theory of adult development, characterized by the identification of one's self with group norms and values.

congregate living facilities Residential complexes in which older adults live independently but take meals together.

conjunctive faith Fifth stage of faith development proposed by Fowler, involving openness to other views, other "faiths"; and to paradox, myth, and metaphor.

connected (desire to be) In Kegan's theory of the development of meaning, to be joined or integrated with others, one of two equal and powerful desires built into all human beings. *Contrast with* independent (desire to be).

conscientiousness According to Costa and McCrae's Big Five personality dimensions, the extent to which a person is disciplined and organized.

conscientious stage Stage proposed by Loevinger following the conformist and the self-aware level, characterized by the creation of individual rules and ideals.

consistency in absolute level Tendency for a person's scores on some measure stay the same over time, independent of the scores of others.

content In the life course transitions perspective, the role one has in relation to other components of one's social system.

contextual validity According to Labouvie-Vief, specialized and pragmatic cognitive structures that adults develop as a replacement for Piaget's formal operational level, trading off deductive thoroughness for openness and paradoxical thinking.

continuing care retirement community Facility that offers a range of services and living arrangements that residents can use as their needs increase.

conventional level In Kohlberg's theory of moral reasoning, the second of three levels, typical of most adolescents and adults in our culture, in which people base moral decisions on internalized rules and expectations from family and peer group members.

conventionally gendered According to Bem, having a world view that is gender polarized.

conventional personality type According to Holland, a worker who prefers structured activities, subordinate roles, clear guidelines, and works best in jobs that involve record keeping and organization.

convoy Term used by Antonucci to describe the set of people with whom each adult has close and intimate relationships and who move through time with the person.

coping Strategies that people use to handle stress.

coping skills Ability to deal effectively with adversities.

coronary heart disease (CHD) General term used by physicians to describe a set of disease processes in the heart and circulatory system, including most noticeably a narrowing of the arteries with plaque (atherosclerosis).

correlation Statistic used to describe the degree to which the scores on two variables covary. A correlation can range from +1.00 to -1.00, with numbers near 1.00 (+ or -) reflecting stronger relationships.

correlational consistency Tendency for a person's scores on some measure to keep the same relative position within a group over time.

countershock phase In Selye's general adaptation syndrome of stress reaction (GAS), the second level of the alarm reaction phase, in which the adrenal cortex secretes increased amounts of adrenaline and body temperature and blood pressure return to normal.

crisis Life transition with demands that overwhelm a person's resources to handle stress.

cross-linking Exchange of DNA material between cells of different types, such as skin and connective tissue cells; results in decrease in efficiency of cell protein.

cross-sectional design Type of research design in which different age groups are compared on the same measures at a single time point.

cross-sequential design Most complex of the set of sequential research designs, involving a set of cross-sectional groups each followed longitudinally.

crystallized intelligence According to Cattell and Horn, intellectual abilities that are learned through specific education or cultural experiences.

culminating phase In Levinson's theory, the last of three substages found within each stage, involving improved and more adaptive efforts.

culture System of customs and meanings shared by some identifiable group or subgroup and transmitted from one generation of that group to the next.

cumulative continuity Fact that our actions produce results that accumulate over time and move us along specific life trajectories.

cyclic GMP Substance released by the brain during sexual arousal and important in males for achieving and maintaining erections.

daily hassles According to Lazarus, common, relatively small sources of stress such as traffic jams and lost keys that may be better predictors of psychological symptoms than major life events.

daily life strain In Pearlin's theory, a type of distress that is chronic, durable, and almost impossible to avoid.

daily uplifts According to Lazarus, common, relatively small sources of pleasure, such as a phone call from a friend.

dark adaptation Ability of the visual system to adapt to changes in available light.

dark night of the soul According to Underhill's writings about mysticism, the fourth of five steps toward mystical experiences, which involves an even deeper exploration of the self than that experienced in previous stages.

decline Term used in this book only as a description of some observed lowering or drop in performance over age on some measure.

defense mechanism In psychoanalytic theories, these are strategies of the ego for coping with anxiety, including such patterns as denial, repression, projection, and intellectualization. May be organized by levels of maturity.

deficiency motives According to Maslow, instincts or drives to correct imbalance or maintain physical or emotional homeostasis, such as getting enough to eat and obtaining love from others. *Contrast with* Being motives.

delayed grieving According to Wortman and Silverman, a type of grieving that involves little initial distress but high levels of stress some months later.

dementia generic term for any broad and systematic deterioration of intellectual abilities, at whatever age. When it occurs in late adulthood, it is typically called *senile dementia.*

demilitarized zone (DMZ) According to Hagestad, mutual but unspoken agreement between parents and children concerning topics not to be discussed.

demographic density Referring to the acquisition of a large number of social roles in young adulthood.

dendrites Treelike branching parts of each nerve cell.

denial In Kübler-Ross's theory of coping with one's impending death, the first of five stages, which involves defending oneself from the threatening information by refusing to believe it.

depression Disturbance of the affect that involves some degree of loss of pleasure and interest in everyday life; in Kübler-Ross's theory of coping with one's impending death, the fourth of five stages, which involves a kind of mourning for oneself.

detribalization According to Levinson, the shift from internal to external definition of the self that occurs at midlife, when one becomes less dependent on the social matrix.

development Term used in this book to refer to any changes with age that appear to involve some systematic improvement, integration, or "growth."

dexterity Skillful use of body or hands.

DHEA Hormone thought to prevent or reverse aging.

Diagnostic and Statistical Manual of Mental Disorders,* 4th edition *(DSM-iv) Handbook published by the American Psychiatric Association as a guide for mental health professionals.

dialectical thought According to Basseches, adult stage of cognitive development that replaces Piaget's stage of formal operations and attempts to describe fundamental processes of change.

disengagement Proposed process in late life involving a healthy withdrawal from social roles and contacts and greater freedom from the rules and expectations of earlier adulthood.

dismissive attachment In adulthood, having a positive internal working model of oneself and a negative internal working model of others.

disorganization and despair According to Bowlby, the third of four phases of grieving, in which the person feels fatigued and depressed.

dream Part of Levinson's theory of adult development. In early adult transition, each person is thought to create a mental picture or fantasy of himself or herself creating a particular kind of life or achieving a particular goal.

early adulthood stage According to Levinson, the time period between 25 and 45 during which a young person works hard to achieve the dream.

early adult transition In Levinson's theory, the phase of reflection and reorientation that occurs in the late teens or early 20s and leads to independence, establishing an identity, and separating from one's family or origin.

eclectic theories In development, explanations that reflect skepticism about stages of adult development.

ecologically significant Relevant to daily living. *Contrast with* Artificial laboratory environments.

ego integrity versus despair Final stage of development proposed by Erikson, confronted in late life, when the adult must come to terms with who she is and has been or face despair.

emotion-focused coping Category of ways to handle stress that involve expressing feelings.

enabling style Types of behaviors that maintain interactions and foster intimacy.

encoding Processes by which information is committed to memory.

enterprising personality type According to Holland, workers who are high in verbal ability and persuasion and work best in sales jobs.

epigentic landscape Visual metaphor suggested by Waddington. Development is depicted as a hill with valleys of various depths and steepness, to convey the idea that some aspects of development are highly "canalized."

equality In relationships, partners treating each other and thinking of each other as equals.

erectile dysfunction (ED) Inability to achieve and maintain an erection adequate for satisfactory sexual performance.

establishment or stabilization stage According to Super, the time period between 25 and 45 during which young people work hard and advance far in their careers.

estrogen Hormones produced chiefly by the ovaries in women and responsible for developing and maintaining reproductive abilities and secondary sexual characteristics.

evolutionary psychology Theory that contemporary human behavior, thought, and emotion are products of a long history of natural selection.

exchange theory Explanation of mate selection that considers the assets each person brings to the relationship.

exhaustion In Selye's general adaptation syndrome of stress reaction (GAS), the last of three stages in which the strategy of the resistance stage breaks down and some of the alarm stage responses reappear, accompanied sometimes by physical exhaustion and even death.

experiment Research design in which the experimenter systematically manipulates one or more variables, assigning subjects randomly to one or more experimental and control groups.

external locus of control According to Rotter, the belief that one's life is controlled by external influences.

external memory aids Ways to help memory function outside the physical memory system, such as lists and calendar entries.

extraversion According to Costa and McCrae's Big Five personality dimensions, the extent to which a person is sociable, enthusiastic, and optimistic.

faith In Fowler's theory of faith development, a person's view of his or her relationship with others and with the universe.

family life cycle Phrase used by family sociologists to describe the series of steps or stages that occur in the life history of any given family from marriage, through birth of first child, through various stages in the child's growth, to the children's departure from the family.

family life stages In Duvall's theory, one of eight changes that occur within a family unit as members are added, taken away, or change roles.

fearful attachment In adulthood, having a negative internal working model of oneself and of others.

filter theories Explanations of mate selection that involve a series of steps that rule out more and more potential mates until only one is left.

flexible goal adjustment According to Brandstädter, personality trait common in older adults that involves change and compromise in pursuit of goals. *Contrast with* Tenacious goal pursuit.

fluid intelligence According to Cattell and Horn, a basic set of intellectual abilities that are not a product of specific education.

formal operational level According to Piaget, the last of four stages of cognitive development featuring abstract thought.

free radicals Molecules or atoms within a cell that possesses an unpaired electron and are thought to be involved in primary aging.

Full-Scale IQ Combination of the verbal IQ score and the performance IQ score on an IQ test.

g Term used by psychologists to denote a central, general intellectual capacity that influences how people approach many different tasks.

gain Term used in this book to describe patterns of change with age that involve increases or rises on some measure.

gendering of poverty Fact that an increasingly larger proportion of people living in poverty in the United States are women.

gender polarized According to Bem, the quality of a person's world view that is distorted by exaggerated gender roles.

gender role "Job description" for the role of a man or woman in a given culture, in a given cohort. These are socially defined and change over time.

gender-role crossover Hypothesized change from masculine roles to feminine roles (or feminine to masculine) as one ages.

gender stereotypes Set of shared cultural beliefs based on gender.

general adaptation syndrome (GAS) Complex sequence of physiological reactions to stressors proposed by Selye, including initial alarm, intermediate resistance, and finally, exhaustion.

generalized anxiety disorder Chronic, persistent, and excessive anxiety and worry.

generational squeeze Situation in middle adulthood typified by responsibilities for one's elderly parents in addition to responsibilities for one's adolescent or young adult children.

generational stake According to Bengston, the emotional value adult children represent to their parents in terms of grandchildren, continuity of the family, and a type of immortality.

generativity versus self-absorbtion and stagnation Seventh stage proposed by Erikson, occurring from perhaps age 25 to 50, when the adult must find some way to rear or support the next generation.

glaucoma Condition common to older people marked by a potentially dangerous buildup of pressure within the eye.

good boy or good girl orientation In Kohlberg's theory of moral reasoning, the first of two stages in the conventional level in which people make moral decisions based on maintaining an image of a "good person."

growth hormone Hormone thought to prevent or reverse aging.

growth motives *See* Being motives.

harm avoidance Personality trait that involves anxiety, depression, or both anxiety and depression.

harm avoidance gene Gene that has been identified and thought to cause both anxiety and depression.

healthy immigrant effect Phenomenon that those who come to the United States as immigrants are in better health than people who were born here.

helplessness According to Seligman, the belief that problems are enduring, due to internal circumstances, and unsolvable.

heritability rating Statistical score that reflects how much variance in a trait is due to genetics.

homogamy In mate selection, the tendency for a person to select a mate who is similar.

hormone replacement therapy (hrt) Practice of supplementing or replacing estrogen and progesterone in women after the natural production decreases due to menopause or surgical removal of the ovaries.

hospice care Relatively new pattern of care for terminally ill patients. The majority of care is provided by family members, with control of care and the setting of care in the hands of the patient and family. May be at home, in special hospital wards, or in separate institutions.

hostile/detached marriages Unsuccessful marriages in which the partners have short but hostile disagreements.

hostile/engaged marriages Unsuccessful marriages in which partners argue long and often without the balance of love and humor found in long-lasting volatile marriages.

hot flash Common symptom of menopause involving a brief, abrupt rise in body temperature accompanied sometimes by sudden sweating and skin flushing.

human factors research Scientific investigation aimed at solving problems people encounter as they interact with the environment.

humanitarian concern According to Schaie, personality trait common in older adults that involves concern for others.

identity Term used in Erikson's theory of development to describe the gradually emerging, and continually changing, sense of self.

identity versus role confusion Fifth stage in Erikson's theory of development, typifying the teenager and young adult, when the person must form specific occupational, gender, and religious identities.

illumination According to Underhill's writings about mysticism, the third of five steps toward mystical experiences, which involves a deeper prolonged awareness of God or some greater reality.

independence According to Helson, a cluster of personality traits that involve feelings of being responsible for oneself.

independent (desire to be) In Kegan's theory of the development of meaning, to be separate or differentiated from others, one of two equal and powerful desires built into all persons. *Contrast with* Connected (desire to be).

individualistic level In Loevinger's theory of development, the transitional point between the conscientious and autonomous stages; the central issue is that of dependence and independence.

individual principles of conscience orientation In Kohlberg's theory of moral reasoning, the second of two stages in the postconventional (or principled) level in which people make moral decisions based on the deepest set of moral principles possible.

individuation Process by which a young adult moves from dependence on family members and others to an independent self.

individuative-reflective faith Fourth stage proposed by Fowler, in which the source of authority for the adult's model of the world shifts from external to internal.

inductive reasoning According to Thurstone and Schaie, one of the five mental abilities identified as primary factors.

influence attempts Among family members, giving advice and persuading others to change their minds.

insomnia Inability to fall asleep or stay asleep.

institutional migration Type of residence change among older adults that involves moving to a nursing home.

instrumental activities of daily living (IADL) Set of activities, including cleaning house, cooking, and shopping, that reflect an adult's ability to live independently. Often used, along with ADLs, to measure the degree of functional disability in older adults.

instrumental roles Social roles based on qualities that are active, competent, and rational.

instrumental values According to Ryff, codes of conduct common in young and middle-aged adults that relate to *being* something, such as ambitious or courageous. *Contrast with* Terminal values.

integrated stage Final stage of adult development proposed by Loevinger, rarely reached, in which the conflicts of the autonomous stage are transcended.

intelligence According to Wechsler, the overall capacity of a person to act purposefully, think rationally, and deal effectively with his or her environment.

interactional continuity The fact that our personalities elicit certain reactions from others which serve to reinforce our basic personality patterns.

interactionist definitions (of stress) Definitions of stress that are based on a person's perception of an event or the extent to which some experience exceeds a person's ability to adapt.

interiority Term used by Neugarten to describe a quality she thought characterized the personalities of older adults, including greater focus on interior processes and less emphasis on trying to change the world.

internal locus of control According to Rotter, the belief that one's life is controlled by internal influences.

internal working model of attachment Internal, cognitive construction or set of assumptions about the workings of relationships, such as expectations of support or affection, or trustworthiness. The earliest relationships may form the template for this internal model.

interpersonal processes Explanations of mate selection that consider the evolving relationship between the people involved.

interview Method of studying behavior by asking people a set of questions (structured interview) or by asking follow-up questions to their initial responses (open-ended interview).

intimacy Comfort and trust that people have in sharing their innermost thoughts and feelings with another person; according to Sternberg, feelings that promote closeness and connectedness.

intimacy versus isolation Sixth stage proposed by Erikson, typically occurring in the early 20s, when the young adult forms several key, intimate relationships.

investigative personality type According to Holland, a worker who is high in organized thought and planning, low in social skills, and works best as a scientist or engineer.

involved grandparents Grandparents who have warm, loving relationships with their grandchildren and take on some of the day-to-day responsibilities for them, such as after-school care or financial assistance.

IQ Abbreviation for intelligence quotient, a score on a test of intelligence that has a mean of 100 and is derived from comparing a person's performance (mental age) with their chronological age.

kinkeeper Social role for promoting and protecting relationships between family members, usually filled by women

kinship migration Type of residence change among older adults, especially widows, that involves moving closer to family members.

late adulthood According to Levinson, the final stage of a person's work life.

learning schema theory Belief that gender stereotypes are the product of learning experiences that begin in childhood.

life change events According to Holmes and Rahe's Social Readjustment Rating Scale, a list of 42 changes, positive and negative, that require some degree of adaptation and therefore can affect one's physical or emotional health.

life course In sociology, a person's unique set of experiences over one's lifetime.

life course markers Life experiences that are highly predictable and widely shared within a culture.

life course transitions Fairly new sociological perspective that attempts to explain the variability of adult life pathways.

life expectancy Average number of years a person of a designated age (e.g., birth, age 65) can still expect to live.

life row According to Butler, a necessary process for the elderly that involves a review of the events of one's life with particular attention to unresolved issues.

life span Theoretical maximum number of years of life for a given species, which is thought will not be exceeded even with improvements in health care.

life span perspective General perspective shared by a number of theorists that emphasizes that development is a lifelong process; that it is multidirectional, involving both gain and loss; and that there is plasticity in human behavior throughout the entire life span.

life structure Concept suggested by Levinson to describe the pattern of existence, combining roles, relationships, and particular personality adaptations created by each person at several points in the adult life.

liking According to Rubin, having feelings of respect and affection toward another person.

limerance According to Tennov, an acute longing that one feels toward another person.

locus of control According to Rotter, the extent to which a person believes that his or her life is controlled by internal or external influences.

longevity Word literally meaning "long life" but used generally in gerontological literature to mean roughly the same as life expectancy.

longitudinal design Research design in which the same people are studied repeatedly over a period of time.

long-term memory In information processing, theoretical location in the perceptual system that stores material transferred from short-term memory for a time period from minutes to a lifetime.

love As defined by Sternberg, includes three elements: intimacy, passion, and commitment.

loving According to Rubin, having feelings of care and intimacy toward another person.

maintenance stage According to Super, the time period between 45 and 60 during which people's careers are going strong but they begin to feel that there is more in life than their careers.

major depressive disorder One of the mental disorders defined by the *DSM-IV* that features extreme and enduring symptoms of depression.

marital homogamy Selection of a spouse from among those similar to the self in social class, background, and race.

maturation Any sequential unfolding of physical changes that is governed by the genetic code or by other biological processes and that is shared by all members of a species.

maturity Increase with age of trust and self-discipline, accompanied by a decrease in impulsiveness, vulnerability, anxiety, and depression; a shift to the use of more mature defense mechanisms.

maximum oxygen uptake (V02 max) Amount of oxygen that can be taken into the bloodstream and hence carried to all parts of the body. A major measure of aerobic fitness, V02 max decreases with age but can be increased again with exercise.

medication nonadherence Failure to take medication as prescribed by one's physician.

memory Ability to retain or store information and retrieve it when needed.

menopause Term used to refer to the female climacteric, that set of physical and hormonal changes associated with the loss of reproductive capacity in women in their 40s and 50s.

mentor Established, senior person on a job who looks after a younger person and helps him or her to advance. According to Levinson, this person also helps with the transition from dependence on parents to independence.

meta analysis Research procedure in which a number of studies are grouped together and reanalyzed as one large study.

middle adulthood stage According to Levinson, the time period between 45 and 60 during which people feel responsible for their own work and also for the work of others.

midera transition In Levinson's theory, the second of three substages found within each stage, involving reflection and reorientation.

midlife transition In Levinson's theory, the phase of reflection and reorientation that occurs around the age of 40, which involves awareness of one's mortality and the possibility the dream may not be fulfilled.

morbidity Illness rate for a particular population.

mortality rate Probability of dying in any one year for all adults in a certain age group.

mutations Genetic errors.

mysticism Referring to a self-transcendent experience.

naive hedonism In Kohlberg's theory of moral reasoning, the second of two stages in the preconventional level in which individuals make moral decisions based on what serves one's own needs of what is negotiated with others according to precise interpretation of rules.

need for power According to McClelland, a motive pattern that predicts certain health outcomes, such as problem drinking and susceptibility to infectious diseases.

neurons Cells comprising the brain and nervous system.

neuroticism According to Costa and McCrae's Big Five personality dimensions, the extent to which a person is emotionally stable.

nonconventionally gendered According to Bem, having a world view that is not gender polarized.

normal grieving According to Wortman and Silverman, a type of grieving that involves relatively high distress and occurs immediately after the loss, followed by rapid recovery.

novice phase in Levinson's theory, the first of three substages found within each stage, involving adjusting to the new demands of that stage.

number According to Thurstone and Schaie, one of the five mental abilities identified as primary factors.

numbness According to Bowlby, the first of four phases of grieving, in which the person experiences shock and is unable to concentrate or think clearly.

observation Method of studying behavior by observing people in their natural surroundings.

obsessive-compulsive disorders Guilt and anxiety over certain thoughts or impulses.

old age Arbitrary period, defined here as the years from 65 to death.

oldest old Phrase now often used to describe those over 85.

"old" jobs Types of jobs, usually held by older people, that are not physically demanding and tend to be more interesting and challenging.

old old Phrase now commonly used by gerontologists to refer to those over 75.

ontogenetic fallacy According to Dannefer, the false assumption made by psychologists that anything that looks like a common pattern of change with age is a basic, normative process of aging.

openness According to Costa and McCrae's Big Five personality dimensions, the extent to which a person is curious and interested in variety.

optimism According to Seligman, the belief that problems are temporary, due to external circumstances, and solvable.

optimization According to Baltes, one of three elements of selective optimization with compensation in which the older person learns new strategies and keeps old skills well practiced.

osteoarthritis Term used generally to describe any significant changes in the bones of the joints of the body associated with the wear and tear of aging.

osteoporosis Changes in bones, including increased brittleness and porousness, resulting from loss of calcium in the bone.

panel studies Form of cross-sequential research design, common among sociologists, in which a large (usually representative) sample, covering many ages, is studied repeatedly over a period of years.

panic disorder Recurring sudden episodes of intense apprehension, palpitations, shortness of breath, and chest pain.

parental imperative Phrase used by David Gutmann to describe a possibly "wired-in" pattern of intensification of gender-role differentiation after marriage and particularly after the first child is born.

passion According to Sternberg, feelings of intense longing for union with another person, including sexual union.

passionate love According to Hatfield, an intense longing for another person that can result in either ecstasy or despair, depending on whether it is returned or not.

perceived control Sense of control over one's life that is predictive of good health.

Performance IQ Subscore for the performance portion of an IQ test.

performance tests Those tests included in many IQ tests that rely less on verbal skills and more on basic analytic or memory processes.

personal competence Person's feeling of self-worth and accomplishment.

personality A person's unique, relatively consistent, and enduring methods of behaving in relation to others and the total environment.

personality traits Relatively enduring ways of thinking, feeling, and acting.

personality trait structures Relatively small number of factors that represent the basic dimensions of personality.

phobias Fears and avoidance out of proportion to the danger.

pink-collar jobs Nonprofessional jobs that are stereotypically "women's jobs," such as secretarial, retail sales, and service jobs.

plasticity Ability to change.

positions In the life course transitions perspective, linking components of social systems, such as teacher and student, parent and child.

postconventional (or principled) level In Kohlberg's theory of moral reasoning, the last of three levels of moral reasoning, typical of only a minority of adults in our society, in which moral decisions are based on underlying reasons behind society's rules.

preconventional level In Kohlberg's theory of moral reasoning, the first of three levels, typical of children under age 9, in which rules are viewed as something outside themselves.

preoccupied attachment In adulthood, having a negative internal working model of oneself and a positive internal working model of others.

presbycusis Common form of deafness among older adults that results from basic wear and tear on the auditory system. More common among adults who have worked in noisy environments.

presbyopia Normal loss of visual acuity with age, especially the ability to focus on objects nearby, resulting from accumulated layers on the lens and accompanying loss of elasticity.

primary aging Term often used to describe those aspects of physical changes with age that are universally shared and inevitable, a result of some basic biological process.

primary memory *See* Short-term memory.

principled level of moral reasoning Third major level of moral reasoning proposed by Kohlberg, in which the adult looks behind the rules of society or family for a set of underlying principles on which to base moral judgments.

problem-focused coping Category of ways to handle stress which involve doing things.

problem solving Complex set of thought processes that a person uses to attain a goal.

process of decentering According to Piaget, the gradual shift seen in cognitive development outward from the self.

pruning In neuropsychology, the ability to shut down neurons that are not needed in order to improve the functioning of the remaining neurons.

psychological openness Willingness to acknowledge and explore the previously unexpressed parts of oneself.

punishment and obedience orientation In Kohlberg's theory of moral reasoning, the first of two stages in the preconventional level, in which people make moral decisions based on what will bring rewards versus punishment.

purification According to Underhill's writings about mysticism, the second of five steps toward mystical experiences, which involves turning inward and examining one's own imperfections.

Q-sort Procedure that involves sorting a set of statements in some order according to how well they apply to the person or topic being investigated.

questionnaire Method of studying behavior by distributing written questions that people can fill out at a time and place convenient to them and then return to the experimenter.

r Symbol used to denote a correlation score.

realistic personality type According to Holland, a worker who is high in aggression and physical strength, low in verbal and social skills, and works best with tools and machines.

recall Type of retrieval process in which some stimulus not currently perceived is retrieved from memory. *Contrast with* Recognition.

reciprocal assistance Extent to which two people in a relationship give help to each other.

reciprocal friendship Most intimate form of friendship proposed by Reisman, characterized by long-term affectional bonds.

reciprocity In relationships, a balance in giving and receiving assistance.

recognition Type of retrieval in which a person remembers a familiar stimulus upon being presented with it again. *Contrast with* Recall.

relationship initiation Promoting and protecting a relationship in the early stages.

relationship maintenance Promoting and protecting a relationship once it is established.

religiosity Degree of a person's religious feeling, regardless of which religious views are held.

remote grandparents Grandparents who interact with their children infrequently, due to physical distance or emotional detachment.

reorganization According to Bowlby, the last of four phases of grieving in which the person takes up his or her usual activities again and finds new relationships.

research analysis In psychology research, the statistical comparison of data gathered for different groups of people.

research design Basic structure of a scientific inquiry or experiment.

research methodology In psychology research, the manner in which behavior is measured and data are gathered for scientific investigation.

resistance In Selye's general adaption syndrome (GAS), the second of three stages of stress reaction, in which the body strives to achieve normality.

resistance resources Personal and social resources that may buffer a person from the potential impact of stress.

restrictive style Types of behaviors that derail interactions.

retirement communities Planned developments restricted to older adults, which feature individual houses and apartments as well as community centers and recreation areas.

retrieval Getting information out of one's memory when it is needed.

role Concept from sociology describing the expected behavioral and attitudinal content of any one social position, such as teacher, mother, or employer.

role conflict Experience associated with occupying two or more roles that are wholly or partially logistically or psychologically incompatible.

role strain Experience associated with occupying a role the demands of which do not match one's own qualities or skills.

role streams Initial adoption of a role and the subsequent experiences that follow.

scheduled life changes According to Pearlin, changes that can be anticipated and prepared for, such as children moving away from home or retirement.

scheduled life strain In Pearlin's theory, a type of distress that is predictable and can be anticipated.

seasonal migration Pattern of residing near family in the summer and spending the winter months in a warmer climate.

secondary aging That part of the changes with age in physical functioning that is not inevitable but may result from widely shared environmental events.

secondary memory *See* Long-term memory.

secure attachment In adulthood, relationship style characterized by accurate and sensitive communication of feelings with partners and optimism about the relationship; having a positive internal working model of oneself and of others.

selection According to Baltes, one of three elements of selective optimization with compensation in which the older person restricts his or her activities and interests so he or she can use limited energy on demands that are central.

selective attrition Risk that people who drop out of longitudinal research studies are different in a systematic way from those who remain until the end, thus confounding the results.

selective optimization with compensation According to Baltes, a process that a person uses to cope with the declines that come with age.

selective theory In explaining the negative health effects of divorce, the theory that people who divorce are less stable than people who stay married.

self-actualization According to Maslow, the highest need experienced by human beings, which can emerge only when other lower needs are satisfied.

self-aware level Step immediately after the conformist level in Jane Loevinger's theory of development; a transitional level in which the person is beginning to define himself or herself apart from external expectations.

self-confidence Trust in oneself and one's abilities.

self-determined motivation Believing that events in one's life are determined largely by oneself.

self-efficacy according to Bandura, a belief in one's own ability to perform some action or control one's behavior or environment.

self-protective stage Fourth stage proposed by Loevinger, typically occurring in middle childhood or adolescence, but found occasionally in adults as well. Characterized by attempts to maximize one's own gain in any situation.

seminal fluid Fluid containing sperm that is ejaculated by males at the climax of a sex act.

semiprofessional jobs Jobs that require college degrees but have relatively low pay and little chance for advancement, such as nursing, social work, and teaching.

senescence In cellular biology, a state that cells enter after dividing a certain number of times.

senile dementia Any deterioration of intellectual abilities in old age that is due to some disorder of the nervous system rather than to the normal aging process.

sensory memory In information processing, theoretical location in the perceptual system that takes in information from the senses, stores it for a second or less, and then either transfers it to short-term memory or ignores it.

sensory store *See* Sensory memory.

sequence Pertaining to the compromise between stage theories and antistage theories, which holds that development may be sequential and systematic, but does not reflect shared changes in internal structures.

sequential designs Family of research designs each of which involves either multiple cross-sectional comparisons or multiple longitudinal comparisons, or both.

settling down In Levinson's theory, the culminating phase that follows the reflection and reorientation of the age-30 transition.

sexual desire According to Freud, the basis of love.

shock phase In Selye's general adaptation syndrome (GAS), the first level of the alarm reaction phase of stress reaction, in which some noxious stimulus is perceived and registered by a drop in body temperature and blood pressure.

short-term memory In information processing, theoretical location in the perceptual system that takes material transferred from the sensory memory and performs an operation on it within 30 seconds, either using it in a response or storing it in long-term memory.

social class Group of people in a given culture who have similar social standing or rank within that culture; typically measured in terms of level of education, occupation, and income.

social clock Usual sequence of life experiences within a given culture.

social contract orientation In Kohlberg's theory of moral reasoning, the first of two stages in the preconventional (or principled) level, in which people make moral decisions based on fundamental principles that may not always agree with the law.

social mobility Movement of people from one social stratum to another within any given society.

social order maintaining morality In Kohlberg's theory of moral reasoning, the second of two stages in the conventional level, in which people make moral decisions based on maintaining the laws of society.

social personality type According to Holland, workers who are high in sociability and need for attention, low in organization, and work best with people.

social readjustment rating scale Holmes and Rahe's list of 42 life change events and rating of their relative stress. Subjects add up stress points for events that have occurred over a certain number of months, and the score predicts the likelihood of physical or emotional illness in the near future.

social role interpretation (theory) Belief that gender stereotypes are the result of division of labor within a culture.

social roles Expected behaviors and attitudes that come with one's position in society.

social status Defined by sociologists as a position within a social structure. Many psychologists use the term more loosely as a roughly synonym of social class.

social support Combination of affect, affirmation; and aid that a person receives from those with whom he or she has relationships.

socioemotional selectivity theory Casternsen's theory that as we age we decrease the number of relationships we have and increase the quality of those relationships.

spatial orientation According to Thurstone and Schaie, one of the five mental abilities identified as primary factors.

speeded tasks Tasks on an I.Q. test that have a time limit.

speed of processing Time it takes for cognitive tasks to be performed.

stage theories Theories that changes in a person's abilities or psychological structures over time are sequential, qualitative, and systematic. *Contrast with* Antistage theories.

stamina Physical strength to withstand fatigue.

storage retaining information in memory over time.

subclinical depression Experience of several symptoms of depression for a limited time.

succorance Caring for others.

synchrony Occurring at the same time and at the same rate.

synthetic-conventional faith Third stage of faith proposed by Fowler, in which a person selects a model (a faith) from among those available in the social system. Authority is external to the person.

t cells Cells produced by the thymus gland that reject and consume harmful or foreign cells as part of the immune system function.

telomeres Lengths of repeating DNA found at the tips of chromosomes and thought to be timekeeping mechanisms that determine how many times a cell will divide before reaching senescence.

temporal progression Sequence of experiences or internal changes that follow a timetable.

tenacious goal pursuit According to Brandstädter, personality trait common in young and middle-aged adults that involves aggression and competition in pursuit of goals. *Contrast with* Flexible goal pursuit.

terminal values According to Ryff, codes of conduct common in older adults that relate to *having* something, such as happiness or independence. *Contrast with* Instrumental values.

testes Male reproductive glands located in the scrotum and involved in the production of sperm and androgen.

testosterone Major male hormone produced in the testes.

thanatology Study of dying.

themes In developmental theory, an alternative to stages.

theories of adult change Explanations of aging based on the assumption that changes over the life span are not necessarily steps toward a higher goal or better state, as opposed to theories of adult *development.*

theories of adult development Explanations of aging based on the assumption that changes over the life span are steps toward a higher goal or better state, as opposed to theories of adult *change.*

theory of mind Understanding that each person has his or her own independent mental state and that behavior can be predicted and explained based on knowledge of those states.

time-lag design Assessment of a series of groups of subjects, each the same age at the time testing occurs but representing different cohorts (e.g., test 20-year-olds in 1970, then another group of 20-year-olds in 1980, then a third group in 1990).

time of measurement effect Risk that people in a longitudinal study are showing the effects of a particular sequence of life events typical of their cohort rather than of a real developmental process.

time-sequential design Variety of sequential design in which parallel cross-sectional studies are completed several years apart (e.g., 20-, 40-, and 60-year-olds might be studied in 1960, then separate groups of 20-, 40-, and 60-year-olds studied in 1980).

tournament Metaphor used by Rosenbaum to describe the course of one's career.

training effect Increase in performance due to an intentional exercise or practice.

transitions Changes that take place with development as people move from one stage to another; times when existing life structures are reassessed and may be altered; in sociology, changes in states that are discrete and limited in duration.

trial stage According to Super, the time period between the ages of 15 to 25 during which young people try to find a fit between jobs available and their own interests and abilities.

tribalization According to Levinson, defining oneself by the group one belongs to and one's position within that group. Contrast with *detribalization.*

type A personality Combination of competitiveness, a sense of time urgency, and hostility or aggressiveness; found to be associated with higher risk of coronary heart disease.

union According to Underhill's writings about mysticism, the last of five steps toward mystical experiences, which involves being one with God or some greater reality.

universality versus diversity Question of whether changes experienced in adulthood happen to most adults or whether they are different.

universalizing faith Highest (sixth) stage of faith proposed by Fowler, involving some loss of the sense of individuality and a commitment to the whole.

unscheduled life changes According to Pearlin, changes that cannot be anticipated and prepared for, such as illness or job loss.

unscheduled life strain In Pearlin's theory, a type of distress that is not predictable and cannot be anticipated.

unspeeded tasks Tasks on an I.Q. test that have no time limit.

vo2 max *See* Maximum oxygen uptake.

validating marriages Long-lasting marriages in which partners express mutual respect even when they disagree.

Verbal IQ Subscore for the verbal portion of an IQ test.

verbal meaning According to Thurstone and Schaie, one of the five mental abilities identified as primary factors.

verbal tests In contrast to performance tests, those measures of intellectual ability that rely heavily on the ability to manipulate verbal symbols.

visual acuity Ability to perceive detail in a visual pattern.

volatile marriages Long-lasting marriages marked by both passionate arguments and expressions of affection, with more positive than negative interactions.

wisdom According to Baltes, an expert knowledge system about the pragmatics of life.

word fluency According to Thurstone and Schaie, one of the five mental abilities identified as primary factors.

working memory The process of holding information in short-term memory while some operation is performed on it.

work patterns Periods during a person's lifetime when he or she was employed, unemployed, or employed part time.

yearning According to Bowlby, the second of four phases of grieving, in which the person longs for the one who has died and also may feel some anger toward those who seem to be responsible for the death.

young adulthood Arbitrary period, defined here as between ages 18 and 40.

"young" jobs Types of jobs, usually held by younger people, that are physically difficult, dirty, and tedious.

young old Term commonly used by gerontologists to refer to those between 60 or 65 and 75.

Ascione, F. & Shrimp, L. (1984). The effectiveness of four educational strategies in the elderly. *Drug Intelligence and Clinical Pharmacy, 18,* 926-931.

Assouline, M., & Meir, E. I. (1987). Meta-analysis of the relationship between congruence and well-being measures. *Journal of Vocational Behavior, 31,* 319–332.

Astone, N. M. (1993). Are adolescent mothers just single mothers? *Journal of Research on Adolescence, 3,* 353–371.

Atchley, R. C. (1989). A continuity theory of normal aging. *The Gerontologist, 29,* 183–90.

Atkinson, R. (1989). *The long gray line.* Boston: Houghton-Mifflin.

Austad, S. N. (1997). *Why we age: What science is discovering about the body's journey through life.* New York: Wiley.

Bakan, D. (1966). *The duality of human existence: An essay on psychology and religion.* Chicago: Rand McNally.

Baker, P. M. (1985). The status of age: Preliminary results. *Journal of Gerontology, 40,* 506–508.

Baker, G. T., III, & Martin, G. R. (1997). Molecular and biologic factors in aging: The origins, causes, and prevention of senescence. In C. K. Cassel, H. J. Cohen, E. B. Larson, et al. (Eds.), *Geriatric medicine (3rd ed., pp. 3–28).* New York: Springer-Verlag.

Balkwell, C. (1985). An attitudinal correlate of the timing of a major life event: The case of morale in widowhood. *Family Relations, 34,* 577–581.

Ball, J. F. (1976–1977). Widow's grief: The impact of age and mode of death. *Omega, 7,* 307–333.

Baltes, P. B. (1987). Theoretical propositions of life-span developmental psychology: On the dynamics between growth and decline. *Developmental Psychology, 23,* 611–626.

Baltes, P. B. (1993). The aging mind: Potential and limits. *The Gerontologist, 33,* 580–594.

Baltes, P. B., & Baltes, M. M. (Eds.). (1990a). *Successful aging: Perspectives from the behavioral sciences.* Cambridge, England: Cambridge University Press.

Baltes, P. B., & Baltes, M. M. (1990b). Psychological perspectives on successful aging: The model of selective optimization with compensation. In P. B. Baltes & M. M. Baltes (Eds.), *Successful aging: Perspectives from the behavioral sciences* (pp. 1–34). Cambridge, England: Cambridge University Press.

Baltes, P. B., & Lindenberger, U. (1988). On the range of cognitive plasticity in old age as a function of experience: 15 years of intervention research. *Behavior Therapy, 19,* 283–300.

Baltes, P. B., & Reese, H. W. (1984). The life-span perspective in developmental psychology. In M. Bornstein & M. E. Lamb (Eds.), *Developmental psychology: An advanced textbook* (pp. 493–532). Hillsdale, NJ: Erlbaum.

Baltes, P. B., Reese, H. W., & Lipsitt, L. P. (1980). Life-span developmental psychology. *Annual Review of Psychology, 31,* 65–110.

Baltes, P. B., Reese, H. W., & Nesselroade, J. R. (1977). *Life-span developmental psychology: Introduction to research methods.* Monterey, CA: Brooks/Cole.

Baltes, P. B., Smith, J., & Staudinger, U. M. (1992). Wisdom and successful aging. In T. B. Sonderegger (Ed.), *Nebraska Symposium on Motivation, 1991* (pp. 123–168). Lincoln, NE: University of Nebraska Press.

Baltes, P. B., Sowarka, D., & Kleigl, R. (1989). Cognitive training research on fluid intelligence in old age: What can older adults achieve by themselves? *Psychology and Aging, 4,* 217-221.

Bandura, A. (1977). Self-efficacy: Toward a unifying theory of behavioral change. *Psychological Review, 84,* 91–125.

Bandura, A. (1982). Self-efficacy mechanism in human agency. *American Psychologist, 37,* 122–147.

Bandura, A. (1986). *Social foundations of thought and action: A social cognitive theory.* Englewood Cliffs, NJ: Prentice Hall.

Bandura, A. (1997). *Self-efficacy.* New York: Freeman.

Bankoff, E. A. (1983). Social support and adaptation to widowhood. *Journal of Marriage and the Family, 45,* 827–839.

Barnes, M. L., & Sternberg, R. J. (1997). A hierarchical model of love and its prediction of satisfaction in close relationships. In R. J. Sternberg & M. Hojjat (Eds.), *Satisfaction in close relationships* (pp. 79–101). New York: Guilford Press.

Barnett, R. C., Marshall, N. L., & Pleck, J. H. (1992). Men's multiple roles and their relationship to men's psychological distress. *Journal of Marriage and the Family, 54,* 358–367.

Bartholomew, K. (1990). Avoidance of intimacy: An attachment perspective. *Journal of Social and Personal Relationships, 7,* 147–178.

Bartholomew, K., & Horowitz, L. M. (1991). Attachment styles among young adults: A test of a four-category model. *Journal of Personality and Social Psychology, 61,* 226–244.

Bass, D. M. (1985). The hospice ideology and success of hospice care. *Research on Aging, 7,* 307–328.

Basseches, M. (1984). *Dialectical thinking and adult development.* Norwood, NJ: Ablex.

Basseches, M. (1989). Dialectical thinking as an organized whole: Comments on Irwin and Kramer. In M. L. Commons, J. D. Sinnott, F. A. Richards, & C. Armon (Eds.), *Adult development: Vol. 1. Comparisons and applications of developmental models* (pp. 161–178). New York: Praeger.

Bateson, M. C. (1989). *Composing a life.* New York: Atlantic Monthly Press.

Baugher, R. J., Burger, C., Smith, R., & Wallston, K. (1989–1990). A comparison of terminally ill persons at various time periods to death. *Omega, 20,* 103–115.

Beal, C. R. (1994). *Boys and girls: The development of gender roles.* New York: McGraw-Hill.

Bearon, L. B. (1989). No great expectations: The underpinnings of life satisfaction for older women. *The Gerontologist, 29,* 772–784.

Beck, R. W., & Beck, S. H. (1989). The incidence of extended households among middle-aged black and white women: Estimates from a 15-year panel study. *Journal of Family Issues, 10,* 147–168.

Bedeian, A. G., Ferris, G. R., & Kacmar, K. M. (1992). Age, tenure, and job satisfaction: A tale of two perspectives. *Journal of Vocational Behavior, 40,* 33–48.

Bell, R. R. (1981). *Worlds of friendship.* Beverly Hills, CA: Sage.

Bellatoni, M. F., & Blackman, M. R. (1996). Menopause and its consequences. In E. L. Schneider & J. W. Rowe (Eds.), *Handbook of the biology of aging (4th ed.* pp. 415–430). San Diego, CA: Academic Press.

Belle, D. (1990). Poverty and women's mental health. *American Psychologist, 45,* 385-389.

Belloc, N. B. (1973). Relationship of health practices and mortality. *Preventive Medicine, 2,* 67–81.

Belloc, N. B., & Breslow, L. (1972). Relationship of physical health status and health practices. *Preventive Medicine, 1,* 409–421.

Belsky, J., Lang, M. E., & Rovine, M. (1985). Stability and change in marriage across the transition to parenthood: A second study. *Journal of Marriage and the Family, 47,* 855–865.

Belsky, J., Spanier, G. B., & Rovine, M. (1983). Stability and change in marriage across the transition to parenthood. *Journal of Marriage and the Family, 45,* 567–577.

Bem, S. L. (1981). Gender schema theory: A cognitive account of sex typing. *Psychological Review, 88,* 354–364.

Bem, S. L. (1993). *The lenses of gender: Transforming the debate on sexual inequality.* New Haven, CT: Yale University Press.

Bender, S. (1989). *Plain and simple: A woman's journey to the Amish.* San Francisco: Harper & Row.

Benfante, R., & Reed, D. (1990). Is elevated serum cholesterol level a risk factor for coronary heart disease in the elderly? *Journal of the American Medical Association, 263,* 393–396.

Bengtson, V. L. (1985). Diversity and symbolism in grandparent roles. In V. L. Bengtson & J. F. Robertson (Eds.), *Grandparenthood* (pp. 11–26). Beverly Hills, CA: Sage.

Bengtson, V. L., Cuellar, J. B., & Ragan, P. K. (1977). Stratum contrasts and similarities in attitudes toward death. *Journal of Gerontology, 32,* 76–88.

Benninger, W. B., & Walsh, W. B. (1980). Holland's theory and non-college-degreed working men and women. *Journal of Vocational Behavior, 17,* 81–88.

Berardo, D. H., Shehan, C. L., & Leslie, G. R. (1987). A residue of tradition: Jobs, careers, and spouses' time in housework. *Journal of Marriage and the Family, 49,* 381–380.

Bergeman, C. S., Chipuer, H. M., Plomin, R., Pedersen, N. L., McClearn, G. E. Nesselroade, J. R., Costa, P. T., Jr., & McCrae, R. R. (1993). Genetic and environmental effects on openness to experience, agreeableness, and conscientiousness: An adoption/twin study. *Journal of Personality, 61,* 159–179.

Berkman, L. F. (1985). The relationship of social networks and social support to morbidity and mortality. In S. Coen & S. L. Syme (Eds.), *Social support and health* (pp. 241–262). Orlando, FL: Academic Press.

Berkman, L. F., & Breslow, L. (1983). *Health and ways of living: The Alameda County Study.* New York: Oxford University Press.

Berkman, L. F., Seeman, T. E., Albert, M. Blazer, D., Kahn, R., Mohs, R., Finch, C., Schneider, E., Cotman, C., McClearn, G., et al. (1993). High, usual, and impaired functioning in community dwelling older men and women: Findings from the MacArthur Foundation Research Network on Successful Aging. *Journal of Clinical Epidemiology, 46,* 1129–1140.

Berlin, J. A., & Colditz, G. A. (1990). A meta-analysis of physical activity in the prevention of coronary heart disease. *American Journal of Epidemiology, 132,* 612–628.

Berman, W. H., Marcus, L., & Berman, E. R. (1994). Attachment in marital relations. In M. S. Sperling & W. H. Berman (Eds.), *Attachment in adults. Clinical and developmental perspectives* (pp. 204–231). New York: Guilford Press.

Berscheid, E. (1983). Emotion. In H. H. Kelley, E. Berscheid, A. Christensen, J. H. Harvey, T. L. Huston, G. Levinger, E. McClintock, L. A. Peplau, & D. R. Peterson (Eds.), *Close relationships* (pp. 63–91). Newbury Park, CA: Sage.

Betz, E. L. (1984). A study of career patterns of women college graduates. *Journal of Vocational Behavior, 24,* 249–263.

Betz, N. E., & Fitzgerald, L. F. (1987). *The career psychology of women.* Orlando, FL: Academic Press.

Bianchi, A. (1993, January–February). Older drivers: The good, the bad, and the iffy. *Harvard Magazine,* pp. 12–13.

Billings, A. G., & Moos, R. H. (1981). The role of coping responses and social resources in attenuating the stress of life events. *Journal of Behavioral Medicine, 4,* 139–157.

Birkhill, W. R., & Schaie, K. W. (1975). The effect of differential reinforcement of cautiousness in the intellectual performance of the elderly. *Journal of Gerontology, 30,* 578–583.

Birren, J. E., & Feldman, L. (1997). *Where to go from here.* New York: Simon & Schuster.

Blackburn, J. A., Papalia-Finley, D., Foye, B. F., & Serlin, R. C. (1988). Modifiability of figural relations performance among elderly adults. *Journal of Gerontology: Psychological Sciences, 43,* P87–P89.

Blair, S. L., & Johnson, M. P. (1992). Wives' perceptions of the fairness of the division of household labor: The intersection of housework and ideology. *Journal of Marriage and the Family, 54,* 570–581.

Blair, S. N., Kohl, H. W., Gordon, N. F., & Paffenbarger, R. S., Jr. (1992). How much physical activity is good for health? *Annual Review of Public Health, 13,* 99–126.

Blakeslee, S. (1994, April 13). A genetic factor may help to explain variations in lung cancer rates. *The New York Times,* p. B10.

Blau, F. D., & Ferber, M. A. (1985). Women in the labor market: The last twenty years. In L. Larwood, A. H. Stromberg, & B. A. Gutek (Eds.), *Women and work: An annual review* (pp. 19–49). Beverly Hills, CA: Sage.

Blau, F. D., & Ferber, M. A. (1991). Career plans and expectations of young women and men: The earnings gap and labor force participation. *Journal of Human Resources, 26,* 581–607.

Blazer, D. G. (1994). Epidemiology of late life depression. In L. Sneider et al. (Eds.), Diagnosis and treatment of depression in late life: Results of the NIH Consensus Development Conference (pp. 9–21). Washington DC: American Psychiatric Press.

Blazer, D. G., Hughes, D. C., & George, L. K. (1987). The epidemiology of depression in an elderly community population. *The Gerontologist, 27,* 281–287.

Blazer, D., & Palmore, E. B. (1976). Religion and aging in a longitudinal panel. *The Gerontologist, 16,* 82–84.

Blieszner, R., & Adams, R. G. (1992). *Adult friendship.* Newbury Park, CA: Sage.

Bliwise, D. L. (1997). Sleep and aging. In M. R. Pressman & W. C. Orr (Eds.), *Understanding sleep: The evaluation and treatment of sleep disorders.* Washington, DC: American Psychological Association.

Bliwise, D. L., Carey, E., & Dement, W. C. (1983). Nightly variation in sleep-related respiratory disturbance in older adults. *Experimental Aging Research, 9,* 77-81.

Bliwise, D. L., Carskadon, M., Carey, E., & Dement, W. C. (1984). Longitudinal development of sleep-related respiratory disturbance in adult humans. *Journal of Gerontology, 39,* 290-293.

Block, J. (1971). *Lives through time.* Berkeley, CA: Bancroft.

Bloom, B. L., White, S. W., & Asher, S. J. (1979). Marital disruption as a stressful life event. In C. Levinger & O. C. Moles (Eds.), *Divorce and separation: Context, causes, and consequences* (pp. 184–200). New York: Basic Books.

Blumenthal, J. A., Emery, C. F., Madden, D. J., Schniebolk, S., Walsh-Riddle, M., George, L. K., McKee, D. C., Higginbotham, M. B., Cobb, R. R., & Coleman, R. E. (1991). Long-term effects of exercise on physiological functioning in older men and women. *Journal of Gerontology: Psychological Sciences, 46,* P352–P361.

Blumstein, P., & Schwartz, P. (1983). *American couples.* New York: William Morrow.

Bolger, N., DeLongis, A., Kessler, R. C., & Wethington, E. (1989). The contagion of stress across multiple roles. *Journal of Marriage and the Family, 51,* 171–183.

Bond, J., & Coleman, P. (Eds.). (1990). *Aging in society.* London: Sage.

Booth, A., & Amato, P. R. (1994). Parental marital quality, parental divorce, and relations with parents. *Journal of Marriage and the Family, 56,* 21–34.

Bornstein, M. H. (1992). Perception across the life span. In M. H. Bornstein & M. E. Lamb (Eds.), *Developmental psychology: An advanced textbook* (3rd ed., pp. 155–210). Hillsdale, NJ: Erlbaum.

Bossé, R., Aldwin, C. M., Levenson, M. R., & Workman-Daniels, K. (1991). How stressful is retirement? Findings from the normative aging study. *Journal of Gerontology: Psychological Sciences, 46,* P9–P14.

Bowlby, J. (1969). *Attachment and loss: Vol. 1. Attachment.* New York: Basic Books.

Bowlby, J. (1973). *Attachment and loss: Vol. 2. Separation, anxiety, and anger.* New York: Basic Books.

Bowlby, J. (1980). *Attachment and loss: Vol. 3. Loss, sadness, and depression.* New York: Basic Books.

Bowlby, J. (1988a). Developmental psychiatry comes of age, *American Journal of Psychiatry, 145,* 1–10.

Bowlby, J. (1988b). *A secure base.* New York: Basic Books.

Bradburn, N. M. (1969). *The structure of psychological well being.* Chicago: Aldine.

Branch, L. G. (1985). Health practices and incident disability among the elderly. *American Journal of Public Health, 75,* 1436–1439.

Brandstädter, J., & Baltes-Götz, B. (1990). Personal control over development and quality of life perspectives in adulthood. In P. Baltes & M. M. Baltes (Eds.), *Successful aging: Perspectives from the behavioral sciences* (pp. 197–224). Cambridge, England: Cambridge University Press.

Brandtstädter, J., & Greve, W. (1994). The aging self: Stabilizing and protective processes. *Developmental Review, 14,* 52–80.

Brandtstädter, J., & Renner, G. (1992). Coping with discrepancies between aspirations and achievements in adult development: A dual-process model. In L. Montada, S. Filipp, & M. J. Lerner (Eds.), *Life crises and experiences of loss in adulthood* (pp. 301–319). Hillsdale, NJ: Erlbaum.

Brandtstädter, J., & Rothermund, K. (1994). Self-percepts of control in middle and later adulthood: Buffering losses by rescaling goals. *Psychology and Aging, 9,* 256–273.

Bray, D. W., & Howard, A. (1983). The AT&T longitudinal studies of managers. In K. W. Schaie (Ed.), *Longitudinal studies of adult psychological development* (pp. 266–312). New York: Guilford Press.

Brennan, K. A., & Shaver, P. R. (1995). Dimensions of adult attachment, affect regulation, and romantic functioning. *Personality and Social Psychological Bulletin, 21,* 267–283.

Breslow, L., & Breslow, N. (1993). Health practices and disability: Some evidence from Alameda County. *Preventive Medicine, 22,* 86–95.

Bridges, W. (1980). *Transitions.* Reading, MA: Addison-Wesley.

Brock, D. B., Guralnik, J. M., & Brody, J. A. (1990). Demography and the epidemiology of aging in the United States. In E. L. Schneider & J. W. Rowe (Eds.), *Handbook of the biology of aging* (3rd ed., pp. 3–23). San Diego, CA: Academic Press.

Brody, E. (1985). Parent care as a normative family stress. *The Gerontologist, 25*(1), 19-29.

Brody, E. M., Litvin, S. J., Hoffman, C., & Kleban, M. H. (1992). Differential effects of daughters' marital status on their parent care experiences. *The Gerontologist, 32,* 58–67.

Broman, C. L. (1988). Satisfaction among blacks: The significance of marriage and parenthood. *Journal of Marriage and the Family, 50,* 45–51.

Brooks, A. M. (1985). *The grieving time: A year's account of recovery from loss.* Garden City, NY: Dial Press.

Brown, S., & Booth, A. (1996). Cohabitation versus marriage: A comparison of relationship quality. *Journal of Marriage and the Family, 58,* 668–678.

Brown, G. W. (1989). Life events and measurement. In G. W. Brown & T. O. Harris (Eds.), *Life events and illness* (pp. 3–45). New York: Guilford Press.

Bryant, S., & Rakowski, W. (1992). Predictors of mortality among elderly African-Americans. *Research on Aging, 14,* 50–67.

Buchner, D. M., Beresford, S. A. A., Larson, E. B., LaCroix, A. Z., & Wagner, E. H. (1992). Effects of physical activity on health status in older adults: II. Intervention studies. *Annual Review of Public Health, 13,* 469–488.

Buck, N., & Scott, J. (1993). She's leaving home: But why? An analysis of young people leaving the parental home. *Journal of Marriage and the Family, 55,* 863–874.

Bumpass, L., Sweet, J., & Martin, T. (1990). Changing patterns of remarriage. *Journal of Marriage and the Family, 53,* 747–756.

Burack, O. R., & Lachkman, M. E. (1996). The effects of list-making on recall in young and elderly adults. *Journal of Gerontology: Psychological Sciences, 51B*(4), P226–P233.

Burkhauser, R. V., Duncan, G. J., & Hauser, R. (1994). Sharing prosperity across the age distribution: A comparison of the United States and Germany in the 1980s. *The Gerontologist, 34,* 150–60.

Burns, E., & Goodwin, J. S. (1997). Changes in immunologist function. In C. K. Cassel, H. J. Cohen, E. B. Larson, et al. (Eds.), *Geriatric Medicine (3rd ed.,* pp. 585–597). New York: Springer-Verlag.

Burr, J. A., & Mutchler, J. E. (1992). The living arrangements of unmarried elderly Hispanic females. *Demography, 29,* 93–112.

Burr, J. A., & Mutchler, J. E. (1993). Nativity, acculturation, and economic status: Explanations of Asian American living arrangements in later life. *Journal of Gerontology: Social Sciences, 48,* S55–S63.

Burton, L. M., & Bengtson, V. L. (1985). Black grandmothers: Issues of timing and continuity of roles. In V. L. Bengtson & J. F. Robertson (Eds.), *Grandparenthood* (pp. 61–78). Beverly Hills, CA: Sage.

Busch, C. M., Zonderman, A. B., & Costa, P. T., Jr. (1994). Menopausal transition and psychological distress in a nationally representative sample: Is menopause associated with psychological distress? *Journal of Aging and Health, 6,* 209–228.

Buss, D. M. (1991). Evolutionary personality psychology. *Annual Review of Psychology, 42,* 459–491.

Buss, D. M. (1994). Personality evoked: The evolutionary psychology of stability and change. In T. F. Hetherton & J. L. Weinberger (Eds.), *Can personality change?* (pp. 41–57). Washington, DC: American Psychological Association.

Busse, E. W. (1987). Primary and secondary aging. In G. L. Maddox (Ed.), *The encyclopedia of aging* (p. 534). New York: Springer.

Busse, E. W., & Maddox, G. L. (1985). *The Duke longitudinal studies of normal aging 1955-1980: Overview of history, design, and findings.* New York: Springer.

Busse, E. W., & Wang, H. S. (1971). The multiple factors contributing to dementia in old age. Proceedings of the 5th World Congress of Psychiatry, Mexico City. (Reprinted in *Normal aging II,* pp. 151–159, by E. B. Palmore, Ed., 1974. Durham, NC: Duke University Press.)

Butler, R. N. (1963). The life review: An interpretation of reminiscence in the aged. *Psychiatry, 256,* 65–76.

Butler, R. N., Lewis, M. I., & Sunderland, T. (1998). *Aging and mental health: Positive psychosocial and biomedical approaches.* Boston: Allyn & Bacon.

Buunk, B. P., & van Driel, B. (1989). *Variant lifestyles and relationships.* Newbury Park, CA: Sage.

Campbell, A. (1981). *The sense of well-being in America.* New York: McGraw-Hill.

Campbell, J. (1986). *The inner reaches of outer space.* New York: Harper & Row.

Caraballo, R. S., Giovino, G. A., Pechacek, T. F., Mowery, P. D., Richter, P. A., Strauss, W. J., Sharp, D. J., Eriksen, M. P., Pirkle, J. L., & Maurer, K. R. (1998). Racial and ethnic differences in serum cotinine levels of cigarette smokers: Third national health and nutrition examination survey, 1988-1991. *Journal of the American Medical Association, 280,* 135-139.

Carey, R. G. (1974). Living until death: A program of service and research for the terminally ill. In *Hospital progress.* (Reprinted in *Death: The final stage of growth,* by E. Kübler-Ross, Ed., 1975. Englewood Cliffs, NJ: Prentice Hall.)

Cargan, L., & Melko, M. (1982). *Singles: Myths and realities.* Beverly Hills, CA: Sage.

Carp, F. M. (1997). Retirement and women. In J. M. Coyle (Ed.), *Handbook on women and aging* (pp. 112–128). Westport, CT: Greenwood Press.

Carstensen, L. L. (1992). Social and emotional patterns in adulthood: Support for socioemotional selectivity theory. *Psychology and Aging, 7,* 331–338.

Case, R. B., Moss, A. J., Case, N., McDermott, M., & Eberly, S. (1992). Living alone after myocardial infarction: Impact on prognosis. *Journal of the American Medical Association, 267,* 515–519.

Caspi, A., Bem, D. J., & Elder, G. H., Jr. (1989). Continuities and consequences of interactional styles across the life course. *Journal of Personality, 57,* 375–406.

Caspi, A., & Elder, G. H., Jr. (1986). Life satisfaction in old age. Linking social psychology and history. *Journal of Psychology and Aging, 1,* 18–26.

Caspi, A., & Elder, G. H., Jr. (1988). Childhood precursors of the life course: Early personality and life disorganization. In E. M. Hetherington, R. M. Lerner, & M. Perlmutter (Eds.), *Child development in life-span perspective* (pp. 115–142). Hillsdale, NJ: Erlbaum.

Caspi, A., Elder, G. H., Jr., & Bem, D. J. (1987). Moving against the world: Life-course patterns of explosive children. *Developmental Psychology, 23,* 308–313.

Caspi, A., Elder, G. H., & Jr., & Bem, D. J. (1988). Moving away from the world: Life-course patterns of shy children. *Developmental Psychology, 24,* 824–831.

Cassileth, B. R., Walsh, W. P., & Lusk, E. J. (1988). Psychosocial correlates of cancer survival: A subsequent report 3 to 8 years after cancer diagnosis. *Journal of Clinical Oncology, 6,* 1753–1759.

Cate, R. M., & Lloyd, S. A. (1992). *Courtship.* Newbury Park, CA: Sage.

Cattell, R. B. (1963). Theory of fluid and crystallized intelligence: A critical experiment. *Journal of Educational Psychology, 54,* 1–22.

Centofanti, M. (1998). Fear of Alzheimer's undermines health of elderly patients. *APA Monitor, 29*(6), 1, 33.

Chamberlain, J. C., & Galton, D. J. (1990). Genetic susceptibility to atherosclerosis. *British Medical Bulletin, 46,* 917–940.

Chambré, S. M. (1993). Volunteerism by elders: Past trends and future prospects. *The Gerontologist, 33,* 221–228.

Chandra, R. K. (1997). Graying of the immune system: Can nutrient supplements improve immunity in the elderly?

Journal of the American Medical Association, 277(17), 1398–1399.

Chao, G. T., & Gardner, P. D. (1992). Formal and informal mentorships: A comparison of mentoring functions and contrasts with nonmentored counterparts. *Personal Psychology, 45,* 616–619.

Chase-Lansdale, P. L., & Hetherington, E. M. (1990). The impact of divorce on life-span development: Short and long term effects. In P. B. Baltes, D. L., Featherman, & R. M. Lerner (Eds.), *Life-span development and behavior* (Vol. 10, pp. 107–151). Hillsdale, NJ: Erlbaum.

Chatters, L. M. (1991). Physical health. In J. S. Jackson (Ed.), *Life in black America* (pp. 199–220). Newbury Park, CA: Sage.

Chatters, L. M., & Taylor, R. J. (1989). Age differences in religious participation among black adults. *Journal of Gerontology: Social Sciences, 44,* S183–S189.

Chen, R., & Morgan, S. P. (1991). Recent trends in the timing of first births in the United States. *Demography, 28,* 513–533.

Cherlin, A. J. (1992). *Marriage, divorce, remarriage.* Cambridge, MA: Harvard University Press.

Cherlin, A. J., & Furstenberg, F. F. (1986). *The new American grandparent.* New York: Basic Books.

Chinen, A. B. (1987). Fairy tales and psychological development in late life: A cross-cultural hermeneutic study. *The Gerontologist, 27,* 340–346.

Chiriboga, D. A. (1984). Social stressors as antecedents of change. *Journal of Gerontology, 39,* 468–477.

Chiriboga, D. A. (1989). Mental health at the midpoint: Crisis, challenge, or relief? In S. Hunter & M. Sundel (Eds.), *Midlife myths: Issues, findings, and practice implications* (pp. 116–144). Newbury Park, CA: Sage.

Chiriboga, D. A. (1997). Crisis, challenge, and stability in the middle years. In M. E. Lachman & J. B. James (Eds.), Multiple pathways of midlife development (pp. 293–322). Chicago: University of Chicago Press.

Chiriboga, D. A., & Cutler, L. (1980). Stress and adaptation: Life span perspectives. In L. W. Poon (Ed.), *Aging in the 1980s: Psychological issues* (pp. 347–362). Washington, DC: American Psychological Association.

Choi, N. G. (1991). Racial differences in the determinants of living arrangements of widowed and divorced elderly women. *The Gerontologist, 31,* 496–504.

Christensen, H., Mackinnon, A., Jorm, A. F., Henderson, A. S., Scott, L. R., & Korten, A. E. (1994). Age differences and interindividual variation in cognition in community-dwelling elderly. *Psychology and Aging, 9,* 381–390.

Cicirelli, V. G. (1982). Sibling influence throughout the lifespan. In M. E. Lamb & B. Sutton-Smith (Eds.), *Sibling relationships* (pp. 267–304). Hillsdale, NJ: Erlbaum.

Cicirelli, V. G. (1983). Adult children and their elderly parents. In T. H. Brubaker (Ed.), *Family relationships in later life* (pp. 31–46). Beverly Hills, CA: Sage.

Cicirelli, V. G. (1989). Feelings of attachment to siblings and well-being in later life. *Psychology and Aging, 4,* 211–216.

Cicirelli, V. G. (1994). Sibling relationships in cross-cultural perspective. *Journal of Marriage and the Family, 56,* 7–20.

Cicirelli, V. G., Coward, R. T., & Dwyer, J. W. (1992). Siblings as caregivers for impaired elders. *Research on Aging, 14,* 331–350.

Clarkson-Smith, L., & Hartley, A. A. (1989). Relationships between physical exercise and cognitive abilities in older adults. *Psychology and Aging, 4,* 183–189.

Clarkson-Smith, L., & Hartley, A. A. (1990). The game of bridge as an exercise in working memory and reasoning. *Journal of Gerontology: Psychological Sciences, 45,* P233–P238.

Clausen, J. A. (1981). Men's occupational careers in the middle years. In D. H. Eichorn, J. A. Clausen, N. Haan, M. P. Honzik, & P. H. Mussen (Eds.), *Present and past in middle life* (pp. 321–354). New York: Academic Press.

Clausen, J. A. (1993). *American lives: Looking back at the children of the great depression.* New York: Free Press.

Clayton, V. P., & Birren, J. E. (1980). The development of wisdom across the life-span: A reexamination of an ancient topic. In P. B. Baltes & O. G. Brim, Jr. (Eds.), *Life-span development and behavior* (Vol. 3, pp. 104–138). New York: Academic Press.

Cohen, L. H. (1998a). Measurement of life events. In L. H. Cohen (Ed.), *Life events and psychological functioning: Theoretical and methodological issues* (pp. 11–30). Newbury Park, CA: Sage.

Cohen, S. (1991). Social supports and physical health: Symptoms, health behaviors, and infectious disease. In E. M. Cummings, A. L. Greene, & K. H. Karraker (Eds.), *Life-span developmental psychology: Perspectives on stress and coping* (pp. 213–234). Hillsdale, NJ: Erlbaum.

Cohen, S., Tyrrell, D. A. J., & Smith, A. P. (1991). Psychological stress and susceptibility to the common cold. *New England Journal of Medicine, 325,* 606–612.

Cohen, S., Tyrrell, D. A. J., & Smith, A. P. (1993). Negative life events, perceived stress, negative affect, and susceptibility to the common cold. *Journal of Personality and Social Psychology, 64,* 131–40.

Cohen, S., & Wills, T. A. (1985). Stress, social support, and the buffering hypothesis. *Psychological Bulletin, 98,* 310–357.

Colby, A., & Kohlberg, L. (1987). *The measurement of moral judgment. Vol. 1: Theoretical foundations and research validation.* Cambridge: Cambridge University Press.

Colby, A., Kohlberg, L., Gibbs, J., & Lieberman, M. (1983). A longitudinal study of moral judgment. *Monographs of the Society for Research in Child Development, 48* (1–2, Serial No. 200).

Coleman, P., & Flood, D. (1987). Neuron numbers and dendritic extent in normal aging and Alzheimer's disease. *Neurobiology of Aging, 8,* 521–545.

Commons, M. L., Armon, C., Richards, F. A., Schrader, D. E., Farrell, E. F., Tappan, M. B., & Bauer, N. F. (1989). A multidomain study of adult development. In M. L. Commons, J. D. Sinnott, F. A. Richards, & C. Armon (Eds.), *Adult development: Vol. 1, Comparisons and applications of developmental models* (pp. 33–56). New York: Praeger.

Conger, R. D., Elder, G. H., Jr., Lorenz, F. O., Conger, K. J., Simons, R. L., Whitbeck, L. B., Huck, S., & Melby, J. N. (1990). Linking economic hardship to marital quality and instability. *Journal of Marriage and the Family, 52,* 643–656.

Connidis, I. A., & McMullin, J. A. (1993). To have or have not: Parent status and the subjective well-being of older men and women. *The Gerontologist, 33,* 630–636.

Cooney, T. M. (1994). Young adults' relations with parents: The influence of recent parental divorce. *Journal of Marriage and the Family, 56,* 45–56.

Cooney, T. M., Schaie, K. W., & Willis, S. L. (1988). The relationship between prior functioning on cognitive and personality dimensions and subject attrition in longitudinal research. *Journal of Gerontology: Psychological Sciences, 43,* P12–P17.

Corcoran, M. (1978). Work experience, work interruption, and wages. In G. D. Duncan & J. N. Morgan (Eds.), *Five Thousand American families: Patterns of economic progress* (Vol. 6, pp. 47–103). Ann Arbor, MI: University of Michigan, Institute for Social Research.

Costa, P. T., Jr., & McCrae, R. R. (1980a). Influence of extraversion and neuroticism on subjective well-being: Happy and unhappy people. *Journal of Personality and Social Psychology, 38,* 668–678.

Costa, P. T., Jr. & McCrae, R. R. (1980b). Still stable after all these years: Personality as a key to some issues in adulthood and old age. In P. B. Baltes & O. G. Brim, Jr. (Eds.), *Life-span development and behavior* (Vol. 3, pp. 65–102). New York: Academic Press.

Costa, P. T., Jr., & McCrae, R. R. (1983). Psychological maturity and subjective well-being: Toward a new synthesis. *Developmental Psychology, 19,* 243–248.

Costa, P. T., Jr., & McCrae, R. R. (1984). Personality as a lifelong determinant of well-being. In C. Z. Malatesta & C. E. Izard (Eds.), *Emotion in adult development* (pp. 141–158). Beverly Hills, CA: Sage.

Costa, P. T., Jr., & McCrae, R. R. (1988). Personality in adulthood: A six-year longitudinal study of self-reports and spouse ratings on the NEO personality inventory. *Journal of Personality and Social Psychology, 54,* 853–863.

Costa, P. T., Jr., & McCrae, R. R. (1994). Set like plaster? Evidence for the stability of adult personality. In T. F. Hetherton & J. L. Weinberger (Eds.), *Can personality change?* (pp. 21–40). Washington, DC: American Psychological Association.

Costa, P. T., Jr., McCrae, R. R., & Norris, A. H. (1981). Personal adjustment to aging: Longitudinal prediction from neuroticism and extraversion. *Journal of Gerontology, 36,* 78–85.

Costa, P. T., Jr., McCrae, R. R., Zonderman, A. B., Barbano, H. E., Lebowitz, B., & Larson, D. M. (1986). Cross-sectional studies of personality in a national sample: 2. Stability in neuroticism, extraversion, and openness. *Psychology and Aging, 1,* 144–149.

Costa, P. T., Jr., Zonderman, A. B., McCrae, R. R., Cornoni-Huntley, J., Locke, B. Z., & Barbano, H. E. (1987). Longitudinal analyses of psychological well-being in a national sample: Stability of mean levels. *Journal of Gerontology, 42,* 50–55.

Cotman, C. W., & Neeper, S. (1996). Activity dependent plasticity and the aging brain. In E. L. Schneider & J. W. Rowe (Eds.), *Handbook of the biology of aging* (4th ed., pp. 283–299). San Diego, CA: Academic Press.

Cotton, C. C., & McKenna, J. F. (1988). Husbands' job satisfaction and wives' income. In S. Rose & L. Larwood (Eds.), *Women's careers: Pathways and pitfalls* (pp. 83–94). New York: Praeger.

Cowan, C. P., & Cowan, P. A. (1987). Men's involvement in parenthood: Identifying the antecedents and understanding the barriers. In P. W. Berman & F. A. Pedersen (Eds.), *Men's transitions to parenthood: Longitudinal studies of early family experience* (pp. 79–109). Hillsdale, NJ: Erlbaum.

Craik, F. I. M. (1997). Age differences in human memory. In J. E. Birren & K. W. Schaie (Eds.), *Handbook of the psychology of aging* (pp. 384–420). New York: Van Nostrand-Reinhold.

Craik, F. I. M., & Jennings, J. M. (1992). Human memory. In F. I. M. Craik & T. A. Salthouse (Eds.), *The handbook of aging and cognition* (pp. 51–110). Hillsdale, NJ: Erlbaum.

Crimmins, E. M., & Ingegneri, D. G. (1990). Interaction and living arrangements of older parents and their children. *Research on Aging, 12,* 3–35.

Crook, T. H. & West, R. L. (1990). Name recall performance across the adult life span. *British Journal of Psychology, 81,* 335–349.

Crook, T. H., & West, R. (1990). Name recall performance across the adult life-span. *British Journal of Psychology, 81,* 335–349.

Crooks, R., & Baur, K. (1990). *Our sexuality.* Redwood City, CA: Cummings.

Crouter, A. C. (1984). Spillover from family to work: The neglected side of the work-family interface. *Human Relations, 37,* 425–442.

Crouter, A. C., & McHale, S. M. (1993). Familial economic circumstances: Implications for adjustment and development in early adolescence. In R. M. Lerner (Ed.), *Early adolescence: Perspectives on research, policy, and intervention* (pp. 71–91). Hillsdale, NJ: Erlbaum.

Cullum, C. M., & Rosenberg, R. N. (1998). Memory loss: When is it Alzheimer's disease? *Journal of the American Medical Association, 279*(21), 1689–1690.

Cumming, E. (1975). Engagement with an old theory. *International Journal of Aging and Human Development, 6,* 187–191.

Cumming, E., & Henry, W. E. (1961). *Growing old.* New York: Basic Books.

Cunningham, W. R., & Owens, W. A., Jr. (1983). The Iowa State study of the adult development of intellectual abilities. In K. W. Schaie (Ed.), *Longitudinal studies of adult psychological development* (pp. 20–39). New York: Guilford Press.

Cutler, S. J., & Grams, A. E. (1988). Correlates of self-reported everyday memory problems. *Journal of Gerontology: Social Sciences, 43,* S82–S90.

Daniels, P., & Weingarten, K. (1988). The fatherhood clock: The timing of parenthood in men's lives. In P. Bronstein & C. P. Cowan (Eds.), *Fatherhood today: Men's changing role in the family* (pp. 36–52). New York: Wiley (Interscience).

Dannefer, D. (1984a). Adult development and social theory: A paradigmatic reappraisal. *American Sociological Review, 49,* 100–116.

Dannefer, D. (1984b). The role of the social in life-span developmental psychology, past and future: Rejoinder to Baltes and Nesselroade. *American Sociological Review, 49,* 847–850.

Dannefer, D. (1988). What's in a name? An account of the neglect of variability in the study of aging. In J. E. Birren & V. L. Bengtson (Eds.), *Emergent theories of aging* (pp. 356–384). New York: Springer.

Davey, G. C. L., Tallis, F., & Hodgson, S. (1993). The relationship between information-seeking and information-avoiding coping styles and the reporting of psychological and physical symptoms. *Journal of Psychosomatic Research, 37,* 333–344.

Davidson, B., Balswick, J., & Halverson, C. (1983). Affective self-disclosure and marital adjustment: A test of equity theory. *Journal of Marriage and the Family, 45,* 93–103.

Dawber, T. R., Kannel, W. B., & Lyell, L. P. (1963). An approach to longitudinal studies in a community: The Framingham study. *Annals of the New York Academy of Sciences, 107,* 539–556.

Dawson-Hughes, B., Harris, S. S., Krall, E. A., & Dallal, G. E. (1997). Effect of calcium and vitamin D supplementation on bone density in men and women 65 years of age or older. *New England Journal of Medicine, 337*(10), 670–676.

Day, A. T., & Day, L. H. (1993). Living arrangements and "successful" aging among ever-married American white women 77–87 years of age. *Ageing and Society, 13,* 365–387.

Deaux, K. (1984). From individual differences to social categories: Analysis of a decade's research on gender. *American Psychologist, 39,* 105–116.

Deeg, D. H. J., Kardaun, J. W. P. F., & Fozard, J. L. (1996). Health, behavior, and aging. In J. E. Birren & K. W. Schaie (Eds.), *Handbook of the psychology of aging* (pp. 129–149). San Diego, CA: Academic Press.

de Graaf, C., Polet, P., & van Staveren, W. A. (1994). Sensory perception and pleasantness of food flavors in elderly subjects. *Journal of Gerontology: Psychological Sciences, 49,* P93–P99.

DeMaris, A., & Leslie, G. R. (1984). Cohabitation with the future spouse: Its influence upon marital satisfaction and communication. *Journal of Marriage and the Family, 46,* 77–84.

Denney, N. W. (1982). Aging and cognitive changes. In B. B. Wolman (Ed.), *Handbook of developmental psychology* (pp. 807–827). Englewood Cliffs, NJ: Prentice Hall.

Denney, N. W., Dew, J. R., & Kihlström, J. F. (1992). An adult developmental study of encoding spatial location. *Experimental Aging Research, 18,* 25–32.

Denney, N. W., & Pearce, K. A. (1989). A developmental study of practical problem solving in adults. *Psychology and Aging, 4,* 438–442.

Denney, N. W., Tozier, T. L., & Schlotthauer, C. A. (1992). The effect of instructions on age differences in practical problem solving. *Journal of Gerontology: Psychological Sciences, 47,* P142–P145.

DeSpelder, L. A., & Strickland, A. L. (1983). *The last dance: Encountering death and dying.* Palo Alto, CA: Mayfield.

deTurck, M. A., & Miller, G. R. (1986). The effects of husbands' and wives' social cognition on their marital adjustment, conjugal power, and self-esteem. *Journal of Marriage and the Family, 48,* 715–724.

Dewit, D. J., Wister, A. V., & Burch, T. K. (1988). Physical distance and social contacts between elders and their adult children. *Research on Aging, 10,* 56–80.

Dickens, W. J., & Perlman, D. (1981). Friendship over the life-cycle. In S. Duck & R. Gilmour (Eds.), *Personal relationships: 2. Developing personal relationships* (pp. 91–122). New York: Academic Press.

Diener, E. (1984). Subjective well-being. *Psychological Bulletin, 95,* 542–575.

Dindia, K., & Allen, M. (1992). Sex differences in self-disclosure: A meta-analysis. *Psychological Bulletin, 112,* 106–124.

Dixon, R. A., & Lerner, R. M. (1988). A history of systems in developmental psychology. In M. H. Bornstein & M. E. Lamb (Eds.), *Developmental psychology: An advanced textbook* (2nd cd., pp. 3–50). Hillsdale, NJ: Erlbaum.

Dixon, R. A., & Lerner, R. M. (1992). A history of systems in developmental psychology. In M. H. Bornstein & M. E. Lamb (Eds.), *Developmental psychology: An advanced textbook* (3rd ed., pp. 3–58). Hillsdale, NJ: Erlbaum.

Doherty, W. J., Su, S., & Needle, R. (1989). Marital disruption and psychological well-being: A panel study. *Journal of Family Issues, 10,* 72–85.

Dohrenwend, B. S., & Dohrenwend, B. P. (1978). Some issues in research on stressful life events. *Journal of Nervous and Mental Disease, 166,* 7–15.

Donelson, F. E. (1999). *Women's experiences.* London: Mayfield.

Dorian, B., & Garfinkel, P. E. (1987). Stress, immunity and illness: A review. *Psychological Medicine, 17,* 393–407.

Doty, R. L., Shaman, P., Appelbaum, S. L., Bigerson, R., Sikorski, L., & Rosenberg, L. (1984). Smell identification ability: Changes with age. *Science, 226,* 1441–1443.

Dreher, G., & Ash, R. (1990). A comparative study of mentoring among men and women in managerial, professional and technical positions. *Journal of Applied Psychology, 75,* 525–535.

Ducharme, F. (1994). Conjugal support, coping behaviors, and psychological well-being of the elderly spouse. *Research on Aging, 16,* 167–190.

Duncan, G. J., & Morgan, J. N. (1985). The panel study of income dynamics. In G. H. Elder, Jr. (Ed.), *Life course dynamics: Trajectories and transitions, 1968–1980* (pp. 50–74). Ithaca, NY: Cornell University Press.

Dura, J. R., & Kiecolt-Glaser, J. K. (1991). Family transitions, stress, and health, In P. A. Cowan & M. Hetherington (Eds.), *Family transitions* (pp. 59–76). Hillsdale, NJ: Erlbaum.

Durlak, J. A. (1972). Relationship between attitudes toward life and death among elderly women. *Developmental Psychology, 8,* 146.

Duursma, S. A., Raymakers, J. A., Boereboom, F. T. J., & Scheven, B. A. A. (1991). Estrogen and bone metabolism. *Obstetrical and Gynecological Survey, 47,* 38–44.

Duvall, E. M. (1962). *Family development.* New York: Lippincott.

Dwyer, J. W., & Coward, R. T. (1991). A multivariate comparison of the involvement of adult sons versus daughters in the care of impaired parents. *Journal of Gerontology: Social Sciences, 56,* S259–S269.

Eagly, A. H. (1987). Sex differences in social behavior: A social role interpretation. Hillsdale, NJ: Erlbaum.

Eames, M., Ben-Schlomo, Y., & Marmot, M. G. (1993). Social deprivation and premature mortality: Regional comparison across England. *British Medical Journal, 307,* 1097–1102.

Eberhardt, B. J., & Muchinsky, P. M. (1984). Structural validation of Holland's hexagonal model: Vocational classification through the use of biodata. *Journal of Applied Psychology, 69,* 174–181.

Edwards, J. N., & Booth, A. (1994). Sexuality, marriage, and well-being: The middle years. In A. S. Rossi (Ed.), *Sexuality across the life course* (pp. 233–259). Chicago: University of Chicago Press.

Eichorn, D. H., Clausen, J. A., Haan, N., Honzik, M. P., & Mussen, P. H. (Eds.). (1981). *Present and past in middle life.* New York: Academic Press.

Eichorn, D. H., Hunt, J. V., & Honzik, M. P. (1981). Experience, personality, and IQ: Adolescence to middle age. In D. H. Eichorn, J. A. Clausen, N. Haan, M. P. Honzik, & P. H. Mussen (Eds.), *Present and past in middle life* (pp. 89–116). New York: Academic Press.

Eilers, M. I. (1989). Older adults and computer education: "Not to have the world a closed door." *International Journal of Technology and Aging, 2,* 56–76.

Elder, G. H., Jr. (1974). *Children of the great depression.* Chicago: University of Chicago Press.

Elder, G. H., Jr. (1978). Family history and the life course. In T. Hareven (Ed.), *Transitions: The family and the life course in historical perspective* (pp. 17–64). New York: Academic Press.

Elder, G. H., Jr., Caspi, A., & Downey, G. (1986). Problem behavior and family relationships: Life course and intergenerational themes. In A. B. Sørensen, F. E. Weinert, & L. R. Sherrod (Eds.), *Human development and the life course: Multidisciplinary perspectives* (pp. 293–340). Hillsdale, NJ: Erlbaum.

Elder, G. H., Jr., Liker, J. K., & Cross, C. E. (1984). Parent-child behavior in the great depression: Life course and intergenerational influences. In P. B. Baltes & O. G. Brim, Jr. (Eds.), *Life-span development and behavior* (Vol. 6, pp. 111–159). New York: Academic Press.

Elman, M. R., & Gilbert, L. A. (1984). Coping strategies for role conflict in married professional women with children. *Family Relations, 33,* 317–327.

Emery, C. F., & Gatz, M. (1990). Psychological and cognitive effects of an exercise program for community-residing older adults. *The Gerontologist, 30,* 184–192.

Erbes, J. T., & Hedderson, J. J. C. (1984). A longitudinal examination of the separation/divorce process. *Journal of Marriage and the Family, 46,* 937–941.

Erdwins, C. J., & Mellinger, J. C. (1984). Mid-life women: Relation of age and role to personality. *Journal of Personality and Social Psychology, 47,* 390–395.

Erdwins, C. J., Tyler, Z. E., & Mellinger, J. C. (1983). A comparison of sex role and related personality traits in young, middle-aged, and older women. *International Journal of Aging and Human Development, 17,* 141–152.

Ericsson, K. A. (1990). Peak performance and age: An examination of peak performance in sports. In P. B. Baltes & M. M. Baltes (Eds.), *Successful aging: Perspectives from the behavioral sciences* (pp. 164–196). Cambridge, England: Cambridge University Press.

Erikson, E. H. (1950). *Childhood and society.* New York: Norton.

Erikson, E. H. (1959). *Identity and the life cycle.* New York: Norton. (Reissued 1980)

Erikson, E. H. (1963). *Childhood and society* (2nd ed.). New York: Norton.

Erikson, E. H. (1980). Themes of adulthood in the Freud-Jung correspondence. In N. J. Smelser & E. H. Erikson (Eds.), *Themes of work and love in adulthood* (pp. 43–76). Cambridge, MA: Harvard University Press.

Erikson, E. H. (1982). *The life cycle completed.* New York: Norton.

Erikson, E. H., Erikson, J. M., & Kivnick, H. Q. (1986). *Vital involvement in old age.* New York: Norton.

Eriksson, P. S., et al. (1998). Neurogenesis in the adult human hippocampus. *Nature Medicine, 4*(11), 1313–1317.

Ernest, J. T. (1997). Changes and diseases of the aging eye. In C. K. Cassel, H. J. Cohen, E. B. Larson, et al. (Eds.), *Geriatric Medicine (3rd ed.,* pp. 683–697). New York: Springer-Verlag.

Ershler, W. B. (1997). The science of neoplasia. In C. K. Cassel, H. J. Cohen, E. B. Larson, et al. (Eds.), *Geriatric Medicine* (3rd ed., pp. 249–255). New York: Springer-Verlag.

Estes, R. J., & Wilensky, H. L. (1978). Life cycle squeeze and the morale curve. *Social Problems, 25,* 277–292.

Ettinger, W. H., Jr., Burns, R., Messier, S. P., Applegate, W., Rajeski, W. J., Morgan, T., Shumaker, S., Barry, M. J., O'Toole, M., Monu, J., & Craven, T. (1997). A randomized trial comparing aerobic exercise and resistance exercise with a health education program in older adults with knee osteoarthritis. *Journal of the American Medical Association, 277,* 25-31.

Evans, L., Ekerdt, D. J., & Bossé, R. (1985). Proximity to retirement and anticipatory involvement: Findings from the Normative Aging Study. *Journal of Gerontology, 40,* 368–374.

Evans, R. I. (1969). *Dialogue with Erik Erikson.* New York: Dutton.

Eysenck, H. J. (1990). Type A behavior and coronary heart disease: The third stage. *Journal of Social Behavior and Personality, 5,* 25–44.

Fackelman, K. (1998), February 28. Valuable vices: Researchers uncover the healthful side of hedonism. *Science News, 153,* 142–143.

Fagenson, E. A. (1989). The mentor advantage: Perceived career/job experiences of protégés vs nonprotégés. *Journal of Organizational Behavior, 10,* 309–320.

Fagenson, E. A. (1992). Mentoring—who needs it? A comparison of protégés' and nonprotégés' needs for power, achievement, affiliation, and autonomy. *Journal of Vocational Behavior, 41,* 48–60.

Farrell, M. P., & Rosenberg, S. D. (1981). *Men at midlife.* Boston: Auburn House.

Farrer, L. A., et al. (1997). Effects of age, sex, and ethnicity on the association between apolipoprotein E genotype and

Alzheimer disease: A meta-analysis. *Journal of the American Medical Association, 278*(16), 1349–1356.

Featherman, D. L. (1983). Life-span perspectives in social science research. In P. B. Baltes & O. G. Brim, Jr. (Eds.), *Life-span development and behavior* (Vol. 5, pp. 1–59). New York: Academic Press.

Feeney, J. A., & Noller, P. (1990). Attachment style as a predictor of adult romantic relationships. *Journal of Personality and Social Psychology, 58,* 281–291.

Feifel, H. (1990). Psychology and death: Meaningful rediscovery. *American Psychologist, 45,* 537–543.

Feifel, H., & Strack, S. (1989). Coping with conflict situations: Middle-aged and elderly men. *Psychology and Aging, 4,* 26–33.

Feld, S., & George, L. K. (1994). Moderating effects of prior social resources on the hospitalizations of elders who become widowed. *Aging and Health, 6,* 275–295.

Ferri, E., & Smith, K. (1996). *Parenting in the 1990s.* York, England: Joseph Rowntree Foundation.

Fiatarone, M. A., & Evans, W. J. (1993). The etiology and reversibility of muscle dysfunction in the aged [Special issue]. *Journals of Gerontology, 48,* 77–83.

Field, D., Schaie, K. W., & Leino, E. V. (1988). Continuity in intellectual functioning: The role of self-reported health. *Psychology and Aging, 3,* 385–392.

Fields, R. B. (1992). Psychosocial response to environment change. In V. B. Van Hasselt & M. Hersen (Eds.), *Handbook of social development: A lifespan perspective* (pp. 503–544). New York: Plenum Press.

Filsinger, E. E., & Thoma, S. J. (1988). Behavioral antecedents of relationship stability and adjustment: A five-year longitudinal study. *Journal of Marriage and the Family, 50,* 785–795.

Finch, C. E. (1986). Issues in the analysis of interrelationships between the individual and the environment during aging. In A. B. Sørensen, F. E. Weinert, & L. R. Sherrod (Eds.), *Human development and the life course: Multidisciplinary perspectives* (pp. 17–30). Hillsdale, NJ: Erlbaum.

Finch, C. E. (1988). Aging in the female reproductive system: A model system for analysis of complex interactions during aging. In J. E. Biren & V. L. Bengtson (Eds.), *Emergent theories of aging* (pp. 128–152). New York: Springer.

Finn, S. E. (1986). Stability of personality self-ratings over 30 years: Evidence for an age/cohort interaction. *Journal of Personality and Social Psychology, 50,* 813–818.

Fischman, J. (1987, February). Type A on trial. *Psychology Today, 21,* 42–50.

Fisk, A. D., & Rogers, W. A. (Eds.). (1997). *Handbook of human factors and the older adult.* San Diego, CA: Academic Press.

Fitzpatrick, J. L., & Silverman, T. (1989). Women's selection of careers in engineering: Do traditional-nontraditional differences still exist? *Journal of Vocational Behavior, 34,* 266–278.

Flavell, J. H. (1970). Developmental studies of mediated memory. In H. W. Reese & L. W. Lipsitt (Eds.), *Advances in child development and behavior* (pp. 181–211). New York: Academic Press.

Fleishman, J. A., & Fogel, B. (1994). Coping and depressive symptoms among people with AIDS. *Health Psychology, 13,* 156–169.

Florio, E. R., et al. (1997). A comparison of suicidal and nonsuicidal elders referred to a community mental health program. *Suicide and Life Threatening Behavior, 27*(2), 182–193.

Floyd, F. J., Haynes, S. N., Doll, E. R., Winemiller, D., Lemsky, C., Burty, T. M., Werle, M., & Heilman, N. (1992). Assessing retirement satisfaction and perceptions of retirement experiences. *Psychology and Aging, 7,* 609–621.

Folkman, S., Lazarus, R. S., Pimley, S., & Novacek, J. (1987). Age differences in stress and coping processes. *Psychology and Aging, 2,* 171–184.

Fordyce, M. W. (1977). Development of a program to increase personal happiness. *Journal of Counseling Psychology, 24,* 511–521.

Fowler, J. W. (1981). *Stages of faith.* New York: Harper & Row.

Fowler, J. W. (1983). Stages of faith: PT conversation with James Fowler. *Psychology Today,* pp. 56–62.

Fozard, J. L. (1990). Vision and hearing in aging. In J. E. Birren & K. W. Schaie (Eds.), *Handbook of the psychology of aging* (3rd ed., pp. 150–171). San Diego, CA: Academic Press.

Fozard, J. L., Metter, E. J., & Brant, L. J. (1990). Next steps in describing aging and disease in longitudinal studies. *Journal of Gerontology: Psychological Sciences, 45,* P116–P127.

Fozard, J. L., Vercruyssen, M., Reynolds, S. L., Hancock, P. A., & Quilter, R. E. (1994). Age differences and changes in reaction time: The Baltimore Longitudinal Study of Aging, *Journal of Gerontology: Psychological Sciences, 49,* P179–P189.

Frable, D. E. S. (1989) Sex typing and gender ideology: Two facets of the individual's gender psychology that go together. *Journal of Personality and Social Psychology, 56,* 95–108.

Frable, D. E. S., & Bem, S. L. (1985). If you're gender schematic, all members of the opposite sex look alike. *Journal of Personality and Social Psychology, 49,* 459–468.

Frankl, V. E. (1984). *Man's search for meaning* (3rd ed.). New York: Simon & Schuster.

Frazier, P. H., & Foss-Goodman, D. (1988–1989). Death anxiety and personality: Are they truly related? *Omega, 19,* 265–274.

Freeman, E. W., & Rickels, K. (1993). *Early childbearing. Perspectives of black adolescents on pregnancy, abortion, and contraception.* Newbury Park, CA: Sage.

Friedman, H. S., Hawley, P. H., & Tucker, J. S. (1994). Personality, health, and longevity. *Current Directions in Psychological Science, 3,* 37–41.

Friedman, M., & Rosenman, R. H. (1974). *Type A behavior and your heart.* New York: Knopf.

Freud, S. (1952). Group psychology and the analysis of the ego. *In The major works of Sigmund Freud* (pp. 664-696). Chicago: Encyclopedia Britannica. (Original work published 1921.)

Fulton, J. P., Katz, S., Jack, S. S., & Hendershot, G. E. (1989, March). *Physical functioning of the aged: United States, 1984.* Vital Health Statistics, Series 10, No. 167. NHHS Publication No. (PHS) 89-1595. Hyattsville, MD: National Center for Health Statistics.

Gallagher, S. K., & Ferstel, N. (1993). Kinkeeping and friend keeping among older women: The effect of marriage. *The Gerontologist, 33,* 675–681.

Gallagher, W. (1993, May). Midlife myths. *The Atlantic Monthly,* pp. 51–68.

Gallagher-Thompson, D., Futterman, A., Farberow, N., Thompson, L. W., & Peterson, J. (1993). The impact of spousal bereavement on older widows and widowers. In M. S. Stroebe, W. Stroebe, & R. O. Hansson (Eds.), *Handbook of bereavement: Theory, research, and intervention* (pp. 227–239). Cambridge, England: Cambridge University Press.

Gannon, L. (1990). Endocrinology of menopause. In R. Formanek (Ed.), *The meanings of menopause: Historical, medical, and clinical perspectives* (pp. 179–237). Hillsdale, NJ: Analytic Press.

Garrison, R. J., Gold, R. S., Wilson, P. W. F., & Kannel, W. B. (1993). Educational attainment and coronary heart disease risk: The Framingham offspring study. *Preventive Medicine, 22,* 54–64.

Gatz, M., Kasl-Godley, J. E., & Karel, M. J. (1996). Aging and mental disorders. In J. E. Birren & K. W. Schaie (Eds.), *Handbook of the psychology of aging* (pp. 365–381). San Diego, CA: Academic Press.

George, L. K. (1990). Social structure, social processes, and social-psychological states. In R. H. Binstock & L. K. George (Eds.), *Handbook of aging and the social sciences* (3rd ed., pp. 186–204). San Diego, CA: Academic Press.

George, L. K. (1993). Sociological perspectives on life transitions. *Annual Review of Sociology, 19,* 353–373.

George, L. K. (1996). Social factors and illness. In R. H. Binstock & L. K. George (Eds.), *Handbook of aging and the social sciences (4th ed.,* pp. 229–252). New York: Academic Press.

George, L. K., Okun, M. A., & Landerman, R. (1985). Age as a moderator of the determinants of life satisfaction. *Research on Aging, 7,* 209–234.

Gesser, G., Wong, P. T. P., & Reker, G. T. (1987–1988). Death attitudes across the life-span: The development and validation of the death attitude profile (DAP). *Omega, 18,* 113–128.

Geyer, S. (1993). Life events, chronic difficulties and vulnerability factors preceding breast cancer. *Social Science and Medicine, 37,* 1545–1555.

Gibson, D. M. (1986). Interaction and well-being in old age: Is it quantity or quality that counts? *International Journal of Aging and Human Development, 24,* 29–40.

Giele, J. Z. (1982). Women in adulthood: Unanswered questions. In J. Z. Giele (Ed.), *Women in the middle years* (pp. 1–36). New York: Wiley.

Gilbert, L. A. (1985). *Men in dual-career families: Current realities and future prospects.* Hillsdale, NJ: Erlbaum.

Gilbert, L. A. (1994). Current perspectives on dual-career families. *Current Directions in Psychological Science, 3,* 101–105.

Gill, B. (1996). *Late bloomers.* New York: Artisan.

Gilligan, C. (1982). *In a different voice: Psychological theory and women's development.* Cambridge, MA: Harvard University Press.

Gilligan, C., & Wiggins, G. (1987). The origins of morality in early childhood relationships. In J. Kagan & S. Lamb (Eds.), *The emergence of morality in young children* (pp. 277–307). Chicago: University of Chicago Press.

Ginsberg, D., & Gottman, J. (1986). Conversations of college roommates: Similarities and differences in male and female friendships. In J. M. Gottman & J. G. Parker (Eds.), *Conversations of friends: Speculations on affective development* (pp. 241–291). Cambridge, England: Cambridge University Press.

Girard, C. (1993). Age, gender, and suicide: A cross-national analysis. *American Sociological Review, 58,* 553–574.

Glassman, M. H. (1995). Housing for the elderly. In W. Reichel (Ed.), *Care of the elderly: Clinical aspects of aging (4th ed.).* Baltimore: Williams & Wilkins.

Glenn, N. D. (1990). Quantitative research on marital quality in the 1980s: A critical review. *Journal of Marriage and the Family, 52,* 818–831.

Glenn, N. D., & Weaver, C. N. (1981). The contribution of marital happiness to global happiness. *Journal of Marriage and the Family, 43,* 161–168.

Glenn, N. D., & Weaver, C. N. (1985). Age, cohort, and reported job satisfaction in the United States. In A. S. Blau (Ed.), *Current perspectives on aging and the life cycle: A research annual; Vol. 1. Work, retirement and social policy* (pp. 89–110). Greenwich, CT: JAI Press.

Glueck, S., & Glueck, E. (1950). *Unraveling juvenile delinquency.* New York: Commonwealth Fund.

Glueck, S., & Glueck, E. (1968). *Delinquents and nondelinquents in perspective.* Cambridge, MA: Harvard University Press.

Goetting, A. (1986). The developmental tasks of siblingship over the life cycle. *Journal of Marriage and the Family, 48,* 703–714.

Gold, D. T. (1990). Late-life sibling relationships: Does race affect typological distribution? *The Gerontologist, 30,* 741–748.

Gold, D. T. (1996). Continuities and discontinuities in sibling relationships across the life span. In V. L. Bengtson (Ed.), *Adulthood and aging: Research on continuities and discontinuities.* New York: Springer.

Goldberg, E. L., Comstock, G. W., & Harlow, S. D. (1988). Emotional problems and widowhood. *Journal of Gerontology: Social Sciences, 43,* S206–S208.

Goldman, N. (1993). The perils of single life in contemporary Japan. *Journal of Marriage and the Family, 55,* 191–204.

Goldman-Rakic, P. S. (1992, September). Working memory and the mind. *Scientific American,* pp. 111–117.

Goldscheider, F., & Goldscheider, C. (1993). Whose nest? A two-generational view of leaving home during the 1980s. *Journal of Marriage and the Family, 55,* 851–862.

Goleman, D. (1994, May 11). Life's small pleasures aid immune system. *The New York Times,* p. B6.

Gonsiorek, J. C., & Weinrich, J. D. (1991). The definition and scope of sexual orientation. In J. C. Gonsiorek & J. D. Weinrich (Eds.), *Homosexuality: Research implications for public policy* (pp. 1–12). Newbury Park, CA: Sage.

Gottman, J. M. (1994a). *What predicts divorce? The relationship between marital processes and marital outcomes.* Hillsdale, NJ: Erlbaum.

Gottman, J. M. (1994b). *Why marriages succeed or fail.* New York: Simon & Schuster.

Gottman, J. M., Katz, L. F., & Hooven, C. (1997). *Meta-emotion: How families communicate emotionally.* Mahwah, NJ: Erlbaum.

Gould, R. (1978). *Transformations: Growth and change in adult life.* New York: Simon & Schuster.

Gould, R. (1980). Transformations during early and middle adult years. In N. J. Smelser & E. H. Erikson (Eds.), *Themes of work and love in adulthood* (pp. 213–237). Cambridge, MA: Harvard University Press.

Gove, W. R. (1972). Sex roles, marital roles, and mental illness. *Social Forces, 51,* 34–44.

Gove, W. R. (1979). SEx, marital status, and psychiatric treatment: A research note. *Social Forces, 58,* 89–93.

Gray, A., Berlin, J. A., McKinlay, J. B., & Longcope, C. (1991). An examination of research design effects on the association of testosterone and male aging: Results of a meta-analysis. *Journal of Clinical Epidemiology, 44,* 671–684.

Greene, A. L., & Boxer, A. M. (1986). Daughters and sons as young adults: Restructuring the ties that bind. In N. Datan, A. L. Greene, & H. W. Reese (Eds.), *Life-span developmental psychology: Intergenerational relations* (pp. 125–150). Hillsdale, NJ: Erlbaum.

Greenough, W. T., Black, J. E., & Wallace, C. S. (1987). Experience and brain development. *Child Development, 58,* 539-559.

Greenstein, T. N. (1986). Social-psychological factors in perinatal labor-force participation. *Journal of Marriage and the Family, 48,* 565–571.

Greenstein, T. N. (1990). Marital disruption and the employment of married women. *Journal of Marriage and the Family, 52,* 657–676.

Greer, D. S., Mor, V., Morris, J. N., Sherwood, S., Kidder, D., & Birnbaum, H. (1986). An alternative in terminal care: Results of the National Hospice Study. *Journal of Chronic Diseases, 39,* 9–26.

Greer, S. (1991). Psychological response to cancer and survival. *Psychological Medicine, 21,* 43–49.

Greer, S., Morris, T., & Pettingale, K. W. (1979). Psychological response to breast cancer: Effect on outcome. *Lancet, 2,* 785–787.

Guralnik, J. M., & Kaplan, G. A. (1989). Predictors of healthy aging: Prospective evidence from the Alameda County Study. *American Journal of Public Health, 79,* 703–708.

Guralnik, J. M., Land, K. C., Blazer, D., Fillenbaum, G. G., & Branch, L. G. (1993). Educational status and active life expectancy among older blacks and whites. *New England Journal of Medicine, 329,* 110–116.

Guralnik, J. M., & Simonsick, E. M. (1993). Physical disability in older Americans [Special issue]. *Journals of Gerontology, 48,* 3–10.

Guralnik, J. M., Simonsick, E. M., Ferrucci, L., Glynn, R. J., Berkman, L. F., Blazer, D. G., Scherr, P. A., & Wallace, R. B. (1994). A short physical performance battery assessing lower extremity function: Association with self-reported disability and prediction of mortality and nursing home admission. *Journal of Gerontology: Medical Sciences, 49,* M85–M94.

Gurin, P., & Brim, O. G., Jr. (1984). Change in self in adulthood: The example of a sense of control. In P. B. Baltes & O. G. Brim, Jr. (Eds.), *Life-span development and behavior* (Vol. 6, pp. 282–334). Orlando, FL: Academic Press.

Gustafson, S. B., & Magnusson, D. (1991). *Female life careers: A pattern approach.* Hillsdale, NJ: Erlbaum.

Gutek, B. A., Searle, S., & Klepa, L. (1991) Rational versus gender role explanations for work-family conflict. *Journal of Applied Psychology, 76,* 560–568.

Gutmann, D. (1975). Parenthood: A key to the comparative study of the life cycle. In N. Datan & L. H. Ginsberg (Eds.), *Life-span developmental psychology: Normative life crises* (pp. 167–184). New York: Academic Press.

Gutmann, D. (1987). *Reclaimed powers: Toward a new psychology of men and women in later life.* New York: Basic Books.

Gwartney-Gibbs, P. A. (1988). Women's work experience and the "rusty skills" hypothesis: A reconceptualization and reevaluation of the evidence. In B. A. Gutek, A. H. Stromberg, & L. Larwood (Eds.), *Women and work: An annual review* (Vol. 3, pp. 169–188). Newbury Park, CA: Sage.

Haan, N. (1976). ". . . change and sameness. . ." reconsidered. *International Journal of Aging and Human Development, 7,* 59–65.

Haan, N. (1981). Common dimensions of personality development: Early adolescence to middle life. In D. H. Eichorn, J. A. Clausen, N. Haan, M. P. Honzik, & P. H. Mussen (Eds.), *Present and past in middle life* (pp. 117–153). New York: Academic Press.

Haan, N. (1982). The assessment of coping, defense, and stress. In L. Goldberger & S. Breznitz (Eds.), *Handbook of stress: Theoretical and clinical aspects* (pp. 254–269). New York: Free Press.

Haan, N., Millsap, R., & Hartka, E. (1986). As time goes by: Change and stability in personality over fifty years. *Psychology and Aging, 1,* 220–232.

Hagestad, G. O. (1979). *Patterns of communication and influence between grandparents and grandchildren in a changing society.* Paper presented at the World Congress of Sociology, Uppsala, Sweden.

Hagestad, G. O. (1984). The continuous bond: A dynamic, multigenerational perspective on parent-child relations between adults. In M. Perlmutter (Ed.), *Minnesota Symposia on Child Psychology* (pp. 129–158). Hillsdale, NJ: Erlbaum.

Hagestad, G. O. (1985). Continuity and connectedness. In V. L. Bengtson & J. F. Robertson (Eds.), *Grandparenthood* (pp. 31–38). Beverly Hills, CA: Sage.

Hagestad, G. O. (1986). Dimensions of time and the family. *American Behavioral Scientist, 29,* 679–694.

Hagestad, G. O. (1988). Demographic change and the life course: Some emerging trends in the family realm. *Family Relations, 37,* 405–410.

Hagestad, G. O., & Neugarten, B. L. (1985). Age and the life course. In R. H. Binstock & E. Shanas (Eds.), *Handbook of aging and the social sciences* (2nd ed., pp. 35–61). New York: Van Nostrand Reinhold.

Haight, B. K. (1988). The therapeutic role of a structured life review process in homebound elderly subjects. *Journal of Gerontology: Psychological Sciences, 43,* P40–P44.

Haight, B. K. (1992). Long-term effects of a structured life review process. *Journal of Gerontology: Psychological Sciences, 47,* P312–P315.

Halford, W. K., Hahlweg, K., & Dunne, M. (1990). The cross-cultural consistency of marital communication associated with marital distress. *Journal of Marriage and the Family, 52,* 487–500.

Hall, D. T. (1972). A model of coping with role conflict: The role behavior of college educated women. *Administrative Science Quarterly, 17,* 471–486.

Hall, D. T. (1975). Pressures from work, self, and home in the life stages of married women. *Journal of Vocational Behavior, 6,* 121–132.

Hall, D., & Zhao, J. (1995). Cohabitation and divorce in Canada: Testing the selectivity hypothesis. *Journal of Marriage and the Family, 57,* 421–427.

Hallström, T., & Samuelsson, S. (1985). Mental health in the climacteric: The longitudinal study of women in Gothenberg. *Acta Obstetricia et Gynecologica Scandanavica, 130* (Suppl.), 13–18.

Hamer, D., & Copeland, P. (1998). *Living with our genes: Why they matter more than you think.* New York: Doubleday.

Handy, B. (1998). The Viagra craze. *Time, 151*(17), 50–57.

Happé, F. G. E., Winner, E., & Brownell, H. (1998). The getting of wisdom: Theory of mind in old age. *Developmental Psychology, 34*(2), 358–362.

Hardy, M. A., & Hazelrigg, L. E. (1993). The gender of poverty in an aging population. *Research on Aging, 15,* 243–278.

Hargrave, T. D., & Hanna, S. M. (1997). *The aging family: New visions in theory, practice, and reality.* New York: Brunner/Mazel.

Haring-Hildore, M., Stock, W. A., Okun, M. A., & Witter, R. A. (1985). Marital status and subjective well-being: A research synthesis. *Journal of Marriage and the Family, 47,* 947–953.

Harman, S. M., & Talbert, G. B. (1985). Reproductive aging. In C. E. Finch & E. L. Schneider (Eds.), *Handbook of the biology of aging* (2nd ed., pp. 457–510). New York: Van Nostrand Reinhold.

Harris, R. L., Ellicott, A. M., & Holmes, D. S. (1986). The timing of psychosocial transitions and changes in women's lives: An examination of women aged 45 to 60. *Journal of Personality and Social Psychology, 51,* 409–416.

Hart, D. A., (1992). *Becoming men: The development of aspirations, values, and adaptational styles.* New York: Plenum Press.

Hatfield, E. (1988). Passionate and compassionate love. In R. J. Sternberg & M. L. Barnes (Eds.), *The psychology of love* (pp. 191–217). New Haven, CT: Yale University Press.

Havighurst, R. J. (1982). The world of work. In B. B. Wolman (Ed.), *Handbook of developmental psychology* (pp. 771–787). Englewood Cliffs, NJ: Prentice Hall.

Hawkins, H. L., Kramer, A. F., & Capaldi, D. (1992). Aging, exercise, and attention. *Psychology and Aging, 7,* 643–653.

Hayflick, L. (1977). The cellular basis for biological aging. In C. E. Finch & L. Hayflick (Eds.), *Handbook of the biology of aging* (pp. 159–186). New York: Van Nostrand Reinhold.

Hayflick, L. (1994). *How and why we age.* New York: Ballantine Books.

Hayslip, B. (1989). Alternative mechanisms for improvements in fluid ability performance among older adults. *Psychology and Aging, 4,* 122–124.

Hayward, M. D., & Hardy, M. A. (1985). Early retirement processes among older men: Occupational differences. *Research on Aging, 7,* 491–518.

Hayward, M. D., & Want, W. (1993). Retirement in Shanghai. *Research on Aging, 15,* 3–32.

Hazan, C., Hutt, M., Sturgeon, J., & Bricker, T. (1991). *The process of relinquishing parents as attachment figures.* Paper presented at the biennial meeting of the Society for Research in Child Development, Seattle, Washington.

Hazan, C., & Shaver, P. (1987). Romantic love conceptualized as an attachment process. *Journal of Personality and Social Psychology, 52,* 511–524.

Hazan, C., & Shaver, P. (1990). Love and work: An attachment-theoretical perspective. *Journal of Personality and Social Psychology, 59,* 270–280.

Heady, B., & Wearing, A. (1989). Personality, life events, and subjective well-being: Toward a dynamic equilibrium model. *Journal of Personality and Social Psychology, 47,* 731–739.

Heaton, T. B., & Pratt, E. L. (1990). The effects of religious homogamy on marital satisfaction and stability. *Journal of Family Issues, 11,* 191–207.

Helson, R. (1993). The Mills classes of 1958 and 1960: College in the fifties, young adulthood in the sixties. In K. D. Hulbert & D. T. Schuster (Eds.), *Women's lives through time: Educated American women of the twentieth century* (pp. 191–210). San Francisco: Jossey-Bass.

Helson, R. (1997). The self in middle age. In M. E. Lachman & J. B. James (Eds.), *Multiple paths of midlife development* (pp. 21–43). Chicago: University of Chicago Press.

Helson, R., Mitchell, V., & Moane, G. (1984). Personality and patterns of adherence and nonadherence to the social clock. *Journal of Personality and Social Psychology, 46,* 1079–1096.

Helson, R., & Moane, G. (1987). Personality change in women from college to midlife. *Journal of Personality and Social Psychology, 53,* 176–186.

Helson, R., & Picano, J. (1990). Is the traditional role bad for women? *Journal of Personality and Social Psychology, 59,* 311–320.

Helson, R., & Stewart, A. (1994). Personality change in adulthood. In T. F. Hetherton & J. L. Weinberger (Eds.), *Can personality change?* Washington, DC: American Psychological Association.

Helson, R., & Wink, P. (1992). Personality change in women from the early 40s to the early 50s. *Psychology and Aging, 7,* 46–55.

Henretta, J. C., O'Rand, A. M., & Chan, C. (1993). Gender differences in employment after a spouse's retirement. *Research on Aging, 15*(2), 148–169.

Herskind, A. M., & McGue, M., Holm, N. V., Sørensen, T. I. A., Harvald, B., & Vaupel, J. W. (1996). The heritability of human longevity: A population-based study of 2872 Danish twin pairs born 1870–1900. *Human Genetics, 97,* 319–323.

Hertzog, C., & Schaie, K. W. (1986). Stability and change in adult intelligence: 1. Analysis of longitudinal covariance structures. *Psychology and Aging, 1,* 159–171.

Hertzog, C., & Schaie, K. W. (1988). Stability and change in adult intelligence: 2. Simultaneous analysis of longitudinal means and covariance structures. *Psychology and Aging, 2,* 122–130.

Herzog, A. R., House, J. S., & Morgan, J. N. (1991). Relation of work and retirement to health and well-being in older age. *Psychology and Aging, 6,* 202–211.

Herzog, A. R., & Rogers, W. L. (1989). Age differences in memory performance and memory ratings as measured in a sample survey. *Psychology and Aging, 4,* 173–182.

Hetherington, E. M., & Camera, K. A. (1984). Families in transition: The process of dissolution and reconstitution. In R. D. Parke, R. N. Emde, H. P. McAdoo, & G. P. Sackett (Eds.), *Review of child development research: Vol. 7. The family* (pp. 398–440). Chicago: University of Chicago Press.

Hetherington, E. M., Cox, M., & Cox, R. (1978). The aftermath of divorce. In J. M. H. Stevens & M. Mathews (Eds.), *Mother/child, father/child relationships* (pp. 149–176). Washington, DC: National Association for the Education of Young Children.

Hetherton, T. F., & Weinberger, J. L. (Eds.). (1994). *Can personality change?* Washington, DC: American Psychological Association.

Higgins, C., Duxbury, L., & Lee, C. (1994). Impact of life-cycle stage and gender on the ability to balance work and family responsibilities. *Family Relations, 43,* 144–150.

Hill, M. S. (1988). Marital stability and spouses' shared time: A multidisciplinary hypothesis. *Journal of Family Relations, 9,* 427–451.

Hill, R. D., Storandt, M., & Malley, M. (1993). The impact of long-term exercise training on psychological function in older adults. *Journal of Gerontology: Psychological Sciences, 48,* P12–P17.

Himes, C. L. (1994). Parental caregiving by adult women. *Research on Aging, 16,* 191–211.

Hinton, J. (1975). The influence of previous personality on reactions to having terminal cancer. *Omega, 6,* 95–111.

Hodgkinson, V., Weitzman, M., & The Gallup Organization Inc. (1988). *Giving and volunteering in the United States: 1988 edition.* Washington, DC: Independent Sector.

Hofferth, S. L. (1987). Social and economic consequences of teenage childbearing. In S. L. Hofferth & C. D. Hayes (Eds.), *Risking the future: Adolescent sexuality, pregnancy, and childbearing. Working papers* (pp. 123–144). Washington, DC: National Academy Press.

Hoffman, L. W., & Manis, J. D. (1978). Influences of children on marital interaction and parental satisfactions and dissatisfactions. In R. M. Lerner & G. B. Spanier (Eds.), *Child influences on marital and family interaction* (pp. 165–213). New York: Academic Press.

Hogan, D. P. (1981). *Transitions and social change: The early lives of American men.* New York: Academic Press.

Holahan, C. J., & Moos, R. H. (1986). Personality, coping, and family resources in stress resistance: A longitudinal analysis. *Journal of Personality and Social Psychology, 51,* 389–395.

Holahan, C. J., & Moos, R. H. (1987). Risk, resistance, and psychological distress: A longitudinal analysis with adults and children. *Journal of Abnormal Psychology, 96,* 3–13.

Holahan, C. J., & Moos, R. H. (1990). Life stressors, resistance factors, and improved psychological functioning: An extension of the stress resistance paradigm. *Journal of Personality and Social Psychology, 58,* 909–917.

Holahan, C. K. (1988). Relation of life goals at age 70 to activity participation and health and psychological well-being among Terman's gifted men and women. *Psychology and Aging, 3,* 286–289.

Holahan, C. K., Holahan, C. J., & Belk, S. S. (1984). Adjustment in aging: The roles of life stress, hassles, and self-efficacy. *Health Psychology, 3,* 315–328.

Holland, J. L. (1973). *Making vocational choices: A theory of careers.* Englewood Cliffs, NJ: Prentice Hall.

Holland, J. L. (1992). *Making vocational choices: A theory of vocational personalities and work environments* (2nd ed.). Odessa, FL: Psychological Assessment Resources.

Holmes, T. H., & Rahe, R. H. (1967). The Social Readjustment Rating Scale. *Journal of Psychosomatic Research, 11,* 213–218.

Holmes, T. S., & Holmes, T. H. (1970). Short term intrusions into life-style routine. *Journal of Psychosomatic Research, 14,* 121–132.

Horn, J. L. (1982). The aging of human abilities. In B. B. Wolman (Ed.), *Handbook of developmental psychology* (pp. 847–870). Englewood Cliffs, NJ: Prentice Hall.

Horn, J. L., & Donaldson, G. (1980). Cognitive development in adulthood. In O. G. Brim, Jr. & J. Kagan (Eds.), *Constancy and change in human development* (pp. 415–529). Cambridge, MA: Harvard University Press.

Horn, J. L., & Hofer, S. M. (1992). Major abilities and development in the adult period. In R. J. Sternberg & C. A. Berg (Eds.), *Intellectual development* (pp. 44–99). Cambridge, England: Cambridge University Press.

Horner, K. W., Rushton, J. P., & Vernon, P. A. (1986). Relation between aging and research productivity of academic psychologists. *Psychology and Aging, 1,* 319–324.

House, J. S., Kessler, R. C., & Herzog, A. R. (1990). Age, socioeconomic status, and health. *Milbank Quarterly, 68,* 383–411.

Houseknecht, S. K. (1987). Voluntary childlessness. In M. B. Sussman & S. K. Steinmetz (Eds.), *Handbook of marriage and the family* (pp. 369–395). New York: Plenum Press.

Houseknecht, S. K., & Macke, A. S. (1981). Combining marriage and career: The marital adjustment of professional women. *Journal of Marriage and the Family, 43,* 651–661.

Hoyert, D. L. (1991). Financial and household exchanges between generations. *Research on Aging, 13,* 205–225.

Hoyert, D. L., & Seltzer, M. M. (1992). Factors related to the well-being and life activities of family caregivers. *Family Relations, 41,* 74–81.

Hu, Y., & Goldman, N. (1990). Mortality differentials by marital status: An international comparison. *Demography, 27,* 233–250.

Hulbert, K. D., & Schuster, D. T. (Eds.). (1993). *Women's lives through time: Educated American women of the twentieth century.* San Francisco: Jossey-Bass.

Hultsch, D. F., Hertzog, C., Small, B. J., McDonald-Miszczak, L., & Dixon, R. A. (1992). Short-term longitudinal change in cognitive performance in later life. *Psychology and Aging, 7,* 571–584.

Hunsberger, B. (1985). Religion, age, life satisfaction, and perceived sources of religiousness: A study of older persons. *Journal of Gerontology, 40,* 615–620.

Hunter, S., & Sundel, M. (Eds.). (1989). *Midlife myths: Issues, findings, and practice implications.* Newbury Park, A: Sage.

Hurwicz, M., Duryam, C. C., Boyd-Davis, S. L., Gatz, M., & Bengtson, V. L. (1992). Salient life events in three-generation families. *Journal of Gerontology: Psychological Sciences, 47,* P11–P13.

Huston, T. L., McHale, S. M., & Crouter, A. C. (1986). When the honeymoon's over: Changes in the marriage relationship over the first year. In R. Gilmour & S. Duck (Eds.), *The emerging field of personal relationships* (pp. 109–132). Hillsdale, NJ: Erlbaum.

Huston, T. L., Surra, C. A., Fitzgerald, N. M., & Cate, R. M. (1981). From courtship to marriage: Mate selection as an interpersonal process. In S. Duck & R. Gilmour (Eds.), *Personal relationships: 2. Developing personal relationships* (pp. 53–90). New York: Academic Press.

Huyck, M. H. (1990). Gender differences in aging. In J. E. Birren & K. W. Schaie (Eds.), *Handbook of the psychology of aging* (pp. 124–132). San Diego, CA: Academic Press.

Huyck, M. H. (1994). The relevance of psychodynamic theories for understanding gender among older women. In B. F. Turner & L. E. Troll (Eds.), *Women growing older: Psychological perspectives* (pp. 202–238). Thousand Oaks, CA: Sage.

Iacocca, L. (1984). *Iacocca: An autobiography.* Toronto: Bantam Books.

Inkeles, A., & Usui, C. (1989). Retirement patterns in cross-national perspective. In D. I. Kertzer & K. W. Schaie (Eds.), *Age structuring in comparative perspective* (pp. 227–262). Hillsdale, NJ: Erlbaum.

Irion, J. C., & Blanchard-Fields, F. (1987). A cross-sectional comparison of adaptive coping in adulthood. *Journal of Gerontology, 42,* 502–504.

Irwin, M., & Pike, J. (1993). Bereavement, depressive symptoms, and immune function. In M. S. Stroebe, W. Stroebe, & R. O. Hansson (Eds.), *Handbook of bereavement: Theory, research, and intervention* (pp. 160–171). Cambridge, England: Cambridge University Press.

Ishii-Kuntz, M., & Seccombe, K. (1989). The impact of children upon social support networks throughout the life course. *Journal of Marriage and the Family, 51,* 777–790.

Jackson, D. J., Longino, C. F., Jr., Zimmerman, R. S., & Bradsher, J. E. (1991). Environmental adjustments to declining functional ability: Residential mobility and living arrangements. *Research on Aging, 13,* 289–309.

Jacobs, S. C., Kosten, T. R., Kasl, S. V., Ostfeld, A. M., Berkman, L., & Charpentier, P. (1987–1988). Attachment theory and multiple dimensions of grief. *Omega, 18,* 41–52.

James, W. (1958). *The varieties of religious experience.* New York: Mentor. (Original work published 1902.)

James, W. H. (1983). Decline in coital rates with spouses' ages and duration of marriage. *Journal of Biosocial Science, 15,* 83–88.

Jaques, E. (1965). Death and the mid-life crisis. *International Journal of Psychoanalysis, 46,* 502–514.

Jarvik, L. F., & Bank, L. (1983). Aging twins: Longitudinal psychometric data. In W. K. Schaie (Ed.), *Longitudinal studies of adult psychological development* (pp. 40–63). New York: Guilford Press.

Jeffrey, R. W. (1989). Risk behaviors and health: Contrasting individual and population perspectives. *American Psychologist, 44,* 1194–1202.

Jendrek, M. P. (1993). Grandparents who parent their grandchildren: Effects on lifestyle. *Journal of Marriage and the Family, 55,* 609–621.

Jensen, A. R. (1998). *The g factor: The science of mental ability.* Westport, CT: Praeger.

Jensen, A. R. (1993). Spearman's hypothesis tested with chronometric information-processing tasks. *Intelligence, 17,* 42–77.

Jette, A. M. (1996). Disability trends and transitions. In R. H. Binstock & L. K. George (Eds.), *Handbook of aging and the social sciences* (4th ed., pp. 94–116). San Diego, CA: Academic Press.

Johansson, B., & Berg, S. (1989). The robustness of the terminal decline phenomenon: Longitudinal data from the digit-span memory test. *Journal of Gerontology: Psychological Sciences, 44,* P184–P186.

John, R., Blanchard, P. H., & Hennessy, C. H. (1997). Hidden lives: Aging and contemporary American Indian women. In J. M. Coyle (Ed.), *Handbook on women and aging* (pp. 290–315). Westport, CT: Greenwood Press.

Johnson, C. L. (1982). Sibling solidarity: Its origin and functioning in Italian-American families. *Journal of Marriage and the Family, 44,* 155–167.

Johnson, D. (1983). *Spirals of growth.* Wheaton, IL: Theosophical Publishing House.

Johnson, L. E., Kaiser, F. E., & Morley, J. E. (1997). Changes in male sexual function. In C. K. Cassel, H. J. Cohen, E. B. Larson, et al. (Eds.), *Geriatric medicine* (3rd ed., pp. 511–525). New York: Springer-Verlag.

Johnson, O. (Ed.) Information please almanac. Boston: Houghton Mifflin.

Just, M. A., & Carpenter, P. A. (1992). A capacity theory of comprehension: Individual differences in working memory. *Psychological Review, 99,* 122–149.

Kagan, J. (1980). Perspectives on continuity. In O. G. Brim, Jr. & J. Kagan (Eds.), *Constancy and change in human development* (pp. 26–74). Cambridge, MA: harvard University Press.

Kahn, R. L., & Antonucci, T. C. (1980). Convoys over the life course: Attachment, roles, and social support. In P. B. Baltes & O. G. Brim, Jr. (Eds.), *Life-span development and behavior* (Vol. 3, pp. 254–86). New York: Academic Press.

Kahn, S. B., Alvi, S., Shaukat, N., Hussain, M. A., & Baig, T. (1990). A study of the validity of Holland's theory in a non-western culture. *Journal of Vocational Behavior, 36,* 132–146.

Kaiser, F. E., Wilson, M-M. G., & Morley, J. E. (1997). Menopause/female sexual function. In C. K. Cassel et al. (Eds.) Geriatirc medicine (3rd ed., pp. 527–539). New York: Springer-Verlag.

Kalish, R. A. (1985). The social context of death and dying. In R. H. Binstock & E. Shanas (Eds.), *Handbook of aging and the social sciences* (2nd ed., pp. 149–170). New York: Van Nostrand Reinhold.

Kalish, R. A., & Reynolds, D. K. (1976). *Death and ethnicity: A psychocultural study.* Los Angeles: University of Southern California Press. (Reprinted 1981, Farmingdale: NJ: Baywood)

Kallman, D. A., Plato, C. C., & Tobin, J. D. (1990). The role of muscle loss in the age-related decline of grip strength: Cross-sectional and longitudinal perspectives. *Journal of Gerontology: Medical Sciences, 45,* M82–M88.

Kane, R. L., Klein, S. J., Bernstein, L., Rothenberg, R., & Wales, J. (1985). Hospice role in alleviating the emotional stress of terminal patients and their families. *Medical Care, 23,* 189–197.

Kane, R. L., Wales, J., Bernstein, L., Leibowitz, A., & Kaplan, S. (1984). A randomized controlled trial of hospice care. *Lancet,* 890–894.

Kannel, W. B., & Gordon, T. (1980). Cardiovascular risk factors in the aged: The Framingham study. In S. G. Haynes & M. Feinleib (Eds.), *Second conference on the epidemiology of aging* (DHHS/NIH Publication No. 80-969, pp. 65–89). Washington, DC: U.S. Government Printing Office.

Kanner, A. D., Coyne, J. C., Schaefer, C., & Lazarus, R. S. (1981). Comparison of two modes of stress measurement: Daily hassles and uplifts versus major life events. *Journal of Behavioral Medicine, 4,* 1-39.

Kaplan, B. (1983). A trio of trials. In R. M. Lerner (Ed.), *Developmental psychology: Historical and philosophical perspectives* (pp. 185–228). Hillsdale, NJ: Erlbaum.

Kaplan, G. A. (1992). Health and aging in the Alameda County Study. In K. W. Schaie, D. Blazer, & J. S. House (Eds.), *Aging, health behaviors, and health outcomes* (pp. 69–88). Hillsdale, NJ: Erlbaum.

Karen, R. (1994). *Becoming attached.* New York: Warner Books.

Karp, D. A. (1988). A decade of reminders: Changing age consciousness between fifty and sixty years old. *The Gerontologist, 28,* 727–738.

Kasl, S. V., & Cobb, S. (1982). Variability of stress effects among men experiencing job loss. In L. Goldberger & S. Breznitz (Eds.), *Handbook of stress: Theoretical and clinical aspects* (pp. 445–465). New York: Free Press.

Keefe, S. E. (1984). Real and ideal extended familism among Mexican Americans and Anglo Americans: On the meaning of "close" family ties. *Human Organization, 43,* 65–70.

Keen, S. (1983). *The passionate life: Stages of loving.* New York: Harper & Row.

Kegan, R. (1980). There the dance is: Religious dimensions of developmental theory. In J. W. Fowler & A. Vergote (Eds.), *Toward moral and religious maturity* (pp. 403–440). Morristown, NJ: Silver Burdette.

Kegan, R. (1982). *The evolving self.* Cambridge, MA: Harvard University Press.

Keith, P. M. (1981–1982). Perception of time remaining and distance from death. *Omega, 12,* 307–318.

Kellehear, A., & Lewin, T. (1988–1989). Farewells by the dying: A sociological study. *Omega, 19,* 275–292.

Kelly, J., & Rice, S. (1986). The aged. In H. Gochros, J. Gochros, & J. Fisher (Eds.), *Helping the sexually oppressed.* Englewood Cliffs, NJ: Prentice Hall.

Kendler, K. S., Neale, M. C., Kessler, R. C., Heath, A. C., & Eaces, L. J. (1992a). A population based twin study of major depression in women: The impact of varying definitions of illness. *Archives of General Psychiatry, 39,* 257–266.

Kendler, K. S., Neale, M. C., Kessler, R. C., Heath, A. C., & Eaces, L. J. (1992b). Major depression and generalized anxiety disorder: Same genes (partly) different environments? *Archives of General Psychiatry, 49,* 716–722.

Kennedy, G. J., Haque, M., & Zarankow, B. (1997). Human sexuality in late life. *International Journal of Mental Health, 26*(1), 35–46.

Kerckhoff, A. C. (1993). *Diverging pathways: Social structure and career deflections.* Cambridge, England: Cambridge University Press.

Kerner, J. F., Dusenbury, L., & Mandelblatt, J. S. (1993). Poverty and cultural diversity: Challenges for health promotion among the medically underserved. *Annual Review of Public Health, 14,* 355–377.

Kessler, R. C., Foster, C., Webster, P. S., & House, J. S. (1992). The relationship between age and depressive symptoms in two national surveys. *Psychology and Aging, 7,* 119–126.

Kessler, R. C., Turner, J. B., & House, J. S. (1988). Effects of unemployment on health in a community survey: Main, modifying, and mediating effects. *Journal of Social Issues, 44,* 69–85.

Kiecolt-Glaser, J. K., & Glaser, R. (1988). Behavioral influences on immune function: Evidence for the interplay between stress and health. In T. M. Field, P. M. McCabe, & N. Schneiderman (Eds.), *Stress and coping across development* (pp. 189–206). Hillsdale, NJ: Erlbaum.

Kiecolt-Glaser, J. K., Glaser, R., Suttleworth, E. E., Dyer, C. S., Ogrocki, P., & Speicher, C. E. (1987). Chronic stress and immunity in family caregivers of Alzheimer's disease patients. *Psychosomatic Medicine, 49,* 523–535.

Kiecolt-Glaser, J. K., Malarkey, W. B., Chee, M., Newton, T., Cacioppo, J. T., Mao, H., & Glaser, R. (1993). Negative behavior during marital conflict is associated with immunological down-regulation. *Psychosomatic Medicine, 55,* 395–409.

Kiernan, K., & Estaugh, V. (1993). *Cohabitation, extramarital childbearing and social policy.* London: Family Policies Study Center.

King, P. M., Kitchener, K. S., Wood, P. K., & Davison, M. L. (1989). Relationships across developmental domains: A longitudinal study of intellectual, moral, and ego development. In M. L. Commons, J. D. Sinnott, F. A. Richards, & C. Armon (Eds.), *Adult development: Vol. I. Comparisons and applications of developmental models* (pp. 57–72). New York: Praeger.

Kirkpatrick, L. A., & Davis, K. E. (1994). Attachment style, gender and relationship stability: A longitudinal analysis. *Journal of Personality and Social Psychology, 66,* 501–512.

Kirkpatrick, L. A., & Hazan, C. (1994). Attachment styles and close relationships: A four-year prospective study. *Personal Relationships, 1,* 123–142.

Kite, M. E., Deaux, K., & Miele, M. (1991). Stereotypes of young and old: Does age outweigh gender? *Psychology and Aging, 6,* 19–27.

Kitson, G. C. (1992). *Portrait of divorce: Adjustment to marital breakdown.* New York: Guilford Press.

Kitson, G. C., Babri, K. B., & Roach, M. J. (1985). Who divorces and why: A review. *Journal of Family Issues, 6,* 255–293.

Kivett, V. R. (1991). Centrality of the grandfather role among older rural black and white men. *Journal of Gerontology: Social Sciences, 46,* S250–S258.

Kivnick, H. Q. (1982). Grandparenthood: An overview of meaning and mental health. *Gerontologist, 22,* 59-66.

Kleemeier, R. W. (1962). Intellectual changes in the senium. *Proceedings of the Social Statistics Section of the American Statistics Association, 1,* 290–295.

Klenow, D. J., & Bolin, R. C. (1989–1990). Belief in an afterlife: A national survey. *Omega, 20,* 63–74.

Kletzky, O. A., & Borenstein, R. (1987). Vasomotor instability of the menopause. In D. R. Mishell, Jr. (Ed.), *Menopause: Physiology and pharmacology* (pp. 53–66). Chicago: Year Book Medical Publishers.

Kliegl, R., Smith, J., & Baltes, P. B. (1990). On the locus and process of magnification of age differences during mnemonic training. *Developmental Psychology, 26,* 894–904.

Kluwe, R. H. (1986). Psychological research on problem-solving and aging. In A. B. Sørensen, F. E. Weinert, & L. R. Sherrod (Eds.), *Human development and the life course: Multidisciplinary perspectives* (pp. 509–534). Hillsdale, NJ: Erlbaum.

Koenig, H. G., & Blazer, D. G. (1992). Mood disorders and suicide. In J. E. Birren, R. B. Sloane, & G. D. Cohen (Eds.), *Handbook of mental health and aging* (2nd ed., pp. 379–407). San Diego, CA: Academic Press.

Koenig, H. G., Blazer, D. G., & Hocking, L. B. (1997). Depression, anxiety, and other affective disorders. In C. K. Cassell et al. (Eds.), *Geriatric Medicine (3rd ed.* pp. 949–965). New York: Springer-Verlag.

Koenig, H. G., Kvale, J. N., & Ferrell, C. (1988). Religion and well-being in later life. *The Gerontologist, 28,* 18–28.

Kogan, N. (1990). Personality and aging. In J. E. Birren & K. W. Schaie (Eds.), *Handbook of the psychology of aging* (3rd ed., pp. 330–346). San Diego, CA: Academic Press.

Kohlberg, L. (1964). Development of moral character and moral ideology. In M. L. Hoffman & L. W. Hoffman (Eds.), *Review of child development research* (Vol. 1, pp. 283–332). New York: Russell Sage Foundation.

Kohlberg, L. (1973). Continuities in childhood and adult moral development revisited. In P. B. Baltes & K. W. Schaie (Eds.), *Life-span developmental psychology: Personality and socialization* (pp. 180–204). New York: Academic Press.

Kohlberg, L. (1976). Moral stages and moralization: The cognitive-developmental approach. In T. Lickona (Ed.), *Moral development and behavior: Theory, research, and social issues* (pp. 31–53). New York: Holt.

Kohlberg, L. (1981). *Essays on moral development: Vol. I. The philosophy of moral development.* New York: Harper & Row.

Kohlberg, L. (1984). *Essays on moral development: Vol. 2. The psychology of moral development.* San Francisco: Harper & Row.

Kohlberg, L., & Kramer, R. (1969). Continuities and discontinuities in children and adult moral development. *Human Development, 12,* 225–252.

Kohlberg, L., Levine, C., & Hewer, A. (1983). *Moral stages: A current formulation and a response to critics.* Basel, Switzerland: Karger.

Kohn, M. L. (1978). The reciprocal effects of the substantive complexity of work and intellectual flexibility: A longitudinal assessment. *American Journal of Sociology, 84,* 24–52.

Kohn, M. L. (1980). Job complexity and adult personality. In N. J. Smelser & E. H. Erikson (Eds.), *Themes of work and love in adulthood* (pp. 193–212). Cambridge, MA: Harvard University Press.

Kohn, M. L., & Schooler, C. (1983). *Work and personality: An inquiry into the impact of social stratification.* Norwood, NJ: Ablex Press.

Kokmen, E., Beard, M., Offord, K. P., & Kurland, L. T. (1989). Prevalence of medically diagnosed dementia in a defined United States population: Rochester, Minnesota, January 1, 1975. *Neurology, 39,* 773–776.

Koplowitz, H. (1990). Unitary consciousness and the highest development of mind: The relation between spiritual development and cognitive development. In M. L. Commons, C. Armon, L. Kohlberg, F. A. Richards, T. A. Grotzer, & J. D. Sinnott (Eds.), *Adult development: Vol. 2. Models and methods in the study of adolescent and adult thought* (pp. 105–112). New York: Praeger.

Kornhaber, A. (1996). *Contemporary grandparenting.* Thousand Oaks, CA: Sage.

Koski, L. R., & Shaver, P. R. (1997). Attachment and relationship satisfaction across the lifespan. In R. J. Sternberg & M. Hojjat (Eds.), *Satisfaction in close relationships.* (pp. 26–55). New York: Guilford Press.

Krause, N. (1987a). Chronic financial strain, social support, and depressive symptoms among older adults. *Psychology and Aging, 2,* 185–192.

Krause, N. (1987b). Understanding the stress process: Linking social support with locus of control beliefs. *Journal of Gerontology, 42,* 589–593.

Krause, N., & Broawski-Clark, E. (1994). Clarifying the functions of social support in later life. *Research on Aging, 16,* 251–279.

Krause, N., Jay, G., & Liang, J. (1991). Financial strain and psychological well-being among the American and Japanese elderly. *Psychology and Aging, 6,* 170–181.

Krause, N., Liang, J., & Yatomi, N. (1989). Satisfaction with social support and depressive symptoms: A panel analysis. *Psychology and Aging, 4,* 88–97.

Kritchevsky, D. (1990). Nutrition and breast cancer. *Cancer (Philadelphia), 66,* 1321–1325.

Krout, J. A. (1983). Seasonal migration of the elderly. *The Gerontologist, 23,* 295–299.

Kübler-Ross, E. (1969). *On death and dying.* New York: Macmillan.

Kübler-Ross, E. (1974). *Questions and answers on death and dying.* New York: Macmillan.

Kunkel, S. R., & Applebaum, R. A. (1992). Estimating the prevalence of long-term disability for an aging society. *Journal of Gerontology: Social Sciences, 47,* S253–S260.

Kurdek, L. A. (1995). Developmental changes in relationship quality in gay and lesbian cohabiting couples. *Developmental Psychology, 31*(1), 86–94.

Kurdek, L. A., & Schmitt, J. P. (1986). Early development of relationship quality in heterosexual married, heterosexual cohabiting, gay, and lesbian couples. *Developmental Psychology, 22,* 305–309.

Labouvie-Vief, G. (1980). Beyond formal operations: Uses and limits of pure logic in life-span development. *Human Development, 23,* 141–161.

Labouvie-Vief, G. (1990). Modes of knowledge and the organization of development. In M. L. Commons, C. Armon, L. Kohlberg, F. A. Richards, T. A. Grotzer, & J. D. Sinnott (Eds.), *Adult development: Vol. 2. Models and methods in the study of adolescent and adult thought* (pp. 43–62). New York: Praeger.

Labouvie-Vief, G., & Gonda, J. N. (1976) Cognitive strategy training and intellectual performance in the elderly. *Journal of Gerontology, 31,* 327-332.

Labouvie-Vief, G., & Schell, D. A. (1982). Learning and memory in later life. In B. B. Wolman (Ed.), *Handbook of developmental psychology* (pp. 828–846). Englewood Cliffs, NJ: Prentice Hall.

Lachman, M. E., & James, J. B. (1997). *Multiple paths of midlife development.* Chicago: University of Chicago Press.

Lamberg, L. (1997). "Old and gray and full of sleep"? Not always. *Journal of the American Medical Association, 278*(16), 1302–1304.

Lamberts, S. W. J., van den Beld, A. W., & van der Lely, A. J. (1997, October 17). The endocrinology of aging. *Science, 278,* 419–424.

Lansdown, R., & Benjamin, G. (1985). The development of the concept of death in children aged 5–9 years. *Child Care, Health and Development, 11,* 13–30.

Larson, E. B., Kukull, W. A., & Katzman, R. L. (1992). Cognitive impairment: Dementia and Alzheimer's disease. *Annual Review of Public health, 13,* 431–449.

Larson, J. H., & Holman, T. B. (1994). Premarital predictors of marital quality and stability. *Family Relations, 43,* 223–237.

Launer, L. J., Dinkgreve, M. A. H. M., Jonker, C., Hooijer, C., & Lindeboom, J. (1993). Are age and education independent correlates of the mini-mental state exam performance of community-dwelling elderly? *Journal of Gerontology: Psychological Sciences, 48,* P271–P277.

Lawrence, R. H., Bennett, J. M., & Markides, K. S. (1992). Perceived intergenerational solidarity and psychological distress among older Mexican Americans. *Journal of Gerontology: Social Sciences, 47,* S55–S65.

Lawton, L., Silverstein, M., & Bengtson, V. (1994). Affection, social contact, and geographic distance between adult children and their parents. *Journal of Marriage and the Family, 56,* 57–68.

Lawton, M. P. (1990). Residential environment and self-directedness among older people. *American Psychologist, 45,* 638–640.

Lazarus, R. S. (1993). Coping theory and research: Past, present, and future. *Psychosomatic Medicine, 55,* 234–247.

Lazarus, R. S., & Folkman, S. (1984). *Stress, appraisal, and coping.* New York: Springer.

Lebowitz, B. D., Pearson, J. L., Schneider, L. S., Reynolds, C. F., III, Alexopoulos, G. S., Bruce, M. L., Conwell, Y., Katz, I. R., Meyers, B. S., Morrison, M. F., Mossey, J., Niederehe, G., & Parmelee, P. (1997). Diagnosis and treatment of depression in late life: Consensus statement update. *Journal of the American Medical Association, 278*(14), 1186–1190.

Lee, G. R. (1988). Marital intimacy among older persons. *Journal of Family Issues, 9,* 273–284.

Lee, G. R., Dwyer, J. W., & Coward, R. T. (1993). Gender differences in parent care: Demographic factors and same-gender preferences. *Journal of Gerontology: Social Sciences, 48,* S9–S16.

Lee, G. R., & Ellithorpe, E. (1982). Intergenerational exchange and subjective well-being among the elderly. *Journal of Marriage and the Family, 44,* 217–224.

Lee, G. R., & Ishii-Kuntz, M. (1987). Social interaction, loneliness, and emotional well-being among the elderly. *Research on Aging, 9,* 459–482.

Lee, G. R., & Shehan, C. L. (1989). Social relations and the self-esteem of older persons. *Research on Aging, 11,* 427–442.

Lee, I., Manson, J. E., Hennekens, C. H., & Paffenbarger, R. S., Jr. (1993). Body weight and mortality: A 27-year follow-up of middle-aged men. *Journal of the American Medical Association, 270,* 2823–2828.

Leean, C. (1985). Working paper of the Faith Development in the Adult Life Cycle Project, The Religious Education Association of the United States and Canada.

Lehman, H. C. (1953). *Age and achievement.* Princeton, NJ: Princeton University Press.

Leigh, G. K. (1982). Kinship interaction over the family life span. *Journal of Marriage and the Family, 44,* 197–208.

Leon, G. R., Gillum, B., Gillum, R., & Gouze, M. (1979). Personality stability and change over a 30-year period: middle age to old age. *Journal of Consulting and Clinical Psychology, 47,* 517–524.

Leonesio, M. V. (1993). Social Security and older workers. *Social Security Bulletin, 56,* 47–57.

Lerner, R. M. (1986). *Concepts and theories of human development* (2nd ed.). New York: Random House.

Lesch, K. P., Bengel, D., Heils, A., Sabol. S. Z., Greenberg, B. D., Petri S., Benjamin, J., Muller, C. R., Hamer, D. H., & Murphy, D. L. (1996). Association of anxiety-related traits with a polymorphism in the serotonin transporter gene regulatory region. *Science, 274,* 1527–1531.

Leserman, J., Petitto, J. M., Perkins, D. O., Folds, J. D., Golden, R. N., & Evans, D. L. (1997). Severe stress, depressive symptoms, and changes in lymphocyte subsets in human immunodeficiency virus-infected men: A 2-year follow-up study. *Archives of General Psychiatry, 54,* 279-285.

LeShan, L. (1966). *The medium, the mystic, and the physicist.* New York: Ballantine.

Lester, D. (1990). The Collett-Lester fear of death scale: The original version and a revision. *Death Studies, 14,* 451–468.

Letzelter, M., Jungermann, C., & Freitag, W. (1986). Schwimmeleistungen im Alter [Swimming performance in old age]. *Zeitschrift für Gerontologie, 19,* 389–395.

Levenson, R. W., Carstensen, L. L., & Gottman, J. M. (1993). Long-term marriage: Age, gender, and satisfaction. *Psychology and Aging, 8,* 301–313.

Levin, J. S. (Ed.). (1994a). *Religion in aging and health.* Thousand Oaks, CA: Sage.

Levin, J. S. (1994b). Investigating the epidemiologic effects of religious experience: Findings, explanations, and barriers. In J. S. Levin (Ed.), *Religion in aging and health* (pp. 3–17). Thousand Oaks, CA: Sage.

Levin, J. S., & Taylor, R. J. (1993). Gender and age differences in religiosity among black Americans. *The Gerontologist, 33,* 16–23.

Levin, J. S., Taylor, R. J., & Chatters, L. M. (1994). Race and gender differences in religiosity among older adults: Findings from four national surveys. *Journal of Gerontology: Social Sciences, 49,* S137–S145.

Levinson, D. J. (1978). *The seasons of a man's life.* New York: Knopf.

Levinson, D. J. (1980). Toward a conception of the adult life course. In N. J. Smelser & E. H. Erikson (Eds.), *Themes of work and love in adulthood* (pp. 265–290). Cambridge, MA: Harvard University Press.

Levinson, D. J. (1986). A conception of adult development. *American Psychologist, 41,* 3–13.

Levinson, D. J. (1990). A theory of life structure development in adulthood. In C. N. Alexander & E. J. Langer (Eds.), *Higher stages of human development* (pp. 35–54). New York: Oxford University Press.

Levinson, D. J. (1996). *The seasons of a woman's life.* New York: Ballantine.

Leviton, R. (1995). *Brain builders! A lifelong guide to sharper thinking, better memory, and an age-proof mind.* Englewood Cliffs, NJ: Prentice Hall.

Levitt, M. J., Weber, R. A., & Guacci, N. (1993). Convoys of social support: An intergenerational analysis. *Psychology and Aging, 7,* 323–326.

Levy, J. (1994). Sex and sexuality in later life stages. In A. S. Rossi (Ed.), *Sexuality across the life course.* (pp. 287–309). Chicago: University of Chicago Press.

Levy, L. H., Martinkowski, K. S., & Derby, J. F. (1994). Differences in patterns of adaptation in conjugal bereavement: Their sources and potential significance. *Omega, 29,* 71–87.

Lieberman, M. A. (1982). The effects of social supports on responses to stress. In L. Goldberger & S. Breznitz (Eds.), *Handbook of stress: Theoretical and clinical aspects* (pp. 764–784). New York: Free Press.

Lieberman, M. A., & Peskin, H. (1992). Adult life crises. In J. E. Birren, R. B. Sloane, & G. D. Cohen (Eds.), *Handbook of mental health and aging* (pp. 119–143). San Diego, CA: Academic Press.

Lieberman, M. A., & Tobin, S. S. (1983). *The experience of old age: Stress, coping, and survival.* New York: Basic Books.

Lieblich, A. (1986). Successful career women at midlife: Crises and transitions. *International Journal of Aging and Human Development, 23,* 310–312.

Liem, R., & Liem, J. H. (1988). Psychological effects of unemployment on workers and their families. *Journal of Social Issues, 44,* 87–105.

Light, L. L. (1991). Memory and aging: Four hypotheses in search of data. *Annual Review of Psychology, 42,* 333–376.

Light, L. L. (1992). The organization of memory in old age. In F. I. M. Craik & T. A. Salthouse (Eds.), *The handbook of aging and cognition* (pp. 111–166). Hillsdale, NJ: Erlbaum.

Lindahl, K. M., Malik, N. M., & Bradbury, T. N. (1997). The developmental course of couples' relationships. In W. K. Halford & H. J. Markman (Eds.), *Clinical handbook of marriage and couples interventions.* New York: Wiley.

Lips, H. M. (1997). *Sex and gender* (3rd ed.) London: Mayfield.

List, N. D. (1988). Cancer screening in the elderly. *Aging (New York), 35,* 113–30.

Litwak, E., & Longino, C. F., Jr. (1987). Migration patterns among the elderly: A developmental perspective. *The Gerontologist, 27,* 266–272.

Livson, F. B. (1976). Patterns of personality development in middle-aged women: A longitudinal study. *International Journal of Aging and Human Development, 7,* 107–115.

Livson, F. B. (1981). Paths to psychological health in the middle years: Sex differences. In D. H. Eichorn, J. A. Clausen, N. Haan, M. P. Honzik, & P. H. Mussen (Eds.), *Present and past in middle life* (pp. 195–221). New York: Academic Press.

Livson, N., & Peskin, H. (1981). Psychological health at 40: Prediction from adolescent personality. In D. H. Eichorn, J. A. Clausen, N. Haan, M. P. Honzik, & P. H. Mussen (Eds.), *Present and past in middle life* (pp. 184–194). New York: Academic Press.

Loehlin, J. C. (1992). *Genes and environment in personality development.* Newbury Park, CA: Sage.

Loevinger, J. (1976). *Ego development.* San Francisco: Jossey-Bass.

Loevinger, J. (1984). On the self and predicting behavior. In R. A. Zucker, J. Aronoff, & A. I. Rabin (Eds.), *Personality and the prediction of behavior* (pp. 43–68). New York: Academic Press.

Longino, C. F., Jr. (1988). Who are the oldest Americans? *The Gerontologist, 28,* 515–523.

Longino, C. F., Jr. (1990). Geographical distribution and migration. In R. H. Binstock & L. K. George (Eds.), *Handbook of aging and the social sciences* (3rd ed., pp. 45–63). San Diego, CA: Academic Press.

Longino, C. F., Jr., Jackson, D. J., Zimmerman, R. S., & Bradsher, J. E. (1991). The second move: Health and geographic mobility. *Journal of Gerontology: Social Sciences, 46,* S218–S224.

Lonky, E., Kaus, C. R., & Roodin, P. A. (1984). Life experience and mode of coping: Relation to moral judgment in adulthood. *Developmental Psychology, 20,* 1159–1167.

Lopata, H. Z. (1973). *Widowhood in an American city.* Cambridge, MA: Schenkman.

Lopata, H. Z. (1979). *Women as widows: Support systems.* New York: Elsevier.

Lopata, H. Z., Heinemann, G. D., & Baum, J. (1982). Loneliness: Antecedents and coping strategies in the lives of widows. In L. A. Peplau & D. Perlman (Eds.), *Loneliness* (pp. 310–326). New York: Wiley.

Lowenthal, M. F., Thurnher, M., & Chiriboga, D. (1975). *Four stages of life.* San Francisco: Jossey-Bass.

Lyell, R. (Ed.). (1980). *Middle age, old age: Short stories, poems, plays, and essays on aging.* New York: Harcourt Brace Jovanovich.

Lyons, N. P. (1983). Two perspectives: On self, relationships, and morality. *Harvard Educational Review, 53,* 125–145.

Maas, H. S., & Kuypers, J. A. (1974). *From thirty to seventy.* San Francisco: Jossey-Bass.

Maccoby, E. E. (1990). Gender and relationships: A developmental account. *American Psychologist, 45,* 513–520.

Maccoby, N. (1980). Promoting positive health behaviors in adults. In L. A. Bond & J. C. Rosen (Eds.), *Competence and coping during adulthood* (pp. 195–218). Hanover, NH: University Press of New England.

Maciel, A. G., Heckhausen, J., & Baltes, P. B. (1994). A life-span perspective on the interface between personality and intelligence. In R. J. Sternberg & P. Ruzgis (Eds.), *Personality and intelligence* (pp. 61–103). Cambridge, England: Cambridge University Press.

Madden, D. J. (1992). Four to ten milliseconds per year: Age-related showing of visual word identification. *Journal of Gerontology: Psychological Sciences, 47,* P59–P68.

Madden, D. J., Blementhal, J. A., Allen, P. A., & Emery, C. F. (1989). Improving aerobic capacity in healthy older adults does not necessarily lead to improved cognitive performance. *Psychology and Aging, 4,* 307–320.

Maeda, D. (1993). Japan. In E. B. Palmore (Ed.), *Developments and research on aging: An international handbook* (pp. 201–219). Westport, CT: Greenwood Press.

Main, M., & Hesse, E. (1990). Parents' unresolved traumatic experiences are related to infant disorganized attachment status: Is frightened and/or frightening parental behavior the linking mechanism? In M. T. Greenberg, D. Cicchetti, & E. M. Cummings (Eds.), *Attachment in the preschool years: Theory, research, and intervention* (pp. 161–182). Chicago: University of Chicago, Press.

Main, M., Kaplan, N., & Cassidy, J. (1985). Security in infancy, childhood, and adulthood: A move to the level of representation. *Monographs of the Society for Research in Child Development, 50*(Serial No. 209), 66–104.

Manton, K. G., Corder, L. S., & Stallard, E. (1993). Estimates of change in chronic disability and institutional incidence and prevalence rates in the U.S. elderly population from the 1982, 1984, and 1989 National Long Term Care Survey. *Journal of Gerontology: Social Sciences, 48,* S153–S166.

Manton, K. G., & Stallard, E. (1997). In L. G. Martin & B. J. Soldo (Eds.), *Racial and ethnic differences in the health of older Americans* (pp. 43–104). Washington, DC: National Academy Press.

Marcia, J. E. (1980). Identity in adolescence. In J. Adelson (Ed.), *Handbook of adolescent psychology* (pp. 159–187). New York: Wiley.

Markides, K. S., & Black, S. A. (1996). Race, ethnicity, and aging: The impact of inequality. In R. H. Binstock & L. K. George (Eds.), *Handbook of aging and the social sciences (4th ed.,* pp. 153–170). San Diego, CA: Academic press.

Markides, K. S., & Kruase, N. (1985). Intergenerational solidarity and psychological well-being among older Mexican Americans: A three-generations study. *Journal of Gerontology, 40,* 390–392.

Markides, K. S., & Mindel, C. H. (1987). *Aging and ethnicity.* Newbury Park, CA: Sage.

Markman, H. J. (1981). The prediction of marital distress: A five-year follow-up. *Journal of Consulting and Clinical Psychology, 49,* 760–762.

Markman, H. J., Renick, M. J., Floyd, F. I., Stanley, S. M., & Clements, M. (1993). Preventing marital distress through communication and conflict management training: A four- and five-year follow-up study. *Journal of Consulting and Clinical Psychology, 61,* 70–74.

Marks, N. F. (1996). Social demographic diversity among American midlife parents. In C. D. Ryff & M. M. Seltzer (Eds.). *The parental experience in midlife.* (pp. 29–75). Chicago: University of Chicago Press.

Marragut, J.; Sala, J.; Masiá, R.; Pavesi, M.; Sanz, G.; Valle, V.; Molina, L.; Serès, L.; Slosua, R.. (1998). Mortality differences between men and women following first myocardial infarction. *Journal of the American Medical Association, 280,* 1405-1409.

Marshall, V. W. (1996). The state of theory in aging and the social sciences. In R. H. Binstock & L. K. George (Eds.), *Handbook of aging and the social sciences* (pp. 12–20). San Diego, CA: Academic Press.

Marshall, V. W., & Levy, J. A. (1990). Aging and dying. In R. H. Binstock & L. K. George (Eds.), *Handbook of aging and the social sciences* (3rd ed., pp. 245–260). San Diego, CA: Academic Press.

Marsiglio, W., & Donnelly, D. (1991). Sexual relations in later life: A national study of married persons. *Journal of Gerontology: Social Sciences, 46,* S338–S334.

Martocchio, J. J. (1989). Age-related differences in employee absenteeism: A meta-analysis. *Psychology and Aging, 4,* 409–414.

Maslow, A. H. (1954). *Motivation and personality.* New York: Harper & Row.

Maslow, A. H. (1968). *Toward a psychology of being* (2nd ed.). New York: Van Nostrand Reinhold.

Maslow, A. H. (1970a). *Motivation and personality* (2nd ed.). New York: Harper & Row.

Maslow, A. H. (1970b). *Religions, values, and peak-experiences.* New York: Viking. (Original work published 1964)

Maslow, A. H. (1971). *The farther reaches of human nature.* New York: Viking.

Matarazzo, J. D. (1972). *Wechsler's measurement of appraisal of adult intelligence* (5th ed.). Baltimore: Williams & Wilkins.

Matt, G. E., Dean, A., Wang, B., & Wood, P. (1992). Identifying clinical syndromes in a community sample of elderly persons. *Psychological Assessment, 4,* 174–184.

Matthews, K. A. (1992). Myths and realities of the menopause. *Psychosomatic Medicine, 54,* 1–9.

Matthews, K. A., Wing, R. R., Kuller, L. H., Meilahn, E. N., Kelsey, S. F., Costello, E. J., & Caggiula, A. W. (1990). Influences of natural menopause on psychological characteristics and symptoms of middle-aged health women. *Journal of Consulting and Clinical Psychology, 58,* 345–351.

Mattox, C., Wu, H. K., & Schuman, J. S. (1995). Ocular disorders of the aged eye. In Reichel, W. (Ed.), *Care of the elderly: Clinical aspects of aging* (pp. 426–440). Baltimore: Williams & Wilkins.

Maylor, E. A. (1993). Aging and forgetting in prospective and retrospective memory tasks. *Psychology and Aging, 8,* 420–428.

McAdams, D. P. (1994). Can personality change? Levels of stability and growth in personality across the life span. In T. F. Hetherton & J. L. Weinberger (Eds.), *Can personality change?* (pp. 299–313). Washington, DC: American Psychological Association.

McAdams, D. P., & de St. Aubin, E. (1992). A theory of generativity and its assessment through self-report, behavioral acts, and narrative themes in autobiography. *Journal of Personality and Social Psychology, 62,* 1003–1015.

McAdams, D. P., de St. Aubin, E., & Logan, R. L. (1993). Generativity among young, midlife, and older adults. *Psychology and Aging, 8,* 221–230.

McCall, P. L. (1991). Adolescent and elderly white male suicide trends: Evidence of changing well-being? *Journal of Gerontology: Social Sciences, 46,* S43–S51.

McAuley, E. (1993). Self-efficacy, physical activity, and aging. In J. R. Kelly (Ed.), *Activity and aging: Staying involved in late life* (pp. 187–205). Newbury Park, CA: Sage.

McAuley, W. J., & Blieszner, R. (1985). Selection of long-term care arrangements by older community residents. *The Gerontologist, 25,* 188–193.

McClelland, D. C. (1991). Is personality consistent? In A. I Rabin, J. Aronoff, A. M. Barclay, & R. A. Zucker (Eds.), *Further explorations in personality* (pp. 87–113). New York: Wiley-Interscience.

McClelland, D. C. (1989). Motivational factors in health and disease. *American Psychologist, 44,* 675–683.

McCrae, R. R. (1989). Age differences and changes in the use of coping mechanisms. *Journal of Gerontology: Psychological Sciences, 44,* P161–P169.

McCrae, R. R., & Costa, P. T., Jr. (1983). Psychological maturity and subjective well-being: Toward a new synthesis. *Developmental Psychology, 19,* 243–248.

McCrae, R. R., & Costa, P. T., Jr. (1984). *Emerging lives, enduring dispositions: Personality in adulthood.* Boston: Little, Brown.

McCrae, R. R., & Costa, P. T., Jr. (1985). Openness to experience. In R. Hogan & W. H. Jones (Eds.), *Perspectives in personality* (pp. 146–172). Greenwich, CT: JAI Press.

McCrae, R. R., & Costa, P. T., Jr. (1987). Validation of the five-factor model of personality across instruments and observers. *Journal of Personality and Social Psychology, 52,* 81–90.

McCrae, R. R., & Costa, P. T., Jr. (1988). Psychological resilience among widowed men and women: A 10-year follow-up of a national sample. *Journal of Social Issues, 44,* 129–142.

McCrae, R. R., & Costa, P. T., Jr. (1990). *Personality in adulthood.* New York: Guilford Press.

McCrae, R. R., & John, O. P. (1992). An introduction to the five-factor model and its applications. *Journal of Personality, 60,* 175–215.

McDonald, P. L., & Wanner, R. A. (1990). *Retirement in Canada.* Toronto: Butterworth.

McEvoy, G. M., & Cascio, W. F. (1989). Cumulative evidence of the relationship between employee age and job performance. *Journal of Applied Psychology, 74,* 11–17.

McGandy, R. B. (1988). Atherogenesis and aging. *Aging (New York), 35,* 67–74.

McGrath, J. E. (1970). *Social and psychological factors in stress.* New York: Holt.

McKinlay, J. B., McKinlay, S. M., & Brambilla, D. J. (1987). Health status and utilization behavior associated with menopause. *American Journal of Epidemiology, 125,* 110–121.

Medina, J. J. (1996). *The clock of ages: Why we age, how we age, winding back the clock.* Cambridge, England: Cambridge University Press.

Meier, S. T. (1991). Vocational behavior, 1988–1990: Vocational choice: decision-making, career development interventions, and assessment. *Journal of Vocational Behavior, 39,* 131–181.

Menaghan, E. G. (1991). Work experiences and family interaction processes: The long reach of the job? *Annual Review of Sociology, 17,* 419–444.

Menaghan, E. G., & Lieberman, M. A. (1986). Changes in depression following divorce: A panel study. *Journal of Marriage and the Family, 48,* 319–328.

Merrill, D. M. (1997). *Caring for elderly parents: Juggling work, family, and caregiving in middle and working class families.* Westport, CT: Auburn House.

Merrill, D. M., & Mor, V. (1993). Pathways to hospital death among the oldest old. *Journal of Aging and Health, 5,* 516–535.

Meyer, B., & Rice, E. (1983). Learning and memory from text across the adult life span. In J. Fine & R. O. Freedle (Eds.), *Developmental studies of discourse.* Norwood, NJ: Ablex.

Mickelson, K. D., Kessler, R. C., & Shaver, P. R. (1997). Adult attachment in a nationally representative sample. *Journal of Personality and Social Psychology, 73*(5), 1092-1106.

Midlarsky, E., & Hannah, M. E. (1989). The generous elderly: Naturalistic studies of donations across the life span. *Psychology and Aging, 4,* 346–351.

Mikulincer, M. & Orbach, I. (1995) . Attachment styles and repressive defensiveness. *Journal of Personality and Social Psychology, 68*(5), 917-925.

Miles, L. E. & Dement, W. C. (1980). Sleep and aging. *Sleep, 3,* 119-120.

Miller, B., McFall, S., & Campbell, R. T. (1994). Changes in sources of community long-term care among African American and white frail older persons. *Journal of Gerontology: Social Sciences, 49,* S14–S24.

Miller, R. A. (1996a). Aging and the immune response. In E. L. Schneider & J. W. Rowe (Eds.), *Handbook of the biology of aging* (4th ed, pp. 355–392). San Diego, CA: Academic Press.

Miller, R. A. (1996b, July 5). The aging immune system primer and prospectus. *Science, 273* 70–74.

Mitchell, J., Mathews, H. F., & Sesavage, J. A. (1993). A multidimensional examination of depression among the elderly. *Research on Aging, 15,* 198–219.

Mobbs, C. V. (1996). Neuroendocrinology of aging. In E. L. Schneider & J. W. Rowe (Eds.), *Handbook of the biolo-*

gy of aging (4th ed. pp. 234–282). San Diego, CA: Academic Press.

Moen, P. (1985). Continuities and discontinuities in women's labor force activity. In G. H. Elder, J. (Ed.), *Life course dynamics: Trajectories and transitions, 1968–1980* (pp. 113–155). Ithaca, NY: Cornell University Press.

Montgomery, R. J. V., & Kosloski, K. (1994). A longitudinal analysis of nursing home placement for dependent elders cared for by spouses vs adult children. *Journal of Gerontology: Social Sciences, 49,* S62–S74.

Moore, K. A., Myers, D. E., Morrison, D. R., Nord, C. W., Brown, B., & Edmonston, B. (1993). Age at first childbirth and later poverty. *Journal of Research on Adolescence, 3,* 393–422.

Moos, R. H. (1988). *Coping Responses Inventory manual.* Palo Alto, CA: Stanford University and Veterans Administration Medical Centers, Social Ecology Laboratory.

Moos, R. H., & Billings, A. G. (1982). Conceptualizing and measuring coping resources and processes. In L. Goldberger & S. Breznitz (Eds.), *Handbook of stress: Theoretical and clinical aspects* (pp. 212–230). New York: Free Press.

Mor, V. (1987). *Hospice care systems: Structure, process, costs, and outcome.* New York: Springer.

Mor, V., Greer, D. S., & Kastenbaum, R. (Eds.). (1988). *The hospice experiment.* Baltimore: Johns Hopkins University Press.

Morgan, D. L. (1988). Age differences in social network participation. *Journal of Gerontology: Social Sciences, 43,* S129–S137.

Morgan, L. A. (1991). *After marriage ends: Economic consequences for midlife women.* Newbury Park, CA: Sage.

Morrell, R. W., & Echt, K. V. (1997). Designing written instructions for older adults: Learning to use computers. In A. D. Fisk & W. A. Rogers (Eds.), *Handbook of human factors and the older adult* (pp. 335–361). San Diego, CA: Academic Press.

Morrell, R. W., Park, D. C., & Poon, L. W. (1988). *Effects of differing labeling techniques on memory and comprehension of prescription information in young and old adults.* Paper presented at the annual meeting of the Gerontological Society of America, San Francisco.

Morrell, R. W., Park, D. C., & Poon, L. W. (1989). Quality of instruction on prescription drug labels: Effects on memory and comprehension in young and old adults. *Gerontologist, 29*(3), 345–354.

Morrison, J. H., & Hof, P. R. (1997, October 17). Life and death of neurons in the aging brain. *Science, 278,* 412–419.

Morrison, N. A., Qi, J. C., Tokita, A., Kelly, P. J., Crofts, L., Nguyen, T. V., Sambrook, P. N., & Eisman, J. A. (1994). Prediction of bone density from vitamin D receptor alleles. *Nature (London), 367,* 284–287.

Morrison-Bogorad, M., Phelps, C., & Buckholtz, N. (1997). Alzheimer's disease research comes of age. *Journal of the American Medical Association, 277,* 837–840.

Mortimer, J. T. (1974). Patterns of intergenerational occupational movements: A smallest-space analysis. *American Journal of Sociology, 5,* 1278–1295.

Mortimer, J. T. (1976). Social class, work and family: Some implications of the father's occupation for family rela-

tionships and son's career decisions. *Journal of Marriage and the Family, 38,* 241–256.

Moss, M. S., Moss, S. Z., & Moles, E. L. (1985). The quality of relationships between elderly parents and their out-of-town children. *The Gerontologist, 25,* 134–140.

Mullins, L. C., & Mushel, M. (1992). The existence and emotional closeness of relationships with children, friends, and spouses: The effect on loneliness among older persons. *Research on Aging, 14,* 448–470.

Mundy, G. R. (1994). Boning up on genes. *Nature (London), 367,* 216–217.

Murray, C., Luckey, M., & Meier, D. (1996). Skeletal integrity. In E. L. Schneider & J. W. Rowe (Eds.), *Handbook of the biology of aging* (4th ed., pp. 431–444). San Diego, CA: Academic Press.

Murrell, S. A., & Himmelfarb, S. (1989). Effects of attachment bereavement and pre-event conditions on subsequent depressive symptoms in older adults. *Psychology and Aging, 4,* 166–172.

Murrell, S. A., & Norris, F. H. (1991). Differential social support and life change as contributors to the social class-distress relationship in old age. *Psychology and Aging, 6,* 223–231.

Murrell, S. A., Norris, E. H., & Grote, C. (1988). Life events in older adults. In L. H. Cohen (Ed.), *Life events and psychological functioning: Theoretical and methodological issues* (pp. 96–122). Newbury Park, CA: Sage.

Murstein, B. I. (1970). Stimulus-value-role: A theory of marital choice. *Journal of Marriage and the Family, 32,* 465–481.

Murstein, B. I. (1976). *Who will marry whom? Theories and research in marital choice.* New York: Springer.

Murstein, B. I. (1986). *Paths to marriage.* Beverly Hills, CA: Sage.

Myers, G. C. (1996). Aging and the social sciences: Research directions and unresolved issues. In R. H. Binstock & L. K. George (Eds.), *Handbook of aging and the social sciences* (4th ed.), (pp. 1–11). San Diego, CA: Academic Press.

Myers, G. C. (1990). Demography of aging. In R. H. Binstock & L. K. George (Eds.), *Handbook of aging and the social sciences* (3rd ed., pp. 19–44). San Diego, CA: Academic Press.

Myers-Walls, J. A. (1984). Balancing multiple role responsibilities during the transition to parenthood. *Family Relations, 33,* 267–271.

Nash, S. C., & Feldman, S. S. (1981). Sex role and sex-related attributions: Constancy and change across the family life cycle. In M. E. Lamb & A. L. Brown (Eds.), *Advances in developmental psychology* (pp. 1–36). Hillsdale, NJ: Erlbaum.

National Center for Health Statistics (1992). *Vital statistics of the United States.* Washington, DC: Public Health Services.

National Institutes of Health. (1992). *Impotence: NIH consensus statement, 10*(4), 1–31. Washington, DC: U.S. Government Printing Office.

Neimeyer, R. A., & Chapman, K. M. (1980–1981). Self/ideal discrepancy and fear of death: The test of an existential hypothesis. *Omega, 11,* 233–239.

Nelson, J. L., & Nelson, H. L. (1996). *Alzheimer's: Answers to hard questions for families.* New York: Doubleday.

Nemy, E. (1991, February 28). Numbers are up, status down for the family of one. *The New York Times,* pp. B1, B5.

Neugarten, B. L. (1968). The awareness of middle age. In B. L. Neugarten (Ed.), *Middle age and aging* (pp. 93–98). Chicago: University of Chicago Press.

Neugarten, B. L. (1970). Dynamics of transition of middle age to old age. *Journal of Geriatric Psychiatry, 4,* 71–87.

Neugarten, B. L. (1977). Personality and aging. In J. E. Birren & K. W. Schaie (Eds.), *Handbook of the psychology of aging* (pp. 626–649). New York: Van Nostrand Reinhold.

Neugarten, B. L. (1979). Time, age, and the life cycle. *American Journal of Psychiatry, 136,* 887–894.

Newtson, R. L., & Keith, P. M. (1997). Single women in later life. In J. M. Coyle (Ed.), *Handbook on women and aging* (pp. 385–399). Westport, CT: Greenwood Press.

Nisan, M., & Kohlberg, L. (1982). Universality and variation in moral judgment: A longitudinal and cross-sectional study in Turkey. *Child Development, 53,* 865–876.

Nolen-Hoeksema, S. (1987). Sex differences in unipolar depression: Evidence and theory. *Psychological Bulletin, 101,* 259–282.

Nolen-Hoeksema, S. (1990). *Sex differences in depression.* Stanford, CA: Stanford University Press.

Norris, F. H., & Murrell, S. A. (1990). Social support, life events, and stress as modifiers of adjustment to bereavement by older adults. *Psychology and Aging, 5,* 429–436.

Norris, J. E., & Rubin, K. H. (1984). Peer interaction and communication: A life-span perspective. In P. B. Baltes & O. G. Brim, Jr. (Eds.), *Life-span development and behavior* (Vol. 6, pp. 356–383). Orlando, FL: Academic press.

Norton, A. J., & Miller, L. F. (1990). *The family life cycle: 1985. Work and family patterns of American women* (Current Population Reports, Series P-23, No. 165). Washington, DC: U.S. Government Printing Office, U.S. Bureau of the Census.

Norton, R. (1983). Measuring marital quality: A critical look at the dependent variable. *Journal of Marriage and the Family, 45,* 141–151.

Nurmi, J., Pulliainen, H., & Salmela-Aro, K. (1992). Age differences in adults' control beliefs related to life goals and concerns. *Psychology and Aging, 7,* 194–196.

Nydegger, C. N. (1991). The development of paternal and filial maturity. In K. Pillemer & K. McCartney (Eds.), *Parent-child relations throughout life* (pp. 93–112). Hillsdale, NJ: Erlbaum.

O'Bryant, S. L. (1988). Sibling support and older widows' well-being. *Journal of Marriage and the Family, 50,* 173–183.

O'Connor, B. P., & Vallerand, R. J. (1994). Motivation, self-determination, and person-environment fit as predictors of psychological adjustment among nursing home residents. *Psychology and Aging, 9,* 189–194.

Ogawa, N., & Retherford, R. D. (1993). Care of the elderly in Japan: Changing norms and expectations. *Journal of Marriage and the Family, 55;* 585–597.

O'Leary, A. (1990). Stress, emotion, and human immune function. *Psychological Bulletin, 108,* 363–382.

Orth-Gomér, K., Rosengren, A., & Wilhelmsen, L. (1993). Lack of social support and incidence of coronary heart disease in middle-aged Swedish men. *Psychosomatic Medicine, 55,* 37–43.

Palmore, E. B. (1970). Health practices and illness. *The Gerontologist, 10,* 313–316.

Palmore, E. B. (1981). *Social patterns in normal aging: Findings from the Duke Longitudinal Study.* Durham, NC: Duke University Press.

Palmore, E. B. (1990). *Ageism: Negative and positive.* New York: Springer.

Palmore, E. B., Burchett, B. M., Fillenbaum, G. G., George, L. K., & Wallman, L. M. (1985). *Retirement: Causes and consequences.* New York: Springer.

Palus, C. J. (1993). Transformative experiences of adulthood: A new look at the seasons of life. In J. Demick, K. Bursik, & R. DiBiase (Eds.), *Parental development* (pp. 39–58). Hillsdale, NJ: Erlbaum.

Parcel, T. L., & Menaghan, E. G. (1994). Parents' jobs and children's lives. New York: de Gruyter.

Park, D. C. (1992). Applied cognitive aging research. In F. I. M. Craik & T. A. Salthouse (Eds.), *Handbook of cognition and aging* (pp. 449–493). Hillsdale, NJ: Erlbaum.

Park, D. C., & Jones, T. R. (1997). Medication adherence and aging. In A. D. Fisk & W. A. Rogers (Eds.), *Handbook of human factors and the older adult* (pp. 257–287). San Diego, CA: Academic Press.

Park, D. C., & Kidder, K. (1995). Prospective memory and medication adherence. In M. Braandimonte, G. Einstein, & M. McDaniel (Eds.), *Prospective memory: Theory and applications* (pp. 369–390). Hillsdale, NJ: Erlbaum.

Park, D. C., Morrell, R. W., Frieske, D., Blackburn, A. B., & Birchmore, D. (1991). Cognitive factors in the use of over-the-counter medication organizers by arthritis patients. *Human Factors, 31*(3), 57–67.

Park, D. C., Morell, R. W., Frieske, D., & Kincaid, D. (1992). Medication adherence behaviors in older adults: Effects of external cognitive supports. *Psychology and Aging, 7,* 252–256.

Parnes, H. S., & Sommers, D. G. (1994). Shunning retirement: Work experience of men in their seventies and early eighties. *Journal of Gerontology: Social Sciences, 49,* S117–S124.

Pearlin, L. I. (1975). Sex roles and depression. In N. Datan & L. H. Ginsberg (Eds.), *Life-span developmental psychology: Normative life crises* (pp. 191–208). New York: Academic Press.

Pearlin, L. I. (1980). Life strains and psychological distress among adults. In N. J. Smelser & E. H. Erikson (Eds.), *Themes of work and love in adulthood* (pp. 174–192). Cambridge, MA: Harvard University Press.

Pearlin, L. I. (1982a). Discontinuities in the study of aging. In T. K. Hareven & K. J. Adams (Eds.), *Aging and life course transitions: An interdisciplinary perspective* (pp. 55–74). New York: Guilford Press.

Pearlin, L. I. (1982b). The social contexts of stress. In L. Goldberger & S. Breznitz (Eds.), *Handbook of stress: Theoretical and clinical aspects* (pp. 367–379). New York: Free Press.

Pendergast, D. R., Fisher, N. M., & Calkins, E. (1993). Cardiovascular, neuromuscular, and metabolic alterations with age leading to frailty [Special issue]. *Journals of Gerontology, 48,* 61–67.

Peplau, L. A. (1991). Lesbian and gay relationships. In J. C. Gonsiorek & J. D. Weinrich (Eds.), *Homosexuality: Research implications for public policy* (pp. 177–196). Newbury Park, CA: Sage.

Peplau, L. A., Bikson, T. K., Rook, K. S., & Goodchilds, J. D. (1982). Being old and living alone. In L. A. Peplau & D. Perlman (Eds.), *Loneliness* (pp. 327–350). New York: Wiley.

Perry-Jenkins, M., & Crouter, A. C. (1990). Men's provider-role attitudes: Implications for household work and marital satisfaction. *Journal of Family Issues, 11,* 136–156.

Perry-Jenkins, M., & Folk, K. (1994). Class, couples, and conflict: Effects of the division of labor on assessments of marriage in dual-earner families. *Journal of Marriage and the Family, 56,* 165–180.

Perun, P. J., & Bielby, D. D. (1980). Structure and dynamics of the individual life course. In K. W. Back (Ed.), *Life course: Integrative theories and exemplary populations* (pp. 97–120). Boulder, CO: Westview Press.

Peskin, H., & Livson, N. (1981). Uses of the past in adult psychological health. In D. H. Eichorn, J. A. Clausen, N. Haan, M. P. Honzik, & P. H. Mussen (Eds.), *Present and past in middle life* (pp. 158–194). New York: Academic Press.

Peterson, C., Seligman, M. E. P., & Vaillant, G. E. (1988). Pessimistic explanatory style is a risk factor for physical illness: A thirty-five-year longitudinal study. *Journal of Personality and Social Psychology, 55,* 23–27.

Pettingale, K. W., Morris, T., Greer, S., & Haybittle, J. L. (1985). Mental attitudes to cancer: An additional prognostic factor. *Lancet,* 85.

Phillips, S. K., Bruce, S. A., Newton, D., & Woledge, R. C. (1992). The weakness of old age is not due to failure or muscle activation. *Journal of Gerontology: Medical Sciences, 47,* M45–M49.

Piaget, J. (1952). *The origins of intelligence in children.* New York: International Universities Press.

Piaget, J., & Inhelder, B. (1969). *The psychology of the child.* New York: Basic Books.

Pillow, D. B., Zautra, A. J., & Sandler, I. (1996). Major life events and minor stressors: Identifying mediational links in the stress process. *Journal of Personality and Social Psychology, 70,* 381–394.

Pleck, J. (1977). The work-family role system. *Social Problems, 24,* 417–427.

Pleck, J. H. (1985). *Working wives, working husbands:* New York: Sage.

Plomin, R., DeFries, J. C., McClearn, G. E., & Rutter, M. (1997). *Behavioral genetics.* New York: Freeman.

Plomin, R., & McClearn, G. E. (1990). Human behavioral genetics of aging. In J. E. Birren & K. W. Schaie (Eds.), *Handbook of the psychology of aging* (3rd ed., pp. 67–79). San Diego, CA: Academic Press.

Pollack, J. M. (1979–1980). Correlates of death anxiety: A review of empirical studies. *Omega, 10,* 97–121.

Poon, L. W. (1985). Differences in human memory with aging: Nature, causes, and clinical implications. In J. E. Birren & K. W. Schaie (Eds.), *Handbook of the psychology of aging* (2nd ed., pp. 427–462). New York: Van Nostrand Reinhold.

Popenoe, D. (1993). American family decline, 1960–1990: A review and appraisal. *Journal of Marriage and the Family, 55,* 527–555.

Posner, R. A. (1996). *Aging and old age.* Chicago: University of Chicago Press.

Post, S. G., Whitehouse, P. J., Binstock, R. H., et al. (1997). The clinical introduction of genetic testing for Alzheimer's disease: An ethical perspective. *Journal of the American Medical Association, 277,* 832–836.

Powell, R. R. (1974). Psychological effects of exercise therapy upon institutionalized geriatric mental patients. *Journal of Gerontology, 29,* 157–161.

Pratt, M. W., Golding, G., & Hunter, W. J. (1983). Aging as ripening: Character and consistency of moral judgment in young, mature, and older adults. *Human Development, 26,* 277–288.

Price, R. H. (1992). Psychosocial impact of job loss on individuals and families. *Current Directions in Psychological Science, 1,* 9–11.

Pyka, G., Lindenberger, E., Charette, S., & Marcus, R. (1994). Muscle strength and fiber adaptations to a year-long resistance training program in elderly men and women. *Journal of Gerontology: Medical Sciences, 49,* M22–M27.

Quinn, J. F., & Burkhauser, R. V. (1990). Work and retirement. In R. H. Binstock & L. K. George (Eds.), *Handbook of aging and the social sciences* (3rd ed., pp. 307–327). San Diego, CA: Academic Press.

Quinton, D., Pickles, A., Maughan, B., & Rutter, M. (1993). Partners, peers, and pathways: Assortive pairing and continuities in conduct disorder. *Development and Psychopathology, 5,* 763–783.

Rabinowitz, J. C. (1989). Age deficits in recall under optimal study conditions. *Psychology and Aging, 4,* 378–380.

Rahman, O., Strauss, J., Gertler, P., Ashley, D., & Fox, K. (1994). Gender differences in adult health: An international comparison. *The Gerontologist, 34,* 463–469.

Raj, B. A., Corvea, M. H., & Dagon, E. M. (1993). The clinical characteristics of panic disorder in the elderly: A retrospective study. *Journal of Clinical Psychiatry, 54,* 150–155.

Rakowski, W. (1988). Age cohorts and personal health behavior in adulthood. *Research on Aging, 10,* 3–35.

Ralston, P. A. (1997). Midlife and older black women. In J. M. Coyle (Ed.), *Handbook on women and aging* (pp. 273–289). Westport, CT: Greenwood Press.

Reed, G. M., Kemeny, M. E., Taylor, S. E., Wang, H. J., & Visscher, B. R. (1994). Realistic acceptance as a predictor of decreased survival time in gay men with AIDS. *Health Psychology, 13,* 299–307.

Reed, D., & Yano, K. (1997). Cardiovascular disease among elderly Asian Americans. In L. G. Martin & B. J. Soldo (Eds.), *Racial and ethnic differences in the health of older Americans* (pp. 270–284). Washington, DC: National Academy Press.

Reese, H. W., & Rodeheaver, D. (1985). Problem solving and complex decision making. In J. E. Mirren & K. W. Schaie (Eds.), *Handbook of the psychology of aging* (2nd ed., pp. 474–499). New York: Van Nostrand Reinhold.

Regier, D. A., Boyd, J. H., Burke, J. D., Rae, D. S., Myers, J. K., Kramer, M., Robins, L. N., George, L. K., Karno,

M., & Locke, B. Z. (1988). One-month prevalence of mental disorders in the United States. *Archives of General Psychiatry, 45,* 977–986.

Reich, J. W., Zautra, A. J., & Guarnaccia, C. A. (1989). Effects of disability and bereavement on the mental health and recovery of older adults. *Psychology and Aging, 4,* 57–65.

Reinke, B. J., Holmes, D. S., & Harris, R. L. (1985). The timing of psychosocial changes in women's lives: The years 25–45. *Journal of Personality and Social Psychology, 48,* 1353–1364.

Reisman, J. M. (1981). Adult friendships. In S. Duck & R. Gilmore (Eds.), *Personal relationships: 2. Developing personal relationships* (pp. 205–230). New York: Academic Press.

Reker, G. T. (1991). *Contextual and thematic analyses of sources of provisional meaning: A life-span perspective.* Paper presented at the biennial meeting of the International Society for the Study of Behavioral Development, Minneapolis, MN.

Reker, G. T., & Butler, B. B. (1990). *Personal meaning, stress, and health in older adults.* Paper presented at the annual meeting of the Canadian Association of Gerontology, Victoria, British Columbia, Canada.

Reker, G. T., & Wong, P. T. P. (1988). Aging as an individual process: Toward a theory of personal meaning. IN J. E. Birren & V. L. Bengtson (Eds.), *Emergent theories of aging* (pp. 214–246). New York: Springer.

Reskin, B. (1993). Sex segregation in the workplace. *Annual Review of Sociology, 19,* 241–270.

Rest, J. R., Davison, M. L., & Robbins, S. (1978). Age trends in judging moral issues: A review of cross-sectional, longitudinal, and sequential studies of the Defining Issues Test. *Child Development, 49,* 263–279.

Rest, J. R., & Thoma, S. J. (1985). Relation of moral judgment development to formal education. *Developmental Psychology, 21,* 709–714.

Rexroat, C. (1985). Women's work expectations and labor-market experience in early and middle family life-cycle stages. *Journal of Marriage and the Family, 49,* 131–142.

Rexroat, C., & Shehan, C. (1987). The family life cycle and spouses; time in housework. *Journal of Marriage and the Family, 49,* 737–750.

Reynolds, C. F., III, Hoch, C. C., Buysse, D. J., Houck, P. R., Schlernitzauer, M., Pasternak, R. E., Frank, E., Mazumdar, S., & Kupfer, D. J. (1993). Sleep after spousal bereavement: A study of recovery from stress. *Biological Psychiatry, 34,* 791–797.

Rhodes, S. R. (1983). Age-related differences in work attitudes and behavior: A review and conceptual analysis. *Psychological Bulletin, 93,* 329–367.

Richardson, J. L., Zarnegar, Z., Bisno, B., & Levine, A. (1990). Psychosocial status at initiation of cancer treatment and survival. *Journal of Psychosomatic Research, 34,* 189–201.

Richardson, V. & Kilty, K. M. (1991). Adjustment to retirement: Continuity vs. discontinuity. *International Journal of Aging and Human Development, 33*(2), 151-160.

Rifkind, B. M. & Rossouw, J. E. (1998). Of designer drugs, magic bullets, and gold standards. *Journal of the American Medical Association, 279,* 1483-1485.

Rikli, R., & Busch, S. (1986). Motor performance of women as a function of age and physical activity level. *Journal of Gerontology, 41,* 645–649.

Riley, M. W. (1976). Age strata in social systems. In R. H. Binstock & E. Shanas (Eds.), *Handbook of aging and the social sciences* (pp. 189–217). New York: Van Nostrand Reinhold.

Riley, M. W. (1983). The family in an aging society: A matrix of latent relationships. *Journal of Family Issues, 4,* 439–454.

Riley, M. W. (1986). Overview and highlights of a sociological perspective. In A. B. Sørensen, F. E. Weinert, & L. R. Sherrod (Eds.), *Human development and the life course: Multidisciplinary perspectives* (pp. 153–176). Hillsdale, NJ: Erlbaum.

Riley, M. W., & Foner, A. (1968). *Aging and society: Vol. I. An inventory of research findings.* New York: Russell Sage Foundation.

Rindfuss, R. R. (1991). The young adult years: Diversity, structural change, and fertility. *Demography, 28,* 493–512.

Ritchie, R. J., & Moses, J. L. (1983). Assessment center correlates of women's advancement into middle management: A 7-year longitudinal analysis. *Journal of Applied Psychology, 68,* 227–231.

Roberts, P., & Newton, P. M. (1987). Levinsonian studies of women's adult development. *Psychology and Aging, 2,* 154–163.

Rodin, J. (1986). Aging and health: Effects of the sense of control. *Science, 233,* 1271–1275.

Rodin, J. (1990). Control by any other name: Definitions, concepts, and processes. In J. Rodin, C. Schooler, & K. W. Schaie (Eds.), *Self-directedness: Cause and effects throughout the life course* (pp. 1–17). Hillsdale, NJ: Erlbaum.

Rodin, J., & Langer, E. J. (1977). Long-term effects of a control-relevant intervention with the institutionalized aged. *Journal of Personality and Social Psychology, 35,* 897–902.

Rogers, R. G. (1991). Health related lifestyles among Mexican-Americans, Puerto Ricans, and Cubans in the United States. In I. Rosenwaike (Ed.), *Mortality of Hispanic populations* (pp. 145–167). New York: Greenwood Press.

Rogers, R. L., Meyer, J. S., & Mortel, K. F. (1990). After reaching retirement age physical activity sustains cerebral perfusion and cognition. *Journal of the American Geriatric Society, 38,* 123–128.

Rollins, B. C., & Feldman, H. (1970). Marital satisfaction over the family life cycle. *Journal of Marriage and the Family, 32,* 20–27.

Rollins, B. C., & Galligan, R. (1978). The developing child and marital satisfaction of parents. In R. M. Lerner & G. M. Spanier (Eds.), *Child influences on marital and family interaction: A life-span perspective* (pp. 71–106). New York: Academic Press.

Roosa, M. W. (1988). The effect of age in the transition to parenthood: Are delayed childbearers a unique group? *Family Relations, 37,* 322–327.

Rose, D. P. (1993). Diet, hormones, and cancer. *Annual Review of Public Health, 14,* 1–17.

Rosenbaum, J. E. (1984). *Career mobility in a corporate hierarchy.* New York: Academic Press.

Rosenfeld, A., & Stark, E. (1987, May). The prime of our lives. *Psychology Today, 21*(5), 62–72.

Rosengren, A., Orth-Gomér, K., Wedel, H., & Wilhelmsen, L. (1993). Stressful life events, social support, and mortality in men born in 1933. *British Medical Journal, 307,* 1102–1105.

Rosenman, R. H., & Friedman, M. (1983). Relationship of Type A behavior pattern to coronary heart disease. In H. Selye (Ed.), *Selye's guide to stress research* (Vol. 2, pp. 47–106). New York: Scientific and Academic Editions.

Rosenthal, C. J. (1985). Kinkeeping in the familial division of labor. *Journal of Marriage and the Family, 49,* 965–974.

Rosow, I. (1985). Status and role change through the life cycle. In R. H. Binstock & E. Shanas (Eds.), *Handbook of aging and the social sciences* (2nd ed., pp. 62–93). New York: Van Nostrand Reinhold.

Rossi, A. S. (1989). A life-course approach to gender, aging, and intergenerational relations. In K. W. Schaie & C. Schooler (Eds.), *Social structure and aging: Psychological processes* (pp. 207–236). Hillsdale, NJ: Erlbaum.

Rossman, I. (1980). Bodily changes with aging. In E. W. Busse & D. G. Blazer (Eds.), *Handbook of geriatric psychiatry* (pp. 125–146). New York: Van Nostrand Reinhold.

Rotter, J. B. (1966). Generalized expectancies for internal versus external control of reinforcement. *Psychological Monographs, 80* (1, Whole No. 609).

Rowe, J. W. (1997, October 17). The new gerontology. *Science, 278.* 367.

Rowe, J. W., & Kahn, R. L. (1998). *Successful aging.* New York: Pantheon.

Rowe, J. W., Wang, S. Y., & Elahi, D. (1990). Design, conduct, and analysis of human aging research. In E. R. Schneider & J. W. Rowe (Eds.), *Handbook of the biology of aging* (3rd ed., pp. 63–71). San Diego, CA: Academic Press.

Rubin, Z. (1973). *Liking and loving: An invitation to social psychology.* New York: Holt, Rinehart & Winston.

Rubinstein, R. L., Alexander, B. B., Goodman, M., & Luborsky, M. (1991). Key relationships of never married childless older women: A cultural analysis. *Journal of Gerontology: Social Sciences, 46,* S270–S277.

Rudinger, G., & Thomae, H. (1990). The Bonn Longitudinal Study of Aging: Coping, life adjustment, and life satisfaction. In P. B. Baltes & M. M. Baltes (Eds.), *Successful aging: Perspectives from the behavioral sciences* (pp. 265–295). Cambridge, England: Cambridge University Press.

Ryff, C. D. (1982). Self-perceived personality change in adulthood and aging. *Journal of Personality and Social Psychology, 42,* 108–115.

Ryff, C. D. (1984). Personality development from the inside: The subjective experience of change in adulthood and aging. In P. B. Baltes & O. G. Brim, Jr. (Eds.), *Life-span development and behavior* (Vol. 6, pp. 244–281). Orlando, FL: Academic Press.

Ryff, C. D. (1989). In the eye of the beholder: Views of psychological well-being among middle-aged and older adults. *Psychology and Aging, 4,* 195–210.

Ryff, C. D., & Baltes, P. B. (1976). Value transition and adult development in women: The instrumentality-terminality sequence hypothesis. *Developmental Psychology, 12,* 567–568.

Ryff, C. D., & Heincke, S. G. (1983). The subjective organization of personality in adulthood and aging. *Journal of Personality and Social Psychology, 44,* 807–816.

Ryff, C. D., Schmutte, P. S., & Lee, Y. H. (1996). How children turn out: Implications for parental self-evaluation. In C. D. Ryff & M. M. Seltzer (Eds.), *The parental experience in midlife* (pp. 383–422). Chicago: University of Chicago Press.

Salthouse, T. A. (1984). Effects of age and skill in typing. *Journal of Experimental Psychology: General, 113,* 345–371.

Salthouse, T. A. (1991). *Theoretical perspectives on cognitive aging.* Hillsdale, NJ: Erlbaum.

Salthouse, T. A. (1994). The nature of the influence of speed on adult age differences in cognition. *Developmental Psychology, 30,* 240–259.

Salthouse, T. A., & Babcock, R. L. (1991). Decomposing adult age differences in working memory. *Developmental Psychology, 27,* 763–776.

Salthouse, T. A., Kausler, D., & Saults, J. S. (1988). Investigation of student status, background variables, and feasibility of standard tasks in cognitive aging research. *Psychology and Aging, 3,* 29–37.

Salthouse, T. A., & Maurer, T. J. (1996). Aging, job performance, and career development. In J. E. Birren & K. W. Schaie (Eds.), *Handbook of the psychology of aging* (4th ed., pp. 353–364). San Diego: Academic Press.

Saluter, A. F. (1992). Marital status and living arrangements: March 1991. In *Current Population Reports, Population Characteristics* (Series P-20, No. 461). Washington, DC: U.S. Government Printing Office.

Sammartino, F. J. (1987). The effect of health on retirement. *Social Security Bulletin, 50*(2), 31–47.

Sanders, C. M. (1989). *Grief: The mourning after.* New York: Wiley-Interscience.

Sanders, C. M. (1993). Risk factors in bereavement outcome. In M. S. Stroebe, W. Stroebe, & R. O. Hansson (Eds.), *Handbook of bereavement: Theory, research, and intervention* (pp. 255–267). Cambridge, England: Cambridge University Press.

Sands, L. P., Terry, H., & Meredith, W. (1989). Change and stability in adult intellectual functioning assessed by Wechsler item responses. *Psychology and Aging, 4,* 79–87.

Sangiuliano, I. (1978). *In her time.* New York: William Morrow.

Sarason, B. R., Sarason, I. G., & Pierce, G. R. (1990). Traditional views of social support and their impact on assessment. In B. R. Sarason, I. G. Sarason, & G. R. Pierce (Eds.), *Social support: An interactional view* (pp. 9–25). New York: Wiley.

Sarton, M. (1993). *Encore: Journal of the 80th year.* New York: Norton.

Savage, R. D., Gaber, L. B., Britton, P. B., Bolton, N., & Cooper, A. (1977). *Personality and adjustment in the aged.* London: Academic Press.

Schafer, R. B., & Keith, P. M. (1984). A causal analysis of the relationship between the self-concept and marital quality. *Journal of Marriage and the Family, 46,* 909–914.

Schaie, K. W. (1983a). What can we learn from the longitudinal study of adult psychological development? In K. W. Schaie (Ed.), *Longitudinal studies of adult psychological development* (pp. 1–19). New York: Guilford Press.

Schaie, K. W. (1983b). The Seattle longitudinal study: A 21-year exploration of psychometric intelligence in adulthood. In K. W. Schaie (Ed.), *Longitudinal studies of adult psychological development* (pp. 64–135). New York: Guilford Press.

Schaie, K. W. (Ed.). (1983c). *Annual review of gerontology and geriatrics.* New York: Springer.

Schaie, K. W. (1989a). The hazards of cognitive aging. *Gerontologist, 29,* 484–493.

Schaie, K. W. (1989b). Individual differences in rate of cognitive change in adulthood. In V. L. Bengtson & K. W. Schaie (Eds.), *The course of later life: Research and reflections* (pp. 65–86). New York: Springer.

Schaie, K. W. (1993). The Seattle Longitudinal Studies of adult intelligence. *Current directions in Psychological Science, 2,* 171–175.

Schaie, K. W. (1994). The course of adult intellectual development. *American Psychologist, 49,* 304–313.

Schaie, K. W. (1995). Perceptual speed in adulthood: Cross sectional and longitudinal studies. *Psychology and Aging, 4,* 443–453.

Schaie, K. W. (1996). Intellectual development in adulthood. In J. E. Birren & W. K. Schaie (Eds.), *Handbook of the psychology of aging (4th ed.,* pp. 265–286). San Diego, CA: Academic Press.

Schaie, K. W., & Hertzog, C. (1983). Fourteen year cohort sequential analyses of adult intellectual development. *Developmental Psychology, 19,* 531–543.

Schaie, K. W., & Parham, I. A. (1976). Stability of adult personality traits: Fact or fable? *Journal of Personality and Social Psychology, 34,* 146–158.

Schaie, K. W., & Willis, S. L. (1986). Can decline in adult intellectual functioning be reversed? *Developmental Psychology, 22,* 223–232.

Schaie, K. W., & Willis, S. L. (1996). *Adult development and aging, 4th ed.* New York: HarperCollins.

Scharlach, A. E., & Fredricksen, K. I. (1994). Eldercare versus adult care: Does care recipient age make a difference? *Research on Aging, 16,* 43–68.

Scheibel, A. B. (1992). Structural changes in the aging brain. In J. E. Birren, R. B. Sloane, & G. D. Cohen (Eds.), *Handbook of mental health and aging* (pp. 147–174). San Diego, CA: Academic Press.

Scheier, M. F., Matthews, K. A., Owens, J. F., Magovern, G. J., Lefebvre, S., Abbott, R. A., & Carver, C. S. (1989). Dispositional optimism and recovery from coronary artery bypass surgery: The beneficial effects on physical and psychological well being. *Journal of Personality and Social Psychology, 57,* 1024–1040.

Schieber, F. (1992). Aging and the senses. In J. E. Birren, R. B. Sloane, & G. D. Cohen (Eds.), *Handbook of mental health and aging* (2nd ed., pp. 252–306). San Diego, CA: Academic Press.

Schneider, E. L., & Guralnik, J. M. (1990). The aging of America: Impact on health care costs. *Journal of the American Medical Association, 263,* 2335–2340.

Schoen, R. (1992). First unions and the stability of first marriages. *Journal of Marriage and the Family, 54,* 281–284.

Schoen, R., & Wooldredge, J. (1989). Marriage choices in North Carolina and Virginia, 1969–71 and 1979–81. *Journal of Marriage and the Family, 51,* 465–481.

Schoenfeld, D. E., Malmrose, L. C., Blazer, D. G., Gold, D. T., & Seeman, T. E. (1994). Self-rated health and mortality in the high-functioning elderly—a closer look at healthy individuals: MacArthur field study of successful aging. *Journal of Gerontology: Medical Sciences, 49,* M109–M115.

Schooler, C. (1984). Psychological effects of complex environments during the life span: A review and theory. *Intelligence, 8,* 259–281.

Schooler, C. (1990). Psychosocial factors and effective cognitive functioning in adulthood. In J. E. Birren & K. W. Schaie (Eds.), *Handbook of the psychology of aging* (3rd cd., pp. 347–358). San Diego, CA: Academic Press.

Schramke, C. J. (1997). Anxiety disorders. In P. D. Nussbaum (Ed.), *Handbook of neuropsychology and aging* (pp. 80–97). New York: Plenum Press.

Schreiber, L. (1990). *Midstream.* New York: Viking.

Schulenberg, J., Goldstein, A. E., & Vondracek, F. W. (1991). Gender differences in adolescents' career interests: Beyond main effects. *Journal of Research in Adolescence, 1,* 37–61.

Schultz, N. R., Jr. Elias, M. F., Robbins, M. A., Streeten, D. H. P., & Blakeman, N. (1986). A longitudinal comparison of hypertensives and normotensives on the Wechsler Adult Intelligence Scale: Initial findings. *Journal of Gerontology, 11,* 169 175.

Schulz-Aellen, M. (1997). *Aging and human longevity.* Boston: Birkhauser.

Schulz, R., & Curnow, C. (1988). Peak performance and age among superathletes: Track and field, swimming, baseball, tennis, and golf. *Journal of Gerontology: Psychological Sciences, 43,* P113–P120.

Schulz, R., Musa, D., Staszewski, J., & Siegler, R. S. (1994). The relationship between age and major league baseball performance: Implications for development. *Psychology and Aging, 9,* 274–286.

Schulz, R., Visintainer, P., & Williamson, G. M. (1990). Psychiatric and physical morbidity effects of caregiving. *Journal of Gerontology: Psychological Sciences, 45,* P181–P191.

Schulz, R., & Williamson, G. M. (1991). A 2-year longitudinal study of depression among Alzheimer's caregivers. *Psychology and Aging, 6,* 569–578.

Schwartz, P. (1994). *Peer marriage: How love between equals really works.* New York: Free Press.

Scott, J. P. (1997). Family relationships in midlife and older women. In J. M. Coyle (Ed.). (pp. 367-384) *Handbook on women and aging.* Westport, CN: Greenwood Press.

Sears, R. R. (1977). Sources of life satisfactions of the Terman gifted men. *American Psychologist, 32,* 119–128.

Seccombe, K. (1986). The effects of occupational conditions upon the division of household labor: An application of Kohn's theory. *Journal of Marriage and the Family, 48,* 839–848.

Seccombe, K. (1987). Children: Their impact on the elderly in declining health. *Research on Aging, 9,* 312–326.

Seiden, A. (1980). Time management and the dual-career couple. In F. Pepitone-Rockwell (Ed.), *Dual-career couples* (pp. 163–190). Beverly Hills, CA: Sage.

Seligman, M. E. P. (1991). *Learned optimism.* New York: Knopf.

Selkoe, D. J. (1997, January 31). Alzheimer's disease: Genotypes, phenotypes, and treatments. *Science, 275,* 630–631.

Selye, H. (1936). A syndrome produced by diverse nocuous agents. *Nature (London), 138,* 32.

Selye, H. (1976). *The stress of life* (rev. ed.). New York: McGraw-Hill.

Selye, H. (1982). History and present status of the stress concept. In L. Goldberger & S. Breznitz (Eds.), *Handbook of stress: Theoretical and clinical aspects* (pp. 7–20). New York: Free Press.

Senchak, M., & Leonard, K. E. (1992). Attachment styles and marital adjustment among newlywed couples. *Journal of Social and Personal Relationships, 9,* 51–64.

Shackelford, T. K., & Buss, D. M. (1997). Marital satisfaction in evolutionary psychological perspective. In R. J. Sternberg & M. Hojjat (Eds.), *Satisfaction in close relationships* (pp. 7–25). New York: Guilford Press.

Shapiro, E. (1983). Impending death and the use of hospitals by the elderly. *Journal of the American Geriatric Society, 31,* 348–351.

Shapiro, G. L., & Farrow, D. L. (1988). Mentors and others in career development. In S. Rose & L. Larwood (Eds.), *Women's careers: Pathways and pitfalls* (pp. 25–40). New York: Praeger.

Sheehy, G. (1996). New passages: Mapping your life across time. New York: Ballantine.

Sheehy, G. (1974). *Passages.* New York: Dutton.

Shelton, B. A. (1990). The distribution of household tasks: Does wife's employment status make a difference? *Journal of Family Issues, 11,* 115–35.

Shelton, B. A., & John D. (1993). Ethnicity, race, and difference: A comparison of White, Black, and Hispanic men's household labor time. In J. C. Hood (Ed.), *Men, work, and family* (pp. 131–150). Newbury Park, CA: Sage.

Shimamura, A. P., Berry, J. M., Mangels, J. A., Rusting, C. L., & Jurica, P. J. (1995). Memory and cognitive abilities in university professors: Evidence for successful aging. *Psychological Science, 6*(5), 271–277.

Shimokata, H., Tobin, J. D., Muller, D. C., Elahi, D., Coon, P. J., & Andres, R. (1989). Studies in the distribution of body fat: I. Effects of age, sex, and obesity. *Journal of Gerontology: Medical Sciences, 44,* M66–M73.

Shipley, M. J., Pocock, S. J., & Marmot, M. G. (1991). Does plasma cholesterol concentration predict morality from coronary heart disease in elderly people? 18 year follow up in Whitehall study. *British Medical Journal, 303,* 89–92.

Shneidman, E. S. (1980). *Voices of death.* New York: Harper & Row.

Shneidman, E. S. (1983). *Deaths of man.* New York: Jason Aronson.

Shneidman, E. S. (1989). The indian summer of life: A preliminary study of septuagenarians. *American Psychologist, 44,* 684–694.

Shock, N. W. (1985). Longitudinal studies of aging in humans. In C. E. Finch & E. L. Schneider (Eds.), *Handbook of the biology of aging* (2nd ed., pp. 721–743). New York: Van Nostrand Reinhold.

Shumaker, S. A., & Smith, T. R. (1995). Women and coronary heart disease: A psychological perspective. In A. L. Stanton & S. J. Gallant (Eds.), *The psychology of women's health: Progress and challenges in research and application* (pp. 25–50). Washington, DC: American Psychological Association.

Siegel, J. M. (1992). Anger and cardiovascular health. In H. S. Friedman (Ed.), *Hostility, coping and health* (pp. 49–64). Washington, DC: American Psychological Association.

Siegler, I. C. (1983). Psychological aspects of the Duke Longitudinal Studies. In K. W. Schaie (Ed.), *Longitudinal studies of adult psychological development* (pp. 136–190). New York: Guilford Press.

Siegler, I. C., George, L. K., & Okun, M. A. (1979). Cross-sequential analysis of adult personality. *Developmental Psychology, 15,* 350–351.

Siegler, I. C., McCarty, S. M., & Logue, P. E. (1982). Wechsler memory scale scores, selective attrition, and distance from death. *Journal of Gerontology, 37,* 176–181.

Simonton, D. K. (1989). The swan-song phenomenon: Last-works effects for 172 classical composers. *Psychology and Aging, 4,* 42–47.

Simonton, D. K. (1991). Career landmarks in science: Individual differences and interdisciplinary contrasts. *Developmental Psychology, 27,* 119–130.

Simpson, J. A. (1990). Influence of attachment styles on romantic relationships. *Journal of Personality and Social Psychology, 59,* 971–980.

Simpson, J. A., Rholes, W. S., & Nelligan, J. S. (1992). Support seeking and support giving within couples in an anxiety-provoking situation: The role of attachment styles. *Journal of Personality and Social Psychology, 62,* 434–446.

Sinnott, J. D. (1986). Prospective/intentional and incidental every day memory: Effects of age and passage of time. *Psychology and Aging, 1,* 110–116.

Sinnott, J. D. (1994). Development and yearning: Cognitive aspects of spiritual development. *Journal of Adult Development, 1,* 91–99.

Skolnick, A. (1981). Married lives: Longitudinal perspectives on marriage. In D. H. Eichorn, J. A. Clausen, N. Haan, M. P. Honzik, & P. H. Mussen (Eds.), *Present and past in middle life* (pp. 270–300). New York: Academic Press.

Small, G. W., Rabins, P. V., Barry, P. P., Buckholtz, N. S., DeKosky, S. T., Ferris, S. H., Finkel, S. I., Gwyther, L. P., Khachaturian, Z. S., Lebowitz, B. D., McRae, T. D., Morris, J. C., Oakley, F., Schneider, L. S., Streim, J. E., Sunderland, T., Teri, L. A., & Tune, L. E. (1997). Diagnosis and treatment of Alzheimer's disease and related disorders: Consensus statement of the American Association for Geriatric Psychiatry, the Alzheimer's Association, and the American Geriatrics Society. *Journal of the American Medical Association, 278,* 1363–1371.

Smeeding, T. M. (1990). Economic status of the elderly. In R. H. Binstock & L. K. George (Eds.), *Handbook of aging and the social sciences* (3rd ed., pp. 362–381). San Diego, CA: Academic Press.

Smelser, N. J., & Erikson, E. H. (Eds.). (1980). *Themes of work and love in adulthood.* Cambridge, MA: Harvard University Press.

Smetana, J. G., Killen, M., & Turiel, E. (1991). Children's reasoning about interpersonal and moral conflicts. *Child Development, 62,* 629–644.

Smith, A. D. (1996). Memory. In J. E. Birren & W. K. Schaie (Eds.), *Handbook of the psychology of aging (4th ed.,* pp. 236–250). San Diego, CA: Academic Press.

Smith, J., & Baltes, P. B. (1990). A study of wisdom-related knowledge: Age/cohort differences in responding to life planning problems. *Developmental Psychology, 26,* 494–505.

Smith, J. P., & Kington, R. S. (1997). Race, socioeconomic status, and health in late life. In L. G. Martin & B. J. Soldo (Eds.), *Racial and ethnic differences in the health of older Americans* (pp. 105–162). Washington, DC: National Academy Press.

Smock, P. J. (1993). The economic costs of marital disruption for young women over the past two decades. *Demography, 30,* 353–371.

Snarey, J. R. (1985). Cross-cultural universality of social-moral development: A critical review of Kohlbergian research. *Psychological Bulletin, 97,* 202–232.

Snarey, J. R., Reimer, J., & Kohlberg, L. (1985). Development of social-moral reasoning among kibbutz adolescents: A longitudinal cross-sectional study. *Developmental Psychology, 21,* 3–17.

Snarey, J. R., Son, L., Kuehne, V. S., Hauser, S., & Vaillant, G. (1987). The role of parenting in men's psychosocial development: A longitudinal study of early adulthood infertility and midlife generativity. *Developmental Psychology, 23,* 593–603.

Social Security Administration. (1997). *Fast facts and figures about Social Security.* Washington, DC: U.S. Government Printing Office.

Solano, L., Costa, M., Salvati, S., Coda, R., Aiuti, F., Mezzaroma, I., & Bertini, M. (1993). Psychosocial factors and clinical evolution in HIV-1 infection: A longitudinal study. *Journal of Psychosomatic Research, 37,* 39–51.

Somers, M. D. (1993). A comparison of voluntarily child-free adults and parents. *Journal of Marriage and the Family, 55,* 643–650.

Sørensen, A. (1983). Women's employment patterns after marriage. *Journal of Marriage and the Family, 45,* 311–321.

South, S. J. (1991). Sociodemographic differentials in mate selection preferences. *Journal of Marriage and the Family, 53,* 928–940.

Spanier, G. B., & Furstenberg, F. F., Jr. (1987). Remarriage and reconstituted families. In M. B. Sussman & S. K. Steinmetz (Eds.), *Handbook of marriage and the family* (pp. 419–434). New York: Plenum Press.

Speece, M. W., & Brent, S. B. (1984). Children's understanding of death: A review of three components of a death concept. *Child Development, 55,* 1671–1686.

Speece, M. W., & Brent, S. B. (1992). The acquisition of a mature understanding of three components of the concept of death. *Death Studies, 16,* 211–229.

Spenner, K. I. (1988). Occupations, work settings and the course of adult development: Tracing the implications of select historical changes. In P. B. Baltes, D. L. Featherman, & R. M. Lerner (Eds.), *Life-span development and behavior* (Vol. 9, pp. 244–288). Hillsdale, NJ: Erlbaum.

Spiegel, D., Bloom, J. R., Kraemer, H. C., & Gottheil, E. (1989, November 18). Effect of psychosocial treatment on survival of patients with metastatic breast cancer. *Lancet, 2,* 888–901.

Spirduso, W. W. (1995). *Physical dimensions of aging.* Champaign, IL: Human Kinetics.

Spitze, G. (1988). Women's employment and family relations: A review. *Journal of Marriage and the Family, 50,* 595–618.

Spitze, G., & Logan, J. (1990). More evidence on women (and men) in the middle. *Research on Aging, 12,* 182–198.

Stack, S. (1992a). The effect of divorce on suicide in Japan: A time series analysis, 1950–1980. *Journal of Marriage and the Family, 54,* 327–334.

Stack, S. (1992b). The effect of divorce on suicide in Finland: A time series analysis. *Journal of Marriage and the Family, 54,* 636–642.

Stack, S., & Wasserman, I. (1993). Marital status, alcohol consumption, and suicide: An analysis of national data. *Journal of Marriage and the Family, 55,* 1018–1024.

Staffa, J. A., Newschaffer, C. J., Jones, J. K., & Miller, V. (1992). Progestins and breast cancer: An epidemiologic review. *Fertility and Sterility, 57,* 473–491.

Stallings, M. C., Dunham, C. C., Gatz, M., Baker, L. A., & Bengtson, V. L. (1997). Relationships among life events and well-being: More evidence for a two-factor theory of psychological well-being. *Journal of Applied Gerontology, 16*(1), 104–119.

Stampfer, M., & Colditz, G. (1991). Estrogen replacement therapy and coronary heart disease: A quantitative assessment of the epidemiologic evidence. *Preventive Medicine, 20,* 47–63.

Stanford, E. P., Happersett, C. J., Morton, D. J., Molgaard, C. A., & Peddecord, K. M. (1991). Early retirement and functional impairment from a multiethnic perspective. *Research on Aging, 13,* 5–38.

Stanford, P., & Du Bois, B. C. (1992). Gender and ethnicity patterns. In J. E. Birren, R. B. Sloane, & G. D. Cohen (Eds.), *Handbook of mental health and aging* (pp. 99–119). San Diego, CA: Academic Press.

Stanley, S. C., Hunt, J. G., & Hunt, L. L. (1986). The relative deprivation of husbands in dual-earner households. *Journal of Family Issues, 7,* 3–20.

Stanovich, K. E. (1998). *How to think straight about psychology.* Reading, MA: Addison-Wesley.

Stanovich, K. E., West, R. F., & Harrison, M. R. (1995). Knowledge growth and maintenance across the life span: The role of print exposure. *Developmental Psychology, 31*(5), 811–826.

Steen, B., & Djurfeldt, H. (1993). The gerontological and geriatric population studies in Gothenburg, Sweden. *Zeitschrift für Gerontologie, 26,* 163–169.

Steinbach, U. (1992). Social networks, institutionalization, and mortality among elderly people in the United States. *Journal of Gerontology: Social Sciences, 47,* S183–S190.

Steindl-Rast, B. D. (1977). Learning to die. *Parabola, 2,* 22–31.

Stephen, E. H., Foote, K., Hendershot, G. E., & Schoenborn, C. A. (1994). Health of the foreign born population: United States, 1989–90: Advance data. *Vital and Health Statistics, 241.*

Stephens, M. A. D., Franks, M. M., & Townsend, A. C. (1994). Stress and rewards in women with multiple roles: The case of women in the middle. *Psychology and Aging, 9*(1), 45-51.

Stephens, M. A. P., & Townsend, A. L. (1997). Stress of parent care: Positive and negative effects of women's other roles. *Psychology of Aging, 12*(2), 376–386.

Stern, Y., Tang, M-X, Albert, M., et al. (1997). Predicting time to nursing home care and death in individuals with Alzheimer disease. *Journal of the American Medical Association, 277,* 806–812.

Sternberg, R. J. (1986). A triangular theory of love. *Psychological Review, 93,* 119–135.

Sternberg, R. J. (1987). Liking versus loving: A comparative evaluation of theories. *Psychological Bulletin, 102,* 331–345.

Sternberg, R. J. (Ed.). (1990a). *Wisdom: Its nature, origins, and development.* Cambridge, England: Cambridge University Press.

Sternberg, R. J. (1990b). Wisdom and its relations to intelligence and creativity. In R. J. Sternberg (Ed.), *Wisdom: Its nature, origins, and development* (pp. 142–159). Cambridge, England: Cambridge University Press.

Sternberg, R., & Hojjat, M. (1997). *Satisfaction in close relationships.* New York: Guilford Press.

Stevens, D. P., & Truss, C. V. (1985). Stability and change in adult personality over 12 and 20 years. *Developmental Psychology, 21,* 568–584.

Stevens, G. (1986). Sex-differentiated patterns of intergenerational occupational mobility. *Journal of Marriage and the Family, 48,* 153–163.

Stevens, J., et al. (1998). The effect of age on the association between body-mass index and mortality. *New England Journal of Medicine, 338*(1), 1–7.

Stevens-Ratchford, R. G. (1993). The effect of life review reminiscence activities on depression and self esteem in older adults. *American Journal of Occupational Therapy, 47,* 413–420.

Stewart, A. J., & Healy, J. M., Jr. (1989). Linking individual development and social change. *American Psychologist, 44,* 30–44.

Stiel, J. M. (1994). Equality and entitlement in marriage. In M. Lerner & G. Mikula (Eds.), *Entitlement and the affectional bond: Justice in close relationships,* (pp. 229-258). New York: Plenum,

Stigsdotter, N. A., & Bäckman, L. (1993). Long-term maintenance of gains from memory training in older adults: Two 3 1/2 year follow-up studies. *Journal of Gerontology: Psychological Sciences, 48,* P233–P237.

Stigsdotter, N. A., & Bäckman, L. (1995). Effects of multifactorial memory training in old age: Generalizability across tasks and individuals. *Journal of Gerontology: Psychological Sciences, 50B,* P134–P140.

Stigsdotter, A., & Bäckman, L. (1989). Comparison of different forms of memory training in old age. In M. A.

Luszca & T. Nettelbeck (Eds.) *Psychological development: Perspectives across the life span.* Amsterdam, The Netherlands: Elsevier.

Stinner, W. F., Byun, Y., & Paita, L. (1990). Disability and living arrangements among elderly American men. *Research on Aging, 12,* 339–363.

Stock, W. A., Okun, M. A., Haring, M. J., & Witter, R. A. (1983). Age and subjective well-being: A meta-analysis. In R. J. Light (Ed.), *Evaluation studies: Review annual* (Vol. 8, pp. 279–302). Beverly Hills, CA: Sage.

Stoller, E. P., Forster, L. E., & Duniho, T. S. (1992). Systems of parent care within sibling networks. *Research on Aging, 14,* 28–49.

Strawbridge, W. J., Camacho, T. C., Cohen, R. D., & Kaplan, G. A. (1993). Gender differences in factors associated with change in physical functioning in old age: A 6-year longitudinal study. *The Gerontologist, 33,* 603–609.

Strickland, B. R. (1992). Women and depression. *Current Directions in Psychological Science, 1,* 132–135.

Stroebe, M. S., Stroebe, W., & Hansson, R. O. (Eds.). (1993). *Handbook of bereavement: Theory, research, and intervention.* Cambridge, England: Cambridge University Press.

Stroebe, W., & Stroebe, M. S. (1986). Beyond marriage: The impact of partner loss on health. In R. Gilmour & S. Duck (Eds.), *The emerging field of personal relationships* (pp. 203–224). Hillsdale, NJ: Erlbaum.

Stroebe, W., & Stroebe, M. S. (1993). Determinants of adjustment to bereavement in younger widows and widowers. In M. S. Stroebe, W. Stroebe, & R. O. Hansson (Eds.), *Handbook of bereavement: Theory, research, and intervention* (pp. 208–226). Cambridge, England: Cambridge University Press.

Stroud, J. G. (1981). Women's careers: Work, family, and personality. In D. H. Eichorn, J. A. Clausen, N. Haan, M. P. Honzik, & P. H. Mussen (Eds.), *Present and past in midlife* (pp. 356–392). New York: Academic Press.

St. Teresa of Avila (1960). *The life of Teresa of Jesus* (E. Allison Peers, Trans.). Garden City, NY: Image Books. (Original work 1562)

St. Teresa of Avila (1960). *Interior castle* (E. Allison Peers, Trans.). New York: Image Books. (Original work 1577)

Sugisawa, H., Liang, J., & Liu, X. (1994). Social networks, social support, and mortality among older people in Japan. *Journal of Gerontology: Social Sciences, 49,* S3–S13.

Sullivan, E. V., McCullough, G., & Stager, M. (1970). A developmental study of the relationship between conceptual, ego, and moral development. *Child Development, 41,* 399–411.

Super, D. E. (1957). *The psychology of careers.* New York: Harper & Row.

Super, D. E. (1971). A theory of vocational development. In H. J. Peters & J. C. Hansen (Eds.), *Vocational guidance and career development* (pp. 111–122). New York: Macmillan.

Super, D. E. (1985). Coming of age in Middletown: Careers in the making. *American Psychologist, 40,* 405–414.

Super, D. E. (1986). Life career roles: Self-realization in work and leisure. In D. T. Hall & Associates (Eds.), *Career development in organizations* (pp. 95–119). San Francisco: Jossey-Bass.

Surra, C. A. (1985). Courtship types: Variations in interdependence between partners and social networks. *Journal of Personality and Social Psychology, 56,* 357–375.

Surra, C. A. (1990). Research and theory on mate selection and premarital relationships in the 1980s. *Journal of Marriage and the Family, 52,* 844–865.

Swensen, C. H., Eskew, R. W., & Kohlhepp, K. A. (1981). Stage of family life cycle, ego development, and the marriage relationship. *Journal of Marriage and the Family, 43,* 841–853.

Syme, S. L. (1990). Control and health: An epidemiological perspective. In J. Rodin, C. Schooler, & K. W. Schaie (Eds.), *Self directedness: Cause and effects throughout the life course* (pp. 213–229). Hillsdale, NJ: Erlbaum.

Szubivacz, M. (1991). Women and retirement. In B. B. Hess & E. W. Markson (Eds.), *Growing old in America* (pp. 293–303). New Brunswick, NJ: Transaction Publishers.

Tait, M., Padgett, M. Y., & Baldwin, T. T. (1989). Job and life satisfaction: A reevaluation of the strength of the relationship and gender effects as a function of the date of the study. *Journal of Applied Psychology, 74,* 502–507.

Tamir, L. M. (1982). *Men in their forties: The transition to middle age.* New York: Springer.

Tamir, L. M. (1989). Modern myths about men at midlife: An assessment. In S. Hunter & M. Sundel (Eds.), *Midlife myths: Issues, findings, and practice implications* (pp. 157–179). Newbury Park, CA: Sage.

Tang, M. X., Stern, Y., Marder, K., Bell, K., Gurland, B., Lantigua, R., Andrews, H., Feng, L., Tycko, B., Mayeux, R. (1998). The APOE-E4 allele and the risk of Alzheimer disease among African Americans, whites, and hispanics. *Journal of the American Medical Association, 279,* 751-755.

Taylor, J. L., Yesavage, J. A., Morrow, D. G., Dolhert, N., Brooks, J. O. I., & Poon, L. W. (1994). The effects of information load and speech rate on younger and older aircraft pilots' ability to execute simulated air-traffic controller instructions. *Journal of Gerontology: Psychological Sciences, 49,* P191–P200.

Taylor, R. J., Chatters, L. M., & Jackson, J. S. (1993). A profile of familial relations among three-generation black families. *Family Relations, 42,* 332–341.

Taylor, R. J., Chatters, L. M., Tucker, M. B., & Lewis, E. (1990). Developments in research on black families: A decade review. *Journal of Marriage and the Family, 52,* 993–1014.

Taylor, R. L. (1997). Who's parenting? Trends and patterns. In T. Arendell, (Ed.), *Contemporary parenting: Challenges and issues* (pp. 68–91). Thousand Oaks, CA: Sage.

Temoshok, L. (1987). Personality, coping style, emotion and cancer: Towards an integrative model. *Cancer Surveys, 6,* 545–567.

Tennov, D. (1979). *Love and limerance.* New York: Stein & Day.

Terkel, S. (1972). *Working.* New York: Avon.

Teti, D. M., Lamb, M. E., & Elster, A. B. (1987). Long-range socioeconomic and marital consequences of adolescent marriage in three cohorts of adult males. *Journal of Marriage and the Family, 49,* 499–506.

Thompson, L., & Walker, A. J. (1984). Mothers and daughters: Aid patterns and attachment. *Journal of Marriage and the Family, 46,* 313–322.

Thornton, A., Young-DeMarco, L., & Goldscheider, F. (1993). Leaving the parental nest: The experience of a young white cohort in the 1980s. *Journal of Marriage and the Family, 55,* 216–229.

Thorslund, M., & Lundberg, O. (1994). Health and inequalities among the oldest old. *Journal of Aging and Health, 6,* 51–69.

Thorson, J. A., & Powell, F. C. (1990). Meanings of death and intrinsic religiosity. *Journal of Clinical Psychology, 46,* 379–390.

Thorson, J. A., & Powell, F. C. (1992). A revised death anxiety scale. *Death Studies, 16,* 507–521.

Thurstone, L. L. (1938). *Primary mental abilities.* Chicago: University of Chicago Press.

Tinetti, M. E., et al. (1997). A multi-factorial intervention to reduce the risk of falling among elderly people living in the community. *New England Journal of Medicine, 331,* 821–824.

Tracey, T. J., & Rounds, J. (1993). Evaluating Holland's and Gait's vocational-interest models: A structural meta-analysis. *Psychological Bulletin, 113,* 229–246.

Troll, L. E. (1985). The contingencies of grandparenting. In V. L. Bengtson & J. F. Robertson (Eds.), *Grandparenthood* (pp. 135–150). Beverly Hills, CA: Sage.

Troll, L. E. (1994). Family connectedness of old women: Attachments in later life. In B. F. Turner & L. E. Troll (Eds.), *Women growing older: Psychological perspectives* (pp. 169–201). Thousand Oaks, CA: Sage.

Tsuya, N. O., & Martin, L. G. (1992). Living arrangements of elderly Japanese and attitudes toward inheritance. *Journal of Gerontology: Social Sciences, 47,* S45–S54.

Tunstall-Pedoe, H., & Smith, W. C. S. (1990). Cholesterol as a risk factor for coronary heart disease. *British Medical Bulletin, 46,* 1075–1087.

Turner, B. F., & Troll, L. E. (Eds). (1994). *Women growing older: Psychological perspectives.* Thousand Oaks, CA: Sage.

Turner, B. F., & Turner, C. B. (1994). Social cognition and gender stereotypes for women varying in age and race. In B. F. Turner & L. E. Troll (Eds.), *Women growing older: Psychological perspectives* (pp. 94–139). Thousand Oaks, CA: Sage.

Uchino, B. N., Cacioppo, J. T., & Kiecolt-Glaser, J. K. (1996). The relationship between social support and physiological processes: A review with emphasis on underlying mechanisms and implications for health. *Psychological Bulletin, 119*(3), 488–531.

Uhlenberg, P., Cooney, T., & Boyd, R. (1990). Divorce for women after midlife. *Journal of Gerontology: Social Sciences, 45,* S3–S11.

Underhill, E. (1961). *Mysticism.* New York: Dutton. (Original work published 1911)

U.S. Bureau of the Census. (1989a). *Current population reports* (Series P-23, No. 162). Washington, DC: U.S. Government Printing Office.

U.S. Bureau of the Census. (1989b). *Statistical abstract of the United States, 1989.* Washington, DC: U.S. Government Printing Office.

U.S. Bureau of the Census. (1990). *Statistical abstract of the United States, 1990.* Washington, DC: U.S. Government Printing Office.

U.S. Bureau of the Census. (1993). *Statistical Abstract of the United States, 1993* (113th ed.). Washington, DC: U.S. Government Printing Office.

U.S. Bureau of Labor Statistics (1996). *Employment and earnings*. Washington, DC: Government Printing Office.

Vaillant, G. E. (1974). Natural history of male psychological health: II. Some antecedents of healthy adult adjustment. *Archives of General Psychiatry, 31,* 15–22.

Vaillant, G. E. (1975). Natural history of male psychological health: III. Empirical dimensions of mental health. *Archives of General Psychiatry, 32,* 420–426.

Vaillant, G. E. (1977). *Adaptation to life: How the best and brightest came of age.* Boston: Little, Brown.

Vaillant, G. E. (1991). The association of ancestral longevity with successful aging. *Journal of Gerontology: Psychological Sciences, 46,* P292–P298.

Vaillant, G. E., & Vaillant, C. O. (1990). Natural history of male psychological health: XII. A 45-year study of predictors of successful aging at age 65. *American Journal of Psychiatry, 147,* 31–37.

van IJzendoorn, M. (1995). Adult attachment representations, parental responsiveness, and infant attachment: A meta-analysis on the predictive validity of the Adult Attachment Interview. *Psychological Bulletin, 117,* 387–403.

Vannoy, D., & Philliber, W. W. (1992). Wife's employment and quality of marriage. *Journal of Marriage and the Family, 54,* 387–398.

Van Velsor, E., & O'Rand, A. M. (1984). Family life cycle, work career patterns, and women's wages at midlife. *Journal of Marriage and the Family, 46,* 365–373.

Vega, W. A. (1990). Hispanic families in the 1980s: A decade of research. *Journal of Marriage and the Family, 52,* 1015–1024.

Verbrugge, L. M. (1989). Gender, aging, and health. In K. S. Markides (Ed.), *Aging and health* (pp. 23–78). Newbury Park, CA: Sage.

Verhaeghen, P., & Marcoen, A. (1993). Memory aging as a general phenomenon: Episodic recall of older adults is a function of episodic recall of young adults. *Psychology and Aging, 8,* 380–388.

Verhaeghen, P., Marcoen, A., & Goossens, L. (1993). Facts and fiction about memory aging: A quantitative integration of research findings. *Journal of Gerontology: Psychological Sciences, 48,* P157–P171.

Verhaeghen, P., & Salthouse, T. A. (1997). Meta-analyses of age-cognition relations in adulthood: Estimates of linear and nonlinear age effects and structural models. *Psychological Bulletin, 122*(3), 231–249.

Veroff, J., Douvan, E., & Kulka, R. A. (1981). *The inner American: A self-portrait from 1957 to 1976.* New York: Basic Books.

Vinokur, A. D., & van Ryn, M. (1993). Social support and undermining in close relationships: Their independent effects on the mental health of unemployed persons. *Journal of Personality and Social Psychology, 65,* 350–359.

Waddington, C. H. (1957). *The strategy of the genes.* London: Allen & Son.

Wagner, E. H., LaCroix, A. Z., Buchner, D. M., & Larson, E. B. (1992). Effects of physical activity on health status in older adults: I. Observational studies. *Annual Review of Public Health, 13,* 451–468.

Walker, A. (1990). Poverty and inequality in old age. In J. Bond & P. Coleman (Eds.), *Aging in society* (pp. 229–249). London: Sage.

Walker, A. J. (1992). Conceptual perspectives on gender and family caregiving. In J. W. Dwyer & R. T. Coward (Eds.), *Gender, families, and elder care* (pp. 34–46). Newbury Park, CA: Sage.

Walker, A. J., & Thompson, L. (1983). Intimacy and intergenerational aid and contact among mothers and daughters. *Journal of Marriage and the Family, 45,* 841–849.

Walker, L. J. (1989). A longitudinal study of moral reasoning. *Child Development, 60,* 157–160.

Walker, L. J., de Vries, B., & Trevethan, S. D. (1987). Moral stages and moral orientations in real-life and hypothetical dilemmas. *Child Development, 58,* 842–858.

Wallace, J. B. (1992). Reconsidering the life review: The social construction of talk about the past. *Gerontologist, 32,* 120–125.

Wallerstein, J. S. (1986). Women after divorce: Preliminary report from a ten-year-follow-up. *American Journal of Orthopsychiatry, 56,* 65–77.

Walsh, W. B., Horton, J. A., & Gaffey, R. L. (1977). Holland's theory and college degreed working men and women. *Journal of Vocational Behavior, 10,* 180–186.

Warr, P. (1994). Age and employment. In M. Dunnette, L. Hough, & J. Triandis (Eds.), *Handbook of industrial and organizational psychology* (Vol. 4, pp. 487–550). Palo Alto, CA: Consulting Psychologists Press.

Warr, P., Jackson, P., & Banks, M. (1988). Unemployment and mental health: Some British studies. *Journal of Social Issues, 44,* 47–68.

Waterman, A. S., & Archer, S. L. (1990). A life-span perspective on identity formation: Developments in form, function, and process. In P. B. Baltes, D. L. Featherman, & R. M. Lerner (Eds.), *Life-span development and behavior* (pp. 30–59). Hillsdale, NJ: Erlbaum.

Waters, E., Merrick, S. K., Albersheim, L. J., & Treboux, D. (1995, April). *Attachment security from infancy to early adulthood: A 20-year longitudinal study.* Poster presented at the biennial meeting of the Society for Research in Child Development, Indianapolis, IN.

Wayne, S., Rhyne, R., Garry, P., et al. (1990). Cell mediated immunity as a predictor of morbidity and mortality in the aged. *Journal of Gerontology, 45,* 45–49.

Webster, J. D. (1997). Attachment style and well-being in elderly adults: A preliminary investigation. *Canadian Journal on Aging, 16*(1), 101–111.

Wechsler, D. (1939). *The measurement of adult intelligence.* Baltimore: Williams & Wilkins.

Wechsler, D. (1955). *Manual for the Wechsler Adult Intelligence Scale.* New York: Psychological Corporation.

Weindrich, R. (1996, January). Caloric restriction and aging. *Scientific American,* pp. 46–52.

Weingarten, H. R. (1985). Marital status and well-being: A national study comparing first-married, currently divorced, and remarried adults. *Journal of Marriage and the Family, 47,* 653–662.

Weishaus, S., & Field, D. (1988). A half century of marriage: Continuity or change? *Journal of Marriage and the Family, 50,* 763–774.

Weiss, R. S. (1982). Attachment in adult life. In C. M. Parkes & J. Stevenson-Hinde (Eds.), *The place of attachment in human behavior* (pp. 171–184). New York: Basic Books.

Weiss, R. S. (1986). Continuities and transformations in social relationships from childhood to adulthood. In W. W. Hartup & Z. Rubin (Eds.), *On relationships and development* (pp. 95–110). Hillsdale, NJ: Erlbaum.

Weiss, R. S. (1990). *Staying the course.* New York: Free Press.

Weisse, C. S. (1992). Depression and immunocompetence: A review of the literature. *Psychological Bulletin, 111,* 475–489.

Werner, H., & Kaplan, B. (1956). The developmental approach to cognition: Its relevance to the psychological interpretation of anthropological and ethnolinguistic data. *American Anthropologist, 58,* 866–880.

West, R. L., & Crook, T. H. (1990). Age differences in everyday memory: Laboratory analogues of telephone number recall. *Psychology and Aging, 5,* 520–529.

White, A. T., & Spector, P. E. (1987). An investigation of age-related factors in the age–job-satisfaction relationship. *Psychology and Aging, 2,* 261–265.

Whitehead, M. I., & Fraser, D. (1987). Controversies concerning the safety of estrogen replacement therapy. *American Journal of Obstetrics and Gynecology, 156,* 1313–1322.

Wickelgren, I. (1997, May 2). Estrogen stakes a claim to cognition. *Science, 276,* 675–678.

Wilkinson, R. T., & Allison, S. (1989). Age and simple reaction time: decade differences for 5,325 subjects. *Journal of Gerontology: Psychological Sciences, 44,* P29–P35.

Willemsen, E. W. (1980). Terman's gifted women: Work and the way they see their lives. In K. W. Back (Ed.), *Life course: Integrative theories and exemplary populations* (pp. 121–132). Boulder, CO: Westview Press.

Williams, D. G. (1988). Gender, marriage, and psychosocial well-being. *Journal of Family Issues, 9,* 452–468.

Williams, D. R. (1992). Social structure and the health behaviors of blacks. In K. W. Schaie, D. Blazer, & J. S. House (Eds.), *Aging, health behaviors, and health outcomes* (pp. 59–64). Hillsdale, NJ: Erlbaum.

Williams, J. E., & Best, D. L. (1990). *Measuring sex stereotypes. A multination study* (Rev. ed.), Newbury Park, CA: Sage.

Willis, S. L. (1996). Everyday problem solving. In J. E. Birren & W. K. Schaie (Eds.), *Handbook of the psychology of aging* (4th ed., pp. 287–307). San Diego, CA: Academic Press.

Willis, S. L., & Schaie, K. W. (1994). Assessing competence in the elderly. In C. E. Fisher & R. M. Lerner (Eds.) *Applied development* (pp. 339-372), New York: MacMillan.

Willits, F. K., & Crider, D. M. (1988). Health rating and life satisfaction in the later middle years. *Journal of Gerontology: Social Sciences, 43,* S172–S176.

Wilson, M. R., & Filsinger, E. E. (1986). Religiosity and marital adjustment: Multidimensional interrelationships. *Journal of Marriage and the Family, 48,* 147–151.

Wilson, R. S., Bennet, D. A., & Swartzendruber, A. (1997). Age related change in cognitive function. In P. D. Nussbaum (Ed.), *Handbook of neuropsychology and aging* (pp. 7–14). New York: Plenum Press.

Wingfield, A., Stine, E. L., Lahar, C. J., & Aberdeen, J. S. (1988). Does the capacity of working memory change with age? *Experimental Aging Research, 14,* 103–107.

Wingo, P.A., Ries, L. A. G., Rosenberg, H. M., Miller, D. S., & Edwards, B. K. (1998). Cancer incidence and mortality 1973-1995. *Cancer, 82,* 1197-1207.

Wink, P., & Helson, R. (1993). Personality change in women and their partners. *Journal of Personality and Social Psychology, 65,* 597–605.

Winstead, B. A., Derlega, V. J., & Rose, S. (1997). *Gender and close relationships.* Thousand Oaks, CA: Sage.

Wolfson, C., Handfield-Jones, R., Glass, K. C., McClaran, J., & Keyserlingk, E. (1993). Adult children's perceptions of their responsibility to provide care for dependent elderly parents. *The Gerontologist, 33,* 315–323.

Wolinsky, F. D., Calahan, C. M., Fitzgerald, J. F., & Johnson, R. J. (1993). Changes in functional status and the risks of subsequent nursing home placement and death. *Journal of Gerontoloty: Social Sciences, 48,* S93–S101.

Wong, B. S. M., & Norman, D. C. (1987). Evaluation of a novel medication aid, the calendar blister-pak, and its effect on drug compliance in a geriatric outpatient clinic. *Journal of the American Geriatrics Society, 35,* 21–26.

Wodruff-Pak, D. S. (1988). *Psychology and Aging.* Englewood Cliffs, NJ: Prentice Hall.

Woodruff-Pak, D. S. (1997). *Neuropsychology of aging.* Malden, MA: Blackwell.

Woollacott, M. H. (1993). Age-related changes in posture and movement [Special issue]. *Journals of Gerontology, 48,* 56–60.

Worobey, J. L., & Angel, R. J. (1990). Functional capacity and living arrangements of unmarried elderly persons. *Journal of Gerontology: Social Sciences, 45,* S95–S101.

Wortman, C. B., & Silver, R. C. (1989). The myths of coping with loss. *Journal of Consulting and Clinical Psychology, 57,* 349–357.

Wortman, C. B., & Silver, R. C. (1990). Successful mastery of bereavement and widowhood: A life course perspective. In P. B. Baltes & M. M. Baltes (Eds.), *Successful aging: Perspectives from the behavioral sciences* (pp. 225–264). Cambridge, England: Cambridge University Press.

Wortman, C. B., & Silver, R. C. (1992). Reconsidering assumptions about coping with loss: An overview of current research. In L. Montada, S. Filipp, & M. J. Lerner (Eds.), *Life crises and experiences of loss in adulthood* (pp. 341–365). Hillsdale, NJ: Erlbaum.

Wortman, C. B., Silver, R. C., & Kessler, R. C. (1993). The meaning of loss and adjustment to bereavement. In M. S. Stroebe, W. Stroebe, & R. O. Hansson (Eds.), *Handbook of bereavement: Theory, research, and intervention* (pp. 349–366). Cambridge, England: Cambridge University Press.

Writing Group for the PEPI Trial. (1996). Effects of hormone therapy on bone mineral density: Results from the Postmenopausal Estrogen/Progesin Interventions (PEPI) Trial. *Journal of the American Medical Association, 276,* 1389–1395.

Yesavage, J., Lapp, D., & Sheikh, J. A. (1989) Mnemonics as modified for use by the elderly. In L. W. Poon, D. Rubin, B. Wilson (Eds.). *Everyday cognition in adulthood and late life.* Cambridge, England: Cambridge University Press.

Yesavage, J. A., Sheikh, J. I., Friedman, L. E., & Tanke, E. (1990). Learning mnemonics: Roles of aging and subtle cognitive impairment. *Psychology and Aging, 5,* 133–137.

Yinger, J. M. (1977). A comparative study of the substructures of religion. *Journal of the Scientific Study of Religion, 16,* 67–86.

Zelinski, E. M., Gilewski, M. J., & Schaie, K. W. (1993). Individual differences in cross-sectional and 3-year longitudinal memory performance across the adult life span. *Psychology and Aging, 8,* 176–186.

Zheng, Y., & Lin, K. (1994). A nationwide study of stressful life events in mainland China. *Psychosomatic Medicine, 56,* 296–305.

CREDITS

Photographs

Title Page Karl Weatherly, PhotoDisc, Inc.

Chapter 1 Page 5 left and right courtesy of the author; p. 9 B. Daemmrich, The Image Works; p. 10 Scott Stewart, AP/Wide World Photos; p. 16 UN/DPI/John Isaac.

Chapter 2 Page 32 UN/DPI PHOTO/Bruno J. Zehnder; p. 38 D. Berry, PhotoDisc, Inc.; p. 51 Grant LeDuc, Monkmeyer Press.

Chapter 3 Page 62 Nourok, PhotoEdit; p. 64 UN/DPI PHOTO/John Isaac; p. 72 Biophoto Associates/Science Source, Photo Researchers, Inc.; p. 75 Dennis Mcdonald, PhotoEdit.

Chapter 4 Page 98 American Cancer Society; p. 108 Martin Rotker, Phototake, NYC; p. 122 left Steve Mason, PhotoDisc, Inc.; p. 122 right Roger M. Richards, Liaison Agency, Inc.

Chapter 5 Page 128 Lawrence Migdale, Lawrence Migdale/PIX; p. 133 Renee Lynn, Photo Researcher, Inc.; p. 144 Susan Holtz; p. 154 left Laima Druskis, Simon & Schuster/PH College; p. 154 right Irene Springer, Simon & Schuster/PH College.

Chapter 6 Page 160 Jeff Greenberg, Omni-Photo Communications, Inc.; p. 177 Steve Mason, PhotoDisc, Inc.

Chapter 7 Page 194 Skjold Photographs, Simon & Schuster/PH College; p. 209 Vermont Travel Division, Vermont Department of Tourism and Marketing; p. 212 Michael Newman, PhotEdit; p. 213 Deborah Davis, PhotoEdit; p. 219 Alice Firgau.

Chapter 8 Page 232 FIND/SVP; p. 234 Laima Druskis, Simon & Schuster/PH College; p. 254 Universal Press Syndicate; p. 262 Methodist Health Care System.

Chapter 9 Page 272 Karen Halverson, Omni-Photo Communications, Inc.; p. 274 left and right courtesy of the author.

Chapter 10 Page 304 Stephen Marks, The Image Bank; p. 327 Richard Hutchings, Photo Researchers, Inc.

Chapter 11 Page 332 UN/DPI PHOTO/Jeffrey J. Foxx; p. 344 SCP Communications, Inc.; p. 355 Laima Druskis, Simon & Schuster/PH College.

Chapter 12 Page 360 Bill Bachmann, Stock Boston; p. 373 top Mike Gallitelli, Simon & Schuster/PH College; 373 bottom Walter E. McGonagill.

Chapter 13 Page 378 Michal Heron, Simon & Schuster/PH College; p. 384 Ron Chapple, FPG International LLC; p. 391 Spencer Grant, Stock Boston; p. 393 James Shaffer, PhotoEdit.

Chapter 14 Page 400 Corbis Digital Stock; p. 415 Russell D. Curtis, Photo Researchers, Inc.; p. 416 Jack Star, PhotoDisc, Inc.

Figures and Tables

Chapter 1 Figure 1.1—From THE INNER AMERICAN by J. Veroff, E. Douvan & R. A. Kulka. Copyright 1981 by Basic Books, Inc. Reprinted by permission of Basic Books, Inc., a member of Perseus Books, L.L.C. Figure 1.2—Table 3, p. 168 from "Genetic and Environmental Effects on Openness to Experience, Agreeableness and Conscientiousness: An Adoption Twin Study" by C.S. Bergeman, H. M. Chipuer, R. Plomin, N. L. Pedersen, G. E. McClearn, J. R. Nesselroade, P. T. Costa, Jr., & R. R. McCrae in *Journal of Personality*, Vol. 61, 1993. Reprinted with permission of Blackwell Publishers. Figure 1.3—Figure 6, p. 224 in THEORETICAL PERSPECTIVES ON COGNITIVE AGING by T. A. Salthouse. Copyright 1991 by T. A. Salthouse. Reprinted by permission of Lawrence Erlbaum Associates, Inc. Figure 1.4—Figure 5, p. 336 in "Social and Emotional Patterns in Adulthood: Support for Socioemotional Selectivity Theory" by L. L. Carstensen in *Psychology and Aging*, Vol. 7, 1992. Copyright 1992 by American Psychological Association. Reprinted by permission of APA. Figure 1.5—From THE INNER AMERICAN by J. Veroff, E. Douvan & R. A. Kulka. Copyright 1981 by Basic Books, Inc. Reprinted by permission of Basic Books, Inc., a member of Perseus Books, L.L.C. Figure 1.6—Data from tables 2 & 3, p. 24 in "Marital Satisfaction over the Family Life Cycle" by B. C. Rollins & H. Feldman in *Journal of Marrriage and the Family*, Vol. 32, 1970. Copyright 1970 by the National Council on Family Relations, 3989 Central Ave., NE, Suite 550, Minneapolis, MN 55421. Reprinted with permission.

Chapter 2 Table 2.1—Derived from E. H. Erikson. (1950). CHILDHOOD AND SOCIETY. New York: Norton; E. H. Erikson. (1959). IDENTITY AND THE LIFE CYCLE. New York: Norton; E. H. Erikson. (1980). "Themes of Adulthood in the Freud-Jung Correspondence" in N. J. Smelser & E. H. Erikson (Eds.), THEMES OF WORK AND LOVE IN ADULTHOOD (pp. 43-76). Cambridge, MA: Harvard University Press; E. H. Erikson, J. M. Erikson, & H. Q. Hivnick. (1986). VITAL INVOLVEMENT IN OLD AGE. New York: Norton. Table 2.2—Material from Ch. 2 on the stages of ego development from EGO DEVELOPMENT by Jane Loevinger. Copyright 1976 by Jossey-Bass Inc., Publishers. Reprinted by permission. Table 2.3—From ADAPTATION TO LIFE by George H. Vaillant. Copyright 1977 by George H. Vaillant. Reprinted by permission of the author. Figure 2.2—From THE SEASONS OF A MAN'S LIFE by Daniel J. Levinson. Copyright 1978 by Daniel J. Levinson. Reprinted by permission of Alfred A. Knopf, Inc. and Sterling Lord Literistic, Inc. Table 2.5—"Stages of Family Life Cycle" from FAMILY DEVELOPMENT by E. M. Duvall. Copyright 1962 by Evelyn M. Duvall. Reprinted by permission of Addison Wesley Longman. Table 2.6—Adapted from Table 1, p. 613 in "Theoretical Propositions of Life-Span Developmental Psychology: On the Dynamics Between Growth and Decline" by P. B. Baltes in *Developmental Psychology*, Vol. 23, 1987. Copyright 1987 by the American Psychological Association. Reprinted with permission of APA. Figure 2.3—Figure 1, p. 102 from "Structure and Dynamics of the Individual Life Course" by P. J. Perun & D. D. Bielby in LIFE COURSE: Integrative Theories and Exemplary Populations ed. by K. W. Back. Copyright 1980 by the authors. Published by Westview Press, Boulder, CO.

Chapter 3 Table 3.1—National Center for Health Statistics, 1993. Figure 3.1—Figure 2.2, p. 27 in "Demography of Aging" by G. C. Myers in HANDBOOK OF AGING AND THE SOCIAL SCIENCES, 3E edited by R. H. Binstock & L. K. George. Copyright 1990 by the Academic Press, Inc. Reprinted by permission of the publisher. Figure 3.2—BMI Index" chart from *www.shapeup.org*. Reproduced with permission of Shape Up America! 6707 Democracy Blvd., Suite 306, Bethesda, MD 20817. Figure 3.3—Photo from p. 685, "Cataracts in Human Eye" in "Changes and Diseases in the Aging Eye" by J. T. Ernest in GERIATRIC MEDICINE 3rd edition ed. by C. K. Cassel, H. J. Cohen, E. B. Larson, et al. Copyright 1997 by the authors. Published by Springer Publishing Company, NY. Table 3.2—U. S. Bureau of the Census (1990, Table 192, p. 119). Figure 3.4—From "The Role of Muscle Loss in the Age-Related Decline of Grip Strength: Cross-Sectional and Longitudinal Perspectives" by D. A. Kallman, C. C. Plato & J. D. Tobin in *Journal of Gerontology: Medical Sciences*, Vol. 45, 1990. Copyright 1990 by The Gerontological Society of America. Reprinted by permission. Figure 3.5—From p. 216 in "Boning Up on Genes" by G. R. Mundy in *Nature*, Vol. 367, 1994. Copyright 1994 by G. R. Mundy. Reprinted by permission of *Nature*. Table 3.3—Derived from S. A. Duursma, J. A. Raymakers, F. T. J. Boereboom & B. A. A. Scheven. (1991). "Estrogen and Bone Metabolism" in *Obstetrical and Gynecological Survey*, Vol. 47; N. A. Morrison, J. C. Qi., A. Tokita, P. J. Kelly, L. Crofts., T. V. Nguyen, P. N. Sambrook & J. A. Eisman. (1994). "Prediction of Bone Density from Vitamin D Receptor Alleles" in *Nature*, London, Vol. 367.; C. Murray M. Luckey, & D. Meier. (1996). "Skeletal Integrity" (pp. 431-444) in E. L. Schneider & J. W. Rowe (Eds.). HANDBOOK OF THE BIOLOGY OF AGING, 4th Ed. San Diego: Academic Press. Figure 3.6—From "Age-Related Decline in VO2 Max for Sedentary and Active Adults" by Larson & Bruce in GERIATRIC MEDICINE, 3rd ed. edited by Cassel, Cohen, Larson et al. Copyright 1997 by Springer-Verlag. Reprinted by permission of the publisher. Figure 3.7—Republished with permission of The Gerontological Society of America, 1030 15th St., NW, Suite 250, Washington, DC 20005. *Age and Simple Reaction Time* (Figure 2, p. 31) by R. T. Wilkinson & S. Allison, *Journal of Gerontology: Psychological Sciences*, 1989, Vol. 44. Reproduced by permission of the publisher via Copyright Clearance Center, Inc. Table 3.4—From "Reproductive Aging" by S. M. Harman & G. B. Talbert in HANDBOOK OF THE BIOLOGY OF AGING 2E edited by C. E. Finch and E. L. Schneider. Copyright 1985 by Van Nostrand Reinhold. Reprinted by permission of the publisher. Figure 3.8—Fig. 6.3, "Peak Performance and Age: An Examination of Peak Performance in Sports" by K. A. Ericsson in SUCCESSFUL AGING: Perspectives from the Behavioral Sciences ed. by P. B. Baltes & M. M. Baltes. Copyright 1990 by the authors. Reprinted by permission of Cambridge University Press. Figure 3.9—E. Palmore, *Social Patterns in Normal Aging*, Figure 6.4, "Frequency of Sex Relations Among Sexually Active Married Men and Women by Age Cohorts (Rounds 1 to 4)", p. 88. Copyright 1981 by Duke University Press. Reprinted with permission. Table 3.5—From THE CLOCK OF AGES: Why We Age, How We Age, Winding Back the Clock by John J. Medina. Copyright 1996 by John J. Medina. Reprinted by permission of Cambridge University Press. Figure 3.10—From LIFE-SPAN DEVELOPMENTAL PSYCHOLOGY: Introduction to Research Methods by P. B. Baltes, H. W. Reese & J. R. Nesselroade. Copyright 1977 by Brooks/Cole Publishing Company, Pacific Grove, CA 93950, a division of International Thomsom Publishing, Inc. By permission of the publisher. Table 3.7—"Calculating Your Own Longevity" from NEUROPSYCHOLOGY OF AGING by D. S. Woodruff-Pak. Copyright 1997 by D. S. Woodruff-Pak. Published by Blackwell Publishers, UK.

Chapter 4 Figure 4.1—U. S. Bureau of the Census, 1993, derived from data in Table 14, p. 15, and Table 127, p. 92. Table 4.1—American Heart Association. Figure 4.2—U. S. Bureau of the Census, 1994. Table 4.2—Republished with permission of The Gerontological Society of America, 1030 15th St., NW, Suite 250, Washington, DC 20005. *Estimating Prevalence of Long-Term Disability in an Aging Society* (Table 3, p. S257) by S. R. Kunkel & R. A. Applebaum in *Journal of Gerontology: Social Sciences*, 1992, Vol. 47. Reproduced by permission of the publisher via Copyright Clearance Center, Inc. Figure 4.3—Republished with permission of The Gerontological Society of America, 1030 15th St., NW, Suite 250, Washington, DC 20005. Physical Disability in Older Americans (Figure 2, p. 5), J. M. Guralnick and E. M. Simonsick, *Journal of Gerontology: Special Issue*, 1993, Vol. 48. Reproduced by permission of the publisher via Copyright Clearance Center, Inc. Table 4.3—From "Gender, Aging and Health" by L. M. Verbrugge in AGING AND HEALTH ed. by K. S. Markides. Copyright 1989 by Sage Publications, Inc. Reprinted by permission of the publisher. Table 4.5—Derived from R. Benfante & D. Reed. (1990). "Is Elevated Serum Cholesterol Level a Risk Factor for Coronary Heart Disease in the Elderly?" *JAMA: Journal of the American Medical Association*, Vol. 263; J. A. Berlin & G. A. Colditz. (1990). "A Meta-Analysis of Physical Activity in the Prevention of Coronary Heart Disease". *American Journal of Epidemiology*, Vol. 132; J. C. Chamberlain & D. J. Galton. (1990). "Genetic Susceptibility to Atherosclerosis". *British Medical Journal*, Vol. 46; J. L. Fozard, E. J. Metter, & L. J. Brant (1990). "Next Steps in Describing Aging and Disease in Longitudinal Studies". *Journal of Gerontology: Psychological Sciences*, Vol. 45; W. B. Kannel & T. Gordon (1980). "Cardiovascular Risk Factors in the Aged: The Framingham Study" in S. G. Haynes & M. Feinleib (Eds.), *Second Conference on the Epidemiology of Aging* (DHHS/NIH Publication No. 80-969, pp. 65-89). Washington, DC: U. S. Government Printing Office; D. Kritchevsky (1990). "Nutrition and Breast Cancer". *Cancer*, Vol. 66; I. Lee, J. E. Manson, C. H. Hennekens & R. S. Paffenbarger, Jr. (1993). "Body Weight and Mortality. A 27-year follow-up of middle-aged men". *JAMA, Journal of the American Medical Association*, Vol. 270; R. B. McGandy (1988). "Atherogenesis and Aging". *Aging*, Vol. 35; D. P. Rose (1993). "Diet, Hormones, and Cancer". *Annual Review of Public Health*, Vol. 14; M. J. Shipley, S. J. Pocock, & M. G. Marmot (1991). "Does Plasma Cholesterol Concentration Predict Mortality from Coronary Heart Disease in Elderly People? 18-Year Follow-Up in Whitehall Study". *British Medical Journal*, Vol. 303. Figure 4.4—Fig. 6 from "Structural Changes in the Aging Brain" by A. B. Scheibel in HANDBOOK OF MENTAL HEALTH AND AGING ed. by J. E. Birren, R. B. Sloane & G. D. Cohen. Copyright 1992 by Academic Press. Reprinted by permission of the publisher. Table 4.5—Figs. 1 & 2 from "The Relationship Between Age and Depressive Symptoms in Two National Surveys" by R. C. Kessler, C. Foster, P. S. Webster & J. House in *Psychology and Aging*, 1992, Vol. 7. Copyright 1992 by American Psychological Association. Reprinted by permission of APA. Table 4.6—From the Beck Depression Inventory. Copyright 1978 by Aaron T. Beck. Reproduced by permission of the publisher, The Psychological Corporation. All rights reserved. Figure 4.6—U. S. Bureau of the Census, 1993, data from Table 137, p. 99. Figure 4.7—Figs. 1 & 3 from "Age, Socioeconomic Status, and Health" by J. S. House, R. C. Kessler, & A. R. Herzog in *Milbank Quarterly*, Vol. 68, 1990. Copyright 1990 by the authors. Reprinted by permission of Blackwell Publishers, Inc. Table 4.7—P. 415 table from "Relationship of Physical Health Status and Health Practices" by N. B. Belloc & L. Breslow in *Preventive Medicine*, Vol. 1, 1972. Copyright 1972 by Academic Press. Reprinted by permission of the publisher. Figure 4.8—From HEALTH AND WAYS

OF LIVING: The Alameda County Study by Lisa Berkman and Lester Breslow. Copyright 1983 by Oxford University Press. Reprinted by permission of Oxford University Press, Inc.

Chapter 5 Figure 5.1—Data from Table 4.5, p. 89 and Table 4.9, p. 100 in "The Seattle Longitudinal Study" A 21-year Exploration of Psychometric Intelligence in Adulthood" by K. W. Schaie in LONGITUDINAL STUDIES OF ADULT PSYCHOLOGICAL DEVELOPMENT ed. by K. W. Schaie. Copyright 1983 by K. W. Schaie. Published by Guilford Press, NY. Figure 5.2—From "The Course of Adult Intellectual Development" by K. W. Schaie in *American Psychologist*, Vol. 48, 1994. Copyright 1994 by American Psychologist Association. Reprinted by permission of APA. Figure 5.3—From "Age Differences in Everyday Memory: Laboratory Analogues of Telephone Number Recall" by R. L. West & T. H. Crook in *Psychology and Aging*, Vol. 5, 1990. Copyright 1990 by American Psychological Association. Reprinted by permission of APA. Figure 5.4—From "Age Deficits in Recall under Optimal Study Conditions" by J. C. Rabinowitz in *Psychology and Aging*, Vol. 4, 1989. Copyright 1989 by American Psychological Association. Reprinted by permission of APA. Figure 5.6—Fig. 2, p. 344 in "Designing Written Instructions for Older Adults: Learning to Use Computers" by R. W. Morrel & K. V. Echt in HANDBOOK OF HUMAN FACTORS AND THE OLDER ADULT ed. by A. D. Fisk & W. A. Rogers. Copyright 1997 by Academic Press. Reprinted by permission of the publisher. Fig. 5.7—Fig. 1, p. 343 in "Designing Written Instructions for Older Adults: Learning to Use Computers" by R. W. Morrel & K. V. Echt in HANDBOOK OF HUMAN FACTORS AND THE OLDER ADULT ed. by A. D. Fisk & W. A. Rogers. Copyright 1997 by Academic Press. Reprinted by permission of the publisher. Table 5.2—Adapted from "The Getting of Wisdom: Theory of Mind in Old Age" by Happe, Winnder & Brownell in *Developmental Psychology*, Vol. 34(2), 1998. Copyright 1998 by American Psychological Association. Reprinted with permission of APA. Fig. 5.8—Fig. 1, p. 321 in "Relation between Aging and Research Productivity of Academic Psychologist" by K. W. Horner, J. P. Rushton & P. A. Vernon in *Psychology and Aging*, Vol. 1, 1986. Copyright 1986 by American Psychological Association. Reprinted with permission of APA. Figure 5.9—Figures 5.13 & 5.14 of "Individual Differences in Rates of Cognitive Change in Adulthood" by K. W. Schaie in THE COURSE OF LATER LIFE: Research and Reflections ed. by V. L. Bengtson & K. W. Schaie. Copyright 1989 by the authors. Reprinted by permission of Springer Publishing Company. Table 5.3—Republished with permission of The Gerontological Society of America, 1030 15th St., NW, Suite 250, Washington, DC 20005. *Correlated Self-Reported Everyday Memory Problems* (Table 1, p. S85), W. B. Cutler & A. E. Grams, *Journal of Gerontology: Social Sciences*, Vol. 43, 1988. Reproduced by permission of the publisher via Copyright Clearance Center, Inc. Figure 5.10—Fig. 2, p. 126 in "After Reaching Retirement Age Physical Activity Sustains Cerebral Profusion and Cognition" by R. L. Rogers, J. S. Meyer, & K. F. Mortel in *Journal of the American Geriatric Society*, Vol. 38, 1990. Copyright 1990 by Williams & Wilkins. Reprinted by permission of the publisher.

Chapter 6 Table 6.1—"Gender Stereotypes" from "From Individual Differences to Social Categories: Analysis of a Decade's Research on Gender" by K. Deaux in *American Psychologist*, Vol. 39, 1984. Copyright 1984 by American Psychological Assn. Reprinted by APA. Figure 6.1—Panels A & B from Fig. 1, p. 496, Panels A & C from Fig. 2, p. 497 and adapted from Fig. 3, p. 498 in "The Young Adult Years: Diversity, Structural Change, and Fertility" by Ronald R. Rindfull in

Demography, Vol. 28, Issue 4 (November 1991). Copyright 1991 by the author. Reprinted by permission of the author and Population Assn. of America. Fig. 6.2—U. S. Bureau of the Census (1995), STATISTICAL ABSTRACT OF THE UNITED STATES, 1995, *National Data Book* (Washington, DC: U. S. Government Printing Office). Figure 6.3—Fig.2, p. 516 from "Recent Trends in the Timing of First Births in the United States" by R. Chen & S. P. Morgan in *Demography*, Vol. 28, 1991. Copyright 1991 by the authors. Reprinted by permission of Population Assn. of America. Figure 6.4—Fig. 1, p. 746 in "The Family Life Cycle and Spouse's Time in Housework" by C. Rexroat & C. Shehan in *Journal of Marriage and the Family*, Vol. 49, 1987. Copyright 1987 by National Council on Family Relations, 3989 Central Ave., NE, Suite 550, Minneapolis, MN 55421. Reprinted by permission. Table 6.2—Table 1, p. 859 from "Stability and Change in Marriage across the Transition to Parenthood" by J. Belsky, E. Lang, & M. Rovine in *Journal of Marriage and the Family*, Vol. 44, 1985. Copyright 1985 by National Council on Family Relations, 3989 Central Ave., NE, Suite 550, Minneapolis, MN 55421. Reprinted by permission. Figure 6.5—From "More Evidence on Women (and Men) in the Middle" by G. Spitze and J. Logan in *Research on Aging*, Vol. 12, 1990. Copyright 1990 by Sage Publications, Inc. Reprinted by permission of the publisher. Figure 6.6—Republished with permission of The Gerontological Society of America, 1030 15th St., NW, Suite 250, Washington, DC 20005. *Gender Differences in Parent Care: Demographic Factors and Same-Gender Preferences* (Table 2, p. S12), G. R. Lee, J. W. Dwyer & R. T. Coward, *Journal of Gerontology: Social Sciences*, vol. 48, 1993. Reproduced with permission of the publisher via Copyright Clearance Center, Inc. Figure 6.7—Fig. 2, p. 8 in "Demography and the Epidemiology of Aging in the United States" by D. B. Brock, J. M. Guralnik & J. A. Brody in HANDBOOK OF THE BIOLOGY OF AGING ed. by E. L. Schneider & J. W. Rowe. Copyright 1990 by the authors. Reprinted by permission of Academic Press. Figure 6.8—Data from Tables 2, 3, 4, 5 & 6 in "Family Life Cycle: 1980" by A. J. Norton in *Journal of Marriage and the Marriage*, Vol. 45, 1983. Copyright 1983 by National Council on Family Relations, 3989 Central Ave., NE, Suite 550, Minneapolis, MN 55421. Reprinted with permission. Figure 6.9—Data from Table 1, p. 359 in "The Economic Costs of Marital Disruption to Young Women over the Past Two Decades" by P. J. Smock in *Demography*, Vol. 30, 1993. Copyright 1993 by the author. Reprinted by permission of Population Assn. of America.

Chapter 7 Table 7.1—Derived from M. Main & E. Hesse (1990). "Parents' Unresolved Traumatic Experiences are Related to Infant Disorganized Attachment Status: Is Frightened and/or Frightening Parental Behavior the Linking Mechanism?" in M. T. Greenberg, D. Cicchetti & E. M. Cummings (Eds.) ATTACHMENT IN THE PRESCHOOL YEARS: Theory, Research and Intervention, Chicago: University of Chicago Press; M. Main, N. Kaplan & J. Cassidy (1985). "Security in Infancy, Childhood, and Adulthood: A Move to the Level of Representation" in *Monographs of the Society for Research in Child Development*, Vol. 50 (Serial No. 209). Table 7.2—From "Love and Work: An Attachment-Theoretical Perspective" by C. Hazan & P. Shaver in *Journal of Personality and Social Psychology*, Vol. 59, 1990. Copyright 1990 by the American Psychological Association. Reprinted by permission of APA. Figure 7.1—Attachment styles from "Attachment-Style and Well-Being in Elderly Adults: A Preliminary Investigation" by J. D. Webster in *Canadian Journal on Aging*, Vol. 16(1), 1997. Copyright 1997 by Canadian Assn. of Gerontology. Reprinted with permission. Table 7.3—From "Liking vs. Loving: A Comparative Evaluation of Theories" by R. J. Sternberg in *Psychologi-*

dence for the Stability of Adult Personality" by P. T. Costa, Jr. & R. R. McCrae, CAN PERSONALITY CHANGE ed. by T. F. Hetherton & J. L. Weinberg. Copyright 1994 by American Psychological Association. Reprinted with permission of APA. Table 9.3—From "Genetic and Environmental Effects of Openness to Experience, Agreeableness, and Conscientiousness: An Adoption/Twin Study" by C. S. Bergeman, H. M. Chipuer, R. Plomin, H. L. Pederson, G. E. McClearn, J. R. Nesselroade, P. T. Costa and R. R. McCrae in *Journal of Personality*, Vol. 61, 1993. Copyright 1993 by Duke University Press. Reprinted by permission of Duke University Press. Figure 9.1—Figs. 1 & 2, p. 228 in "As Time Goes By: Change and Stability in Personality over Fifty Years" by N. Haan, R. Millsap, & E. Hartka in *Psychology and Aging*, Vol. 1, 1986. Copyright 1986 by American Psychological Association. Reprinted with permission of APA. Figure 9.2—Adaptation of Fig. 8.5 in "The AT&T Longitudinal Studies of Marriages" by D. W. Bray & A. Howard in LONGITUDINAL STUDIES OF ADULT PSYCHOLOGICAL DEVELOPMENT ed. by K. W. Schaie. Copyright 1983 by the authors. Reprinted by permission of Guilford Press. Figure 9.3—From Table 2, p. 601 in "Personality Change in Women and Their Partners" by P. Wink & R. Helson in *Journal of Personality and Social Psychology*, Vol. 65, 1993. Copyright 1993 by American Psychological Association. Reprinted by permission of APA. Figure 9.4—From ADAPTATION TO LIFE by George E. Vaillant. Copyright 1977 by George E. Vaillant. Reprinted by permission of the author. Figure 9.5—Fig. 3, p. 229 of "As Time Goes By: Change and Stability in Personality over Fifty Years" by N. Haan, R. Millsap, & E. Hartka in *Psychology and Aging*, Vol. 1, 1986. Copyright 1986 by American Psychological Association. Reprinted with permission of APA. Figure 9.6—Fig. 3, p. 67 in "The Aging-Self: Stabilizing and Protective Processes" by J. Brandstadter & W. Greve in *Developmental Review*, Vol. 14, 1994. Copyright 1994 by the authors. Reprinted by permission of Academic Press. Figure 9.7—Derived from E. Midlarsky & M. E. Hannah (1989). "The Generous Elderly: Naturalistic Studies of Donations across the Life Span" in *Psychology and Aging*, Vol. 4; V. Hodgkinson, M. Weitzman & The Gallup Organization, Inc. (1988). GIVING AND VOLUNTEERING IN THE UNITED STATES: 1988 Edition. Washington, DC: Independent Sector as reported in U. S. Bureau of the Census, 1989a, Table 615, p. 371. Figure 9.8—Fig. 2, p. 214 from "Personality Change in Adulthood" by R. Helson & A. Stewart in CAN PERSONALITY CHANGE? ed. by T. F. Hetherton & J. L. Weinberger. Copyright 1994 by American Psychological Association. Reprinted by permission of APA. Original data by P. Wink & R. Helson. Table 9.4—From "The Timing of Psychosocial Transitions and Changes in Women's Lives: An Examination of Women Aged 45 to 60" by R. L. Harris, A. Ellicott, & D. S. Holmes in *Journal of Personality and Social Psychology*, Vol. 51, 1986. Copyright 1986 by American Psychological Association. Reprinted with permission of APA. Figure 9.9—Fig. 3, p. 216 of "Personality Change in Adulthood" by R. Helson & A. Stewart in CAN PERSONALITY CHANGE? ed. by T. F. Hetherton & J. L. Weinberger. Copyright 1994 by American Psychological Association. Reprinted by permission of APA. Figure 9.10—From MOTIVATION AND PERSONALITY 3rd ed. by Abraham H. Maslow. Copyright 1954, 1987 by Harper & Row, Publishers, Inc. Reprinted by permission of Addison Wesley Educational Publishers, Inc. Table 9.5—From TOWARD A PSYCHOLOGY OF BEING 2nd ed. by Abraham H. Maslow. Copyright 1968 by Abraham H. Maslow. Published by Van Nostrand Reinhold/ John Wiley & Sons.

Chapter 10 Figure 10.1—Republished with permission of The Gerontological Society of America, 1030 15th Street, NW, Suite 250, Washington, DC 20005. "Age Differences in Religious Participation Among Black Adults" by L. M. Chatters & R. J. Taylor in *Journal of Gerontology:Social Sciences*, Vol. 44, 1989. Reproduced with permission of the publisher via Copyright Clearance Center, Inc. Table 10.1—"Stages of Moral Development" from ESSAYS ON MORAL DEVELOPMENT: The Psychology of Moral Development Vol. II by Lawrence Kohlberg. Copyright 1984 by Lawrence Kohlberg. Reprinted by permission of HarperCollins Publishers, Inc. Figure 10.2—Derived from A. Colby, L. Kohlberg, J. Gibbs & M. Lieberman (1983). "A Longitudinal Study of Moral Judgement" in *Monographs of the Society for Research in Child Development,* Vol. 48 (1-2, Serial No. 200); M. Nisan & L. Kohlberg, (1982). "Universality and Variation in Moral Judgement: A Longitudinal and Cross-Sectional Study in Turkey" in *Child Development,* Vol. 53; J. R. Snarey, J. Reimer, & L. Kohlberg (1985). "Development of Social-Moral Reasoning among Kibbutz Adolescents: A Longitudinal Cross-Sectional Study" in *Developmental Psychology*, Vol. 21. Figure 10.3—Table B.3, p. 318 from STAGES OF FAITH: The Psychology of Human Development and the Quest for Meaning by James W. Fowler. Copyright 1981 by James W. Fowler. Reprinted by permission of HarperCollins, Publishers, Inc. Figure 10.4—*Contextual and Thematic Analyses of Sources of Provisional Meaning: A Life-Span Perspective* by G. T. Reker. Paper presented at the biennial meeting of the International Society for the Study of Behavioral Development, Minneapolis, MN, 1991. Table 10.2—Derived from STAGES OF FAITH by J. W. Fowler, 1981, New York: HarperCollins, Publishers, Inc.; ESSAYS ON MORAL DEVELOPMENT: The Psychology of Moral Development, Vol. II by L. Kohlberg, 1984, New York: HarperCollins, Publishers, Inc.; EGO DEVELOPMENT by J. Loevinger, 1976, San Francisco: Jossey-Bass Publishers, Inc.; MOTIVATION AND PERSONALITY 3rd ed. by A. H. Maslow, 1954, New York: HarperCollins Publishers, Inc.

Chapter 11 Table 11.1—Reprinted from *Journal of Psychosomatic Research*, Vol. 14, 1970, "Short Term Intrusions in Life-Style Routine" by T. S. Holmes & T. H. Holmes. Copyright 1967 by Pergamon Press Ltd. Reprinted with permission of Elsevier Science. Figure 11.1—B. S. Dohrenwend & B. P. Dohrenwend (1980). "What is a Stressful Life Event?" in H. Selye (Ed.) SELYE'S GUIDE TO STRESS RESEARCH, Vol. I. New York: Van Nostrand Reinhold. Figure 11.2—Data from Table 1, p. 1103 in "Stressful Life Events, Social Support and Mortality in Men Born in 1933" by A. Rosengren, K. Orth-Gomer, H. Wendel, & L. Wilhelmsen in *British Medical Journal,* Vol. 307, 1993. Copyright 1993 by the authors. Reprinted with permission of BMJ Publishing Group. Figure 11.3—Adapted from Fig. 1, p. 609 in "Psychological Stress and Susceptability to the Common Cold" by S. Cohen, D. A. J. Tyrell, & A. P. Smith in *The New England Journal of Medicine*, Vol. 325, 1991. Copyright 1991 by the Massachusetts Medical Society. All rights reserved. Figure 11.4—Figure 4.3, p. 130 from HEALTH AND WAYS OF LIVING: The Alameda County Study by Lisa Berkman & Lester Breslow. Copyright 1983 by Oxford University Press. Used by permission of Oxford University Press, Inc. Figure 11.5—From Table 1, p. 432 of "Social Support, Life Events, and Stress as Modifiers of Adjustment to Bereavement by Older Adults" by F. H. Norris & S. A. Murrell in *Psychology and Aging*, Vol. 5, 1990. Copyright 1990 by American Psychological Assn. Reprinted by permission of APA. Figure 11.6—Republished with permission of The Gerontological Society of America, 1030 15th St. NW, Suite 250, Washington, DC 20005. *Emotional Problems in Widowhood* (Table 1, p. S207), by E. L. Goldberg, G. W. Comstock, & S. D. Harlow in *Journal of Gerontology: Social Sciences*, Vol. 43, 1988. Reproduced by permission of the publisher via Copyright Clearance Center, Inc. Figure 11.7—From Table 1, p. 323 in "Changes in Depression Following Divorce: A Panel Study" by E. G. Menaghan & M. A. Lieberman in *Journal of Marriage and the Family*, Vol. 48, 1986. Copyright 1986 by National Council on Family Relations, 3989 Central Ave., NE, Suite 550, Minneapolis, MN 55421.

Chapter 12 Figure 12.1—Republished with permission of The Gerontological Society of America, 1030 15th St. NW, Suite 250, Washington, DC 20005. "The Status of Age: Preliminary Results" (Figure 1, p. 507) by P. M. Baker, *Journal of Gerontology: Social Sciences*, Vol. 40, 1985. Reproduced by permission of the publisher via Copyright Clearance Center, Inc.

Chapter 13 Table 13.1—Text excerpt from p. 205 in DEATH AND ETHNICITY: A Psychocultural Study by R. A. Kalish & D. K. Reynolds. Copyright 1976 by the authors. Reprinted by permission of Baywood Publishing Company, Inc. Fig. 13.1—Republished with permission of The Gerontological Society of America, 1030 15th St. NW, Suite 250, Washington, DC 20005. *"Stratum Contrasts and Similarities in Attitudes Toward Death"* (Figure 1, p. 80) by V. L. Bengtson, J. B. Cueller & P. K. Ragan in *Journal of Gerontology*, Vol. 32, 1977. Reproduced by permission of the publisher via Copyright Clearance Center, Inc. Table 13.2—Table 1, p. 45 from "Psychological Response to Cancer and Survival" by S. Greer in *Psychological Medicine*, Vol. 21, 1991. Copyright 1991 by the author. Reprinted by permission of Cambridge University Press. Table 13.2—Table 1, p. 45 in "Psychological Response to Cancer and Survival" by S. Greer in *Psychological Medicine,* Vol. 21, 1991. Copyright 1991 by S. Greer. Reprinted by permission of Cambridge University Press. Figure 13.2—From *OMEGA—Journal of Death and Dying*, Vol. 18, No.1, 1987 (Fig. 13.2, p. 43) "Attachment Theory and Multiple Dimensions of Grief" by Selby C. Jacobs, Thomas R. Kosten, Stanislav V. Kasl, Adrian M. Ostfeld, Lisa Berkman & Peter Charpentier, pp. 41-52 (1987-1988, Baywood Publishing Company, Amity, NY 11710).

Chapter 14 Table 14.1—Derived from T. C. Antonucci (1991). "Attachment, Social Support, and Coping with Negative Life Events in Mature Adulthood" in E. M. Cummings, A. L. Greene & K. H. Karraker (Eds.) LIFE-SPAN DEVELOPMENTAL PSYCHOLO-GY: Perspectives on Stress and Coping. Mahwah, NJ: Erlbaum; E. Diener (1984). "Subjective Well-Being" in *Psychological Bulletin*, Vol. 95; L. K. George (1990). "Social Structure, Social Processes and Social-Psychological States" in R. H. Binstock & L. K. George (Eds.) HANDBOOK OF AGING AND THE SOCIAL SCIENCES, 3rd ed. San Diego: Academic Press; D. M. Gibson (1986) "Interaction and Well-Being in Old Age: Is it Quantity or Quality That Counts?" in *International Journal of Aging and Human Development*, Vol. 24; H. G. Koenig, J. N. Kvale & C. Ferrell (1988). "Religion and Well-Being in Later Life" in *The Gerontologist,* Vol. 28; AGING AND ETHNICITY by K. S. Markides & C. H. Mindel, 1987. Newbury Park, CA: Sage Publications, Inc.; S. A. Murrell & F. H. Norris (1991). "Differential Social Support and Life Change as Contributors to the Social Class-Distress Relationship in Old Age" in *Psychology and Aging*, Vol. 6; F. K. Willits & D. M. Crider (1988). " Health Rating and Life Satisfaction in the Later Middle years" in *Journal of Gerontology: Social Sciences*, Vol. 43. Table 14.2—Derived from P. T. Costa, Jr. & R. R. McCrae (1980a). "Influence of Extraversion and Neuroticism on Subjective Well-Being: Happy and Unhappy People" in *Journal of Personality and Social Psychology*, Vol. 38; P. T. Costa, R. R. McCrae, & A. H. Norris (1981). "Personal Adjustment to Aging: Longitudinal Prediction from Neuroticism and Extraversion" in *Journal of Gerontology*, Vol. 36. Table 14.3—Derived from G. E. Vaillant (1975), "Natural History of Male Psychological Health, III. Empirical Dimensions of Mental Health" in *Archives of General Psychiatry*, Vol. 32; G. E. Vaillant & C. O. Vaillant (1990). " Natural History of Male Psychological Health, XII: A 45-year Study of Predictors of Successful Aging at Age 65" in *American Journal of Psychiatry*, Vol. 147.

AUTHOR INDEX

SUBJECT INDEX